Advance Praise for *The*

"*The Fairshare Model* is an important work. The larger context is even more important: 'reimagining' the funding process from cradle to grave, as the existing ones all have serious flaws. That said, I see two challenges associated with early-stage IPOs:

1. Companies need the counter-balancing opinions that (good) VC's provide entrepreneurs–will investors be able to provide that once an early-stage venture is publicly traded?

2. Most important–and, most obvious–there is a general lack of interest in (actually, strong resistance to) creative solutions that undermine the interests of established players.

"Fight on and good luck, Karl. Your work IS important."

–Ken Wilcox, Chairman Emeritus,
Silicon Valley Bank

"It's time to reassess the alignment of interests in early-stage companies. How do you allow for the fact that investors are subject to valuation risk and have to 'pay' now for assumed future performance that may never happen? How do you let founders and their employees keep more of their company? How do you get everyday people to share in the benefits of capitalism? How do you avoid insane valuations of companies going public? It may be time to look at the ideas set out in *The Fairshare Model.*"

–Sara Hanks, CEO, CrowdCheck, Inc.
and Managing Partner, CrowdCheck Law, LLP

"For some financiers, pay-for-performance might sound like it's just too far out to be relevant in the near-term. This book shows how it can be relevant, what it would take, and why it would make a difference."

–Gordon Feller, San Francisco
Board Member of four VC-funded tech start-ups,
former Director-level positions at Cisco Systems

"This book is a manifesto for those whose life philosophy is: 'Why not?' Why not reimagine the relationship between investors and company employees to be one that is fairer and benefits both? Why not re-structure the financial industry to broaden opportunities to benefit millions more people? What sacred cows need to be put out to pasture? The result of the author's deep research and profound thought is an intriguing model for capitalism based on fairness, reciprocity, empathy, compassion. The author passionately appeals to the hearts and challenges the minds of readers with a tantalizing vision that declares: 'YES, IT COULD WORK!' "

–Po Chi Wu, Ph.D., Senior Partner, Futurelab Consulting, LLC
Adjunct Professor, School of Business & Management,
Hong Kong University of Science & Technology Visiting Professor & Industry Fellow,
Sutardja Center for Entrepreneurship & Technology,
University of California–Berkeley

THE Fairshare Model

A performance-based capital structure
for raising venture capital via an IPO

 Investors

Employees

The Fairshare Model doesn't present a better way to value future performance at an IPO. It says, don't even try to project it–assign no value to it. Instead, figure out how to reward actual performance.

–from Chapter 4, "Fairshare Model Q&A"

The Fairshare Model upends precepts about capital formation and resets the traditional relationship between capital and labor.

It is a *disruptive innovation* in finance that will unsettle venture capital firms, as well as Wall Street banks that make boatloads of money selling shares in venture-stage companies to public investors–"the high-profit-margin customers."

–from Chapter 7, "Target Companies for the Fairshare Model"

A conventional capital structure enables insiders to profit when public investors don't–the Fairshare Model does not.

–from Chapter 22, "Blockchain and Initial Coin Offerings"

Karl Sjogren

*Reimagining
Capitalism
at the
DNA Level*

The
Fairshare
Model

A Performance-Based

Capital Structure

for Venture-Stage

Initial Public Offerings

Fairshare Model Press, Oakland, California, USA
info@fairsharemodel.com
fairsharemodel.com

Book design by Lorna Johnson | LornaJohnsonPrint.com

Cover design by Matt Hinrichs | matthinrichs.com

M.C. Escher's "Ascending and Descending" © 2018 The M.C. Escher Company-The Netherlands. All rights reserved. mcescher.com.

Screen Bean images created by A Bit Better Corporation are property of Microsoft Corporation, and licensed for use under the Creative Commons Attribution-Share Alike 4.0 International license.

All other illustrations are by Henry White

Library of Congress Control Number: 2019907625

The Fairshare Model: Reimagining Capitalism at the DNA Level—A Performance Based Capital Structure for Venture-Stage Initial Public Offerings / Karl Sjogren—1st ed.

ISBN 978-1-950732-00-5 paperback

ISBN 978-1-950732-01-2 ebook

Dedication

To John Gilbert Wilson of San Antonio, Texas,
who conceived the Fairshare Model and introduced me to it in 1995.

Also, to my parents, who encouraged me to be curious.

Foreword

What is a dream worth?

Of all the things that we teach business school students, corporate valuation is given very little time or attention. When a business needs to be valued because it is being bought or sold, the task is relegated to accountants who are asked to render their opinion whether the price is "fair." Accountants plug data about earnings and assets into established formulas and come up with a value. But what if there is little or no data? What if the business has no earnings or assets?

When I first started on Wall Street in the 1970s, a company could not go public until it had earnings and indeed was operating profitably. That began to change in the 1980s. By the dotcom era of the late 1990s, earnings were not required. A company needed only a good story about how it would use this new thing called the internet to make money. Not surprisingly, a great many of those dotcom companies that had no earnings failed.

With any IPO the value is often based on a significant amount of perception. There is an old saying on Wall Street that brokers "sell the sizzle, not the steak." Still, there was always a belief that there had to be some "meat" in the company for any investment to make sense.

Regardless of how an investment banker prices an offering, it still must sell that price to investors. The investors must believe that the company will succeed and prosper. The risk that the company will not perform as advertised always falls on the investors.

Venture capital firms are often dealing with companies that have little more than an idea that they want to bring to market. These companies do not have earnings or assets. If they are lucky, they have a patent for their product or process. The value of a patented but untried product is very difficult to value.

Intellectual property like patents, copyrights, and trademarks are very hard to value at the time they are obtained. No author knows that they have a bestseller on the day their book is published. Few know that their book will be made into a movie or that anyone will pay to see it. So what is the "value" of any book on the day before the manuscript goes to the publisher?

As an exercise, I used to ask my students if they could identify the most valuable intellectual property that was in use in the 20th century. It was always an interesting discussion. What we were talking about, after all, was the value of an idea written on a few pieces of paper or an image originally produced on a single sheet—something that was untried when it began but took off when it finally hit the market. The question was always how to spot a winner.

The purpose of the exercise was to impress upon the students how very difficult it is to value something as intangible as an idea, especially if the market has not yet had an opportunity to purchase the product that will be based upon it. A lot of inventors and entrepreneurs think that their idea will hit a home run. The truth is very few will even get to first base. Placing a value on an idea or a company that is pre-revenue is very difficult, especially if you ask the entrepreneur, who is likely to be dreaming big.

The JOBS Act and crowdfunding gave entrepreneurs the ability to fund their startups directly with small investors, bypassing investment banks and venture capitalists. The result has been an explosion of new start-ups and a lot of not-so savvy investors faced with decisions about investing in them.

The Fairshare Model is important because it takes a fresh look at this problem. It attempts to shift the risk of the future performance of a company away from the shareholders and place it upon the insiders who can best control how well the company actually performs. That may seem simple and even obvious, but it isn't.

I had the pleasure of a two-hour conversation with the author in January 2017, while he was still writing this book. At that point, we had been interacting on LinkedIn for more than a year. This is not an academic tome. It is a "roll up your sleeves and let's get it done" approach written by someone who has worked with finance and financial statements for a long time. It is a well-reasoned attempt to help those small companies and small investors. It is a new approach to corporate finance for the new world of direct-to-investor IPOs.

Year after year, my students would reach the conclusion that the most valuable piece of intellectual property in use in the 20th century was the formula for Coca-Cola. The image of Mickey Mouse was second. In neither case, could any investor know that when first presented to the public either would grow into the iconic product that it has.

This book is important for any finance professional, any entrepreneur seeking investors, and any investor who wants to look at the risks of investing in a new way. Every chapter is well-thought-out, thought-provoking, and full of hidden gems. Pour yourself a Coke and get ready for something new and different, something that finance professionals never dreamed was possible—a book about finance that is actually enjoyable to read.

–Irwin Stein

Irwin G. Stein is a highly experienced securities attorney. He began his long career at large brokerage and investment banking firms. Before the age of forty, he was General Counsel for a $1.5 billion real estate firm. For nine years, he was an Adjunct Assistant Professor at Golden Gate University, teaching business courses such as "Law, Economics, and Finance."

He has counseled investors—including those defrauded by scam artists—entrepreneurs, mainstream firms, and financial advisors. He has also been an expert witness in securities arbitrations and complex financial litigation.

Irwin blogs at *Law and Economics in the Capital Markets* (laweconomicscapital.com) and is a well-respected commentator on LinkedIn.

In 2015, he authored a book, *Investment Schemes, Scams & Strategies Retirees Should Avoid.* Every baby boomer should read it—every millennial should buy a copy for their parents. Irwin says:

> Many books offer strategies on how to invest your money or which specific investments to buy. I tell you which investments and strategies that you would do well to avoid.

> What happens to retirees in the financial markets is a national disgrace—many of them suffer devastating investment losses.

I worked as an attorney in and around the financial markets for 40 years, helping thousands of investors who were victims of financial fraud and unsuitable investments. Retirees have made up a disproportionate number of them because they are targeted in the financial markets. They are easy marks--many know just enough about investing to get themselves into serious trouble.

Plus, financial sharks are more prevalent than you might think. The person from whom you seek financial advice is the key person who will be responsible for determining how much money you have to spend between the time that you retire and the time that you die.

I show you how to avoid the many bad actors in the markets, and how to find a financial advisor who will be good for you.

The proceeds from sales of his book are used to fund cancer research. Irwin has this to say about cancer:

I woke up one morning in 2011 with a bad stomachache.

Three hours later they told me that I had leukemia. They also told me to put my affairs in order. I was fortunate to get world-class treatment from the doctors, nurses, and staff at the University of California San Francisco Medical Center.

I learned that cancer is not for wimps. I fought my cancer. A lot of people with cancer do the same. I do not feel that it is right to call us cancer survivors.

I prefer the term cancer conquistadors, instead.

"Just for once I'd like to see all these things sort of straightened out, with each person getting exactly what he deserves. It might give me some confidence in this universe."

–Joseph Heller, *Catch-22*

"One of the things I learned the hard way was that it doesn't pay to get discouraged. Keeping busy and making optimism a way of life can restore your faith in yourself."

–Lucille Ball

"Some men see things as they are and ask why. Others dream things that never were and ask why not."

–George Bernard Shaw

"The men were perfectly content to fly as many missions as we asked them as long as they thought they had no alternative. Now you've given them hope, and they're unhappy. So the blame is all yours."

–Joseph Heller, *Catch-22*

Contents

Introduction

I come to capital markets via Main Street, not Wall Street. My 35-year financial career began at Fortune 500 manufacturing companies in the Midwest region of the United States. In 1983, I moved to California's Silicon Valley, the hotbed of what was then called "high technology." My first job there was with a personal computer company that had just had its initial public offering (IPO). It filed for bankruptcy nine months after I started. It was my initiation into a world more exciting and volatile than anything I had previously known. Nowadays, we call it the New Economy.

I then worked for a variety of companies before embarking on a career path as a consulting chief financial officer where I helped companies improve their performance and sometimes, raise money. In 1996, the insights I obtained led me to cofound a company that sought to make it easier for young companies to market IPOs without a broker-dealer. We built an online community of 16,000 valuation-savvy investors called Fairshare and it is the genesis of this book, The Fairshare Model.

My experience is detailed in Chapter 9, "Fairshare Model and the Future." What's important here, at the start of the book, is to know that we placed the interests of average investors–Main Street–first. That means the ideas presented herein are unlike those you can get elsewhere. Normally, views on capital markets are based on the perspective of entrepreneurs, investors in the private capital market, investment bankers or their best customers, the ones who manage to get shares in hot IPOs. Traditionally, the interests of average investors are relatively unimportant. I would like to change that.

That makes this a movement book. It seeks to rouse debate about a better way to structure ownership interests in companies that raise venture capital via an IPO. To set the stage for that, the book needs to help readers better understand capital structures. It must also promote awareness of the importance of valuation and expose a little secret–*no one* knows how to reliably value a startup. This knowledge will lead to a revolution in how public venture capital is raised because it will encourage investors to demand better deals than they get now.

> No cause was won that wasn't first mocked, no gate stands wide that wasn't at first locked.

In Spring 2014, a few months after I began writing this book, I was awakened from a nap by a phone call. I thought I was in a dream state when I heard the caller's opening words: "Whatever happened to Fairshare?" He told me he was from Wisconsin and had become a Fairshare member in 1998. I knew I wasn't dreaming when he said that he looked at his member binder from time to time. As we began our membership drive, some people said that it was difficult to absorb all the information on our website–hyperlinks could confuse those new to the internet. Those who printed pages felt overwhelmed by the challenge of organizing them. There were enough requests for printouts that we experimented with binders for premium members. More than a dozen years later, this gentleman still had his.

I told him Fairshare was too early and met its demise in 2001. I also said that I had decided to write a book about its core concept because the time seemed right for it. He replied: "I always thought it was a good idea."

The Purpose of This Book

The purpose of this book is to spark a movement to reimagine capitalism at the DNA level. A capital structure is a company's DNA–it defines ownership interests and voting rights–so everything that capitalism is (or can be) flows from the expression of qualities that originates in its capital structure.

The Fairshare Model is an idea for a performance-based capital structure for companies that raise venture capital via an *initial public offering*. Its mission is to balance and align the interests of investors and employees; to offer public investors a deal comparable to what venture capitalists get.

It has two classes of stock. One trades, the other cannot; both vote. Investors get the tradable stock, which I call "Investor Stock." For past performance, employees get it too. For future performance, employees get the non-tradable stock, which I call "Performance Stock." Based on milestones, Performance Stock converts into Investor Stock. The model's structure is simple–its complexity flows from a question that is both philosophical and practical: "What is performance?" How that question is answered will vary–it can be whatever a company's shareholders say it will be.

The idea behind the Fairshare Model is simultaneously radical and ordinary.

It is radical because the model presents a different philosophy about how to structure ownership interests in public companies whose value chiefly comes from their uncertain promise of future performance. Such companies have raised venture capital for decades via Wall Street IPOs. Recent changes in securities law will accelerate such activity. Another unique aspect of the Fairshare Model is that it presents a way for middle class investors to participate in venture capital investing on terms comparable to what venture capitalists get.

The Fairshare Model is ordinary because it encourages the public capital markets to work the way most markets work, where sellers compete for buyers by offering a better deal (i.e., lower prices and better terms). Remarkably, this isn't common with a conventional capital structure; companies don't currently compete for public investors by offering lower valuations and better protections.

This reflects weak market forces. IPO issuers and Wall Street firms do not want to compete on deal terms, valuation, and investor protections. In addition, many public investors are unsure what valuation is, let alone how to calculate or evaluate one. Oftentimes, "market forces" is a phrase used to explain adverse developments for the middle class, but they *can* bring better deals to average investors. One way to reimagine capitalism is with *stronger market forces* that result in a better product and increased competition for public capital. The Fairshare Model promotes this in a win-win manner–with significant benefits for investors and employees.

So, how does one go about changing the DNA of capitalism? By popularizing a new philosophy about the relationship between companies and their IPO investors. The key idea? Treat public venture capital like private venture capital. That is, provide IPO investors price protection, comparable to what venture capital firms get in a private offering. Then reward well-performing entrepreneurial teams with more ownership than they would get if the financing were from a venture capital firm.

I hope you will discuss the Fairshare Model with others. To generate buzz among hives of people with interest in entrepreneurial companies is the job of this book. As the model's philosophy  gains traction, experts from a range of fields will evaluate how to implement it for different companies—but that will only happen if there is clear investor interest in the model.

The San Francisco Bay area, where I have lived for the past 35 years, is renowned for sourdough bread. Think of the process of popularizing the Fairshare Model as the process of baking. This book will serve as the "starter," the yeast culture that gives the bread its unique flavor and texture.

Readers like you will contribute ingredients to make the dough, but instead of flour and water you will provide ideas and enthusiasm.

Experts in various matters—law, tax, accounting, organizational development, and other areas—will knead it. Once the dough rises, early adopters will bake it.

The aroma of a fresh approach to capital formation will attract more people to the kitchen who will contribute more ideas on what to make.

Often, after I'm exposed to a new idea, I see other things in a new light. I get pleasure when that happens—it's a reward for being curious.

> "I would rather have questions that can't be answered than answers that can't be questioned."
>
> –Richard Feynman

I trust that you feel similarly. And so, I seek to engage you in new thinking about capital markets, stimulating the interplay of concept and possibility, analysis, and imagination.

And I hope you will inspire others to do the same.

So, let's begin to explore how to reimagine capital structures, the DNA of capitalism!

At some level, I hope to fortify your sense that it is possible for people who are not wealthy or powerful to promote change in how established systems work—to make them work better for more people.

The Fairshare Model is an attempt to do that in capital markets. It harnesses two forces that many see as incompatible—market forces and cooperation.

I solicit your help to strengthen market forces. A way to do this is to encourage companies to compete for public capital. That can happen if they are required to disclose the valuation that they have given themselves when they sell stock. Chapter 16, "Valuation Disclosure," explains this further and what you can do to help.

The other way to change capital markets is to enhance the rewards available to the providers of capital and labor when they cooperate and collaborate. That is what the Fairshare Model does. As support for it grows, so too will the opportunities to see companies explore the benefits of cooperation between investors and employees.

Vision

My vision for the Fairshare Model is that average investors will be able to make venture capital investments *on terms that are comparable to those that venture capitalists get in a private offering.*

Goal

My goal is to popularize a deal structure that can:

1. expand entrepreneur access to capital,

2. offer liquidity to investors who support private companies, and

3. create an attractive, yet prudent, option for average investors to be "mini-angel investors."

Note the self-renewing cycle. Entrepreneurs are more likely to attract capital if investors feel fairly treated for the risks they assume. Angel investors are more likely to invest in a company when they believe it can attract investors to the next round of capital and there is the prospect of liquidity–the ability to sell shares. Public investors are more likely to provide that capital and liquidity if they, too, feel fairly treated.

Within a generation, I hope the Fairshare Model will present an attractive approach for companies that raise venture capital in a public offering. This will happen if it helps them raise capital and provides a competitive advantage in attracting employees and managing them.

Why not more quickly? It takes time for innovation to take root in a tradition-bound market.

While I proselytize about the Fairshare Model, I acknowledge there may be other ways to achieve the above three goals, and I welcome debate about the relative merits of alternative approaches.

In the simplest sense, my goal is to give average investors a more sophisticated understanding of venture capital. The more they know, the more they will want better deals when it is raised via a public offering. The effect will be to encourage entrepreneurs to offer them.

Audience

This is a book for thinkers. People who like Big Ideas but who are also practical; they like innovative ideas but also want a way to put them into practice.

My principal target audience is composed of investors who might want to invest in a public startup company someday. Some of them see a problem–such companies are notoriously difficult to value. For them, the Fairshare Model is a solution because it avoids the need to value future performance.

My secondary target audience is comprised of entrepreneurs willing to consider a public offering as an alternative to a private finance round from a venture capital fund–a VC.

There is another important audience made up of attorneys, accountants, investment bankers and others involved in the startup ecosystem. They are not my focus, but their involvement will be critical for companies that seek to implement the Fairshare Model. Their interest will naturally build as investor and entrepreneur interest in the concept builds.

Most readers will be new to capital structures or unsure how to define one, while a sizable proportion will be expert in them. In my mind's eye, my reader is in their late teens to early forties and has invested in or worked for a venture-stage company or aspires to. More to the point, I sense three age-related clusters of readers. Those over 50 years of age will use their wisdom and experience to critically evaluate the Fairshare Model. The ones in their 30s and 40s will have the ambition to put it into practice—they will be the wellspring of entrepreneurs and investors who determine the adoption rate. Readers under 30 will provide the energy required to strengthen this movement.

Whatever their age, background or ambition, this book will appeal to people drawn to these topics:

- economic philosophy and behavioral finance,
- valuation (concepts, calculation, and evaluation),
- corporate governance and organizational behavior,
- how to align the interests of investors and employees,
- how to resolve the conflict between expanding access to venture investments for average investors and protecting their interests,
- the intersection of social/impact investing and capital markets,
- economic growth,
- a partial solution to income inequality that does not rely on taxes,
- game theory, and
- blockchain and initial coin offerings (ICOs)

All readers will want to better understand how economies work—some will want to change how they work. This book explores how venture capital formation works from the perspective of public investors; it also shows how it can be made friendlier to them.

Geographically, my focus is on the US capital market and my perspective is that of an American, however, the Fairshare Model is not US-centric. I anticipate that it will be adopted in other countries, possibly more quickly or with greater success.

Encouragement and a Compass

> Every page or two, I hope to give you a "Ha!" or an "Aha!"

There may be times when my points are unclear to readers who are unfamiliar with capital structures. I offer two things to deal with those moments when you feel disoriented.

The first is encouragement. Stick with me and matters that seem obscure will come into focus. You will acquire a credible view of how capital formation works in a capitalistic economy. I make technical points in simple language. Philosophy, analogy, and humor are in my toolbox. Make this journey, and you'll have a better understanding of a complex socio-economic process that affects many aspects of life. If you don't already have one, you will acquire a coherent point of view about the IPO market for early stage companies. If you already have such a perspective, I may challenge it. Either way, if you like ideas, this book will be fun!

The second thing that I offer is a conceptual compass. With respect to how capital formation works, between where we are now and where I imagine we can be, is unexplored terrain. When you wonder where I am headed, where I will turn, how I think a matter should be settled, look to my compass.

On it, True North is the interests of public investors who buy stock from a venture-stage company in an IPO. The interests of entrepreneurs, private investors and investors in the secondary market are important, but not as central as those of the IPO investor; there is only one True North.

Public IPO investors occupy that position for the Fairshare Model because if they make money, there will be more money for entrepreneurs and better liquidity options for their private investors.

In the Fairshare Model's hierarchy of interests, IPO investors are at the top. So the answer to any question about how to make the Fairshare Model work will be found by asking, "What is best for the IPO investors?" while considering the interests of the other key constituencies.

This ranking hierarchy is on display below.

Fairshare Model's Hierarchy of Interests

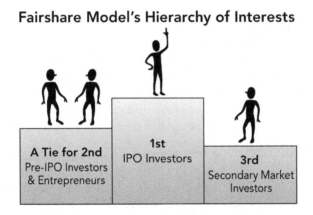

- The interests of IPO investors are at the top, in first place.
- The interests of pre-IPO investors and the entrepreneurial team are in a tie for second place.
- In third place are the interests of secondary market investors.

Your Mindset

A reviewer of this book, Po Chi Wu, is a blockchain expert with a background in venture capital. He is also an educator—he is an Adjunct Professor in the School of Business at Hong Kong University of Science & Technology and a Visiting Professor in the College of Engineering at the University of California-Berkeley. He recommends that, at the outset, I encourage readers to approach this material with an open mind.

I know that some of you will sense conflict with what you already know. For example, if you believe that venture capital is only raised from venture capital firms, you will resist the idea that it can be raised in an IPO. You may be skeptical that average investors can cause innovation to take hold in capital markets. Then too, you may doubt capitalism can be changed for the better, or question whether is necessary to do so.

Major change to The-Way-Things-Are is rare, but it happens. For example, the competitive landscape for computer operating systems was upended in 1991 when Linus Torvald made the kernel logic for Linux available as open source code. The effect of a viable alternative to traditional proprietary operating systems was profound—Linux-based systems are now pervasive on all manner of computing devices. I hope that the Fairshare Model has a similar effect on the IPO market in the decades to come. It is open source idea for a capital structure—there will be variation in how it is implemented.

So, taking Dr. Wu's advice, I ask you to nurture that part of you that is open to possibilities. We all have one. Some feed it by reading science fiction. Others do it by watching sports, movies, or magic acts. Political activism is a form of it—a spirited debate about ideas can be, at its best. The Fairshare Model relies on the imagination of those willing to explore new ideas about how to structure ownership interests in companies that raise capital via an IPO.

To prime your imagination, here are thoughts that Professor Wu shared with me as he reflected on what he had read.

> The words that come to my mind when I [Po Chi Wu] think of [the Fairshare Model] is "decoupling/uncoupling" because I think those words help us understand why understanding does not come easily.
>
> Of course, the subject matter is complex, but the conventional mindset is rigid in how the basic concepts of "power," "ownership," and "value/valuation" are linked together inseparably because of all the assumptions and expectations we have about how the world works. We cannot think of one without being reminded of its connection with the other two.
>
> You are asking—What if we could deal with these three aspects separately? Let value/valuation be directed by market forces. Power should be held primarily by those who are doing the hard work of building the business. Governance considerations will add some nuance to this idea. Ownership can reflect contributions of money and/or labor.
>
> To break up this "unholy trinity," you suggest decentralized mechanisms for each feature. In a way, I think that blockchain implementation could actually make your ideas easier to understand because of the fundamentally distributed framework.[1]
>
> To change someone's mindset, we have to bring them into a fresh context, one that doesn't have the usual baggage.

That is my goal—to present a fresh context that opens up your thinking about how companies can raise capital from public investors.

How This Book Is Organized

As Professor Wu notes, capital structures and markets are complex matters. To enhance your understanding of them, I avoid overwhelming detail. Instead, I present core ideas in a manner that helps you associate them with things that you already know—I emphasize breadth over depth.

---

[1] The Fairshare Model is designed for an IPO, but the underlying idea—that no value should be placed on future performance when equity is raised—can be applied to blockchain projects. This is discussed in Chapter 22, "Blockchain and Initial Coin Offerings."

Strategically, I trust this approach will encourage you to consider the implications of these ideas further, in your way.

To aid navigation, each chapter opens with a list of its subtopics.

Stylistically, I favor a light manner. I also provoke; being inspired by Diogenes, the ancient Greek philosopher to whom the following is attributed:

> "Of what use is a philosopher who never offends anybody?"

I serve up ideas using a literary adaptation of "pointillism," a technique of painting in which dots define and fill an image. Here, ideas from a range of sources serve as dots, and I share images that I see. You will surely see dots too as you consider the images they form. Ask yourself "What is really going on here?" Then, ask yourself "Is there a better way?"

To simplify ideas, I sometimes use a conceptual equation. This approach is inspired by Chip Conley's 2012 book *Emotional Equations*. Chip founded the *Joie de Vivre* chain of boutique hotels in the US before going on to head strategy at Airbnb, a startup in the vanguard of the "sharing economy." He came to his book in an effort to analyze emotions he struggled with. A friend suggested that he find a way to express a feeling as a formula, to focus his attention on the variables that cause the emotion.

For example:

Anxiety = Uncertainty x Powerlessness

This emotional equation states that anxiety is a multiple of uncertainty and powerlessness. It suggests that one can reduce anxiety by reducing uncertainty, the sense of powerlessness, or both. My favorite equation was suggested by a caller when Chip was interviewed on a radio program.[2]

Happiness = What is Happening − Expectations

This states that happiness can be increased by improving what's happening, by reducing your expectations, or both.

Substantively, these emotional equations are insightful. Stylistically, they de-tangle a complex subject. So, occasionally, I repurpose the concept as a conceptual equation like this:

Performance = Results − Expectations

This formula states that performance has a positive value when results exceed expectations, which helps shed light on a slippery question: "What is performance?"

Organizationally, a river of thought meanders through the five sections. That is, you can proceed straight through or jump around to topics that interest you because key concepts presented early on are repeatedly touched on later in the book. Before you do that, however, read Chapter 1, "The Fairshare Model," Chapter 2, "The Big Idea and Thesis" and Chapter 4, "Fairshare Model Q&A."

---

[2] Chip Conley. January 11, 2012. Accessed May 7, 2018. fairsharemodel.com/Conley. Author of "Emotional Equations" interview on KQED's *Forum* radio program.

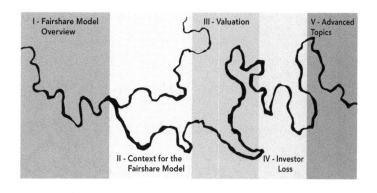

The first section, Fairshare Model Overview, covers micro-economic points. It is written for those knowledgeable about capital structures but in a way that a novice can follow.

The second section considers the macroeconomic context for the Fairshare Model—its chapters cover economic growth, job creation, income inequality and the potential for cooperation to be a tool for competition. If the first section seems too technical for you, skim it, move to the second section, and then return to the first one.

The third section has four chapters on valuation—concepts, calculation, evaluation, and a call for a valuation disclosure requirement. Valuation disclosure can strengthen market forces in a way that benefits all investors.

The fourth section discusses the causes of investor loss—fraud, failure, and investing in an overvalued company. It also considers the objections some have to participation in venture capital by average investors.

The fifth section, Advanced Topics, begins with a deeper dive into the investor risk concepts that are touched on in Chapter 2, "The Big Idea and Thesis." It goes on to cover game theory, then blockchain and initial coin offerings. The Fairshare Model was conceived for IPOs, but the idea of a performance-based capital structure makes sense for ICOs too.

The epilogue revisits what needs to happen to make this movement to reimagine capitalism move forward. Before you put the book down for good, please read it.

Finally, there is an appendix with tables that show the valuation of a company based on how much ownership new investors get for their money.

Throughout the book, footnotes provide context to text on the same page. Some chapters conclude with endnotes that list source material referenced in the chapter. Footnotes are numbered consecutively within each chapter. Endnotes are identified with a letter that is unique to the chapter. That is, the first endnote in each chapter that has one is an "A," the second is a "B," and so on.

Website links can go bad. If you encounter one, write me at info@fairsharemodel.com and I will fix it.

Mini-Glossary

Terms with Conventional Meanings

Capital: Money raised from external sources in the form of debt or equity financing. Capital can also be in the form of intellectual property, rights, or services.

Issuer: A company that issues or sells a security to investors.

Security: Generally, a security is either a debt or equity instrument. Debt is a loan, and it conveys no ownership interest—the issuer is obligated to repay what is owed. Equity represents an ownership interest in the issuer, who is not obliged to repay it, unless it was sold illegally. Securities include exotic financial instruments that are neither debt or equity—derivatives like warrants, options, forward contracts, investment contracts and digital tokens.[3] The definition of a security is broad and can vary by securities regulator.

Securities regulator: All developed economies regulate securities. In the US, the Securities and Exchange Commission—the SEC—is the federal securities regulator; states and US territories have regulators too. There are also non-governmental regulators, not-for-profit organizations like FINRA and stock exchanges that are a self-regulated organization—an SRO.

Capital market: The market for financial instruments. Generally, to buy a security in the private capital market, one must be an accredited investor. In a public capital market, anyone can invest.

Initial public offering (IPO): When a company first sells equity or stock in a way that any investor can buy.

Secondary offering: A public offering by a company whose shares are already publicly traded.

Original issue market: Where investors buy new shares from the issuer, as opposed to other shareholders.

Secondary market: Where investors buy issued shares from other shareholders, not the issuer.

Shareholder: Someone who has an ownership interest in a company.

Creditor: Someone who provides capital in exchange for an issuer's promise to repay it, or goods or services in exchange for a promise to be paid.

Accredited Investor: The designation for investors who meet a wealth and income standard defined by the SEC that fewer than 10 percent of US households meet.

Non-accredited investors: Anyone who is not an accredited investor (over 90 percent of US households). They are often referred to as average investors.

Deal terms: The terms of an investment agreed to by an issuer and investor or creditor.

Debt capital: Capital provided in exchange for the issuer's promise to repay it, along with interest and fees. A convertible note is a debt instrument with terms that allow it to convert into equity. Debt holders don't have voting rights. If a company is liquidated—sold or dissolved—creditors are entitled to be paid before money is distributed to shareholders.

Debt seniority: Creditors rank in seniority, based on deal terms. The more senior the debt, the better positioned the creditor is, legally, to be repaid.

Equity capital: Capital provided for stock, which provides an ownership interest and, usually, voting rights.

Stock class: An issuer can have a single class of stock, where all shares have the same rights, or multiple classes of stock, where some classes have rights that others don't. Private companies tend

---

[3] "Digital token" is defined in Chapter 22, "Blockchain and Initial Coin Offerings."

to have complex capital structures: common stock and multiple classes of preferred stock. Public companies tend to have a simple capital structure: a single class of stock, common.

Common stock: The basic form of stock issued by a corporation.

Preferred stock: A class of stock senior to common stock in designated rights. Multiple classes of preferred stock are frequently present in private companies with professional investors.

Registered offering of securities: An offering that is legal to sell in the jurisdiction of a regulator. Large IPOs, those sold by Wall Street broker-dealers, are frequently registered with the SEC using a Form S-1.

Offering exempt from registration: A legal offering exempt or excused from full registration requirements. Exemptions are created by legislatures to reduce the regulatory burden for issuers. They affect all private offerings, which are largely limited to accredited investors, and certain public offerings. The most amount that can raised in a public exempt offering—a Reg. A+ offering—is $50 million.

Other offerings: An offering that is not registered or exempt from registration may be illegal.

Digital token: A financing device that has emerged from blockchain technology. Just how digital tokens (or coins) fit into the regulatory scheme is evolving. Often, they convey no ownership interest or voting rights. They appeal to investors who are neither shareholders nor creditors but who are willing to bet that token will rise in value. Chapter 22, "Blockchain and Initial Coin Offerings," defines other terms that are unique to initial coin offerings.

Capital structure: Refers to how a company is financed; the composition of debt and equity, taking note of the rights attached to each financial instrument.

Exit: An event that allows an investor to convert an investment back to money.

Venture capitalist: A general partner of a venture capital fund. VC firms invest in early-stage private companies in the hope that they can sell their position at a profit if the company is acquired or becomes publicly traded. Limited partners are a fund's investors; they usually provide 99 percent of the capital while general partners provide one percent. General partners run the fund in exchange for management fees and about 20 percent of any profit earned.

Private equity firms: Private equity firms are VCs that invest in more established companies. Sometimes, they buy all the stock of a public company and take it private. To finance their deals, PE firms rely heavily on debt, secured by the assets of the companies they invest in. To repay it, they sell off assets and improve the performance of what remains. Their goal is to sell the company or take it public at a higher valuation.

Broker-dealer: A regulated seller of securities that can charge a commission.

Funding portal: An online intermediary authorized by the JOBS Act of 2012 that can advertise offerings of securities but cannot (a) solicit transactions, (b) provide investment advice, (c) compensate parties for the sale of securities, or (d) either hold or manage investor's money or securities.

Offering platform: A website authorized by the JOBS Act that is operated by a broker-dealer to facilitate the sale of securities. An offering platform can do what a funding portal cannot.

Terms with Unconventional Meanings

Failure risk: The risk that a company will fail to fully deliver the operational performance that investors expect. A company can fall short of these expectations and have investors view an investment a success.

Valuation risk: The risk that an investor overpays for an ownership position.

Venture capital: Capital provided to a venture-stage company, *whether in a private or public offering.* It is unconventional to say that venture capital is raised in an IPO; many feel it is limited to capital provided by a VC or PE firm. I find that definition unnecessarily restrictive and inaccurate. Venture capital should be defined by what the investment is, not by who makes it.

Venture-stage company: A company that has significant risk with respect to performance. Examples include startups and other companies that require future infusions of capital to survive.

Price protection: Deal terms that limit valuation risk. They are provided to sophisticated investors in the private capital market, but rarely to public investors. Price protection comes in a variety of forms. For example, a price ratchet, which is a form of an anti-dilution clause. It requires that a company issue more shares for free to an investor with this protection, if a later investor gets stock at a lower price than allowed. A liquidation preference is another form of price protection. In a liquidity event, it entitles an investor to a recover its investment, or a multiple of it, before other investors share in what remains.

Conventional capital structure: This term is explained at length in Chapter 5, "The Problem with a Conventional Capital Structure," but mentioned before that. A conventional capital structure places a value on future performance at the time of an equity investment. It is used in some private offerings and in virtually all public offerings. The Fairshare Model is the opposite of a conventional capital structure–it places no value on future performance at the time of an equity investment.

Modified conventional capital structure: A modified conventional capital structure is also called the VC Model because it is used by venture capital and private equity funds. It also places a value on future performance at the time of an equity investment, but it has deal terms that provide the investor with price protection. Thus, the VC Model limits valuation risk.

Investor Stock: This is a Fairshare Model term. It refers to common stock issued to investors for capital and to employees for actual–not projected–performance.

Performance Stock: This is also a Fairshare Model term. It is preferred stock (or non-tradable common stock) issued to employees and others for future performance. It converts to Investor Stock as performance milestones are achieved.

Ownership interest: The percentage of share ownership an investor has in a company.

Ownership payoff: The proportion of total proceeds that a shareholder receives when there is a liquidity event. A shareholder's ownership payoff can differ from their ownership interest due to price protections they or other shareholders have.

SECTION 1:

Fairshare Model Overview

This section presents the Fairshare Model and addresses an array of questions you will have about it. It delves into the problem that a conventional capital structure has for public investors and explains how the Fairshare Model differs from crowdfunding.

The types of companies that will be attracted to the Fairshare Model are described, as is the quality that enables it to work, a multiclass capital structure.

The section ends with a chapter that provides more information about who I am and what led me to write this book. It also describes how I expect the Fairshare Model movement to evolve.

Chapters in this section:

Chapter 1:

The Fairshare Model

What's Included in This Chapter

- Introduction
- The Problem
- The Fairshare Model
- Where the Fairshare Model is Positioned in Capital Markets
- Chicken vs. Egg
- What's Next?

Introduction

The Fairshare Model can be described in a few sentences, but its implications are vast. So, it takes more than a page to appreciate the problem that it addresses, and the implications it could have for investors, employees, and the economy. This chapter prepares you for an exploration of the economics of capital formation for startup companies. It is about philosophy as much as finance.

The Problem

The core problem with a conventional capital structure is that it provides a weak model for a self-renewing cycle of capital—one that encourages investment. The reason is that it requires that a value be set on future performance when equity capital is raised. But it is hard to reliably estimate the value of future performance, especially for a venture-stage company. All entrepreneurs and investors share this problem.

The good news is that there are ways to resolve it. A company can modify a conventional capital structure to provide investors with price protection—deal terms that can protect them from buying in at an excessive valuation.

The bad news is that such terms are commonly provided only to investors in a private offering, not a public one. But public investors also assume significant risk that a company's performance will fall short of the expectations it promotes. Once upon a time, companies went public only after they were profitable. Nowadays, its unremarkable to see companies with dubious prospects have an initial public offering (IPO), so the valuation problem is pervasive–both private and public investors face it. But only private investors are usually provided with terms that can mitigate the problem.

This disparity is unfair. After all, a dollar is worth a dollar, whether it comes from a private or public investor. Furthermore, when IPO investors assume high failure risk, shouldn't they get protection from valuation risk comparable to what private investors get? I say "yes!" But rights aren't necessarily parceled out based on fairness. Sometimes, they must be demanded.

The fundamental reason IPO investors don't get price protection is that too few of them insist on it. These two conceptual formulas show why this is the case.

$$\text{Private Venture Capital Round} = \text{Investors are Valuation Aware} + \text{Valuation is Negotiated} + \text{Price Protection}$$

versus

$$\text{Public Venture Capital Round (IPO)} = \text{Many Investors Are Valuation Unaware} + \text{Issuer Sets Valuation} + \text{No Price Protection}$$

The first formula states that in a private round of venture capital, investors are valuation-aware, they negotiate the valuation with the company selling stock, and secure deal terms that protect them from overpaying. The second formula states that in a public round of venture capital–which many IPOs are–many investors are valuation-unaware. Plus, the valuation is set by the company and no price protection is offered. So, while the valuation problem is universal, it falls heaviest on public investors–compared to private investors, they get a bad deal.

Before public investors can solve this problem, they must realize that they have one. This book helps them do that. Next, investors need to support ways to get better deals. This book presents two different, but complementary, ways to do this–two calls for action.

One is to petition members of the US Congress and the chair of the Securities Exchange Commission (SEC) to require that all offering documents of stock disclose the valuation the issuer has given itself. This will encourage issuers to compete for public capital, and that can lead to better deals. The case for this requirement is made in Chapter 16, "Valuation Disclosure."

The other call to action is to promote the Fairshare Model.

By the way, entrepreneurs also face a problem with a conventional capital structure–it links voting power to valuation. For any investment amount, the valuation offered to investors climbs as the proportion of ownership retained by insiders grows. For entrepreneurs, retaining control over their company can be a paramount concern. It is their vision, their baby, after all.

Many of them recognize that their plan may need to change after they raise capital. The original idea may prove too costly. Market conditions might shift. Employee turnover may change what can be accomplished. There are many reasons why a pivot may be called for and sometimes, founders oppose them. Major changes require approval by the board of directors and some may be significant enough that a shareholder vote is called for. Unhappy directors or shareholders may favor management changes.

Entrepreneurs want protection from changes they don't like. With a conventional capital structure, they maintain control by limiting how much money they raise or by increasing the valuation of the company to new investors. The former can lead a company to raise less than it needs. The latter makes it less likely that new investors will make money because later investors may not accept a premium valuation.

These options are unappealing if the business is capital-intense or its expected profitability is low or uncertain. It may be capital intense because a large investment is required for research and development, for manufacturing, or for marketing. Expected profitability may be low for businesses that focus on social good and it may be doubtful for those that are vulnerable to competition.

> "By the time startups are three years old, 50 percent of founders are no longer CEO, and by the IPO fewer than 25 percent still lead their company."
>
> –Noam Wasserman,
> "The Founder's Dilemma,"
> *Harvard Business Review*, February 2008

Founders want to maintain control over a business. To do that, a conventional capital structure requires them to choose between the amount of capital they raise and the attractiveness of the deal they offer investors. To raise what they need, it is tempting for entrepreneurs to use optimistic projections that make the deal look more appealing. The Fairshare Model avoids this tradeoff because it:

- creates an attractive opportunity for IPO investors by not linking valuation to projected performance, and

- decouples voting rights from valuation.

The Fairshare Model

The Fairshare Model is for a company (an "issuer" of securities) that raises venture capital via an IPO. There are two classes of stock. Both can vote, but only one can trade.

I refer to the tradable stock as **Investor Stock**; it is sold to investors to raise equity capital for the company. From a legal perspective, Investor Stock is common stock.

I refer to the non-tradable stock as **Performance Stock**; it is issued to employees, consultants, directors, and others. From a legal perspective, Performance Stock is a senior security–preferred stock.

Investor Stock has at least 50 percent of the voting power, even when it represents less than 50 percent of the total shares issued.

Ability to Trade

- Investor Stock
- Performance Stock

Voting Control (at IPO)

- Investor Stock
- Performance Stock

At the IPO, there is far more Performance Stock than Investor Stock—enough to envision years of robust performance. Even so, as a class, Investor Stock has half the voting power. So even if Performance Stock is 80 percent of total shares, and Investor Stock is 20 percent, Investor Stock has 50 percent of the voting power. Should Performance Stock represent less than 50 percent of total shares, voting is based on issued shares, not class. Therefore, if Performance Stock represents 40 percent of total shares, it has 40 percent of the vote and Investor Stock has 60 percent.

As Performance Stock converts to Investor Stock, employees who keep their Investor Stock (as opposed to selling it) will vote those shares in the Investor Stock class. They will also have voting rights through their Performance Stock.

"Investor Stock" and "Performance Stock" are not legal or technical terms; I use them to aid comprehension. Investors get tradable stock for money—the Investor Stock. Employees get Performance Stock for future performance. Again, a company that adopts the Fairshare Model will likely use its common stock as Investor Stock and preferred stock as Performance Stock.

Based on performance milestones agreed to by the two classes of stock, Performance Stock converts to Investor Stock. There will be variation in how companies define and measure their performance based on:

- industry: software, manufacturing, services, biotech, etc.;
- stage of development: pre-revenue, early growth, late growth, mature, etc.;
- corporate purpose: a socially-conscious issuer may have non-traditional goals such as impact in a location or marketplace;
- geography: countries and regions may favor certain approaches (i.e., what is favored on the West Coast, East Coast and in the Midwest, may differ—and then there's Texas); and
- the personalities of the entrepreneurial team and their investors.

The performance criteria will be stated in an issuer's incorporation document and described in its offering document (i.e., prospectus, registration statement). It can change whenever and however, provided both classes of stock agree to change it.

Ordinarily, an offer to acquire the company must be approved by both classes of stock. Such an event may cause substantial conversion of Performance Stock.

Where the Fairshare Model Is Positioned in Capital Markets

As we begin, it's helpful to establish the positioning of the Fairshare Model in capital markets. The diagram on the following page provides high-level perspective—it shows there are two pathways to improve access to capital for companies—the private sector and government.

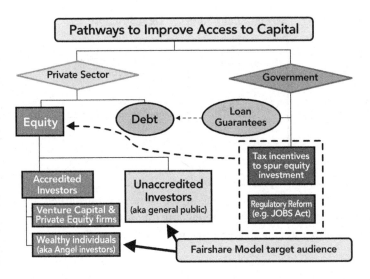

Companies raise capital from the private sector in the form of equity or debt. Stock is issued for equity—shares of stock convey an ownership interest in the issuing company.[1] The value of an equity position grows as the company grows in value. Debt is a loan, but it may be called a corporate bond, promissory note, or royalty agreement. A company is obligated to repay debt, usually with interest. Debt does not have the potential to appreciate the way equity does because debt does not have an ownership interest in the company.

In the US, equity capital is raised from the private sector, in either a private or public offering. Only accredited investors may invest in a private offering, but anyone can invest in a public one. Accredited investors are wealthy individuals or institutional investors, who invest in individual companies—or in venture capital and private equity funds that do so. The Fairshare Model is for an initial public offering, which is available to all investors, accredited or not.

The diagram indicates that capital is available from government, but it is usually in the form of a loan guarantee—rarely debt or equity.[2] Indirectly, government can improve the availability of capital in the private market using tax and regulatory policies.

Next, we'll use a series of charts to drill down to the forms of capital raised in the private sector. The first chart (see following page) presents four characteristics about capital markets. It indicates that:

1. There are two kinds of capital for companies: debt or equity.

2. There are two ways to raise that capital: in a private offering or a public one. Again, only accredited investors can invest in a private offering, but anyone can invest in a public one.

3. Two kinds of companies raise capital:

   a. those with an established operational track-record and profitable, and

   b. venture-stage companies, which are rarely profitable and hard to reliably value. They are startups or companies in a turnaround situation.

4. There are two kinds of deal structures for equity capital: those that provide investors with price protection, and those that do not.

---

[1] Digital tokens can covey ownership interests. This is discussed in Chapter 21, "Blockchain and Initial Coin Offerings."

[2] Government support can also be in the form of grants or contracts. Neither affect a capital structure, however.

Kind of Capital	How Raised	Development Stage	Deal Structure
Debt	Private Offering (accredited investors only)	Established	No price protection; high valuation risk
Equity	Public Offering (open to anyone)	Venture-stage	Price protection; valuation risk mitigated

The following chart shows how a conventional capital structure is positioned. On occasion, it is used to raise equity capital in a private offering, usually when the investors are unsophisticated. It is routinely used in public offerings, however. A conventional capital structure is used for established and venture-stage companies and it offers investors no price protection.

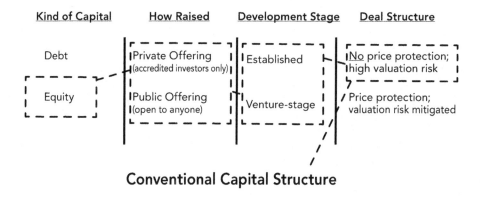

Conventional Capital Structure

The next chart shows the positioning of a modified conventional capital structure. It is used to raise equity capital in a private offering for venture-stage companies using deal structures that provide price protection. I call it the "VC Model" because venture capital funds use it when they invest in a company.

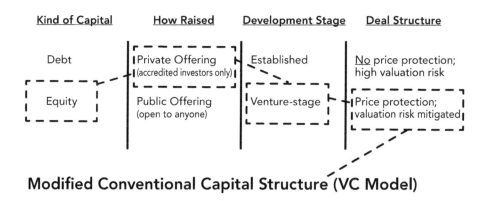

Modified Conventional Capital Structure (VC Model)

The next chart has the Fairshare Model–it is for raising equity capital in a public offering for venture-stage companies, using deal terms that provide price protection.

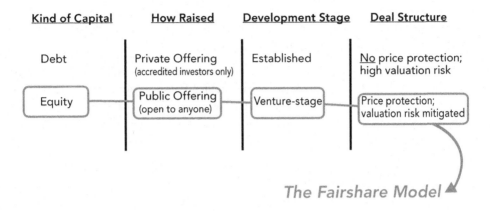

The Fairshare Model

The final chart has the key point–the Fairshare Model applies the VC Model to a public offering.

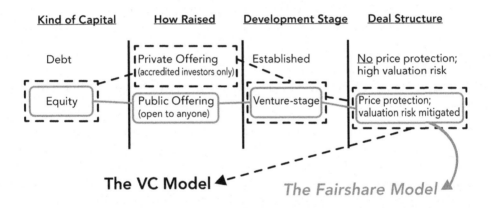

The VC Model *The Fairshare Model*

Chicken vs. Egg

No company has used the Fairshare Model. It's entirely conceptual at this point. I have no anecdotes about how it has worked. What I can tell you is that about twenty years ago, in 1996, I cofounded a company called Fairshare, Inc. that promoted the Fairshare Model, and a plan to implement it. We had some success–a robust website and 16,000 opt-in members–before we slipped under the waves in 2001, in the wake of the dotcom and telecom busts.

I describe my Fairshare adventure in Chapter 9, "Fairshare Model History & the Future." One lesson that I learned is how to address the Chicken vs. Egg conundrum. Companies will adopt a new capital structure if there is an audience for it. Investors want to see companies using it before they get enthusiastic about it.

The movie *Field of Dreams* has a line to describe such a challenge: "If you build it, they will come." In our case, was "it" an opportunity to invest in a specific company that used the Fairshare Model? Or, was "it" an audience of investors interested in the Fairshare Model? Which comes first?

For a couple of reasons, we decided that it was most practical to build the audience first. The most important one was that the kind of companies we wanted to attract could raise capital in other ways. There would be no reason for them to craft an offering using our novel structure before there were investors who liked it. Also, garnering support for an idea *before it is implemented* has an advantage. Once an idea is implemented, attention is directed to the attributes of the implementer itself and away from the concept that inspired the implementation.

All companies have shortcomings so having some become the "poster children" for the Fairshare Model risked making their flaws the focal point, distracting attention from the Big Idea. This issue comes up in politics, which is why politicians prefer to campaign on a Big Idea rather than on a specific proposal—you're more likely to hear "I'm for a balanced budget" than "I want to cut these programs or raise these taxes."

Some suggested another option—persuade venture capitalists and investment bankers to support the Fairshare Model. Well, that would be greeted with the interest that a high-end retailer has for a competing discount store. In fact, when I pitched the Fairshare concept to a prominent San Francisco-based VC in the 1990s, his response was: *"Why would I be interested in THAT?"*

Much has changed since then but not that sentiment, I'm sure. However, fast forward some years from now. Once the Fairshare Model's effectiveness is demonstrated, a new breed of VC is likely to consider using it. It could be to fund a new round for a portfolio company that is a "single or double" in baseball-speak, not a "triple or home run."

It might be to bring in public investors to co-invest. This would limit the amount of capital a VC needs to put up, allow customers to have a piece of the action, and provide liquidity for the VC's limited partners—those who provide the fund's capital. There is similar potential for an investment bank to use the Fairshare Model.

For such things to happen, VCs, investment bankers, and broker-dealers need to see that there is a market for the Fairshare Model and that there is money to be made using it. This will take time and experience, but it will happen, I'm certain, because it is problematic to apply a conventional capital structure to a startup. That's why VCs insist on a modified conventional capital structure when they invest. As public investors become savvier, many will want a better deal too!

So, I lead with an idea because it's all I've got. If enough people visualize the egg, intrepid (not-so-chicken) entrepreneurs will give it a go. A community of experts will grow to help other companies figure out how to make the Fairshare Model work for them. Supportive infrastructure will develop. A self-sustaining community of integrated interests will form—organically, if you will.

How many people are needed to give the Fairshare Model the traction that it needs? Half of a small fraction of those who supported the Occupy Wall Street protests in 2011. There were enough of them to attract wide attention to their dissatisfaction with The-Way-Things-Are. It doesn't take many to spark a revolution—the Boston Tea Party wasn't large either.

When protestors demonstrate (it doesn't matter why), they channel Howard Beale, the fictional television anchor in the 1976 movie, *Network*. One night, Beale snaps. He's enraged that his network is abandoning "hard news" for news that generates high ratings. On a live broadcast, he exhorts his audience to stop being mere observers of the problems that define their existence. In part, he says:

> So, I want you to get up now. I want all of you to get up out of your chair. I want you to get up right now and go to the window.

Open it, and stick your head out, and yell: "I'M AS MAD AS HELL, AND I'M NOT GOING TO TAKE THIS ANYMORE!"

Beale's speech expresses anger and frustration–negative energy. It mobilizes, which is why political campaigns favor negative ads. Ironically, though, negative energy is the opposite of what will turn things around. To build something better, one requires positive energy–optimism, creativity, and cooperation.

I rely on positive energy to solve my chicken and egg puzzle. I use a bit of negative energy because people tend to be more energized by it. At my core, however, I'm a builder, a practical optimist, not a bomb thrower. How many people might have to express interest in the Fairshare Model to get it onto the proving grounds? My guess is 20,000, but it could be less than ten thousand. That could be no big deal. In 2014, a guy raised $55,000 from 7,000 people on Kickstarter to make a potato salad. On the other hand, capital markets are not as easy to change as a potato salad recipe!

If there is investor interest in the Fairshare Model, some companies will try to raise capital using it. Should enough of them have a good result, more will come. That's because there is a connected, worldwide constituency for examples on how to reimagine capitalism, how to support entrepreneurial efforts in ways that promote innovation and opportunity–even social good. Being the social creatures that we are, with the ability to connect over the internet, lessons learned by those who put the Fairshare Model into practice will be absorbed by a larger audience. And those who create wealth for IPO investors and employees using the Fairshare Model will inspire others to try to do so as well.

What's Next?

The next chapter describes the big idea that the Fairshare Model is based on and the thesis of this book.

Chapter 2:

The Big Idea and Thesis

What's Included in This Chapter

- Introduction
- Why I Focus on Valuation
- The Big Idea
- Thesis
- The Macroeconomic Benefit of the Fairshare Model
- The Fairshare Model is Well-Suited for "Fifth Era" Economies
- What's Next?
- Chapter Endnotes

Introduction

This chapter introduces the Big Idea behind the Fairshare Model, that there are two fundamental risks for investors in venture-stage companies—failure risk and valuation risk. It also presents the thesis of the Fairshare Model, which states that it is possible (and desirable for economic vitality) to reduce valuation risk in initial public offerings (IPOs) of companies with high failure risk.

Why I Focus on Valuation

Throughout this book, I emphasize the importance of valuation for public investors. A *Wall Street Journal* article succinctly states why the buy-in—or purchase—valuation deserves to be emphasized. [Bold added for emphasis.]

> An enormous body of academic research has proved time and again that **your long-term investment returns will overwhelmingly depend upon** just two things: asset allocation—how you spread your money between investments like stocks and bonds—and **the value of those investments when you buy them.**

News stories that mention valuation are more common nowadays. Unfamiliar with the term? Don't worry, you'll develop a refined understanding of it as you continue reading.

What is important to know is:

- The valuation for a company is the presumed price to buy it. It is calculated by multiplying the number of shares outstanding by the current share price.

- A valuation is set whenever shares of a company's stock are sold. It doesn't matter whether the stock is sold by the company in a private or public offering or sold by a shareholder to someone else.

- As with anything, there can be a difference between price and worth. Valuation is price, not necessarily worth.

- A conventional stock structure requires a valuation when an equity investment is made.

- *No one* knows how to reliably value a venture-stage company (i.e., a startup).

The Big Idea

In the minds of many, venture capital is associated with venture capitalists—investment professionals who manage funds that invest in private companies.

But venture capital is not the exclusive province of VCs, or their cousins, private equity firms. It can be raised in either a private or a public offering. In fact, Wall Street IPOs are routinely used to raise it. Many technology IPOs are for companies that are unprofitable and rely on new capital to survive. Ditto for biotech IPOs—some are for companies that lack significant revenue.

A central premise of this book is that venture capital is properly defined by the risks presented by the company, not by how it raises capital—in a private or public offering—or by who invests—accredited or average investors.

Venture capital investors face two fundamental risks. The first is that a company will fail to meet operational expectations—failure risk. That is, management says it will do "X" but achieves less than that. It may achieve 90 percent of X, 50 percent of it, or be a complete dud. Anything less than X is a measure of failure.

The second risk is that the investor will overpay for a position—valuation risk. It can happen even if the company meets all operational expectations. Put another way, one can invest in a successful company but lose money (or make less than expected) because the buy-in valuation is too high.

These twin risks underpin all others. Those related to market, technology, and management are but a blend of the two. It is also true for fraud, which is a serving of failure and valuation risk, garnished with false or inadequate disclosure.

> Practice Fusion, a startup in the electronic medical records market, was acquired January 2018 for $100 million, two years after bankers were expecting to take the company public at a $1.5 *billion* valuation.

Failure risk is omnipresent in a venture-stage investment—it can't be eliminated. Investors can mitigate it through due diligence. Once they invest, they might be able to limit it by using oversight—if they have influence. If the company is private, they are stuck with the failure risk. However, if it is public, they can sell their stock.

Valuation risk is different. VCs mitigate it using deal terms that provide price protection by retro-actively reducing their buy-in valuation if it turns out to be too high. Price protection—lower valuation risk—is a terrific idea. It increases the likelihood that investors will profit from an investment in a company with high failure risk.

The problem is that companies only offer it to private VCs, not to public VCs (a.k.a. the general public). Since public VCs buy in at far higher valuations than their private counterparts, they get a bigger dose of valuation risk—a higher buy-in and no price protection.

The big idea behind the Fairshare Model is to reduce valuation risk for IPO investors, to make it more likely that they will make money when they invest in a company with high failure risk. And if that happens, more public investors may take a chance and invest in a startup. Since they are the engine of economic growth and job creation, the Fairshare Model can therefore be good for the economy too.

Thesis

Average investors lack an attractive way to invest in young companies. The opportunity to innovate in this space reveals itself when one considers venture capital from the perspective of public investors. Normally, it is viewed from the perspective of entrepreneurs, VCs, angel investors, and Wall Street firms. But assume the view of public investors and it looks arrestingly different, like the shift from black and white to color that occurs in the classic movie *The Wizard of Oz*.

Make this shift in perspective and the Fairshare Model will be intuitive, even to those who know little about venture capital. Those with knowledge about capital formation will recognize similarities between the Fairshare Model and how VCs construct their deals.

As you contemplate The-Way-Things-Are, a question will form in your mind. *Why are public investors who invest in venture-stage companies treated so unfairly?* Another question will follow. *What can be done to change this?*

The Fairshare Model is an innovation in deal structure that treats IPO investors as venture partners as opposed to inhabitants at the bottom of the capital market food chain. To achieve its goals, it adopts a different approach to IPO valuation. It extends the concept of price protection from the private VC market to the public VC market. To continue with the Oz metaphor, investors must see capital markets *in color* to appreciate this idea, which is what this book will help them do.

Early-stage companies are hard to value because virtually all their value comes from future performance, which is steeped in uncertainty. A conventional capital structure demands that a value be placed on future performance each time new stock is sold. VCs skirt this problem by securing deal terms that retroactively lower their buy-in valuation if expectations are not met. IPO investors don't get a similar deal when they buy shares in a venture-stage company.

For public investors, the risk of buying stock at an excessive valuation has been around a long time, and it will grow due to the JOBS Act of 2012 because more unproven companies will seek capital from them. This risk can be reduced with the Fairshare Model because it eliminates the need to value undelivered performance.

The model was conceived to solve a *microeconomic* problem—how to let public investors invest on terms comparable to VCs. As a by-product, it offers ideas on *macroeconomic* challenges such as slow economic growth and rising income inequality.

> The key question for public investors is: "Would you prefer to invest in a company that uses a conventional IPO model or the Fairshare Model?"

Therefore, the Fairshare Model reimagines capitalism in both a small and large sense. Its challenges rest on human behavior, not technical matters.

For companies, the promise of the Fairshare Model is twofold. First, it will make it easier for them to raise money because they can offer investors a better deal than they could with a conventional capital structure. Second, they will have a competitive advantage when recruiting and managing employees.

The following pages visually present the thesis. They compare the Fairshare Model to a conventional IPO.

The vertical axis in the chart to the right represents a company's valuation, the horizontal axis indicates time and the vertical line is when its IPO takes place.

What drives the rise in valuation that often occurs as a company approaches its IPO? Is it performance?

Or, is it something else?

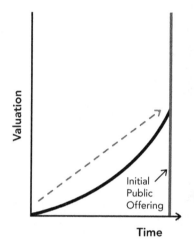

From the perspective of public investors, what is the valuation risk of an IPO valuation? The next chart shows that it can be a good deal if the stock climbs in price. If it remains stable, the investor is unlikely to be pleased. If it falls, the IPO valuation was a bad deal.

All venture stage companies present high failure risk.

When they use a conventional capital structure, they also present new investors with high valuation risk.

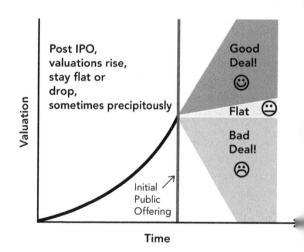

Sonos will attempt to avoid the same fate suffered by fellow hardware companies FitBit and GoPro, whose share prices have dropped 80% since they went public.

—*Business Insider,* August 7, 2018

In this chart, the company has its IPO in its sixth year. However, even if it were sooner, the valuation curve would look similar when a conventional capital structure is used.

That's because companies tend to be valued higher when they are public. So, private companies rise in value as expectations of a public offering heighten.

Note that only investors who meet the accredited investor standard may invest in a private offering.

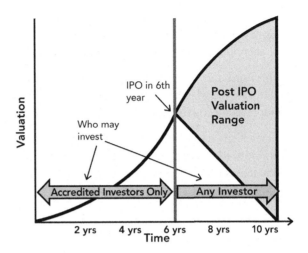

The Fairshare Model encourages venture-stage companies to offer IPO investors a low valuation, the kind a VC might get. In the chart below, the issuer goes public sooner, in its second year of existence, at a much lower valuation.

The reduced valuation risk makes it more likely that IPO investors make money.

If the company performs, the investors and employees share in the increase in valuation.

If it doesn't perform, IPO investors lose less because their buy-in valuation was lower.

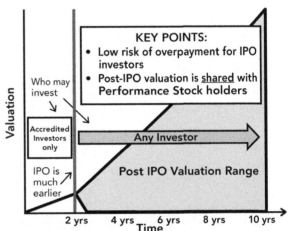

What is the issuer's incentive to offer a low IPO valuation when using the Fairshare Model? One reason is that a well-performing team can wind up owning more of the company than they would if a VC provides the round of capital. Another is that the company can be more competitive in attracting and managing human capital.

The Macroeconomic Benefit of the Fairshare Model

The Fairshare Model does not reduce the *risk of failure* for IPO investors. Rather, it reduces the *cost of failure* when measured by the cost to own a given percentage of a company.

It is analogous to the casino game of roulette. Imagine that each chip represents ownership in a young company. The Fairshare Model does not change the odds that a bet will pay off. Instead, it reduces the cost of a chip. This allows the player to place bets on more numbers for the same money. More bets on startups could pay off in a macroeconomic sense because they are the engines of economic growth and job creation.

The Fairshare Model reduces the cost of a bet because the IPO investor does not pay for future performance when the investment is made. When the performance is delivered, it is shared with employees using the rules that shareholders of Investor and Performance Stock agree upon.

This activity has a less obvious social benefit. Even when ventures fail, they contribute to a risk-taking, innovation-seeking culture. Such a culture is richer, more vibrant, and more productive overall than one that is timid. The national psyche is healthier when it pursues possibilities and accepts failure.

Another benefit of the Fairshare Model is that it's a private sector approach to reduce income inequality because it improves prospects for average investors who invest in a company that uses it. It also enables employees of that company to share more fully in the wealth they create for investors with their money.

Put another way, we live in a time when the return on capital exceeds the return on labor, and this dynamic is unlikely to change. The Fairshare Model addresses income inequality because it provides a vehicle for those whose income is largely defined by the return on labor—employees and average investors—to participate in the higher return on capital.

> "If America is to continue to be the place where ordinary people find stimulation, challenge, novelty, and fulfillment, our business sector will need more dynamism and inclusion than it has shown lately.
>
> "This will require a restructuring of the financial sector to serve business innovation. The tiny band of 'angel investors' and venture capitalists can't do it all."
>
> —Professor Edmund S. Phelps,
> Director of Columbia University's Center on Capitalism and Society,
> and winner of the 2006 Nobel Prize in Economics

The Fairshare Model rethinks capitalism, but it needs your interest, and that of thousands of others to get off the ground.

The Fairshare Model is Well-Suited for "Fifth Era" Economies

There is another way to see how the Fairshare Model fits our times. In their 2017 book, *Build Your Fortune in the Fifth Era: How Angel Investors, VCs, and Entrepreneurs Prosper in an Age of Unprecedented Innovation*, Matthew C. Le Merle and Alison Davis share three observations about today's world.

1. The world's population is larger than ever.
2. Economic activity in the world is higher than ever before.
3. The world is more connected than ever before.

As a result, they say that "addressable markets are larger, and new technologies have the opportunity to capture more profits by serving more people from the moment they launch."[A]

Le Merle and Davis refer to the period we're in as "The Fifth Era," to distinguish it from four earlier ones—the hunter-gatherer, agrarian, mercantile and industrial eras. They say that all of them share four common themes:[B]

1. Disruptive innovations change the essence of the way most people spend their time.

2. New, and very different wealth-creation opportunities surface as economies adjust to new activities that emerge.

3. Wealth-creation does not automatically accrue to the best positioned and most successful players of the prior era.

4. One can see a new era coming and position themselves for wealth-creation, only to discover that prior wealth-creation strategies are less relevant than they were before.

The authors identify a number of Fifth Era characteristics for investors. The ones below are particularly relevant for the Fairshare Model.[C]

• A revaluation of what humans value and what makes us happy.

• The Industrial Era corporate model of organization will be challenged.

• Public capital markets will evolve to address their shortcomings, for example, short-termism.

• Sustainability will become an essential part of doing business, with a clear focus on the broader societal impacts of company strategies, including the quality of jobs, the impact of products and services on society and other external considerations.

• Most innovation will come from small, emerging players, with large corporations being the "go-to market" partners for innovators.

• There will be a global war for talent as regions try to keep their innovators home and attract new ones from elsewhere to strengthen their own economies.

• Traditional philanthropy and the for-profit model will come closer together as non-profits look to adopt sustainable social entrepreneurship models and for-profit corporations aim for outcomes that go beyond profits.

With their book, Le Merle and Davis seek to encourage more accredited households to participate in angel investing. It follows, therefore, that they include this in their list of Fifth Era characteristics.

"Private capital will drive the initial stages of development for most emerging innovations, capturing much of the value of new disruptive innovations."

I have a somewhat different perspective and goal on this one. I agree that private capital is critically important for venture-stage companies, that there is a need for more angel investors, and that attractive wealth-creating opportunities exist for them.

However, I seek to *change* where public capital fits in the venture capital ecosystem. I want to see far more of the value of new disruptive innovations captured by unaccredited investors, and by employees. As that happens, prior wealth-creation strategies of private investors will weaken in relevance.

Aside from that difference, there is congruence between the Fairshare Model and the other Fifth Era characteristics. [Note: Le Merle and Davis authored their book before they knew of The Fairshare Model.]

What's Next?

The next chapter is for readers who think that a book about capital structures will be too difficult or boring.

Chapter Endnotes

Contextual references for material in this chapter appear as numbered footnotes on the page where the reference is made. **Source references** for material in this chapter appear below as endnotes with capital letter identifiers.

A Le Merle, Matthew C., and Alison Davis. *Build Your Fortune in the Fifth Era: How to Prosper in an Age of Unprecedented Innovation.* Fifth Era, 2017. Pages 78 – 79.

B Ibid. Page 14.

C Ibid. Pages 64 – 66.

Chapter 3:

Orientation

What's Included in This Chapter

- Introduction
- Capital Structures as Art
- Why Capital Structures Deserve Your Attention
- Capital Structures and Sex
- Fairshare Model–The Movie
- Summation
- What's Next?
- Chapter Endnotes

Introduction

If you are well-versed in capital formation matters, you'll be intrigued by the Fairshare Model. But, I want to reach people who know little about this subject as well.

Having two dissimilar target audiences places me on the horns of a dilemma. Which one determines how I present the case for the Fairshare Model?

This chapter reassures readers who are new to capital structures that they just might enjoy this book.

If you are familiar with capital structures, you may wish to proceed to the next chapter.

Clearly, capital formation is a large topic, one that interweaves finance, ideas about the economy, competitiveness, and human behavior. Just as a newspaper has one front page, the front section of a book is limited. As a result, I have made judgments on where to place material, and it may not match your interests. If that is the case, graze! The first two chapters and the next two provide foundational material–the material in the other chapters can be consumed à la carte.

Capital Structures as Art

I encourage you to consider capital structures as art, not as an obscure, technical thing that you need special expertise to consider.

I love art, though I have an affinity for some forms over others. For instance, I particularly like sculpture, especially those that portray realism and ideas. When inspired, my father–a tool and die maker by trade–created such works, so I appreciate the skill, sensitivity, and imagination required. I enjoy paintings, too. When I look at a piece in a museum, I first step back from it. Then I shift my position, getting in close, sometimes inches away in order to evaluate the artist's technique–it's a habit that can strike those around me as a bit peculiar. Finally, I take the time to read the placard about the artist's time and life.

In taking this time to *appreciate* art, my accumulated sense of it–history, human nature, and experience itself–is richer than if I view pieces as mere objects. On occasion, this perspective gives me insight into matters wholly unrelated to art. That's because a broad base of reference points–dots if you will–enables me to draw richer connections.

Here is an image that I want you to contemplate.

The investor's simple question suggests others, such as: "What is the valuation of the company?" and "How was it determined?"

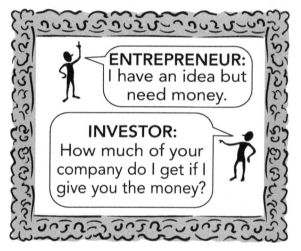

Answer those questions and others emerge. How likely is it that the valuation is unfair to either the entrepreneur or investor? And, if the odds are high, doesn't that cast the answers to the two questions in a new light?

Now, keep going. Assume that time itself is a perspective that you can use to evaluate the question. Might they decide to set the valuation later? That is, after the company's performance can be assessed?

If so, that leads to another question: What issues might that approach raise? That's what this book explores!

Another perspective will come into focus as these questions are considered–fairness.

Companies routinely provide private investors with terms that effectively allow their buy-in valuation to be decided *long after* an investment is made. Should comparable terms be provided to public investors? Or, should they continue to get dramatically worse terms than private investors?

The overarching question is this: How might–how should–one contemplate a capital structure?

If you view the structuring of ownership interests as art, Sister Wendy Beckett has a brilliant answer. Sister Wendy is a British nun. She is also an art critic. Her views on art appear in a series of programs on the BBC. In the US, the Public Broadcasting System (PBS) has a series too: *Sister Wendy's American Collection.*

Here's how Sister Wendy advises one to appreciate art:

I would tell them to go to a museum and look at no more than two or three works, perhaps even two or three taken at random.

- Look at them. Walk backwards and forwards between them.

- Go and have a cup of coffee. Come back again.

- Wander around the museum. Come back again.

- Go to the shop. Buy postcards of them.

- Look again and go home.

- At home, look at the postcards. Borrow from the library books on these artists. Go back again.

Eventually you will find they open up like one of those Japanese paper flowers in water.

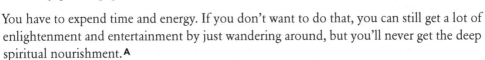

You have to expend time and energy. If you don't want to do that, you can still get a lot of enlightenment and entertainment by just wandering around, but you'll never get the deep spiritual nourishment. **A**

If you invest the time and energy to connect the dots that constitute the ideas in this book with your own experience and news reports, you'll form images that open up like a Japanese paper flower.

> "To see what is in front of one's nose needs a constant struggle."
>
> –George Orwell

You will view capital markets differently, especially if you assume the perspective of a public investor, and that will lead you to ask questions about a company's capital structure such as:

- How is voting power allocated?

- Is stock compensation spread broadly or concentrated in top management?

- Is stock compensation earned by performance or over the passage of time?

- If there are unusual features in the capital structure, who benefits from them?

- Are deal attributes appropriate for the company's stage of development?

- What does the deal structure say about how the company views new investors?

All this is to say that you'll develop an intuitive feel for the Fairshare Model if you contemplate deal structures as an appraiser of art who assumes the perspective of a public investor.

Why Capital Structures Deserve Your Attention

If you are an entrepreneur who needs investors, you spend a lot of time contemplating capital structures. If you are not one, why might you want to pay attention to them?

First, any examination of human behavior can be fascinating, and capital structures reflect how people rank in importance in the minds of those who create them.

Second, the pace of new company formation is positively associated with an inventive, adaptive society. Improving opportunity for new things is good for the economy and makes life more interesting. In his 2014 book, *How We Got to Now,* which was the subject of a PBS television series,[B] Steven Johnson explores how inventiveness led to aspects of life that we now take for granted. Three examples he offers are:

1. For ages, humans were unaware how common farsightedness was (poor close-up vision). The invention of the printing press changed that for it caused people to want to read more. That, in turn, prompted glassmakers to learn how to craft eyeglasses. Lens-making led to telescopes, which made it possible for Galileo to conclude that the Earth revolves around the sun, which was a monumental change in perspective. Conventional thinking was that the sun (and all else) revolved around the Earth.

2. Urbanization first led to waste of all kind being disposed on city streets. Sewers were invented to move sewage, but they also contaminated water supplies with the bacteria that cause the deadly disease, cholera. Discovery of how cholera spread led to water treatment technology that makes dense city living possible without the threat of this disease. That technology led to ultrapure water refinement, something needed to make the electronics that defines our modern lives.

3. The invention of air conditioning made it possible for vast areas in the southern US to be comfortably habitable. This encouraged older people, who tend to prefer warmth and often favor more conservative politics, to migrate to southern and western states. Political maps were thus arguably transformed, at least in part, as the result of air conditioning.

The dots that Johnson connects show how innovation in one area can ripple elsewhere, altering society in profound ways. He observes: "We make our ideas, and they make us in return."[C]

The Fairshare Model is an innovation that balances and aligns the interests of capital and labor. If it becomes popular, what changes might it effect in the decades to come?

> "Learn how to see. Realize that everything connects to everything else."
>
> —Leonardo da Vinci

> "Eventually everything connects—people, ideas, objects—the quality of the connections is the key."
>
> —Charles Eames

Capital Structures and Sex

If I haven't yet inspired you to explore capital structures, let me try a classic Madison Avenue strategy to get your interest. Sex. Seriously! It works for beer and cars.

If you were to ask people at random to define a capital structure or describe aspects of capital formation, the conversation would likely resemble a person-on-the-street interview about sex and sexuality in the 1950s, before the dawn of the sexual revolution.

Back then, sex education consisted of a talk about "the birds and the bees," a phrase so indirect that it conveys *nothing.* What was thought to be "understood" turned out to be based on ignorance, hearsay, and poor research. The perspective of heterosexual men framed *the entire matter.* Female sexuality was largely an undiscovered and ignored concept, and homosexuality was a forbidden zone. This is the lens through which our popular understanding of capital formation is seen, for it is significantly influenced by traditions that are convenient for those who benefit from The-Way-Things-Are.

Back to sex and sexuality. Think about where we are with it nowadays. Discussions are franker, information is better, and attitudes are broader. Consider how life changed as women asserted their interests. Look at how much has changed in the US regarding marriage; couples are no longer expected to share a religion or ethnicity–they can even be the same sex. Marvel at how the Roman Catholic Church has evolved in its acceptance of gays and lesbians.

Those changes are the result of *ideas*–not physiology or technology. There was just a willingness to look at something familiar from an unfamiliar perspective.

Now, take the concept of change through ideas–change that results from a new perspective–and view capital formation as sex between a company and its investors. Here, "conception" requires agreement on valuation and the determination of one is routinely referred to as an "art." I've heard it promoted as a "black art," which is as transparent as "the birds and the bees."

The process used to set a valuation is described in such an obscure way for four reasons:

1. No one knows how to do it "right." No method or process is inherently best.

2. There is no intrinsic value to a startup; that destination is as mythical as Camelot.

3. An assessment of what others might pay is central to the process. That means a valuation reflects opportunism. That is, *perceived* value is important, since it is so difficult to assess actual value. This leads some to consider it impolite to discuss valuation–they shun frank talk about it just as some avoid discussion about sex.

4. Dressing up valuation with mysticism inspires awe and discourages questions. Similarly, shamans rely on mysticism when they proclaim how the stars, moon, and sun foretell events.

Capital formation is, more than anything else, about perspective, not science. It takes place in a variety of ways. Furthermore, when discussing valuation, it is not unusual to hear executives describe the needs of public investors as a secondary consideration that is less important than their needs, or those of their pre-IPO investors. Such a perspective is reminiscent of how classic 1950s-era males talked about sex–their needs and desires were more important than that of women.

Today, popular knowledge about capital formation is comparable to what it was about sex and sexuality in the 1950s. That's where this book comes in. I aspire to enhance popular understanding of venture capital just as a 1969 book by David Reuben improved understanding of sexuality: its title, *Everything you always wanted to know about sex* (*but were afraid to ask)*.

The precursor of the 1960s sexual revolution was *information*. Researchers like Alfred Kinsey, William Masters, and Virginia Johnson broke ground by asking, from a medical perspective: "What is going on here?" Writers, musicians, and filmmakers asked that question from a cultural perspective. Information and discussion converged into waves of change that profoundly altered social conventions. It wasn't always easy, and it was often downright uncomfortable.

Like dating, capital formation is rife with awkwardness. Entrepreneurs are uneasy asking for capital and investors are uncomfortable when asked to provide it.

It is easier to talk about products, markets, and management teams (the dating equivalent of long walks on the beach, talking about pets, and how close you are to your parents) than to get to the point of valuation (In 1950s date-speak, "wanna make out?" In the 70s, it was "get down." Nowadays, "doing it").

Thankfully, when it comes to capital formation, change is occurring. For instance, college graduates have traditionally aspired to secure jobs in large companies, but that allure has dimmed. Now, it is acceptable, even laudable, to plan to join or launch a startup. Some young people even aspire to become venture capitalists, "the new superhero of the modern world." Both factors promote curiosity about how entrepreneurial ambition mates with capital from investors.

There are other signs. Over the past two decades, angel investors have grown in number and organized themselves in ways once hard to imagine. Business incubators and accelerators now pepper the landscape. Companies have executives whose responsibility it is to encourage innovation. Universities offer courses—even degrees—in entrepreneurship, innovation, and social networking. People from a range of backgrounds see opportunities outside of large corporations, consulting firms, and government. "Disruptive" has acquired a positive connotation, when not long ago it was principally associated with something undesirable.

In 1963, Bob Dylan released a song about the gathering winds of change: "The Times They Are A-Changin'." The theme applies today. The internet, blockchain technologies, and new business models are bringing disruptive change to financial services; "Fintech" is the term used to capture it.

Technology, in the form of the birth control pill, also played a powerful role in the sexual revolution.[1] In an essay in *Time* magazine, Nancy Gibbs put it this way:

> The 1950s felt so safe and smug, the '60s so raw and raucous, the revolutions stacked one on top of another, in race relations, gender roles, generational conflict, the clash of church and state—so many values and vanities tossed on the bonfire, and no one had a concordance to explain why it was all happening at once.

> Thus did Woodstock, caked in muddy legend, become much more than a concert, and leaders become martyrs, and the pill become the Pill, the means by which women untied their aprons, scooped up their ambitions and marched eagerly into the new age.◻

Change has roiled our times—and it will keep on coming. In capital markets, it feels like 1960, when the Pill was approved. Our ability to discuss sexuality has come a long way since the 1950s, and the Fairshare Model makes a similar call to get valuation out of the closet and secure better terms for public investors. The discussion that ensues will have ramifications for how companies are financed and how ownership interests are set.

Most people would agree that the women's movement has been good for men and families, even when it has posed challenges. A movement to promote the interests of public investors similarly promises to be good for entrepreneurs and society at large, though it will, of course, have its own set of challenges to conquer.

Changing The-Way-Things-Are always involves challenges. It has been observed that *"Change occurs when the pain associated with doing things differently is less than the pain of continuing*

---

1 The birth control pill was approved for use in 1960.

to do it the way it's been done." That suggests that public investors should channel Howard Beale (he is mentioned in Chapter 1). That is, they should make their discontent known so clearly that venture-stage companies think twice about whether they are offering public investors an attractive deal with their IPO.

I propose positive energy to effect change in capital markets. Help develop a better way. Reformulate the observation above to *"Change occurs when the advantage of doing things differently is greater than the challenge of doing it the same way."*

How can you help create the positive energy that effects change in capital markets?

- Talk about the Fairshare Model.

- Help identify ways to make it work in industries and communities you care about.

- When companies adopt the Fairshare Model, consider investing in *them* and be a supportive shareholder.

- Support a valuation disclosure requirement for companies when they offer stock to investors.

Capital formation is undergoing profound changes that will ripple into parts of socio-economic life that affect you and people you care for. Even if you have little interest in the subject now, this book will prepare you to engage in the lively discussions that lie ahead.

How? Simply follow Sister Wendy's advice.

Take a look.

Walk away.

Come back.

Repeat.

Fairshare Model—The Movie

Finally, if I were to pitch the Fairshare Model to a movie producer, I'd need a simple story. A good one has a hero, a villain, and conflict. Here is what I would say:

The slumbering hero in this story is the Middle Class. For just over a century, he has been growing, coming into his own. His quality of life steadily improved until the 1970s, when its foundation began to weaken. He has felt better at times, but his decline has progressed and become more apparent to him. He feels anxious. The options he sees deaden his spirit and dull his expectations for the future.

The conflict in this story is the lack of a promising solution, and our hero regards this with two minds. He can appeal to his community to change how resources are shared (though this creates discord), or he can create a new solution. His internal struggle is to re-discover his pluck, and his ability to change the world around him.

The Fairshare Model covers an early part of the hero's journey, not the full story. Here, he learns that he has a latent power to shape capital markets by asserting his interests. Exercising this power has risks, and it requires him to develop new skills. The hero has self-doubts, but the potential to overcome them energizes his spirit as he searches for ways to use his developing power. Some of his optimism flows from the recognition that he may be able to help his entire community.

The villain in the story is The-Way-Things-Are-Done-Now, an immensely large and powerful ogre known as a conventional capital structure—but it has a key weakness.

The dramatic question is "What will our hero do?"

It may sound a bit crazy to use a Hollywood storyline to describe a book about capital structures, but I suspect that you'll come to agree that the comparison is apt as you contemplate what's really going on. You'll get a sense of it in Chapter 5, "The Problem with a Conventional Capital Structure."

Summation

Even if you are unfamiliar with capital structures, your confidence that you can understand them can be bolstered by the recognition that they are as much an expression of philosophy and human behavior as anything else. Hang in there with me!

What's Next?

The next chapter covers a broad range of questions about the Fairshare Model.

Chapter Endnotes

Contextual references for material in this chapter appear as numbered footnotes on the page where the reference is made. **Source references** for material in this chapter appear below as endnotes with capital letter identifiers.

A "Meet Sister Wendy." PBS. Accessed May 07, 2018. fairsharemodel.com/SisterWendy.

B "How We Got to Now." PBS. Accessed May 07, 2018. fairsharemodel.com/Now.

C Genzlinger, Neil. "Just History, Not Common and Not Core." Oct. 14, 2014, *The New York Times,* fairsharemodel.com/Johnson.

D Gibbs, Nancy. "The Pill at 50: Sex, Freedom and Paradox." *Time*. April 22, 2010. Accessed May 08, 2018. fairsharemodel.com/Pill.

Chapter 4:

Fairshare Model Q&A

What's Included in This Chapter

- Introduction
- What Is a Public Offering?
- How Expensive Is a Public Offering?
- What Is a Direct Public Offering?
- What Is Venture Capital?
- What Is a Venture-Stage Company?
- Is the Fairshare Model "Equity Crowdfunding?"
- Is the Fairshare Model for Average Investors?
- What Is a Company's "Valuation?"
- What Is a Capital Structure?
- What Is a Class of Stock?
- Investor Stock, Performance Stock – What Are These Names?
- What Is a Conventional Capital Structure?
- What Leads a Capital Structure to Change?
- What Does Complexity Contribute to a Capital Structure?
- Is a Stock Option that Vests Based on Performance the Same as Performance Stock?
- Who Gets Performance Stock?
- How Might the Fairshare Model Affect an IPO Valuation?
- Has the Fairshare Model (or Anything Like It) Been Used Before?
- Must Securities Laws Change to Make the Fairshare Model Work?
- What Is the Attraction of the Fairshare Model for Public Investors?
- What Kinds of Companies Might Want to Use the Fairshare Model?
- What Appeal Does the Fairshare Model Have for Pre-IPO Investors?

- What Is the Bargain Between a Fairshare Model Issuer and Its Investors?
- What Is the Bargain Between the Company and its Workforce?
- How Does a Stock Option Compare to an Interest in Performance Stock?
- How Does Restricted Stock Compare to an Interest in Performance Stock?
- Can a Company that is Already Public Adopt the Fairshare Model?
- What Tax and Accounting Issues Does the Fairshare Model Raise?
- What Challenges Does the Fairshare Model Face?
- Fairshare Model Principles
- What Constitutes an "Equitable" Split of Voting Power?
- What's Next?
- Chapter Endnotes

Introduction

Conceptually, the Fairshare Model is simple and intuitive, but it has myriad facets. So does a conventional capital structure. Few of us contemplate them, though, because we don't sense an alternative. But the Fairshare Model presents one! In a question and answer format, this chapter covers a broad range of questions you may have about capital structures.

What Is a Public Offering?

What constitutes a public offering? Surprisingly, the question isn't always easy to answer. It can be like asking whether a food should be labeled "organic." In many cases, it is obvious, but sometimes it isn't.

Regulators sometimes rule that an offering that a company feels is private is, effectively, public. Or a private offering can cause an issuer to be subject to rules for public companies based on the number of shareholders it has. Apart from what regulators say, some people feel that a "real public offering" must be a minimum size and sold by a broker-dealer—and underwritten by an investment bank. They feel that a small offering *sold directly, by the issuer, to public investors* (a.k.a. direct public offering or DPO) isn't a "real IPO" even when it literally is the company's initial offering of stock to the public.

Securities law and practices are complex, and industry jargon often fails to convey clear meaning. From a lay perspective (I'm not an attorney), *a public offering has three basic qualities.*

First, a public offering has **disclosure requirements:** regulators seek to ensure that things an investor ought to consider are disclosed. For example, financial statements, risk factors, and other disclosures are required for a public offering. Private offerings have no such requirements. Why? Securities law presumes that anyone wealthy enough to be an accredited investor is smart enough to protect their interests. Some people assume that a public offering must meet a quality standard. They believe that securities regulators only allow promising companies to sell stock to the public; that they are like food and drug regulators. In truth, the US Securities and Exchange Commission and many states enforce a disclosure standard. The presumption is that if a company clearly discloses sobering aspects of its business, investors will not be misled. A former SEC examiner summarized the idea to me this way: "You can sell stock in a dead horse...so long as you disclose that it's dead!" All states apply the disclosure standard, but some apply a "merit review" standard too; they might not allow stock in a dead horse to be sold to its residents.

Second, securities in a public offering may be legally **sold to anyone in the US.** That requires the offering to be registered with the relevant regulators or qualify for an exemption from registration. Large offerings are registered. Small ones often rely on an exemption that has less rigorous requirements. The foundation of US securities regulation, the Securities Act of 1933, authorized the first exemption, befittingly named Regulation A, known as "Reg. A" for short. Before the JOBS Act of 2012, this form of offering could be used to raise up to $5 million in what some call a "mini-IPO." The JOBS Act increased the limit to $50 million, causing it to be renamed "Reg. A+." A new exemption is Rule CF, the equity crowdfunding rule, which went into effect in 2016. It allows an issuer to raise up to about $1 million in a public offering with unaudited financials, provided they are reviewed by an independent accountant.

Third, securities sold in a public offering may be **resold to anyone in the US.** Those sold in a private offering may not be resold, at least not to non-accredited US investors—it is possible to resell them to either an accredited or foreign investor. Of course, one may have the *right* to resell but have trouble finding a buyer, which investors in small-cap stocks often discover.[1]

How Expensive Is a Public Offering?

The cost of a public offering varies based on the complexity of the disclosures, the amount of money to be raised and how the stock will be sold. Companies that raise capital via a Wall Street IPO often spend millions for legal, accounting, commissions, printing, and a road show to pitch the deal to large investors.

A public offering can be completed for far less, however. The internet allows an issuer to save on selling expense, which can run from 6 to 15 percent or more of an offering, by enabling them to directly reach investors. Legal and accounting expense can be modest for startups if they have little history to disclose. For a simple, newly formed company, the cost of a direct public offering might begin at $35,000. Issuers that have been in business longer, or have complex matters to disclose, will spend more for legal and accounting work. The minimum annual cost to be a small public company can be $300,000 to $800,000. That covers legal, accounting, and audit work, as well as director and officer insurance and the pay premium for employees who can handle such responsibilities.

It takes time, money, effort, and skill to attract investors. That's why issuers hire broker-dealers; they have relationships with investors that issuers lack. What does it take for an issuer to find investors? Having a pre-existing relationship with them is incredibly valuable—they can include customers or a community of supporters. It also takes money. Darren Marble, CEO of CrowdfundX, a Los Angeles-area crowdfunding marketing firm, recommends that issuers spend five percent of the offering size to promote it. That is, $50,000 per $1 million offered or $500,000 to raise $10 million.

---

[1] Stock sold by a company using Rule CF is subject to resale restrictions for a year. Effectively, Rule CF is a private offering that is open to anyone, but the shares become publicly tradable after a year.

Generating investor interest in an offering can be expensive; a company must create awareness as well as comfort. The Fairshare Model has the potential to ease the cost of that for two reasons:

1. As investor interest in the Fairshare Model grows, there will be a deal-centric affinity group eager to see offerings that use it.

2. Prospective investors will be comfortable with a Fairshare Model IPO because the issuer:

   a. demonstrates confidence in its ability to perform,

   b. offers a low IPO valuation, and

   c. has a unique, powerful tool—Performance Stock—to attract and motivate the employees it will need to build value for investors.

What Is a Direct Public Offering?

Traditionally, companies hire a securities broker-dealer—sometimes referred to as an investment banker or underwriter—to market their offering to investors. They do that for the reasons someone with real estate hires a real estate broker-dealer to sell it. A broker-dealer has greater access to buyers and experience in selling. It can also be legally paid a success fee or commission.

A direct public offering (DPO) is a public offering that is directly sold to investors by the issuer, without a broker-dealer. It's akin to a home owner putting up a "For Sale by Owner" sign. The selling effort is similarly challenging for a company selling stock, but it is easier given the internet and the investment portals that began to operate in 2015. A DPO can be an initial or a secondary public offering.

What Is Venture Capital?

Venture capital investing is popularly construed to be the exclusive province of institutions and wealthy individuals who invest in private offerings. I define it more broadly; as an *investment in a venture-stage company, be it private or public.*

A foundational concept of the Fairshare Model is that capital provided to a venture-stage company is venture capital regardless of its source; it doesn't matter if it is supplied by accredited or average investors.

Put another way, *whether or not an investment is venture capital is a question of What, not Who.* That is, it is decided based on whether the company presents venture-stage risks, not by who invests.

Raising venture capital in a public offering wasn't always popular with investors—it was viewed as too risky. That mindset began to change in the 1970s. Since then, it's no longer odd to see a company raise venture capital via an IPO.

What Is a Venture-Stage Company?

A venture-stage company has the following risk factors:

- Market for its products/services is new or uncertain.
- Unproven business model.

- Uncertain timeline to profitable operations.

- Negative cash flow from operations; which means *it requires new money from investors to sustain itself.*

- It expects to continue to have negative cash flow from operations; its future depends on its ability to raise more money later.

- Little or no sustainable competitive advantage.

- Execution risk; the team may not build value for investors.

Venture-Stage Deals

Many public companies list such risk factors in their offering documents, so unaccredited investors have been public venture capitalists for decades!

Therefore, the pertinent question isn't whether average investors should be allowed to be venture capitalists. It's whether they should get the type of deal that wealthy investors get in a private offering! (The discrepancy is the subject of Chapter 5, "The Problem with a Conventional Capital Structure.")

Is the Fairshare Model "Equity Crowdfunding?"

The Fairshare Model is not "equity crowdfunding" as you may understand it. In the US, the term refers to a public offering that qualifies under SEC Rule CF. Such an offering, which can be up to about $1 million, may be sold directly by an issuer, by a broker-dealer, or through a funding portal. It also has lower disclosure requirements; for example, audited financial statements may not be required. But that's not new—small public offerings with reduced disclosure requirements have been authorized for years; a Small Company Offering Registration (SCOR) has been available in many states for decades. Rule CF breaks new ground by allowing someone other than the issuer, or a broker-dealer, to market shares (i.e., a funding portal).

Thus, equity crowdfunding is best understood as an innovation in the *distribution* of stock. In contrast, the Fairshare Model is an innovation in the *structure* of stock.

A company that adopts the Fairshare Model can distribute its shares like a conventional offering; the Fairshare Model does not innovate in how stock is sold. Furthermore, it is not limited in offering size—the Fairshare Model can be used to raise $100 million or more. There are only *two defining attributes* to a Fairshare Model offering. One is that the issuer is a venture-stage company. The other is that it is used to raise capital via an IPO.

> The success standard for many crowdfunding enthusiasts is "how much money was raised?"
>
> It should be "are investors well-positioned to make money?"

How innovations in distribution differ from innovations in substance is illustrated in these analogies.

- In food, highly processed products are conventional, while fresh, minimally processed food is an innovation in substance. Farmer's markets in urban areas are an innovation in distribution.

- Netflix began as an innovator in how movies are distributed. It began by delivering DVDs by mail, then added internet streaming. Now, it also innovates in substance, creating original content, which was once the exclusive domain of movie and television studios.

- Tesla Motors innovates in substance: electric cars. It also seeks to innovate in distribution by selling directly to customers, outside the dealer franchise model that dominates the auto industry. Interestingly, some states do not allow manufacturers to sell direct to consumers—they require the use of dealers.

Another way to draw a distinction is that the Fairshare Model emphasizes valuation protection for IPO investors while creating incentives for employees to deliver the performance investors expect. Equity crowdfunding is all about making it easier for companies to sell shares to non-accredited investors—there is no emphasis on making deal structures more investor-friendly.

Is the Fairshare Model for Average Investors?

The Fairshare Model is for average investors, but not exclusively.

Philosophically, the interests of average investors inform everything about the Fairshare Model. It is designed to make investments in venture-stage companies more appealing to them by making it more likely that they will make money. By necessity, the vehicle is an IPO because companies are restricted from selling stock in a private offering to non-accredited investors.

That said, the Fairshare Model is not just for average investors. It could be used in a public offering sold exclusively to wealthy investors. The model simply adapts concepts that are common in private offerings to an IPO. Each company that adopts it will decide to whom it will sell its shares.

What Is a Company's "Valuation?"

Valuation is the price to buy the entire company, given the price of its stock. If the price of a share is $1 and the company has one share outstanding, its valuation is $1. If there are ten million shares outstanding, its valuation is $10 million. As Chapter 14, "Calculating Valuation," shows, the figure is calculated differently when just a fraction of the company—a share of ownership—is for sale.

The central question this book raises is whether IPO investors pay a price that is too high. It is convention to include the value of future performance in the price. Put aside the fact that it is hard to figure out what that should be. If it's convention, why is that an issue? Because venture capital firms, who invest before the IPO, get deal terms that protect them from that value being set too high. IPO investors don't get similar protections, and that's unfair. Then too, public investors buy in at much higher valuations than VCs. So, they are more likely to overpay for a position.

The Fairshare Model doesn't present a better way to value future performance at an IPO It says, don't even try to project it; assign no value to it. Instead, figure out how to reward actual performance.

This idea will be explored in depth. For now, just bear in mind that (a) valuation is price, and (b) price is not necessarily worth. You already know and apply this insight when you evaluate the price of things you regularly buy. You may, however, be unfamiliar with how to apply it to investing in companies.

There is a little secret you'll come to appreciate as you progress through this book. *No one,* no matter what their experience or credentials are, knows how to reliably value a venture-stage company. But those who are savvy know that deal terms can provide protection from buying in at an excessive valuation.

What Is a Capital Structure?

A capital structure defines how financial interests in a company are ordered. It refers to the mix it has of debt and equity financing. Capital market theory considers how the mix may affect its market value. In this book, I use the term more narrowly, to describe how equity interests are structured.

If a company is a corporation, its incorporation document defines roles in governance matters and the rights of every class of shareholder. That document is to a corporation what a constitution is to a nation and shareholders must approve changes to it using the rules set forth in the incorporation document.

The document's name varies by where the corporation is legally formed or domiciled, but *articles of incorporation* is a common term. If there is ligation that involves shareholders, the lawsuit will be heard where the company is incorporated, even if it is headquartered elsewhere. In October 2015, more than half of publicly traded US companies were incorporated in the state of Delaware, but very few had significant facilities there.[A]

What Is a Class of Stock?

When a company has a single class or type of stock, it's typically called common stock. One might expect shareholders in such a company to adopt the "all for one and one for all" motto from Alexandre Dumas' novel, *The Three Musketeers*, because all have the same rights in proportion to how much stock they control.

Frequently, however, a line from George Orwell's book, *Animal Farm*, best captures a capital structure: "All animals are equal, but some animals are more equal than others." That is, some shareholders have special rights. It's common in private companies but happens in public ones too.

If some shareholders are to have special rights, a unique class of stock must be created for them. One might say their shares are *un*common. Indeed, a class of preferred stock is usually created for them, but it could be separate class of common. It doesn't matter what it is called, it just needs to be distinct from what others have. A capital structure becomes more complex as the number of classes increases, because each class is likely to have different rights.

When there are multiple classes of stock, they vary in rank or seniority. All members within a class are treated alike, but rights vary by class. Think of a ship where the quality of passage–and possibly access to lifeboats–reflects a passenger's class–senior classes have superior ability to protect their interests. Classes of stock can have similar effect.

Investor Stock and Performance Stock – What Are These Names?

Again, I use these names to aid comprehension. They are not legal or technical terms. Investors get Investor Stock, which is tradable, for money or other consideration. Employees get Performance Stock for future performance, which is not tradable. Performance Stock converts into Investor Stock based on the performance milestones that both classes agree to.

That concept is what is important, not what the classes of stock are called. Name-wise, a company that adopts the Fairshare Model may

- refer to its common stock as "Investor Stock" and preferred stock as "Performance Stock," just as I do;

- give its common stock and preferred stock the qualities described but not refer to them at all as Investor and Performance Stock; or

- have two classes of common stock (e.g., Class A and Class B), one for investors, the other for employees that acts like Investor Stock and Performance Stock.

In the basic version of the Fairshare Model, both classes have equal voting rights at the IPO, even though there will be many more shares of Performance Stock than Investor Stock. However, voting rights could be defined differently. Founders, for example, could have preferential voting rights if investors accept it.

The defining quality of the Fairshare Model is not about voting rights, it's that IPO investors do not pay for undelivered performance.

What Is a Conventional Capital Structure?

In their best-selling book *Freakonomics,* Stephen Dubner and Steven Levitt write that famed economist John Kenneth Galbraith coined the term "conventional wisdom" to describe a convenient and comfortable point of view. They add that is often false.

There is conventional wisdom about how to organize ownership interests in a corporation. One bit of conventional wisdom is the notion that a venture-stage company should be valued substantially higher when it is public than when it is private. Another is that public investors should not get price protection, even though private investors do.

> A conventional deal structure is the nemesis of the Fairshare Model,
> which is decidedly unconventional with respect to IPO valuation.

The defining quality of a conventional capital structure is that a value must be set for future performance when a company issues new stock. For example, assume that I form a new company and sell you half of it for $1.00. Implicitly, we agree that my future performance is worth $1.00. Put another way:

My share (50%) + Your share (50%) = Total ownership (100%)

or

My idea ($1.00) + Your money ($1.00) =   Value of the company

after you invest ($2.00)[2]

---

[2] It may help to recognize that you break even if we sell the company for $2.00 – I get half for my idea and you get half for your investment.

The problem is that neither of us knows if my performance will be worth $1.00. It could be worth nothing, $0.05, $0.10, $0.50 or more than $1.00. Add zeros to the amounts to make them more realistic–the principle remains. *A conventional capital structure demands that the parties set a value for future performance when an equity investment is made, and this is hard to do in a reliable manner.*

You might ask, isn't that the way it must be? Mustn't investors and a company agree on a value for future performance when an investment is made?

The answer is no–for two reasons. First, investments can be structured to defer a valuation. This is discussed in "Ways to Defer a Valuation of Startups" in Chapter 13, "Valuation Concepts."

Second, in a private offering of equity, *savvy investors get price protection.* How this is done is covered in the next chapter: "The Problem with a Conventional Capital Structure."

For now, just know that there are three basic capital structures for equity:

1. A *conventional capital structure,* which requires that a value be placed on future performance at the time of an equity investment. It has a single class of stock.

2. A *modified conventional capital structure,* which provides certain shareholders with price protection. It requires multiple classes of stock, one for each investment round. If there are four rounds, for instance, the company will have five classes of stock; the one sold to employees and the four that are sold to investors.

3. *The Fairshare Model capital structure,* which places no value on future performance at the IPO–it uses a multiclass capital structure.

Public companies generally use a conventional capital structure. However, a trend is emerging among hot technology companies to use modified conventional structures for their IPO. But these modifications do not provide valuation protection; rather, they create super-voting power for some pre-IPO shareholders.

The inspiration for this comes from Ford Motor Company. When it prepared to go public in 1956, Henry Ford and other shareholders wanted to both create wealth for themselves and maintain control of the company. They accomplished this with a dual-class stock structure. Class A common stock was sold to the public and Class B super-voting common stock–which was entitled to special dividend income–went to insiders. In 2010, the holders of the Class B stock held 2 percent of all the Ford shares but controlled 40 percent of the votes.[B] If that strikes you as unfair, consider that Ford was a profitable and growing company at its IPO; there was no question about its future ability to perform.

When it went public in 2004, Google was an unprofitable challenger to the dominant search companies, so its future performance was less assured than Ford's, but it also adopted a dual class structure. The Class A stock it sold to the public had one vote per share while some pre-IPO shareholders got a Class B common stock with ten votes per share.

LinkedIn, Groupon, Yelp, Zynga, and Facebook followed with similarly structured IPOs. Ever the innovator, Google created Class C common shares in 2014 with no voting rights at all! I call it "silent partner stock," and it demonstrates the flexibility issuers have when setting a capital structure. By the way, at that point, Google's founders controlled more than 55 percent of the vote despite owning only 15 percent of the total shares.[C]

The apogee of this trend for insiders–and the nadir for public investors–may be Snap's February 2017 IPO that raised $3.4 billion selling a stock with zero voting rights![D] It raises the question,

"What is a stock?" Classic thinking holds that it is an ownership interest and that owners have a say in corporate governance. That idea may be quaint if investors continue to buy stocks that have no voting power.

Perhaps we should not view equity as necessarily representing an ownership interest. Rather, we should merely say that a stock has a residual claim on net assets upon liquidation of a company. And, that it may have the ability to trade in the market.[3]

Multiple classes of stock can provide equal rights for each class (separate but equal) but they usually grant *super-rights* to some classes (separate and unequal).

The Fairshare Model uses multiple classes to balance and align the interests of IPO investors and employees. The classes are designed to be "separate but equal" rather than "separate and unequal." Chapter 8, "The Tao of the Fairshare Model," describes how it is done.

What Leads a Capital Structure to Change?

Capital structures evolve. They become more complex as the issuer accepts investments on terms that differ from what prior investors have. On occasion, a capital structure is transformed. A liquidity event–an IPO, being acquired or dissolved–is the principal reason.

No transformation occurs when a company with a conventional capital structure has a liquidity event because everyone has the same stock–common–before and after the event.

How a Conventional Capital Structure Transforms at IPO or Acquisition

Before IPO or acquisition
Common stock

New investors (if IPO)

At close of IPO or acquisition
If IPO, the common stock of issuer. If acquisition, the acquiring company's common stock.

But if that company has a Fairshare Model IPO, its capital structure will change when it closes on the IPO. It will divide its common stock into two sets. Stock issued to investors or to employees for delivered performance will remain common stock (Investor Stock). Stock issued for future performance will be reissued as a preferred stock (Performance Stock).

Conventional Capital Structure Transforms to Fairshare Model

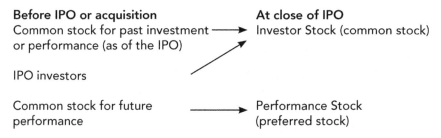

Before IPO or acquisition
Common stock for past investment or performance (as of the IPO)

IPO investors

Common stock for future performance

At close of IPO
Investor Stock (common stock)

Performance Stock (preferred stock)

---

[3] Digital tokens, the things sold in an initial coin offering are similar in this regard–they can trade but often have zero voting rights. This is covered in Chapter 22, "Blockchain and Initial Coin Offerings."

Many private companies, certainly the ones with VC or PE investors, have a modified conventional capital structure; employees have common stock and each round of investors have a distinct class of preferred stock. Simultaneous with the close of an IPO or a deal to be acquired, the preferred classes convert into common stock based on the deal terms. If there is an IPO, new investors also get the common stock. If there is an acquisition, the consideration paid is divvied among shareholders.

Modified Conventional Capital Structure Transforms at IPO or Acquisition

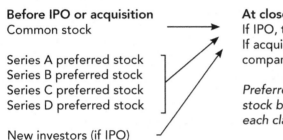

Before IPO or acquisition
Common stock

Series A preferred stock
Series B preferred stock
Series C preferred stock
Series D preferred stock

New investors (if IPO)

At close of IPO or acquisition
If IPO, the common stock of issuer. If acquisition, the acquiring company's common stock.

Preferred stock converts to common stock based on the deal terms for each class.

Deal terms can profoundly change the percentage allocation of total shares. They can result in a set of investors with, say, twenty percent of shares before a liquidity event, having a majority of the shares when the event occurs. It can happen if the investors have a liquidation preference with a high multiple.

A modified conventional capital structure will transform differently for a Fairshare Model IPO. The common stock will be divided into shares earned for actual performance and shares for future performance. Shares for future performance will be reissued as Performance Stock (preferred stock). Shares issued for actual performance will be Investor Stock (common stock). The preferred stock held by pre-IPO investors will be reissued as Investor Stock based on terms they agree to.

Modified Conventional Capital Structure Transforms to Fairshare Model IPO

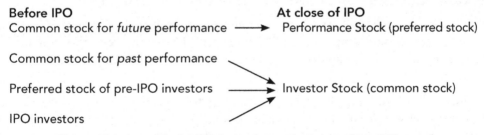

Before IPO
Common stock for *future* performance

Common stock for *past* performance

Preferred stock of pre-IPO investors

IPO investors

At close of IPO
Performance Stock (preferred stock)

Investor Stock (common stock)

Since a Fairshare Model IPO is an alternative to a private VC round, an issuer is likely to have fewer classes of preferred stock to convert.

If a Fairshare Model issuer accepts an offer to be acquired, a transformation is required to divvy up the shares or cash to be paid the acquirer. The question will be: "How much Performance Stock (preferred stock) should convert to Investor Stock (common stock)?"

The determination will be made by the two classes of shareholders, guided by the conversion rules they agreed to. This topic is discussed in Chapter 7, "Target Companies for the Fairshare Model."

For now, just understand there are four sources of Investor Stock at the time of an acquisition:

1. Investor Stock outstanding after the close of the IPO
   (i.e., what is issued to pre-IPO and IPO investors,
   plus what is issued to employees for pre-IPO performance),

2. Investor Stock sold *after the IPO*
   (i.e., stock option exercise, secondary offering),

3. Investor Stock issued due to pre-acquisition conversions
   of Performance Stock, and,

4. Performance Stock that converts based on acquisition price.

Fairshare Model Transforms When Issuer is Acquired After IPO

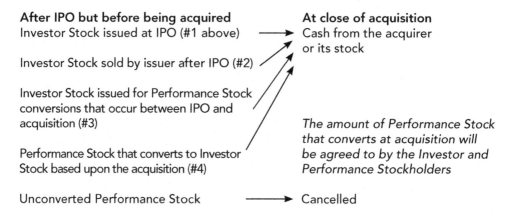

After IPO but before being acquired
Investor Stock issued at IPO (#1 above) ⟶ **At close of acquisition** Cash from the acquirer or its stock

Investor Stock sold by issuer after IPO (#2)

Investor Stock issued for Performance Stock conversions that occur between IPO and acquisition (#3)

The amount of Performance Stock that converts at acquisition will be agreed to by the Investor and Performance Stockholders

Performance Stock that converts to Investor Stock based upon the acquisition (#4)

Unconverted Performance Stock ⟶ Cancelled

What Does Complexity Contribute to a Capital Structure?

A multiclass capital structure allows a company to treat some shareholders differently than others, which can be a good thing. Employees and investors have different interests; then too, there are differences in interests among employees (i.e., founders vs. non-founders) and among investors (i.e., early vs. later).

The downside of a complex capital structure is that it can be more difficult to assess the economic positions of the classes. That's because claims to a company's value is defined by the rights accorded to the different classes of stockholders, not by their share ownership percentage. In other words, you might think that a class of shareholders that owns a quarter of the shares in a company valued at $100 million would have a position worth $25 million. But that could easily be wrong. If there is a liquidity event that causes all shares to convert to the same class, the terms for that class could result in a position that is quite different.

Complexity can obscure reality, but the benefits of complexity can outweigh the negatives. If that were not the case, complex capital structures would not be popular.

The real question is: who benefits from the complexity? It's notable that multiclass structures are routinely used to protect the interests of investors in private offerings, but rarely, if ever, to protect the interests of investors in public offerings. The reasons are explored in the next chapter: "The Problem with a Conventional Capital Structure."

The Fairshare Model uses complexity to benefit IPO investors. The goal of that complexity is stated in the first chapter: *to foster a self-renewing cycle for public venture capital, one that benefits entrepreneurs and both pre-IPO and IPO investors.*

Contemplate what was just described, the transformation that occurs in the capital structure of a VC-backed private company at IPO. The preferred stock held by investors converts to the common stock held by employees, the same stock public investors buy.

That company, when going public, would mimic the Fairshare Model if it:

- registered its preferred stock (the one held by pre-IPO investors) instead of registering its common stock for trading with the SEC;

- sold new preferred stock to IPO investors to raise capital; and

- allowed the unregistered/non-tradable common stock held by employees to convert to the tradable preferred stock based on performance.

The Fairshare Model is no more complex than how private companies are financed. What makes it conceptually different is that IPO investors are the prime beneficiaries of the complexity.

Is a Stock Option that Vests Based on Performance the Same as Performance Stock?

No. A stock option is not a stock, it is a contract to sell a stock. As such, an option does not have voting rights or rights to residual asset value. Performance Stock does.

Who Gets Performance Stock?

Each company will decide how to divvy up interests in its Performance Stock. It can be distributed narrowly or broadly to employees; just to management or among the entire workforce. Pre-IPO investors and/or strategic partners might get some. It can also be issued to contract employees and consultants.

Companies are likely to use dynamic equity splitting—a way to reward actual contributions to performance over time. The opposite is a static or fixed equity split, where awards are set before work is performed. Fixed splits routinely rely on vesting provisions to help protect the employer from making an award that is overly generous.

In his 2012 book, *Slicing Pie: Fund Your Company Without Funds,* Mike Moyer describes a model for dynamic equity splitting among employees of a startup that can't pay market value for work. He points out the problem with a fixed equity split: It is impossible to reliably predict the value of an employees' work before it is delivered. He says attempts to do so are based on "estimates, rules of thumb, industry standards (i.e., this role normally gets X%), darts, guessing…." Such methods are likely to deliver results that are unfair in the minds of employees. That can foster a toxic environment, one where employees want to renegotiate the split, which makes work less fun or rewarding.

Moyer calls his alternative approach "Slicing Pie"–it provides a way to compensate employees based on the market value of their actual contributions. It assumes that all contributions of time, money, ideas, relationships, facilities, supplies, or anything else should be compensated fairly. Here is an example of how the Slicing Pie model credits interest in the equity pool:

- The base rate for the equity pool is 1 unit for every dollar of salary paid per month (i.e., 1,000 units for every $1,000 paid).
- Credit for foregone compensation is double what is earned for paid salary.
  - ◦ Example: Say an employee who can earn $8,000 a month elsewhere is paid $5,000; they sacrifice $3,000 a month to work at the startup. Each month, the employee is credited with 5,000 units for salary paid (i.e., $5,000 times 1 unit) and 6,000 units for below-market pay (i.e., $3,000 times 2 units)–a total of 11,000 units in the equity pool for compensation.
- Equity pool units are earned for ideas, based on what they turn out to be worth.
- Credit can be provided to non-employees too. For example, to a landlord for cheap rent or to a supplier for assistance.
- Units are earned for expenses paid on behalf of the company. They can have a multiplier rate higher than 1, like foregone compensation.

The Slicing Pie model focuses on the bootstrap phase of a startup's existence–it terminates once it is paying fair value in money for contributions. However, I think it offers a good framework for a Fairshare Model issuer to use to allocate interests in its Performance Stock. It is a rational, practical model for how to allocate equity among employees fairly over time. There are sure to be other ideas, for example, awards based on votes by those in the Performance Stock pool.

What is the role of a leader?

The principal responsibility of a CEO is to *"be the Chief Meaning Officer. To let everyone in the place know where you are going, why you are going there, and most importantly, what's in it for them to get there with you. People like to talk about where they are going, why they are going there. But they always leave out the third thing."*

–Jack Welch, former CEO of General Electric

How Might the Fairshare Model Affect an IPO Valuation?

Virtually all companies use a conventional capital structure when they have an IPO and their goal is to get the highest IPO valuation it can. This maximizes the cash raised for a given percentage of ownership, or alternatively, minimizes how much of the company must be sold for a set amount of money. And, of course, maximizing the valuation maximizes the wealth of pre-IPO shareholders and the prospective wealth of employees with stock options.

If the company has investment bankers, their valuation goal is somewhat different–to balance the interests of the issuer with those of the investors they gather to buy the IPO shares. Their solution is to get the issuer to accept a valuation that the bankers feel is 15 to 20 percent below what will be sustained in secondary market trading.

Regardless of whether an issuer sells its IPO directly to investors—a direct public offering or DPO—or through broker-dealers, when it uses a conventional capital structure, the expected value of future performance accounts for most of the valuation.

A Fairshare Model issuer will approach the matter quite differently. It will not factor the value of future performance into IPO valuation, as no Investor Stock is issued for it. Indeed, if a rise in the market capitalization is a measure of performance, company management will want to give IPO investors a low valuation.[4] Crazy low. For example, if the valuation of comparable companies is $100 million, a Fairshare Model issuer may go public at a valuation of $10 million. Secondary market investors are likely to bid the price of Investor Stock up if they see it as undervalued. If that happens, Performance Stock will convert.

The eventual market value of an issuer may be lower than that of comparable enterprises, reflecting a discount for potential dilution from conversions. On the other hand, it may be higher, reflecting a premium for a remarkably motivated and focused workforce.

The valuation for a Fairshare Model IPO will not affect how much money is raised. In this example, the issuer can raise the same amount at an IPO valuation of $10 million as it can if it is $100 million. Also, voting power is decoupled from valuation. Performance Stock has voting power, but it doesn't affect the market cap because it can't trade. With a conventional capital structure, there is a direct relationship between voting power of employees and the valuation—the greater the percentage of employee ownership, the higher the valuation.[5]

One thing is certain about the Fairshare Model; public investors are better positioned to make money than with a conventional capital structure. Here are two reasons why:

1. The value of uncertain future performance is baked into the valuation of a conventional IPO. With the Fairshare Model, it's not.

2. Employees that work for a Fairshare Model issuer have greater incentive to perform, which makes it more likely that investors will profit.

Has the Fairshare Model (or Anything Like It) Been Used Before?

Not in a way that benefits average investors. However, the underlying concept of the Fairshare Model, price protection, is not new. It has been the bedrock of private equity transactions for decades.

For example, when a VC or private equity investor likes a company, a principal concern is that the buy-in valuation will turn out to be too high. Thus, they require price protection, in the form of terms that can retroactively reduce their share price if the company fails to perform as expected.

Acquirers—companies that purchase other companies—also rely on this concept, albeit in different forms. One is an earn-out clause, which allows a seller to get a higher price if the company performs well after it is acquired (i.e., price protection for the seller). Another form is a claw-back clause, which allows a buyer to recover some of the price agreed to at acquisition if the seller's company does not perform well enough (i.e., price protection for the buyer).

---

[4] Valuation being the number of shares of Investor Stock outstanding times the IPO share price.

[5] The direct relationship between employee voting power and valuation can be altered by a multiclass stock structure, which enables a modified conventional capital structure.

So, the idea of price protection is well-accepted. What makes the Fairshare Model novel, even radical, is that it extends the concept to public investors.

Must Securities Laws Change to Make the Fairshare Model Work?

No securities laws must change for the Fairshare Model to work. It would be helpful, though, if regulators require issuers to disclose the valuation that they give themselves in an offering. This would help investors be more valuation-savvy and encourage issuers to offer better deals. Valuation transparency would cause IPOs based on the Fairshare Model to be conspicuous in the market because more people would know that they offer superior value. Chapter 16, "Valuation Disclosure," describes the importance of such a requirement and how you can help make it happen.

What Is the Attraction of the Fairshare Model for Public Investors?

I've described the two fundamental risks that venture-stage investors face—failure and valuation. The attraction of the Fairshare Model for public investors is that it greatly reduces valuation risk.

Fairshare Model issuers will offer IPO investors a relatively low valuation, which increases the likelihood that they will make money. Over the years, as the number of Fairshare Model IPOs grows, it will be easier for investors to reduce failure risk in their venture-stage portfolio by diversifying their holdings; studies have shown diversification reduces overall risk and improves returns, even when all of the investments are high risk.

Potentially, Investor Stock will be less susceptible to "pump-and-dump" schemes by unethical promoters. They occur when a stock, often a thinly traded one, is hyped on behalf of those with stock they want to sell. Often, pump and dumpers get cheap stock as an incentive to promote it in the marketplace. Owners of Investor Stock pay market price when they buy or earn it via Performance Stock conversions. Arguably, they are inclined to be in for the long-term, not be flip-oriented. Put another way, stock promotion is all about short-term expectations while the Fairshare Model is about long-term performance. Since actual performance will result in Performance Stock conversions that dilute the position of Investor Stockholders, there is less incentive to hype expected performance.

What Kinds of Companies Might Want to Use the Fairshare Model?

Companies that seek an alternative to a VC round and are prepared to raise it via an IPO will be interested in the Fairshare Model. Some of them will not like VC deal terms. Others will have poor access to VC money. But all will be confident in their ability to perform.

Undoubtedly, all will sense benefit from having Performance Stock to attract and motivate employees and possibly from broadly distributing their equity to customers. In addition, their executives will see public investors as partners, just as those who raise private capital see VCs as partners. Too often, companies see public investors as targets; Fairshare Model issuers will certainly not.

The categories of companies that will be drawn to the Fairshare Model are discussed in Chapter 7, "Target Companies for the Fairshare Model." I call one type a "Feeder," it aspires to be acquired. SmartThings, Inc. was such a company. In 2012, it raised $1.2 million using rewards-based crowdfunding and leveraged this support to raise $16 million in equity from VCs. In 2014, Samsung acquired SmartThings for $200 million. Oculus VR charted a similar course. In 2012, it raised $2.4 million in reward- and contribution-based crowdfunding, then raised $91 million from VCs before being acquired by Facebook for $2 billion in 2014.

There will be companies that believe they can parlay an early IPO into a handsome gain for investors in such a manner. For them, the appeal of the Fairshare Model will be that insiders can have more control, and the opportunity to own a greater share of the wealth, than they would with VCs. They will share equity with their public supporters, something neither SmartThings nor Oculus VR did.

Another factor may make the prospect of a VC-led private round less alluring to entrepreneurs—"most CEOs are fired or leave their position between raising VC money and the eventual IPO of the firm."[E] Research by Harvard Business School professor Noam Wasserman indicates that "by the time startups are three years old, fifty percent of founders are no longer CEO and by the IPO, fewer than twenty-five percent still lead their company."[F]

What Appeal Does the Fairshare Model Have for Pre-IPO Investors?

Pre-IPO investors may like the Fairshare Model because their company can get capital on better terms. When a VC-backed company struggles, the position of some investors may be squeezed—reduced or even eliminated. That doesn't happen with the Fairshare Model; investors are diluted by positive developments—employees performing. There is also the appeal of a liquidity option; investors can sell enough shares to recovery their investment and hold the rest as an upside.

What Is the Bargain Between a Fairshare Model Issuer and Its Investors?

If the company performs, investors will be diluted *on a percentage basis*—their slice of the ownership pie will be reduced. If the performance is good, they will experience heavy dilution. *On an economic basis,* however, if the performance translates into a higher valuation, investors will not suffer dilution, they will have a smaller piece of a more valuable company.

VCs like to say: "I'd rather own a small slice of a big pie than a large slice of a small pie." It's the same idea.

What Is the Bargain Between the Company and its Workforce?

In addition to their salary, employees may have an interest in their employer's Performance Stock. When they perform well enough as a team, they earn Investor Stock.

How Does a Stock Option Compare to an Interest in Performance Stock?

A stock option is a contract; the right of an employee to purchase shares in the future at a set price. It is not an issued security, as Performance Stock is, and has no voting rights or claim on the company's assets.

A Fairshare Model issuer can grant options on its Investor Stock. They are more likely to pay off for employees than if the company has a conventional capital structure because, at the IPO, Investor Stock is not priced to include future performance, which makes it likely that it will appreciate, if for no reason other than that secondary market traders anticipate performance.

Stock options can attract and motivate employees. They work when employees believe the value of the company will climb. They don't work well if they sense it will take an Act of God to keep the stock at its current price, let alone increase it. Ironically, that's when a company most needs motivated talent.

An over-valued stock eventually falls in price. If it levels off below an option's exercise price, it is worthless as an incentive. In the argot of finance, it is "underwater." When this happens to enough employees, companies reset the exercise price of the affected options to the lower market price. Investors may resent this because they can't reset the cost of their position, but there isn't an acceptable alternative; workers are likely to leave if their options are unlikely to pay off.

This is a fundamental problem with stock options; it is hard to align the interests of investors and employees, especially when the company's stock price is volatile. The alignment problem stems from the valuation problem—no one knows how to reliably value a venture-stage company.

By avoiding the valuation problem, the Fairshare Model avoids the investor-employee misalignment problem.

Obviously, investors want the price of their stock to go up in value. Employees may too, but they don't control the price. The premise of an option plan is that the stock will appreciate if employees perform well. Work that logic back and you have an incentive program that is tied to increasing the stock price. It doesn't work when a company is overvalued or when its stock is falling. (See "Employee Stock Options" in Chapter 21, "Game Theory.")

Another way to understand the alignment problem is that options promote a *direct* connection to what employees have no control over, and an *indirect* connection to what they do influence— operational performance. If a direct solution is more effective than an indirect one, options that vest over time provide less employee motivation than options that vest based on performance. The former *indirectly* links reward to profitability while the latter does so *directly*.

This indirect linkage creates inefficiencies that intensify once a company is public. Employees at newly public companies are routinely urged to focus on their work, not their prospective wealth. It can be a hard message to get across since the relationship between one's work and the stock price is fuzzy. Another reason inefficiencies increase is that the stock price is typically higher after a company is public and new grants, which are pegged to that price, often have less payoff potential. Nonetheless, employees with options at a high exercise price are expected to work as hard as those with low ones.

Valuations often get ahead of actual performance.

Startups known as "unicorns" exemplify this, but it happens with "horses" (established companies) and "ponies" (ordinary startups) as well.

With that understanding, let's look at how stock options "vest." That word describes how employees earn the right to exercise the option to buy the stock at an old price. By and large, they vest over three to five years of employment[6] and must be exercised before employment ends (or shortly thereafter) or the option is canceled.

Performance Stock doesn't vest, per se. It is issued, subject to terms set by the company, which could include its right to repurchase the shares under circumstances like a cessation in employment. Then

---

[6] Stock options that vest based on performance tend to be issued to senior executives.

again, it could be that an employee does not lose Performance Stock when they leave the company. An issuer could have more than one class of Performance Stock, with one going to founders and another for other employees. There might be a class for pre-IPO investors and another for suppliers. How Performance Stock is administered will vary and it isn't important at this point—investor support for the Fairshare Model is.

The question here is: How does a stock option compare to an interest in Performance Stock? The answers below show important differences and similarities.

- Performance Stock votes, stock options don't.

- Stock options generally vest over time. Performance Stock can convert on this basis too.

- Stock options can vest based on performance, but they usually don't.

- An array of measures can cause Performance Stock conversions—the price of Investor Stock, operational achievements such as product release, financial measures like sales and profit, the price paid if the company is acquired, and even measures of social good.

- Options tend to be granted to a small fraction of a company's employees. Performance Stock programs are likely to cover more of them.

- To exercise an option, an employee must buy the stock from the employer at the exercise price. No purchase is required when Performance Stock converts, however. That's because the Performance Stock, which is senior to the Investor Stock, is already issued. The Performance Stock is purchased at the close of the IPO by employees or a trust designated by the company to administer it. The price is so low as to be free, like stock sold to founders. Employees will appreciate not being required to buy stock if they are about to end their employment. If they are laid-off, for example, using cash that would provide a safety net to exercise an option creates stress. If they choose not to exercise their option, the incentive that motivated them to work as hard as they did, possibly for below-market pay, vaporizes—they get nothing for it.

- Companies become increasingly stingy with options once they are public; they pay more in salaries and benefits to motivate employees, the opposite of what investors want.[7] Fairshare Model issuers have reason to broadly distribute interests in Performance Stock and doing so may make employees less likely to seek generous pay and benefits, as it may hamper their collective ability to meet profitability measures that trigger conversions.

The "secret sauce" of the Fairshare Model is its potential to help companies out-compete other companies for human capital and to encourage their employees to work collaboratively to meet performance goals.

A company that uses it can say to them: "If we, as a team, deliver the performance that our Investor Stockholders expect, you will get shares of Investor Stock." Thus, the Fairshare Model encourages the feelings associated with being part of a team with common purpose, regardless of what the stock price is.

---

[7] Once public, they favor stock purchase programs that allow employees to purchase tradable stock at a discount from the market price which, again, focuses attention on stock price.

How Does Restricted Stock Compare to an Interest in Performance Stock?

Restricted stock is stock that is issued but cannot trade until the restrictions are released. Like stock option vesting, this may be a function of time or achievement of goals. Voting rights may or may not be restricted—there is no uniform answer. To answer the question, let's assume the restricted shares enjoy full voting rights but are restricted from trading.

There are similarities in the way restricted stock and Performance Stock align the interests of investors and employees. Both provide voting rights while denying liquidity until certain conditions are met. How is Performance Stock different from restricted stock? There are three ways:

1. The timing of investor dilution for future performance differs. With restricted stock, investors buy in at a valuation that assumes no restrictions as it's the same class of stock that investors have. Whatever the criteria to remove the restriction, valuation wise, it's assumed to be met before it is delivered. With the Fairshare Model, the buy-in valuation does not assume future performance because the employees have a different, non-tradable class of stock. Should Performance Stock convert, an investor's ownership percentage is diluted, after the investor invests.

2. Restricted stock is generally issued only to senior executives. Interests in Performance Stock are likely to be distributed broadly, possibly to all employees, and even to contractors, suppliers, and strategic partners.

3. Psychologically, there is a difference. Restricted stock becomes tradable when its restrictions expire—it may be a passive act. Performance Stock converts when conversion criteria are met—it is likely to be an active act. Tone-wise, the inertia is different. Restricted stock requires a company to say: "You didn't earn it" to the grantee to alter course. With a Performance Stock conversion, the company says: "You earned it!" when a conversion occurs. The former has negative energy while the latter has positive energy.

Another way to look at this is to realize that the two approaches have different purposes. Restricted stock solves a compensation challenge—but it doesn't make an investment more appealing as the valuation assumes the restrictions will come off. The Fairshare Model makes a company more appealing to IPO investors. Its approach to compensation is a by-product of this, not the main goal.

Therefore, if you consider this question simply in terms of compensation, a case can be made that restricted stock is an alternative way to achieve what the Fairshare Model can.

Can a Company that is Already Public Adopt the Fairshare Model?

It isn't obvious how a company that is already public would adopt the Fairshare Model because tradable stock has already been issued for future performance. To make it work, ownership granted for future performance would have to be separated into one class of stock from ownership granted for capital and actual performance. That would be like trying to separate a beaten raw egg into yolk and white.

Pre-IPO, it is easy to separate the two, especially if a modified conventional capital structure has been used. That's because investors and employees already have separate classes of stock—employees have common and investors have preferred. The challenge will be to allocate the common stock issued to employees into two categories—shares issued for actual performance would get Investor Stock while the balance would be converted to Performance Stock.

What Tax and Accounting Issues Does the Fairshare Model Raise?

The tax and accounting implications of a capital structure rarely are of interest to investors. However, the Fairshare Model faces issues worth mentioning. How they are resolved will affect its acceptance by companies. Tax matters are the most important as they affect the pockets of employees. I'm most concerned about how the Internal Revenue Service will view these three issues.

- The cost of Performance Stock will be so miniscule as to be free, like the common stock that is issued to founders. When Performance Stock converts into Investor Stock, will gains realized from selling that Investor Stock be taxed at a low capital gain rate or at the higher rate for ordinary income?
  - General partners typically provide just one percent of the capital in a venture capital firm and earn at least twenty percent of the profit on its investments, which is called their "carried interest." The IRS treats this income as a capital gain, even though it is earned by the labor of the general partners, not their capital. To be fair, those who profit from converted Performance Stock should get similar treatment. Call it "carried interest for employees."

- Will the IRS rule that the increase in value that occurs when Performance Stock converts to Investor Stock is taxable income? Or, will it rule that it is taxable income when the Investor Stock is sold?
  - It will be a fatal blow to the Fairshare Model if employees earn income when their Performance Stock converts. That's because employees will be pressured to sell their Investor Stock right away to have money to pay the tax. This will cause founders to reject the Fairshare Model—they will not want a capital structure that discourages them and other employees from being long-term shareholders.
  - The conversion of a senior security to a junior one is often non-taxable. So, if an issuer constructs its Performance Stock to be senior to Investor Stock, it seems unlikely that the IRS will view it as a transaction that creates taxable income.

- Will the purchase date of Performance Stock establish the acquisition date for converted Investor Stock or will the conversion date be the acquisition date?
  - An investor who owns a stock at least a year has any gain taxed at the taxpayer's long-term capital gain rate. If it is sold within a year, it is taxed as ordinary income, which can be at a rate that is nearly twenty percent higher.
  - There is reason for the IRS to set the purchase date for Investor Stock as the date the employee acquires the underlying Performance Stock. This would mean that employees whose Performance Stock converts after years of work will be taxed at their long-term capital gain rate, even if they sell it immediately.
  - If Performance Stock is bought by a trust that administers interests in it for employees, will an employee's purchase date be when the trust acquires the Performance Stock or when the employee earns an interest in it?

The accounting questions center around the guidance auditors will apply to Performance Stock transactions. Complex accounting standards exist for stock-based compensation. It applies to employee stock options, restricted stock, stock warrants, and other securities. Using these rules, an estimate of the potential gain is recognized as a non-cash expense on the issuer's income statement.[8]

When applied to a Fairshare Model issuer, it is possible that these rules will result in an enormous charge—again, a non-cash expense—that is surprisingly large, for two reasons.

1. The company will have enough Performance Stock issued to cover potential performance for a long time—say, ten years beyond the IPO. That's a lot of shares!

2. If the performance that generates conversions increases the value of the company, the price of Investor Stock will increase, which will increase the estimated value of future conversions.

The details of the expense calculation are unimportant here. What is? Awareness that the Fairshare Model could result in so much stock-based compensation expense that a company that uses it may *never have income* using generally accepted accounting principles or GAAP. Some companies may find this prospect unappealing or dislike the prospect of having to explain to readers of financial statements how it is possible that it is performing well enough to have earnings-based conversions while its audited financials show that it is losing money.

There is reason to believe this will not be a big deal, however. That's because no one seems to pay attention to stock-based compensation expense. In earnings calls with stock analysts, public companies focus on non-GAAP measures of profitability that exclude it. Creditors do the same thing when evaluating a company's creditworthiness. I have yet to identify anyone who benefits from a disclosure of stock-based compensation expense other than the valuation, software, and auditing firms that earn fees to measure and opine on it.

The accounting rule arose from political pressure in the 1990s. The idea was that companies would be less likely to lavishly compensate executives with stock options if doing so made the company less profitable. At the same time, accountants argued there was real value to stock options and the like because if there wasn't, companies would not offer them. And, they added, this value wasn't captured in financial statements.

The development of mathematical models to estimate the value of put and call options in the secondary market—the Black-Scholes model—led to a confluence of support to require recording an expense for stock-based compensation in audited financial statements.

It didn't curtail excessive executive compensation. And it didn't make financial statements more useful—virtually every serious reader of one makes a pro-forma adjustment to remove the expense. Thus, the sole effect of the rule is counterproductive—a costly toll levied on companies that issue stock-based compensation and need audited financial statements.

The Fairshare Model may do a better job of containing executive compensation that doesn't correlate with performance. It will certainly improve the ability of all employees to benefit from stock compensation. Both these outcomes are sure to be welcomed by politicians who support the accounting requirement. However, the appeal of the Fairshare Model will be hindered if those rules lead to financial results that are expensive to measure and hard to explain.

---

[8] Depreciation of fixed assets and amortization of intangible assets are other forms of non-cash expense.

What Challenges Does the Fairshare Model Face?

Broadly, there are three challenge phases for the Fairshare Model.

The initial one is to establish that there are many investors who would consider investing in a company that adopts it. Before companies think about how to make the Fairshare Model work for them…

A LOT of you need to make a little bit of noise…

…like, like, well…

…like the tiny residents of Whoville in Dr. Seuss's children's book *Horton Hears a Who!* [9]

That means many voices are needed to create some significant buzz.

You—yes You, Dear Reader—can cause others to take note and join in.

People who like the Fairshare Model must combine their small voices and shout…

We Are Here!

We Are Here!

We Are Here!!

We Are Here!!!

---

[9] In the story, Horton the elephant hears a small speck of dust talking to him. He discovers that it is actually a tiny planet, home to a microscopic community called Whoville, where the Whos reside. The Mayor of Whoville asks Horton (who, though he cannot see them, can hear them with his large ears) to protect them from harm, which Horton agrees to do, because "even though you can't see or hear them at all, a person's a person, no matter how small." Other animals in the jungle ridicule him for believing that there is anyone on that speck of dust because they are unable to see or hear them. The animals cage Horton and threaten to drop him in boiling oil if he does not drop the speck of dust into it. Horton tells the Whos that they need to make themselves heard to the other animals. The Whos accomplish this by **ensuring that all members of their society play their part in creating enough noise** to be heard by the other jungle folks. Convinced of the Whos' existence, Horton's neighbors vow to help him protect the tiny community.

In other words, Main Street investors must first promote the Fairshare Model because Wall Street bankers and K Street lobbyists are not going to.

The second challenge is to fine-tune the Fairshare Model. This will be done by entrepreneurs, attorneys, angel investors and others with expertise in capital markets, corporate governance, compensation, tax, and financial reporting. Many types of people will contribute.

The big questions that must be addressed are the "Ponderables," some of which are listed below.

- How might performance be defined?
- Who should define performance?
- How might it be measured?
- Who should measure it?
- How should the rewards of performance be allocated?
- Who should administer the Performance Stock, and how?
- What might be the tax and accounting implications of the Fairshare Model?

The best answers to these questions will emerge from discussion and experience. Finding them will reveal beguiling thoughts about how to square human nature with the Fairshare Model. It will be a playground for researchers in decision science, behavioral finance, and organizational development.

America's founding fathers engaged in similar discussions as the structure of government was debated. These pathfinders sought an alternative to dynastic, feudal forms of government. Their first product was the Articles of Confederation, which proved to have serious flaws—its strong state-model inhibited the ability of the states to function in a united form.

The Federalist Papers, a series of pamphlets written by James Madison, Thomas Jefferson, and John Jay fed public discourse on how to redefine the structure into what emerged. In 1788, twelve years after the American Revolution began, James Madison described the central challenge of defining a stronger central (federal) government:

> But what is government itself, but the greatest of all reflections on human nature?
>
> If men were angels, no government would be necessary.
>
> If angels were to govern men, neither external nor internal controls on government would be necessary.
>
> In framing a government which is to be administered by men over men, the great difficulty lies in this: you must first enable the government to control the governed; and in the next place oblige it to control itself.**G**

Therefore, the third challenge for the Fairshare Model will be time and experience.

The product of the founder's second round of deliberations was the US Constitution. Yet, they didn't get it right when it was first drafted, as witnessed by the number of times it was amended—*ten times before it was ratified* and more than thirty times since. One measure of how difficult it is for people to produce a set of durable rules that fits their needs and the times they live in is that there have been more than 11,500 proposed Constitution amendments.

The time it takes to define rules does not cover the challenge of applying them. Again, the Constitution is instructive. Over the years, there has been conflict over how to apply its meaning—as a strict constructionist or through interpretation of what the founders might intend if presented with a contemporary situation.

The founders of the American experiment had admirable character and remarkable fortitude. The entrepreneurial teams that first adopt the Fairshare Model will surely have similar qualities.

For the Fairshare Model to gain widespread acceptance, pacts comparable to those between the government and the governed must be formed between investors (the providers of capital), and the providers of labor (management and others). It must make money for both—more than a conventional model.

Sustaining goodwill among these groups is **the central challenge** for companies that adopt the Fairshare Model. It will be harder for a large company, where constituencies are diverse, than for a startup, where common interests are easy to identify. Early implementations of the model may reveal flaws in its approach to "government." If so, fixes will be adopted, as flaws in the Articles of Confederation were corrected by the Constitution, as amended.

Also, there will be variations on the Fairshare Model, just as there are variations on a conventional capital structure and variation in how capitalism and democracy are practiced. Ultimately, it will present a laboratory to study human behavior and variation in organizational behavior.

Reaction to the Fairshare Model from a prominent Silicon Valley securities attorney

"I think your [Fairshare Model] concept is very interesting. My first reaction was, and still is, that it is not us (corporate and securities lawyers) who you need to convince, but investors. Besides the investors, you also need to find the companies that want to be forerunners – always hard to find.

"Everything in venture capital, or corporate finance for that matter, is about not re-inventing the wheel. Investors want stability more than new approaches. Further, venture capital as an investment class is not a very innovative industry, in my mind. You find a lot of cookie cutter people out there who are afraid to step outside a 'normal' Delaware C-Corp capital structure, even when it makes sense. I think you may find more interests from hedge fund folks.

"Anyway, very interesting work!"

Fairshare Model Principles

The five principles that guide the Fairshare Model are:

1. **Wealth Creation, Not Wealth Transfer:** Corporate insiders don't become wealthy because public investors supply the venture capital. Rather, they become wealthy by delivering performance.

2. **Valuation:** IPO investors get a deal comparable to what pre-IPO investors get.

3. **Share Distribution:** The issuer allows a significant proportion of its IPO shares to be purchased by average investors.

4. **Incentive:** If they perform well, insiders can acquire most of the tradable shares.

5. **Control:** Voting power is "equitably shared" between investors and employees.

What Constitutes an "Equitable" Split of Voting Power?

The fifth Fairshare Model principle calls for an equitable sharing of voting power between investors and employees. That one has more squishiness than the others because what is equitable is open to debate. For the following reasons, I feel an even split in voting power at IPO between Investor Stock and Performance Stock is appropriate.

- If the issuer has a record of good performance, employees will have Investor Stock at the IPO. Their voting power will reflect those shares and what they have with Performance Stock.

- If the issuer lacks such a record, employees should equally share voting power with investors and it can grow if they perform well, due to conversions. That's fair. It's also a far better deal than employees get when they raise capital in a private offering from a VC.

Naturally, entrepreneurs want super-voting rights—few want to share power or be accountable to investors if they fall short of expectations. In recent years, we have witnessed an emerging trend in which issuers offer IPO shares with inferior—even zero—voting rights. I sense three reasons for this.

1. Seemingly, public investors do not care about voting rights—they just want a stock they think it will rise in price. It may be that they feel their vote can't affect anything anyway. It could be that they don't want to bother with matters that require a vote. Either way, they can sell their shares if they are unhappy.

2. Issuers want to simplify corporate governance. The state in which they are incorporated may have requirements that make a shareholder vote expensive or cumbersome to comply with. If investors have no-vote shares, that's not an issue.

3. Issuers may believe that their exposure to shareholder lawsuits is lessened if voting power is concentrated in the hands of a few.

The debate over voting rights mirrors those about government—is it better to have accountability for leaders or a system that enables them to act decisively? A case can be made for either. But a concern arises here if employees have superior voting rights without having earned them via performance. If they have it, they can make it easier for Performance Stock to convert to Investor Stock. The appeal of the Fairshare Model is undercut if either class of stock can unilaterally redefine the conversion criteria.

Earlier, I compared the evolution of the Fairshare Model to that of representative government. I think democracy is at its best when everyone can vote. But sometimes, I question whether that results in good government.

John Adams, a US Founding Father and its second President, expressed a grimmer view of democratic rule in 1814, having observed how it had evolved in America and in Europe.

> Democracy never lasts long. It soon wastes, exhausts, and murders itself. There never was a democracy yet that did not commit suicide.

> It is in vain to say that democracy is less vain, less proud, less selfish, less ambitious, or less avaricious than aristocracy or monarchy. It is not true and nowhere appears in history.

> Those passions are the same in all men, under all forms of simple government, and when unchecked, produce the same effects of fraud, violence, and cruelty. When clear prospects are opened before vanity, pride, avarice, or ambition, for their easy gratification, it is hard for the most considerate philosophers and the most conscientious moralists to resist the temptation.

> Individuals have conquered themselves. Nations and large bodies of men, never.[H]

Adams' sobering assessment of the prospects for democracies was not an endorsement for concentrated power as much as a reminder that any scheme to allocate power has potential downsides.

That said, a determinant of the ability of Fairshare Model issuers to thrive will be how they define voting power. It will be fascinating to see how various practices play out. If a company strays from the 50/50 baseline that I advocate, markets will reveal the extent to which investors care about voting power. Since they will get an attractive valuation, they may not care. But limiting the voting power of IPO shares is not a straight-forward proposition. Pre-IPO investors may be unwilling to accept that type of stock and employees will certainly not want to convert their voting Performance Stock to such a stock.

A solution might be to have multiple classes of Investor Stock. One for IPO investors with inferior voting rights. Another with superior rights for pre-IPO investors that Performance Stock will convert into. That's complicated, however. Also, an issuer that takes such an approach signals that it is not confident of its ability to perform well.

In closing, my principal concern about deviating from the baseline assumption of equal voting power for each class of stock at IPO is that the conversion criteria could be changed in a non-democratic manner. That could be mollified by:

- requiring Investor Stock approval for any change to the conversion criteria, OR
- requiring ample notice of any change so that Investor Stockholders have opportunity to sell their shares before it is put into effect.

What's Next?

The next chapter will discuss a conventional capital structure—the status quo—which has strengths as well as weaknesses. The weaknesses become apparent when applying it to venture-stage companies.

Chapter Endnotes

Contextual references for material in this chapter appear as numbered footnotes on the page where the reference is made. **Source references** for material in this chapter appear below as endnotes with capital letter identifiers.

A Vega, Suzanne. "Why Are the Majority of U.S. Companies Incorporated in Delaware?" *Mental Floss.* March 11, 2016. Accessed May 07, 2018. fairsharemodel.com/Delaware.

B Muller, Joann. "Ford Family's Stake Is Smaller, But They're Richer And Still Firmly In Control." *Forbes.* August 11, 2011. Accessed May 07, 2018. fairsharemodel.com/FordFamily.

C Waters, Richard. "Google Founders Look to Cement Control with Novel Share Split." *Financial Times.* April 02, 2014. Accessed May 07, 2018. fairsharemodel.com/GoogleControl.

D Ibid.

E Korver, Clint. "If You Don't Want to Be Fired From Your Startup, Founders Should Remember These 3 Things." *Entrepreneur.* August 15, 2017. Accessed June 21, 2018. fairsharemodel.com/Founders.

F Ibid.

G Hamilton, Alexander or Madison, James. "Federalist No 51." *Yale Law School Avalon Project – Documents in Law, History and Diplomacy.* Accessed May 08, 2018. fairsharemodel.com/Federalist51.

H Adams, John. "From John Adams to John Taylor, 17 December 1814." *National Archives–Founders Online.* Accessed October 02, 2018. fairsharemodel.com/Adams.

Chapter 5:

The Problem with a Conventional Capital Structure

What's Included in This Chapter

- Introduction
- Quick Comparison of Capital Structures
- Praise for a Conventional Capital Structure
- The Fundamental Problem: Valuation
- Private Investors Get a Valuation Cushion
- Public Investors Bear the Weight of the Valuation Problem
- You May Ask Yourself…
- "The Next Guy" Theory of Pricing
- Market Forces
    - First Hypothesis: Its Considered Normal
    - Second Hypothesis: Key Players Like The-Way-Things-Are
    - Third Hypothesis: A Bigger Neighborhood
    - A Unifying Thesis for Weak Market Forces: Wholesale/Retail Valuations
- Public Investors Bear the Weight of the Valuation Problem – Redux
    - #1 The basis for an IPO valuation is speculative
    - #2 Public investors have the most to lose from an excessive valuation
    - #3 Public investors have no price protection
    - #4 IPO allocations are undemocratic
- Must the Valuation Problem Persist for Public Investors?
- Bird's-Eye View of Possible Outcomes: Conventional vs. Fairshare Model
- Are Capital Markets Rigged?
- Is There a Moral Question?
- Does Valuation Unfairness Promote Vibrant Private Capital Markets?

- Summation
- What's Next?
- Chapter Endnotes

Introduction

A conventional deal structure demands a valuation when an investment is made, but it's difficult to arrive at one that is both rational and fair. When the negotiating parties settle on one, it is fraught with uncertainty.

Private investors have ways to modify a conventional capital structure so to cushion themselves from valuation risk. IPO investors do not–unless the issuer adopts the Fairshare Model. This chapter discusses the underside of a conventional capital structure and how it is that public investors get a lousier deal than private investors would accept.

Its goal is to expose the belly of the beast, to spark discussion about who is served by traditions in public venture capital–and who isn't.

Quick Comparison of Capital Structures

A key concept to bear in mind is that there are three basic capital structures for equity; a conventional model, a modified conventional model, and the Fairshare Model. This table characterizes their key attributes. The shaded rows deal with valuation, and they are important because they identify

1. *when a value is placed* on future performance, and
2. whether there is *price protection* for new investors.

	Conventional Capital Structure	Modified Conventional Capital Structure	Fairshare Model Capital Structure
Where used	IPOs and some private offerings	Private offerings with VC investors	IPOs
When a value for future performance is set	At time of investment	At time of investment	Once delivered
Price protection available?	No	Yes	Yes
Classes of stock	Single	Multiple	Multiple

The key point is that a conventional capital structure and a modified capital structure both set a value on future performance at the time of an equity investment. That's why they are "conventional." The Fairshare Model doesn't—it sets a value on performance after it has been delivered.

A conventional capital structure is the subject of this chapter, as it is used in virtually all initial public offerings. Chapter 8, "The Tao of the Fairshare Model," compares a modified conventional capital structure to the Fairshare Model.

Praise for a Conventional Capital Structure

Before preparing to bury "Caesar"—here in the form of a conventional capital structure—let me first praise him (or it). A conventional capital structure has many advantages, such as:

- It has been utilized for a long time and applied to a range of situations.
- It's simple to understand.
- Private investors, particularly VC and private equity firms, are comfortable with how to modify the structure to protect their interests.
- In the IPO market, it works well for companies, investment banks, and investors.
- It is understood by service providers (i.e., legal, tax, accounting, and valuation firms), who work for companies or investors.
- It is familiar to stock analysts.
- Securities regulators are accustomed to it.
- Few people question whether it is possible to improve it.

Not bad for complex socio-economic process!

Gahan Wilson sets the tone for the rest of this chapter. In a cartoon called "Is nothing sacred?" he draws a scene where a character enters an area where priests are paying homage to an unseen deity called "Nothing." That character asks a worshiper—who is clearly annoyed by the intrusion—"Is nothing sacred?" You may be able to view it online by searching for "Gahan Wilson, Is nothing sacred?"

The Fundamental Problem: Valuation

Praise aside, a conventional capital structure has a fundamental problem, an Achilles' heel. At the time of an equity financing, an issuer and its investors must set a value on future performance. For venture-stage companies, this is exceptionally hard to do in a reliable manner.

You can test this assertion even if you are new to capital structures. Ask someone who has raised money for a company or invested in one: "What was the valuation?" Follow that up with: "Why did that make sense?"

> "HorseConnect, The Social Network for Horses, Bought for $1 Billion"
> —The Onion [a satirical news website]

Chances are that you will see uncertainty and anxiety play across their face. It may be that they don't know the valuation. Perhaps they know it, but not how to calculate it. Or they know what it is and how to calculate it, but they are not comfortable justifying it.

This is the problem with a conventional capital structure; the need to settle a matter—the value of future performance—before there is evidence of what it should be. **The Fairshare Model attacks the conventional structure where it is weak, on valuation. It does so by establishing a valuation for performance *after* it is delivered, using standards that shareholders agree on.**

The chapters in Section 3 discuss valuation in depth, including how to calculate it. Here, all you need to know is that the valuation is what a buyer and seller agree the entire company is worth, based on the price for a piece of it. Investors who want to make a profit

> Slack's valuation in its $120 million round is based almost as much on speculation as on traditional metrics. "One billion is better than $800 million because it's the psychological threshold for potential customers, employees, and the press," the CEO said.
>
> —"How to get a $1 billion valuation in just eight months," *Fortune*, January 22, 2015

should pay attention to it since they only make money if they sell their stock to someone who feels the company is worth more.

The underlying problem is that it is hard to reliably determine what the value of a company should be, especially if it is venture-stage. Nonetheless, a conventional capital structure demands a valuation. That's the source of the uncertainty for your conversation partner. You're asking about something important that they don't understand well or have trouble justifying.

How hard is it to produce a rational valuation? Imagine that you are required to assess a class of elementary school children for who will be a success in life. Define "success" any way you like. You have as much information as you want about the kids, so you have clues about who may achieve success. Still, you struggle because you know life is

> "It's tough to make predictions, especially about the future."
>
> —Yogi Berra

uncertain and takes unpredictable turns. Qualities that will be important in each child's future may be unknown to you, or difficult to evaluate.

If you were forced to make this assessment, it would be hard. Time would reveal you were wrong in many instances. The success of a child is difficult to predict reliably because it does not lend itself to prediction. It reveals itself over time and with perspective.

Entrepreneurs and investors are similarly challenged when setting a valuation, but from different perspectives. Entrepreneurs *always* think their future looks bright. Their backers do too, but they don't know if the entrepreneur's confidence will be borne out. Nonetheless, even though the company's success will take time to reveal itself, the players must set a valuation when new stock is sold. The amount is set somewhat arbitrarily; some dress up the price-setting process in mystery and complexity.

So, the *central problem* for a conventional capital structure is that it does not reflect the way life plays out. It requires a decision on what is difficult to assess, and like any prediction, it is likely to be wrong.

A *derivative problem* is the lack of transparency in valuation. The figure is not a required disclosure for issuers—investors must calculate it. Chapter 16, "Valuation Disclosure," proposes a straightforward way for regulators to make valuation transparent to investors.

Frankly, many entrepreneurs care more about voting control than valuation. For them, the problem with a conventional capital structure is that voting power and valuation are linked. To maintain a given percentage of ownership while increasing the amount of money raised, the valuation must climb. The Fairshare Model decouples valuation from voting power. It does that by providing employees Performance Stock, which has significant voting rights but does not affect a company's valuation.

Private Investors Get a Valuation Cushion

When investing in a startup, venture capitalists sidestep the valuation problem by requiring terms like anti-dilution provisions, a non-intuitive term for price protection. Investors with price protection may get more shares from the issuer for free if later investors buy shares at a lower price or one that isn't high enough to deliver the VC's target return on investment. When that happens, the valuation that the price-protected investors bought in at is retroactively reduced—more shares for the same money means a lower price per share.

Merchants of consumer goods sometimes offer buyers price protection by offering to match another store's price. It's an inducement to get shoppers to buy from them. Buyers get a deal on a product that they can use or consume. Economists call this value "utility."

Investments are different. Stocks don't have utility; you can't use or consume one. An investor buys one with the hope that it will increase in value. But, it's hard to know what a company's value is unless and until there is a liquidity event. That is, until there is a buyer for the shares.

VCs and private equity firms require price protection from companies they invest in. Put another way, to mitigate valuation risk, they rely more on getting the right terms than on getting the right valuation. To mitigate failure risk, they rely on due diligence and voting rights.

Public Investors Bear the Weight of the Valuation Problem

The weight of the valuation problem falls the heaviest on public investors. Four interlinked facets explain why:

1. Venture-stage valuations are highly speculative.

2. Public investors buy-in at far higher valuations than private investors.

3. VC and PE investors get price protection, but IPO investors do not.

4. Allocations of IPO shares are undemocratic.

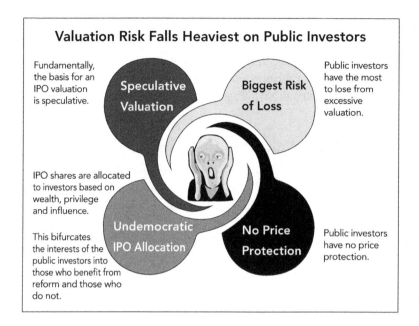

These four facets are discussed at the end of this chapter. But before that, let's step back and consider why the valuation problem falls the heaviest on public investors to begin with. Two concepts explain why.

1. *The Next Guy theory* of pricing. A simple, yet remarkably sturdy explanation—I think—for what investors are willing to pay for an asset.

2. *Weak market forces.* If they were stronger, issuers would compete for public investors based on valuation and terms. That they don't is *prima facie* evidence of weak market forces for public venture capital.

But before we discuss them, ask yourself the questions that follow.

You May Ask Yourself...

An IPO establishes a benchmark for a company's market value—but what does that value reflect when the company is a startup? It's performance? It's potential? It's risk? That there are more buyers to bid for shares? That many of them are not valuation-savvy? It's a bit of all of that.

Going public is not a controlled experiment on value. An IPO does not compare what wealthy pre-IPO investors feel the issuer is worth to what wealthy public investors feel it is worth.

A new active ingredient is added to the mix when a company goes public—average investors who have been unable to invest earlier. Their involvement effervesces the valuation for two reasons.

1. Generally, they are valuation-unaware.

2. They are enthusiastic, as it is their first opportunity to invest in the company.

These factors create demand that is relatively price insensitive—what economists call "price inelastic demand"—for the shares. Competition for them by eager, valuation-unaware investors bids the valuation up from whatever the issuer decided to set it at to begin with.

You may ask yourself, is there an intrinsic value for a venture-stage company? For example, if its founders have a plan for how to acquire customers and generate profit–but nothing more than a plan–what is the idea worth?

If there isn't intrinsic value, how about a fair value? One established by investors with similar information and opportunity to invest?

Is a company's value measured fairly in a private offering, where investors have price protection?

Is it measured more fairly in the IPO price or in the secondary market trading that follows?

If each of these is a fair measure, what explains the remarkable increase in valuation that typically occurs in the quarters leading up to an IPO?

What explains what happens to the price in secondary market trading?

You may ask yourself, is it performance or is it something else?

Then, you may ask yourself:

"How did I get here?" [1]

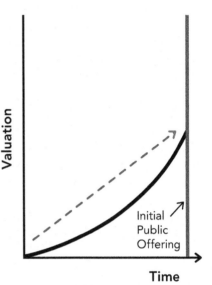

"The Next Guy" Theory of Pricing

In the 1990s, to simplify valuation for Fairshare members, I described my Next Guy theory of asset pricing.[2] The economic climate has changed, but the idea still makes sense, and it doesn't require a fancy equation.

The Next Guy theory is that for an investment, the price is no more than what the buyer believes the Next Guy will pay, less a discount. Here it is in a formula.

Expected Price a Future Buyer Will Pay	$ XXX
− Discount Required	(YYY)
= Price Buyer Will Pay for an Investment	$ ZZZ

So, if an investor believes the Next Guy will pay $10 per share and the buyer's target return is 25 percent, she will pay no more than $7.50; the $2.50 discount is the 25 percent expected return.

The Next Guy theory does not explain the price that a buyer will pay for necessities (food, medical care, fuel, shelter), pleasure (fashion, travel, entertainment), or a gift, or for another non-investment

---

[1] With a nod and smile to the Talking Heads and their song "Once In A Lifetime." fairsharemodel.com/TalkingHeads

[2] My experience as CEO of Fairshare, Inc. led to this book and it is described in Chapter 9, "Fairshare Model History and the Future."

purpose (vanity, status, guilt). These have utility, status, or emotional value. An investment rarely has such qualities. People smitten with their iPhone need not be emotional about Apple's stock.

The theory neatly explains buyer behavior when evaluating an investment. Consider real estate. A key determinant of price is what the buyer expects to get when he sells the property later. The buyer may have non-investment motivations too. They need a place to live (consumption), they may love aspects of the property (pleasure) and there may be other factors. But if investment is the sole motivation, the price a rational buyer will pay will be a discount from what they expect the Next Guy to pay.

Ditto for cars, art, and jewelry. Although here, like in some investments, the concept of utility can influence the price. You may, for example, be willing to pay a premium for something that reflects your social sensibilities, the image you want to project and so on.

For companies, the Next Guy theory plays a significant role in explaining pre-IPO valuations. Performance plays a role, but it's not as significant as who is expected to be the next buyer—public investors. Put another way, when a conventional capital structure is used, valuation is a function of "who" is buying, not "what" is sold. The idea is expressed in these concept equations.

$$\text{Valuation} = f \ [\textit{Who} \text{ the investor is}]$$

$$\text{Valuation} \neq f \ [\textit{What} \text{ the company's performance is}]$$

Another idea in finance, the greater fool theory, says that an investor will pay a foolish price if he thinks a greater fool will pay more. It assumes that anyone willing to pay more than a sensible price is a fool.

The Next Guy theory encompasses that. It also recognizes that there are smart investors who see value that others do not. Smart companies have been known to pay more than market to acquire a company.

Market Forces

The Next Guy theory can apply to products that have utility, like clothing or food, where wholesale/retail pricing models are used. Similarly, the wholesale/retail concept offers a way to understand the venture capital market. Let's break down the components of trading in goods, then reassemble them in a novel way. It will provide reason to believe that market forces are weak when it comes to capital formation.

Here, the "product" is equity in a venture-stage company, and, it is sold to investors in both the private and the public capital markets. The "manufacturer" is the issuer, and it sells its product to private investors at wholesale and to public investors at retail. As the prior chart illustrates, the rise in valuation as a company approaches an IPO can be substantial. So, there is different pricing for a comparable product—the issuer's stock.

Wait! Check that last thought! The products are *not comparable;* there is a crucial difference. *The product sold at wholesale is better* than the retail version. Remember, the stock sold to pre-IPO investors has price protection. The product sold to IPO investors doesn't. So the retail buyer gets an *inferior product…*and *pays more* for it!

Can you think of another market—a competitive one—where that happens? I can't.

Let's put that general point to the side and focus on possible answers to the question: "What accounts for the increase in the price of the issuer's equity–it's product–as it approaches an IPO?" The Next Guy theory provides insight, but *why are market forces weak?* What are the drivers?

I offer three overlapping hypotheses:

1. It's considered normal.
2. Key players like The-Way-Things-Are.
3. There is a bigger neighborhood of investors.

First Hypothesis: It's Considered Normal

Everyone thinks its normal for a company's value to increase when is public. Could it be that "normal" means "it happens all the time" as opposed to "it makes sense?" One could say the first is a statistical measure while the other is a moral/ethical question.[A]

Should a startup that raises capital in an IPO be worth more than one that raises it in a private one? One reason a public stock *should be* worth more than a private one is that the shares are tradable. How much more valuable they should be is debatable. I think a liquidity premium is worth 15 to 30 percent and that *it is awarded when shares are tradable,* not in advance of the IPO. So, the fact that private company valuations climb in anticipation of an IPO undermines the liquidity premium argument.

It's easier to argue it is normal, in a statistical sense, for a company to be worth far more when it is public, than it is to make a moral/ethical case for it.

Second Hypothesis: Key Players Like The-Way-Things-Are

There is high demand for venture capital; companies struggle to raise it. There is also a robust supply of investors with interest in them, as witnessed by demand for IPOs. So, why don't companies compete for public capital? Why don't they say: "We're having a sale!" or "Our terms are better!" like sellers in other markets? If competitive forces were strong, issuers would compete for investors by offering lower valuations and better terms. Why doesn't it happen in public venture capital?

My second hypothesis for why market forces are weak, as far as public investors are concerned, is that issuers, investment bankers and the privileged investors who get allotments of IPO shares benefit from The-Way-Things-Are; average investors who would benefit from greater competition are not well-positioned to change things.

> Arguably, public venture capital is a rigged market; one in which average investors are relegated to the bottom of the capital food chain.

On the sell side, issuers lack incentive to offer lower valuations because it reduces the wealth and control of its shareholders–its pre-IPO investors and employees. They view a discounted valuation the way a cat views a bath.

Investment bankers are uninterested in competition for public capital because it complicates their business model. They would rather say "We represent fine companies" than "this IPO is a better deal" because doing so draws attention to the terms of their other deals. Companies with brand names feel similarly about discounting their products, but some made factory outlet stores work. Similarly, full service retailers sell merchandise at full price in their traditional stores and offer discounted items at their off-price stores. Broker-dealers could adopt the concept, but traditionalists will shun the idea because it makes the Next Guys more valuation conscious.

On the buy side, Wall Street IPO investors don't insist on better terms because they are bifurcated into two groups. Many who receive allocations of shares flip or quickly re-sell them in the secondary market. They care about getting in front of the Next Guy, period. The other group, buy and hold investors, may not sense they can have the influence to get better deals. Undoubtedly, that's because too many of them are unsure of what an issuer's valuation is, how to calculate it or how to evaluate one. Thus, issuers don't feel much pressure to offer public investors better deals.

> **Future IPO Outlet Stores?**
> Goldman Sachs' "Off Wall Street"
> "Sprouts" from Morgan Stanley
> Credit Suisse's "Emergence Zone"

As more people become valuation-savvy, issuers are more likely to see their valuations challenged. Some companies will respond earnestly, providing context and rationale for the figure, but many more are likely to rely on obfuscation because valuations can be hard to justify.

Wouldn't it be nice to see a CEO eschew answers that employ smoke and mirrors? Wouldn't it be refreshing to see one simply use a variation of the tag line uttered by the actors who promote L'Oreal hair products in ads?

> *"L'Oreal.* It costs more, but I'm worth it!"

Third Hypothesis: A Bigger Neighborhood of Investors

My third hypothesis for why a valuation climbs in anticipation of an IPO is that one represents a gateway into a much bigger neighborhood of investors. A concept equation for the effect on valuation is:

More Potential Buyers = Higher Potential Demand = Higher Potential Price

To apply it, imagine a work of art. Physically, it is no different in a small town than if it is in a large city. But there are more potential buyers in a city, so the object sells for more there. City buyers anticipate exposure to a greater number of Next Guys when they are ready to sell than those in a small town.

Imagine how this can play out in stocks. Moving from the private market to the public market is akin to moving art from a small market to a big one. Of course, some public markets are more attractive than others (i.e., NASDAQ is better that the pink sheets). Nonetheless, the expectation that a stock will trade can explain the non-performance-related rise in valuation for venture-stage companies.

From a *fundamental perspective,* this presents a distinction where there is no difference. That is, the transition from private to public does not improve a company's revenue or profits. Nor does it meaningfully reduce its failure risk, which is what the following conceptual equation conveys.

Failure Risk for a Private Venture-Stage Co. ≈ Failure Risk for a Public Venture-Stage Co.

It's a different story with respect to valuation risk because from a *market perspective,* a venture-stage company can be worth more public than private. Interestingly, the premium is awarded upon *entry* to the public market and can erode over time. This helps explain why private equity funds will take a public company private. After reinvigorating its performance potential, the PE firm will have an investment banker take it public again (or find a buyer). The PE fund profits in two ways–the fundamental premium earned for better performance plus the market premium associated with the public market.

Investment bankers and others like to say that they "build value" when they help companies go public. But an IPO doesn't make a venture-stage company fundamentally better or less risky–it moves it into a different plane of valuation. It takes work to get there, but the reward reaped by those who help issuers go public is often outsized compared to the rewards earned by those who invent, design, or manufacture an issuer's products, expand its market, or improve its operations.

Thus, the value-add claim of those who usher a company to the public market rests more on weak market forces than on the actual work required. Their compensation reflects their ability to help issuers arbitrage the private and public markets as much as anything.

From a public investor's perspective, movement from private to public doesn't change a business any more than moving a caterpillar from one place to another makes it a butterfly–that transformation takes time. It also takes effort and luck.

A Unifying Thesis for Weak Market Forces: Wholesale/Retail Valuations

A thesis emerges for why market forces are weak in public venture capital. One that unifies the hypotheses that high public valuations are considered normal, that key players like The-Way-Things-Are, and that a larger pool of investors drives prices up.

There is a wholesale and retail valuation in capital markets–wholesale for private investors and retail for the public. For that reason, valuations climb to a level not explained by performance–to a list or retail price. (Of course, in the New Economy, no one wants to pay retail!)

Wholesalers don't transform a product–they buy it in quantity, store it and ship fractions of it to retailers who charge a higher price. Similarly, private investors invest earlier than public investors and write larger checks. The support they provide has value even if isn't evident from a company's operational performance. For one thing, it allows the company to get to the point where it can have an IPO.

This wholesale/retail concept can explain why market forces support IPO valuations that are far higher than what the private market would pay. It suggests that competition can benefit investors, just as it has consumers. Discount stores, internet sites and warehouse outlets improved consumer access to better products at lower prices. Might venture capital be subject to similar competitive forces?

We've seen innovation in how investors invest. Many now invest in funds rather than individual stocks. The 1970s saw the advent of broker-dealers that charge lower commissions. The 1980s brought innovation to the debt market in the form of junk bonds, the below-investment grade bonds that provided low-cost capital for up-starts in the telecom, cable television and media industries. In 2001, stock prices in the US switched from fractional to decimal pricing. The JOBS Act led to innovative ways for companies to sell shares. The next frontier may be in how public offerings are structured.

Another factor is that markets can be inefficient, even nuts, when they involve investors who are not valuation-savvy. Exhibit A could be the April 2017 market capitalization of Tesla Motors, relative to General Motors and Ford Motor Company, each of whom dwarf Tesla in terms of vehicles produced and financial performance.

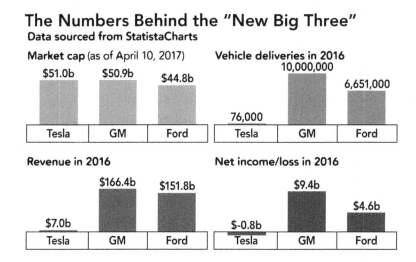

The Numbers Behind the "New Big Three"
Data sourced from StatistaCharts

Market cap (as of April 10, 2017)

Tesla	GM	Ford
$51.0b	$50.9b	$44.8b

Vehicle deliveries in 2016

Tesla	GM	Ford
76,000	10,000,000	6,651,000

Revenue in 2016

Tesla	GM	Ford
$7.0b	$166.4b	$151.8b

Net income/loss in 2016

Tesla	GM	Ford
$-0.8b	$9.4b	$4.6b

Public Investors Bear the Weight of the Valuation Problem – *Redux*

The bottom line is that the weight of the valuation problem falls heaviest on public investors. With the Next Guy theory and the weak market force argument in mind, let's revisit the four reasons why.

#1 The basis for an IPO valuation is speculative.

No one knows how to reliably value a venture-stage company. Nonetheless, a conventional capital structure—the kind used in virtually all IPOs—demands one.

#2 Public investors have the most to lose from an excessive valuation.

While all venture-stage investors face failure risk, private investors face more since they invest at earlier stages. On the other hand, public investors assume greater valuation risk than private investors.

Who is the Next Guy for Unaccredited Investors?

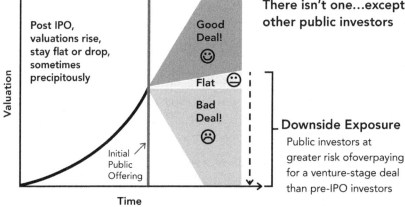

#3 Public investors have no price protection.

VCs get terms that modify a conventional capital structure in ways that provide a safety net in case the valuation they buy in at proves to be excessive. Public investors don't get this protection.

#4 IPO allocations are undemocratic.

Share allocation schemes are designed to benefit the business models of investment banks, which reflect a wholesale/retail perspective on capital markets.

Must the Valuation Problem Persist for Public Investors?

This state of affairs need not be permanent. Time and time again, we have seen markets evolve as sellers compete by offering buyers better value. Examples are:

- food and drugs: branded vs. private label

- clothing: designer labels vs. look-alikes

- stores: department vs. warehouse

- real estate: broker multi-listing service vs. web-listings

Can similar dynamics affect IPOs?

> Warehouse clubs like Costco disrupted the consumer goods market by offering warehouse prices to the mass market.
>
> The Fairshare Model is similarly disruptive because it encourages companies to offer IPO investors a "wholesale price," what private investors would pay for its stock.

Sure! Especially if the Securities and Exchange Commission requires issuers of equity securities to disclose their valuation.[3] To be valuation-savvy, one must be valuation-aware. Also, as more investors become valuation-aware, issuers will be more inclined to compete for capital by offering better terms.

For public investors, a conventional capital structure has an essential problem. They assume much more valuation risk than private investors. Four interlocking conditions provide the foundation for the problem.

M.C. ESCHER, ASCENDING AND DESCENDING (1960 LITHOGRAPH)

1. Public investors pay "retail" for venture-stage investments but don't know it.

2. They are not offered a better deal because they don't demand it.

3. Public investors don't demand better deals because they are not valuation-savvy.

4. They aren't valuation-savvy because securities regulators don't require valuation disclosure, and companies see no benefit in voluntarily stating what the valuation is.

"So it goes," Kurt Vonnegut might say—it was a recurring line in his novel, *Slaughterhouse-Five*.

---

3 More on this in Chapter 16, "Valuation Disclosure."

Bird's-Eye View of Possible Outcomes: Conventional vs. Fairshare Model

Before concluding this chapter, let's revisit the charts that show how public investors are positioned in a conventional capital structure versus the Fairshare Model.

The first one illustrates the possible outcomes for public investors with a conventional capital structure. It assumes the issuer goes public six years after it's formed. At IPO, the valuation is based on anticipation; it reflects newness as well as the dynamics discussed in this chapter. Gradually, its valuation as a public company is guided by how it performs.

Possibilities: Conventional Model

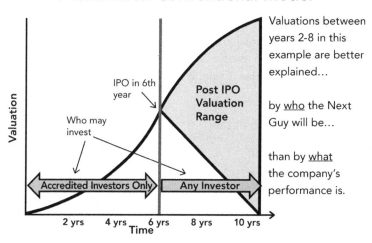

The next one shows how the Fairshare Model is different. The issuer goes public sooner, here in year two, and at a lower valuation. If it performs well, investors and employees share the increase in valuation. If it doesn't perform well, public investors lose less because the valuation was lower at the IPO.

Possibilities: Fairshare Model

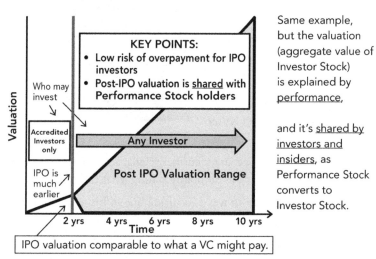

Are Capital Markets Rigged?

So, there is unfairness in how valuation risk is allocated—it is mitigated in private offerings but escalated in public ones. This prompts a question. Are capital markets rigged to benefit investors who are wealthy and/or privileged?

I'm hesitant to say they are rigged. That suggests a degree of intentionality that I'm uncomfortable with; also, more control than anyone likely has.

It is more accurate, I think, to say they are *tilted* against average investors. The Fairshare Model offers a way to level them.

To get there, public investors must indicate interest in it. Enough to encourage companies to try it. If enough of these issuers raise the money they need, and the well-performing ones have good outcomes for their investors and employees, others will try it.

The Fairshare Model presents a path that can encourage capital markets to be fairer and more efficient.

Thought Experiment

It is easy to see why companies prefer a conventional capital structure.

Can you think of reasons for new investors to prefer one? I can't.

Is There a Moral Question?

In a related vein, some may feel that the unfairness of how valuation risk is distributed rises to a moral issue. I think not. Companies don't have an obligation to new investors regarding valuation. Indeed, they have incentive to get as high a price as they can. Also, investors are free to buy, or not.

Market power isn't offered, it is taken. So to get a better deal, investors need to routinely favor companies that offer them one.

There is rising investor interest in supporting sustainability—investments in companies that conduct business in ways that benefit more people or is less harmful to our planet. For a comparable movement to take hold regarding valuations, public investors must understand that they get a lousy deal now—one that a VC would never accept.

Does Valuation Unfairness Promote Vibrant Private Capital Markets?

It is possible to look at the unfairness in valuation risk as beneficial to capital markets. One could argue that it encourages investment in private companies, the most successful of which may go public. If companies go public at lower valuations, investors will have less incentive to assume the failure risk that is inherent in venture-stage companies.

This is a trickle-down argument, the kind used to argue that low income tax rates for the wealthy translate into more spending and investment that benefit those who earn less. The evidence that the economy works that way is, at best, arguable.

Summation

This chapter argues why public investors should be interested in upending tradition in public venture capital. It exposes you to a conventional capital structure–the nemesis of the Fairshare Model.

How do you feel about The-Way-Things-Are?

You may feel there are reasons to support the status quo. There are good arguments for a traditional perspective on many things, after all.

On the other hand, if your reaction is to proclaim: "I'm mad as hell, and I'm not going to take it anymore!", reflect on the challenges facing the Fairshare Model–they are listed at the end of Chapter 4, "Fairshare Model Q&A."

Whatever your reaction, I imagine you feel capital structures are more interesting than you did before you picked up this book!

Thought Experiment

Imagine that, starting tomorrow, shares in Wall Street IPOs are allocated by lottery, not based on wealth, privilege, or connections.

Will investors who have routinely been able to get shares at the IPO price remain content with a conventional capital structure?

If they must buy shares in the secondary market from those who win the lottery, might these well-connected investors clamor for a deal structure that reduces valuation risk?

What's Next?

The next chapter discusses crowdfunding.

Chapter Endnotes

Contextual references for material in this chapter appear as numbered footnotes on the page where the reference is made. **Source references** for material in this chapter appear below as endnotes with capital letter identifiers.

A Knobe, Adam, and Joshua Knobe. "Opinion | The Normalization Trap." *The New York Times*. January 28, 2017. Accessed May 13, 2018. fairsharemodel.com/Normalization. An interesting article on what constitutes "normal."

Chapter 6:

Crowdfunding and the Fairshare Model

What's Included in This Chapter

- Introduction
- Deal Access vs. Deal Quality
- Innovation in Distribution vs. Innovation in Structure
- Crowdfunding Is Not a New Idea
- Equity Crowdfunding Is Such a Vague Term
- Substantively, Equity Crowdfunding Is Not a New Idea
- Prospects for Crowdfunding Via Wall Street
  - A Word About Etsy: The Times, They May Be A-Changing (a bit)
- The Intermediary Problem for DPOs
- Funding Portals – Intermediaries Who Are Not Broker-Dealers
- What Is a Self-Regulatory Organization?
- Funding Portals May Need an SRO of Their Own
- Perspective on Intermediaries Who Are Not Broker-Dealers
- Summation
- What's Next?
- Chapter Endnotes

Introduction

Crowdfunding describes the phenomena of large numbers of people providing money for projects that they want to support, typically online. This chapter describes how the Fairshare Model compares to equity crowdfunding and considers policy issues equity crowdfunding raises.

Deal Access vs. Deal Quality

The JOBS Act of 2012 authorized the SEC to make profound changes to securities law. With the economy mired in the Great Recession, there was decisive support for improving access to capital for entrepreneurs. The debate surrounding the JOBS Act centers on the wisdom of making it easier for startups to sell stock to average investors as they generally lack the sophistication needed to evaluate deals, as well as the capacity to absorb losses.

I like the idea of making it easier for average investors to invest in these types of companies, but fear that few will make money doing so. I'm not overly concerned about the failure risk; it is possible to have success in this space with luck and skill. Plus, developing the skills to do so is fun and beneficial.

My concern arises from the high valuation risk public investors assume. The deal structures they typically get are lousy—they take on far more valuation risk than a VC would accept, even when failure risk is similar. And it isn't necessary, it's just tradition.

My vision for the Fairshare Model is to popularize the extension of the VC-proven idea of price protection to IPOs. As stated in this book's introduction, that vision is that…

Average investors will be able to make public venture capital investments on *terms that are comparable to those that venture capitalists get.*

Enthusiasts for the JOBS Act embrace the first part of that sentence, arguing that there are plenty of smart, savvy, public investors who want to invest in young companies. However, relatively few of these supporters similarly promote initiatives to protect public investors from loss.

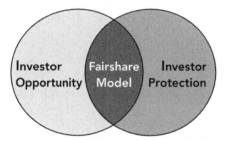

Thus, the Fairshare Model occupies unique territory, one between support for average investor opportunity and advocacy for better investor protection.

One might say that the Fairshare Model seeks to make a risky activity safer.

Innovation in Distribution vs. Innovation in Structure

Equity crowdfunding is an innovation in distribution, how offerings are sold. The Fairshare Model is an innovation in how offerings are structured; it replicates protections available to VCs for IPO investors.

Therefore, the Fairshare Model is not equity crowdfunding as you may understand it. It can be used to raise any amount, not just $1 million. Additionally, an IPO based on it can be sold like any other—direct by the issuer, through a funding portal, or by broker-dealers. Interestingly, even though it is designed to benefit average investors, it could be used for IPOs that are only sold to accredited investors.

So, if the offering size doesn't matter, nor how the shares are sold, or to whom, what defines a Fairshare Model offering? There are simply two qualities:

1. The issuer is a venture-stage company, and

2. The offering is an IPO.

Simply put, the Fairshare Model is a *much bigger* idea than equity crowdfunding, however you define it.

Crowdfunding Is Not a New Idea

Crowdfunding has existed for a long time in three forms: reward, donation, and credit.**A** Let's touch on examples of each before discussing a fourth one, equity.

In the early 1700s, a founding father of the United States of America, Benjamin Franklin, wanted to start a printing business, but he didn't have the money to buy printing presses. The enterprising young man used **rewards-based crowdfunding;** he raised the money by offering the reward of future printing services at a discount. This form of crowdfunding is used to raise money to develop a new product or service. Contributors don't get stock, so they have no stake in the company's success. The money is at-risk, meaning it is not repaid if the product or service isn't produced or doesn't meet expectations. If it is not at-risk (it can be refunded), the money is a deposit. The incentive for someone to "invest" is transactional but it may be infused with the kind of emotions that fuel donation-based crowdfunding.

Donation-based crowdfunding is the collection of money to support a cause or project—it too, has been done for ages. Intriguingly, the Statue of Liberty was the result of donation-based crowdfunding campaigns in France and the United States.

The Statue of Liberty Was Crowdfunded![B]

French writer Edouard de Laboulaye proposed the idea for a statue that would celebrate liberty as he anticipated the centennial of the United States of America. He conceived it as a gift from the people of France to the people of the young nation. Enthused by the concept, sculptor Frédéric-Auguste Bartholdi designed the statue and helped to promote building it.

In France, an organization named the *French-American Union* was formed in 1875 to raise money for the project. It was to be paid for by the French people, not by their national government, and the Americans were to pay for the pedestal base. Over the following five years, tens of thousands of French citizens donated the money to build the statue.

In the US, it was hard to raise money for the statue's base. Leading newspapers, particularly *The New York Times*, often criticized the effort as folly and vehemently opposed spending any money on it. In 1885, newspaper publisher Joseph Pulitzer argued in his paper, *New York World*, that it was important to raise the $100,000 needed to complete the base for the statute. Here is what he said:

> We must raise the money! *The World* is the people's paper, and now it appeals to the people to come forward and raise the money. The $250,000 that the making of the statue cost was paid in by the masses of the French people—by the working men, the tradesmen, the shop girls, the artisans—by all, irrespective of class or condition. Let us respond in like manner. Let us not wait for the millionaires to give us this money. It is not a gift from the millionaires of France to the millionaires of America, but a gift of the whole people of France to the whole people of America.

Credit-based crowdfunding is also an old practice, particularly in communities that have poor access to affordable lending. A popular form occurs when a group of people contribute money to build a pool of capital that is available to help those in need of credit. The loans are often interest free—but borrowers are expected to repay it.

In the 1800s, Jonathan Swift, author of *Gulliver's Travels,* reportedly had such a fund for those suffering from the Irish potato famine. In the 1970s, Muhammad Yunus developed concepts for micro-credit lending and founded Grameen Bank to implement it, initially, in Bangladesh. He was awarded the Nobel Peace Prize for his pioneering work.

Non-institutional credit-based crowdfunding has been in place for generations where institutions are weak or expensive. Kiva.org has made more than two million micro-loans totaling about a billion dollars with close to a 100 percent repayment rate.

Why would someone give money to such an effort? To support those who need it, of course, but there's more to it. It combines the altruism of donation-based crowdfunding with the satisfaction that one is getting something for it, a self-renewing resource that encourages industrious activity that, in turn, can reduce the need for charity.

Equity Crowdfunding Is Such a Vague Term

Let us now turn to "equity crowdfunding." It is a maddeningly ambiguous term. I'll preface my explanation for that assessment with context.

In 1996, I cofounded a company named Fairshare, Inc. To my knowledge, we were the first to promote the concept of equity crowdfunding as a systematic way for companies to sell stock via the internet, even though we didn't use the term "crowdfunding."[1] We built an online membership of people with interest in investing in venture-stage companies by providing community and education about capital formation. Once we reached critical mass, we planned to let companies with legal offerings pitch our members for free. To qualify, an issuer would have to pass a due diligence review, use the Fairshare Model, and let members invest as little as $100.

People were intrigued by the concept. We attracted plenty of visitors to our website, 16,000 of whom signed up for membership. A third were so supportive that they paid $50 or $100 for one–the rest had free memberships. We told paid members that we hoped to give them special privileges but were unsure of what we could deliver, given the uncertainties inherent in our revolutionary plan. For that reason, the membership fees represented a mix of rewards- and donation-based crowdfunding. All Fairshare members, however, hoped to participate in equity crowdfunding.

As an innovator, we encountered regulatory challenges. Ultimately, though, our problem was that interest sagged after the dotcom and telecom bubbles burst. When equity crowdfunding entered the popular lexicon, around 2010, I thought it was a cool name for what Fairshare had wanted to do.

In 2016, the SEC issued Rule CF (for crowdfunding), which defines a new type of offering that can be used to raise around $1 million from public investors. The name seemingly narrows the meaning of crowdfunding to be that particular form of an offering. Before Rule CF was released, many people felt that the word crowdfunding meant a way to sell offerings without a broker-dealer.

So, the difficulty I have with "equity crowdfunding" is that the term is imprecise. Does it refer to a what, a how, or a who?

- *If it's a **What**,* it refers to the legal form of an offering–it is one under Rule CF, which is limited to about $1 million.

---

1 My Fairshare experience is detailed in Chapter 9, "Fairshare Model History and the Future."

- *If it's a How,* crowdfunding refers to the way an offering is sold—it describes one sold directly by the issuer or through a funding portal. That definition excludes broker-dealers.

- *If it's a Who,* crowdfunding means that average investors get to invest. Is there a minimum proportion of the offering they should get? By the way, I have seen arguments that online funding portals for accredited investors provide "crowdfunding for angels," which implies that crowdfunding can exclude the proletariat, the "unwashed masses."

Substantively, Equity Crowdfunding Is Not a New Idea

To me, equity crowdfunding occurs when an issuer makes a "significant portion" of its offering available to average investors, no matter how it is sold.

Thus, I feel that *any public offering* can be crowdfunded, not just one under Rule CF, and that *any selling method* can be used. And it makes little sense to say that a private offering can be crowdfunded. After all, less than 10 percent of the US population meet the accredited investor standard, and they don't constitute a crowd of people who heretofore have lacked opportunities to invest.**C**

"Equity crowdfunding" is best understood as an outcome, not as a process.

What constitutes a significant portion of an offering for average investors? More than they ordinarily get, which equals anything more than 15 percent of the amount raised. And it only needs to be offered. That means if average investors get the chance to invest at least $1.5 million in a $10 million offering, it should qualify as crowdfunded, even if they invest less than that.

Virtually all direct public offerings meet this criterion. The pre-internet DPO pioneer was Real Goods Trading Corporation, a California solar equipment retailer. In 1991, it raised $4.6 million in two offerings by soliciting its mail order customers, winding up with 5,000 investors. The internet-era trailblazer was Spring Street Brewing Company, a New York microbrewer of beer. In 1996, it posted its DPO documents on its website and advertised on its six-packs. It raised $1.6 million from about 3,500 investors.**D**

By my way of thinking, broker-dealers can crowdfund an offering. But, as an idealistic entrepreneur discovered, Wall Street investment banks are not keen on giving average investors access to shares. In 1995, Boston Beer Company, maker of Samuel Adams beer, raised $75 million in an underwritten IPO. Founder James Koch said they had to overcome strong resistance from its investment banks and had to go through difficult regulatory hoops to make it possible for its customers to buy a few shares at the offering price (about a $500 investment). Here is what Koch told *The New York Times.*

> "You really have to fight the whole system: the investment bankers, the SEC, the current regulations," said Mr. Koch, noting that Goldman, Sachs, one of his underwriters, refused to handle the consumer deal. "The entire regulatory system is not set up to allow shares to be available for consumers."**E**

Have things changed in the decades since Boston Beer did a Wall Street version of the song, *Fight the Power?***F** Is it easier to crowdfund an underwritten IPO?

Prospects for Crowdfunding Via Wall Street

Koch said securities regulations complicated Boston Beer's crowdfunding effort. But changes have taken place over the past two decades, and the mindset of regulators has evolved since then. More change may be called for, but the most significant barrier to equity crowdfunding may come from the financial services industry.

The SEC states: "it does not regulate the business decision of how IPO shares are allocated." A post on its website titled "Initial Public Offerings: Why Individuals Have Difficulty Getting Shares" makes the following points.**G** [Bold added for emphasis.]

- **Underwriters and the company** that issues the shares control the IPO process.

- *Most* **underwriters target institutional or wealthy investors** in IPO distributions.

- Brokerage firms must consider if the IPO is appropriate for individual investors in light of their income and net worth, investment objectives, other securities holdings, risk tolerance, and other factors. **A firm may not sell IPO shares to an individual investor unless it has determined the investment is suitable** for that particular investor.

- Even if the firm decides that an IPO is an appropriate investment for an individual investor, the brokerage firm may sell the IPO only to selected clients. For example, before you can purchase an IPO, **some firms require that you have a minimum cash balance in your account, are an active trader with the firm, or subscribe to one of their more expensive or "premium" services.** In addition, **some firms impose restrictions on investors who "flip" or sell their IPO shares** soon after the first day of trading to make a quick profit.

These comments touch on how average investors are disadvantaged in IPO allocations. Bear in mind that their disadvantage goes beyond share allotments. The big story is that public investors assume far more valuation risk than private investors. They buy in at higher valuations and don't get price protection like private investors.

As the SEC states, issuers, and their broker-dealers—underwriters or investment banks—decide who gets IPO shares. Allocations are not an issue in a direct public offering. DPO shares are as easy to get as a seat in a restaurant that isn't busy. Shares in hot IPOs are as difficult to get shares in as a table at an exclusive restaurant; you must be a prized customer, know someone, or be a celebrity.

Those allocations favor accredited investors, but the reason has at least as much to do with the investment bank business model as with any suitability screen. After all, such standards are not similarly enforced in the secondary market. A broker-dealer may determine that an IPO is unsuitable for a customer but accept an order from the same customer to *buy the same stock* in secondary trading.

The business model of investment banks also explains why crowdfunding has little appeal to them. They want more demand than supply for shares they broker. That allows their issuer-client to sell all IPO shares, and their investor-customers to make money. Ideally, the underwriter pegs the market right, and the issuer offers an IPO valuation at a 15 to 20 percent discount to that. If the aftermarket pop is less, IPO investors are unhappy. The issuer will be unhappy if it is more, as it indicates the IPO was underpriced.

The key is to forecast the secondary market, but this can be hard to do. Historically, underwriters have been willing to game the aftermarket to ensure that everything worked out, even when doing so was illegal. For example, Morgan Stanley and Goldman Sachs both paid a $40 million penalty to settle charges that they violated SEC regulations. The practices they were charged with engaging in during 1999 and 2000 include:**H**

- encouraging customers to place orders to buy shares in the immediate aftermarket of offerings they underwrote in exchange for allocations of other over-subscribed IPOs,

- suggesting what price customers should bid in the secondary market to obtain good allocations of other hot IPOs,

- allocating IPO shares to customers only if they promised to buy additional shares in the aftermarket, and

- soliciting customers to place aftermarket orders before all IPO shares were distributed.

These actions created upward pressure on the stock price—what average investors paid. Even though it was illegal, top-shelf investment banks engaged in them, which indicates just how powerful the motivation is for broker-dealers to see the price climb in the secondary market. Talk to those with experience in small-cap stocks, and you'll hear that such market conditioning is as rare as shoplifting.[1]

The importance of an attractive IPO pop suggests crowdfunding has little appeal to underwriters for it erodes their ability to reward favored customers. Also, if average investors can satiate their appetite for shares with what they are allocated, the zest of aftermarket trading may flatten, making it harder to sustain a good pop.

Another impediment to crowdfunding may be the Financial Industry Regulatory Authority (FINRA), the industry's self-regulating organization or SRO.[2] It sets suitability and other requirements to protect investors and reduce legal exposure from disgruntled investors, but they also have the effect of inhibiting broker-dealers from crowdfunding.

Cynical reasons for FINRA to impede crowdfunding are:

- There is a duality to SROs; they exist to keep government from directly regulating an industry but can act like a trade guild, protecting the interests of its members.

- Many FINRA officials come from the industry they regulate and may be protective of its business model, consciously or not.

- Regulators are motivated more by fear of looking bad than a desire to innovate.

But suspend cynicism. Presume that FINRA and government regulators are neutral on how its broker-dealers distribute IPO shares. Boston Beer is not the only issuer who has felt hindered when they sought to crowdfund an IPO.

So, what is going on? Is it hard to allocate IPO shares to average investors?

Or, is it not in the interest of underwriters?

Hmmmmm...investment banks have lots of resources. Plus, they hire bright people and pay them well. So, I'm guessing that the obstacle to crowdfunding isn't that it's too hard to do.

I'm going to go with the second choice—it isn't in the interest of underwriters.

---

2 FINRA is the Financial Industry Regulatory Authority, the SRO that resulted from the 2007 merger of the regulatory arms of the NYSE and the National Association of Securities Dealers (NASD). The NASD is no more, but the NASDAQ echoes its name—the National Association of Securities Dealers Automated Quotations.

Thought Experiment

What do you think the explanation is for why an IPO sold by Wall Street underwriting firms is not crowdfunded?

 a. Investment banks are frustrated because issuers reject their recommendations to make a significant portion of their IPOs available to average investors.

 b. Crowdfunding a portion of an IPO is disadvantageous to an issuer.

 c. Crowdfunding weakens the ability of investment banks to reward customers with whom they want to curry favor.

 d. Other reasons.

A Word About Etsy: The Times, They May Be A-Changing (A Bit)

In April 2015, Etsy, Inc., a New York-based online marketplace for hobbyists and participants in the "maker's movement," had an IPO that raised $270 million. Its management made sure that fifteen percent of the new shares were available to investors who invested between $100 and $2,500.[J]

That qualifies as equity crowdfunding; a significant portion of the new shares are available to average investors. Morgan Stanley and other broker-dealers administered the IPO.[K] That is noteworthy, as this plan of share distribution cuts against their business model. Morgan Stanley even waived conventional fees for new customers who invested between $100 and $1,500.

Etsy sensed benefit from marketing via a distribution of its equity—it relies on word-of-mouth to attract users and spur loyalty. The investment banks saw benefit too. First and foremost, their client wanted it. Secondarily, it signals sensitivity to concern about income inequality and willingness to experiment with crowdfunding. All of this is a good thing. And if Etsy's experience is positive, more Wall Street IPOs may be crowdfunded. The initial reaction was good; the stock doubled from the $16 offering price to $32. Over the next year, it fell as low as $7 but, as of this writing, it is above $73.

The data for this graphic about Etsy's financing history is from Pitchbook Data-graphics.[L] Note how the valuation curve resembles the chart that describes the thesis of this book (see Chapter 2, "The Big Idea and Thesis").

It rises in anticipation of an IPO. Etsy's history suggests that performance was not the principal reason.

Its pre-IPO climb, I think, is best explained by the Next Guy theory.

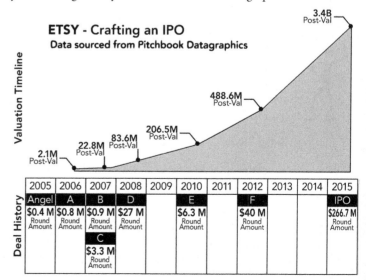

ETSY - Crafting an IPO
Data sourced from Pitchbook Datagraphics

	2005	2006	2007	2008	2009	2010	2011	2012	2013	2014	2015
	Angel	A	B	D		E		F			IPO
	$0.4 M Round Amount	$0.8 M Round Amount	$0.9 M Round Amount	$27 M Round Amount		$6.3 M Round Amount		$40 M Round Amount			$266.7 M Round Amount
			C								
			$3.3 M Round Amount								

The Intermediary Problem for Direct Public Offerings

What are the prospects for equity crowdfunding? If it were potentially profitable for underwriters, surely, they would promote it. If they felt it was simply the right thing to do, more of them would support issuers who want to do it. If there was requirement to do so, they would, but there isn't one and unaccredited investors are not organized to make that happen.[3]

If Wall Street banks are going to support crowdfunding, it will be because issuers like Boston Beer and Etsy press them to do it. And if that is what it takes, my forecast for crowdfunding for hot IPOs is "cloudy with a chance of disappointment." However, broker-dealers that focus on IPOs that are under $50 million are a different matter. They are likely adopters of crowdfunding because such offerings are unlikely attract institutional investors and, hence, to oversubscribe.

What about direct public offerings? Crowdfunding was conceived to be an intermediary-free transaction. But issuers can underestimate how difficult it is to sell an offering without an intermediary. Their challenge compares to that of a real-estate seller who tries to sell a property without a real estate broker-dealer. In both cases, the seller must make potential buyers aware of their deal. In real estate, this is easier if buyers are actively looking in the seller's neighborhood. Investors are rarely so motivated to find a stock. Those who are have many places to look, which makes it hard for a DPO issuer to be noticed.

In real estate, buyers may shy away from even viewing a property without an agent; an intermediary can make them feel more comfortable. One can also help a buyer evaluate an opportunity and perform due diligence.

> *Stocks are sold, not bought* means that investors buy-in response to a persuasive pitch; they don't shop on their own for a stock to buy.

The box below shows some areas where it is uncontroversial to use an intermediary. It is human nature to want one, even when we decide how to proceed ourselves. They can make introductions, reduce awkwardness, and provide information and perspective on how to evaluate something.

Intermediaries for Non-Regulated Transactions

Cars: third parties who review the design, performance, and reliability of vehicles

Colleges: websites that collect data on schools and suggest options to consider

Services: rating services that compile measures of buyer satisfaction

Dating: third parties who identify potential matches and facilitate communication

Dining: websites and publications that identify restaurants and review/rank them

---

The overarching problem for direct public offering issuers is that the opportunity to use *intermediaries who are not broker-dealers* is often closed, narrow, or uncertain. Therefore, while securities law allows for DPOs, in practice, companies are nudged into hiring a broker-dealer, which can be expensive.

---

[3] As discussed in Chapter 5, "The Problem with a Conventional Capital Structure," the interests of public investors are split between those who get IPO allocations and those who buy shares in the secondary market.

Funding Portals – Intermediaries Who Are Not Broker-Dealers

Should parties who are not broker-dealers be allowed to facilitate securities offerings?[4] Put differently, should websites not operated by a broker-dealer be allowed to screen companies, share due diligence on them, and otherwise help issuers market their stock?[5]

This is what the equity crowdfunding debate is partly about. It doesn't matter if the security is a stock or a digital token, which are discussed in Chapter 22, "Blockchain and Initial Coin Offerings."

The question bears on whether one thinks society is better served when broker-dealers have an exclusive franchise to facilitate offerings or when they have competition. The question would not interest so many people if Wall Street IPOs were allocated in a democratic manner. The question would not be significant if innovative companies were satisfied with their access to, and cost of, capital.

The JOBS Act answered the question with a qualified "yes" by authorizing a new online intermediary, "funding portals." They can advertise offerings but cannot:

- offer investment advice or recommendations;
- solicit purchases, sales, or offers to buy the securities displayed on its platform;
- compensate employees, agents, or other persons for such solicitation or based on the sale of securities displayed or referenced on its platform; or
- hold, manage, possess, or handle investor funds or securities.[M]

An organization that intends to engage in any of those activities must register with the SEC as a broker-dealer. To operate, a broker-dealer must also be a member of FINRA, the major self-regulating organization for the financial services industry. Similarly, funding portals must be a member of FINRA or another SRO. Websites operated by broker-dealers to facilitate offerings are called "offering platforms" and they can do what a funding portal cannot.

What Is a Self-Regulatory Organization?

Self-regulatory organizations play a key role in regulating providers of goods and services in several sectors in the US economy. Before discussing FINRA, let's touch on where SROs fit in a regulatory scheme.

There are three models for government oversight of activities that individuals and organizations engage in.

- The default is no oversight at all. One is free to think anything, to say, or write just about anything.
- The direct oversight model covers most activity. People and organizations are subject to criminal and civil sanctions if there is a violation of law that comes to the attention of government (e.g., police, courts, agencies).

---

[4] *Facilis,* the Latin root of facilitate, means to make easy.

[5] Attorneys, accountants, and financial advisors may facilitate introductions and due diligence, but this isn't a practical approach for those who plan to invest a modest amount.

- The third model is to augment direct government oversight with industry self-regulation. This happens where there is a need for more oversight than government usually provides. Organizationally, self-regulation can occur via an industry group, trade association or self-regulated organization—an SRO. All are not-for-profit organizations. Some trade associations and groups are essentially a club for members, while others—especially an SRO—act as a non-governmental regulator. Private sector organizations that practice self-regulation are not a replacement for government; executive departments and agencies retain the ability to form and enforce rules. Rather, they add oversight. An SRO is the most powerful form of it—they have the power to license someone to practice an activity, authority to create and enforce rules of behavior for participants, and to discipline those who violate the rules. The National Association of Realtors is an SRO for real estate brokers and agents—national stock exchanges are SROs for those who have a seat to trade on one. FINRA is the SRO for securities broker-dealers.

Models for How Government Oversight Is Performed

The bargain that a self-regulated industry makes with government is that it can limit direct oversight by establishing and enforcing standards of behavior on its members that are in the public interest. This allows government to avoid spending resources to manage activities at a level of detail it is ill-equipped to perform. It's a way to balance the need for oversight against desire to limit government involvement.

Funding Portals May Need an SRO of Their Own

Funding portals must register with the SEC. Essentially, that's what state regulators wanted Fairshare to do twenty years ago—operate as a regulated entity, not as an unregulated one. (More on that in a moment.)

A portal must also be a member of FINRA or another self-regulatory organization. When you consider the duality of SROs, the choice may be important for the fledgling portal sector and anyone interested in encouraging competition in the financial services industry. Again, SROs are expected to provide oversight that is protective of the public interest, but they are susceptible to behaving like a trade guild to protect the interests of its members.

Two young industry associations exist for portals, the Crowdfund Intermediary Regulatory Advocates (CFIRA) and Crowdfunding Professional Association (CfPA)—they are essentially clubs, as they lack the authority to issue government-like sanctions. Registered portals—there are about 40 at this writing—find it difficult to fund a costly SRO.[6] That's because they are, at best, marginally profitable—they can't charge a commission unless they are a broker-dealer. Absent a viable SRO that is focused on the portal business, they must join FINRA, the one for the very profitable broker-dealer business.

FINRA is a private non-profit organization, not a government agency. Its website points out that it has 3,400 employees in 20 offices who oversee 4,100 securities firms with 640,000 brokers. The SRO is funded by membership fees and fines it collects from members who violate its rules; it levied $75 million in fines and restitution from fraudulent traders in 2013. *The argument for* requiring funding portals to be FINRA members rest on these robust capabilities.

The arguments against FINRA as the regulatory authority for funding portals include:

- FINRA has conflicts of interest as large Wall Street banks and broker-dealers heavily influence it. It is, therefore, unlikely to manage oversight of portals in a way that allows them to undermine the interests of its most powerful members.

- FINRA may smother portals with requirements designed for large broker-dealers.

- FINRA regulators may handicap portals with innovative business models because they don't "get it"—it's too different from what they normally see.[7]

In industry, concentration of power often hinders competition, stifles innovation, and leads to higher prices. Concentration of power in rulemaking and enforcement can have a similar effect.

That last point is buttressed by this passage from a report titled *Improving Entrepreneurs' Access to Capital* by Heritage Foundation senior fellow David Burton.

Large broker-dealers and other regulated financial professionals benefit from reduced competition, from the barrier to entry caused by needlessly complex and expensive laws and from legal provisions that *de facto* or *de jure* force issuers to use broker-dealers;

- The securities bar has a strong interest in complexity because it generates large legal fees; and

- The accounting profession benefits from fees generated by securities laws that require internal control reporting and from needlessly complex financial accounting and laws that require the generation and reporting of information that is, at best, peripherally related to the needs of investors.[N]

If the options for oversight by an SRO are unappealing for portals, an alternative solution is *direct oversight* by the SEC. The agency does this for registered investment advisors who provide services to help others manage their investments; they include money managers, investment consultants, financial planners, and hedge funds. For compensation, investment advisors opine on the value of

---

[6] An SRO must maintain an office, pay officers, attorneys, and other full-time staff to fulfill its responsibilities.

[7] Dividend Reinvestment Plans (DRIPs) are a way for shareholders to buy additional stock directly from the company, without a broker-dealer. These types of programs are about a century old. Here's a thought experiment: If DRIPs were a new idea, would FINRA promote or hinder it?

securities and advisability of buying or selling them. That's something that portals are not allowed to do. So, the oversight work should be much less than what the SEC performs for investment advisors.

Another solution is for FINRA to help fund a portal-focused SRO for a decade or two, enough time to see if it has the ability to affect the financial services industry the way that Walmart altered the retail business or discount brokers like Charles Schwab and E-Trade redefined the brokerage business.

Perspective on Intermediaries Who Are Not Broker-Dealers

For decades, accredited investors have joined to educate themselves about investing, to screen deals and pool due diligence on them. In 1994, a dozen individuals in San Francisco formed the Band of Angels, possibly the first organized angel investor group. The popularity of this form of interaction grew. In 2000, the Keiretsu Forum was formed in the San Francisco Bay area to build on this concept.[8] Today, it is the world's largest angel investor network with nearly 3,000 members in more than fifty chapters. The growth in the number of such groups led to the formation of the Angel Capital Association in 2004; it has nearly 300 angel groups and more than 13,000 accredited investor members.

Angel groups facilitate investments by providing education, community, deal screening and a pooling of due diligence. Before the JOBS Act, such activity risked violating securities regulations because they were not regulated. As a result, meetings routinely began with a benediction like this: "Nothing we discuss here is to be construed to be an offering of securities, which can only be made by a broker-dealer." Then, they went on to facilitate investments!

The need for this fan dance weakened in 2013, when the SEC allowed non-broker-dealers to facilitate investments by accredited investors online. Now, so-called angel investor portals may list private offerings, provide matchmaking services, and facilitate due diligence. But, a portal may not charge success-based compensation—a commission. To do that, some affiliate with, or become, a broker-dealer.

For unaccredited investors, investment clubs provide similar benefits involving securities in the secondary market. The National Association of Investors Corporation—also known as **BetterInvesting. org**—has a membership of 50,000 individuals, most of who are in an investment club. Formed in 1951, the organization reached a peak membership of 400,000 in 1999. Investment clubs are like book clubs, but they discuss investment concepts and stocks. The internet has reduced the appeal of formal investment clubs because there are many websites that provide education about investing and facilitate due diligence of public stocks.

Facilitation of direct public offerings by non-broker-dealers has been controversial because it involves unaccredited investors and does not fit the regulatory framework. An anecdote illustrates this.

Earlier, I mentioned Fairshare, the company I cofounded in 1996 to offer services like those provided by angel groups, but to any investor interested in IPOs by venture-stage companies that used the Fairshare Model. Fairshare said it would charge no commission nor handle anyone's stock or money.

---

8 The Keiretsu Forum describes itself this way. "Keiretsu is a Japanese term for a group of affiliated corporations with broad power and reach. Keiretsu Forum is a conglomeration of individuals or small companies that are organized around private equity funding for mutual benefit. Keiretsu Forum believes that through a holistic approach that includes interlocking relationships with partners and key resources, they can offer an association that produces high quality investment opportunities." fairsharemodel.com/Keiretsu.

A few months into our membership drive, the California Department of Corporations, the state's securities agency, issued a Cease and Desist Order that forbade Fairshare from offering memberships to California residents. It ruled that a Fairshare membership was a security, an investment contract, and since they were not registered as a security, we could not offer them there.

The regulator's website–**dbo.ca.gov/ENF/decisions/**–identifies that ruling as a *Precedent Decision,* which means it is significant and likely to recur in a similar circumstance. California's position is unique. Regulators in Texas, Ohio, and Colorado looked at Fairshare's program but rejected the idea that a membership was an investment contract. The SEC also disagreed with California.

So, five regulatory agencies see the same evidence. One finds that a Fairshare membership is a security and four don't. The movie *Forrest Gump* has a line that captures this situation–"Life's like a box of chocolates, you never know what you're going to get."

Life is a learning experience, and here is what I learned:

- It is easy to create an investment contract in California. For a free Fairshare membership, we just required a name and contact information. A paid membership promised only our best efforts to do what we said we hoped to do, while cautioning that we might be unsuccessful.

- Texas, Ohio, and Colorado wanted to see a regulated entity–not necessarily a broker-dealer– deliver services that facilitate an offering. Investor education and community interaction were not a problem but the services we planned to provide–deal screening, due diligence, and share allocation guidance–tested the boundaries of unregulated activity. Their concern relaxed when we created a subsidiary that registered with the SEC as an investment advisor. Curiously, about a year later, the SEC informed us that our subsidiary did not qualify to be an investment advisor because it was not engaged in activities that required it to be one!

My Fairshare adventure is more fully described in Chapter 9, "Fairshare Model History & the Future." Here, I simply want to share three points:

1. The JOBS Act led the SEC to authorize funding portals, a new type of regulated entity that can provide services that resemble what Fairshare proposed to deliver about two decades earlier.

2. Without the JOBS Act, it is unlikely that an alternative to broker-dealers would be allowed. A reason may be that regulators are loath to innovate if it increases risk, and making it easier for average investors to invest in venture-stage companies carries the potential for them to lose money.

3. There is an inherent tension between rules to protect investors and efforts to spur economic growth. It is a challenge for policymakers to strike the right balance.

Summation

The key takeaway of this chapter is that the Fairshare Model is bigger than equity crowdfunding, which is merely an innovation in selling small offerings that use a conventional capital structure. The Fairshare Model is an innovation in deal structure that can be used in an IPO of any size. Such an offering can use crowdfunding, but it need not.

The distinguishing quality of the Fairshare Model is that the IPO valuation does not factor in future performance.

I like policy initiatives that can make it less expensive for companies to raise capital from public investors. However, I don't have high expectations for equity crowdfunding. The reasons are:

- However one defines equity crowdfunding—a Rule CF offering, a way of selling offerings, or by who has a chance to invest—it will likely involve a conventional capital structure, which creates high valuation risk. Since companies that use equity crowdfunding are bound to have high failure risk as well, public investors are unlikely to make money.
  - ° Note: when a crowdfunded offering uses the Fairshare Model, I will be more enthusiastic about the prospects for investors.
- Equity crowdfunding, as I define it, calls for better access to IPO allocations by average investors, even in those sold on Wall Street, and that's not in the traditional interests of investment banks.
- FINRA may be the only viable SRO for funding portals, but its members are likely to view them as undermining their business interests, especially if the Rule CF offering size is increased or portals are allowed to facilitate Reg. A+ offerings. Should either occur, FINRA might impede portals.

What's Next?

The next chapter will discuss the types of companies that are likely to use the Fairshare Model.

Chapter Endnotes

Contextual references for material in this chapter appear as numbered footnotes on the page where the reference is made. **Source references** for material in this chapter appear below as endnotes with capital letter identifiers.

A Tip of the hat to Kim Kaselionis, founder of Breakaway Funding, LLC (breakawayfunding.com) for pointing out to me the heritage of crowdfunding.

B Robert MacNamara, "Who Paid for the Statue of Liberty?" ThoughtCo.com and the US National Park Services. May 18, 2018. Accessed October 18, 2018. fairsharemodel.com/Liberty.

C Scharpf, Elizabeth. "This Is Not a Typo: Only 3% of Americans Are Legally Allowed to Invest in Startups." *Quartz*. June 22, 2015. Accessed May 08, 2018. fairsharemodel.com/WhoCanInvestInStartups.

D Sjostrom, William K., Jr. "Going Public Through an Internet Direct Public Offering: A Sensible Alternative for Small Companies?" November 2005. fairsharemodel.com/InternetDPOs.

E "Boston Beer: The Sad Fall of an I.P.O. Open to All"; by Reed Abelson, Nov. 24, 1996; *The New York Times*, fairsharemodel.com/Boston-Beer-IPO.

F The song "Fight the Power" by Public Enemy was used to conspicuous effect in the opening credits of Spike Lee's 1989 film, "Do The Right Thing." fairsharemodel.com/FightThePower.

G "Initial Public Offerings, Why Individuals Have Difficulty Getting Shares." *SEC.gov*. November 24, 1999. Accessed May 08, 2018. fairsharemodel.com/IPO-Shares.

H "SEC Sues Morgan Stanley and Goldman Sachs for Unlawful IPO Allocation Practices." SEC.gov. October 2005. Accessed January 25, 2018. fairsharemodel.com/Unlawful-IPO-Practices.

I A study found that shoplifting "was more common among those with higher education and income." Rainey, Clint, and Allegra Hobbs. "Been Caught Stealing." *New York Magazine.* December 8, 2013. Accessed May 08, 2018. fairsharemodel.com/Shoplifting.

J Driebusch, Corrie. "Etsy Inc. Prices IPO at $16 Share." *The Wall Street Journal.* April 15, 2015. Accessed May 08, 2018. fairsharemodel.com/Etsy-IPO.

K Wursthorn, Michael. "Etsy Vendors to Get a Piece of IPO." *The Wall Street Journal.* April 13, 2015. Accessed May 08, 2018. fairsharemodel.com/Etsy-Vendors-Get-IPO-Shares.

L The original Etsy infographic is viewable here fairsharemodel.com/Etsy-Infograph.

M "Registration of Funding Portals." SEC.gov. January 18, 2017. Accessed May 08, 2018. fairsharemodel.com/FundingPortals.

N Burton, David R. "Improving Entrepreneurs' Access to Capital: Vital for Economic Growth." February 14, 2017. *The Heritage Foundation.* Accessed May 08, 2018. fairsharemodel.com/Heritage.

Chapter 7:

Target Companies for the Fairshare Model

What's Included in This Chapter

- Introduction
- The Appeal of the Fairshare Model
- Common Qualities
- Categories of Companies – Overview
    - Feeders (Strategic Category)
        - Sidebar on the Cost of Being a Public Company
    - Aspirants (Strategic Category)
    - Pop-Ups (Non-Strategic Category)
    - Spin-Outs (Non-Strategic Category)
    - Rejuvenators (Non-Strategic Category)
- Possible Variants
- It Can Be Difficult to Assign a Company to a Category
- What's Next?
- Chapter Endnotes

Introduction

What companies might adopt the Fairshare Model? This chapter contemplates five basic categories of prospects.

The Appeal of the Fairshare Model

A conventional capital structure is beset with the valuation challenge, that's why venture capital and private equity funds use a modified conventional capital structure. As public investors understand that they are the Next Guy for dicey IPO valuations, they are likely to express interest in deal structures that offer them price protection too.

If enough investors do this, what might motivate companies to consider adopting the Fairshare Model for their IPO? To begin with, they will respond to the fact that they can attract investors if they do! Additionally, these companies will:

- seek an alternative to a VC round,
- have shareholders who like having tradable shares,
- believe that the Fairshare Model can help them attract and motivate employees, and
- like the idea of using the Fairshare Model to create awareness and support for the company and its products.

Common Qualities

Companies that adopt the Fairshare Model will share two essential qualities. They will be venture-stage companies, and so, present significant failure risk. They will also seek capital via an IPO but, auspiciously, present less valuation risk than those that use a conventional capital structure.

Beyond that, they will be confident that they can deliver the performance investors expect. Those who aren't confident will not adopt a capital structure that ties the wealth of employees to performance. Possibly, a team will be *overly* confident. Confidence is good, but no guarantee. But, would you rather invest in an overly confident team using a conventional capital structure, or one that uses the Fairshare Model?

Of course, an issuer that adopts the Fairshare Model may have trouble attracting private capital, but that can be true for any IPO issuer. Some feel that a company that seeks capital from average investors is desperate—willing and needing to go for unsophisticated money. They believe there is an abundance of private capital available, and if a company can't attract it, there must be a problem with it.

There can be a measure of truth to this. A company that has trouble raising capital is likely to be desperate. No money means failure to launch an initiative.[1] It can also lead to a death spiral. Such pressure may lead management to overstate their prospects, or to understate and/or omit disclosures about unflattering information. Most venture-stage companies are desperate for capital at some point—even those with VC backing. That's because they do not generate enough cash from operations to sustain themselves. And yes, there are VC-backed companies that struggle to find investors for a subsequent round. Some are desperate squared; desperate for capital and desperate to avoid a down round.

So, it's haughty and provincial to dismissively paint all companies that try to raise venture capital in a public offering as desperate. That notion presumes capital markets are efficient in the sense that entrepreneurs with attractive opportunities find the capital they need. Geographically, that's untrue: VCs concentrate in certain cities and favor opportunities within an hour from their office. Industry wise, that's also untrue: VCs flock to market sectors that are hot because they have the potential

---

[1] A startup CEO who appeared to be an exemplar of personal and professional virtue once urged me to "go to the dark side" when dealing with a prospective angel investor because he badly wanted her money. That is, he wanted me to downplay risks the project faced and say only say positive things about the opportunity.

to generate a 30X return on investment (i.e., a dollar investment grows to thirty dollars in value). In Chapter 9, "Fairshare Model History & the Future," I describe an environmental technology startup that led me to co-develop the Fairshare Model. It had promising potential, but that industry sector didn't attract VC interest in the 1990s–internet-related companies did.

Those who pre-judge companies that seek capital from average investors as desperate demonstrate a world view like the one satirized in an iconic *The New Yorker* magazine cover known as "A New Yorker's View of the World." Reimagine it as "A VC's View of the World." Make Manhattan the home base for VCs. The buildings in the foreground are companies that promise to be worth at least thirty dollars for every dollar invested within three to five years. Companies outside that neighborhood are in the land that begins on the other side of the Hudson River and stretches to the other side of the Pacific Ocean. They may be nice, but the VCs will say: "there's just so little time, and there is so much to do here in New York City!"

In passing, I'll note that private capital isn't available to management teams of all backgrounds. Those who attended schools that VCs favor are more likely to get funded while companies lead by women and minorities are significantly underrepresented in VC portfolios.

My point is that VCs don't fully cover the universe of opportunity. Also, companies that pursue an early IPO are *not inherently inferior* to those backed by VCs.

That said, many of the most promising companies will indeed prefer VC backing. But some of them will also consider an IPO if it is beneficial to do so. In any case, a debate about whether the quality of a company is based on whether they raise venture capital via an IPO is of no consequence to average investors. That's because they can only invest in a public offering. For them, the relevant question is whether it is better to invest in an IPO that uses a conventional capital structure or the Fairshare Model.

A company that uses the Fairshare Model will have four characteristics:

1. It cannot attract private capital *on terms it is satisfied with.*

2. The entrepreneurial team is confident in its ability to perform well.

3. The issuer is willing to treat IPO investors as venture partners, not the ultimate Next Guy at the end of a series of private rounds of financing.

4. It believes that Performance Stock will give it a competitive advantage when recruiting and managing employees.

Note that there is no minimum level of revenue or profitability for a company to have an IPO. If you question that, think about biotech companies that have a Wall Street IPO before they have a product to sell. Also know that a company can have an IPO right after it is formed. In fact, an early IPO makes for less expensive offering documents because there is less to disclose.

For example, a company with a large offering–say, over $100 million–is normally required to provide three years of audited financial statements and five years of select financial information. But that doesn't mean it must have at least three years of history before it can go public. If it has been in operation for nine months at the IPO, it need only provide audited statements for the first six months.

Before we proceed to the categories of companies likely to adopt the Fairshare Model, I want to make three points about how *any company* that uses it will raise capital.

1. Normally, issuers target investors who have an affinity for where it is based, what it seeks to accomplish and/or who runs the company. Fairshare Model issuers will have an additional group to pitch—those who will look at any deal that uses the Fairshare Model.

2. A Fairshare Model IPO is more likely to attract buy-and-hold investors. One that uses a conventional capital structure is more likely to attract investors who intend to flip their shares.

3. Some Fairshare Model issuers will target average investors. Some will just sell to accredited investors—offering shares that can be resold in the secondary market. Most will likely use a hybrid approach. They will target wealthy investors for the minimum needed to close the offering, then allow time for average investors to get on board. These scenarios are in the chart below.

Issuer's IPO Share Distribution Scheme

A Fairshare Model issuer might sell small stakes to a large number of unaccredited investors, large stakes to a few accredited investors or some combination of both.

It may surprise you that an option for Fairshare Model issuers is to sell their shares exclusively to accredited investors. After all, it is designed to provide opportunity for average investors. But issuers are in control of their offering and, understandably, they want to raise the money as quickly as possible. If unaccredited investors are slow to buy, an issuer will want to do what it can to close the offering quickly, and that may involve selling the shares to wealthy investors.

The investor mix is not an issue for the Fairshare Model because it is a practical form of idealism. It creates opportunity for average investors, but it doesn't rely on them. Those who matter the most are IPO investors because they supply the capital—it doesn't matter if they are wealthy or not.

In April 2018, Spotify, a leading streaming music company, had a successful IPO that didn't raise any money for the company. It registered shares it had sold to private investors and employees for public trading. Shares opened up trading at $148 and climbed to $180 in two months.

A company might use the Fairshare Model to similar effect, especially if it aspires to have a large customer base. For instance, it could raise the capital it truly needs privately, then raise a modest amount in an IPO, using small allotments to maximize the number of investors. This could expand the customer base, and enhance their loyalty, providing incentive to promote the company to others. Pre-IPO investors would have liquidity at the secondary market trading price. As a bonus, they might have Performance Stock.

Categories of Companies – Overview

So, what type of companies might adopt the Fairshare Model? Five are in the table below and discussed in the pages ahead. Two of them are strategic—I refer to them as "Feeders" and "Aspirants." If they were race cars, a Feeder is a dragster that goes down a straight track as fast as it can—the race is seconds long. An Aspirant is a Formula One car that races for hours over a course with curves. The non-strategic categories are "Pop-Ups," "Spin-Outs" and "Rejuvenators."

Category of Company	Strategic for Fairshare Model?	Goal	Likely IPO Size (in USD millions)	LIkely to be an SEC Reporting Company?	Expectation of Performance Stock Conversion
Feeder	Yes	Launch a product, be acquired	$3 to $10	Maybe	High
Aspirant	Yes	Build a company that lasts	$5 to $20+	Yes	High
Pop-Up	No	Offer equity in a project	Less than $5	Maybe	Low
Spin-Out	No	Alternative to a new VC round	$5 to $20+	Yes	High
Rejuvenator	No	Fund a turnaround	$20+	Yes	High

The table shows the goal of each category of company and the likely size of their IPO. Feeders, for example, are likely to have IPOs between three and ten million dollars. Rejuvenators will seek at least twenty million dollars.

A column refers to the likelihood that an issuer will be an SEC "reporting company"—one that files periodic shareholder reports like a Form 10-Q or 10-K.[A] Expensive legal and accounting work is required to be a reporting company and some Feeders and Pop-Ups might elect to minimize the expense. There are consequences, however. Secondary market investors avoid companies that are not current in their regulatory filings. An issuer's rationale for not being a reporting company could be sensible to IPO investors, however. It may want to maximize the funds available to meet a critical goal, like launching a product. If the value of the stock hinges on a development effort, not quarterly financial activity, it could be a poor use of capital to have lawyers and accountants opine on past progress for an SEC filing. For example, investors in a biotech company with a drug in clinical trials might feel that it is a waste of money to be a reporting company before it is known whether the trials are successful. A non-reporting company strategy is more likely for issuers with a small offering. One that contemplates such a course should disclose it in its IPO documents.

The column for Performance Stock conversions indicates the expectation for conversions. Note that Pop-Ups are the lone category where there isn't necessarily a high expectation.

The secondary market that a stock trades in will be affected by multiple factors, including the number of shareholders. A rule of thumb is the larger the offering size, the better the venues for trading. Shares in small offerings are likely to trade on the pink sheets (the bulletin board), where liquidity can be slim to none. Offerings larger than $20 million may qualify to trade on a NASDAQ platform.

Feeders (Strategic Category)

Feeder fish inspire this moniker. Aquariums use them as food for the larger fish in their collection–big fish eat little fish. The Feeder category is strategic for the Fairshare Model because these companies will most quickly reap its advantages, and their successes will lead others to adopt it.

A Feeder seeks capital to develop something other companies will pay a premium to acquire. For entrepreneurs, this strategy minimizes the cost, risk, and stress of building long-term infrastructure (i.e., employees, facilities, systems) because Feeders focus on product and market development. For investors, such an issuer can generate a return faster than an Aspirant, which is a build-for-the-long-haul company.

Here are a few indicators that Feeders are common:

- In a thirteen-month period, Yahoo acquired twenty startups.[B]

- From its 2006 inception through mid-2013, Twitter made 31 acquisitions.[C] In April 2014, it acquired a year-old company that had raised $1.5 million.[D]

- In August 2014, Samsung acquired SmartThings for $200 million. In 2012, SmartThings used rewards-based crowdfunding to raise $1.2 million from nearly 5,700 backers to launch its product–an average of $210 per person. It went on to raise $16 million from VCs before Samsung bought it.[E]

For a Feeder, the Fairshare Model is an alternative to a VC round. To see how it could work, imagine a company raises $2 million from 100 angel investors who invest $20,000 each. It then raises $10 million in an IPO where half comes from accredited investors who also invest $20,000 each and half from unaccredited investors in $200 allocations.

	Investors Accredited	Investors Unaccredited	Total Capital Raised	Total Investors
Private offering	$2,000,000		$2,000,000	
Average investment	$20,000			
Number of investors	100			100
Initial public offering	$5,000,000	$5,000,000	$10,000,000	
Average investment	$20,000	$200		
Number of investors	250	25,000		25,250
Total after IPO			$12,000,000	25,350

As shown above, the company has more than twenty-five thousand investors who can be evangelists for the company. Some of whom can direct the attention of a potential acquirer to it–a startup can't have too many friends. By *spreading its shares* in this manner, this Feeder spawns interest in its success. By contrast, a company that relies on VC backing *must spend capital* to generate such awareness. And, advertising is unlikely to sustain that interest the way that allowing target customers to own its stock does.

Might an investment of $200 move shareholders to promote the interests of the Feeder? Yes, for two reasons. First, people like to have a team to root for, and they favor those with whom they share an affinity. Second, because the IPO uses the Fairshare Model, the investment is at a *wholesale valuation,* not the retail valuation the public normally gets. The retail valuation could easily be 5 times higher than what the Feeder sold its IPO shares for. In other words, they get a $1,000 stock for $200![2] There is a glee factor in that.

And the interests of Investor and Performance Stockholders are aligned—they both want the company to be acquired. Say there is an offer for $40 million. How might the holders of Investor and Performance Stock decide to split that? We'll look at charts that illustrate two scenarios. Before we do, note that both classes of stockholders must agree on how much Performance Stock converts.

One approach is to decide by prior agreement, to rely on a formula set forth in the issuer's incorporation document.[3] Another is to have the classes negotiate the split.

Failure of the classes to agree means no deal. That invites the problems of divided government, something the US had from 2010 to 2014. Republicans controlled the House of Representatives and Democrats had the Senate and the Presidency. In 2013, the two legislative bodies could not agree on a budget, which threatened a government shutdown. To avoid that, the Congress agreed to a clause to implement automatic budget cuts (a.k.a. sequestration) if they later failed to pass a budget. That forged approval for high-level budget parameters when there was no agreement on specifics.

If the Investor and Performance Stock don't agree on how to share a buyout offer, they face a comparable situation, but the consequence is that they may lose the deal. In addition, if new capital is needed to continue as an independent company, they must agree on the terms. If they don't, both classes are at risk of harm.

Should there be such an impasse, a potential acquirer might propose separate deals to the holders of Investor and Performance Stock, offering employment agreements for enough employees to swing the votes needed. In other words, it may be possible to get a deal done when there is a lack of goodwill among shareholders. If not, the acquirer might come back with a lower price when the company is desperate for new capital, which could be bad for both shareholder groups.

In the two scenarios that follow, there is prior agreement that Performance Stock equal to 2 percent of the Investor Stock outstanding as of the IPO converts each quarter (i.e., 8 percent per year). This "presumed performance" enhances the appeal of Performance Stock for employees and simplifies the issues of defining and measuring performance.[4]

---

[2] The rise in the price of Investor Stock is a measure of performance for this Feeder—it generates conversions of Performance Stock to Investor Stock.

[3] The incorporation document is to a corporation what a constitution is to government. The agreement is first defined by the company and its initial investors. Subsequent amendments require shareholder approval.

[4] A presumed performance conversion clause can be constructed in a variety of ways.

The following chart has the first scenario; the acquisition offer comes *three years after the IPO*. The light grey area shows the proportion of Investor Stock *outstanding at the close of the IPO*. The dark grey area is the proportion of Investor Stock that results from Performance Stock conversions. Note how the origin of Investor Stock changes over the three years; the proportion that results from conversions starts at zero percent and climbs.

Of course, the number of shares of Investor Stock increases as conversions occur, but the chart does not plot this; it does not present the number of shares. Rather, it maps the origin of Investor Stock. The variables in this conceptual equation are for the totality of the Investor Stock.[5]

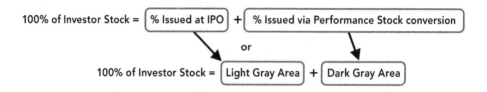

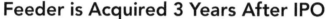

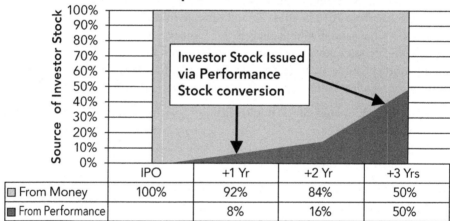

In the chart above, one year after the IPO, the portion of Investor Stock that results from Performance Stock conversion is 8 percent (i.e., 2 percent per quarter times 4 quarters).[6] Two years after the IPO, cumulative presumed performance conversions total 16 percent (i.e., 8 percent for year one + 8 percent for year two). Three years after the IPO, when the offer comes in, it is 24 percent (i.e., add 8 percent for year three to the cumulative total in year two of 16 percent).

Here, the two classes of stock happen to agree to a fifty-fifty split of the $40 million offer—it could otherwise. So enough Performance Stock converts in year three—at the close of the acquisition—to make the cumulative conversion 50 percent and all remaining Performance Stock is cancelled.

---

5 There is no offering after the IPO. The number of shares of Investor Stock issued for money is unchanged.

6 It was 2% one quarter after the IPO, 4% after two quarters, 6% after three quarters and 8% after four quarters.

NOTE: Any deal can be cut, so long as the classes agree. The Big Idea is that the final split of wealth between investors and employees is set after the value of actual performance is apparent, not when investors invest.

In this scenario, the employees make more than if the company had raised the IPO money from VCs.[7] VCs demand a higher return than non-professional investors. Their limited partners–the institutional funds and wealthy individuals who provide the capital expect an attractive return. The general partners who manage the fund want a big payday too.

The entrepreneurial team also has more control than if VCs provide the $10 million. Their voting power is based on Investor Stock they have for performance, plus the Performance Stock. For them, the ability to chart and hold a course may be more important than the financial payoff.[8]

The company's angel investors benefit as well–they didn't have to pony up the money provided by public investors, and it was on friendlier terms than a VC would offer.[9] In addition, the angels have a liquidity option after the IPO; they can sell some or all of their shares, something they could not easily do if the company had remained private; some may sell enough to recover their principal.

In the second scenario, the $40 million acquisition offer comes *one year after the $10 million IPO*. Arguably, Performance Stockholders deserve more because an acquisition happens sooner. In the chart below, the horizontal axis shows time in four quarters, not three years like the last one. As before, presumed performance results in quarterly conversions of 2 percent of what is outstanding after the close of the IPO, or 8 percent per year. Thus, one quarter after the IPO, converted Performance Stock accounts for 2 percent of all Investor Stock, 4 percent after two quarters, and 6 percent after three quarters. It would be 8 percent at the end of four quarters, but the acquisition offer changes that.

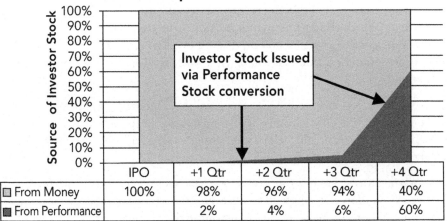

Feeder is Acquired 1 Year After IPO

Source of Investor Stock

Investor Stock Issued via Performance Stock conversion

	IPO	+1 Qtr	+2 Qtr	+3 Qtr	+4 Qtr
☐ From Money	100%	98%	96%	94%	40%
■ From Performance		2%	4%	6%	60%

Time Since Fairshare Model Offering

---

[7] This is in addition to salaries and what employees make on options on the Investor Stock.

[8] The CEO defines the vision. For simplicity, I assume all employees share that vision.

[9] In a VC deal, early investors can be compelled to invest in a new round or lose much of their ownership.

Here, the two classes decide that the Performance Stock deserves 60 percent of the Investor Stock issued as of the IPO. So, 40 percent or $16 million of the $40 million price goes to the Investor Stock, 60 percent or $24 million goes to the Performance Stock. The unconverted Performance Stock is cancelled.

The takeaway is that companies with a Feeder strategy will like the Fairshare Model because its employees can earn more of the appreciation than VCs will allow.

Sidebar on the Cost of Being a Public Company

Before moving to the next category, Aspirants, let's touch on the expense of being a public company. Broadly, these are legal and accounting costs to file public disclosures with the SEC about financial statements, significant changes in ownership, management changes and anything else that investors may consider relevant to their decision to buy, hold, or sell its stock. An issuer that meets these requirements is a reporting company and being one is a requirement for companies that want their stock to trade on stock exchanges. The alternative is unattractive—over-the-counter markets known as the pink sheets or the bulletin board.

The cost of being a public company begins with what it takes to prepare the IPO documents. The more history there is to disclose, the more expensive it is to prepare. If a startup has little history, it has little to disclose. Thus, an offering can be prepared for $20,000 to $60,000. If a broker-dealer is hired, the commission may run 6 to 12 percent of what is sold, plus expenses. Regardless of whether a broker-dealer is used, issuers who need to attract investor attention should expect to spend $50,000 for every $1 million to advertise and market the offering.[10]

Even for a startup, the annual cost to be a reporting company can run $400,000 to $1,000,000 when one considers the fees for legal, audit, investor relation services, the extra compensation for employees knowledgeable about reporting requirements, and premiums for director and officer liability insurance. The JOBS Act reduces some obligations for small public companies, but the cost of compliance remains significant. Much of the cost is fixed, so it falls more heavily on a company that raises $5 million than on one that raises $50 million. The cost can especially burdensome for a troubled company, as the disclosure and accounting issues can be more complex.

These costs will be a concern for Feeders. Some will be a reporting company, but some will choose not to be in order to maximize the funds available for product development and operations. Hopefully, an issuer that takes the latter route will disclose its intent upfront, perhaps by including a statement like this in its offering document:

> Your investment is a chip in a game of chance. The odds of a payoff are not high, and they are not improved if we spend a significant portion of the money that we raise from you to be a reporting company. To maximize the resources available for product development and launch, we may elect to "go dark"—not be a reporting company. If we do that, it may be more difficult for you to find a buyer for your shares. If we are not a reporting company, we intend to periodically notify shareholders of business

---

[10] Estimate provided by Darren Marble of CrowdfundX, a Los Angeles-based marketing firm for public offerings.

developments and of actions that require their approval. Financial statements we provide might be unaudited. Should we not be a reporting company, Performance Stock conversions will be suspended and our directors and management pledge to not sell their Investor Stock until we are again a reporting company for at least 30 days.

Essentially, I suggest two ways for Fairshare Model issuers to deal with the costs of being a reporting company. Plan A is to view the expense as a cost of doing business. Plan B is to decide not to be a reporting company but forewarn investors, and don't allow insiders to acquire or sell Investor Stock while the condition persists.

Aspirants (Strategic Category)

The Fairshare Model is designed for a company with what I call an Aspirant strategy. It aspires to build for the long-term. If it's to be a party to an acquisition, it intends to be the acquirer, not the acquired.

The metaphor for an Aspirant is a Formula One race car because it needs to maneuver through a more complex course for a longer time than a Feeder. That's a way to say that Aspirants have the challenge of defining and measuring performance over several years, during times that are good and bad. Ideas for how to do this will emerge in the shake-down phase of the Fairshare Model.

Feeders is a strategic category for the Fairshare Model because a Feeder's path to success is simple: raise money, demonstrate potential, then get acquired. They provide a limited, straight-forward test. Aspirants is a strategic category because issuers provide a complete test of the Fairshare Model—can organizations create durable incentives for labor and capital? Time and experience will produce evidence. Eventually, a record of accomplishment will be established that encourages companies to use the Fairshare Model in large IPOs.

Compared to a Feeder, an Aspirant's two classes of shareholders have greater need to collaborate because adjustments to conversion rules may be proposed. How they view performance will evolve as the company and its market opportunity does. Their ability to cooperate will be tested by external factors (e.g., economic conditions, market shifts, competition, price of supplies) and internal factors (e.g., leadership attitude, employee turnover, changes in priority). Changes within each shareholder class will play a role; investors who bought their stock at the IPO may have different perspectives on performance than those who invest later. Overall, Aspirants face greater challenges than Feeders.

In each of the five categories, there will be variation based on industry, stage of development, geography, and the personalities of the principals. That's why there is much to learn from the shake-down phase of the Fairshare Model and from the experience of early adopters. Nonetheless, some ideas on how to define performance can be sketched out now.

For a startup, revenue and profitability can be inadequate measures as some issuers will have an IPO before they have product to sell. Other indicators of performance like strategic partnerships and other important relationships may take time to contribute to the bottom line. Cash burn rate is a vital operational measure but difficult to define for Performance Stock conversions. The same can be said for product release, quality, market penetration, and growth in the customer base.

Non-traditional measures of value-creation such as environmental impact and job creation are similarly challenged.

You might think that performance should be easy to define and measure, but it isn't. Think about attractive concepts like peace, justice, fairness, quality, and effectiveness. How easy is it to produce a shared definition? Think about things that are viewed in a negative light—it may be easier to find a consensus definition for harm, injustice, unfairness, and so on.

Often, we are like US Supreme Court Justice Potter Stewart when he issued an opinion in 1964 on whether material was pornographic. He said that he would not attempt to define what the word meant, but said: "I know it when I see it." When it comes to performance, many feel similarly, which presents a significant challenge—can holders of Investor and Performance Stock agree on how to define and measure it?

That said, performance should include raising additional capital on favorable terms. Funding operations is the most important task for a venture-stage company. It is eventually kaput if it fails to do so. When it happens on favorable terms, it's evidence that employees have created value. Another indicator is the market value of the Investor Stock. If it climbs, one can infer performance. But this logic has limits—a drop in the stock price can occur even when employees perform well.

The difficulty of defining and measuring performance makes a case for "presumed performance," the presumption that employees are productive. Most employee stock option plans do this—option grants vest (or are earned) over time, generally three to five years, not based on performance milestones. Such plans avoid the need to define and measure performance. A Fairshare Model issuer might combine this approach—conversions based on presumed performance—with performance-based conversions.

A hybrid solution may be attractive. IPO investors get a deal on the Investor Stock—a deep discount from what the valuation would be if the issuer used a conventional capital structure. They will know that Performance Stock will convert regularly and, as they decide to sell or hold, be able to weigh its dilutive effect on ownership against the prospect that the Investor Stock will rise in price. New investors will also make an assessment. For the issuer, predictable conversions will help recruit, manage, and motivate employees.

There is plenty to think about. The three following charts depict Aspirants over a seven-year period (longer than the earlier ones). The first assumes no Performance Stock conversion. The second chart presumes performance for two years with no milestone performance. The third one presumes performance for two years and strong actual performance after. Collectively, they show how performance conversions might be addressed.

On the following page is the first of the charts. There is neither presumed nor actual performance—the most adverse scenario for employees. Metaphorically, this Formula One race car fueled up with IPO cash but didn't complete a lap of the track. It may due to a bad car, bad driver, or bad weather—whatever the reason, it was a dud. The chart shows no Investor Stock issued via Performance Stock conversions. Thus, all Investor Stock is held by those who paid money for shares or earned them with pre-IPO performance.

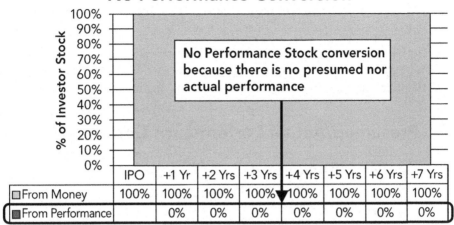

No Performance Conversion

No Performance Stock conversion because there is no presumed nor actual performance

	IPO	+1 Yr	+2 Yrs	+3 Yrs	+4 Yrs	+5 Yrs	+6 Yrs	+7 Yrs
☐ From Money	100%	100%	100%	100%	100%	100%	100%	100%
■ From Performance		0%	0%	0%	0%	0%	0%	0%

Time Since Fairshare Model Offering

Such a situation presents an interesting question. What might happen to such a company when it is about to run out of money? The possibilities are:

1. New capital is raised.

2. The company is acquired.[11]

3. The company dissolves.

I mentioned earlier that the shake-down phase of the Fairshare Model will occur once investors express interest in it. At that point, ideas will emerge about how Performance Stock might work in these scenarios. Of course, a conventional capital structure must deal with them too.

The next chart has presumed performance conversions for two years after the IPO and no measured performance thereafter. As before, presumed performance is eight percent per year of the Investor

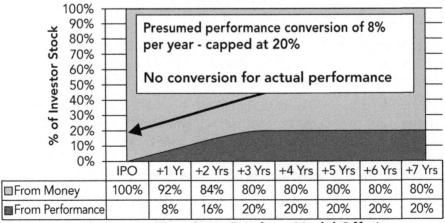

Only Presumed Performance Conversion

Presumed performance conversion of 8% per year - capped at 20%

No conversion for actual performance

	IPO	+1 Yr	+2 Yrs	+3 Yrs	+4 Yrs	+5 Yrs	+6 Yrs	+7 Yrs
☐ From Money	100%	92%	84%	80%	80%	80%	80%	80%
■ From Performance		8%	16%	20%	20%	20%	20%	20%

Time Since Fairshare Model Offering

---

[11] It is not obvious, but a defunct public company has intrinsic value to a private company that wants to become publicly traded via a "reverse merger." You can learn more about this type of transaction online.

Stock outstanding at the close of the IPO (or two percent per quarter) and it is capped at twenty percent. So, presumed performance conversions cease after three and a half years. There are no conversions after that because actual performance is insufficient to trigger them.

In the final Aspirant chart, conversions in the first two years are based on the same presumed performance rule, eight percent per year (two percent per quarter) of the Investor Stock at the close of the IPO. After that, there are conversions based on actual, measured performance.

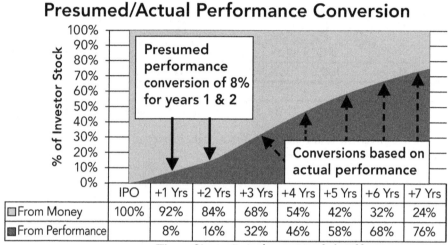

Presumed/Actual Performance Conversion

	IPO	+1 Yrs	+2 Yrs	+3 Yrs	+4 Yrs	+5 Yrs	+6 Yrs	+7 Yrs
☐ From Money	100%	92%	84%	68%	54%	42%	32%	24%
■ From Performance		8%	16%	32%	46%	58%	68%	76%

Time Since Fairshare Model Offering

The reason for the increase in year three is that measured performance begins to exceed presumed performance. This scenario could describe a company that uses its IPO money to develop products, then has a spurt of accomplishment that tails off in subsequent years.

Bear in mind that some employees have Investor Stock at the IPO for pre-IPO performance (i.e., what's in the light grey area). Therefore, an entrepreneurial team that adopts the Fairshare Model can wind up with more ownership than they will when VCs finance their company, provided they perform as their Investor Stockholders expect.

Like the two preceding charts, this one assumes that the company does not issue new Investor Stock. If it does, new investors are sure to buy-in at a higher valuation. As a result, all owners of Investor Stock are happy, regardless of whether they bought their shares or earned them via performance.

The range of scenarios is beyond the scope of this book. It will take time to identify the dos, don'ts and gotcha's that may be important for an Aspirant. One thing is certain, however; the CEOs of Aspirants will have superior ability to communicate, inspire, and manage. They will have keen insight into human behavior and group dynamics. They will also be able to strike a balance between their ego and willingness to be accountable to both classes of shareholders.

What works at one company may not work at others. There will be variation based on industry, stage of development, and geography (i.e., what works in Texas may not work in California). There will also be legal, tax, and accounting issues that all issuers must address. The good news is that there will be legal, tax, financial, and organizational specialists who are eager to help. And, importantly, the benefits promise to exceed the costs of making the Fairshare Model work.

Pop-Ups (Non-Strategic Category)

The term "Pop-Up" is inspired by pop-up stores and restaurants, those that lease space for a few months. The property owner rents space short-term while waiting for a long-term tenant. In the US, retailers who specialize in Halloween goods pop-up in September then go away in November. This activity is not new, but the term Pop-Up is of recent vintage—it reflects rising interest in entrepreneurship, and an opportunity for entrepreneurs to see if they might be onto something.

In the context of the Fairshare Model, a Pop-Up is a company that uses an IPO to fund a project. It could be a product, a movie, a game, mine exploration, or an oil well. It might be a cause; to fund research, improve a city, or a new agricultural practice—use your imagination. At present, this type of money is raised via a contribution- or rewards-based crowdfunding campaign. The difference here is that the people who provide the money get more than a good feeling—they will get tradable stock.

From an investor's perspective, a Pop-Up has dubious traditional appeal because it will need capital later and it is questionable whether others will provide it. Those who provide it are sometimes known as "impact" or "social" investors.

From an entrepreneurial perspective, a Pop-Up is a bud of hope, an indication that investors share the sense that it could eventually be financially viable.

So, investors and entrepreneurs share a view of the worthiness of the project but not necessarily a perspective on the prospect for financial reward. If backers are willing to support the project without equity, they act more like a philanthropist than a traditional investor.

Pop-Ups are not a strategic category for the Fairshare Model because they lack significant investor appeal. They are unlikely to be acquired or be a reporting company hence, their performance is unlikely to generate a financial return for shareholders, and the money raised is more like a contribution than an investment.

> **Game developer raises $51 million via contribution- and rewards-based crowdfunding**
>
> When *Star Citizen* first went on Kickstarter, it had a goal of $0.5 million; it raised $2.1 million by November 2012.
>
> "Sales and members of our community are the two main fund-raising sources," game creator Chris Roberts said. By December 2014, it raised $65 million via reward-based crowdfunding.
>
> Roberts said *"Star Citizen* isn't a normal game. It's not being developed like a normal game and it's not being funded like a normal game. I've had to toss aside a lot of my knowledge from the old way of developing and embrace a completely new world. There is no publisher. There is no venture capitalist wanting a massive return in three years."
>
> Source: *Star Citizen* website

Nonetheless, Pop-Ups will be early adopters because entrepreneurs will conclude that if they offer stock, more investors will contribute, and the Fairshare Model is a more appealing structure than a conventional one.

Spin-Outs (Non-Strategic Category)

A Spin-Out is a company that has raised capital from a VC fund but is not a candidate for another round. VCs refer to these types of investments as the "living dead" or "zombies." In a baseball analogy, they only get to first or second base—VCs seek "triples" and "home runs."

The Fairshare Model may interest VCs because it offers the opportunity to spin-out such companies from their portfolio—public investors fund the next round. An IPO allows them to distribute shares to their limited partners—institutional, or wealthy individual investors. The pre-IPO investors get Investor Stock, and possibly Performance Stock too. The combination provides a VC with liquidity and an upside.

Spin-Outs are a non-strategic category for the Fairshare Model because they will not happen unless Feeders and Aspirants find success with it. In addition, time and experience are not the only barriers to adoption—Spin-Outs mess with two elements of the VC model.

The first is the idea that public investors should pay a high valuation for a promising story. VCs are accustomed to seeing later investors pay high valuations for potential successes. VCs agree with the valuation ideas behind the Fairshare Model—they insist on them in their own deals. That said, few will welcome the idea that IPO investors should get price protection too. Some might even think it is self-destructive to offer them a low valuation because it could affect investor expectations for deal terms on the IPOs of other companies. Similar sensibilities once led retailers of brand-name consumer goods to eschew discount stores, but premium outlet stores show that it is possible to maintain retail pricing in traditional stores and discount pricing elsewhere.

The second element in the VC model threatened by Spin-Outs is the relationship that a fund's general partners have with their limited partners.[12] Adoption of a Spin-Out strategy might invite scrutiny of general partner compensation by the limited partners. Nonetheless, some VCs will explore Spin-Outs—if Feeders and Aspirants have good experiences with the Fairshare Model.

Clayton Christensen suggests a reason to believe that this will be true in his 1997 book, *The Innovator's Dilemma: When New Technologies Cause Great Firms to Fail.* Christensen describes how new entrants in an industry attack the dominant players from the low-end of the market, offering products that are cheaper and/or better in quality, design, etc. For instance, somnolence on the part of US and European automakers created an opening for Japanese manufacturers in the 1960s and 1970s—they ignored the low end of their markets. Korean automakers later adopted a similar strategy to take market share from American, European, and Japanese companies.

Christensen's book provides examples in computers, steel, and even milkshakes. Below is an excerpt from a 2013 interview that he had with Jeff Howe of *Wired* magazine where they discuss a 1996 meeting he had with Andy Grove, then-CEO of Intel Corporation about disruptive innovations.[F] [Bold added for emphasis]

> **Clayton Christensen:** You could see how, in each generation [of computer disk drives], an established company would start focusing on bigger, more powerful disks for the top end of the market and then just get wiped out when the lower end of the market found a way to make smaller, cheaper disks, even though those had lower profit margins. It made my thesis. Smart companies fail because they do everything right. They cater to high-profit-margin customers and ignore the low end of the market, where disruptive innovations emerge from.
>
> **Jeff Howe (Wired):** Is this around the time that Intel CEO Andy Grove heard about your work?

---

[12] A VC fund's general partners manage the fund and its investments—they provide labor. The limited partners provide virtually all the capital.

Christensen: This was before the book came out. I'd published two papers on my theory, and a woman who worked in the bowels of Intel's engineering department went to Andy and said: "You have to read this article. It says Intel is going to get killed." I hadn't even mentioned Intel, but the implications were there. So Grove called me up, and he's a very gruff man: "I don't have time to read academic drivel from people like you, but I have a meeting in two weeks. I'd like you to come out and tell me why Intel's going to get killed." It was a chance of a lifetime. I showed up there. He said: "Look, I'll give you 10 minutes. Explain what you think of Intel." I said: "I don't know anything about Intel. I don't have an opinion. But I have a theory, and I think my theory has an opinion on Intel." I described the idea of disruptive innovations, and he said: "Before we discuss Intel, I need to know how this worked its way through another industry, to visualize it." So I described how mini mills killed off the big steel companies. They started by making rebar cheaper than the big mills did, and the big mills were happy to be rid of such a low-margin, low-quality product. The mini mills then slowly worked their way upward until there was nothing left to disrupt.

Howe: What did Grove say?

Christensen: He cut me off before I could finish. "All right. I got it," he said, and then he described the whole thing. Instead of the mini mills, there were two microprocessor companies, Cyrix and AMD, making cheap, low-performance chips. Grove says: "What you're telling me, Clay, is that we have to go down and kill them, set up our own business unit, and launch our own low-end competitor." I didn't say anything. I wasn't going to be suckered into telling Andy Grove what he should do with Intel. I knew nothing about semiconductors. Instead of telling him *what* to think, I told him *how* to think.

Howe: What did Intel wind up doing?

Christensen: They made the Celeron Processor. They blew Cyrix and AMD out of the water, and the Celeron became the highest-volume product in the company. The book came out in 1997, and the next year Grove gave the keynote at the annual conference for the Academy of Management. He holds up my book and basically says: "I don't mean to be rude, but there's nothing any of you have published that's of use to me except this."

The Fairshare Model is a *disruptive innovation* in finance that will unsettle VCs and Wall Street banks that make boatloads of money selling shares in venture-stage companies to public investors–"the high-profit-margin customers." But VCs are cut from the same cloth as Andy Grove; they are smart, alert to threats and they adapt. For those reasons, some of them, as well as some private equity firms, may experiment with using the Fairshare Model with the singles and doubles in their portfolios, once it has demonstrated that it performs well with Feeders and Aspirants.

Wall Street banks will continue to focus on IPOs for the triples and home runs in venture portfolios because it works well for them. Even so, as interest in the Fairshare Model grows, investment bankers may see investor resistance to the idea of paying handsomely for undelivered performance without price protection.

Thus, the model could eventually have a "trickle up" effect on capital markets. That is, an idea that takes root in small IPOs may influence how larger ones are structured later.

Rejuvenators (Non-Strategic Category)

A "Rejuvenator" is a financially distressed medium-to-large company that seeks to renew its prospects by executing a turnaround—rejuvenating its performance. They can raise capital with a conventional capital structure, but that doesn't have Performance Stock.

Rejuvenators is a non-strategic category for the Fairshare Model—before it is adopted by established companies in a turnaround situation, Aspirants must demonstrate that it helps them attract and manage human capital. It is also a whimsical category as it has the potential to do something big—rejuvenate the relationship of labor and capital in established companies. The category conjures up those that failed to adapt to evolving conditions because they were not imaginative or bold enough. Think of General Motors, Sears & Roebuck, US Steel, Eastman Kodak, and many others.

Here's something to consider: Think about the myriad challenges that GM faced, starting in the 1970s, when the era of rising fuel prices began—low mileage products, uncompetitive manufacturing costs and quality. Now, imagine its response if its capital structure had been based on the Fairshare Model. Surely, if employees had Performance Stock, their response to these developments would have been different because:

1. They could vote on shareholder matters (i.e., the board of directors, which hires and fires officers, sets executive compensation, and proposes dividends).

2. They could benefit financially if the company met performance targets agreed to by the holders of Investor Stock.

Had the interests of capital and labor been better balanced and aligned, the quality of communications, the sense of urgency, responsibility, and commitment among all levels of the organization would surely have been better. It seems likely that the United Auto Workers would have approached contract matters differently had its members been more concerned about GM's vitality. The union might have been more interested in enhancing worker training and involvement in process improvement than in maximizing wages and benefits. It seems likely that management would have relied more on collaboration and knowledge-based authority than on position-based authority. There also may have been more willingness to take product risks, like becoming competitive with high-mileage cars.

Simply put, had GM used the Fairshare Model, it is difficult to imagine the decades-long decline that led to its 2009 bankruptcy.

The standard prescription for an underperforming company is to hire a turnaround CEO who will fix or cull money-losing products and cut expenses (jobs), among other things. There are good reasons for such a move, but it often happens so late in the game that desperate, painful actions are necessary.

The Fairshare Model has the potential to help low-performing companies recognize and arrest their decline earlier and, thus, minimize the havoc associated with a turnaround. Balance and alignment between capital and labor does not avoid the need for painful adjustments, but it can help organizations spot problems earlier and address them in an effective manner.

Possible Variants

Once the conversation about the Fairshare Model gets rolling, the categories of companies are sure to be expanded and refined. To light up your imagination, I offer two ideas and some general thoughts.

The first idea is inspired by Kim Kaselionis, CEO of Breakaway Funding, an investment advisory firm based in Sausalito, California.**G** Before founding Breakaway, she led a bank that had been designated by regulators as failing to achieve fifty-three consecutive profitable quarters. Kim sees potential for equity crowdfunding to help small banks attract capital, enabling them to make loans to businesses in their community. A bank that utilizes the Fairshare Model in such an effort could have investors that define performance in non-traditional ways, such as lending to underserved markets.

The second idea is a public venture fund that raises capital using a Fairshare Model IPO. Securities law allows a company to raise capital to invest in other companies. If the issuer has a target company in mind for an investment, disclosures must be made about the specific candidate. However, if there is no target company, the disclosures are general, describing how management will use the capital. Such a public offering is referred to as a "blind pool" or "blank check" offering, and the issuer is called a "special purpose acquisition company," a SPAC. Venture funds are restricted to accredited investors when the money is raised using a private offering. But if it were raised in a public offering, average investors could participate.

A SPAC's investment criteria could be defined to appeal to investors with specific interests. Below are some possible focus areas:

- *geo-centric:* investments in companies located in a geographic area,
- *university-centric:* funds go to startups with a tie to a school (e.g., license intellectual property from it, founders are alumni, or come out an affiliated incubator).
- *industry-centric:* companies in sectors that have difficulty attracting interest VC funds might be favored. They are likely to have societal value but low commercial appeal (e.g., agricultural, resource conservation, alternative energy, services for the aged, grocery stores that provide healthy foods in poor neighborhoods), and
- *demographic-affinity:* A fund might target companies based on demographic qualities of the entrepreneurs or who their target customers are. Segments might be defined by gender, age, ethnicity, etc.

Should the Fairshare Model be used to raise IPO money for a VC fund, the principals will need to decide how to distribute Performance Stock and how to define the conversion criteria. If such a fund plans to invest in companies with a quasi-charitable focus, it raises the possibility that the Performance Stock would vote but have little chance of converting to Investor Stock.

It Can be Difficult to Assign a Company to a Category

One can't always tell what kind of strategy companies will pursue—they can be shapeshifters. A Feeder may tell you it's a Feeder—but it might tell you that it's an Aspirant. A Pop-Up may believe it's a Feeder or an Aspirant. A Spin-Out can't remain a Spin-Out—it evolves into a Feeder or an Aspirant. And, an Aspirant may wind up being a Feeder after all.

Think of these categories like martial arts moves—a kick, a blow, a block. It is best to learn them separately, as they can appear seamless in actual fighting. Business tactics can have this quality too. A product feature or price, even an acquisition of a company can contemporaneously appear to have aggressive, defensive, or exploratory qualities. Then, in retrospect, the same act may be viewed differently.

The point is that the Fairshare Model has the potential to balance and align the interests of investors and employees in companies in a range of circumstances. Before an issuer adopts it, what-if scenarios must be considered by experts in corporate governance, organizational behavior, and game theory. However, the ability of an issuer to succeed with the model will rest on the ability of its shareholder classes to cooperate.

Regardless of the category they are in, early adopters of the Fairshare Model will be intrepid entrepreneurs who are prepared to tackle their Ponderables.[13] They will be practical idealists who focus on how to make the model work for them. Some of them will be intrigued by the opportunity to reinvent capitalism. What they experience will interest others because the Fairshare Model upends precepts about capital formation and resets the traditional relationship between capital and labor.

Three closing thoughts:

1. Undoubtedly, some companies that use the Fairshare Model will fail. Some of them may report that their experience with it was bad, which will discourage others from adopting it. As failures occur, I hope for fair and balanced analysis of the causes: I feel that any difficulties with the Fairshare Model can be overcome.

2. Fair-to-good experiences with the Fairshare Model will encourage experimentation.

3. Good-to-great experiences with the Fairshare Model will usher in a new era of venture capital, and, it will prod mature companies to seek ways to better align the interests of their investors and employees.

What's Next?

The next chapter will examine the quintessential difference between a conventional capital structure and the Fairshare Model—how they deal with uncertainty. It will also discuss the causes of uncertainty.

Chapter Endnotes

Contextual references for material in this chapter appear as numbered footnotes on the page where the reference is made. **Source references** for material in this chapter appear below as endnotes with capital letter identifiers.

A   In December 2007, the SEC adopted scaled down reporting company rules for issuers that have a public float valuation of less than $75 million. fairsharemodel.com/Reporting-Rules.

B   Indvik, Lauren. "The 20 Startups Marissa Mayer Has Acquired at Yahoo." *Mashable*, July 31, 2013. Accessed May 08, 2018. fairsharemodel.com/YahooAcquisitions.

C   Casti, Taylor. "The 31 Startups Twitter Has Acquired." *Mashable*, September 18, 2013. Accessed May 08, 2018. fairsharemodel.com/TwitterAcquisitions.

---

13 The Ponderables (challenges) for the Fairshare Model at the end of Chapter 4, "Fairshare Model Q&A."

D Tate, Ryan. "Twitter Just Bought a Startup That Could Remake the Service." *Wired*. April 09, 2014. Accessed May 08, 2018. fairsharemodel.com/TwitterBoughtStartup.

E Alois, JD. "SmartThings Raised $1.2 Million on Kickstarter, 2 Years Later the Company Is Acquired by Samsung for $200 Million." *Crowdfund Insider*. August 16, 2014. Accessed May 08, 2018. fairsharemodel.com/SmartThings.

F "Howe, Jeff. "Clayton Christensen Wants to Transform Capitalism." *Wired*. February 12, 2013. Accessed May 08, 2018. fairsharemodel.com/Christensen.

G For more information about Breakaway Funding, visit breakawayfunding.com.

Chapter 8:

The Tao of the Fairshare Model

What's Included in This Chapter

- Introduction
- A Different Approach to Uncertainty
- Uncertainty Illustrated
- The Treatment for Uncertainty – Multiple Classes of Stock
  - Ownership Payoffs Using Single Class Stock
  - Ownership Payoffs Using Multiclass Stock
  - Structural Characteristics That Can Lead to a Bizarre Ownership Payoff
- Negative vs. Positive Energy – The Allure of the Fairshare Model
- Summation
- What's Next?
- Chapter Endnotes

Introduction

Taoism (or Daoism) is an ancient Chinese philosophy about indefinable truths underlying the universe, which are revealed in the natural order of things. Tao (or Dao) has multiple meanings but, broadly, it is a path, an appropriate way to behave and to lead others. One's tao is about balance, sensing what is missing and restoring it. Everyone has his or her own tao and finding it requires meditative and moral exploration.

This chapter describes the tao of the Fairshare Model—its approach to living in harmony with the uncertainty that is inherent when bringing equity capital into a venture-stage company. The Fairshare Model's tao—its sense of the natural order of things—is at odds with the tao of a conventional capital structure, at least the kind presented to IPO investors. That's because such a deal structure offers public investors far less protection from uncertainty than it offers private investors.

On the other hand, the tao of the Fairshare Model is like the tao of capital structures used by venture capitalists—a modified conventional capital structure. Both seek to balance performance uncertainty with ownership uncertainty. Each does it differently, but that's because their audiences are different–the VC model is for private investors, while the Fairshare Model is for public investors.

This chapter contrasts how the performance uncertainty is addressed in the VC model and the Fairshare Model. It shows how the Fairshare Model relies on positive energy to align the interests of investors and employees. And, it will discuss *the most astonishing aspect of the Fairshare Model—it causes entrepreneurs to be indifferent about their IPO valuation. In fact, it gives them reason to make it low.*

As we begin, think of performance uncertainty for investors as having two components: failure risk and valuation risk.

Performance Uncertainty = Failure Risk + Valuation Risk

A capital structure cannot reduce failure risk, but it can reduce valuation risk.

A Different Approach to Uncertainty

The Fairshare Model is for an IPO, one that anyone can invest in. Its goal is to emulate the deal structure that VCs (and private equity investors) rely on when they invest in a private offering. The VC model is a conventional capital structure, modified to provide price protection or less valuation risk.

VC Model = Conventional Capital Structure + Deal Terms that Reduce Valuation Risk

The Fairshare Model differs from a conventional capital structure in how it deals with uncertainty. *Uncertainty is inescapable* when balancing ownership interests and performance risk. And an issuer's shareholders and prospective investors both struggle to agree on who bears the risks of uncertainty. As they work toward agreement, the two groups resolve this question: *Is it better to define the ownership interests of insiders before or after performance is delivered?* Put another way, *who should bear the risk of valuation uncertainty, insiders—that is, employees and existing investors—or new investors?*

There are those who feel that ownership interests should be *set before performance is delivered.* They believe the uncertainty of future performance should be borne by new investors. People who feel this way don't understand how VC investments are structured, or they believe that private investors ought to get a better deal than IPO investors. Accordingly, those in this camp favor a conventional capital structure for an IPO.

> With a conventional capital structure, the bet is on what future performance will be.
>
> With the Fairshare Model, the bet is on human behavior; will shareholders agree on how to reward performance?

Then there are those who feel ownership interests should be *set after performance is delivered.* They believe what's good for VCs is good for IPO investors too. People in this camp will like the Fairshare Model.

So the essential difference between the VC Model and the Fairshare Model is *when* the ownership split is decided–before or after performance is delivered. We'll consider the distinction with a simple example and visual device.

Assume that newly formed ABC Company raises $5 million in exchange for half the company. Using a conventional capital structure, the new investors and employees agree on a $5 million *pre-money* valuation (i.e., pre-investment). After the money is raised, the *post-money* valuation is $10 million. Here is how it breaks down.

	Valuation	Ownership
Pre-Money Valuation (Employees)	$ 5 million	50%
Money (New investors)	5 million	50%
Post-Money Valuation (Combined)	$ 10 million	100%

A puzzle? Not to worry! This narrative explains what you need in order to contemplate the tao of the Fairshare Model. These terms are further explained in Section 3, Valuation.

The parties—the founders and investors—have established certainty with respect to ownership—they agree the new investors get half of the equity. In doing so, the parties effectively agree that the *present value* of the company's future performance is $5 million, even though it is just an idea.[1] The post-money valuation of $10 million is the value of future performance—$5 million—plus the $5 million investment, the money.

However, no one knows what the performance will be. Nor do they know what the valuation will be in the next round, when more money is needed. The bet, the uncertainty, hinges on whether the company will meet expectations and what market conditions will be. It doesn't matter how the parties came to value the future performance at $5 million, it only matters that they did.

So, there is certainty regarding ownership and uncertainty about what the future performance will be worth. If the company is worth less than $10 million in the next round, the value of the new investors position erodes. Why? Their $5 million was worth that amount before they invested. If the next round valuation is less than $10 million, the future performance was worth less than the $5 million pre-money valuation they accepted.

Of course, the investors may also feel that they overpaid if the next valuation isn't more than $10 million. After all, they invested $5 million with the expectation that the company would make it more valuable. A $10 million pre-money valuation for the next round represents no appreciation. Then too, if the appreciation—measured by the valuation in subsequent rounds—is below the investor's target rate of return, they will be unhappy.

Performance uncertainty affects the founders too. They may have wistful regret if their idea/performance turns out to be worth much more in the second round. For instance, if the second-round valuation is $20 million, they may ask, *Weren't we worth more than $5 million in the first round? Did we sell too cheap?*

Chances are, though, that the founders will not beat themselves up too much about the first-round valuation because it is water under the bridge. Besides, there are ways to rationalize it. They may not have gotten where they did without that money. It may have been the best available option.

---

[1] "Present value" is the value today of a future stream of income or cash, discounted for risk and time. A dollar that you get in five years is worth less than a dollar today. Today's value of that future dollar is the present value.

"Investors are reportedly begging Warby Parker to let them invest at a billion-dollar valuation."

Source: *Business Insider,* March 2015

"This is certainly not the fabulous exit that Fab was hoping for. The ecommerce service once valued at nearly $1 billion has been acquired for about $15 million."

Source: *Mashable,* March 2015

"Nextdoor, which runs a social network for people to interact with others who live in their physical neighborhoods, is the latest private tech company to join the swelling ranks of the billion-dollar valuation club."

Source: *Techcrunch,* March 2015

Uncertainty Illustrated

To grasp the tao of the Fairshare Model, imagine a long balloon, the kind that looks like a hot dog and can be twisted into animal shapes. But instead of air, this balloon is full of uncertainty. The left end of this balloon represents ownership interests in a venture-stage company, while the right end represents the value of its future performance.

Ownership side   Performance side

And what is a venture-stage company? Again, regardless of whether it is privately held or publicly traded, it is one that has the following risk factors for investors:

- market for its products/services is new or uncertain,
- unproven business model,
- uncertain timeline to profitable operations,
- negative cash flow from operations–*requires new money to sustain itself,*
- little or no sustainable competitive advantage,
- execution risk; team may not build value for investors.

Pressing down on the balloon creates certainty, but it does not eliminate uncertainty, it simply moves it. A weight symbolizes certainty in our imagery. Placing the weight at one end of the balloon creates certainty there but causes uncertainty to bulge on the other end.

This is a way to show that when a venture-stage company raises equity capital, uncertainty can be moved but it can't be eliminated. This is true whether the funds come from accredited investors in a private offering or from public investors in an IPO.

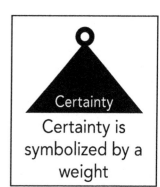

Certainty is symbolized by a weight

The next three balloons will help you visualize the essential difference between a conventional capital structure, a modified conventional capital structure, and the Fairshare Model. It is all about *when* the ownership split for investors and employees is decided–*before or after performance* is established.

The following balloon portrays what happens in a conventional capital structure. Ownership interests are established at the time of an equity financing–the ownership split between employees and investors is set. It is symbolized by the certainty on the ownership end of the balloon. The creation of certainty there pushes uncertainty to the performance end of the balloon.

Conventional Capital Structure
Where the Uncertainty Is

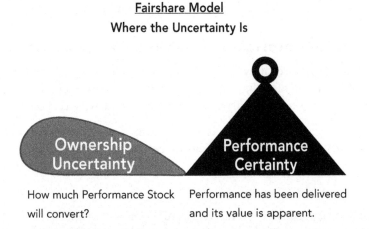

Ownership interests are set   Will performance be delivered?
when there is financing.   How valuable will it be?

Will the company deliver its new product as expected? How will the market respond to it? The answers to these questions would surely influence the deal if they were known when the investment is made. But, in a conventional capital structure, the kind offered to IPO investors, ownership interests must be decided before the answers are known, when the investment is made.

What happens in the Fairshare Model, as the next balloon shows, is that performance has been delivered and its value is more apparent. That is why the weight of certainty is on the performance end of the balloon. Placing it there moves uncertainty to the ownership end.

Fairshare Model
Where the Uncertainty Is

How much Performance Stock   Performance has been delivered
will convert?   and its value is apparent.

Here, the uncertainty centers on how much Performance Stock will convert. Will the criteria to convert Performance Stock match the performance delivered? If there is disagreement between the shareholders of Investor Stock and Performance Stock, how will it be resolved? If either or both classes believe the conversion criteria should change, will they be able to agree on a new set?

In the Fairshare Model, employees don't get Investor Stock for *future performance,* they get it for *past performance.* [Note: Future performance can be presumed, as described in Chapter 7, "Target Companies for the Fairshare Model," but the conversions happen quarterly, not as an up-front, lump-sum total, as in an IPO that uses a conventional capital structure.]

As the final balloon illustrates, when VCs invest in a private offering, they modify a conventional capital structure with deal terms that suspend certainty about ownership until there is certainty about performance.

For employees, they require vesting schedules for stock issued for ideas and future performance. Shares already owned by employees may be subject to buyback or forfeiture agreements.[2]

A VC's deal terms can create uncertainty for other investors too. They may find that their ownership interest or payout is reduced or even wiped out to increase what the VC gets.

My purpose here isn't to argue whether VCs treat employees and other private investors fairly or not. It's to point out that *VCs use complex capital structures to deal with uncertainty.* And that leads to a question. If companies offer VCs complex capital structures, shouldn't they offer them to public investors too?

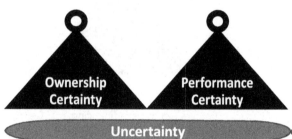

Modified Conventional Capital Structure

Used by VCs in Private Offerings

VCs suspend the weight of ownership certainty until there is performance certainty. Their deal terms enable them to retroactively increase ownership if a company falters and expand their ownership when it looks like a winner.

An IPO based on a conventional capital structure is simple to understand because it has a single class of stock. But is simple better? The smart money doesn't think so. We'll see why next.

The Treatment for Uncertainty – Multiple Classes of Stock

There is no panacea for the uncertainty that is inherent in a venture-stage investment, but there is a way to treat it. It involves the use of multiple classes of stock to structure control and economic interests. VC and private equity firms require companies they invest in to have such a capital structure.[3]

It is unusual for an issuer to have multiple classes of stock in an IPO, however. When it happens, it is to create preferential voting or dividend rights for certain pre-IPO shareholders—to provide them,

---

[2] There are vesting schedules for stock options too.

[3] Private Equity (or PE) is a superset of venture capital. All VC firms are a form of PE, but VCs focus on private, early-stage companies while PE firms invest in established businesses, both private and public.

not IPO investors, with a better deal. *The Fairshare Model is novel because it uses a multiclass capital structure to protect the interests of IPO investors.*

To understand how, one must distinguish an *ownership interest,* the proportion of total shares owned by a shareholder, from an *ownership payoff,* which is the proportion of value the shareholder receives when there is a liquidity event–the company goes public or is acquired.

When a company has a conventional capital structure, it has a single class of stock, which means there is no difference between a shareholder's ownership interest and any ownership payoff. Shareholders with half the ownership receive half the proceeds from an acquisition, for example.

When a company has a modified conventional capital structure, it has multiple classes of stock. In such a situation, as these conceptual formulas indicate, ownership interests and ownership payoffs are likely to differ.

Conventional capital structure (which has a single-class of stock)	*Means that*	Ownership interest	=	Ownership payoff
Modified conventional capital structure (which has multiple classes of stock)	*Means that*	Ownership interest	≠	Ownership payoff

Again, IPOs almost always use a conventional capital structure and VC/PE funds require a modified conventional capital structure when they invest in a private company. When there is a liquidity event, its capital structure converts to a conventional one. The process is described in Chapter 4, "Fairshare Model Q&A," under the heading "What Leads a Capital Structure to Change?"

Let's return to ABC Company, our example earlier in this chapter. Having raised $5 million at a pre-money valuation of $5 million, it has a post-money valuation of $10 million–employees and investors each own half. We're about to see how shareholders with a 50 percent ownership interest can wind up with a quite different ownership payoff when the company is acquired a year later

Ownership Payoffs Using Single-Class Stock

The following table shows the ownership payoff for investors and employees if ABC Company has a single-class of stock in three scenarios–an acquisition price that is good ($30 million), mediocre ($12 million) and poor ($2 million).

	Good Price	Mediocre Price	Poor Price
Acquisition Price	$30 Mil	$12 Mil	$2 Mil
Less: post-money valuation	(10 Mil)	(10 Mil)	(10 Mil)
Valuation increase/(decrease)	20 Mil	2 Mil	(8 Mil)
Investors (non-VC)			
50% ownership interest (split)	$15 Mil	$6 Mil	$1 Mil
Less: cash investment	(5 Mil)	(5 Mil)	(5 Mil)
Ownership payoff	$10 Mil	$1 Mil	($4 Mil)
Employees			
50% ownership interest (split)	$15 Mil	$6 Mil	$1 Mil
Less: cash investment	de minimis	de minimis	de minimis
Ownership payoff	$15 Mil	$6 Mil	($1 Mil)

Put off by a table of numbers? Then skim this and the others. The numbers are not important here, the narrative is.

Note that in each scenario, the ownership payoff for employees is better than for investors. That's because investors paid cash for their ownership and that must be netted out of their gross split of the proceeds. Employees, on the other hand, paid a trivial or *de minimis,* amount of money for their stock.

In the good scenario, the acquisition price is $30 million, which is $20 million over the $10 million post-money valuation ABC Company had after its $5 million raise. Investors net $10 million as their ownership payoff, after deducting their $5 million investment from the $15 million they get for their ownership interest. The ownership payoff for employees is equal to their $15 million ownership interest.

In the mediocre scenario, the appreciation is $2 million ($12 million acquisition price less $10 million post-money valuation). The ownership payoff for investors is $1 million after deducting their $5 million investment from their $6 million ownership interest. The ownership payoff for employees is $6 million, the same as their ownership interest.

In the poor scenario—there is an $8 million loss in enterprise value ($10 million post-money valuation less $2 million acquisition price). The ownership payoff for investors is a loss of $4 million after deducting their $5 million investment from their $1 million ownership interest. The ownership payoff for employees is $1 million, the same as their ownership interest.

Overall, the good-price scenario makes sense because the value of the company tripled, from $10 million to $30 million in one year. The employees delivered, either through performance or by offering investors a low buy-in price.

The outcomes in the mediocre- and poor-price scenarios, however, are best described as bizarre for investors who made it possible for the employees to be paid for their work. Despite that, in the mediocre scenario, they make $1 million while employees make $6 million. In the poor scenario, investors lose $4 million while employees make $1 million.

Ownership Payoffs Using Multiclass Stock

The next table has the same set of acquisition prices and the same ownership scenario, half is owned by those who invested $5 million and half is owned by employees. The difference is that ABC Company raised the $5 million from a VC using a multiclass capital structure. It also assumes that the VC has a "liquidity preference" for twice the amount of its investment.

In his 2011 book, *The Business of Venture Capital,* Mahendra Ramsinghani says that "liquidation preferences, often seen as an opportunity to juice up the returns, are rights to receive a return prior to [other] shareholders" when there is a liquidation event.[4] An acquisition is a liquidation event. Multiples of one or two are common but they are sometimes as high as ten.[5] Another popular way for a VC to boost its ownership payout is to secure a dividend or management fee—effectively, interest on their investment that is paid when there is a liquidity event. But, for simplicity, those are not assumed here.

---

[4] Ramsinghani, Mahendra. *The Business of Venture Capital: Insights from Leading Practitioners on the Art of Raising a Fund, Deal Structuring, Value Creation, and Exit Strategies.* Hoboken, NJ: John Wiley & Sons, 2014. page 239.

[5] Ibid.

This 2X liquidity preference gives the VC a priority claim to the first $10 million of the price (i.e. $5 million investment with 2X liquidation preference.) What is left is split evenly between the VC and employees. In the case of the $2 million poor price, there isn't enough to cover the preference, so there is nothing for the employees, which is fitting.

	Good Price	Mediocre Price	Poor Price
Aquisition Price	$30 Mil	$12 Mil	$2 Mil
Less: VC's 2X liquidity preference	($10 Mil)	($10 Mil)	($2 Mil)
Available for 50-50 ownership split	$20 Mil	$2 Mil	None
VC investor			
Liquidation preference (from above)	$10 Mil	$10 Mil	$2 Mil
50% ownership split	10 Mil	1 Mil	None
Less: investment	(5 Mil)	(5 Mil)	(5 Mil)
Ownership payoff	$15 Mil	$6 Mil	($3 Mil)
Non-VC investor outcome in prior table	$10 Mil	$1 Mil	$(4 Mil)
Better for VC than single class by:	$5 Mil	$5 Mil	$1 Mil
Employees			
50% ownership split	$10 Mil	$1 Mil	None
Less: investment	None	None	None
Ownership payoff	$10 Mil	$1 Mil	None
Employee outcome in prior table	$15 Mil	$6 Mil	$1 Mil
Worse for employees than single class by:	$(5 Mil)	$(5 Mil)	$(1 Mil)

Note that in both the good and mediocre scenario, the VC makes $5 million more that the non-VC investors did in the single-class capital structure table. That comes out of what the employees had. It can, and often does, also come out of the ownership payoff of other investors, like angel investors.

Also, in the poor scenario, the $2 million price doesn't cover the liquidation preference, so the VC gets the entire price—there is nothing to divide with others.

A multiclass structure allows VCs to deal with performance uncertainty, which involves failure and valuation risk, by creating uncertainty for the *ownership interests* of other shareholders. It also allows them to increase their *ownership payout* above what's suggested by their *ownership interest*.

Structural Characteristics That Can Lead to a Bizarre Ownership Payoff

A single-class stock structure—a conventional capital structure—will deliver a bizarre ownership payout when the performance outcome is mediocre or poor. A multiclass capital structure—a modified capital structure, the kind used by VCs—can ensure that this doesn't happen.

The next table, on the following page, shows why. It lists three characteristics that enable bizarre ownership payouts, and the capital structures that have them.

Capital structure characteristics that enable bizarre ownership payouts	Conventional Capital Structure (IPOs)	Modified Conventional Capital Structure (Private Offerings)	Fairshare Model (IPOs)
Type of capital structure →	Single-class	Multi-class	Multi-class
1. Ownership interests are issued upfront for future performance.	Yes	Yes	Yes
2. Significant value placed on future performance when investment is made.	Yes	Yes	No
3. The same type of ownership interest issued for future performance as for capital	Yes	No	No

All three capital structures share the first characteristic—ownership interests are issued upfront for future performance. With either conventional capital structure, employee stock issued upfront may be subject to restrictions, such as vesting over time or via performance. With the Fairshare Model, Performance Stock is issued upfront to establish ownership interests in the form of voting rights and the potential for conversions into Investor Stock. Companies are likely to issue Performance Stock to a trust to administer for the benefit of employees.

The second characteristic is that significant value is placed on future performance. This is the defining quality of both a conventional structure and a modified conventional structure. The price of any stock issued—common or preferred—assumes a value for future performance. The Fairshare Model does not have this quality—Performance Stock has no market value because it is not tradable and it does not have a significant claim on the issuer's assets. It has the right to vote, and the potential to convert to Investor Stock. That's it.

The third characteristic is that the same ownership interest is issued for future performance as for capital. With a conventional capital structure, companies sell investors the same common stock that employees get for future performance. Neither a modified conventional capital structure nor the Fairshare Model has this characteristic because each uses a multiclass capital structure.

With a modified conventional capital structure, a different type of stock from what employees get allows investors to secure price protection. That is, terms that protect them from accepting too high a valuation—the second characteristic.

With the Fairshare Model, tradable Investor Stock is issued for capital and past performance while employees get non-tradable Performance Stock for future performance.

So the tao of the Fairshare Model is about reflecting how life truly is. For a person, meaning and purpose are revealed over time. For a company, value is revealed by performance.

By changing *when* the ownership split between investors and employees is decided, the Fairshare Model encourages public investors to support risky ventures. It does that by replicating investor protections VCs insist on for themselves. It is merely a novel application of a proven idea.

A fairer deal for public investors can foster more equity funding for venture-stage companies. This, in turn, enables more entrepreneurs to pursue the good life.[6] Vicariously, it helps public investors do the same thing. As such, the Fairshare Model makes them partners, both in substance and spirit.

Negative vs. Positive Energy – The Allure of the Fairshare Model

All involved in venture capital know that investors want a low valuation and entrepreneurs want a high one. Reaching an agreement can involve a contest of wills. The agreed-upon valuation may have terms that make the deal less attractive if the founders totally understand them.

On the other side, an entrepreneurial team may oversell or deceive investors. The negotiation would be one thing if there were a right valuation, a truth that can be revealed at that point. But, it is actually quite another thing because neither side knows what the value will turn out to be.

Ultimately, if a deal is done, interests are aligned. They fall out of alignment if things don't progress as expected. Then, the battle over valuation can be renewed and devolve into a struggle for control. The entrepreneurs may lose ownership. Investors may lose some as well to other investors who have price protection. So, in a conventional model, parties assume opposing positions and may return there if things don't go well. The process has negative energy.

> An interesting conflict can arise in an "inside round," a private offering financed by existing investors. They will favor a lower valuation than it would be if the money came entirely from new investors. Employees will want higher one than that. The conflict can be avoided if a new investor added and made responsible for pricing the round.

In the Fairshare Model, pre-money valuation isn't a battle, the process has positive energy.[7] There's no struggle between a company and its investors because they don't begin on opposite sides of the table with respect to valuation. Investors want the valuation to be low, of course. But–*and this is the amazing part*–entrepreneurs don't mind providing one. In fact, they will want the IPO valuation low! Ridiculously low in the minds of those using a conventional model; alarmingly low, to those at comparable companies.

If a company adopts the Fairshare Model, its directors, executives, and other employees don't care what their pre-money IPO valuation is. They are indifferent as to whether it is $500,000 or $5,000,000 or $500,000,000–because it doesn't affect their financial position or voting power. **What matters to them is what it takes for Performance Stock to convert.**

If a rise in valuation–the market value of all the Investor Stock–is a measure of performance, a low IPO valuation is in the interest of both new investors and employees. New investors like it–after all, a low buy-in is the first part of "buy low, sell high."

---

6 The Aristotelian concept of a Good Life is discussed in Chapter 10, "The Macroeconomic Context – Growth."

7 This dichotomy evokes a famous comedy routine performed by the late George Carlin that contrasts baseball and American football. You are sure to laugh even if you have little interest in sports. To view it, do a web search for "Carlin baseball football" or use this link fairsharemodel.com/Carlin. Transcript here fairsharemodel.com/CarlinText.

Employees like a low IPO valuation of Investor Stock too because it makes it easier to meet a valuation performance measure. It also makes it more likely that stock options on Investor Stock will be in the money because they will have a low exercise price.

What about those who invest before a Fairshare Model IPO? How might those investors think about a low IPO valuation? Not at all well, one might think. After all, they also want to "buy low, sell high" so "buy low, sell a bit higher" can be expected to have little appeal. However, there are reasons why a company's pre-IPO investors might support a low valuation with a Fairshare Model IPO.

1. The company gets the capital it needs, and pre-IPO investors don't need to provide it.

    ° Many early investors dread having a company that will need more money than they can provide, one that struggles to find investors for the next round.

2. Pre-IPO investors can avoid the ownership squeeze that VCs inflict when there is a down round of financing or other performance targets are not met. Two examples:

    ° A VC's anti-dilution provisions provide price protection. If a later transaction lowers the company's valuation, the VC gets more shares for free, reducing its overall price per share and increasing its ownership share. That provision, known as a price ratchet, can be invoked if a single shareholder sells shares to a family member at a price that is lower than the VC paid.

    ° A "pay-to-play" right allows a VC who invests in a new round to force other shareholders to do so too or lose the ownership position that they have.

3. The secondary market price is likely to be substantially higher than the IPO price. A Fairshare Model IPO will reflect market value the way a Black Friday sale reflects the value of a consumer product.[8] In one, a television normally priced at $2,500 might be sold for $500. The dynamics of a low valuation and small allotments may cause the share price of an issuer's Investor Stock to climb in the secondary market, even if it is a "penny stock."[9]

4. Pre-IPO investors might have Performance Stock as a sweetener for supporting the deal.

5. If pre-IPO investors have warrants on the Investor Stock, they can profit from the delta between the warrant exercise price and the price of Investor Stock in secondary trading. Essentially, a warrant is a stock option for non-employees; it is the right to buy stock in the future at a set price. If the exercise price is below the price later set in the secondary market, warrant-holders can profit.

6. By enlarging an issuer's network of investors, a Fairshare Model IPO fosters vibrant secondary market trading, which is conducive to a rising stock price.

7. By making it possible for many customers to be investors, an issuer promotes loyalty and favorable word-of-mouth reviews without an expensive advertising campaign—and that can lead to better operational results.

---

[8] *Wikipedia:* Black Friday is the Friday following Thanksgiving Day in the US and regarded as the beginning of the Christmas shopping season. Many retailers open early and offer sales to kick off the shopping season. Violence sometimes occurs among shoppers competing for access to the limited supply of deeply discounted items.

[9] *Wikipedia:* Penny stocks are shares of public companies that trade at low prices per share. In the US, a penny stock is one that trades below $5 per share, is not listed on a national exchange, and fails to meet other criteria.

8. Employees are motivated to deliver the performance that triggers conversions. This enhances the ability of the company to attract and retain employees.

For these reasons, the most likely objectors to a low IPO valuation—investors in the issuer's private offerings—may be inclined to support one if the Fairshare Model is used.

But how about after the IPO? What if things don't go well? After all, a company can encounter rough seas, just as ships do. Will the positive energy created by the IPO dissipate? Can a capital structure make a difference in how well difficulties are weathered? If so, which is better equipped to navigate the challenge, an issuer with a conventional capital structure or the Fairshare Model?

It's speculative to say at this point, as is the ability of companies to raise money using the Fairshare Model. That said, when things don't go well for a company, the Fairshare Model relies on positive energy to address the problem. Management will feel pressure to take corrective action from investors regardless of the deal structure but if the Fairshare Model is used, other employees will also be a vocal constituency. Their ability to convert Performance Stock depends on working through the trouble, turning lemons into lemonade.

Troubles may lead to a reexamination of the conversion criteria. This may be difficult, but achievable targets will result because positive energy helps identify pathways to success.

The potential to create alignment between investors and employees is the most exciting aspect of the Fairshare Model. If the owners of Investor and Performance Stock agree to change the conversion rules, it makes a company a remarkably agile competitor. This may be more significant than its potential to help companies raise capital.

The Achilles heel of the Fairshare Model may be that it is too difficult to efficiently reach consensus on how to adjust conversion rules. This topic is explored a bit in Chapter 12, "Cooperation as the New Tool for Competition," as well as in Chapter 18, "Failure." While the issue is hard to forecast, it is safe to say that some types of leaders are better suited for the Fairshare Model than others.

For contrast on that last point, consider how a company with a conventional capital structure is equipped to deal with adverse conditions. Negative energy is likely to define decision-making because of the importance of valuation. If events suggest that it was too high, blame is cast and factions form.

If a modified conventional capital structure is used, shareholders without price protections may feel that those with protective terms are using the foul weather to extract advantage at their expense.

By contrast, the energy in the Fairshare Model focuses on how to generate conversions—it leads people to be forward-looking, it channels positive energy.

The Fairshare Model recasts conventional ideas about corporate governance, giving employees a voice in it. Is this wise?[10] Will it promote better capitalism? A more effective culture? Can a strong

---

[10] In Europe, many companies give employees the right to appoint a member of the board of directors.

CEO be effective if employees have a say in corporate governance? Such questions will be asked as interest in the Fairshare Model builds.

My sense is that giving employees a vote in corporate governance can be a good thing at any phase of development, startup or mature, high growth or distress. It provides board members with perspective that is not controlled by the CEO. This can help a CEO too, because employees are a source of wisdom, and their input can result in a better solution and more complete buy-in to the charted course.

There will be much discussion about how voting rights should be distributed in the Fairshare Model and variation in how companies implement it. For example, some companies may have two classes of Performance Stock, one that votes and one that doesn't.

In politics, comparable questions arose as feudal forms of rule were challenged. In England, the *Magna Carta* established the notion of a constitutional monarch–the idea that royalty ruled with the consent of the governed (the lords, in this case, not the ordinary people). The formation of the United States of America radically transformed the relationship between those who govern and those who are governed. The French Revolution had similar aspirations–*Liberty, Equality, Fraternity*– but their experiment descended into a morass that presaged, in some ways, the authoritarian mess that became known as communism more than a century later.

Nations have conducted who-can-vote experiments over time–companies that adopt the Fairshare Model will do the same.

Summation

This chapter discussed the tao of the Fairshare Model, which is to balance and align the interests of entrepreneurial companies and public investors. And it identified how, structurally, this is accomplished. It also examined the most remarkable aspect of the Fairshare Model–it creates incentive for an issuer to offer a low IPO valuation.

What's Next?

The next chapter describes the history of the Fairshare Model and speculates on what it will take for it to become the New Normal for startup companies raising public venture capital.

Chapter 9:

Fairshare Model History & the Future

What's Included in This Chapter

- Introduction
- My Path to the Fairshare Model
    - My Sensibilities
    - My Personality
    - My Work Experience
    - A New Direction
- How the Fairshare Model Will Emerge
- The Concept Gap
- Summation
- What's Next?
- Chapter Endnotes

Introduction

This chapter describes my path to the Fairshare Model and how I think it will emerge to be the New Normal for how companies raise venture capital in a public offering.

My Path to the Fairshare Model

For the first three quarters of the 20th century, Michigan's Detroit metropolitan area was the equivalent of "Silicon Valley" in California's San Francisco Bay area. I grew up in the former and spent most of my adulthood in the latter. Both inform and inspire my aspirations for the Fairshare Model. Unsurprisingly, my path to the Fairshare Model begins with the sensibilities I formed growing up, my personality, and my work experiences.

My Sensibilities

I was born in Detroit in 1953 and raised in a nearby suburb. Our family went to Detroit for church, shopping, dining, and cultural events, so I have an emotional connection to the Motor City and its devolution over the past half-century leaves me with a heavy heart. From when I was born to when

I graduated from high school, it was the nation's fifth largest city by population but by 2014, it had fallen to eighteenth. A few years into the 21st century, San Jose, California–the center of Silicon Valley–overtook Detroit in population. A few years later, it was the country's wealthiest city and Detroit was bankrupt.

History provides lessons on the impermanent nature of power and fortune. In *Ozymandias*, Percy Bysshe Shelley offered it in poetry. For most people, economic upheaval is something to dread but for those who are philosophically minded, adverse change in an economy can represent a form of creative destruction that invites reinvention and renewal. (A renewal process began in Michigan and other Midwestern states a few years ago. My fondest hope is that the Fairshare Model will contribute to it by helping startups raise money and use Performance Stock to create competitive advantage.)

The juxtaposition of fortune between Detroit and San Jose feeds my interest in how economies adapt to change. That will be apparent in Section 2–its chapters examine the socio-economic context for the Fairshare Model.

My Personality

The Fairshare Model also reflects my personality. I was anything but precocious. I didn't speak until I was three years old. This was a cause for parental anxiety, but my first word encouraged them. We were at a waterfall when I pointed to the flowing water and uttered "river."

As a child, I liked reading, even though I had dyslexia.[1] I also favored exploring the woods that surrounded the river behind our house over organized activities. I was undistinguished as a student. My late November birthdate put me at the tail end of my class. So by age and other signs of maturation, I lagged my peers. That began to change in high school as I participated in competitive swimming, which led me to overcome my awkwardness. As a junior, I developed a willingness to attempt big things, like organizing a 500-mile swimming relay that took seven days to complete. It was an odd endeavor–nothing presaged that I would propose such a thing. I had read of a 100-mile relay making the *Guinness Book of World Records* and thought it would be fun to surpass it. Once my coach agreed to support it, I recruited kids to sign-up. That was a challenge, but a bigger one was to ensure that they showed up, and that someone was swimming all the time. The adventure produced multiple anecdotes and one lasting insight. The night before the final day, my co-manager and I gazed at the stars outside the natatorium as we reflected on the week. I was happy about the imminent success, of course. But it was revelatory to realize that I took even greater satisfaction from finding solutions to the difficulties we had faced.

Other key events that formed my personality involve the junior college I attended, Schoolcraft College. I was on the swimming team and was nudged by someone who had been active in student government, Mark McQuesten, to participate in it myself. Mark also led me to get involved in the 1972 primary election, supporting Senator George McGovern in his bid to be the Democratic Party nominee for president. At eighteen-years old, I came close to being selected a delegate to the national convention.

I applied myself academically at Schoolcraft, which enabled me to transfer to Michigan State University, where I earned my BA degree in business/pre-law with high honors. I aspired to go to law school and

---

[1] Early on, I was drawn to comic books and books with illustrations, as they helped me visualize a story or setting. Over time, I came to enjoy books that evoked images, like science fiction, in particular.

business school—I imagined teaching at a college at some point. But I didn't get into the law schools I wanted, and I wasn't ready to work, so I decided to get my MBA degree in finance at MSU too. While there, I changed my mind about law school and upon graduation, was hired by the Ford Motor Company.

By then, my friend Mark had been elected to the board of trustees at Schoolcraft College, and he encouraged me to run for one of three open seats. As a twenty-three-year old, I became one of nine candidates for a position that was viewed as a springboard to higher elected office.

Campaigning was an amazing challenge and an intense experience. The voting area was as large as a congressional district. There were messages to craft, literature to design, events to attend and doors to knock on. I lost, but the effort delivered an emotional high that rivaled what I felt during the swim relay. I better understood myself because of that experience: I was an introvert who was comfortable being extroverted when I had something to say.

I enjoyed my flirtation with possible public service but concluded it wasn't in the cards for me at that point. I see the Fairshare Model as a form of it, though, albeit in the private sector—a way to address socio-political-economic problems, utilizing ideas formed out of my work experience. (Interestingly, Mark ultimately decided to change his form of service. He became a Roman Catholic priest.)

My Work Experience

Following my electoral failure, I reconsidered my future at Ford. It was an attractive place for a recent graduate to be, but I now questioned whether it was a good fit. Campaigning required me to be creative and action-oriented regarding strategy and tactics. My job didn't. Also, I didn't feel a collective sense of urgency at Ford to respond to the challenges that it faced; people liked their pay but were not invigorated by their work. As a result, I didn't see any role models. My superiors noticed my attitude and questioned whether Ford was the place for me.

Relieved to acknowledge the misfit, I left and landed an analyst job at Gould, Inc., a Fortune 500 manufacturer of electrical products headquartered in the Chicago area. I loved everything about the place. Dynamism pervaded, and I found something to admire in everyone there. After a year, I was on the corporate audit staff, traveling to factories and distribution centers in cities and towns across the country. When I hear of communities that have suffered economic decline, some of those places come to mind.

My final job at Gould was as financial planning and analysis manager at a division headquartered in Saint Louis, Missouri. My prior jobs dealt with historic data—this one emphasized projections. That led me, in 1980, to use personal computers. At work, I used a Radio Shack TRS-80 and VisiCalc, the first spreadsheet program. Outside of work, a friend and I played with the Apple II, exploring the idea of selling time and billing systems to law offices.[2]

My next change emerged from three things. Gould sold my division, my girlfriend moved to San José and my interest in the technology sector blossomed. When a PC manufacturer offered me a job, I headed to Silicon Valley and got married. My new employer had gone public shortly before I started, and it filed for bankruptcy nine months later. That signaled that I was in a new world.

---

2 My first hard drive had a capacity of 10 megabytes and weighed eighteen pounds.

My next employer of significance was a telecom equipment manufacturer, Granger Associates, Inc. (not W.W. Grainger, Inc.), which had just been acquired by a Texas company. Granger had a remarkable performance-driven culture that had been put in place by a renowned turnaround CEO, Q.T. Wiles. Insights I acquired there are in later chapters. I had three jobs there, but the opportunities eventually shrank as operations were moved out of California. That led me to a job with a hot laptop computer startup called Dynabook Technologies, Inc.

Dynabook had every advantage one could hope for—plenty of money from top-shelf VCs, executives with impressive accomplishments in the PC industry, a compelling product for a rapidly growing market and a distribution agreement with a leading retailer. Nonetheless, supply chain problems emerged as shipments were about to begin. The window of opportunity to begin an ascent like that of Compaq Computer closed. Dynabook downsized to focus on designing a new model. About a year later, it was sold to another computer company. Post-sale, I worked out of the lead VC's office while performing accounting clean-up work and had incidental exposure to aspects of the world of venture capital.

A New Direction

It was the early 1990s, I was in my late 30s and realized I was more attracted to companies in transition than to those that were stable. It could be a startup seeking to get off the ground or an established business trying to avoid hitting it—both held appeal for me because they offered an opportunity to make a difference. Had I been a physician, I suppose I would have been attracted to emergency room work!

I could look for a new startup, but Dynabook had taught me that it was hard to foretell the future. So, I decided to offer consulting chief financial officer and controller services to startups in the hope that it would help me identify where I wanted to land as an employee. My skill set strengthened from exposure to a range of situations, more than I would get at one company. That, in turn, flattened my learning curve when I encountered something new—the more I saw, the more I learned, the better I got at assessing a situation and creating an appropriate plan of action. Flexibility on when and where I worked was a bonus. This was valuable as my wife worked, and we had three kids to care for.

When I began consulting, my understanding about the capital formation process was based more on theory than on practical exposure. Many of the companies I interacted with had a tenuous relationship with capital. They were seeking it then or planned to later. So, consulting gave me insights that would have been difficult to get without being in the financial services industry.

I learned that capital formation is rife with challenges and inefficiencies; I saw many promising companies struggle with it. A notable one was Zap-It Technologies, Inc., the first startup to license intellectual property from the Lawrence Livermore National Laboratories. The patents covered the use of a high-energy electron beam to transform toxic volatile organic compounds into harmless ones. Zap-It planned to develop machines that could, for example, blast fumes from petroleum or coal, in a manner that caused them to recombine as water, carbon dioxide, hydrogen, and salt.

It was important stuff. There was an immense potential market. Nevertheless, environmental technologies were uninteresting to VCs because no one had made big money on them. As a result, Zap-It relied on selling stock to accredited investors known to the founders and board members. This made for lumpy cash flows that contributed to inefficiencies, which along with other factors, led the company to need more money than it had estimated. After putting in nearly $2 million, its investor pool was tapped out. Desperate, the company engaged a broker-dealer to raise about $0.7 million using convertible debt where interest was paid monthly. That meant that some of the capital raised had to be retained for future interest payments.

As I discussed the challenges with another Zap-It consultant, John G. Wilson from San Antonio, Texas, he told me about a long-standing vision he had for a way to raise equity capital. It involved public offerings, average investors, investment clubs and a performance-based capital structure–what came to be the Fairshare Model. The idea was to create a system that would help venture-stage companies pitch vetted, investor-friendly deals to large numbers of average investors.

It was both beguiling and fanciful–like a bridge that connected clouds in the sky. It was wonderful to imagine, yet unclear how it could be put into practice. We worked to identify issues but shelved the effort when we realized that the cost to print and mail offering documents was a showstopper. It would cost an issuer $15 to $25 per packet–too much given that the average investment would be small, and likelihood wasn't high that a given mailing would yield one. Also, some states required that an offering be cleared by their regulators before it could be presented to its residents. They regulated the offer of securities and charged a fee to perform the review. All these factors undermined the feasibility of John's concept.

In October 1995, the clouds parted. The SEC announced that it would adapt its rules to the Internet Age. Two changes altered the economics for John's idea. The SEC said documents could be emailed instead of mailed, and that the sale of securities would be regulated, not the offer. These changes led the states to follow suit. As a result, the cost to send a document to a prospective investor was miniscule and one didn't need to first pay and wait for a state review. It was a game changer.

In 1996, we formed a company named Fairshare, Inc. and worked to implement John's core idea. We had some success before Fairshare sank about five years later, in the wake of the dotcom and telecom busts. As it turns out, Fairshare was a forerunner for the idea of equity crowdfunding. Another way to say that is that we were too early with a concept that later became popular.

There was significant interest in the potential to invest using the Fairshare Model. We had 16,000 opt-in members, a third of whom were enthusiastic enough to buy a paid membership ($50 or $100); the rest signed up for a free membership. Of course, more people visited our website than joined, so we could tell that we had struck a chord with our target market.

We received satisfaction from seeing interest in the Fairshare Model from entrepreneurs and investors–especially from investors experienced in venture-stage investing. The unsatisfying element was the difficulty we faced with securities regulators. It took a lot of time and money to find a place where they seemed satisfied with what we planned to do. The core problem was that we had positioned Fairshare to operate as an unregulated entity. That fostered disquiet among some regulators.

We published our plan on our website. It was to build an internet-based community that, once it reached critical mass, could attract companies who wanted to pitch a public offering to our members. We would allow an issuer to do that for free so long as they:

- had a legal offering,
- passed a due diligence review,
- adopted the Fairshare Model, and
- allowed Fairshare members to invest as little as $100.

Fairshare declared that it would not handle anyone's cash or stock. If we were to do that, we would need to be a regulated entity. Charging a commission or success fee would also require us to be regulated, but we were not going to do that. We hoped to influence an issuer's allocation of shares, so that our paid members had better access than free members, but we were unsure that we could.

Our plan was to make money from membership fees and advertising. In retrospect, we wanted IPOs to be to Fairshare as books are to Amazon.[3] Amazon reduced the cost of selling books. We aimed to reduce the cost of selling IPOs. Since our plan touched on regulated areas, I mailed it to the SEC and solicited feedback on it—we didn't hear back.

We began by creating a community on the web—offering education on deal structures and valuation, calculators to calculate valuation in multiple ways, and chat rooms that could be used to pool due diligence. Our content was designed to help investors make smarter decisions, not to help companies promote an offering. We aspired to be a variant of *Consumer Reports* magazine, except our focus was IPOs from venture-stage companies, not products.

In November 1998, about eight months after we launched our membership drive, the securities regulator for California, the Department of Corporations, ordered us to cease and desist from offering memberships to California residents. The department said that a membership—even a free one—was itself a security, an investment contract.

Seemingly, the script for getting members in California was now written by the Hungarian surrealist Franz Kafka. Education and chat rooms wasn't the sort of things that were subject to regulatory approval and our membership information stressed that we might not be able to provide anything more than that. We said there were challenges that could take years to address before we could deliver an IPO. We offered free and paid memberships and said that even if we could deliver an IPO, we couldn't say that a paid member would be better positioned to invest than a free member.

Nonetheless, the regulator's position was that a Fairshare membership was an investment contract. To offer one in California, we would have to file a registration statement that, among other things, disclosed risk factors associated with a membership—I couldn't imagine any that we hadn't already made clear. Then there was this—generally, a broker-dealer must be engaged to offer a security to the public. So prospectively, in California, we would be required to hire one to offer memberships—even free ones. That would be akin to a demand that Amazon only offer user accounts through brick and mortar book stores.

We appealed the Department of Corporations order to its administrative law court, which upheld the order. On its website, the department identifies its decision as precedent-setting. You can see the list here dbo.ca.gov/ENF/decisions/default.asp and read the ruling of the department's administrative law judge here dbo.ca.gov/ENF/decisions/288.pdf. It is identified as follows:

> Respondents: Fairshare, Inc., a.k.a. Fairshare Capital Markets; Karl M. Sjogren
>   and John G. Wilson
> Dept. file number: ALPHA
> OAH file number: N-1998110288
> Law(s) involved: Corporations Code §§ 25019, 25110, 25532
> Date of Decision: January 26, 1999

---

[3] That said, I lament that Amazon has caused a steep reduction in the number of retail booksellers. Innovations can have a downside.

Summary: Desist & Refrain order issued under Corporations Code § 25532 upheld based on finding that "membership interests" in "internet-based" organization were "investment contract" securities under both "traditional" and "risk capital" analyses.

In the ensuing months, Fairshare had requests for information from regulators in Ohio, Colorado, and Texas. When I described California's position, all said that they did not view a Fairshare membership as a security.[4] However, they all wanted to see a regulated entity involved when an offering was presented to members and allocations of shares set.

We had no idea how long it would take to have an offering for members, but knew we had to quell the concerns of these states. If we didn't, they might issue cease and desist orders too. To do that, we formed a Fairshare subsidiary that registered as an investment advisor with the SEC and all fifty states. We planned to ask California to review its cease and desist order but first had to deal with a more pressing concern—we were running out of money.

I was tired. Consulting had remained my day job during this four-year effort. That allowed me to preserve our capital for critical expenses and for others who needed to be paid. John and I were also increasingly frustrated with each other's view on how the company should develop.

John saw Fairshare as a closed system where only direct public offerings that used the Fairshare Model were presented to members. He did not want to see broker-dealers present offerings because he felt they would be based on a conventional capital structure, and would therefore, provide an inferior deal. He also wanted to see the administration of Performance Stock for all issuers controlled by a single trust—a legal entity administered by a board of trustees.

His view was akin to a strong central government model or, to use a tech reference, a "walled garden." A walled garden described the experience that America Online provided to its subscribers—they could only browse the content that AOL curated, not everything on the internet. Apple's closed approach to applications provides a contemporary comparison. John channeled the sentiment expressed in Apple's iconic "1984" Super Bowl ad, but to him, the enemy of the people was Wall Street, not IBM.

In contrast, my view was that Fairshare should adopt a strong local government model, or, to use a tech reference, the open approach used by Microsoft's operating system. I agreed with John that members would prefer offerings that used the Fairshare Model but felt they would be more interested in an investor-oriented community that had access to any public offering that passed due diligence.

So, I was open to the idea of offerings being presented to our members that used a conventional capital structure and/or were sold by a broker-dealer. If we could organize the buyers and help them be savvier investors, I felt that market forces would move issuers to provide better deals—to adopt the Fairshare Model.

I saw a walled garden as inhibiting what investors wanted—a wide choice of offerings in an environment that was investor-oriented. I also saw a central trust to administer Performance Stock as an unnecessary complication. Issuers should be free to choose who would administer their program.

---

[4] SEC staff who I presented the matter to felt similarly—a membership was not a security under federal law.

We debated our perspectives as we explored options to raise more capital. Then, a year after it accepted our subsidiary's registration as an investment advisor, the SEC notified us that it intended to rescind it. The reason? We did not qualify to be a regulated investment advisor because we did not manage anyone's money or stock and we didn't offer fee-based advice!

Joseph Heller's novel, *Catch-22*, came to mind.[5]

Our business model was to be a trusted financial intermediary—we didn't want to be a broker-dealer. But, we were willing to be an investment advisor because it was an easy, inexpensive way to deal with regulatory concerns.

Clearly, we sought to operate in unfamiliar territory. I viewed California as a regulatory outlier whose position could be addressed with time and expense. By forming our investment advisor subsidiary, we addressed the concern of states that seemed to be in the mainstream—which was that we would facilitate investments without being a broker-dealer. But now, the solution that promised to satisfy state regulators was at risk of being rescinded by the SEC because we were **not** engaged in activities that required us to be regulated!

Our round peg did not fit in the federal agency's square hole and state regulators wanted us to find a regulated place for our peg.

We were in no-man's land.

Why didn't Fairshare want to be a broker-dealer?

We would be compelled by a FINRA predecessor, the National Association of Securities Dealers, to raise millions of dollars in capital for reserves, and to incur expenses associated with a broker-dealer business that were unnecessary for our "no commission" business model.

Indeed, we believed we would be viewed with puzzlement or even hostility by the NASD—either of which would be a hindrance. Government regulators had already reacted as if I had three legs when I described our business model.

There was no capital requirement to be an investment advisor and supervision was via the SEC, not the NASD, which had conflicts of interest, given its ties to the broker-dealer business.

We entered discussions with an investment group about buying the company. The principal investor was a member of a nationally-known family with powerful political connections. He had experience in the securities business and was prepared to recast Fairshare as a broker-dealer.

Two days before we were to close the deal, we learned that the SEC was preparing an inquiry into Fairshare's operations. It took four months for the investigation to conclude.[6] No action resulted, but our prospective buyer lost interest, so we ceased operations in 2001.

---

[5] In Joseph Heller's novel, *Catch-22*, US bomber crews flying over WW II Italy are told they must fly additional missions before they may rotate to safe duty. Increasingly cognizant of the risks of being exposed to the ferocious German defenses, Capt. John Yossarian asks the doctor to excuse him because he has become crazy with fear. The rule is that anyone who is crazy is not allowed to fly missions. The doctor explains that he can't excuse Yossarian from flying because of the catch-22 provision, which states it is a mark of sanity to be afraid. By claiming to be crazy with fear, Yossarian proves he is sane, for only someone crazy would willingly go into such danger.

[6] Our lawyer advised that such investigations usually took at least six months.

This may seem quite odd, but even though it failed, I viewed Fairshare as the most interesting and fulfilling business endeavor that I had ever been involved in. It was more than a business failure to me—it was a magnificent failure!

Fast-forward to now:

- The Great Recession triggers a cascade of anxiety about how to spur economic growth.
- Young companies are recognized as job-creating engines.
- Entrepreneurship is considered cool—so is innovation.
- Fallout from the slow economic recovery is expressed as concern about rising income inequality.
- Online communities have emerged as powerful social networks.
- A lot of money has been raised via crowdfunding.
- Policy sensibilities about capital formation are changing, as witnessed by the JOBS Act, especially the authorization of online platforms that can market offerings.

These factors led me to reprise the Fairshare Model as a book. It intrigued a lot of people. It presents a solution to the valuation challenge, something that will become more significant as interest in equity crowdfunding grows.[7]

Fairshare, Inc. may have been too early, but the Fairshare Model continues to be relevant to economic matters that are on the minds of many people.[A]

"There are decades where nothing happens; and there are weeks where decades happen." – Vladimir Ilyich Lenin	"There are no bad ideas, only early ones." – VC Marc Andreessen

How the Fairshare Model Will Emerge

The Fairshare Model has the potential to be widely adopted, at least by early stage companies that have an initial public offering. But how long will it take?

An article in *The New York Times* showed household penetration rates between 1900 and 2005 for innovative technologies such as electricity, stoves, telephones, autos, refrigerators, clothes washers, clothes dryers, dishwashers, TVs, microwave ovens, cell phones and the internet.[B] The article points out that it took twenty-five years for sixty percent of households to have a clothes dryer. Personal computers, invented in 1977, took about twenty years to get to that penetration rate. The internet and cell phones each took about fifteen years. So it takes time for innovations to be accepted, though it's not taking as long as it used to. A large part of the reason is that it takes time for innovative products to become affordable to mass markets. Another is that it takes time for traditions to change.

How long will it take for the Fairshare Model to be used in sixty percent of IPOs? The answer can be thought of as a recipe that combines one-part technical matters with two parts of tradition.

---

[7] Chapter 22, "Blockchain and Initial Coin Offerings" considers how the Fairshare Model addresses the valuation challenge for initial coin offerings (ICOs).

How Companies Structure Ownership Interests	=	One Part: Technical Matters	+	Two Parts: Tradition

The Fairshare Model can help companies raise capital—the technical matter—but that's insufficient to encourage broad adoption. For that to happen, investors need to make money—the more the better—and employees at well-performing companies need to be better off than those who raise venture capital from VC firms and/or who do so with a conventional IPO. Also, issuers that use the Fairshare Model must outperform competitors who don't.

On paper, a conventional capital structure has technical vulnerabilities that the Fairshare Model is positioned to exploit, but that's not enough to create change. Traditions must weaken, which means the Fairshare Model needs multiple successes. That will take years.

Then again, each time a valuation bubble pops, interest in the Fairshare Model will increase. I see acceptance of it as inevitable because the problems with a conventional capital structure are profound. The best evidence of that is that VCs will not accept one when they invest.

The saying "What's good for the goose is good for the gander" suggests that public investors will want an alternative to a conventional capital structure once they realize how lousy of a deal they get with one, relative to what private investors get with a modified conventional capital structure. Is there a modified conventional capital structure that could provide a better deal for IPO investors? Possibly. Meanwhile, I offer the Fairshare Model for consideration. It is *unconventional* because, unlike a conventional capital structure or a modified conventional capital structure, it places *no value on future performance when an equity investment is made.*

The Concept Gap

How might the Fairshare Model become more than an idea? Geoffrey A. Moore's 1991 book, *Crossing The Chasm*, provides a framework that helps us visualize the answer.

Moore uses a "technology adoption life cycle," shown below, to explain how customer acceptance of a technology product evolves. The time scale begins at the left, when a product is introduced. The market expands in the growth phases until it reaches maturity, when the adoption rate declines.

Technology Adoption Life Cycle

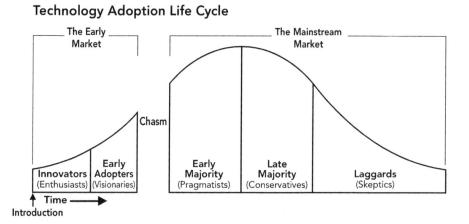

The early market is comprised of "Innovators" who are enthusiasts for the technology and a larger group of "Early Adopters" who can imagine how they might benefit from it.

The mainstream market has three different groups of customers. There is an "Early Majority" whose pragmatic concern–"What's in it for me?"–must be addressed before they buy. Then, the "Late Majority" who is conservative when it comes to purchasing a new technology–they want evidence that it meets their needs. And, the final group of customers will be the "Laggards," who are generally skeptical about new solutions.

Moore says that there is a gap in the adoption cycle between the early market and the mainstream market. He called it the "Chasm," and says that products that successfully cross it can go on to expand their market. Those that fail to do so are likened to a train that falls off a trestle bridge that spans the gap. Moore's Technology Adoption Life Cycle explains why some products grow from niche to mainstream markets, while others that do well with early customers fail to catch on with larger numbers of them.

The Fairshare Model has a chasm to cross before it is put into practice by companies. I call it a Concept Gap, and to cross it, investors must signal that they like the Fairshare Model and professionals in the capital formation and organizational matters must be prepared to advise companies on how to make it work. The Concept Gap is shown here and below it, each phase is described. The time scale is subject to Hofstadter's Law, which is named after cognitive scientist, Douglas Hofstadter.

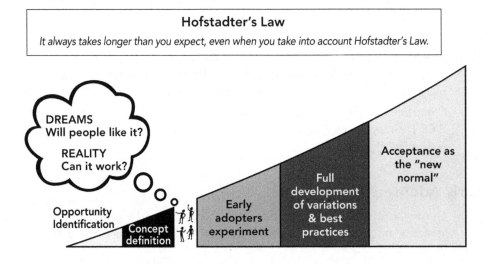

Fairshare Model – Opportunity Identification and Concept Definition

- First Try
  - In the 1980s, John G. Wilson begins to think about how to better match up average investors and entrepreneurial companies, which leads to the genesis of Fairshare Model.
  - In 1994, John and I meet at a Silicon Valley startup that struggles to find the capital it needs. We determine that his idea isn't feasible due to the cost of mailing offering documents.

- **Second Try**
  - In 1995, the SEC announces that it will regulate the *sale* of securities, not the *offering* of securities, and, that electronic documents are the equivalent to printed ones. State regulators follow.
  - In 1996, John and I form Fairshare, Inc. With the help of a small team, we develop our message, and membership program. We underestimate the challenge of fitting in the regulatory framework, however. The dotcom and telecom busts dim investor interest in the concept—Fairshare goes under in 2001.

- **Third Try**
  - In the wake of the Great Recession, the Jobs Act of 2012 is made law. The buzz is about new ways to sell offerings; no one is proposing new ways to structure them. In 2014, I conclude that no one else is likely to do that and begin to write this book.

The Concept Gap

a. The Fairshare Model is published in 2019. It provokes discussion about the potential for innovation in venture capital.

b. A critical mass of investor interest begins to form.

c. Experts in the capital market ecosystem evaluate how to implement the Fairshare Model for their client companies. (Think of the Fairshare Model as an architectural design and the work of these experts as the engineering.)

d. Companies consider using the Fairshare Model to raise venture capital via an IPO. Their biggest challenge is to identify how to define and measure their performance.

Early Adopters Experiment

a. Those who advise companies explore how to implement the Fairshare Model— how to adapt price protection concepts that are used in private offerings to IPOs.

b. Early adopter companies use the Fairshare Model and experiment with ways to manage Performance Stock.

Full Development of Variations and Best Practices

a. Early Adopter companies are studied to gain insight on opportunities, pitfalls, best practices, and areas to explore.

b. Broker-dealers find ways to benefit from offerings that use the Fairshare Model.

c. As tradition erodes, VC firms advise portfolio firms that are not on track for an attractive investor exit to consider the Fairshare Model if they need capital.

Acceptance as the New Normal

Having established that the Fairshare Model can help companies attract and manage human capital, companies begin to consider the possibility that a conventional capital structure is a disadvantage. A new era in how capitalism is practiced emerges.

Summation

This chapter demonstrates that a new idea can encounter difficulties if it emerges too soon. It also explains why this may be the right time for the Fairshare Model.

What's Next?

This chapter concludes Section 1. Section 2 discusses the macroeconomic context for the Fairshare Model.

Chapter Endnotes

Contextual references for material in this chapter appear as numbered footnotes on the page where the reference is made. **Source references** for material in this chapter appear below as endnotes with capital letter identifiers.

A Ritholtz, Barry. "Marc Andreessen Answers the Tech Valuation Question." *Bloomberg.com*. May 22, 2017. Accessed May 08, 2018. fairsharemodel.com/AndreessenValuation.

B Cox, W. Michael, and Alm, Richard. "Opinion | You Are What You Spend." *The New York Times*. February 10, 2008. Accessed May 08, 2018. fairsharemodel.com/WhatYouAre.

SECTION 2:

Context for the Fairshare Model

This section is markedly different from the last one.

For readers unfamiliar with capital structures, Section 1 moved briskly. Metaphorically, it surveyed capital formation from an altitude of 10,000 feet: too high to see details but low enough to see objects. It was broad enough to escape matters that must be addressed before the Fairshare Model is put into practice but focussed enough to see how it might work.

Section 2 ascends to 50,000 feet, where one can see the curvature of our planet and the topology below.

The analogy indicates that this section contemplates how the Fairshare Model might address concerns about economic growth, job creation and income inequality. It considers the capacity of humans to cooperate and provides high-level perspective on how the Fairshare Model can harness it.

The Fairshare Model is a tool to solve the on-the-ground challenge of valuation, which is a microeconomic problem. It calls into question the premise of a conventional capital structure—that a value must be set for future performance at the time of an equity financing. As such, it incidentally raises questions about traditions that rest on a conventional capital structure. For instance, what is the purpose of a corporation? And, are stock options the most effective way to align employee and investor interests?

Quite by accident, I realized that the Fairshare Model provides a new way to think about macroeconomic challenges that are often viewed dogmatically, through a political lens. Few people will say that valuation isn't a real, microeconomic challenge. The Fairshare Model offers a promising solution to it. It turns out that it also provides a prism that allows us to view macroeconomic problems in a new light. There is a saying: "where there is agreement on what a problem is, solutions become self-evident."

To that end, the music is about to slow down for readers who are unfamiliar with capital structures. The ensuing chapters provide grist for reflection and conversation about the matters of slow economic growth and rising income inequality—the challenges of the New Economy.

Many thoughtful people are discussing these issues and this section heavily samples the ideas of others. By doing so, I hope to contribute to your ability to find connections between things that are seemingly disparate.

Section 3 will return to a microeconomic matter: valuation.

Chapters in this section:

Chapter 10: The Macroeconomic Context – Growth

Chapter 11: The Macroeconomic Context – Income Inequality

Chapter 12: Cooperation as the New Tool for Competition

Chapter 10:

The Macroeconomic Context – Growth

What's Included in This Chapter

- Introduction
- What Policies Hold Promise for Economic Growth?
- What About Job Growth?
- Four Prescriptions for Economic Growth – Better Capitalism
- Cultural Factors Affect Economic Growth Too
- Another Prescription for Better Capitalism – Restore Dynamism
- Summation
- What's Next?
- Chapter Endnotes

Introduction

The Fairshare Model addresses a microeconomic concern—how to mitigate valuation risk for investors in the initial public offerings of venture-stage companies. This chapter discusses its implications for the macroeconomic challenge of spurring economic growth.

What Policies Hold Promise for Economic Growth?

A major question facing America and all other countries is, how to generate economic growth? Auguste Rodin's sculpture *The Thinker* can be used to illustrate the basic options available to policymakers.

To varying degrees, the United States has pursued each policy avenue since the Great Recession. None have been remarkably effective; the downturn exposed structural issues for which there are no obvious solutions in the playbook of economists. Advocates of any given approach argue that the policies they support haven't been adopted with sufficient vigor. In response, their opponents argue that the lack of success is evidence that it's not the right approach at all. Political gridlock about what to do makes "just wait out the cycle" the default response.

So it goes.

How did we get here, and what policy initiatives hold the most promise? The following explanation is from Robert E. Litan's and Carl J. Schramm's 2012 book, *Better Capitalism*.[1] [Bold added for emphasis.]

> The 1950s and 1960s were the halcyon days of "managerial capitalism," when large firms such as General Motors, Ford Motor Company, US Steel, IBM, and AT&T (in its previous monopoly incarnation), among others, were the driving forces of the US economy.
>
> Taking advantage of the pent-up demand for consumer goods during World War II, large firms expanded their reach into new markets at home and abroad. They used their economies of scale, access to internal capital, and in-house research labs to generate new products, drawing on technologies that had been developed during or before World War II.
>
> This managerial capitalism delivered rapid growth and thus rising living standards for almost three decades after the end of the war. Indeed, our particular brand of this capitalism was not only envied but feared. In the late 1960s, European intellectual Jean-Jacques Servan-Schreiber warned European governments and citizens that, without aggressive counter measures, the multinational companies birthed and headquartered in America—the quintessential managerial capitalists—would dominate the world economy.
>
> But then the US economy hit the proverbial wall in the early 1970s. Inflation had been edging up throughout the Vietnam War, eventually leading to a run on the dollar that forced the United States to quit exchanging gold at the price fixed after World War II. Soon thereafter, the fixed exchange rate system that had governed world currency markets and international trade that had been in place since World War II came undone. The coup de grace was the quadrupling of oil prices in 1973, which pushed both inflation and the unemployment rate nearly into double digits, then post-Depression highs. Even though growth later resumed, and the unemployment rate fell back to near 6 percent, inflation stayed uncomfortably high until the economy was hit by yet another oil shock, this one in 1979 during the Iranian hostage affair. From 1973 to 1980, stock prices dropped in real terms (adjusted for inflation) by roughly 40 percent, reflecting a loss of faith in the managerial capitalism that, at least until the first oil shock, had produced such rapid growth and widely shared prosperity.
>
> There was ample reason for the loss of faith. **Big Auto and Big Steel—along with steadily Bigger Government—that helped define managerial capitalism proved too**

---

[1] At publication of *Better Capitalism*, Litan was vice president for research and policy at the Ewing Marion Kauffman Foundation, and a senior fellow at the Brookings Institution. Schramm was a visiting scientist at MIT and had been president of the Kauffman Foundation for a decade. Both are fellows of the Bush Institute.

bureaucratic and uninventive to withstand the seeming onslaught of cheaper (and often better) imports from Japan and elsewhere. While many Americans feared the United States was thus losing out to the Japanese on the economic front, they had also been steadily losing faith in government.

The US military not only suffered its first-ever defeat in Vietnam, but the Watergate scandal that ultimately forced President Nixon to resign shocked Americans of both political parties. The decade ended with the seizure of the American Embassy in Iran and the humiliation of US government employees being held hostage for over a year, unable to be rescued by the one failed military attempt to do so.

In one narrative, what saved America and rejuvenated its economy was the election of the optimistic, anticommunist, free market enthusiast Ronald Reagan to the presidency in 1980.

Rather than wade into contentious political waters about the correctness of this explanation, we suggest here that an uncontroversial but important contributing reason for **the economic turnaround was the transformation of the US economy from managerial to entrepreneurial capitalism.**

This apparently new form of capitalism was not new at all but is in fact what powered the American economy from Revolutionary times until the early 1900s: the cleverness and hard work of waves of entrepreneurs of all types whose efforts gradually lifted the living standards of American citizens.

Entrepreneurs began to take center stage in the US economy again in the 1970s (before Reagan was elected) with the formation of such companies as Intel, Microsoft, Apple, Federal Express, and Southwest Airlines, among others. But **entrepreneurial capitalism really took off in the 1980s and 1990s and flowered under presidents of both major parties.A**

Here is another passage from *Better Capitalism:*

We [Litan and Schramm] **argue that the "better capitalism" the United States needs now more than ever is one that fosters continuous entrepreneurial revolution**–the economic equivalent of what Thomas Jefferson called for when he famously uttered: "Every generation needs a new [political] revolution."

Whether or not that statement is appropriate for governing, it could not be more relevant today as an economic proposition. **For countries at the technological frontier like the United States, sustained rapid growth is only possible through the continued commercialization of new, disruptive–and, yes, revolutionary–technologies, products, and services.**

We are not sufficiently clairvoyant to predict what those technologies will be. Futurists in the past have missed the mark, and no doubt their heirs today will be equally unsuccessful.B

What About Job Growth?

In the late 1990s, I saw a presentation by the head of the US Small Business Administration that said that since the late 1970s, young companies had been responsible for more net job growth than all Fortune 500 companies! My first reaction was "I wouldn't have thought to compare the two." My second was: "That's amazing!"

In June 2010, Tim Kane, a senior fellow at the Kauffman Foundation, authored a report, "The Importance of Startups in Job Creation and Job Destruction," which makes the following statement. [Bold added for emphasis.]

> **"Without startups, there would be no net job growth in the US economy.** This fact is true on average, but also is true for all but seven years for which the United States has data going back to 1977."[c]

The report includes the chart below, which shows startups adding about 3 million jobs each year from 1977 to 2005, and existing firms shedding jobs.

There is no obvious solution to the persistent job losses at existing firms. However, it is abundantly clear that startups have been a consistent source of good news on this front.

One way to encourage job creation, therefore, is to improve access to capital for venture-stage companies.

That isn't controversial, but where the capital should come from is. Some want average investors to be able to help provide it.

Others feel that is unwise, that the capital should entirely come from wealthy investors who can afford to lose their money.

As I say in Chapter 2, "The Big Idea and Thesis," investors in venture-stage companies face substantial failure and valuation risks.

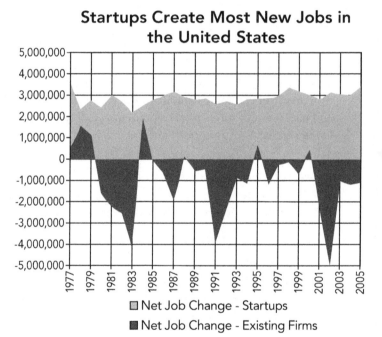

Startups Create Most New Jobs in the United States

☐ Net Job Change - Startups
■ Net Job Change - Existing Firms

The Fairshare Model reduces valuation risk, which makes it more likely that IPO investors will make money. That alone isn't reason for average investors to invest—there is still failure risk. However, it does encourage capital, be it from wealthy or average investors, to flow to the engines of job creation.

Four Prescriptions for Economic Growth – Better Capitalism

The Ewing Marion Kauffman Foundation is one of the largest foundations in the world devoted to entrepreneurship. Its website—kauffman.org—has a set of engaging video sketchbooks. If you go there and search for "Better Capitalism," you'll see an animation that explains Robert Litan's and Carl Schramm's four strategic policy initiatives to spur entrepreneurship and reinvigorate long-term economic growth.[2]

---

[2] Better Capitalism video sketchbook. fairsharemodel.com/StartupJobCreation.

1. Encourage immigration by high-skilled foreigners.
2. **Improve access to capital for new firms.**
3. Speed up commercialization of innovations at universities.
4. Undertake regulatory reform.

This book, of course, is all about a way to contribute to the second initiative–improve access to capital for new firms. Let's briefly discuss the other three.

Traditionally, the US and other countries have benefited from encouraging immigration by high-skilled foreigners and there is little reason to think that should not continue to be the case. Litan and Schramm write the following in their book:

> Readers will surely recognize the names of these outstanding immigrants, and the companies they founded and helped launch, but we'll bet not many realize that these individuals were all born in other countries: Alexander Graham Bell (AT&T), Levi Strauss (Levi Strauss & Co.), Andrew Carnegie (US Steel), Herbert Dow (Dow Chemical Company), E.I. du Pont (DuPont), Charles Pfizer (Pfizer), David Buick (Buick Motors, later purchased by General Motors), Adolph Coors (Coors Beer), Henry Heinz (H.J. Heinz Company), James Kraft (Kraft Foods), William Proctor and James Gamble (Proctor & Gamble), Eberhard Anheuser and Adolphus Busch (Anheuser-Busch), Samuel Goldwyn and Louis Meyer (MGM), Marcus Goldman (cofounder of Goldman Sachs), and even Ettore Boiardi (Chef Boyardi). Add Sergey Brin (Google), Andrew Grove (Intel), Jerry Yang (Yahoo!), and Pierre Omidyar (eBay).[D]

President Barack Obama made a similar point when advocating for congressional action on immigration reform:

> In recent years, one in four of America's new small business owners were immigrants. One in four high-tech startups in America were founded by immigrants. Forty percent of Fortune 500 companies were started by a first- or second-generation American. Think about that–almost half of the Fortune 500 companies were started by first–or second–generation immigrants.

> So, immigration isn't just part of our national character. It is a driving force in our economy that creates jobs and prosperity for all our citizens.[E]

The Fairshare Model complements Litan's and Schramm's third recommendation–speed up commercialization of innovations at universities, because it can help improve access to capital by startups that license technology. Additionally, an institution might be interested in receiving a licensee's Investor Stock and/or Performance Stock as part of its compensation for intellectual property.

The fourth recommendation, regulatory reform, is beyond the scope of this book. I will say, however, that companies in a financial turnaround situation must rethink strategy and processes. The same is true for nations in an economic turnaround. Starting in 1991, Japan's theretofore phenomenally successful economy entered recession. Its failure to address regulatory reform is why some problems persist.

Better Capitalism was published in 2012 as the sequel to a book that Litan and Schramm issued with William J. Baumol in 2007, *Good Capitalism, Bad Capitalism, and the Economics of Growth and Prosperity*. The later book, *Better Capitalism*, was written because the world changed dramatically shortly after *Good Capitalism, Bad Capitalism* came out and the authors felt "we need an even stronger dose of entrepreneurial capitalism" than first proposed.

Here is an excerpt of a review of *Good Capitalism, Bad Capitalism* that appeared in *The Economist*, a few months before the 2007 collapse of Lehman Brothers, the investment bank that precipitated the financial crisis [Bold added for emphasis].

> **The fall of the Berlin Wall in 1989 may have proved once and for all that capitalism is better than communism, but it did nothing to settle the debate about which model of capitalism is the best. Or, to be precise, the debate about whether the American model will continue to outdo all comers, or instead be replaced at the top of the economic heap by a rival.**
>
> "Good Capitalism, Bad Capitalism" helpfully moves the debate on from competing national models to the underlying structures that shape the relative effectiveness of different sorts of capitalism. Written by three economists, including 85-year-old William Baumol, arguably the leading thinker about the economics of innovation since Joseph Schumpeter [an Austrian economist of the first half of the 20th century], it identifies four main varieties of capitalism.
>
> 1. State-guided capitalism, in which government tries to guide the market, typically by supporting certain industries that it expects to become "winners."
>
> 2. Oligarchic capitalism, in which the bulk of the power and wealth is held by a small group of individuals and families.
>
> 3. Big-firm capitalism, in which the main economic activities are carried out by established giant enterprises.
>
> 4. Entrepreneurial capitalism, in which a major role is played by small innovative firms.
>
> **The only thing that all four of these models of capitalism have in common is that they recognize the right of private property ownership.**
>
> Nor is there any single country that has exactly any one of the models described; in most national economies there is some blend of at least two. Moreover, the blend changes over time, and with it, the performance of the economy. Less than two decades after the fall of communism, Russia is already moving rapidly from oligarchic capitalism to an authoritarian state-guided capitalism.
>
> **What works best, argue the authors, is a mix of big-firm capitalism and entrepreneurial capitalism.** And this happens to describe America's economy during the past 20 years, during which time it has reversed its seemingly inevitable long-term decline and delivered a "productivity miracle."
>
> **The possibility of change is at the heart of *Good Capitalism, Bad Capitalism*.** The authors are skeptical—for the most part, plausibly—of claims that the growth rates of economies are largely predestined by culture or geography, as books such as *The Wealth and Poverty of Nations* by David Landes or Jared Diamond's *Guns, Germs and Steel* suggest. There are no quick fixes, but over time the right policies can make a big difference, as can the wrong policies.

The authors argue that continental Europe and Japan, currently dominated by big-firm capitalism, can increase the role of entrepreneurial capitalism—perhaps, ironically, by learning from the incremental approach to reform of the Chinese government. And **America, they say, is in danger of stifling its own entrepreneurial capitalism through the same increased regulation and risk-aversion that led to the dominance of big-firm capitalism in America in the 1960s and 1970s. If so, it risks losing its capitalistic crown, not as a result of any external threat, but through its own fault.[F]**

More from Better Capitalism

It was Karl Marx, capitalism's most famous critic, who coined the word "capitalism."

It described an economic system he believed was dominated by a few "capitalists"—owners of buildings, equipment, and the dreaded corporations—whom he believed exploited the masses.

But Marx the wordsmith was cleverer than Marx the economist. The emerging economic system that he decried for enslaving the poor turned out instead to be the greatest anti-poverty force the world has ever known, lifting living standards for ever-growing numbers of people beyond what they could have imagined.

Cultural Factors Affect Economic Growth Too

How capitalism is practiced is not fully defined by government—cultural factors play an important role too. In his 1905 book, *The Protestant Ethic and the Spirit of Capitalism,* German sociologist Max Weber argues that the Protestant Reformation—Calvinism and Lutheranism—were largely responsible for the development of capitalism.

He focuses on the Calvinists, who believed there were a set number of places in heaven and that they could secure one of those seats by being productive beings, living a good life. Thus, they worked hard and lived modestly, reinvested their profits, and contributed to their community through their work. Weber argues that this "Protestant ethic" spurred the growth of capitalism in northern Europe and, eventually, throughout the world—that its early impetus was from a theological source.[3][G]

Weber's treatise overlooks the fact that non-Protestant nations, like Italy, had more wealth than Germany and other Protestant countries. Also, that there were prosperous non-Christian countries. Then too, the behaviors he ascribes to a Protestant ethic—thriftiness and industriousness—are conducive to economic growth, independent of any religious connotation, or lack thereof.

That is clear when one considers that secular countries tend to be richer than religious ones. That observation led a set of researchers—Damian J. Ruck, R. Alexander Bentley, and Daniel J. Lawson—to ask which came first, "the secular chicken or the economic egg?" In the July 2018 issue

---

3 Christoph Stueckelberger, a Professor of Ethics at the University of Basel, advocates reading John Calvin's words, not just Max Weber's writings on Calvinism. He says: "Calvin did not invent exploitive capitalism, but defended the interests of the weak and the poor in his concept of a socially responsible economy."

of *Science Advances,* they report that in the 20th century, nations generally experienced a rise in secularization *before* economic growth, not *after,* as some believe.

While the researchers acknowledge it's foolish to attribute the course of an economy to a single cause, their work led them to conclude that economies improve when the rights of individuals are respected. In an article that summarized their findings, Ruck writes:

> A respect for the rights of individuals is the moral triumph of the humanitarian revolution and might provide the "leg up" that societies need to reach economic prosperity. A respect for individual rights requires tolerance of homosexuality, abortion and divorce and we showed that secular societies only become prosperous once they have evolved a greater respect for these individual rights.
>
> If we zoom in on different regions of the world, we see some rich countries that are religious and some poor ones that are secular. Countries like the US and the Catholic countries of Europe have become economically prosperous, yet religion remains important. Conversely, the former Communist countries of Eastern Europe are some of the most secular on Earth but have middling economic performance.
>
> It turns out that it's a respect for individual rights that separates the rich from the poor countries.
>
> Though we shouldn't ignore the role of religion. It's easy to see why individual rights flower once religious influence has withered. That said, there's no reason why individual rights can't exist in a religious world.
>
> If religious institutions can become less of a conservative force and embrace modern cultural values, then they could provide moral guidance for the economically prosperous societies of the future.[H]

Another cultural factor that affects how a country practices capitalism is considered next—the capacity of a society to nurture a spirit of innovation. It requires values that are not part of the Protestant ethic—a willingness to explore, to experiment, and to dare in the face of unknowability.

Another Prescription for Better Capitalism – Restore Dynamism

A broader, more elemental perspective on what ails the economies of the US and other developed nations comes from Professor Edmund Phelps, director of Columbia University's Center on Capitalism and Society. A Nobel laureate, he was awarded the economics prize in 2006 for his work on unemployment and microeconomics.

His 2013 book, *Mass Flourishing: How Grassroots Innovation Created Jobs, Challenge and Change,* presents a wide-ranging assessment on what leads economies to thrive. His diagnosis of what's wrong with the economy is fundamental and delivered in a genteel manner. (He strikes me as a mild-mannered version of Howard Beale from the movie *Network,* who is referenced in Chapter 1.)

Professor Phelps emphasizes the importance of dynamism—the willingness and capacity of an economy to innovate—a quality he says that has been in decline for decades for two reasons. The first is rising hostility to what he calls "modern values." The second is movement away from a modern notion of the ancient Aristotelian concept of the "good life" and toward a self-destructive fixation on money-making and materialism.

Before elaborating on his thesis, let's get the politics out of the way. Some of what he says appeals to the political Left and some of it is off-putting to them. The same is true for those on the political Right. His iconoclastic view is disorienting to anyone who largely views problems and solutions through a politically partisan lens.

In part, it is because both ends of the spectrum benefit from what he sees as a key problem—corporatism. It is an uncommon word that refers to the control of a state or organization by large interest groups. Phelps sees the Democratic Party pursuing corporatism that goes well beyond the New Deal or Great Society. He despairs at the Republican enthrallment of "traditional values" that suppress individual self-expression, which he associates with a rise in materialism and a desire to amass wealth. He also wants to move beyond their superficial argument that freedom will return economies to those of the past.

> Corporatism is a political and economic system in which planning and policy are controlled by major interest groups.

There is pervasive use of the word "modern" in *Mass Flourishing;* modern era, modern society, modern economies and modern values, attitudes, and beliefs.[4] The word generally means relating to the present time or using recent ideas or designs, but Phelps embraces another meaning—modern is the untraditional, novel, disruptive or even subversive.

The tableau Phelps works with begins in antiquity. He writes: "some ideas that we think of as modernist existed in ancient times but were not widespread or they were driven out in the Middle Ages." He marks the beginning of the *modern era* at around 1500, when the Renaissance period began. It is hard to say with precision when *modern society* was ushered in, but Phelps notes that English historian Paul Johnson puts it between 1815 and 1830. In his 1991 book, *The Birth of the Modern,* Johnson says the matrix of the modern world was formed then: the US became a global power, Russia expanded rapidly, Britain penetrated the Middle East, Latin America threw off Spain's yoke, and an international order which would endure for a century took shape.[I]

Modern economies are what emerged first in Britain, then America, followed later by France and Germany. Phelps writes that their economies somehow developed *dynamism*—the appetite and capacity for indigenous innovation (i.e., homegrown, as opposed to copied from another country). What followed was a breakout of prosperity that fired imaginations and transformed working lives. The emancipation of women and abolition of slavery widened the flourishing. Scientists, business people and pioneering end-users drove the creation of new methods and new products. Phelps says: "the epic story of the West is the development in the 19th century of a mass prosperity the world had never seen and its near-disappearance in one nation after another in the 20th."[J]

Modern values, according to Phelps, are the attitudes that began to be formulated in the modern era, accelerated with modern society, and are the foundation of a modern economy. They remain prevalent in Western nations, even though they differ significantly by country. Examples of modernist values that he cites are:

- thinking and working for yourself,
- self-expression,
- readiness to accept change caused or desired by others,

---

4 The permutations of Professor Phelps' use of "modern" are in Chapter 11, "Income Inequality."

- eagerness to work with others,

- desire to test one's self against others, thus to compete, and

- the willingness to take the initiative, to go first.

He adds that, *"Modern attitudes* are the desire to create, explore and experiment, the welcoming of hurdles to surmount, the desire to be intellectually engaged, and the desire to have responsibility and to give orders. Behind these desires is a need to exercise one's own judgment, to act on one's own insights, and to summon up one's own imagination. This spirit does not involve a love of risk. It is a spirit that views the prospect of unanticipated consequences that may come with voyaging into the unknown as a valued part of experience and not a drawback. Self-discovery and personal development are major vitalist values."[K]

Phelps goes on to say that, *"Modern beliefs* include some distinctive ideas about what is right: the rightness of having to compete with others for positions of higher responsibility, the rightness of greater pay for greater productivity or responsibility, the rightness of orders from those in responsible positions and the rightness of holding them accountable, the right of people to offer new ideas, and the right of people to offer new ways of doing things and to offer new things to do. All this stands in contrast to traditionalism with its notions of service, obligation, family and social harmony."[L]

Phelps says Western nations lost half or more of their dynamism in the 20th century: Britain and Germany in the 1940s, France in the early 1960s and America in the 1970s. He is skeptical of the ability of the technology sector to raise the economy because its financial benefits are concentrated geographically, like in the San Francisco Bay area, and the revenues from many tech innovations are insubstantial. What's needed, he believes, is an approach that has broader impact on more sectors of the economy.

Mass Flourishing identifies institutions and policies that block innovation. They include a short-term perspective in big business and finance, under-taxation that gives people inflated perceptions of their wealth, and a minefield of patent and regulatory risks.

But Phelps says the more fundamental problem is that the desire to innovate has been dampened by waning belief in modern values and a rise in traditional values. He advocates a reembrace of modern values because they encourage the innovation that people need to thrive—and when they thrive, productivity and satisfaction are likely to improve.

Phelps defines innovation as "new knowledge that leads to new practices." He points out that scientists and engineers tend to view innovation as new knowledge and assume that it will lead to new practices, but economists view new knowledge and its adoption as separate phenomena.

In other words, innovations (and innovative societies) depend on systems—innovative people and companies are the beginning. There must also be people with the ability to effectively judge whether to attempt to develop or to finance a new thing. And, once the new thing is developed, there must be those who decide it is worth trying; early adopters are important for economic innovation.[5]

A trio of conceptual equations reflects this notion. They show how a *willingness to embrace new practices* provides the glue between innovation and a modern economy.

---

[5] This underscores how critical buzz about the Fairshare Model is to its adoption by pioneering entrepreneurs.

Innovation = New Knowledge that Leads to <u>New Practice</u>

<u>New Practice</u> = Origination of New Thing (Concept & Development) + Pioneering Adoption

<u>Embrace of New Practices</u> = Dynamism = Modern Society = Modern Economy

Let's return to Phelps' use of the word *dynamism*. He describes it as the willingness and capacity to innovate and says the difference between innovation and imitation is fuzzy. Historically, nations relied on their own ability to innovate (indigenous innovation). Increasingly, however, they adopt innovation originated elsewhere (exogenesis innovation)–call it false innovation or copying. He uses this insight to distinguish economic *dynamism* from economic *vibrancy*, which is the alertness to opportunities, a readiness to act.

This leads him to make an intriguing point. **The economic growth rate is NOT a useful measure of dynamism** and an economy with little or no dynamism may regularly have the same or better growth in productivity and/or real wages that a dynamic one has.

How? Partly, by trading with a dynamic economy. Mainly, by being vibrant enough to imitate the new practices of a dynamic economy. In fact, an economy with low dynamism might for a time show a faster growth rate than a modern economy does with its high dynamism.

Innovation can be bad news for those who earn a living from what is being disrupted.

Phelps supports safety nets that cushion the effect of disruption because they encourage public support for policies that encourage dynamism and reduce support for corporatism.

Professor Phelps offers three alternate ways to measure the effect of dynamism in an economy.**M**

1. **Consider the strength of the forces and facilities that are its inputs:**
   - drive to change things,
   - talent to change things,
   - receptivity to new things, and
   - institutions that enable change.

2. **Estimate its output**

   Start with . . . . . Gross Domestic Product growth that is NOT due to growth in the supply of capital or labor.

   Add or Subtract. . Unusual market conditions.

   Subtract. . . . . . . False innovations–those that are copied from other countries; from a global perspective, that's not innovation.

   Equals . . . . Growth in income earned from an economy's indigenous dynamic qualities.

3. **Assess circumstantial evidence**

- new company formation,

- employee turnover (i.e., higher turnover = higher dynamism),

- turnover in the list of large companies in an economy,

- turnover of retail stores, and

- mean life of universal product codes (i.e., UPC barcode life is a proxy for dynamism, how rapidly new products displace older ones).

A key question emerges. *If an economy with little or no dynamism can have growth that equals or exceeds one that has it, and, if economic dynamism risks disruption, why encourage it?*

Phelps argues persuasively that dynamism is positively correlated with growth. He acknowledges that dynamism can lead to bad luck but emphasizes that **the central reward of a modern economy is that its participants have the opportunity to pursue the Aristotelian concept of the good life.**

This string of ideas can be expressed conceptually this way:

Modern Beliefs, Attitudes, and Values → Modern Economy → The Good Life

The Good Life = **The *intellectual growth* that comes from actively engaging the world** + **The *moral growth* that comes from creating and exploring in the face of great uncertainty**

The singer Tony Bennett popularized a song about romance called "The Good Life" that has the line "It's the good life to be free and explore the unknown." That reflects a sentiment Phelps says Aristotle had in mind about what made a life fulfilling and, by extension, what makes an interesting job satisfying. For him, the good life is something that people would choose once their need for essentials were comfortably met.

A similar notion was expressed by 20th century psychologist Abraham Maslow in his theory of human motivation, illustrated in this diagram.

His hierarchy of needs has self-actualization—a form of the good life—as the highest need, sought once other lower ones are satisfied. I feel that belonging and love are components of the good life but take comfort from the idea that these psychological needs are below self-actualization in Maslow's hierarchy.

Mass Flourishing highlights the thoughts of many thinkers on what brings people the greatest satisfaction in life. One of them is Jacques Barzun, a historian of Western thought who

Self-actualization: achieving one's full potential, including creative activities — Self-fulfillment needs

Esteem needs: prestige and feeling of accomplishment — Psychological needs

Belongingness and love needs: intimate relationships, friends

Safety needs: security, safety — Basic needs

Physiological needs: food, water, warmth, rest

dubbed self-discovery and personal growth as "vitalism." If there is a doctrine of vitalism, its most succinct expression may be "to boldly go." That was the motto of the US space agency, NASA, in the early days of its project to go to the moon and it opened *Star Trek* episodes on television. Phelps adds this:

> The difference between the pragmatist take on the good life and the vitalist take is striking. The word 'hurdle' is in the lexicon of both schools, but hurdles come up in contrasting ways.
>
> In the **vitalist** view, people are *looking for* hurdles to overcome, problems to solve: if you do not happen to meet any, you change your life so that you start meeting them.
>
> In the **pragmatist** view, people *encounter* hurdles in the course of being pragmatic—of working in an industry or profession that seems to offer the best prospects of success. Pragmatists do not specify what humankind wants to succeed at. They only say that, whatever a person's career is aimed at, the person—unless very unlucky—will meet innumerable problems and solve a great many of them.
>
> Their *engagement* in problem-solving is an intellectual side of the good life. The resulting mastery is another part of the good life: the part called *achievement*. The value of engagement and mastery could be seen as part of what Aristotle had in mind.[N]

Phelps observes: "Vitalism is enjoying a revival after decades of pragmatism," then considers how Aristotle might apply *eudaimonia*—ancient Greek for happiness or flourishing—to contemporary times. He cites research, saying "many Americans want to feel embarked on a mission *to make a difference.*"[O]

So, what might constitute a vibrant economy? Phelps offers this:

> A society seeks and builds an economy to provide mutual benefits for its citizens.
>
> So, as a life in pursuit of the highest good, or benefit, is termed by Aristotle the "good life," an economy enabling people's mutual pursuit of the highest good may be termed a *good economy*. An economy is good if and only if it permits and fosters the good life.[P]

What can be done to restore economic dynamism? Phelps sees a significant role for government, provided it rescinds old interventions at least as actively as it initiates new ones. He makes these recommendations.[Q]

- Government must be aware of the importance of dynamism in a modern economy.
- To take well-judged actions, governments must have a sense of the way forward. They need an elementary understanding of how the business sphere of a well-functioning modern economy generates dynamism. It is not mechanical; it is organic. It is not an ordered system; it is topsy-turvy. Legislators and regulators should ask of every bill or directive; "How would it impact the dynamism of our economy?"
- Policymakers should disabuse themselves of the notion that economic growth is increased by policies that stimulate some industries over others through subsidies, mandates, private-public partnerships, or government-sponsored enterprises.

- Shrink or terminate policies that promote a corporatist economy. Much special interest legislation exists in the form of tax deductions, exemptions, and carve-outs. "The US tax code runs to 16,000 pages. The French have a tax code with only 1,900 pages."[R]

- Stop paying CEOs very high short-term salaries as this induces short-term thinking. Corporations should not be able to use their capital for golden parachute payments.

- Don't allow mutual funds to threaten a CEO with dumping her company's stock if she doesn't fix her attention on hitting the next quarter's earnings target.

- Overhaul the banking industry to provide vastly more credit for innovative projects and startups. Specifically, restructure the behemoths into smaller units with narrower lines of business, leaving risky assets to markets with the appropriate expertise.

- Reexamine the ability of labor unions and professional associations to inhibit innovation or restrict new entrants into markets.

- Reintroduce to secondary and higher education the main ideas of modern thought, such as individualism and vitalism (i.e., a creative and venturesome spirit).[6]

Summation

This chapter presents context for the Fairshare Model regarding the challenge to invigorate the economy. The economists cited share the belief that something different is called for. Robert Litan and Carl Schram narrow their recommendations to immigration reform, improved access to capital, more rapid commercialization of university intellectual property, and regulatory reform. Edmund Phelps argues for steps that restore dynamism.

The Fairshare Model seeks to improve the odds that public investors will make money when they invest in venture-stage companies—the kind that play an outsized role in America's economic growth, its ability to engage in mutually beneficial trade with other nations, and to create engaging, fulfilling jobs. The Fairshare Model also promotes an innovative social compact between investors and workers—a form of dynamism.

Professor Phelps suggests that the assumption of risks enlivens what it means to be human. Entrepreneurs are more likely to fail than succeed, and as they strive, they assume costs in the form of foregoing stable employment, loss of savings, increased debt, and lost time. Their struggles can fray relationships and create a stigma of failure. Still, many try. Investors who back them are likely to lose money, but there are those who want to provide it, including non-accredited ones. Those who have had success in the past are not immune from suffering loss; and there are those who have had little success but continue to strive, nonetheless. Early adopters of a technology often pay a price for being in the first wave, but they are willing to take the leap.

Bad outcomes can result for everyone in the entrepreneurial ecosystem, for all those who contribute to a dynamic economy. But that doesn't keep them from trying. To strive is to hope, and when we do, we are likely to self-actualize. Thus, it is possible to view this activity apart from the prospect to make money—to see it as a pursuit of the good life. As an expression of support by investors to an obsessive entrepreneurial team with a quirky idea that is unlikely to generate a financial return for investors. They all dream of what may be possible, and their existence is a vital asset to the economy.

---

[6] Exposure to Greek, Roman and other mythology as well as philosophers, adventure novels, etc.

And if the investment doesn't pay off? If the investor didn't invest more than she could afford to lose, didn't overpay, and wasn't misled, it is possible that the investor was in pursuit of the good life. The lessons learned may make success more likely down the road.

Chapter 18, "Causes of Investor Loss: Fraud, Overpayment & Failure," discusses fraud in depth. But for now, reflect on how the ability of anyone to invest in venture-stage companies, with low valuation risk, might help the economy restore its innovative engine and strengthen its *mojo*— a power that may seem magical and that allows someone to be very effective, successful, etc.

> "It is only in adventure that some people succeed in knowing themselves— in finding themselves."
>
> –Andre Gide

What's Next?

The next chapter explores another macroeconomic issue that creates context for the Fairshare Model: income inequality.

Chapter Endnotes

Contextual references for material in this chapter appear as numbered footnotes on the page where the reference is made. **Source references** for material in this chapter appear below as endnotes with capital letter identifiers.

A Litan, Robert E., and Carl J. Schramm. *Better Capitalism Renewing the Entrepreneurial Strength of the American Economy*. New Haven: Yale University Press, 2012. Pages 5 - 6.

B Ibid, page 7.

C Kane, Tim. "The Importance of Startups in Job Creation and Job Destruction." *Ewing Marion Kauffman Foundation*. July 2010. Accessed May 08, 2018. fairsharemodel.com/Startup-job-creation. Page 2.

D *Better Capitalism*, by Robert Litan and Carl Schramm, page 110.

E "Obama on Immigration (transcript)." June 11, 2013. *Politico*. Accessed May 08, 2018. fairsharemodel.com/Immigration.

F "America Still Wears the Crown." *The Economist*. July 05, 2007. Accessed May 08, 2018. fairsharemodel.com/AmericaCrown.

G Stueckelberger, Christoph. Lecture at Nanjing Union Theological Seminary titled "Why the new interest in Max Weber's 'The Protestant Ethic and the Spirit of Capitalism' in Southeast Asia today?" ChristophStueckelberger.ch. April 26, 2005. Accessed October 11, 2018. fairsharemodel.com/Weber.

H Ruck, Damian. "This Is the Link between Religion and Economic Development." *World Economic Forum*. August 3, 2018. Accessed October 10, 2018. fairsharemodel.com/Religion.

I From the publisher's summary of *Mass Flourishing*.

J "Mass Flourishing: How It Was Won, Then Largely Lost," lecture delivered by Phelps Oct. 9, 2013.

K Phelps, Edmund S. *Mass Flourishing: How Grassroots Innovation Created Jobs, Challenge, and Change.* Princeton, NJ: Princeton University Press, 2015. Pages 98 – 99.

L Ibid.

M *Mass Flourishing,* page 21.

N *Mass Flourishing,* pages 283-284.

O Ibid, page 285.

P Ibid, page 288.

Q Ibid, pages 316-324.

R Ibid, pages 164-165.

Chapter 11:

The Macroeconomic Context – Income Inequality

What's Included in This Chapter

- Introduction
- Piketty's R > G
- Conservative Perspectives on Income Inequality
- My Take: R > L
- Common Ground?
- Is the Fairshare Model Capitalism?
- Economic Justice in the New Issue (IPO) Market
- An Allegory for What Troubles Developed Economies
    - A Political Scientist Reflects on Regulation, Politics, and Income Inequality
- Summation
- What's Next?
- Chapter Endnotes

Introduction

Income or wealth inequality is the handmaiden of slow economic growth and, increasingly, people feel it also is the result of a system that is gamed to favor the wealthy and connected. To identify solutions that can get broad support, we need discussion about what Edmund Phelps refers to as a "good economy"–*one that enables people's mutual pursuit of the highest good.* Then, we need to consider how best to achieve it. Clearly, it is an enduring challenge, made more difficult by the declining quality of public dialogue and the influence of corporatism.

In the long-run, the Fairshare Model offers a *partial* solution to the problem. I say partial, because its benefits go directly to those with skin in the entrepreneurial game–investors and employees. To the extent these investors are not accredited they, like the employees of the companies they invest in, largely rely on the return on their labor. The Fairshare Model positions them to participate in the higher return on capital–specifically, in venture-stage companies, the asset class responsible for much of the wealth earned in equities. This notion, presented earlier, is delved into in this chapter.

Before that, from a high-level perspective, we'll consider the drivers of rising income inequality.

Thought Experiment

Imagine that the Fairshare Model had been used for decades.

What might our socio-economic challenges look like now?

Piketty's R > G

In 2014, French economist Thomas Piketty published *Capital in the 21st Century*, which examines how income has been distributed in capitalistic economies. This summary is from *The New Yorker*:[A]

> Using tax records and other data, [Picketty] studied how income inequality in France had evolved during the twentieth century and published his findings in a 2001 book. A 2003 paper that he wrote with Emmanuel Saez, examined income inequality in the United States between 1913 and 1998.
>
> It detailed how the share of US national income taken by households at the top of the income distribution had risen sharply during the early decades of the twentieth century, then fallen back during and after the Second World War, only to soar again in the nineteen-eighties and nineties.
>
> With the help of other researchers, Piketty expanded his work on inequality to other countries, including Britain, China, India, and Japan. The researchers established the World Top Incomes Database, which now covers some thirty countries. They also updated their US figures, showing how the income share of the richest households continued to climb during and after the Great Recession, and how, in 2012, the top one percent of households took 22.5 percent of total income, the highest figure since 1928.

The book's central argument captured considerable attention; the growth in the size of the middle class in the 20th century was a historic anomaly, and rising income inequality is a return to normalcy.

In other words, income inequality has been a persistent economic reality. And, the 20th century experience of a large and growing middle class was a remarkable phenomenon that is unlikely to persist. Professor Piketty uses this formula to explain why:

Return on capital > Growth in the economy

expressed as

R > G

The formula means that the rate of return on capital (abbreviated as "R" in the following chart) has tended to exceed the growth rate in the economy (abbreviated as "G").[B]

Piketty's measurement period is about two thousand years, year 0 to 2012. Over this time, he concludes that R has averaged 4 to 5 percent per year and G has been about 0 percent–0.1 percent.

The difference in income is magnified over time, in part because it accumulates in the form of wealth, and in part, because invested wealth earns the higher rate of return–R.

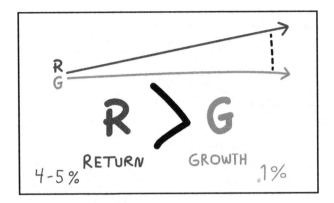

In contrast, those whose income is chiefly derived from their labor see their income grow at the lower rate, G, and have less opportunity to acquire wealth.

Thus, Piketty's formula neatly explains why the rich get richer over time. The components of the two rates are identified below.

R = Return on capital = Interest + Dividends + Capital Gains + Rent Income

G = Growth in the economy = Productivity Rate x Change in Population Size

The components of the term "R" are straightforward. The components of G merit explanation. It's intuitive to associate productivity with growth. When the productivity rate climbs, so does economic growth. The reverse effect is also clear.

Less obvious is why an increase in population promotes economic growth, or why a decrease in population contributes to a shrinking economy. It happens because people need to find ways to make economic transactions to support themselves—the best that they can, anyway. An increase in the number of people transacting for food, clothing, shelter and so on contributes to an increase in economic activity. It works the opposite way when the population shrinks; a reduction in the number of people making such transactions contributes to a decline in economic growth.

The chart on the following page illustrates Piketty's long-view conclusions about R and G, starting in year 0 through his projections through the end of our current 21st century. The vertical axis shows the annual rate of economic growth, and the horizontal axis measures time, in irregular blocks.[1] The return on capital after taxes and loss of capital (due to fire, war, spoilage, etc.), R, is the dark line that begins at 4.5 percent. The lighter line that begins at zero percent is G, the growth rate of the world's economic output.

---

[1] The first vertical line marks the rate of return (or growth rate) between year 0 and 1000 (a 1,000-year period). Subsequent ones' mark returns between 1000 and 1500 (500 years later), between 1500 and 1700 (200 years later), between 1700 and 1820 (120 years later), between 1820 and 1913 (97 years later); between 1913 and 1950 (47 years later); and between 1950 and 2012 (62 years later) before projecting the balance of this century.

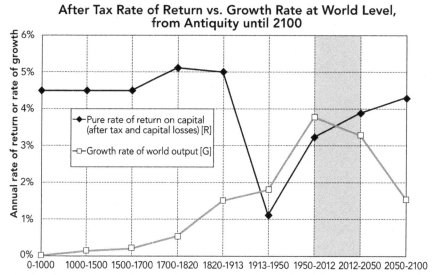

After Tax Rate of Return vs. Growth Rate at World Level, from Antiquity until 2100

The rate of return on capital (after tax and capital losses) fell below the growth rate during the 20th century, and may again surpass it in the 21st century. Source - piketty.pse.ens.fr/files/capital21c/en/pdf/F10.10.pdf

For the first 1,500 years, from year 0 through the Roman Empire and the end of the Middle Ages, the return on capital (R), averaged 4.5 percent. [Recall that Edmund Phelps marks 1500 as the start of the Modern Era.] It climbed to about 5 percent by 1700, sparked by the discovery of the New World and other European Renaissance developments. It remains there during the 1820-1913 measurement period. [Phelps identifies 1815-1830 as the start of the Modern Society.] In the 1913-1950 period, R plunged 80 percent, from 5 to 1 percent, due to loss of asset value during two world wars and an economic depression.

Turn now to the economic growth rate, G. It hovers above zero from year 0 to 1500, an epoch defined by a rise in agricultural productivity and mercantile trade. It is barely higher the first 200 years of the Modern Era, between 1500 and 1700. But in the period from 1700 to 1820, G climbs significantly, to 0.5 percent. From 1820–the dawn of Modern Societies–to 1913, just before WWI, G triples to 1.5 percent.

This is what Phelps calls an age of mass flourishing, propelled by productivity improvements from the Industrial Revolution and rising populations. Economic growth increases to nearly 2 percent between 1913 and 1950. Note that then, for the first time, G exceeds R; growth exceeds the return from capital by about 0.75 percent.

During the postwar period to the present, 1950 to 2012, R and G climb in tandem. Economic growth is nearly 1 percent higher than the return on capital in 1950, but that advantage narrows a bit over the next six decades. More significantly, economic growth, the factor that enabled the formation of a growing middle class in America, grows to about 3.9 percent–a historic high.

Piketty speculates how these trends will play out over the 21st century. Absent adoption of tax policies that tax capital gains and inherited wealth at higher rates, or, tax rates on income from salaries and wages at lower rates, he thinks that it's likely that R, the return on capital, will begin to exceed G, economic growth. This occurs in the shaded portion of the graph, midway between 2012 and 2050.

After that, between 2050 and 2100, he expects that the worldwide return on capital will continue to grow toward the pre-Renaissance norm, and the global economic growth will slide from its 2012 peak of 3.8 percent to the 1.5 percent last seen before 1820.

He anticipates rapid expansion in the use of non-human producers of economic output–computers, robots, or biological processes–plus a decline in population size. Absent changes in tax policies, Piketty expects that the economic benefits generated by non-human forms of production will disproportionately go to the owners of capital.

With respect to his historic analysis, economists across the political spectrum express admiration for his work. That said, some disagree with his dystopian projection for labor and there is a predictable divide on his prescription for higher taxes on the wealthy. Piketty reports that Microsoft founder Bill Gates told him: "I love everything that's in your book, but I don't want to pay more tax." Recognizing the charitable work that the Bill and Melinda Gates Foundation does, and the efficiency with which it operates, Piketty said: "I understand his point. I think he sincerely believes he's more efficient than the government, and you know, maybe he is sometimes."[c]

In his blog, Gates encourages others to read Piketty's book or a good summary of it.[D] Below are some of the points that he makes in the full piece:

> I [Bill Gates] agree with Piketty's most important conclusions, and I hope his work will draw more smart people into the study of wealth and income inequality. I very much agree that
>
> - High levels of inequality are a problem–messing up economic incentives, tilting democracies in favor of powerful interests, and undercutting the ideal that all people are created equal.
>
> - Capitalism does not self-correct toward greater equality–that is, excess wealth concentration can have a snowball effect if left unchecked.
>
> - Governments can play a constructive role in offsetting the snowballing tendencies if and when they choose to do so.
>
> Extreme inequality should not be ignored–or worse, celebrated as a sign that we have a high-performing economy and healthy society. Yes, some level of inequality is built into capitalism. The question is, what level is acceptable? And when does it do more harm than good? That's something we should have a public discussion about, and it's great that Piketty helped advance that discussion in such a serious way.
>
> At the core of his book is a simple equation: $R > G$, where R stands for the average rate of return on capital and G stands for the rate of growth of the economy. The idea is that when the returns on capital outpace the returns on labor, over time the wealth gap will widen between people who have a lot of capital and those who rely on their labor.
>
> Other economists have cast doubt on the value of $R > G$ for understanding whether inequality will widen or narrow. I'm not an expert on that question. What I do know is that $R > G$ doesn't adequately differentiate among different kinds of capital with different social utility.
>
> I agree that taxation should shift away from taxing labor. It doesn't make any sense that labor in the United States is taxed so heavily relative to capital. It will make even less sense in the coming years, as robots and other forms of automation come to perform more and more of the skills that human laborers do today.

But rather than move to a progressive tax on capital, as Piketty would like, I think we'd be best off with a progressive tax on consumption. Like Piketty, I'm also a big believer in the estate tax. Letting inheritors consume or allocate capital disproportionately simply based on the lottery of birth is not a smart or fair way to allocate resources.

The debate over wealth and inequality has generated a lot of partisan heat. Even with its flaws, Piketty's work contributes at least as much light as heat. And now I'm eager to see research that brings more light to this important topic.

If it isn't clear, Piketty is considered politically liberal, and his policy recommendation to use taxes to remedy the inequity reflects this. Again, his analysis of historic evidence is respected by economists across the political spectrum.

I will get to the relevancy of Piketty's analysis for the Fairshare Model and sample conservative perspectives on the drivers of income inequality. Before that, I'll mention that in 2013, Hedrick Smith wrote a thoroughly researched book by about the drivers of income inequality in the US, *Who Stole the American Dream*. Here is the summary from *Booklist,* the review journal of the American Library Association (bold added for emphasis).

[Hedrick] Smith, Pulitzer-Prize–winning reporter, explains how the middle-class prosperity after WWII was reversed [after] the 1980s because of a long period of sweeping transformations both in Washington's policies and in the mindset and practices of American business leaders.

American corporations paid high wages and good benefits after the war; millions of workers spent their money; and business investment increased, which led to growth, expansion, and higher living standards. The 1980s ushered in the era of job losses and a lid on average pay scales; hence, consumer spending declined, and the nation's economy was negatively affected.

We learn the top 1 percent (3 million people) got two-thirds of the US economic gain between 2002 and 2007, and the 99 percent (310 million) got one-third. Smith concludes, we are at a defining moment for America.

Piketty's expansive research has largely been subject to praise, but elements of it has attracted criticism from other economists. If you have interest in the debate, here are links to some material to get you started.

- A liberal and a conservative economist debate Piketty's theory in a May 2104 PBS *NewsHour* segment "Why do the rich get richer?" at fairsharemodel.com/RichGetRicher

- Piketty clarifies aspects of his work in a May 2015 America Economic Review paper called "About Capital in the Twenty-First Century" at fairsharemodel.com/AER.

- "Review and Critique of Piketty's Capital in the Twenty-First Century" (June 2016) by Mark J. Warshawsky, senior research fellow at the Mercatus Center at George Mason University, at fairsharemodel.com/Mercatus.

Piketty's Political Proclivity

Paul Solman (PBS *NewsHour*): Thomas Piketty's recent US press tour was likened to Beatlemania, with standing-room-only events. Nobel laureates on stage with him piled on the praise especially ones tilting [politically] left, who share concern for the global trend the 42-year-old Parisian has definitively documented: growing economic inequality.

So our first question, when we sat down with him, was about his political slant.

Capital–*Das Kapital*–the name of Karl Marx's famous work, so are you a French Marxist?

Piketty: Not at all. No, I am not a Marxist. I turned 18 when the Berlin Wall fell, and I traveled to Eastern Europe to see the fall of the communist dictatorship. And, you know, I had never had any temptation for communism or, you know, Marxism.

–from PBS *NewsHour*, May 12, 2014

Conservative Perspectives on Income Inequality

This succinct summation of the conservative view on income inequality was made in November 2013 by liberal journalist Timothy Noah from the *New Republic*.[E]

> The usual conservative approach to income inequality (besides simply ignoring it) is to try to argue that it doesn't really exist, or to argue that if it does exist, it's mooted by upward mobility, or to argue that it's good for you.

To me, Noah repurposes conservative talking points about climate change that are more widely believed in the US than elsewhere in the world.[F] At any rate, conservatives may find his summation suspect since he's not one of them.

So let's check in with Matthew Continetti, a journalist with established conservative bona fides. In a November 2011, *Weekly Standard* article called "About Inequality," he concedes that the inequality trend is probably real and that it's a nasty business. But he doesn't think it's the government's place to do anything about it. Here's what Continetti had to say:[G]

> The way out is to reject the assumption that government's purpose is to redress inequalities of income. Inequalities of condition are a fact of life.
>
> Some people will always be poorer than others. So too, human altruism will always seek to alleviate the suffering of the destitute.
>
> There is a place for reasonable and prudent actions to improve well-being. But that does not mean the entire structure of our polity should be designed to achieve an egalitarian ideal.
>
> Such a goal is fantastic, utopian even, and one would think that the trillions of dollars the United States has spent in vain over the last 50 years to promote "equality as a fact and equality as a result" would give the egalitarians pause.

Another conservative thinker, Charles Murray of the American Enterprise Institute, expressed a somewhat different perspective in his 2012 book, *Coming Apart: The State of White America*. In a review of the book called "A Conservative Take on America's Economic Divide," Niall Ferguson wrote:[H]

> Murray is no apologist for Wall Street. Looking at the explosion in the value of the total compensation received by the chief executives of large corporations, he pointedly asks if the boards of directors of corporate America—and nonprofit America, and foundation America—[have] become cozy extended families, scratching each others' backs, happily going along with a market that has become lucrative for all of them, taking advantage of their privileged positions—rigging the game, but within the law.

In his review of Murray's book, *New York Times* columnist David Brooks, another conservative writer, wrote [bold added for emphasis]:[I]

> I'll be shocked if there's another book this year as important as Charles Murray's "Coming Apart." I'll be shocked if there's another book that so compellingly describes the most important trends in American society. Murray's basic argument is not new, that America is dividing into a two-caste society. What's impressive is the incredible data he produces to illustrate that trend and deepen our understanding of it.
>
> His story starts in 1963. There was a gap between rich and poor then, but it wasn't that big. a house in an upper-crust suburb cost only twice as much as the average new American home. The tippy-top luxury car, the Cadillac Eldorado Biarritz, cost about $47,000 in 2010 dollars. That's pricey, but nowhere near the price of the top luxury cars today.
>
> More important, the income gaps did not lead to big behavior gaps. Roughly 98 percent of men between the ages of 30 and 49 were in the labor force, upper-class and lower-class alike. Only about 3 percent of white kids were born outside of marriage. The rates were similar, upper class and lower class. Since then, America has polarized. The word "class" doesn't even capture the divide Murray describes. You might say the country has bifurcated into different social tribes, with a tenuous common culture linking them.
>
> The upper tribe is now segregated from the lower tribe. Today, Murray demonstrates, there is an archipelago of affluent enclaves clustered around the coastal cities, Chicago, Dallas and so on. If you're born into one of them, you will probably go to college with people from one of the enclaves; you'll marry someone from one of the enclaves; you'll go off and live in one of the enclaves.
>
> **Worse, there are vast behavioral gaps between the educated upper tribe (20 percent of the country) and the lower tribe (30 percent of the country). This is where Murray is at his best, and he's mostly using data on white Americans, so the effects of race and other complicating factors don't come into play.**
>
> Roughly 7 percent of the white kids in the upper tribe are born out of wedlock, compared with roughly 45 percent of the kids in the lower tribe. In the upper tribe, nearly every man aged 30 to 49 is in the labor force. In the lower tribe, men in their prime working ages have been steadily dropping out of the labor force, in good times and bad. People in the lower tribe are much less likely to get married, less likely to go to church, less likely to be active in their communities, more likely to watch TV excessively, more likely to be obese.

Murray recommends that the upper tribe be more outspokenly judgmental about non-productive behaviors of the lower tribe and that they reduce their self-imposed geographic isolation of living in wealthy enclaves or "Super Zips" (the 900 or so zip codes of affluent communities).

Murray's book was published nearly four years into the Great Recession. The stubbornly slow recovery created resentment over the 2008 bank bailouts across the political spectrum. The Tea Party movement and Occupy Wall Street protests were both expressions of anxiety about the future. Broad dissatisfaction about The-Way-Things-Are-Done was evident. With that in mind, fast-forward from David Brooks' 2012 book review to his 2014 column, "The Inequality Problem."[J]

> Suddenly the whole world is talking about income inequality. But, as this debate goes on, it is beginning to look as though the thing is being misconceived. The income inequality debate is confusing matters more than clarifying them, and it is leading us off in unhelpful directions.
>
> In the first place, to frame the issue as income inequality is to lump together different issues that are not especially related.
>
> Second, it leads to ineffective policy responses.
>
> Third, the income inequality frame contributes to our tendency to simplify complex cultural, social, behavioral, and economic problems into strictly economic problems.
>
> Fourth, the income inequality frame needlessly polarizes the debate.

Brooks makes a good point: if income inequality is an issue, there is risk that the debate about economic policies will become even more difficult than it is. That said, there is little argument that income inequality has been growing and that it presents a threat to the well-being of society in America and elsewhere.

On *Fox News*, whose audience is reliably conservative, media pundit Howard Kurtz said the following in January 2015:[K]

> Suddenly, leading Republicans are openly embracing the notion that income inequality is a clear and present danger that must be addressed. That is such a tectonic shift that it moves the national debate several degrees to the left.
>
> It's not that congressional Republicans are going to pass sweeping legislation to boost the income of the lower and middle classes. But it tells you something about how they read the mood of the country. What agile politicians do is try to co-opt issues that the other side views as strengths. Real change is often preceded by an evolution in the way politicians frame an issue.
>
> In the past, when Democrats pounded away at the gap between rich and poor, many Republicans accused them of class warfare. Obviously, the GOP would explore a different mix of incentives and reject pitches to tax the rich and Wall Street to finance lower levies for the middle class. But after being pilloried as the party of the 1 percent, several of its biggest names are now saying the 1 percent have too much of the pie.

My Take: R > L

Like many, I've contemplated the relationship between the distribution of wealth/income and social stability. Piketty provides scholarly evidence that income inequality is increasing and a perspective as to why.

Before Piketty's book came out, I had already formulated an "armchair explanation" for income inequality. That is, one based on lay observation—I'm not an economist. I asked myself: "What is going on here?" Coincidently, the explanation I came up with resembles Piketty's formula—I think income inequality has been increasing because the return on capital exceeds the return on labor. This concept formula expresses the idea:

$$\text{Return on Capital} > \text{Return on Labor}$$

expressed as

$$R > L$$

My R term is similar to Piketty's—asset appreciation, rents, and interest. My L is the return on labor, which is a bit different from Piketty's G. To measure it, one might take real wages (i.e., inflation-adjusted) and add proxies for a sense of security, belonging, and purpose. Admittedly, they are nebulous, but so is consumer confidence and investor sentiment, and they are regularly mentioned in economic commentaries. My return on labor is this sort of measure, part quantifiable, part sensed. It is a measure of economic vitality and optimism and a barometer of social stability.

My analysis could be dubbed "economic impressionism" because it relies on observation and contemplation, not detailed analysis of data. My conclusion was that the return on labor has been in decline for three reasons—technology, economic theory, and the end of the Cold War. Their effect came into play in the 1980s and have gathered strength since then.

The relative strength of the return on capital is heightened on an after-tax basis because tax rates on income from labor are higher than income from capital.

Technology

Computer and telecom technologies made it easier to perform all manner of work, to be more productive. However, and significantly, it also made it easier to relocate where it is performed—it could be in another local office or in another country. Once digitized, work took far less time and effort to recreate. And it was easily shared, willingly or not.

It is difficult to identify jobs where the income potential has not been adversely affected by the ability to move work elsewhere—they range from factory workers to radiologists who evaluate x-ray images. Robotics and other forms of machine learning represent a permutation of the trend—they move work away from humans altogether.

Economic Theory

Philosophers provide ideas, the intellectual framework, for movements to coalesce around. Technology encouraged the idea that businesses didn't need to do everything in-house—that companies should focus on their core competencies, what they do well. An expression of this idea was outsourcing, which first affected support functions like computer operations and payroll.

It migrated to those once thought to be central, like manufacturing and customer support. Offshoring was just a skip and a hop away.

Outsourcing and offshoring were propelled by two theories from economic philosophers. One was that countries are net beneficiaries of free-trade. The other was that management's principal duty is to maximize the wealth of shareholders. The next chapter, "Cooperation as the New Tool for Competition," discusses the latter idea.

Lean organizational philosophies are a variant of the idea that companies need not do everything themselves and they are popular among emerging companies. That may foretell the future of work, given that these types of businesses are responsible for most job creation.

End of the Cold War

In 1990, when president George H. W. Bush proclaimed that a *New World Order* was emerging, he was expressing optimism about the future—especially, the prospects for nuclear disarmament, the reunification of Germany and European integration. However, the battle for the commanding heights of the world economies was not ending, it was merely shifting—from one based on political ideology to one driven by market economies.[L]

The Soviet Union dissolved in 1991. With the end of the Cold War, Russia, along with China, sought to transition from a centrally controlled economy to one that was more market-oriented, while minimizing political instability.[2] Countries indirectly affected by the Cold War, like India, had adjustments to make as well. As they began to trade with the developed economies, an emerging low-cost pool of labor became increasing responsible for products consumed in the West.

In 1992, the European Union was formed. Member countries came to share a currency; citizens were free to travel, live and work within the EU and commerce within it was free of restrictions and border taxes. In part, EU countries sought to emulate the United States of America. They also sought a way to respond to rising imports from Japan and the so-called Asian Tiger countries—Hong Kong, Singapore, South Korea, and Taiwan.

Similar trade concerns led to the 1993 NAFTA[3] trade agreement between the US, Canada, and Mexico. "Globalization" was coined to describe the increasing integration of economies around the world.

> In the early 1990s, I was struck by a story about how gravestone cutters in the US faced competition from China. If cemetery-related workers were affected by those on other side of the globe, I thought, few markets would be untouched by globalization.

The collective effect of these drivers was to lower the return on labor in developed economies. The political landscape looks startlingly different once you recognize that. Technology made it easier

---

[2] A fundamental question was whether to first redistribute state-owned property (everything was state-owned) and then deregulate prices, or to first deregulate prices and then redistribute property. Russia opted for the former approach. China chose the latter and controlled price increases to minimize social disruption.

[3] NAFTA (or Nafta) is the acronym for the North American Free Trade Agreement.

to move work. Economic theory led to a management ethos that it *should* move work to the lowest cost labor. And the end of the Cold War expanded the supply of low-cost labor in distant lands.

Their combined effect was to erode opportunity for those in developed economies who rely on the return on labor.

Little can be done to affect the global supply of labor and few are willing to forego the benefits that technology has brought. That leaves changes in economic theory as the best way to improve the return on labor or slow its decline.

> In the face of these three drivers, is it possible for today's job market to look much better for workers than it does now?

Hence, we have more people rejecting traditional notions about free trade or challenging dogma about corporate purpose. Those who do hold disparate political beliefs about a range of economic policy prescriptions.

What unites them is the desire to improve the return on labor.

New business models also created turmoil for those who rely on the return on labor, but they emerge from the three drivers—technology, economic theory, and less expensive labor. For example, airline deregulation in the 1970s led to upstart carriers, like Southwest Airlines, and changes in financial service regulations led to the rise of discount brokerages like Schwab. Deregulation is a change in economic theory—innovative thinking that leads to new business strategies. Big Box retailers leveraged low-cost producers and supply-chain technology to do that. The internet enabled newcomers in a range of industries to upend incumbents that employed many people.

Whatever the combination of the three drivers, few markets have avoided movement toward making labor a commodity.

- The winners were consumers, who got lower prices, businesses that reduced costs, and investors who made good bets on innovative companies.
- The losers were workers and suppliers who were not competitive, and the communities where they were based. Investors in non-innovative firms saw losses too.[4]

Labor intensive industries like textiles and furniture were among the first to be affected, but capital-intensive industries like tires and steel followed because reducing the variable cost of labor positioned them to cover their fixed costs faster.[5] Looser regulatory requirements for manufacturers in developing economies provided incentive to relocate work, but I suspect that lower labor costs were a more significant factor.

The three drivers created a new world order for those who rely on the return on labor. Increasingly, labor became a commodity. Those not directly affected by the trend nonetheless felt more insecure because they knew their world could change quickly.

---

[4] "Buy and hold stock for the long term" increasingly sounds like quant advice from less volatile times.

[5] These emerging exporters also had help from their governments—weak environmental laws, subsidies and currency exchange rates managed so to provide a cost advantage. The fact that the dollar has served as the dominant world currency has also boosted its value, making US exports more expensive.

Focusing on the relative rates of return on capital and labor can help one grasp the root cause of diminishing optimism in developed economies.

In 2011, Robert B. Reich, a former US Secretary of Labor, wrote an op-ed piece in *The New York Times* called "The Limping Middle Class." It included this chart, which underscores how the return on labor has stagnated in recent decades and how income gains have become increasingly asymmetrical.[M]

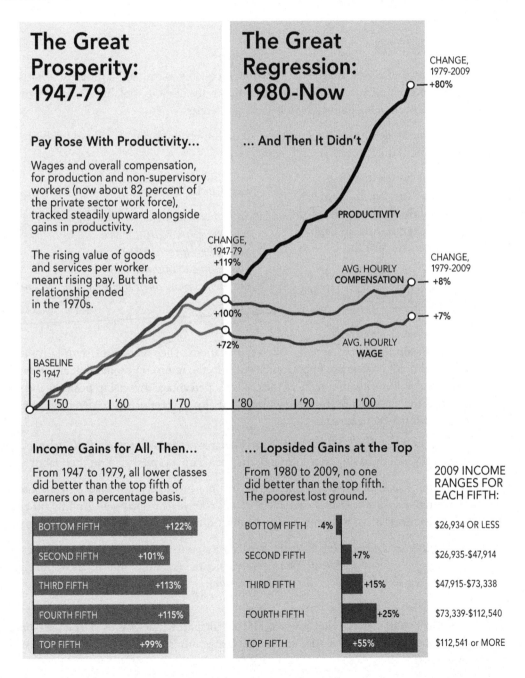

This is from *The New York Times* in September 2018. "Data from the Federal Reserve show that over the last decade and a half, the proportion of family income from wages has dropped from nearly 70 percent to just under 61 percent. It's an extraordinary shift, driven largely by the investment profits of the very wealthy. In short, the people who possess tradable assets, especially stocks, have enjoyed a recovery that Americans dependent on savings or income from their weekly paycheck have yet to see. Ten years after the financial crisis, getting ahead by going to work every day seems quaint, akin to using the phone book to find a number or renting a video at Blockbuster."[N]

Common Ground?

Liberals and many conservatives agree that income inequality is real and a problem. That suggests that policymakers can find ways to address it. Tax policy is the obvious tool, but it's also a contentious one, and vulnerable to being defined by self-serving interests.

With the Fairshare Model, I propose an additional path to explore, one that should appeal to those whose politics are on the left, center, and right.

Call it the "Paul McCartney Solution" because his song "Let 'Em In" captures the idea—**expand the opportunities for workers to earn the return on capital.** Besides, everyone likes Sir Paul!

The Fairshare Model helps workers get in on the higher return on capital in two ways:

"Let 'Em In" chorus

Someone's knockin' at the door
Somebody's ringin' the bell
Someone's knockin at the door
Somebody's ringin' the bell
Do me a favor, open the door and let 'em in

–Paul McCartney

1. It helps average investors to invest in venture-stage companies at lower valuations. They rely on the return on their labor and don't have many opportunities to earn the return on capital that are attractive and fun. A lower valuation reduces the cost of a percentage ownership position and increases the odds of a profitable investment. It also makes it easier to diversify a venture-stage portfolio—reducing risk.

2. Employees "capitalize" the value of their collective performance when Performance Stock converts. Without having to risk capital, they can earn a capital gain on their labor.

The ability of the Fairshare Model to ameliorate income inequality will take generations to test because the outcomes for companies that adopt it will take years to play out. And it will only pay off for those who invest in, or work for, a successful venture. Therefore, it is not a general panacea.

Still, it's something to contemplate. Policymakers chart a course to where they want the economy and society to be in a few decades. If it's an entrepreneurial economy that offers opportunity for more people, it's sensible to support the Fairshare Model.

Reflect how much money could flow to these two groups of workers—average investors and employees in the companies that they invest in. If the Fairshare Model was used by large companies, the capital gains earned could rival the returns that hedge funds deliver to their wealthy investors—billions of dollars!

Is the Fairshare Model Capitalism?

A guy I chatted with told me that the Fairshare Model smacks of communism or socialism. I found it odd. Those top-down systems focus on macroeconomic matters while the Fairshare Model focuses on a microeconomic issue—when a value for performance is set, and it is a bottom-up solution, determined by shareholders, not government. Puckishly put, two guys named "Karl" say quite different things:

> Karl Marx said: "From each according to his abilities, to each according to his needs."

> I, Karl Sjogren, say: "Fairly share the rewards of building a business between those who provide capital and those who make it worth more with their labor."

The Fairshare Model is a solution for companies that seek public venture capital—it is not a broad set of socio-economic policies. By adopting it, an issuer encourages investors to invest by reducing their valuation risk. It also positions its employees to earn the return on capital and to have a voice in governance—which is provocative. Such empowerment makes it a Rorschach test of sensibilities about the relationship between capital and labor. It confronts conventional thinking about public venture capital by presenting a radically different way to approach ownership interests.

The Fairshare Model will evoke skepticism from traditionalists, as well as from those who feel the human behavior challenges it faces will be difficult to resolve. Hostility will come from those who see bets on valuation as the essence of capitalism[6] and from those who profit from The-Way-Things-Are.

However, those who seek to make capitalism work better for more people will like the Fairshare Model. They will see benefits at the microeconomic level from better alignment of interests between investors and employees. They will sense macroeconomic benefits too: greater emphasis on wealth generated by long-term performance, and less on wealth derived from opportunistic trading. More capital gains will go to workers and average investors. Psychologically, it promises to boost vitalism in an economy by emphasizing the opportunity to be rewarded by activities that generate economic growth.

Another way to make that last point is to say that the Fairshare Model seeks to feed society's animal spirits, which is good for capitalism. John Maynard Keynes coined this term to describe the emotional mindset of an economy's participants—their level of confidence in investing or spending. In 2009, George A. Akerlof and Robert J. Shiller, each of whom is a winner of the Nobel Prize, published *Animal Spirits: How Human Psychology Drives the Economy and Why It Matters for Global Capitalism*. Below are some of the book's takeaway points, as identified in *The Economist:*[O]

- Conventional economic analysis confines itself to rational, quantifiable facts. However, economic decision makers are often intuitive, emotional, and irrational.

- Confidence or lack of it can drive or hamper economic growth.

- Fairness matters greatly in setting wages, but classical economic models ignore it.

- People tend to reach irrational conclusions about money; this is the "money illusion." For example, they ignore inflation and believe their savings maintain their value; or they resist pay cuts when prices fall—even if their jobs may be at stake.

---

[6] These types are likely to enjoy a sporting event more if they know the betting spread set by odds makers.

- Stories of corruption and broken trust can contribute to economic depressions.

- Minorities have a different story of America than whites do. Their story depicts an unfair society offering less opportunity than the majority perceives.

- Economists and policymakers need to shed the untenable theory of rational, efficient, self-correcting markets and pay appropriate attention to animal spirits.

> "Education: the path from cocky ignorance to miserable uncertainty."
>
> —Mark Twain

Economic Justice in the New Issue (IPO) Market

In *Mass Flourishing*, Edmund Phelps writes of John Rawls, a philosopher who explored concepts of economic fairness and justice and offers this quote from Rawls's 1971 work, *A Theory of Justice*.[P]

> A society is a cooperative venture for mutual advantage.
>
> There is an *identity of interests,* since social cooperation makes possible a better life for all than any would have if each were to live solely by his own efforts.
>
> There is a *conflict of interests,* since persons are not indifferent as to how the greater benefits produced by their collaboration are distributed, for in order to pursue their ends they each prefer a larger to a lesser share.
>
> A set of principles is required for choosing among the various social arrangements, which determine this division of advantages and for underwriting an agreement on the proper distributive shares.
>
> These…are the *principles of social justice.*

Phelps says: "The classic defenders of capitalism…have sought an economy having few 'interferences' with what they see to be the good in capitalism–the 'freedoms' and the 'growth'–*without a thought for what a just economy is.* In the premise of some of these classic defenders, each participant receives in pay the value of his or her contribution to the national product, exactly as if each worked in isolation, so it is difficult if not impossible to see what moral claim one sort of participant might have to the pay of other sorts. But *this premise is untenable.*"[Q]

He adds that other defenders of capitalism "while conceding that the low earners benefit the high earners, jump in to say that the high earners, through their capital investment and innovation, greatly benefit the low earners–pulling up their wages and employment. They see no reason why the high earners should dig into their pockets to pay subsidies aimed at further benefiting the low earners. But this view of a market economy is as mistaken as the previous one. The free market sets wages that send signals and present incentives serving *efficiency*–in some rough and ready way, at any rate–*not* any ideas of *equity.*"[R]

Phelps's comments address the economic justice of after-tax wages, but the ideas behind them apply to capital markets. He notes that "A modern economy is striking for the *extraordinary income*–oversize profits and capital gains in anticipation of profits–that accrues to those whose new idea or whose entrepreneurial development or marketing of a new idea led to a successful adoption in the marketplace."[5] He could be describing the IPO valuations of venture-stage companies—after all, they represent wealth delivered in anticipation of future performance.

The process that begins with a VC investment and ends with a Wall Street IPO is discussed in Section 1. It allocates wealth based on efficiency rather than equity—it reflects market power, not economic justice. That is, a VC's dollar buys more than an angel investor's in that VCs get better terms. And the dollar of those privileged enough to get hot IPO shares get a better deal than investors who don't.

Rawls identified two principles that lead to a just and moral society. The first is that each person has liberty that is compatible with the liberty of others. The second is that social and economic positions are designed to everyone's advantage and open to all. In other words, Rawls said economic justice improves when open opportunity expands and corporatism—rules and practices that privilege certain players—is reduced.

He conducted experiments in which study subjects were told they would play a social-economic game after they defined the rules. When participants knew in advance what their position in the game would be, they advocated rules that benefited someone in that position. When they did not know what position they would occupy, they designed rules that did not favor any type of player over another. Rawls allowed that a justly functioning system could have unjust outcomes—he found that participants based their assessment of the fairness of the system on whether it appeared to be justly functioning, not on the outcome.

Now, with all this in mind, reflect again on the thought experiment presented at the end of Chapter 5, "The Problem with a Conventional Capital Structure."

Thought Experiment

Imagine that, starting tomorrow, shares in Wall Street IPOs are allocated by lottery, not based on wealth, privilege, or based on connections.

Will investors who have routinely been able to get shares at the IPO price remain content with a conventional capital structure?

If they must buy shares in the secondary market from those who win the lottery, might these well-connected investors clamor for a deal structure that reduces valuation risk?

The Fairshare Model focuses on valuation, making it fairer and driven more by performance than by speculation about the Next Guy. What if those who now occupy a preferred position in the capital formation process had to redesign it in a Rawlsian thought experiment? The study participants would include entrepreneurs, angel investors, VCs, underwriters, and their favored customers for IPO allocations, as well as average investors.

Importantly, no person designing the process would know in advance what position they would occupy in the game. For example, a real-life VC might be assigned the role of an entrepreneur, an angel investor, or an average investor. An investment banker might be made an IPO investor, or a secondary market investor. A secondary market investor could wind up being a VC, and so on. As a result, no player would have reason to design the process so that it favors a given role because they wouldn't have advance knowledge of the role they would occupy when the game was played.

I think that the rules for valuation that would emerge from such an experiment would resemble the Fairshare Model, don't you? Also, don't you think that the rules for share allocations would include a significant allocation of IPO shares for average investors?

Why would these approaches to valuation and share allocation prevail? Because they make it more likely that there will be more winners when the game is played. Who would lose if the rules are based on the Fairshare Model? Traders in the secondary market–those who "buy on the rumor and sell on the news," or, buy on talk of performance and sell when it is announced. They lose because more of the increase in a company's market capitalization goes to those who deliver it–the employees.

Arguably, this is consistent with a just, well-functioning system. While secondary market investors provide something useful–liquidity–they don't invent or make anything. And they don't provide the capital to those who do–they buy shares from shareholders, not new shares from the company.

An Allegory for What Troubles Developed Economies

The Fairshare Model offers a solution for income inequality that can work for employees of, and investors in, companies that adopt it. Admittedly, that is a small community of interests–a tribe. But that's okay, tribal solutions are more likely to get support nowadays than big solutions.

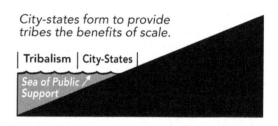

City-states form to provide tribes the benefits of scale.

Tribes were an early form of social order for humans. Often, tribal affiliation reflected familial connection; it always reflected shared interests. Advantages of scale led to city-states, where tribal affiliation weakened in importance. Ancient Athens and Rome were city-states; similar clusters were common in Europe in the Renaissance era.

Over time, nation-states supplanted city-states because larger affiliations of common interests promoted economic and political influence. Metaphorically, the tide of support rose to the nation-state level and remained there until the late 1980s.

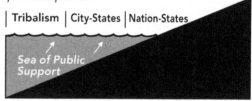

Nation-states displace city-states because they offer potential for more economic and political power.

That is when the effect of technology, economic theory and the expanding supply of labor began to be apparent to developed economies.

These forces, depicted here as rising moons, created a tide of support for transnational pacts like the European Union and NAFTA. The idea was that the best way to compete with the growing Asian economies was to make trade within Europe and North America more attractive.

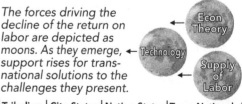

The forces driving the decline of the return on labor are depicted as moons. As they emerge, support rises for transnational solutions to the challenges they present.

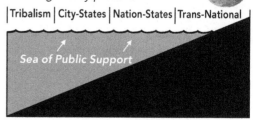

Both pacts were controversial because, like any trade agreement, there were winners and losers. It is striking, however, that those who opposed these alliances didn't offer an alternative way to address the declining return on labor.

The highwater mark for transnational solutions is depicted by the moons that cause the tide to recede. It was reached in 2016, when the UK voted to exit the EU—Brexit, it was called.

Shortly thereafter, Donald Trump was elected US president. He withdrew from the negotiations for the Trans-Pacific Trade Agreement and threatened to exit NAFTA if Canada and Mexico didn't agree to make it more beneficial to the US.

As the strength of the forces is revealed, support from transnational solutions recedes from those who rely on the return of labor.

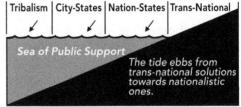

The tide ebbs from trans-national solutions towards nationalistic ones.

Trump summed up his approach as "America First," which mirrored his campaign slogan, "Make America Great Again." In France, the leader of the nationalistic and populist National Front party, Marine Le Pen, was a finalist in the 2017 presidential contest, which she lost to Emmanuel Macron. Politicians who similarly supported weakening ties to the EU showed signs of support in the Netherlands and Italy.

"We are in what the political scientist Ian Bremmer calls a 'G-Zero' world; one in which no country or bloc can shape or direct global events. The era of the cacophony is upon us."

—Angela Merkel, Chancellor of Germany

Each of these outcomes surprised pundits. Collectively, they suggest a dynamic—loss of confidence in transnational solutions. because they didn't protect voters from the forces that pressured the return on labor. It was easier to overlook their effect before the Great Recession, which caused credit to tighten, asset values to fall, and jobs to be lost. The pain that resulted was felt widely and it led to less optimism about the future.

Dissatisfaction with the pace of the recovery left voters mad as hell—but, in a peculiar way. They knew what they were against, and what they wanted, but they were not sure how to achieve it. Politicians were similarly adrift. Theories burnished over decades by thinkers across the political spectrum about government spending, taxes, regulation, and trade policy prescribed responses that struck voters as impotent, irrelevant, or too divisive.

"When inequality becomes too large to ignore, everyone starts acting strange. It divides us, makes us believe weird things and erodes our trust in one another."

—Keith Payne,
author of *The Broken Ladder: How Inequality Affects the Way We Think, Live and Die*

Economic growth is measured by the growth in gross domestic product (GDP), but it comes from increases in population and/or improvements in productivity. Few countries see a larger population as their engine for economic growth. And it is hard to increase productivity when work can be so easily moved elsewhere or, increasingly, to machines. It seems like a game of musical chairs—a winner-take-all contest—rather than a game that increases opportunity for all players.

This helps explain why an undertow of tribalism colors so much talk about economic growth and income inequality. It also suggests that protectionist trade policies may gain popular support, unless and until they result in too much political pain, due to the cost to consumers or the cost to producers who are affected by retaliatory actions from countries affected by the trade barriers.

> "Suffering has its limit,
> but fears are endless."
>
> —Pliny the Younger

Eventually, I expect the debate about protectionist policies to focus on one of the three moons—economic theory—as there isn't much that can be done to affect the other two—technology and the supply of labor. It will be a remarkable debate—in part because economies are interconnected more than ever, which makes it difficult to implement trade barriers, and in part because it will confront the grand premise of the dogmas of deregulation, free trade, and shareholder wealth maximization.

A premise of deregulation and free trade is that economies work best when government gets out of the way of its participants. Managed trade undercuts that notion because it relies on government intervention. The idea that shareholder wealth maximization should be a company's goal will be similarly challenged because protectionism calls on companies to favor domestic production, even when it isn't the lowest cost option.

So, it's okay that the Fairshare Model approaches the challenges of economic growth and income inequality from a tribal perspective. Small-bore solutions fit our times. If it works well for the tribes that adopt it, that community will expand. As adoption of the Fairshare Model widens, its benefits will percolate up into the broader economy.

A Political Scientist Reflects on Regulation, Politics, and Income Inequality

On The Media is a WNYC radio program carried on NPR. The September 14, 2018 episode, "Doomed to Repeat," focuses on the ten-year anniversary of the 2008 financial crisis and it considers how financial regulatory policy, politics, and income inequality entwine. One of the people interviewed is Mark Blyth, a well-humored professor of international political economy at Brown University and author of the 2013 book, *Austerity: The History of a Dangerous Idea.* Here's how Blyth summarizes his book's thesis.

> Politicians today in both Europe and the US have succeeded in casting government spending as reckless wastefulness that has made the economy worse. In contrast, they have advanced a policy of draconian budget cuts—austerity—to solve the financial crisis. We are told that we have all lived beyond our means and now need to tighten our belts.

> This view conveniently forgets where all that debt came from. Not from an orgy of government spending, but as the direct result of bailing out, recapitalizing, and adding liquidity to the broken banking system. Through these actions private debt was rechristened as government debt while those responsible for generating it walked away scot free, placing the blame on the state, and the burden on the taxpayer.

> That burden now takes the form of a global turn to austerity, the policy of reducing domestic wages and prices to restore competitiveness and balance the budget. The problem is [Mark Blyth argues] here is that austerity is a very dangerous idea.

First of all, it doesn't work. As the past four years and countless historical examples from the last 100 years show, while it makes sense for any one state to try and cut its way to growth, it simply cannot work when all states try it simultaneously: all we do is shrink the economy. In the worst case, austerity policies worsened the Great Depression and created the conditions for seizures of power by the forces responsible for the Second World War: the Nazis and the Japanese military establishment.

The arguments for austerity are tenuous and the evidence thin. Rather than expanding growth and opportunity, the repeated revival of this dead economic idea has almost always led to low growth along with increases in wealth and income inequality. Written for all of us with an interest in how we've come to our current disastrous economic situation, this book demands that we recognize austerity for what it is, and what it costs us. T

My transcription of the exchange between Professor Blyth and *On The Media* host, Brooke Gladstone follows.U [Bold for added emphasis.]

Brooke Gladstone, *On The Media:* So my first question involves a kind of lightening round of putative causes (for the financial crisis) that are popular with different groups for different reasons. [A *Jeopardy*-like quiz show music theme is evoked.] Are you ready?

Mark Blyth: Let's go! Let's play the game!

Gladstone: The first named cause, "The crisis was caused by handing out subprime mortgages to unreliable would-be householders. People who could not afford to pay back the loans."

Blyth: Subprime mortgages were the trigger that lit the dynamite that was those complex (financial) derivatives. But at the end of the day, what matters is how the explosion traveled through the system and why it blew up elsewhere in places where you didn't have subprime mortgages. And that was to do with the size of the banks, and the way that many of themselves were structured, with very little capital and a huge amount of liabilities that were paradoxically called assets.

Gladstone: Number two. It was caused by "complex instruments."

Blyth: So this narrative is popular with academics who like to show they are very clever about understanding what these credit instruments are. Don't get me wrong, asset-based financial paper is an important part of the plumbing for what happened. This is [what] everything flowed through. But you can tell the story without getting involved in the plumbing.

Gladstone: That is was about "excessive leverage."

Blyth: Leverage is simple. When you have an income of $100,000 and you get a mortgage of $300,000, you have leverage of 3 to 1. You want to know how bad it was in the financial crisis? There were four banks in Iceland that lent enough to the rest of the world to be 1,000 percent of the GDP of Iceland.

Gladstone: Wow!

Blyth: Yeah, financial leverage as a narrative is popular with bank regulators because what they want to do is have the banks have less leverage. And that would have been good, but that would mean banks earn less money.

Gladstone: Some say "It was about inequality and credit." [Clip from a newscast is played saying "Since the top 1 percent now command more than one third of the wealth, how's the bottom 99 percent supposed to keep up with the Jones, if not the Kardashians? By borrowing!"]

Blyth: And there is something to this! When you have wage stagnation for the majority of Americans for most of, if not in some cases more than, a generation. How do you fill in the gap? People rolled up on credit, on the expectation that they would pay it off with higher wages. But they didn't have the higher wages, they just had a ton of debt. So when they become unemployed, they become insolvent, like the banks, and they drag each other down.

Gladstone: Who is in favor of this narrative?

Blyth: I would say everyone from Bernie Sanders on to the (political) Center. The concern with inequality has become one of the touchstone issues of our generation. Given the fact that is has actually been raising to historic levels. The financial crisis exacerbated that rather than reset it.

Gladstone: How about "The crisis was caused by Alan Greenspan, head of the Federal Reserve from 1987 to 2006, holding interest rates down for too long?" [Greenspan clip– "It was our job to unfreeze the American banking system if we wanted the economy to function. This required that we keep interest rates modestly low."]

Blyth: Essentially, he gave asset protection to everyone in the world. The economy hits a bump, that means you are going to earn less money. [Imitating Greenspan] "Don't worry! I'll make your borrowing cheaper, so you don't actually lose any money!"

Gladstone: With whom is this narrative popular with?

Blyth: The Greenspan narrative is popular with people who write books about Greenspan, obviously. It's also popular with the journalistic community because the thing about journalism is that you want to attach it to personality. So, if you can point to someone who looks like Yoda (from Star Wars) and sounds like Yoda, and say he screwed up, that's kind of popular!

Gladstone: Last in our lightning round, "The banking crisis was caused by greed!"

Blyth: You can't explain a variable with a constant. [Gladstone laughs.] You know, just imagine that in 2005, we were all Mother Teresas, then we all got greedy and caused the crisis. It doesn't sound too convincing, does it?

Gladstone: So I imagine it's possible that, taken all together, maybe they create the right narrative?

Blyth: Exactly! We're always looking for *The Cause*. But when you have the generator being the entire global economy, why would you think one cause is what matters?

Gladstone: A particular narrative about a cause that irks you more than any other is the one that says we spent too much money and now we have to pay.

Blyth: Federal debt was down from 2000 to 2006. And it was the same in Europe. So there was no orgy of spending. What happened is that these giant banks are massively over-levered and about to blow up the whole world. So you have to save them. That was the "too big to fail" argument. And so to do that you give more money to recapitalize the banks, you run big government deficits, you hold your breath for six months, suddenly, there is a lot more debt. So there was no additional spending on schools, doctors and hospitals and anything fluffy—it all went to soothing the financial sector. They didn't want that to stick as the narrative, so they were quite happy to have it be an enormous bait and switch where particularly politicians on the Right use it as an excuse to kill programs they never liked in the first place.

Gladstone: I'm wondering about the tagline, "too big to fail." That is, if the government didn't do something, some terrible things would happen, and they would happen to ordinary Americans.

Blyth: It's a very convenient story and it may also be a true story. That's the most frustrating part about it. We built this system whereby that if any of the big banks went down, it would take down the whole system. Now, we managed to save that, and it *only* cost us $17 trillion in central bank bailouts, and liquidity and all this sort of stuff. Being too big to fail, it could have been worse, absolutely. But at the same time, what we're saying is that if you are a giant institution, you can take unbelievable risks, and the taxpayer will come and bail you out. This is what annoyed the Tea Party, and they were absolutely right in this. The Tea Party is the canary in the coal mine when we think about the populism of the moment—when we think about Trump now, and Europe.

Gladstone: What's Europe have to do with any of this? One of the sustaining narratives is that this is fundamentally an American problem, a problem with American banks.

Blyth: Oh, well that's what we thought at first. The German finance minister said: "This is a problem of Anglo-Saxon capitalism." Then about six months later he found out that German banks, and French banks, and Belgian banks, and British banks had bought 70 percent of the crappy mortgages. And suddenly it was on European bank balance sheets. And it turns out that European banks are twice as leveraged as the Americans at this point.

Gladstone: There is a piece in *The New York Times* this week, as part of their Lehman Brothers collapse anniversary coverage, "The Policymakers Saved the Financial System. And America Never Forgave Them." I gather you would expand that to Europe as well? As evidenced by the turn towards the (political) Right?

Blyth: Absolutely. And a very simple way to think about this is the following. British wages have been as stagnant for most Brits as American wages, prior to the crisis. So companies have been making a profit. GDP and other measures of the economy have been going up. Then there is a giant crisis. Millions are made unemployed. People's incomes fall. The real terms, the value of their assets fall with them. It's taken them in Britain, and in most of Europe, a whole decade to get back to where they started in terms of their incomes. So, (policymakers are) saying, "We saved the system!" Yeah, but it cost me (the average person) a decade of income and a hell of a lot of stress. Well, of course, there is going to be a political reaction to that.

Gladstone: Why did (politics) turn to the Right instead of towards the Left?

Blyth: But it didn't! If you look at southern Europe, all the countries that are debtor countries–the Spanish, the Italians, the Greeks, the Portuguese–they've all got Left-wing governments.

Gladstone: Well, the Italians?

Blyth: It's a coalition because they have Five Star (a nationalist party) in the south and they have the Right in the north. Portugal, Greece, and Spain all have Left-leaning coalition governments. When you go to the [northern EU countries], it's all the Right ones. And the Right ones in the creditor countries have been fed a diet of, "We are the hard-working people and *they* (in the south) are the ones that spend all the money!" And then when you have a migrant crisis that comes and exposes many people in those (creditor) countries to the idea that there's no money for them for hospitals or schools or training or whatever. They had a whole decade of austerity. And guess what? A bunch of foreign people show up, and there is need for language training, schools, et cetera. This is the type of dynamite that Right-wing populists thrive on!

Gladstone: If you take a step back from 2008, as you've described in your book, it seems to be a **thirty-year history of workers being squeezed by low wages which leads to ballooning debt.**

Blyth: It's all about inflation because we had super tight labor markets, and big unions, and the ability to push prices up. **So we spend thirty years deregulating our markets, making labor markets flexible, beating down on unions, globalizing our markets. And what you end up with is that labor has no ability to affect price. And indeed, most companies have no ability to affect price,** if you take out Amazon and these big giants. **So what does that mean? It means that profits then do not get split evenly between capital and labor–it goes all to capital! And that's the inequality issue.** So, we've made it to a point whereby that issue has become so gross, that even bailing it out with lots of credit has reached it limit. Think student loans. What are you going to do? Another trillion dollars in student loan (relief)? So we reached the limit of credit to finance growth–we didn't change the system. We built the banks back up again and said, "please do it again!"

Gladstone: Just this week there is news from the Census Bureau that household income in the US had finally reached its 2007 pre-recession level of $61,372. The growth in the last few years is not from increased pay, it's from increased employment. What does that tell you?

Blyth: It tells me we still have the Bill Gates problem: Bill Gates walks into a bar then–*on average*–everyone in it is a millionaire.

Gladstone: Right. And in 2015, Wall Street bonuses were $32 billion.

Blyth: And everyone on minimum wage in the whole country, added together, got precisely half of that.

Gladstone: So if nothing has changed, and we still have American workers crushed by low wages, are we setting ourselves up for more personal debt, more borrowing from banks, and the same amount of 'no regulation of their bigness?' Are we doomed to repeat this?

Blyth: (Your view will) depend on where you are in the income distribution. If you are in the top 20 percent, you are not being touched. If you are in the top 10 percent, you are getting a massage! If you are above that—well, I can't even think of a metaphor! [Laughter] But when the next generation—the millennials—can't afford assets—they are not buying houses, they're not buying cars—because they are too busy paying back (student loan) debt—debt earlier generations didn't have to accrue because things were "free," then you've got a problem.

Gladstone: Mark, thank you very much. Mark Blyth is a professor at Brown University and author of *Austerity: The History of a Dangerous Idea.*

Summation

The Fairshare Model is designed to encourage public investors to invest in venture-stage companies. As it grows in popularity, it can help ameliorate income inequality by:

a. improving access to capital for job-creating startups,

b. improving the potential for capital gains for average investors, and

c. bolstering the ability of employees to participate in the return on capital.

What's Next?

The next chapter considers how the Fairshare Model promotes a new vector of economic competition: the ability to cooperate and collaborate.

Chapter Endnotes

Contextual references for material in this chapter appear as numbered footnotes on the page where the reference is made. **Source references** for material in this chapter appear below as endnotes with capital letter identifiers.

A Cassidy, John. "Forces of Divergence." *The New Yorker.* March 31, 2014. Accessed May 08, 2018. fairsharemodel.com/Divergence.

B "How Piketty's Inequality Theory Explains Mr. Darcy's Wealth." PBS *NewsHour.* May 13, 2014. Accessed May 08, 2018. fairsharemodel.com/Darcy. The image used to explain Thomas Piketty's finding.

C Strachan, Maxwell. "Thomas Piketty: Bill Gates Told Me He Doesn't Want To Pay More in Taxes." *Huffington Post.* January 04, 2015. Accessed May 08, 2018. fairsharemodel.com/GatesTaxes.

D Gates, Bill. "Why Inequality Matters." *Gatesnotes: The Blog of Bill Gates.* October 13, 2014. Accessed May 08, 2018. fairsharemodel.com/GatesInequality.

E Noah, Timothy. "An Honest Conservative Take on Income Inequality." *The New Republic.* November 13, 2011. Accessed May 08, 2018. fairsharemodel.com/Conservatives-on-inequality.

F St. Fleur, Nicolas. "Where in the World Is Climate Change Denial Most Prevalent?" *The New York Times.* December 12, 2015. Accessed July 29, 2018. fairsharemodel.com/Climate.

G Continetti, Matthew. "About Inequality." *The Weekly Standard.* November 14, 2011. Accessed May 08, 2018. fairsharemodel.com/WeeklyStd.

[H] Ferguson, Niall. "A Conservative Take on America's Great Economic Divide." *Newsweek.* January 16, 2012. Accessed May 08, 2018. fairsharemodel.com/ConservativeView.

[I] Brooks, David. "The Great Divorce." *The New York Times.* January 30, 2012. Accessed May 08, 2018. fairsharemodel.com/GreatDivorce.

[J] Brooks, David. "The Inequality Problem." *The New York Times.* January 16, 2014. Accessed May 08, 2018. fairsharemodel.com/InequalityProblem.

[K] Kurtz, Howard. "The GOP's 2016 Playbook? Republicans Rip Income Inequality." *Fox News.* January 22, 2015. Accessed May 08, 2018. fairsharemodel.com/GOP2016Playbook.

[L] A terrific examination of how the 20th century progressed to globalization is provided by Daniel Yergin and Joseph Stansilaw in their 2002 book, *The Commanding Heights: The Battle for the World Economy*, a PBS program based on the book, can be streamed here fairsharemodel.com/CommandingHeights.

[M] Reich, Robert B. "Jobs Will Follow a Strengthening of the Middle Class." *The New York Times.* September 3, 2011. Accessed May 13, 2018. fairsharemodel.com/MiddleClassChart. Charts at fairsharemodel.com/MiddleClass.

[N] Schwartz, Nelson D. "The Recovery Threw the Middle-Class Dream Under a Benz." *The New York Times.* September 12, 2018. Accessed September 12, 2018. fairsharemodel.com/Benz.

[O] "Animal Spirits: How Human Psychology Drives the Economy, and Why It Matters for Global Capitalism." *Get Abstract.* Accessed May 08, 2018. fairsharemodel.com/AnimalSpirits.

[P] Mass Flourishing, pages 289.

[Q] Ibid, pages 289.

[R] Ibid, pages 290.

[S] Ibid, page 293.

[T] Blyth, Mark. *Austerity: The History of a Dangerous Idea.* MarkBlyth.com. Accessed September 16, 2018. fairsharemodel.com/Austerity.

[U] Gladstone, Brooke. "Doomed to Repeat." WYNC Studios *On the Media.* September 14, 2018. Accessed September 16, 2018. fairsharemodel.com/Doomed.

Chapter 12:

Cooperation as the New Tool for Competition

What's Included in This Chapter

Introduction

This chapter considers the potential to improve economic growth and lessen income inequality by harnessing the potential of investors and employees to cooperate.

Set-Up

John Donne was an English poet, satirist, lawyer, and priest who died in 1631. He wrote this piece, which has always touched me:

> No man is an island, entire of itself; every man is a piece of the continent, a part of the main. If a clod be washed away by the sea, Europe is the less, as well as if a promontory

were, as well as if a manor of thy friend's or of thine own were: any man's death diminishes me, because I am involved in mankind, and therefore never send to know for whom the bell tolls; it tolls for thee.

Those who benefit from the return on capital have a stake in addressing the social anxiety that the diminishing return on labor is unleashing. Few would challenge that, yet there is little agreement on what to do about it. No matter what policies are adopted, technology will make it easier to relocate work, and the supply of low-cost labor will grow, which will continue to pressure the return on labor. Protectionist trade policies—import tariffs and quotas—are an intuitive reaction but they are not a long-term solution for developed economies; higher productivity is.

Can a high labor cost economy be more productive than a low labor cost one? Yes, it can happen due to leadership, workers, quality, and technology, as well as the physical and legal infrastructure, including intellectual property protections. Agility can be important too, which can involve suppliers.

The Fairshare Model adds a dimension—the ability of investors and employees to cooperate. Some view this as a weakness, but I see it as a strength. It can create advantage when it comes to attracting and motivating employees. As you progress through this chapter, note that it builds on ideas presented earlier and weaves in benefits that can result from investors and employees cooperating. Those benefits include

1. better matching of capital with entrepreneurial opportunity, which promotes economic growth and job creation (Chapter 10, "The Macroeconomic Context – Growth"),

2. strengthening of an economy's indigenous ability to innovate (Chapter 10),

3. expansion of the ranks of those who participate in the return on capital (Chapter 11, "The Macroeconomic Context – Income Inequality"),

4. more people have an opportunity to pursue the good life (Chapter 10), and

5. IPO distributions that are less gamed to favor wealthy and connected investors (Chapter 5, "The Problem with a Conventional Capital Structure") and more in line with John Rawls' *Theory of Economic Justice* (Chapter 11).

The Fairshare Model is a Big Idea, but it is not a Big Solution to the macroeconomic problems of capitalism. Rather, it is a market-driven microeconomic idea to promote the interests of public investors in the IPOs of venture-stage companies. They are the most important constituency for the Fairshare Model because they provide capital to the issuer.

Cooperation vs. Collaboration

Cooperation and collaboration have different meanings, but I use them synonymously. Please forgive me but the distinction is not obvious, and I don't want to bog down the discussion.

What's the distinction? When they cooperate, people perform together. They *co-operate*, work selfishly to achieve goals they have in common.

When they *collaborate*, people work together too. They co-labor—they work jointly to achieve shared goals.

In the Fairshare Model, the Investor and Performance Stock classes cooperate to establish conversion criteria and the employees collaborate to meet as many as they can.

Of secondary importance are the interests of entrepreneurs and their pre-IPO investors. Of tertiary importance are the interests of secondary market investors, as they buy stock from other shareholders, not the issuer.

Collectively, investors in Fairshare Model IPOs will not be a lot of people—thousands per year in the early adopter phase. Hundreds more than that will be required for it to enter the mainstream. Ideas lead to change, but it takes time.

The Fairshare Model is not a utopian notion—it is a practical way to promote innovation and growth in the economy. It can help capitalism work better for those who invest in and work for issuers that use it. It can benefit communities where these companies do business by expanding the vectors of competition to include alignment of capital and labor. In this unexplored country the emphasis is on productivity, not labor costs.

The Fairshare Model plays to the strengths of developed economies, which can include trusted capital markets, legal, and accounting standards, intolerance of corruption, skilled workers, infrastructure, open societies, acceptance of immigrants, optimism, and tolerance for risk.

Big Solutions to Big Problems Are Hard to Find

Philosophers have long puzzled: "What systems most benefit society?" The question lurks as gripes about how capitalism operates increase. The discussions focus on how things end up, whether it's due to slow growth, wealth concentration, wage levels, inflation, healthcare, environmental issues, or other concerns. These are Big Problems.

For some, the solution to a Big Problem is a Big Solution. But the problem with a Big Solution is that it can be Too Big to gain enough support to be approved. Those that are invariably encounter implementation issues because, well, Big Problems involve complex, dynamic issues. Also, the political debate that frames problems and solutions is influenced by special interests. Thus, government often has two responses to problems—it either ignores them or overreacts.

All indications are that it will be difficult to find broad support for Big Solutions to the Big Problems of weak economic growth and rising income inequality.

Of course, objections to Big Solutions can melt in the face of a common threat because it promotes common cause. In America, the Wall Street Crash of 1929 led to a body of securities laws. The Patriot Act ushered in transformative changes in banking and travel after the 9/11 terrorist attacks. The Sarbanes-Oxley Act strengthened financial reporting controls after a series of scandals at large firms. The Dodd-Frank Wall Street Reform and Consumer Protection Act and the Affordable Care Act are other examples.

Concerns about how the benefits of capitalism are distributed are mounting but they haven't risen to the level of a broadly perceived threat, so there are no broadly supported responses.

Common values can foster common cause, but not always effective action. Some societies that share values—some northern European countries and Canada come to mind—seem less likely to need Big Solutions because they try to address issues before they become Big Problems. Others seem crippled by shared values. The desire to avoid disharmony helps explain why Spain, Greece, and Japan struggle to respond effectively to economic problems.

For a variety of reasons, it's increasingly difficult for communities that share common values to find common cause and that's ironic, given that any of us can reach more people, more rapidly, with more information than ever before. *Don Quixote*, Miguel de Cervantes's fictional character, undertook a quest to change the world. He sought to right all wrongs while practicing respect and promoting civility toward others. Quixote would surely despair at the current state of social dialogue. It was captured by an observer who suggested that the most frequent sentence used over the internet is "You're an idiot!" with the second being "It's a hoax!"[A] It is symptomatic of alienation, marginalization, social disengagement, and pessimism about the future.

Sociologist Robert Putnam examines this phenomenon in his 2001 book, *Bowling Alone: The Collapse and Revival of American Community*. He notes that civil society is breaking down as Americans become more disconnected from their families, neighbors, communities, and the republic itself. Organizations that gave life to democracy are fraying.

Putnam adopts bowling as a metaphor, observing that thousands of people once belonged to bowling leagues but nowadays, they're more likely to bowl alone. He writes:[B]

> Television, two-career families, suburban sprawl, generational changes in values—these and other changes in American society have meant that fewer and fewer of us find that the League of Women Voters, or the United Way, or the Shriners, or the monthly bridge club, or even a Sunday picnic with friends fits the way we have come to live.

> Our growing social-capital deficit threatens educational performance, safe neighborhoods, equitable tax collection, democratic responsiveness, everyday honesty, and even our health and happiness.

The potential for solutions inspired by a common threat is unclear too. In his 2017 book, *The Great Leveler,* historian Walter Scheidel says that economic inequality developed after the rise of agrarian societies for they allowed wealth to be amassed, and passed on, and used to acquire political influence. It led to concentrations of wealth and power that continued until a violent shock upended the established order and leveled out the inequality. He describes four forms of levelers.

Levelers of Inequality	How the Levelers Reduce Inequality
Collapse of states (Grecian, Roman, Mayan and Tang China empires)	Everyone suffers when law and order unravel but the rich have more to lose.
Massive disease epidemics (medieval Europe plagues)	Fewer workers results in a rise in real wages and the value of capital assets fall.
Mass mobilization warfare (WW I and WW II)	Value of assets fall; trade is disrupted; high taxes on the wealthy to fund war and recovery; government intervention in the economy; full employment due to conscription and high demand for labor; and an increase in social and labor solidarity.
Transformative revolution (Bolshevik Russia, Maoist China, Cuba, Vietnam, Cambodia)	Assets are nationalized, private wealth reduced. Price and wages are controlled by the state.

Scheidel sees little prospect that any of these levelers will occur soon and wonders whether other mechanisms might reduce inequality. On that count, he says: "The past should teach us not to promise too much, to be realistic; that it might be much harder to effect real change than we think. It doesn't mean we should throw up our hands and surrender. It simply means we need to think hard and not just fall back on recipes that seem to have worked in the past, because they may no longer be feasible. And we don't want to stifle economic growth."[C]

Scheidel continues: "Many would say it's unfair, but it does seem inequity goes hand-in-hand with growth. And it may well be necessary for growth. If everybody's income were exactly the same, there wouldn't be much incentive for people to innovate, or even work hard. That's one of the problems that communist regimes have faced. The question is: how much inequality is needed? You have capitalist economies in Scandinavia with very low levels of inequality that work just fine. The real question is what level of inequality is pernicious. At what point does it become a real problem in terms of both discouraging economic growth due to widespread alienation and social and political stability?"[D]

Neither common cause nor common threat seems likely to lead to a Big Solution to the problems of economic growth and income inequality. There is no commonly perceived threat and it is difficult to find common cause based on philosophy, values, or beliefs in what capitalism should deliver, even though it is generally viewed to be the best system, or at least the one most likely to endure.

The question, "What is the best system?" has lingered for a long time. Around 380 B.C., in a dialogue known as *The Republic*, the Greek philosopher Plato presented a utopian idea, one where citizens who completed fifty years of rigorous training would be "philosopher-kings" with the wisdom to fairly distribute resources so there was no poverty. *Wikipedia* reports that The Republic "has few laws, no lawyers and rarely sends its citizens to war, but hires mercenaries from among its war-prone neighbors (these mercenaries were deliberately sent into dangerous situations in the hope that the more warlike populations of all surrounding countries will be weeded out, leaving peaceful peoples)."[E]

Wikipedia also notes that the word "utopia" was coined nearly two thousand years later by Sir Thomas More for his 1516 book, *Utopia*, which described a fictional island society in the Atlantic Ocean. Then it adds:

> The word comes from the Greek: οὐ ('not') and τόπος ('place') and means 'no-place.' The English homophone *eutopia*, derived from the Greek εὖ ('good' or 'well') and τόπος ('place'), means "good place."

Homophones are words that sound the same but are spelled differently and have different meanings (e.g., assistance and assistants; sear and seer; fair and fare). Knowing that, you may be amused that *Wikipedia* points out, deliciously, that "because of the identical English pronunciation of 'utopia' and 'eutopia,' it gives rise to a double meaning." That is, it sounds like both "no place" and a "good place."

Utopia may be a mythical place, but the desire to find it can have great consequence. In the 20th century, the most spectacular example was the monumental contest over whether the world economies would be controlled by an idealized state or by imperfect markets. It was a battle over whether communism or capitalism would most benefit mankind. It began intellectually, with competing ideas about what was the "best system" for society, then manifested into physical and economic combat.

That struggle was the subject of the 1998 book, *The Commanding Heights: The Battle for the World Economy* by Daniel Yergin and Joseph Stanislaw. It was made into a 2002 PBS series by the same name that I highly recommend to anyone with interest in the role that economics has played in modern world history. Here is how the first episode opens: **F**

> **Program Narrator:** This is the story of how the new global economy was born, a century-long battle as to which would control the commanding heights of the world's economies—governments or markets; the story of intellectual combat over which economic system would truly benefit mankind; the story of epic political struggles to implant those ideas on the nations of the world.

> **Jeffrey Sachs, Professor, Harvard University:** Part of what happened is a capitalist revolution at the end of the 20th century. The market economy, the capitalist system, became the only model for the vast majority of the world.

> **Narrator:** This economic revolution has defined the wealth and fate of nations and will determine the future of the planet.

> **Daniel Yergin, Author, *Commanding Heights:*** This new world economy is being driven by technological change and by political change, but none of it would have happened without a revolution in ideas.

Ultimately, communism failed everywhere. No country could make it work remotely close to its ideal, let alone as a sustainable system. This is evidence that capitalism is a better system, but it doesn't mean it can't be improved. *Good Capitalism, Bad Capitalism,* a book mentioned in Chapter 10, points out that there is variation in how it is practiced; the dynamics in the US differ from what they are in Canada, Germany, Great Britain, Sweden, Japan, Australia, and South Korea, for instance.

What will define the epic struggle of our 21st century? Imagine what answers might have been offered about the 20th century before WWI. Few would have guessed that it turned out to be what it was because there was no compelling, competing ideology to capitalism.

It seems that this century will be defined by competition for resources and spheres of influence, stoked by conflict regarding values, beliefs, and attitudes—traditional versus modern. The damage that modern society wreaks on the planet seems certain to be the epic struggle, however, and it may involve nuclear devastation, be it by accident, war, or terrorism.

But these conflicts are not about economics. If the question focuses on that, the answer may be that the defining challenge of the 21st century will be "How can the benefits of capitalism best be shared?"

The Fairshare Model provides fresh perspective on how to answer that because it offers a revolutionary idea about ownership interests in corporations.

Cooperation as a Model for Competition

I posit that the ability to cooperate will emerge as an important form of competition in the 21st century. By that, I mean cooperation within and between networks—not at the broad-based societal level because that relies on an overly optimistic view of human nature.

Micro-networks exist within an enterprise, its supply chain and its customer base. Within an enterprise, they exist between shareholder classes, within a shareholder class, between directors and management, and among management, other employees, and even non-employees. These micro-networks layer upon each other and interact like themes in a musical fugue. They are partnerships with shifting and overlapping interests that center on how well the company is doing.

Micro-networks that interact in positive, self-renewing ways seem to be associated with successful companies. Those that generate negative, discordant energy are likely to be found in companies that are prone to dysfunction and eventual failure.

How might the benefits of capitalism best be shared? To be broadly supported, an answer must be practical, and it must appeal to people with diverse philosophical views. Since micro-networks are narrow, self-selecting associations, it is easier to define an approach that can be tailored to various ends than one for an entire society.

In other words, rather than a Big Solution, I propose a mosaic of Small Solutions to the Big Problem facing contemporary capitalism, writ large.

Micro-solutions suit our times. Common ties are weaker, and worldviews are increasingly fractured; there is more talk about succession than about coming together. Smaller definitions of common interest are acquiring traction while the one John Donne advanced is at risk of losing popular support. Many will bemoan that assessment, but I suspect that few will disagree with it.

To be sure, there are good-hearted souls who wish to change that. While they work on it, I'll recognize the course we're on and argue that the ability to cooperate could be a competitive tool for those who invest in, or work for, companies that adopt the Fairshare Model.

The Size of the Prize (or the Economic Pie)

If cooperation is to be a mean of competition, what is the competition for? What is the size of the prize, the economic pie?

It has two components.

1. economic growth that results from increasing productivity, and
2. expanding the ability of working-class people to participate in the increase in valuation that occurs in venture-stage companies.

The first one is straightforward. As discussed earlier, new companies are the engine of economic growth and job creation. In his 2013 book, *Rebooting Work*, Maynard Webb makes this interesting observation:

> The speed at which companies come and go, succeed and fail, is different from even a short while ago.
>
> The half-life of a company is diminishing incredibly quickly. One-third of the companies listed in the 1970 Fortune 500 were gone by 1983. (They were acquired, merged, or split apart.) The average life expectancy of a company in the S&P 500 has dropped from seventy-five years (in 1937) to fifteen years today.[G]

Despite the shortened life-expectancy of companies, the US economy has grown, fueled by new companies that offer ways to be more productive. Improving their ability to raise equity capital can make a positive contribution to economic growth.

The size of the second component is immense yet hard to quantify—but its significance is apparent when you think about it. It's the wealth earned by betting on the valuation of venture-stage companies and it has two elements:

1. the increase in valuation that takes place when a company is privately held, between its formation and when it is acquired or goes public, and

2. the increase in valuation that occurs in the secondary trading market.

The collective amount of wealth generated in recent decades by these two segments has gone to a small portion of society. The Fairshare Model can enlarge the pool of beneficiaries because it provides a better deal structure for unaccredited investors, and that can lead to better returns than such investors can get otherwise.

Also, when Performance Stock converts to Investor Stock, a portion of the wealth created by an increase in the company's valuation goes to employees. At present, it goes to investors who bought shares from the company or from other investors in the secondary market. The latter group, secondary market investors, don't provide the company with capital, they trade based on information. When a company uses the Fairshare Model, more of this wealth goes to the people whose work leads to the increase in valuation.

That is, more goes to those who create value through their contribution of capital or labor to a business, less to those who reap profits based on trading the stock.

More to makers, less to traders. That is a good thing.

The Power of Cooperation as a Model for Competition

Toyota Motor Company demonstrated that the ability to cooperate could create a competitive advantage. The so-called lean manufacturing concept it pioneered is associated with collaboration with employees and suppliers and it led to concepts like zero defects and just-in-time inventory management. In such a system, micro-networks cooperate and collaborate.

In contrast, the scientific management philosophy once favored by US companies relied on a command-and-control style that emphasized time-study efficiency and fostered workplace alienation.

In his 2008 book, *The Toyota Way to Healthcare Excellence: Increase Efficiency and Improve Quality with Lean*, John Black writes:[H]

> Sakichi Toyoda, who founded the Toyota Group, was the inventor of a loom that would stop automatically if any of the threads snapped. His invention reduced defects and raised yields, since a loom would not continue producing imperfect fabric and using up thread after a problem occurred. The new loom also enabled a single operator to handle dozens of looms, revolutionizing the textile industry.

> The principle of designing equipment to stop automatically and call attention to problems immediately is crucial to the Toyota Production System (the foundation of Lean Manufacturing). This is the system of 'jidoka,' the intelligent use of both people and technology, with the ability (even the obligation) to stop any process at the first sign of an abnormality.

> When the Toyota Group set up an automobile manufacturing operation in the 1930s (replacing the Toyoda family's 'd' with a 't'), Sakichi's son, Kiichiro headed the new venture.

He traveled to the US to study Henry Ford's system in operation. He returned with a strong grasp of Ford's conveyor system, and an even stronger desire to adapt that system to the small volumes of the Japanese market.

Soon thereafter, the first Toyota system of manufacturing was born. To say that Toyota copied Ford is not accurate–Toyota learned from Ford, especially from Ford's mistakes. This demonstrated the power of the Toyota system: continuous improvement. It was in some ways a revolution, just as Ford's had been–but the differences were often striking.

The scientific management approach has lost favor since the 1980s. Increasingly, many organizations have adopted so-called "lean" principles, including those outside of the manufacturing sector. As Black's book title indicates, that includes healthcare, which may surprise many; it affects design of operating rooms, nurse stations, management of supplies, accounting practices, etc.

The table below highlights how the old-school scientific management approach and new school lean approach differ in addressing the Big Problem of how to build quality products and control costs.

	Old-School *Scientific Management*	New-School *Lean*
Relies on	Command and control	Cooperation and communication
Viewpoint	*Discrete* or separate view of quality and cost—manage them to target levels	*Integrated* view of quality and cost that relies on constant improvement
Approach to Product Quality	• Set acceptable defect rate • Find and fix defects • Fix the underlying problem if the savings will generate an acceptable return on the cost to do so	• Zero defect standard • Internal process improvement • Careful worker and vendor selection process • Extensive worker and vendor training
Approach to Product Cost	• Win price concessions from vendors and employees or replace them with lower cost equivalents • Find more efficient vendors and/or employees	• Empower workers and vendors to improve process controls and reduce costs • Incentives to improve quality and reduce cost

In a scientific management mindset, the Big Problem is the defect, not the process that creates it. The solution is to inspect for quality and repair defects. Process improvements require justification via cost/benefit analysis (i.e., there must be payoff for the investment). Workers are replaceable cogs;

they are to keep production going, not change process. If they don't keep up, they are fired. Companies flex their buying power to force suppliers to lower their price—there is no collaboration on how to do it.

In a lean system mindset, the Big Problem is a process that creates defects; a defect is a symptom of a Big Problem. Workers are empowered to stop a process if they see a defect. What follows is a search for the cause and a way to prevent it from recurring. Suppliers are trusted partners who are transparent about their process—they collaborate with their customer on ways to improve processes so that costs decrease and/or quality improves.

These two approaches differ in the importance of cooperation—the relationships they promote between an employer and its employees, and between a company and its suppliers. Scientific management discounts the humanity of relationships; the lean approach leverages it.

My admiration for what Toyota accomplished is enhanced by my background. I grew up in the Detroit area, exposed to labor strife. My first job after college was at Ford Motor in 1977, when the scientific management approach was dominant. I performed cost/benefit analysis on changes to vehicle transmission design and manufacturing. A few years later, in 1984, my then-spouse, Diane, helped bring up the accounting department at New United Motor Manufacturing, Inc. (NUMMI) in Fremont, California, a joint venture between Toyota and General Motors that explored the portability of the Toyota system to the US.[1]

After a stint in purchasing, where Diane worked with NUMMI suppliers, she left to work for the United Auto Workers union. So, I had the opportunity to observe and hear about this unique enterprise from different perspectives. One takeaway was appreciation for the many constituencies that a business has—shareholders, lenders, employees, customers, suppliers, and the community— and how well NUMMI balanced them. Another was recognition that those who advocate on behalf of a single interest, like unions and special interest groups, have a less complex job than businesses do because they have fewer constituencies to satisfy.

Another experience informs my perspective on the power of cooperation. In the 1980s, I worked for a Silicon Valley telecom manufacturer called Granger Associates, Inc. Just before I was hired, it had been acquired by a company with a centralized command and control style.

Like all companies, Granger Associates used a financial planning process, but its version differed from what most used. It was established by a seasoned turnaround executive named Quentin Thomas Wiles (everyone referred to him as "Q.T."), who was also chairman of a San Francisco investment firm, Hambrecht & Quist. His long and impressive record of revitalizing companies in turnaround situations led him to be known as "Dr. Fix-It." In an article called "The Green Berets of Corporate Management," he was quoted as saying, "I think I can fix anything."

Q.T. left Granger when the transaction took place, so I never met him, but virtually every executive I initially worked with had worked for him. Through them and other study, I came to understand his philosophy and methods for performance definition, measurement, and reward. Also, I learned that he applied the same structure in other companies, and that many managers worked for him at more than one of them.

---

[1] The NUMMI joint venture was liquidated in 2010 and its former facility is now the main factory of Tesla Motors.

Q.T. expanded the number of operating units a company had and sized them to the opportunity—he combined managerial focus with resource fluidity; employees and facilities could be assigned where they were needed. The financial planning system was remarkable. The focus was the next quarter, with slight attention to subsequent quarters; there was no multi-year plan. Q.T. had said: "A company makes its annual numbers one quarter at a time, so focus on the one in front of you."

A key product of the quarterly planning process was to identify the "Five Most Important Tasks" for each bonus-eligible manager. In Q.T.'s system, one's salary was about 80 percent of the market rate. If they earned their full quarterly bonus, their compensation could be 120 percent—or more—of the market rate. So the company had 20 opportunities a year—five tasks times four quarters—to align employee behavior with business targets. The tasks were a blend of shared goals for the company as well as those a manager had direct responsibility for. As you might imagine, this system had a powerful effect on behavior. As quarter-end approached, those who were not on-track to meet their goals became focused on how to do it, if feasible. Management monitored the situation and took steps to offset shortfalls in one division with overachievement in others, if possible.

The theme of this chapter is cooperation and it existed at Granger—the *esprit de corps* was high. But the spirit of cooperation did not flow from an overly optimistic view of human nature. Rather, it flowed from understanding risks and opportunities, goal setting, effective communications, accountability, and the authority to act. This spirit of cooperation flowed from trust and confidence in oneself and in others. This was the result of Q.T.'s organizational philosophy.[1]

Granger Associates usually made its quarterly targets. There was a vitality and dynamism in that organization that was the best I've ever seen. Compared to the annual plan process used by Granger's parent and most companies, Q.T.'s approach unleashed the equivalent of what John Maynard Keynes might have described as an organization's "animal spirits," a sense of purpose in the face of uncertainty. A significant reason was that managers had input on what their goals were and had the ability to meet them.

After Granger Associates, one of Q.T.'s turnarounds became his Waterloo. MiniScribe Corporation, a publicly traded disk drive manufacturer based in Longmont, Colorado, became infamous for fraudulent financial reporting. To meet quarterly targets, some managers falsified their performance, which came to light in an audit. A senior Granger Associates manager, who knew Q.T. and several MiniScribe managers, told me that the system worked well when people shared an ethos that kept them from doing something wrong. It failed at MiniScribe, he said, because some did not understand where the lines were drawn.

These anecdotes illustrate three important points about cooperation in the workplace.

1. Cooperative micro networks help companies of all sizes succeed. They were critical to Toyota's ascent to become the world's largest automaker. Its approach to creating a collaborative workforce and its supply chain practices are popular with startups.

2. Reward systems can evoke and channel cooperation. This is particularly true when the goals are specific and relevant to employees, when the incentive goes deep into the organization and the reward for achievement is issued frequently enough to maintain the incentive.

3. A good system can deliver a bad result. Wiles' system had an impressive record: MiniScribe did not invalidate it. Other popular approaches to motivate employees have had bad

results too, or simply delivered insubstantial results. Similarly, if a company applies the Fairshare Model ineffectively, that will not invalidate it. It's a promising approach if you believe that cooperative micro-networks can be a game-changer in the tough business of growing a business; it's not a utopian solution, however.

Few will question the idea that the ability to cooperate can yield competitive advantage. However, does the proposition rely on an idealized notion of human society?

Many will argue it's our nature to compete, to be selfish, to be sneaky or aggressive to advance our interest. That undercuts the notion that micro-networks of investors and employees will cooperate in ways that enables the Fairshare Model to compete with a conventional capital structure.

Time and experience will provide the proving grounds. And the balance of this chapter will challenge that view of human nature; the idea that cooperation and fairness—indeed, empathy and compassion, qualities that John Donne expressed—are not natural human qualities.

Cooperation in Animals

Some readers may accept the benefits of cooperation but be skeptical about the potential to achieve it.

"Humanity is actually much more cooperative and empathic than its given credit for," says Frans de Waal, a biologist known for his work on primate behavior. In 2007, *Time* magazine named him one of The World's 100 Most Influential People Today. In 2011, Discover magazine had him among 47 all-time Great Minds of Science. Professor de Waal has a TED talk, "Moral Behavior in Animals," on the capacity of primates to reconcile, share, and cooperate.[J] My edit of the transcript is below.

> I [Frans de Waal] discovered that chimpanzees are very power hungry and wrote a book about it. And at that time, the focus of animal research was on aggression and competition. I painted a whole picture of the animal kingdom, humanity included, that said deep down we are competitors, we are aggressive, and we're all out for our own profit, basically.
>
> But in the process of researching power, dominance, and aggression, I discovered that chimpanzees reconcile after fights. And so, what you see here [pointing to the screen] are two males who have had a fight. They ended up in a tree, and one of them holds out a hand to the other. And about a second after I took the picture, they came together in the fork of the tree and they kissed and embraced each other.
>
> Now this is very interesting because at the time everything was about competition and aggression, and this didn't make sense. The only thing that matters is that you win or that you lose. But why would you reconcile after a fight? That doesn't make any sense.
>
> The principle we found is that when you have a valuable relationship that is damaged by conflict, you need to do something about it. So, my whole picture of the animal kingdom, including humans, started to change.
>
> So, we have this image in political science, economics, the humanities, and philosophy that man is like a wolf—deep down, our nature is nasty. I think it's a very unfair image for the wolf. The wolf is, after all, a very cooperative animal; that's why many [people] have a dog, which has these characteristics also.

And it's unfair to humanity, because it is more cooperative and empathic than its given credit for. So, I started getting interested in those issues and studying that in other animals.

If you ask, 'What is morality based on?' two factors always come out.

- One is reciprocity and associated with it is a sense of justice and a sense of fairness.
- And the other one is empathy and compassion.

Human morality is more than this, but if you would remove these two pillars, there would not be much remaining–they're absolutely essential.

[VIDEO OF TWO EXPERIMENTS ARE SHOWN
TO DEMONSTRATE THE POINT.]

We also published an experiment where the question is, 'Do chimpanzees care about the welfare of somebody else?' It's been assumed that only humans worry about the welfare of others. We found that the chimpanzees care about the well-being of others–especially, members of their group.

The final experiment that I want to mention is about fairness. It has been performed in many ways. I'm going to show you the first experiment that we did with capuchin monkeys, but it has been done with dogs, birds, and chimpanzees.

We put two monkeys in a test chamber side-by-side, so they see each other. These animals know each other. Each has a simple task to do to get a reward–hand us back a rock. The reward is a piece of cucumber. As you can see, they're perfectly willing to do this repeatedly. Cucumber is fine for them, but they prefer grapes. If you give one monkey cucumber and the other a grape, you create inequity between them. That's the fairness experiment.

In the videotape, the one on the left gets cucumber for returning the rock to the researcher.

[MONKEY ON THE LEFT GETS ROCK FROM RESEARCHER,
RETURNS IT AND GETS A CUCUMBER REWARD.]

The first cucumber is perfectly fine as a reward for the one on the left. The first piece she eats.

[MONKEY ON THE RIGHT GETS ROCK FROM RESEARCHER,
RETURNS IT AND GETS A GRAPE REWARD.]

Then she sees the other one on the right get a grape for the same task. Watch what happens.

[MONKEY THAT GOT CUCUMBER SHOWS ENVY
OF THE ONE THAT GOT A GRAPE.]

The one on the left again gets the rock, gives it back, and gets a piece of cucumber.

[AUDIENCE HOWLS WHEN THE MONKEY THROWS THE CUCUMBER
BACK AT THE RESEARCHER.]

[MORE LAUGHTER AS THE MONKEY EXTENDS HER ARM
FOR THE OUT-OF-REACH GRAPE DISH. FRUSTRATED AND ANGRY,
SHE SHAKES HER CAGE AND SLAMS HER HAND ON THE TABLE
TO GET THE ATTENTION OF THE RESEARCHER.]

[CONTINUED LAUGHTER WHEN THE SEQUENCE IS REPEATED–
THE MONKEY EXPRESSES ANGER AT GETTING CUCUMBER
WHEN THE OTHER GETS GRAPE FOR PERFORMING THE SAME TASK.]

So, this is basically the [Occupy] Wall Street protest that you see here.

[AUDIENCE LAUGHS UPROARIOUSLY]

Let me tell you a funny story about this. This study became famous, and we got a lot of comments, especially from anthropologists, economists, and philosophers. They didn't like this at all. Because they had decided that fairness is a very complex issue and that animals cannot have it.

One philosopher wrote that he would believe it had something to do with fairness if the one who got grapes refused them. Now the funny thing is, an experimenter who used chimpanzees had instances where, indeed, the one offered the grape refused it until the other also got one.

So we're getting very close to the human sense of fairness. And I think philosophers need to rethink their philosophy. I think morality is much more than what I've been talking about, but it would be impossible without these ingredients that we find in other primates, which are empathy and consolation, pro-social tendencies and reciprocity and a sense of fairness.

Thus, Professor de Waal provides reason to believe that humans–the most highly developed primates–naturally have the social qualities that are necessary for the Fairshare Model to work.

What Does Adam Smith Say About Human Nature?

In 1776, the year America declared its independence, Scottish economist and philosopher Adam Smith published *An Inquiry into the Nature and Causes of The Wealth of Nations*. This book, also known as *The Wealth of Nations*, is the cornerstone of classic economic thought, which likens market forces to an "invisible hand." Less known is Smith's 1759 book, *The Theory of Moral Sentiments*, which explores the moral underpinnings for commerce, the "system" that came to be known as "capitalism."

Economist Russ Roberts is a fellow at Stanford University's Hoover Institution. In 2014, he authored a book, *How Adam Smith Can Change Your Life: An Unexpected Guide to Human Nature and Happiness*. In it, he writes that *The Theory of Moral Sentiments* "was Adam Smith's attempt to explain where morality comes from and why people can act with decency and virtue even when it conflicts with their own self-interest. It's a mix of psychology, philosophy, and what we now call behavioral economics, peppered with Smith's observations on friendship, the pursuit of wealth, the pursuit of happiness, and virtue. Along the way, Smith tells his readers what the good life is and how to achieve it."[K]

Defenders of convention in the capital formation process–today's high valuations and the way Wall Street IPOs are allocated–may be taken aback when Roberts reports that "Smith wrote on the futility of pursuing money with the hope of finding happiness."[L]

To those who believe capitalism is about self-interest and that "greed is good," Roberts lets it be known that there is nothing about that in *The Wealth of Nations* and the opposite is true in *Theory of Moral Sentiments,* which minimizes the importance of constantly seeking fame, power, and money. He offers this quote from the first page of *Theory of Moral Sentiments* which leads me to think that Adam Smith and John Donne shared views about human nature.

> How selfish soever man may be supposed, there are evidently some principles in his nature, which interest him in the fortune of others, and render their happiness necessary to him, though he derives nothing from it except the pleasure of seeing it.[M]

Roberts says that Smith felt that, deep down, what humans really want is to love, to be loved and to be admired—and that these motivations are the foundation of civilization. By the way, Roberts is rather hip for an economics professor. He hosts *Econtalk,* a podcast on economic matters. He also helped create a YouTube video in which dueling views on the nature of economic cycles are delivered in rap-style.

From a personal perspective, he writes, "Smith helped me understand why Whitney Houston and Marilyn Monroe were so unhappy and why their deaths made so many people so sad. He helped me understand my affection for my iPad and my iPhone, why talking to strangers about your troubles can calm the soul, and why people can think monstrous thoughts but rarely act upon them. He helped me understand why people adore politicians and how morality is built into the fabric of the world."[N]

Roberts also writes "Economics helps you understand that money isn't the only thing that matters in life. Economics teaches you that making a choice means giving up something. And economics can help you appreciate complexity and how seemingly unrelated actions and people can become entangled."[O]

Isn't "Maximization of Shareholder Value" the Common Purpose?

I mentioned earlier that after seeing material about the Fairshare Model, a fellow asked me "Are you a communist, a socialist?" The idea that employees could vote on shareholder matters and share in the return on capital prompted his question.

I'm neither of those. And frankly, I find that arguments based on "-isms" (i.e., capitalism, socialism, libertarianism) generate more heat than light. I associate them with sophomoric thinking for they are frequently shallow and pointless—they erode the quality of discourse. Ironically, it was communist leader, Deng Xhou-Peng, who best expressed why dogmatic thinking should be abandoned as he moved China toward a market-driven model. He said that, "It doesn't matter if a cat is black or white so long as it catches mice." More irony is apparent when one contemplates that the Communist Party of China runs its market-driven economy while ism-based arguments animate discussions in the US.

Oh well. If *-ism* thinking is important to you, consider me a capitalist who wants to address flaws in capital markets that discourage public investors from investing in venture-stage companies. What I think we need is *better capitalism.* One way to get there is to increase valuation competition in capital markets. Another way is the Fairshare Model; it encourages greater fairness, embraces empathy, and promotes cooperation—and it has the potential to help its adopters outperform competitors.

A company's constituencies are its shareholders, top management, other employees, customers, suppliers, and the communities it operates in. The question posed by that gentleman—"Are you a communist...a socialist?"—begs a better one: "How should corporate stakeholders rank in importance?"

If you think shareholders are unquestionably the most important stakeholders, consider what happens when a company enters a "zone of insolvency," when its ability to fully pay creditors in the ordinary course of business is imperiled. When this occurs in the US, a company's board of directors and management is legally obligated to place the interests of creditors, which can include employees, before those of shareholders.

Interestingly, many venture-stage companies reside in the zone of insolvency at times. Their ability to move to a better neighborhood can depend on new investors or creditors, or existing creditors willing to restructure what they are owed. If such a corporation were a real person, it might be cast as Blanche DuBois, the character in Tennessee William's *A Streetcar Named Desire* who utters the line, "I have always depended on the kindness of strangers."[2]

Put that thought to the side. There is a deeper question to contemplate: "How do the stakeholder's rank in priority when a company is not financially distressed?" Jack Ma, the CEO of Alibaba, famously said that his ranking is, "Customers first, employees second, and shareholders last." He didn't have a place for creditors, probably because in 2014, his Chinese company had the largest IPO in history. (Actually, a Cayman Island affiliate of Alibaba had the IPO.)

There are management teams who operate as if their interests trump everyone else's—they're more important than customers, other employees, creditors, or shareholders. This worldview is rarely articulated. But when it is, it is usually as a justification for some exposed behavior. I don't recall a CEO advancing, "It's all about me!" as a legal or business theory, but I've seen evidence that some believe it.

With that prelude, common wisdom is that a corporation's highest duty is to maximize the interests of its shareholders. *Washington Post* business columnist Steven Pearlstein challenges that orthodoxy in a brilliant 2013 essay entitled "How the Cult of Shareholder Value Wrecked American Business." I recommend that you read the full piece.[P] The following is excerpted from his article because it perfectly complements our discussion about corporate purpose [bold added for emphasis].

> **In the history of management ideas, few have had a more profound—or pernicious— effect than the one that says corporations should be run in a manner that "maximizes shareholder value."** Indeed, you could argue that much of what Americans perceive to be wrong with the economy these days — the slow growth and rising inequality; the recurring scandals; the wild swings from boom to bust; the inadequate investment in R&D, worker training and public goods — has its roots in this ideology.
>
> The funny thing is that this **imperative to "maximize" a company's share price has no foundation in history or in law. Nor is there any evidence that it makes the economy or the society better off.** What began in the 1970s and '80s as a corrective

---

[2] In his 2012 presidential campaign, Mitt Romney declared that "corporations are people too"—a position consistent with the US Supreme Court's 2010 decision in the *Citizen's United* case which found that corporations have a constitutional right to exercise free political speech (i.e., give unlimited money to political causes).

to managerial mediocrity has become a **corrupting, self-interested dogma peddled by finance professors[3], money managers and over-compensated corporate executives.**

[Apparently, no law requires] that executives and directors owe a special fiduciary duty to shareholders. How then did "maximizing shareholder value" evolve into such a widely accepted norm of corporate behavior? The most likely explanations are globalization and deregulation, which together rob many major American corporations of the outsize profits they earned during the "golden" decades after World War II. Those profits were enough to satisfy nearly all the corporate stakeholders. But in the 1970s, when increased competition started to squeeze profits, it was easier for executives to disappoint shareholders than their workers or communities.

No surprise, then, that by the mid-1980s, companies with lagging stock prices found themselves targets for hostile takeovers by rivals or corporate raiders using newfangled 'junk' bonds to finance their purchases. Disgruntled shareholders were willing to sell. And so it developed that the threat of a possible takeover imbued corporate executives and directors with a new focus on profits and share prices, tossing aside inhibitions against laying off workers, cutting wages, closing plants, spinning off divisions and outsourcing production. Today's "activist investor" hedge funds are the descendants of these 1980s corporate raiders.

While it was this new "market for corporate control" that created the imperative to boost near-term profits and share prices, an elaborate institutional infrastructure has grown up to reinforce it. This infrastructure includes business schools that indoctrinate students with the shareholder-first ideology and equip them with tools to manipulate earnings and share prices. It includes lawyers who advise against any action that might lower the share price and invite shareholder lawsuits, however frivolous. It includes a Wall Street that is fixated on quarterly earnings, quarterly investment returns and short-term trading. And most of all, it is reinforced by pay packages for executives that are tied to the short-term performance of the company stock.

The result is a self-reinforcing cycle in which corporate time horizons have become shorter and shorter. The average holding periods for stocks, which for decades was six years, is now less than six months. The average tenure of a public company CEO is less than four years. And the willingness of executives to sacrifice short-term profits to make long-term investments is rapidly disappearing.

The real irony surrounding this focus on maximizing shareholder value is that it hasn't, in fact, done much for shareholders. One thing we know is that less and less of the wealth generated by the corporate sector was going to frontline workers. Another is that more of it was going to top executives. **Almost all of that increase came from stock-based compensation.**

---

3 The seminal role university finance professors played in promoting the policies that led to the Great Recession was highlighted in Charles Ferguson's Academy Award-winning 2010 movie, *Inside Job*. It reports how eminent academics have made fortunes from Wall Street since the 1980s while advocating its interests in regulatory proceedings, the courts and in the media. Some who were promoted to positions based on their expertise failed to disclose that they earned considerable sums from those who benefit from their policy prescriptions. Ferguson draws an ethical comparison to a physician who promotes the benefit of a drug as a medical expert, while failing to disclose that he has been paid a large sum by the company making the drug.

One problem is that it's not clear which shareholders it is whose interests the corporation is supposed to optimize. Should it be the hedge funds that are buying and selling millions of shares every couple of seconds? Or mutual funds holding the stock for a couple of years? Or the retired teacher in Dubuque, Iowa, who has held it for decades?

"There's a lot of lip service that 'people are our most important asset.' Every executive will tell you that. Very few seem to act like it in terms of investing in their people."

–Rick Wartzman, author of *The End of Loyalty: The Rise And Fall of Good Jobs n America*

Even as [corporations] proclaim their dedication to shareholders, they have been doing everything possible to minimize and discourage shareholder involvement in corporate governance. This hypocrisy is recently revealed in the effort by the business lobby to prevent shareholders from voting on executive pay or to nominate a competing slate of directors.

For too many corporations, "maximizing shareholder value" has provided justification for bamboozling customers, squeezing suppliers and employees, avoiding taxes, and leaving communities in the lurch. For any one profit-maximizing company, such behavior may be perfectly rational. But when competition forces all companies to behave in this fashion, it's hardly clear that society is better off. Perhaps the most ridiculous aspect of "shareholder über alles" is how at odds it is with every modern theory about managing people. David Langstaff, CEO of TASC, a government contracting firm, put it this way:

> *"If you are the sole proprietor of a business, do you think that you can motivate your employees for maximum performance by encouraging them simply to make more money for you? Of course not. But that is effectively what an enterprise is saying when it states that its purpose is to maximize profit for its investors."*

These days, economies have been scrambling to explain the recent slowdown in the pace of innovation and the growth in worker productivity. Is it possible it might have something to do with the fact that workers now know that any benefit from their ingenuity or increased efficiency is destined to go to shareholders and top executives?

The defense you usually hear of "maximizing shareholder value" from CEOs is that most of them don't confuse this week's stock price with shareholder value. They acknowledge that no enterprise can maximize long-term value for its shareholders without attracting great employees, producing great products and services, and doing their part to support effective government and healthy communities. In short, they argue, there is no inherent conflict between the interests of shareholders and those of other stakeholders.

But if optimizing shareholder value requires taking care of customers, employees, and communities, then you could argue that "maximizing customer satisfaction" would require taking good care of shareholders, employees, and communities. And, indeed, that is the suggestion made by Peter Drucker, the late, great management guru.

"The purpose of business is to create and keep a customer," [he] wrote.

It is no coincidence that companies that maintain a strong customer focus—think Apple, Johnson & Johnson, and Proctor & Gamble—have done better for their shareholders than companies which claim to put shareholders first. The reason is that customer focus minimizes risk taking and maximizes reinvestment, creating a larger pie from which everyone benefits.

Most executives would be thrilled if they could focus on customers rather than shareholders. In private, they chafe under the quarterly earnings regime forced on them by asset managers and the financial press. They fear and loathe "activist" investors who threaten them with takeovers. And they are disheartened by their low public esteem.

If it were the law that was at fault, that would be easy to change. **Changing a behavioral norm—one reinforced by so much supporting infrastructure—turns out to be much harder. The challenge facing the "corporate social responsibility" movement is that it exhibits an unmistakable liberal bias that makes it easy for academics, investment managers and corporate executives to dismiss it as ideological and naïve.**

My guess is that it will be a new generation of employees that finally frees the American corporation from the shareholder-value straitjacket. Young people – particularly those with skills that are in high demand – today are drawn to work that not only pays well but also has meaning and social value. As the economy improves and the baby boom generation retires, companies that have reputations as ruthless maximizers of short-term profits will find themselves on the losing end of the global competition for talent. **In an era of plentiful capital, it will be skills, knowledge, creativity, and experience that will be in short supply, with those who have it setting the norms of corporate behavior.**

Diversity in Common Purpose

How might people respond to debate about what the common purpose for a corporation should be? For some, it will be disorienting to consider that maximizing shareholder value isn't the sole answer. For others, it will be liberating.

The ability—the responsibility—to define common purpose is daunting. It is more stressful to have a choice than to have it predefined. In this sense, those who use maximize shareholder value have had it easy. What's clear is that more than one definition of what common purpose should be is possible, and that the rationale for the conventional answer is not as strong as many people think.

Milton Friedman, a Nobel Prize-winning economist at the University of Chicago, originated the idea that the *only* purpose of a corporation is to advance the interests of its shareholders. In a 1970 essay called "The Social Responsibility of Business Is to Increase Its Profits," he argued that making shareholders richer made markets more efficient for everyone, and that it was heresy for management to spend company dollars

Thought Experiment

If a large employer in your community who sells something that you need is acquired by a foreign company, might that affect your view of what its priorities should be?

Would you support layoffs and/or price hikes designed to maximize shareholder wealth?

on anything other than increasing profits. He called corporate philanthropy "pure and unadulterated socialism," and argued that the appropriate way to create social change is to give profits to investors, who could choose which—if any—causes to support, and to pay taxes to government, which could use that money to make an impact.

Increasingly, people want new thinking about corporate purpose, which is an expression of common purpose. They are like those who see value in athletics that goes beyond winning. In a 2005 paper titled "Sacrificing Corporate Profits in the Public Interest," Harvard University's Einer Elhauge argues that profit maximization is too restrictive as a goal when shareholders share social concerns.[Q]

In a 2017 paper called "Companies Should Maximize Shareholder Welfare Not Market Value," Oliver Hart of Harvard, a Nobel laureate, and Luigi Zingales of Chicago express a similar idea. They say that companies should prioritize *shareholder welfare*, not *shareholder value*. They believe that Friedman was too narrow in his focus on corporate support of socially beneficial causes because, Zingales says, in many instances, it makes more sense for a company to act rather than leave it to individual shareholders.[R]

Such sentiment is echoed by Lawrence Fink, CEO of BlackRock, the world's largest asset manager. In a January 2017 open letter to CEOs, he said society is demanding that companies—public and private—"serve a social purpose," benefiting not just shareholders but also employees, customers, and neighbors. He announced that henceforth, BlackRock is "eager to participate in discussions about long-term value creation and work to build a better framework for serving all your stakeholders."[S]

A "benefit corporation" is yet another expression of this energy. It's a new class of corporation, one whose charter encompasses a duty to benefit society. Since the first US state codified it in 2010, about thirty have authorized them. The accounting and tax rules are the same as for a regular corporation, which is known as a "C corp."

What's different about a benefit corporation is that its directors are empowered to consider the interests of non-shareholders. This provides a defense if shareholders file a lawsuit against directors charging that they decided a matter in a manner that did not maximize shareholder wealth.

Another manifestation of this idea is "B corp" certification, which can be issued to any form of company—a sole proprietorship, C corp, a benefit corporation—anywhere in the world. B corp certification is to business what Fair Trade certification is to coffee and cacao or what USDA Organic certification is to milk.

In 2013, Rally Software, a B corp, went public with a valuation of $315 million, raising $84 million.

In 2015, Etsy became the largest B corp to have an IPO; it raised $267 million at a valuation of $1.8 billion.

Companies qualify for a B corp designation by meeting standards for social sustainability, environment performance and corporate governance established by a non-profit organization, B Lab.

B corp companies consider the interests of all stakeholders—shareholders, employees, suppliers, customers, community, and the environment—when deciding matters. By late 2018, approximately 2,700 companies in 60 countries had earned a B corp designation.

An article by James Surowiecki in *The New Yorker* expands on this:[T]

> Whereas a regular business can abandon altruistic policies when times get tough, a benefit corporation can't. Shareholders can sue its directors for not carrying out the company's social mission, just as they can sue directors of traditional companies for violating their fiduciary duty. Becoming a B corp raises the reputational cost of abandoning your social goals. It's what behavioral economists call a "commitment device"–a way of insuring that you'll live up to your promises. Being a B corp also insulates a company against pressure from investors.
>
> Since the nineteen-seventies, the dominant ideology in corporate America has been that a company's fundamental purpose is to boost investor returns: as Milton Friedman put it, increased profits are the "only social responsibility of business." Law professors still debate whether or not this is legally true, but most CEOs feel huge pressure to maximize shareholder value.
>
> At a B corp, though, shareholders are just one constituency. [The clothing company] Patagonia doesn't need to worry about investors' opposing its environmental work, because that work is simply part of the job. For similar reasons, benefit corporations are far less vulnerable to hostile takeovers. When Ben & Jerry's was acquired by Unilever, in 2000, its founders didn't want to sell, but they believed that fiduciary duty required them to. A benefit corporation would have had an easier time staying independent.

In his full article, "How the Cult of Shareholder Value Wrecked American Business," Steven Pearlstein argues for tax and regulatory reforms that "help the corporate ecosystem become more heterogeneous." Biodiversity is good for the planet and social diversity creates a more vibrant, interesting society. It makes similar sense to support diversity in the purpose of capitalist enterprises. Pearlstein says we ought to encourage "different companies taking different approaches and adopting different priorities." Because, "In the end, 'the market'–not just the stock market, but product markets and labor markets as well–would sort out which worked best."

How companies with a conventional capital structure go about adjusting to this changing landscape will be interesting to watch. Those that adopt the Fairshare Model when going public have a unique tool to define, measure and reward the social good they achieve–Performance Stock.

The Fairshare Model supports heterogeneity in how common purpose is defined. It does not require a corporation to be "good"–it simply calls for agreement by two groups of shareholders on how performance is defined, measured, and rewarded.

Common Purpose is What You Make It

You may believe that cooperative micro-networks provide competitive advantage and that people naturally want to cooperate but be unclear on what the objectives of the cooperation might be.

In the Fairshare Model, common purpose is the criterion that causes Performance Stock to convert to Investor Stock. It can be whatever the two shareholder classes want it to be, and they can change it whenever they agree to do so. Here, common purpose is not a top-down Big Solution, it's a bottoms-up Small Solution that is agreed to by those affected. A solution for the divisive times that we live in!

The performance criteria may vary by company. They will reflect an issuer's industry, stage of development and the personalities of the players. Thus, the Fairshare Model will support diversity in corporate purpose. The basic performance categories will likely be valuation, operational measures, financial measures, and in some cases, social measures.

1. Valuation performance may be improvement from the IPO valuation, measured by the
    a. average quarterly market value of Investor Stock,
    b. valuation when additional capital is raised, and
    c. valuation when the company is acquired, while
2. operational performance could be expressed as product release, intellectual property development, regulatory milestones, market share, customer satisfaction, significant contracts, etc.,
3. financial performance will be measures such as revenue and profitability, and
4. measures of social good that are relevant.

These areas will form the common purpose *between* the Investor and Performance Stockholders. Helmuth von Moltke, a 19th century German military strategist, observed that "no battle plan survives first contact with the enemy." An analog is that few business plans survive engagement with the market. Thus, a key test for the Fairshare Model will be the ability of shareholder classes to change the conversion criteria, as needed. Some issuers will do it better than others.

What about common purpose *within* the Performance Stock pool? How hard will it be for employees to agree on how to allocate Performance Stock?[4] Investor Stockholders are unlikely to care who has Performance Stock, but it is a significant question, and there is sure to be variation in how it is answered. For now, contemplate how Performance Stock might be used to build common purpose.

- **Employees** –The effectiveness of team-building and creative thinking exercises fade over time. Performance Stock will elicit more enduring motivation to accomplish specific goals.

- **Suppliers**–If suppliers have an interest in an issuer's Performance Stock–it could be a non-voting class–that would encourage collaboration in novel ways. Vendor negotiations that have a short-term winner-loser quality could be replaced by those that have a long-term win-win flavor.

- **Investors**–Performance Stock could be a "sweetener" for pre-IPO investors, providing incentive to support a low IPO valuation, and the conversion rules.

Summation

This chapter was about cooperation, collaboration, and common purpose. There is evidence that people (and animals) do best when it exists. The same can be said for companies–those whose micro-networks have a high degree of these qualities are likely to outperform those who have less.

What's Next?

This concludes Section 2, which is broad in scope and high-level in its perspective. Section 3 descends from those lofty heights to the central matter when companies raise venture capital: valuation.

---

4 See "Who Gets Performance Stock?" in Chapter 4, "Fairshare Model Q&A."

Chapter Endnotes

Contextual references for material in this chapter appear as numbered footnotes on the page where the reference is made. **Source references** for material in this chapter appear below as endnotes with capital letter identifiers.

A Malady, Matthew J.X. "I've Discovered the Internet's Most Internet Sentence, and Your [sic] an Idiot If You Disagree." *The New Republic*. February 26, 2014. Accessed May 09, 2018. fairsharemodel.com/Idiot.

B Putnam, Robert D. *Bowling Alone: The Collapse and Revival of American Community*. New York, NY: Simon & Schuster, 2007. Page 367.

C Scheidel, Walter. "The Only Conquerors of Inequality Are the Four Horsemen of the Apocalypse." PBS *NewsHour*. June 16, 2017. Accessed May 09, 2018. fairsharemodel.com/Horsemen.

D Ibid.

E "Utopia." *Wikipedia*. May 15, 2018. Accessed May 15, 2018. fairsharemodel.com/Utopia.

F *The Commanding Heights* may be streamed here fairsharemodel.com/Commanding-Heights.

G Webb, Maynard, and Carlye Adler. *Rebooting Work Transform How You Work in the Age of Entrepreneurship*. San Francisco, CA: Jossey-Bass, 2013. Page 52.

H Black, John R., David Miller, and Joni Sensel. *The Toyota Way to Healthcare Excellence: Increase Efficiency and Improve Quality with Lean*. Chicago, IL: HAP/Health Administration Press, 2016. Pages 28-29.

I "Company Doctor - Q. T. Wiles." *Inc*. February 01, 1988. Accessed May 09, 2018. fairsharemodel.com/QT.

J de Waal, Frans. "Moral Behavior in Animals." *TED*. Accessed May 09, 2018. fairsharemodel.com/Morality.

K Roberts, Russ. *How Adam Smith Can Change Your Life an Unexpected Guide to Human Nature and Happiness*. New York, NY: Portfolio/Penguin, 2015. Page 3.

L Ibid.

M Ibid.

N Ibid., page 5.

O Ibid., page 13.

P Pearlstein, Steven. "How the Cult of Shareholder Value Wrecked American Business." *Washington Post*. September 09, 2013. Accessed May 09, 2018. fairsharemodel.com/ShareholderValue.

Q Elhauge, Einer. "Sacrificing Corporate Profits in the Public Interest." *NYU Law Review*. June 2005. Accessed November 23, 2018. fairsharemodel.com/Elhauge.

R Schoenberger, Chana R. "Why We're All Impact Investors Now." *Chicago Booth Review*. August 28, 2018. Accessed November 23, 2018. fairsharemodel.com/Impact.

S Ibid.

T Surowiecki, James. "Companies with Benefits." *The New Yorker*. August 4, 2014. Accessed May 09, 2018. fairsharemodel.com/Bcorp.

SECTION 3:

Valuation

Someone with experience in crafting Hollywood stories, consumer advertising, and marketing messages for financial products advised me to forgo my emphasis on valuation. He warned:

> It's a snoozer! People want to engage at an emotional level. Just tell them the Fairshare Model will make them rich!

Here's what he recommended that I should do instead of writing about valuation: make the benefits of the Fairshare Model the focus.

> Start with a story about a young couple that wants financial security before they start a family.

> The husband has stock options, but his company can't raise the money it needs unless it has an IPO. It can't have an IPO because it's too expensive. As a result, his options are worthless.

> Because his options are worthless, he and his wife can't afford to have a baby.

> No IPO–no baby!

> Then say…the Fairshare Model can change that!!

Man! Did he make me laugh!

The pitch has nothing to do with the Fairshare Model.

It relies on emotion and fuzzy association, not relevant issues. But it was hilarious—he combined kitsch with insight into human nature. He knew that the best way to evoke interest in something is to *promote a positive outcome as the likely reward*.[1]

After all, ideas are boring to some people. They just want to hear that there will be a happy ending! You have interest in ideas, however—you wouldn't be here otherwise.

This section explores ideas about valuation in more depth, but not enough to be eye-glazing. It has four chapters:

Chapter 13: Valuation Concepts

Chapter 14: Calculating Valuation

Chapter 15: Evaluating Valuation

Chapter 16: Valuation Disclosure

---

[1] His script reminds me of commercials for DirecTV, a satellite provider of TV. One of them shows a man watching cable TV (fairsharemodel.com/directv). He can't find anything he wants to see. He gets depressed and attends a motivational seminar that makes him feel like a winner. Feeling like a winner, he decides to go to Las Vegas. He loses all his money and winds up sleeping on the streets. To get money, he pulls out his hair and sells it to a wig shop.

With that visual sequence in mind, the following voiceover for the commercial will make sense:

"When you have cable and can't find something good to watch, you get depressed.

When you get depressed, you attend seminars.

When you attend seminars, you feel like a winner.

When you feel like a winner, you go to Vegas.

When you go to Vegas, you lose everything.

And when you lose everything, you sell your hair to a wig shop.

Don't sell your hair to a wig shop.

Get rid of cable, and upgrade to DirecTV!"

Chapter 13:

Valuation Concepts

What's Included in This Chapter

- Introduction
- Points to Bear in Mind
- What Is the Value of an Idea?
- Startup Valuation Technology – Illustrated
- Valuation Is a Challenge for Established Companies
- Valuation Is a Challenge for Wall Street
- Valuation Is a Challenge for VCs
- Ways to Defer a Valuation of Startups
- Valuation of Sustainable Companies
- What's the *Microeconomic* Harm of Getting Valuation Wrong?
- What's the *Macroeconomic* Harm of Getting Valuation Wrong?
- Why Is a Valuation Necessary?
- Summation
- What's Next?
- Chapter Endnotes

Introduction

This chapter addresses questions like: How might one think about valuation? How do the smartest guys in the room think about it? What's the harm of getting it wrong? Why does a company need to have one?

Points to Bear in Mind

1. Two valuations determine an investor's profit or loss—the buy-in and the exit.
2. Valuation is price; price is not necessarily worth.

3. A valuation may seem reasonable, but it is speculative if no one is prepared to pay that to buy the company. Plus, what seems reasonable in a heated market may be untenable as it cools.

4. A company's valuation is set whenever its stock is bought or sold.

   a. In a private offering where there is a lead investor, the valuation is set via negotiation between that investor and the issuer. If there is no lead investor, the company sets and presents it as a take it or leave it proposition.

   b. In a brokered public offering, the valuation is determined by the broker-dealer and issuer.

   c. In a direct public offering (no broker-dealer), the valuation is set by the issuer.

   d. In the secondary market, the most recent buyer and seller set it.

   e. In an acquisition, the valuation is set by negotiation between the seller and buyer (the acquiring company).

What Is the Value of an Idea?

Typically, the value of a venture stage company rests heavily on the potential value of an idea. Entrepreneurs differ on how much time, thought, and effort they put into getting an idea ready-to-fund without being (fairly) paid—the "sweat equity."

So, what is the value of an idea? Entrepreneurs and their friends and family are most likely to have the highest assessment.

Savvy investors, I think, will smile at Derek Sivers' thoughts on this subject, which are below. On his website, he says "I'm a musician, programmer, writer, entrepreneur, and student—though not in that order. I'm fascinated with the usable psychology of self-improvement, communication, business, philosophy, and cross-cultural relativism. I love seeing a different point of view." This is from his blog.

Ideas Are Just a Multiplier of Execution[A]

It's so funny when I [Derek Sivers] hear people being so protective of ideas. (People who want me to sign a Non-Disclosure Agreement to tell me the simplest idea.) To me, ideas are worth nothing unless executed. They are just a multiplier. Execution is worth millions.

Explanation:

Value of an Idea			Value of Execution		
Awful Idea	=	-1	No Execution	=	$1
Weak Idea	=	1	Weak Execution	=	$1,000
So-So Idea	=	5	So-So Execution	=	$10,000
Good Idea	=	10	Good Execution	=	$100,000
Great Idea	=	15	Great Execution	=	$1,000,000
Brilliant Idea	=	20	Brilliant Execution	=	$10,000,000

To make a business, you need to multiply the two.

- The most brilliant idea, with no execution, is worth $20.
- The most brilliant idea takes great execution to be worth $20,000,000.

That's why I don't want to hear people's ideas. I'm not interested until I see their execution.

Many people would agree with Sivers on the importance of execution, *but a conventional capital structure requires that a valuation be set for future performance when an equity investment is made.*

"Vision without execution is hallucination."

–Thomas Edison

"You can't build a reputation on what you're going to do."

–Henry Ford

Can one reconcile his sentiment with a conventional capital structure? Sure! If it involves a modified conventional capital structure–the kind VCs use in a private offering. If it's a public offering, though, the answer is "no" because virtually all IPOs use a conventional capital structure. That creates the opportunity–the need–for the Fairshare Model.

Startup Valuation Technology – Illustrated

Time magazine annually selects a Person of the Year, the person who had the most impact that year. The first, in 1927, was Charles Lindbergh. In 1938, it was Adolf Hitler. Joseph Stalin made it twice, in 1939 and 1942. George Marshall did too, first in 1943 as US Army Chief of Staff and then in 1947 as Secretary of State and progenitor of the Marshall Plan to rebuild war-torn Europe. In 1982, remarkably, *Time* broke its tradition by naming a non-person, the personal computer, Person of the Year. It signaled that technology was poised to powerfully alter everyday life, the economy, and more.

The next year, 1983, I moved to the Santa Clara Valley, which is at the south end of the San Francisco Bay. A few years earlier, the term "Silicon Valley" had been popularized by a newspaper columnist who covered technology companies in the area. It was a play on the region's fertile agricultural heritage that had led it to be called the Valley of Heart's Delights. The name Silicon Valley captured the transition to an economy based on semiconductors. Publications like *Electronics News, Computer News,* and *High Technology* shed light on technology developments. Over time, reporters began to cover startup culture, financing, and consumer behavior.

The fusion of these elements created the ferment that led *Wired* magazine to launch in 1993. Less known now is *Upside,* a magazine "for Silicon Valley about Silicon Valley" that started in 1989. That's because it went upside down in 2002, a casualty of the precipitous drop in advertising revenue that followed the dotcom and telecom busts.

A regular *Upside* feature was a cartoon strip called "The VC" that satirized the rapidly growing venture capital industry. It was the creation of then-VC Robert von Goeben and artist Kathryn Siegler. Some of their strips are archived at thevc.com. The one on the following page is characteristic.

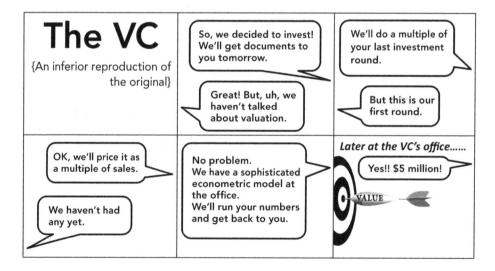

As the Internet Era dawned, VCs had concerns about rising pre-money valuations for companies that targeted this space. They were so different from the ventures that VCs were accustomed to that it was hard to figure out how to price a deal. What was reasonable?

The VC website does not have my favorite strip, which was on valuation. So, with apologies to von Goeben and Siegler, I offer this re-creation of it.

The joke is that VCs, the Masters of the Universe of venture capital, didn't have an objective way to evaluate a valuation. Rules of thumb that had been developed for companies were ignored by a new wave of VCs willing to accept higher valuations to secure a deal. This, in turn, encouraged companies to hold out for even higher valuations. (VC terms began to be more important than valuation in this era.) And, it was paying off! IPO valuations were climbing to remarkable heights, especially for internet-related companies.

Bill Reichert, managing director of Garage Technology Ventures tells a story about how he became a Silicon Valley software entrepreneur right out of graduate school in the 1980s. For reasons that mystified him, VCs gave his neophyte team the capital they needed to launch a software company. It met with success and was eventually acquired.

The same thing happened again with another company. And then again. As an entrepreneur, he assumed that VCs had insight and techniques into how to value an early stage company. So, in the late 1990s, as he prepared to join their ranks by heading up Garage, a boutique VC firm, he asked his VC friends, "What's the secret?"

He was told that the secret was that there is no secret. That VCs fund a deal because they fall in love. They fall in love with the company's market, its technology, and its team. And, they feel, if they love a company's potential, surely others will love it too! In other words, a valuation can reflect emotion more than a "sophisticated econometric model at the office."

Valuation Is a Challenge for Established Companies

The book, *The Art of M&A*, is a joint effort of Stanley Foster Reed, the founder of *Mergers and Acquisitions* magazine and Lane Edison, a law firm well known for its merger, acquisition, and leveraged buyout transactions. The authors report that executives at established companies struggle with their valuation, relative to that of an enterprise they want to acquire, even when there is abundant data to evaluate. The valuation chapter opens with this declaration.

> No factor counts more than price in closing a transaction. Yet very few operating executives have any notion as to how much their or anyone else's companies are worth, except from the stock tables. Very few know how to go about answering that question when they buy or sell.[B]

Presumptively, the valuation is the price to buy the entire company, but an acquirer may offer a price that is quite different from the valuation offered to investors. If executives at established companies have difficulty assessing the relative value of another established business, expect that executives who deal with venture-stage companies struggle even more.

Valuation Is a Challenge for Wall Street

Does a company (and, by extension, a stock) have an intrinsic value? The answer to that question has been the Holy Grail in the development of financial market theory, the effort to explain credibly and consistently what is known or observed.

In his 1992 book, *Capital Ideas: The Improbable Origins of Modern Wall Street*, Peter L. Bernstein examines the evolution of theories of how capital markets work. He says the idea of time value of money was well understood by the 1930s and that it led to the development of the dividend discount model to evaluate the true value of a stock. It assumes that a stock's value comes from its future dividend stream, discounted at a rate that reflects the time value of money and the risk associated with it. It is analytically sound and intuitive to say that the value of an investment is derived from the income that it produces. The problem is that this idea doesn't explain prices.

Columbia University's Benjamin Graham believed the difficulties of the dividend discount model were insurmountable.[1] While he believed that investors should base their decisions on the intrinsic value of a security, he felt it was "an elusive concept."

In their 1934 book *Security Analysis,* Graham and David Dodd use an analogy to suggest that an *approximate measure* of intrinsic value is good enough:

> Inspection [can reveal] whether a woman is old enough to vote without knowing her age, or that a man is heavier than he should be without knowing his exact weight.[c]

And they defined intrinsic value as "that value justified by the facts, e.g., the assets, earnings, dividends, definite prospects." To approximate it, most people rely on fundamental analysis–an analytic assessment of financial history and projections.

When an established company is evaluated, the analysis looks at history to provide a baseline for expectations. With a venture-stage company, the focus can be entirely on projections since there is little history that is meaningful. In addition, an analyst evaluates the model that produced the projections to see if it is well thought out, considers the drivers for success, uses prudent assumptions, and doesn't have computational or logic errors.

Another way to glean intrinsic value is a form of gestalt known as technical analysis. It focuses on price trends, not the underlying worth of the asset, relying on charts to discern if a stock price appears too high, too low, or just right. Like readers of tea leaves, analysts look for patterns in the trendline, for shapes such as "heads and shoulders," "candlesticks," and "cup and handles." They also compare the price-earnings ratio to what it has been, as well as to comparable companies.

Stock prices have a long history of defying traditional measures of value, but during the bull market of the 1990s, they rendered them utterly irrelevant for internet companies. Wall Street analysts looked for novel ways to rationalize what was going on. One was to use a multiple of "eyeballs"–internet users who visited a website–to identify value. The idea was that companies with high traffic websites should be worth more because they were better positioned to convert visitors to customers who generate revenue and profit. This inspired some to take that logic further, to argue that the companies with high marketing expense should be valued higher than competitors that did not spend as aggressively. Absurd, but it illustrates two things. One is how elastic explanations can get. The other is how challenging it can be to make sense of capital markets.

Keep intrinsic value in mind as we proceed. On the one hand, it makes sense that there is one. Theoretically, if market participants had equal access to information, knowledge, and the skill to exercise it, there would be agreement on what it is. Any price change would reflect additional information.

On the other hand, it is difficult to establish an intrinsic value because it is derived from expectations about the future, which is hard to get consensus on. Also, no one has demonstrated the ability to be reliably right. Thus, if one is intent on building wealth via the public capital markets, two paths present themselves.

1. The bright path involves vision, work, discipline, and the ability to assess risk well.

    a. Luck and fortunate timing often proves to be helpful.

---

[1] Graham is considered the father of "value investing." His most famous student is billionaire Warren Buffet.

b. No one gets this reliably right, so diversification is prudent. And, one's ability to maximize diversification in a portfolio is enhanced with attractive buy-in (purchase) valuations.

2. The dark path relies on gamed systems, inside information, manipulation of perception, deception and/or cheating.

Valuation Is a Challenge for VCs

VCs are the savviest investors in the venture-stage space. They are smart, connected, and disciplined. They usually invest in market sectors that they have expertise in, where they have contacts to help vet a concept, business model, and management team. Oh, and they have trouble with valuation too!

Nonetheless, a valuation must be set in an equity financing deal. VCs negotiate the lowest valuation they can without alienating the entrepreneurs. They will accept a higher-than-comfortable valuation in exchange for terms that protect their interests. Frankly, they rely more on getting the right deal terms than getting the valuation right. Put another way, a VC will tell the entrepreneur, "I'll give you your price, if you give me my terms."

In real estate, that expression captures a way to bridge a valuation gap between a buyer and seller. The buyer will pay more than she feels the property is worth at that time if the seller agrees to a payment plan that is long enough to make that price workable. That minimizes the cash outlay the buyer must make upfront when uncertainty is high about its future value. If the value doesn't rise enough, the buyer can walk away without losing much.

To provide price protection, issuers must use a modified conventional capital structure. The deal terms that protect a VC from overpaying include:

1. A *liquidation preference* which, if the company is sold, entitles a VC to get a multiple of its investment back before other shareholders share in the proceeds. As shown in Chapter 8, "The Tao of the Fairshare Model," this can make a valuation meaningless when ownership payouts are set.

2. An *anti-dilution clause* (i.e., a price ratchet) will retroactively adjust the price paid by a VC downward if a subsequent transaction is at a valuation that is lower than allowed. A company puts it into effect by issuing more shares to the VC for free.

3. A *redemption right* requires a company to buy back a VC's investment if there isn't an investor exit (i.e., IPO or acquisition). If the issuer can't provide an investor exit, the equity investment converts to debt, which enables the VC to foreclose on the assets. To avoid this, companies have been known to offer more shares at little or no cost.

4. *Conversion rights* enable a share of a VC's preferred stock to convert into common stock when there is a liquidity event. If the conversion ratio is higher than 1 for 1, the VC's ownership share increases without further investment.

In addition, a VC will seek terms related to corporate governance and control that enable it to "minimize risks, protect against any downside, and thereby amplify the upside."[D] Control of the board of directors allows VCs to replace management, set priorities, and make major business decisions.

The point is, that as important as the valuation is for any investor, VCs can give ground on one if they secure rights that will retroactively reset the deal if performance fails to meet their expectations.

One might say that VCs negotiate the appearance of a valuation when they invest, rather than the actual valuation.

The illusory quality of a VC valuation is reported on in a March 2015 *Bloomberg* article titled "The Fuzzy, Insane Math That's Creating So Many Billion-Dollar Tech Companies," which is excerpted below. [Bold added for emphasis]

> Snapchat, the photo-messaging app raising cash at a $15 billion valuation, probably isn't worth more than Clorox or Campbell Soup. So where did investors come up with that enormous headline number?
>
> **Here's the secret to how Silicon Valley calculates the value of its hottest companies: The numbers are sort of made-up.** For the most mature startups, investors agree to grant higher valuations, which help the companies with recruitment and building credibility, in exchange for guarantees that they'll get their money back first if the company goes public or sells. They can also negotiate to receive additional free shares if a subsequent round's valuation is less favorable. Interviews with more than a dozen founders, venture capitalists, and the attorneys who draw up investment contracts reveal **the most common financial provisions used in private-market technology deals today.**
>
> The backroom agreements are becoming more common as tech companies stay private longer, according to the interviews and financial documents obtained by "Bloomberg Business." The practice **obfuscates the meaning of a valuation, which can become dangerous down the road because private investors aren't taking the same risks a public-market shareholder would.**
>
> Some VCs defend the practice by saying valuations are just a placeholder number, part of an equation fueled by other, more important factors. Those can include market share, growth projections and a founder's ego. The number is typically set by the company and negotiated alongside various provisions designed to protect a new backer's money. That often comes at the expense of employee shareholders and earlier investors, whose holdings are diluted to make room for new entrants.
>
> "These big numbers almost don't matter," says Randy Komisar, a partner at venture firm Kleiner Perkins Caufield & Byers. **"Those numbers are just a middling shot at a valuation, and then it's adjusted later"** through various legal techniques, if an earlier valuation was too high, he says.
>
> A founder often starts off with a number in mind, based on the startup's last valuation, the valuations of competitors, and, for good measure, the valuation of the company's neighbor down the street. It can become a sort of arms race.
>
> Startups [have] all sorts of provisions [in their financing documents] that reward investors for accepting these mega-valuations. The practice is more regular and egregious in financing rounds for mature companies. Their capital requirements tend to be much larger, so they must turn to more sophisticated investment firms that demand these kinds of terms. Startups that are generous with these guarantees can garner much higher valuations.[E]

Ways to Defer a Valuation of Startups

There are two ways that startups use to kick the proverbial valuation can down the road that merit mention—convertible promissory notes and a peculiar investment structure know as a SAFE or a KISS.

A convertible note is a loan that gives the lender the option to be repaid or convert to stock. That is, an investor invests as a creditor who has the option to become a shareholder. Generally, the price of the stock at conversion is a discount from what it is then being sold at—say twenty to thirty percent less—because the money was provided earlier. Convertible notes are a popular way to structure an investment without establishing a valuation—rather than set it at the time of investment, it is based on what the Next Guy gets. [The Next Guy theory of valuation is in Chapter 5, "The Problem With a Conventional Capital Structure."] Noteholders that do not convert remain creditors, with the right to sue if they are not repaid. Often, noteholders have a security interest in the company's assets, which gives them the ability to obstruct their sale. Convertible notes are not relevant for average investors, so there is no need to delve into them further. Companies that are considering them will find a 2015 *Xconomy* article, "Seven Surprises About Convertible Notes That Founders Should Know" by James Geshwiler of interest.**F**

A less established way to defer a valuation for an equity investment is called a Simple Agreement for Future Equity, which goes by the acronym SAFE, even though it's not "safe," or a similar vehicle called a Keep It Simple Security, which goes by KISS for short. With each, the investor's money is like a non-refundable deposit on a future equity position—the price is not set at the time of investment. Like a convertible note, the price will be based on what future equity is priced at. Unlike a loan, the company need not be obligated to pay it back.

A SAFE or a KISS are forward contracts, agreements to deliver shares in the future if a funding event occurs—typically an equity investment by a VC. If a VC doesn't invest, the investor might not get anything—no stock or repayment. So, investors in such an instrument should be prepared to kiss their money away since their investment isn't safe.

Convertible notes, SAFE and KISS investments encourage an equity-oriented investor to invest by deferring a valuation until the Next Guy invests—here, a VC. And VCs use a modified conventional capital structure to protect themselves from overpaying, based on the valuation their Next Guy gets.

So it goes—until IPO investors buy in. The dynamics change then, however, as described in Chapter 5, "The Problem with a Conventional Capital Structure."

Valuation of Sustainable Companies

There is growing interest in so-called sustainable economies and companies. There may not be a common, practical definition of what constitutes a sustainable, socially responsible company, but those that aspire to be one seek investors who have non-traditional perspectives on valuation.

New phrases have entered the vernacular of financial markets such as "socially responsible investing," "impact investing," "conscious capitalism," "circular economy," and "Environmental, Social and Governance" or ESG for short. All are expressions of interest in alternatives to the idea that a corporation's principal responsibility is to maximize shareholder wealth. It is a significant and growing movement.

How might being socially responsible affect a company's valuation? Will it drive it higher because investors will pay a premium for a company that aspires to do good? Or, will it suppress it because social, nonfinancial considerations are given weight in corporate governance?

The breadth and scope of interest in this sector suggests that a socially responsible focus can help a company attract capital. That said, it is too early to suggest what its impact on valuation may be. I suspect that its strongest effect will be on customers. The cachet can translate into greater sales and higher margins. If it does, that will attract investors and higher valuations. In other words, being socially responsible may be more about defining a customer brand than an investor valuation.

The Fairshare Model provides a rich platform for investors and entrepreneurs as they get creative with capitalism because achievement of social good can be a trigger for Performance Stock conversion. The challenge is to define what that performance is and how to measure it.

Thoughts on how to define and apply alternative measures of value are being developed. The United Kingdom government has a publication, *A Guide to Social Return on Investment (SROI)*, which explores how to determine a SROI for investors.[G] It identifies six stages to establish a community-centric valuation:

1. Establish scope and identify stakeholders.
2. Map target outcomes.
3. Define what constitutes evidence of the outcomes and what each is worth.
4. Establish impact of meeting target.
5. Calculate the SROI.
6. Communicate the SROI to stakeholders and embed the measurement and monitoring of it within the organization.

The Seven Principles of Social Return on Investment

1. Involve stakeholders
2. Understand what changes
3. Value the things that matter
4. Only include what is material
5. Do not over-claim
6. Be transparent
7. Verify the result

Source: *A Guide to Social Return on Investment*

What's the *Microeconomic* Harm of Getting Valuation Wrong?

What is the harm of accepting a valuation that is too high? From an investor perspective, it reduces the likelihood of a future return. Less obvious is that entrepreneurs face challenges when they raise capital at an excessive valuation.

John Huston, founder of Ohio Tech Angels, describes why in a video that used to be on an angel investor website, Gust.com.

> If I [John Huston] think back over the greatest ideas I've seen that have gone "splat" and were never really brought to market, it's because they fumbled the funding plan.

> The most prevalent way they've done that is that they go out to raise the most money at the highest valuation, and they take checks from "mullets," as we call them, who are just hobbyist angels who don't know what the current market valuation is, they don't know about terms and conditions. And if an inadequate amount of capital is raised to take out the risk to justify the valuation that they raised the money on, by definition, the next round [of capital will be] a "down round." If you are an angel investor who sees a deal or two a day, why would you look at a down round?

A down round occurs when a private company raises capital at a lower pre-money valuation than the prior post-money valuation, which suggests it was overvalued earlier or that it failed to perform as expected. Rumors of weakness float about when a down round takes place. A company loses its shine in the eyes of its shareholders; confidence in management diminishes. If the exercise price of stock option grants are re-priced to a lower value, it fosters a sense that the pain of the overvaluation is borne only by early investors, not the employees.

A down round only applies to a private company because shareholders lack the ability to sell their shares before a lower valuation is set. When a public company raises capital below its IPO post-money valuation, it isn't called a down round because shareholders can sell their shares anytime.

In any case, Huston's point applies whether a company is private or public. If a company is overvalued, there is an eventual price to pay.

> "We don't know if we're investors until the exit occurs—until then we're merely donors."
>
> – John Huston,
> speaking at the 2013
> Angel Capital Association Summit
> in San Francisco, California

> "He who lives by the crystal ball will eat shattered glass."
>
> – Ray Dalio, *Principles: Life and Work*

What's the *Macroeconomic* Harm of Getting Valuation Wrong?

There is a broad harm that can result from valuation unawareness—it fuels asset valuation bubbles that wreak havoc. There is a long history of these occurring, as explained in the PBS *Nova* program, "Mind Over Money: Can markets be rational when humans aren't?" Here is an excerpt from it.[H]

> The first financial bubble involved something highly unlikely.

> **Justin Fox (Harvard Business Review):** In the 1630s, in the Netherlands, people were buying and selling tulip bulbs...complete, mass insanity in Holland, for a couple of years there, where hundreds of people, artisans, would leave their workshops and set up

business as "florists," they called themselves, although, for the most part, they were tulip bulb traders. And it was a real financial market.

Robert Shiller (Yale University): The price of tulips in Holland rose to such a level that the value of one tulip bulb would sometimes be that of an entire house.

Narrator: Over a three-year period, the price of tulip bulbs rose and rose, and then began to soar. By some accounts, almost half of all the money in the Dutch economy was caught up in trades involving tulips.

Fox: To a lot of historians, this is really the first example of a financial bubble, even though it was, basically, tulips.

Shiller: People were buying them, not primarily because they liked tulips, but they were buying them because they thought that the price was going up, and they could resell them to someone else at a higher price.

Narrator: On February 5, 1637, the most expensive bulb in Holland failed to sell, and tulip investors panicked.

Shiller: Then it burst, because prices start falling. And then they're falling more, and then you start thinking, "You know, I remember I doubted that tulips could possibly be worth so much. Maybe I better get out fast." And then everyone starts dumping, and then it just drops.

Narrator: As the prices plunged, leading citizens found themselves bankrupt. Some historians estimate it took a generation for the Dutch economy to recover. There have been many bubbles and crashes since, but the most famous happened closer to home.

The year 1929 began with optimism. Stock prices had been rising for eight years, and in '29 they were soaring.

Fox: The 1920s was a great decade economically. The economy was booming, industry was booming, and toward the latter part of the decade, financial markets just sort of went from reflecting that boom to, kind of, creating it. It was just boom times all over. By the late 1920s, there was just this feeling of a new era.

Narrator: Observers described feverish emotions, as thousands of investors paid ever-higher prices for stocks.

Shiller: In the so-called "Roaring '20s" the stock market went through an enormous bubble; people thought it would never end.

Narrator: But then, on October 29th, prices suddenly dropped, and the mood turned to one of panic and fear. Over 9,000 American banks failed, wiping out the life savings of millions.

Shiller: It led to a depression that lasted over 10 years.

More recently, there were the dotcom and telecom bubbles in the 1990s. Investors saw IPOs from young companies that promised to transform facets of life. Many had questionable prospects but went up in price anyway. The accelerant for this hot market was that many public investors were unfamiliar with valuation and how to evaluate one.

Now, valuation awareness does not, in and of itself, prevent bubbles. Investors may be valuation aware but be unsure about how to evaluate one. Or, they may decide that FOMO–*Fear Of Missing Out*–trumps prudence. When enough people share this sense, bubbles grow, until they bust. It's a cycle we've seen for generations in securities and real estate.

Cheerleaders are the handmaidens of bubbles because they promote ways to rationalize hard-to-explain valuations. As mentioned earlier, internet company valuations were justified in the 1990s based on their website traffic and what they spent on marketing. These notions influenced how other capital-hungry companies thought about how to operate. The CEO of a small public company told me that he would attract investors by spending heavily on marketing–he was later fired.

Valuations of venture-backed startups have been blossoming in recent years and cheerleaders are evident. For example, in an August 2014 opinion piece in the *Wall Street Journal*, the CEO of a business valuation firm, asserts that: [I]

- The majority of startups and small businesses are not overvalued,

- It is the startups that create new markets that can ask for larger premiums,

- We should do more to create new companies and not worry as much if the companies being created are overvalued or not. As a country, we should focus on helping them have better knowledge and access to capital.

Tellingly, this view is advanced by someone whose firm charges companies to opine on what they are worth. Similarly, arguments advanced about eyeballs or marketing expense were made by analysts affiliated with the underwriters of the companies they rationalized high value for.

Strikingly, the author of this article presumes future performance and deems it valuable enough to command a premium when the company plans to create a new market. Put another way, *if no one has done what a company hopes to do, it is worth more!*

The most provocative part of this valuation expert's argument is that *we should not be much concerned if companies appear to be overvalued–just make it easier for them to raise capital!*

Opposing perspectives come to mind when I contemplate that op-ed. On the positive side, an entrepreneurial culture thrives when capital is available on attractive terms, and such a culture feeds an innovative economy. So, yes, we need to improve access to capital, as the author suggests. On the negative side, yikes! Do we not learn from history? Are we destined to repeatedly relive boom-bust cycles?

Economist Hyman Minsky considered this question and concluded that financial markets are inherently vulnerable to them. Early in 2008, before the downturn was called the Great Recession, *The New Yorker* summarized Minsky's financial-instability hypothesis this way: [J]

> [In the early 1980s,] when most economists were extolling the virtues of financial deregulation and innovation, a maverick named Hyman P. Minsky maintained a more negative view of Wall Street; in fact, he noted that bankers, traders, and other financiers periodically played the role of arsonists, setting the entire economy ablaze. Wall Street encouraged businesses and individuals to take on too much risk, he believed, generating ruinous boom-and-bust cycles.
>
> Many of Minsky's colleagues regarded his 'financial-instability hypothesis,' which he first developed in the nineteen-sixties, as radical, if not crackpot. There are basically five stages in Minsky's model of the credit cycle: displacement, boom, euphoria, profit taking, and panic.

A displacement occurs when investors get excited about something—an invention, such as the internet, or a war, or an abrupt change of economic policy.

As a boom leads to euphoria, Minsky said, banks and other commercial lenders extend credit to ever more dubious borrowers, often creating new financial instruments to do the job. During the nineteen-eighties, junk bonds played that role. More recently, it was the securitization of mortgages, which enabled banks to provide home loans without worrying if they would ever be repaid. Then, at the top of the market, some smart traders start to cash in their profits. The onset of panic is usually heralded by a dramatic effect.

Contrary to what that CEO of a valuation firm wrote in his *WSJ* article, there is reason to believe that venture-stage companies are overvalued, and, that the combination of cheerleaders, valuation unsavvy investors, and FOMO are a recipe for a boom-bust cycle.

This tempers my enthusiasm for equity crowdfunding, as it is popularly defined, especially when a conventional capital structure is used. Not because investors will lose money—that cannot be avoided with companies that have high failure risk. *What bothers me is that public investors will incur far more valuation risk than private investors do. That's because investors in a conventional IPO don't get the price protection that VCs do. Plus, they invest at much higher valuations.*

Venture-stage investing is like roulette. The more numbers you place bets on, the more likely you are to have a winner. It is easy to lose one's head betting. But one is less likely to be harmed if the chips are inexpensive (i.e., valuations are low).

The overall harm of getting valuations wrong is that it encourages speculation that leads to boom-bust cycles. Speculation that supports adventurism—more bets—is desirable because it supports innovation. The trick is to encourage adventurism with realistic valuations. Thus, I like equity crowdfunding—provided public investors get the type of deal a VC gets.

Why Is a Valuation Necessary?

Why is it necessary to set a valuation? Can't people just provide the money a company needs and reward employees when they perform well as a team? Such questions may come to mind to readers unfamiliar with capital structures.

The answer rests on what someone wants from a company in exchange for their money. If it is an ownership interest, a valuation establishes what it is, relative to the interests of others. If no ownership interest is provided, no valuation is needed. Thus, no valuation is needed for a loan or a gift.

The Fairshare Model addresses valuation differently than a conventional capital structure because:

- It decouples ownership interests from voting rights, and
- It places no value on undelivered performance.

A pre-money valuation is required for a Fairshare Model IPO, but it will be relatively cheap if a rise in the market capitalization is a basis for conversion of Performance Stock.

Summation

The smartest people in the room have trouble with valuation whether a company is a startup or established. For this reason, even if you are new to this subject, there are two questions you can ask of anyone who is raising money for a company that will make you appear to be an incisive questioner–even if you are not! For fun, ask, "What is the valuation?" You may sense discomfort in their expression. It will magnify when you ask the follow-up question: "Why does that valuation make sense?"

Venture-stage companies are particularly difficult to value. Nonetheless, the beast known as a conventional capital structure demands a valuation of future performance at the time an equity investment is made. The question for financial professionals is, how will valuation theory change if the villagers–public investors–realize that they don't have to feed the beast? That, like VCs, they can demand deal terms that reduce valuation risk, and thereby increase the odds that they will make money.

What's Next?

We next look at how to calculate a company's valuation: the mechanics.

Chapter Endnotes

Contextual references for material in this chapter appear as numbered footnotes on the page where the reference is made. **Source references** for material in this chapter appear below as endnotes with capital letter identifiers.

A Sivers, Derek. "Ideas are just a multiplier of execution." *Sivers.org*. August 16, 2005. Accessed October 17, 2016. fairsharemodel.com/Sivers.

B Reed, Stanley Foster., and Lane Edson P. C. *The Art of M & A: A Merger Acquisition Buyout Guide*. Homewood, IL: Dow Jones-Irwin, 1989. page 63.

C Bernstein, Peter L. *Capital Ideas: The Improbable Origins of Modern Wall Street*. Hoboken, NJ: John Wiley & Sons, 2006. page 158.

D Ramsinghani, Mahendra. *The Business of Venture Capital: Insights from Leading Practitioners on the Art of Raising a Fund, Deal Structuring, Value Creation, and Exit Strategies*. Hoboken, NJ: Wiley, 2011. page 230.

E Frier, Sarah, and Eric Newcomer. "The Fuzzy, Insane Math That's Creating So Many Billion-Dollar Tech Companies." *Bloomberg.com*. March 17, 2015. Accessed May 09, 2018. fairsharemodel.com/Fuzzy.

F Geshwiler, James. "Seven Surprises About Convertible Notes That Founders Should Know." *Xconomy*. January 12, 2015. Accessed August 03, 2018. fairsharemodel.com/Cnotes.

G Nicholls, Jeremy, Eilis Lawlor, and Tim Goodspeed. "A Guide to Social Return on Investment." *U.K. Cabinet Office: Third Sector*. Accessed May 9, 2018. fairsharemodel.com/SROI.

H "Mind Over Money." PBS *Nova* episode. April 26, 2010. Accessed May 09, 2018. fairsharemodel.com/NovaMindMoney.

I Carter, Michael. "A Look at Startup Valuations Then and Now." *The Wall Street Journal*. August 29, 2014. Accessed May 09, 2018. fairsharemodel.com/StartupValuations.

J Cassidy, John. "The Minsky Moment." *The New Yorker*. February 4, 2008. Accessed May 10, 2018. fairsharemodel.com/Minsky.

Chapter 14:

Calculating Valuation

What's Included in This Chapter

- Introduction
- Pre-Money vs. Post-Money Valuation
- Calculating Valuation – Share Method
- Calculating Valuation – Percentage Method
- Valuation Is Not Intuitive
- Price Per Share Is Not Valuation
- Valuation – Primary and Fully-Diluted Shares
- Valuation Calculation Using the Fairshare Model
- What's Next?
- Chapter Endnotes

Introduction

This chapter explains how to calculate a company's valuation.

Pre-Money vs. Post-Money Valuation

"Valuation" is a slippery word because it can be understood to mean something different, depending on the context. The last chapter opened with some points to keep in mind when contemplating valuation issues. The most important one is that valuation is price, and that price is not necessarily worth. That's an idea that makes sense even if you don't know how to calculate a valuation.

If you are going to calculate or evaluate one, it is similarly important to be mindful of the difference between a company's pre-money and post-money valuation. The difference is the money–the amount raised in the offering. But there is also a difference in relevance–for investors, the pre-money valuation is the one that is important.

To help make the distinction between pre-money and post-money valuation clear, imagine a pair of pants offered for $20. You put $20 in the pants pocket. What is the value of the pants?

	Value
Price of the pants	$20
Money that you put in the pants pocket	$20
Value of pants with your money	$40

The first thing that you ask yourself is, "When?" Before or after you put your money in the pocket? The $20 price is the analog of "pre-money valuation." The $20 that you put in the pants pocket is the "money" and the $40 is the "post-money valuation."

- The pants are worth $40 after your $20 is in the pocket…*if the pants are worth $20 to begin with.*

- If the pants are only worth $15 before the money (i.e., they are overpriced, not worth $20), they are worth $35 now.

- If the pants are worth $25 before the money (i.e., they are underpriced, a good deal, at $20), they are worth $45 now.

So the answer to the question—What is the value of the pair of pants?—depends on the context. Before or after the money? Also, **the important figure is the pre-money valuation**—what the pants are worth *before* your money is put in the pocket. That is true for companies too.

With that analogy in mind, let's return to the example in Chapter 8, "The Tao of the Fairshare Model," where a company raises $5 million from investors in exchange for half the ownership. The parties agree that the company's pre-money valuation is $5 million. The table below summarizes the deal. The post-money valuation of $10 million is equivalent to the value of the pants *with your money*. As with the pants, the figure to focus on is the pre-money valuation. The question: is the company worth $5 million before the $5 million is raised from investors?

	Valuation	Ownership
Pre-Money Valuation (Employees)	$5 million	50%
Money (New Investors)	$5 million	50%
Post-Money Valuation (Combined)	$10 million	100%

This chapter answers the question: "How does one *calculate* the pre-money valuation?" Or, in the example, "How can you tell that the pre-money valuation is $5 million?" It makes no judgment about whether the amount is high, low, or reasonable.

Calculating the pre-money valuation is a mechanical process. All you need is a formula, a calculator, and a few moments. Evaluating the attractiveness of a pre-money valuation is a complex matter; the next chapter discusses that.

There are two ways to calculate a valuation—the share method or the percentage method.

Calculating Valuation – Share Method

This is the formula to calculate a pre-money valuation using the outstanding shares method.

PreMoney Valuation	=	Number of Shares Outstanding Before the Offering	X	Price of a New Share

If a company has 10 million shares outstanding before an offering and plans to sell new shares for $1, its pre-money valuation is $10 million. It doesn't matter how many new shares are offered, its pre-money valuation is $10 million. What matters is the number of shares outstanding before the offering and the price of a new share.

Let's apply this formula to a fresh example. ABC Company has 10 million shares outstanding and plans to raise $5 million. To do so, it decides to issue 1 million new shares at $5 per share. With these terms, ABC gives itself a $50 million valuation (e.g., 10 million shares X $5).

ABC Company's Pre-Money Valuation Using Share Method				
PreMoney Valuation	=	Number of Shares Outstanding Before the Offering	X	Price of a New Share
$50 Million	=	10 Million Shares	X	$5 per share

Here is the relationship between ABC's pre-money and post-money valuation.

ABC Company's Pre-and Post-Money Valuation	
$50 Million	Pre-money valuation (10 million shares x $5 per share)
+ $5 Million	Money raised in the offering (1 million shares X $5 per share)
$55 Million	Post-money valuation (11 million shares X $5 per share)

After the offering, if someone sells a share of ABC stock for $6, or $1 higher than the offering price, the company's valuation—its market capitalization—will rise from $55 million to $66 million (11 million shares X $6).

Conversely, if the most recent share price is $4, ABC's valuation falls to $44 million (11 million shares X $4).

Whether a company is privately held or publicly traded, the calculation assumes that stock is sold at market value and that the most recent price is the value of all the other shares. Thus, it is presumably what someone would pay to buy the entire company.

Calculating Valuation – Percentage Method

You can also calculate the pre-money valuation if you know the percentage of the company that the money buys. The formula is:

$$\text{Pre-Money Valuation} = \left(\frac{\text{Investment Amount}}{\text{Percentage of the Company Bought}} \right) - \text{Investment Amount}$$

As you'll see in a moment, it is nothing more than a variation of the simple formula you've seen. Stepwise, first calculate the post-money valuation. That is what you get by dividing the investment amount by the percentage of the company the money buys.

$$\text{Post-Money Valuation} = \frac{\text{Investment Amount}}{\text{Percentage of the Company Bought}}$$

Let's apply this to a fresh example. Say that 10 percent of XYZ Company is offered for $10 million. What is the pre-money valuation? First, calculate the post-money valuation, so, divide $10 million by 10 percent. The result is a post-money valuation of $100 million.

$$\$100,000,000 \text{ [XYZ's Post-Money Valuation]} = \frac{\$10,000,000 \text{ Investment}}{0.010 \text{ [10\% of XYZ]}}$$

The second step is to subtract the amount of the new investment from the post-money valuation. That is the pre-money valuation.

$$\text{Post-Money Valuation} - \text{Investment Amount (Money)} = \text{Pre-Money Valuation}$$

To calculate XYZ's pre-money valuation, subtract the $10 million investment from the $100 million post-money valuation. The result is its pre-money valuation, $90 million.

$$\underset{\text{[XYZ's Post-Money Valuation]}}{\$100,000,000} - \underset{\text{Investment}}{\$10,000,000} = \underset{\text{[XYZ's Pre-Money Valuation)}}{\$90,000,000}$$

You can prove that $90 million is the pre-money valuation because $10 million buys 10 percent of XYZ: $10 million is 10 percent of the $100 million post-money valuation.

XYZ Company	Valuation	Ownership
Pre-Money Valuation	$90 million	90%
Money	$10 million	10%
Post-Money Valuation	$100 million	100%

Valuation Is Not Intuitive

Unless you are a math whiz, you'll need a calculator to compute valuation, particularly using the percentage method. If you think you can eyeball it, be careful. To understand why, consider how the pre-money valuation changes as the percentage of ownership that new investors get changes.

The table below shows that a pre-money valuation climbs as the percentage of the company retained by insiders grows and, conversely, how it falls as the percentage sold to new investors grows. Also, that the pre-money valuation changes in a non-linear manner as the percentage changes. Here we have the valuation range of XYZ Company, the one we just calculated the $90 million pre-money valuation for, given that $10 million buys 10 percent of the company. Its pre-money valuation is presented at multiple points, ranging from 1 to 100 percent, assuming $10 million is raised.

Valuation is Non-Linear
Assume Investment is $10 Million
As the Percentage of Company the Investment Held by Insiders Falls, the Pre-Money Valuation Falls

Percentage to Insiders	99%	90%	80%	70%	60%	50%	40%	30%	20%	10%	0%
Percentage to New Investors	1%	10%	20%	30%	40%	50%	60%	70%	80%	90%	100%
Pre-Money Valuation	$990M	$90M	$40M	$23M	$15M	$10M	$7M	$4M	$3M	$1M	$0M
+ Money Investment	10M	$10M	$10M	$10M	$10M	$10M	$10M	$10M	$10M	$10M	$10M
= Post-Money Valuation	$1,000M	$100M	$50M	$33M	$25M	$20M	$17M	$14M	$13M	$11M	$10M

The first column shows that if 1 percent is sold for $10 million—99 percent of the company is retained by insiders—its pre-money valuation is $990 million and its post-money valuation is $1,000 million or $1 billion. The column on the far right shows that its pre-money valuation is zero if insiders get nothing—the post-money value is the amount of the new money. Between these extremes, pre-money valuations appear for deciles of ownership percentages—10%, 20%, 30%, etc.

Look at the second column, where 10 percent of the company is sold for $10 million—90 percent is held by insiders. The pre-money valuation is $90 million and the post-money valuation is $100 million, just as calculated on the prior page.

Compare that to the third column, to see what happens to the pre-money valuation when the percentage purchased by new investors doubles, from 10 to 20 precent—it falls disproportionately, from $90 million to $40 million.

Let's double the ownership to investors again—look at the column where 40 percent is purchased and compare it to the 20 percent column. Again, the change in pre-money valuation is disproportionate. The ownership percentage doubles, but the pre-money valuation is not halved—it goes from $40 million to $15 million.

Do it again. Double the percentage of the company purchased for $10 million from 40 percent to 80 percent. Just as before, the inverse change in the pre-money valuation is disproportionate, it drops from $15 million to $3 million.

> The appendix has tables that show the pre-money valuation for a range of investment amounts and percentages of the company purchased. Check out how a change in one variable affects the pre-money valuation. Also, an Excel workbook that will calculate pre-money valuation using variables you enter is available for download at fairsharemodel.com/resources.

Could you calculate these pre-money valuations in your head? Most people need a calculator.

A takeaway point from the valuation tables in the appendix is that when half a company is offered, the pre-money valuation is equal to the investment. For example, if half the company is sold for $5 million, its pre-money valuation is $5 million. If half is sold for $20 million, the pre-money valuation is $20 million. If half is sold for $30 million, the pre-money valuation is $30 million and so on.

Another takeaway is that, for the most part, valuation is not intuitive—it needs to be calculated. The following chart shows why. It illustrates the non-linear relationship between the pre-money valuation, and the percentage of the company sold for a given amount of money.

The chart assumes the investment amount is $10 million. On the low end, if it buys 1 percent of the company, the post-money valuation is $1 billion and the pre-money valuation is $990 million. On the high end, if it buys the entire company, the post-money valuation is $10 million and the pre-money valuation is zero. If it buys half the company, the post-money valuation is $20 million and the pre-money valuation is $10 million, the same as the investment.

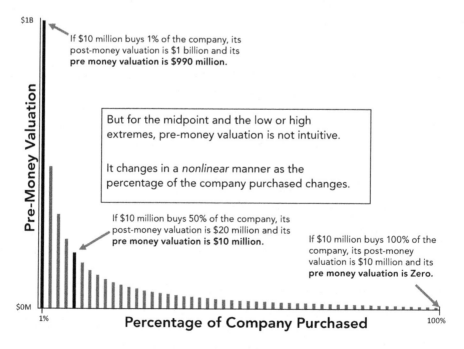

The curve is the same for any other amount of investment.

Price Per Share Is Not Valuation

Valuation or market capitalization is the number of shares outstanding multiplied by the current share price. That means an increase in the number of shares outstanding will increase the valuation unless there is an offsetting drop in the share price.

Valuation is a quintessential measure but many people focus on half of what determines it–share price. Stock price behavior after a stock split suggests this is true. For example, a two-for-one stock split gives shareholders two shares in exchange for each one they own. In a rational market, the post-split stock would trade at half pre-split price; after all, it's the same company with twice as many shares. When splits occur, however, it is not unusual to see the price climb without rational reason.

IPO pricing also suggests that many investors focus on share price. Valuation is often not disclosed– the subject of the next chapter–while share prices are tailored to fit into the equivalent of a baseball strike zone, between $14 and $18 per share. Psychology influences this, just as it does in retail pricing of consumer products.[A] For instance, items sell better if priced at $19.95 instead of $20.00 or $20.05. To be in this zone and in order to hit a valuation target, issuers will adjust the number of their shares outstanding.

In addition to psychology, stock marketers utilize razzle-dazzle. There is also the influence of others, be they trusted cohorts or simply voices one is exposed to. Two factors determine how persuasive such things are: whether the product has utility, and how valuation-savvy the potential buyer is.

Items with utility can be eaten, worn, or otherwise used–examples include food, clothing, and transport. Buyers tend to be valuation-savvy about these because they have experience with them and, significantly, sellers compete by offering better deals. Nonetheless, razzle-dazzle and the influence of others can persuade many buyers, even valuation-savvy ones, to overpay.

Items that lack utility, like stocks, cannot be used or consumed. Three factors make it likely that someone will overpay for one:

1. Buyers don't purchase them often.
2. Intrinsic value is hard to discern.
3. Sellers avoid competition based on valuation.

Buyers who don't calculate a valuation, or understand its significance, are very vulnerable to razzle-dazzle and the influence of others. Weirdly, they can influence markets more than valuation-savvy ones do. The effect depends on the stock involved. If the company is established and has significant trading volume, investors are less likely to overpay. The opposite is true if the issuer is venture-stage, newly public, or thinly traded.[1]

> The market can stay irrational longer than you can stay solvent.
>
> –Wall Street wisdom

---

[1] "Thinly traded" refers to securities that cannot be easily sold or exchanged for cash without a significant change in price. They have low trading volumes because there are few buyers and sellers for them. Their price, therefore, is subject to volatile change when a transaction is for more than a nominal number of shares. To trade on a major exchange, a stock must meet the minimum trading volume set by the exchange.

Valuation – Primary and Fully-Diluted Shares

Valuation calculations focus on shares that are outstanding–those held by investors and employees. Complications are introduced when a company is committed to issuing additional shares in the future. For instance, the holders of convertible promissory notes have the right to convert what they are owed into stock. Stock warrants and employee stock options can also cause additional shares to be issued.

> Stock warrants are like stock options, but for non-employees–usually investors and creditors. Both grant the right to buy shares at a preset price in the future. Sometimes, the warrant exercise price is higher than the value of the stock when it is granted. In contrast, the exercise price for a stock option is at or below the stock price when granted. Chapter 22, "Blockchain and Initial Coin Offerings," explains warrants further.

These are examples of contingently issuable shares or share equivalents–stock that is not outstanding but might be construed to be. When a company reports its earnings per share, there are two measures: "primary" and "fully diluted."[2] Primary EPS is the earnings for the period divided by the average number of shares outstanding during that period. Fully-diluted EPS is the same calculation except that the denominator adds shares that may be issued, per the company's agreements.

There is no uniform answer for how to deal with contingently issuable shares when calculating valuation.

- Some investors ignore contingently issuable shares or selectively include them.
- There are public stock investors who use only issued shares to calculate the valuation and focus on the shares available to trade–the "float." They ignore unissued shares because they will not affect the near-term trading market.
- Investors negotiating a hard deal have been known to include all contingently issuable shares in the valuation they accept. For example, they treat stock that could be issued in the future from the exercise of stock options and warrants as already issued. That causes the dilution that will result from exercise to be absorbed by other shareholders.
- VCs sometimes include *unissued* employee stock options in the valuation they negotiate. These are shares that are not yet contingently issuable because no agreement to do so has been formed. When this happens, a VC effectively says to other shareholders "all dilution that will result from a new option plan to motivate employees will come out of your share of ownership." This provides the VC with a sweeter deal–a lower valuation.

A deeper dive into contingently issuable securities is beyond the scope of this book. Once significant investor interest is expressed in the Fairshare Model, this will be a topic of discussion for those involved in financial reporting.

---

2 "As converted" is a scenario for defining outstanding shares when there is debt that can convert to shares in the future. Typically, investors assess private companies on this basis as well; it falls between actual shares outstanding and fully-diluted shares. It's unlikely to be relevant in the Fairshare Model. Pre-IPO investors will most certainly prefer to convert their debt to tradable Investor Stock.

Valuation Calculation Using the Fairshare Model

In the Fairshare Model, an exceptionally large block of Performance Stock is outstanding at the IPO. For example, if there are one million shares of Investor Stock outstanding after the IPO, there could be ten or twenty million shares of Performance Stock. Why such a high ratio of Performance Stock to Investor Stock? The Performance Stock is to motivate performance for many years, say a decade. Plus, it may be impractical to issue new Performance Stock after the IPO for tax or other reasons.

The number of Performance Stock shares outstanding is unimportant if the IPO is structured as described in this book. That's because Performance Stock is capped at 50 percent of the total vote. Regarding dilution of Investor Stock, what matters are the conversion rules, not the total number of shares of Performance Stock. To illustrate that, imagine a dam holding back a body of water, which represents Performance Stock. From the perspective of the town below the dam–the Investor Stock, in this analogy–it doesn't matter how much water is behind the dam. What matters is the release rate.

How much Performance Stock will convert? That depends on the company's performance, the conversion rules established by the two classes of shareholders and the terms that are agreed to in any acquisition. Broadly speaking, it is likely that some of it will convert, but not all of it.

When calculating pre-money valuation, I believe that Performance Stock should be excluded from the basic valuation calculation based on primary or issued shares because they can never trade, and any liquidation preference it has is *de minimis*–or trivial–value. For a fully-diluted valuation calculation, one may want to assume Performance Stock conversions, but an estimate of the value of the performance associated with those conversions ought to be considered too.

This is a complex topic in which expert opinions may vary. The issues are arcane to my target audience, many of whom are not focused on valuation. What they care about, I believe, is how to make it possible for *middle-class investors to make venture capital investments on terms comparable to those that professional investors get.* That's the prize that all eyes should be set on.

What's Next?

If you know a company's valuation, how do you evaluate it? How do you identify what is reasonable? What's a deal? What's out of line?

Chapter Endnotes

Contextual references for material in this chapter appear as numbered footnotes on the page where the reference is made. **Source references** for material in this chapter appear below as endnotes with capital letter identifiers.

A In his 1957 book, *The Hidden Persuaders,* Vance Packard compared the use of motivational research and other psychological techniques to "the chilling world of George Orwell and his Big Brother." Severo, Richard. "Vance Packard, 82, Challenger of Consumerism, Dies." *The New York Times.* December 13, 1996. Accessed May 10, 2018. fairsharemodel.com/Packard.

Chapter 15:

Evaluating Valuation

What's Included in This Chapter

- Introduction
- It's in the Eye of the Beholder
- The Next Guy Theory Tells You All You Need to Know
- Is There an Intrinsic Value?
- How Valuation Experts Approach Valuation
- Weakness of Approaches Used by Valuation Experts
- Rules of Thumb
- Non-Quantifiable Factors – the Power of Love, Reputation, and Charisma
- Quantifiable Factors for Evaluating Valuation
- How VCs Evaluate a Valuation
- How Angel Investors Evaluate a Valuation
- Valuation Evaluation – As Seen on TV!
- How Private Equity Investors Evaluate a Valuation
- Evaluating the Valuation of a Company that Uses the Fairshare Model
- Summation
- What's Next?
- Chapter Endnotes

Introduction

To get a sense of whether stock market valuations are attractive overall, Warren Buffett, the world's most famous investor, compares the value of a country's stock market to its annual economic output. If the stock market value exceeds 100 percent of the gross domestic product or GDP, he feels the market is overvalued. If it is less than 50 percent, it is undervalued. He said, "It is probably the best single measure of where valuations stand at any given moment."[A]

Buffett favors established companies with a history of profitable operations, but his comment begs a question. Might there be a similar rule for venture-stage investors? A Goldilocks-like one that helps them assess whether the valuation that a company gives itself is high, low, or, just about right?

That question summons yet another; if there has been no performance, is the company worth anything at all? This chapter provides an overview of approaches for assessing a valuation.

It's in the Eye of the Beholder

Value, like art, is a concept, especially if the object has little utility. It is more in the eye of the beholder than an objective measure. In addressing *the difference between price and value*, Peter Bernstein, author of *Capital Ideas*, put it the following way [bold added for emphasis]:[B]

> From Adam Smith, the eighteenth-century author of *The Wealth of Nations*, all the great economists have wrestled with this problem in one form or another; it plays a central role in Karl Marx's model of capitalism.

> Economists agree that "value" refers to something that lies behind, or beneath, the prices observed in the marketplace; prices gyrate around "true value." But what is "true value?"

> The question is not unlike the exchange between three baseball umpires trying to describe how they distinguish between a ball and a strike. "I call them as I see them," said the first. "I call them as they are," replied the second. "They ain't nothing till I call them," declared the third.

> **Is value a subjective quantity? Or is it a quality that cannot be measured except by some objective standard? Or does value emerge only when a transaction takes place in which buyers and sellers agree on a price?**

> The reason stock prices jump around so much, and the reason stocks are considered such a risky investment, is that there is nothing clear-cut about their value. Is [General Motors] worth $50 a share because the accountants, in their wisdom, add up GM's assets, deduct its liabilities and find that the difference is $50? Or is worth only $40 because a security analyst applying the [Discounted Cash Flow] model finds $40 to be the discounted present value of GM's future cash flows? Or is it perhaps worth $60 because there is a rumor that the hot mutual fund manager or the latest takeover artist is buying it, and everyone knows that what they buy is bound to go higher?

> The most pessimistic and disturbing—and the most amusing—answer to these questions came from [economist John Maynard] Keynes, who was no mean speculator in his own right. Published in 1936, Keynes' sarcastic indictment of the stock market appears in a chapter in *General Theory of Employment, Interest and Money*, in which he uses the phrase **"prospective yield" to refer to the intrinsic value of an asset:**

>> It is not sensible to pay 25 for an investment of which you believe the prospective yield [ought] to justify a value of 30, if you also believe that the market will value it at 20 three months hence…

>> Human nature desires quick results, there is a particular zest in making money quickly, and remoter gains are discounted by the average man at a very high rate.

It is, so to speak, a game of Snap, of Old Maid, of Musical Chairs—a pastime in which **he is the victor** who says Snap neither too soon or too late, who passes the Old Maid [card] to his neighbor before the game is over, **who secures a chair for himself when the music stops.**

The Next Guy Theory Tells You All You Need to Know

Peter Bernstein's perspective is instructive for venture-stage companies. Valuation is a straight-forward measure to calculate, but evaluating whether one is high, low, or approximately right is a highly subjective matter. Keynes zeroed in on the importance of the "prospective yield" in determining the "intrinsic value" of a stock. Essentially, this is the Next Guy theory of pricing described in Chapter 5, "The Problem With a Conventional Capital Structure," as:

> For an investment, the price is no more than what the buyer believes the Next Guy will pay, less a discount.

No matter how one evaluates a valuation, it boils down to an effort to figure out what the Next Guy might pay. It may be driven by a mathematical exercise, but ultimately it is a bet on human behavior.

To appreciate this, let's first examine quantifiable issues that affect how a valuation is evaluated. Then, we'll look at some of the non-quantifiable, emotional ones.

Is There an Intrinsic Value?

A way to define and assess an intrinsic value for a company has long been the highest goal of financial market theorists. If one could discern it, one would know which stocks to sell or to avoid buying because they were overvalued. If a stock was selling below its intrinsic value, it might be promising to buy it. If investors knew a company's intrinsic value, they would be less susceptible to FOMO—*Fear Of Missing Out*—which causes valuations to rise on a speculative basis.

Peter Bernstein writes "the most rigorous and influential method for determining intrinsic value was published in 1938 by John Burr Williams," in his dissertation for a doctoral degree in economics.[c] Adding that Williams's "solution continues to be applied to almost all valuation problems…it provides the only formal method for determining what a price/earnings ratio or a dividend yield should be. Comparing that ratio or yield gives an indication of whether the asset is cheap or expensive."

Williams developed a theory of intrinsic value that "rests on the proposition that an asset is worth only what its owner can get out of it," which he defines as the sum of its future cash flows discounted to its present value for the time value of money. By extension, the present value of a company, its intrinsic value from an *operating point of view*, is today's value of the cash flows it generates in the future.[1] An operating point of view assumes the business continues to operate—it is a "going concern." On the other hand, a *liquidation perspective* considers value from the point of view of a buyer of the entire company or its assets, which can differ significantly from its going concern value.

---

[1] It is convenient to use net income as a proxy for cash flow, but there is a difference. Non-cash related expenses include the accrual of liabilities and the amortization (depreciation) of assets. Investors care more about cash flow—cash generated or consumed—than income as defined by accounting standards.

Money expected in the future is never worth as much as money on-hand because of the time value of money, which is the interest that one could earn if the money were available now. Then too, there is the risk that the money will not be there when expected. Bernstein says, "The process of giving future payments a haircut to allow for uncertainty and the passage of time is known as discounting, and investors call this valuation technique the Dividend Discount Model [or Discounted Cash Flow (DCF) model]. The model is applicable to any kind of investment that is designed to produce cash flows to its owner in the future. Few investors perform the elaborate calculations required by the model. Yet, no other formula for determining intrinsic value makes sense."

The cornerstone of a DCF valuation is the cash flow forecast. When a company is being valued, such a projection is made for each of the next three to five years. It could be longer, but each year beyond the present one is increasingly speculative. That's not the case when valuing a debt security, given that a debtor's loan payments can be more reliably forecast than their cash flows. Thus, DCF is much better suited for valuing a debt instrument than a company. For aside from a questionable forecast, one must estimate an enormously speculative figure called the "terminal value." There are two ways to do this. One is to estimate the average annual cash flow beyond the years that are individually forecast and assume it will be that each year thereafter, in perpetuity. The other is to project a valuation at an IPO or acquisition.

A terminal value is a necessary exercise in make-believe that accounts for a substantial portion of a present value. It is necessary because a terminal value is needed to make the DCF model work. It is make-believe for these reasons.

1. Few things have perpetual value. In Chapter 12, "Cooperation as the New Tool for Competition," Maynard Webb describes how the half-life of a company is diminishing quickly—that a third of the Fortune 500 companies operating in 1970 no longer existed in 1983. That's because product life cycles are increasingly rapid and dominance in one phase is no assurance of continued success. The turbulence is significant for large companies and severe for startups.

2. Even for things perpetually in demand like oil and housing, a terminal value is hard to predict. So it is hard to reliably peg the terminal value of an oil well or housing project. Items that are not in perpetual demand—things made by startups—are impossible to accurately project.

3. A terminal value based on an IPO can be useful. After all, public investors do accept higher valuations than private ones. But this isn't useful for most readers of this book—average investors—because they can't invest in private offerings. Got that? A terminal value for a private company based on an IPO can work if investors like you will pay a premium. But there isn't a clear Next Guy for average investors in public stock, is there?

4. A terminal value based on being acquired someday is a dicey basis for a buy-in valuation.

For these reasons, *the most rigorous and most influential method for determining intrinsic value for a company—DCF—is unlikely to establish a realistic valuation for investors.*

Mathematicians who theorize about intrinsic value of financial assets in markets have long recognized this problem, which is acute for "growth stocks"—companies whose earnings and dividend streams are expected to rise continuously (i.e., many tech companies). In 1957, David Durand, a MIT professor of economics, wrote:

Growth stocks...seem to represent the ultimate in difficulty of evaluation. The very fact that [the problem of unrealistic results resulting from extrapolating growth] has not yielded a unique and generally acceptable solution to more than 200 years of attack by some of the world's greatest intellects suggests, indeed, that the growth-stock problem offers no great hope of a satisfactory solution.

Thus, one of the key takeaways you should take from this book is that those who make a living setting or opining on corporate valuations, especially those for venture-stage companies, don't have special knowledge about how to reliably evaluate one.

Another takeaway is that a big reason capital markets work the way they do is that public investors are willing to pay outsized valuations. Many of them do so unwittingly, which is no surprise.

One can, therefore, infer that those who benefit from The-Way-Things-Are are unlikely to be enthusiastic about efforts to help make public investors become more valuation-savvy.

> **Thought Experiment**
>
> What is the intrinsic value of a company that is acquired for stock (versus cash) by a company that is itself overvalued?

How Valuation Experts Approach Valuation

Despite the challenges, the question, "What is a company worth?" often demands an answer. Those negotiating an acquisition have an acute need for one. Those who opine on the accounting for a transaction need an answer too, albeit less urgently.

Interestingly, those who negotiate an acquisition rarely rely on people certified in business valuation to set the price. That sounds curious because isn't that what you would expect such experts do?

The truth is, valuation experts are not the deal makers who set price; their principal job is to assess how to account for an agreed upon price on financial statements. When they determine that the price exceeds what an asset is worth, they recommend a write-down of its value on the acquirer's balance sheet. When that happens, some of the price is reported as an expense.

So, how do valuation experts evaluate a company's worth? Like art, they evaluate it from multiple perspectives—the *asset approach*, the *income approach*, and the *market approach*.

The *asset approach* to valuation considers what another party might pay for a company's assets or what it would cost to replace them. It is more relevant for an established business than a startup as new companies rarely have assets with significant value.

For a venture-stage company, the *income approach* is the most significant. To apply it, a discounted cash flow (DCF) calculation is applied to a company's projections.[2] Experts will assess the assumptions used in the financial model, as many of them require subjective judgment. They also look for computational and logic errors.

---

2 DCF measures the present value of the cash flow associated with an investment. When applied to a company, cash flow is the sum of net income, adjustments for noncash expenses and changes in working capital. In practice, however, net income is frequently used for startups out of convenience because there may be little difference between it and cash flow.

Next, a discount rate is selected. That requires a risk-free interest rate for the time value of money, which is usually the rate on a US Treasury note. Then risk is quantified. That requires judgment about failure risk—the likelihood that projections will not be met—and valuation risk. Higher risk calls for a higher risk premium. The risk-free rate and the risk premium are added together to get a discount rate.

Discount rate = Risk-free interest rate + Risk premium rate

So, if the risk-free interest rate is three percent and the risk premium is fourteen percent, the discount rate is seventeen percent. This is the "cost of capital," the minimum rate of return required to attract risk-aware investors. There are tables that express a discount rate into factors that are applied to the earnings stream to calculate its present value, which is the goal of the *income approach*.

The *market approach* looks at the valuation of comparable companies.

A valuation expert will evaluate the results from these three approaches—asset, income, and market—and judge how to weigh them for a composite valuation.

Weakness of Approaches Used by Valuation Experts

The combination of these three different approaches is intellectually impressive, but they frequently don't deliver practical value. If they did, valuation experts would be heavily relied upon by those who negotiate deals.

Furthermore, there is a fundamental problem with applying these approaches to startups, for they operate outside the relevant range of these measures. That is, these approaches work for bonds that pay interest, stocks that pay dividends, and income-generating companies. Venture-stage companies, however, have little asset value and uncertain income. If there is income, the stock pays no dividends and speculation fuels its market value. Furthermore, the very existence of such entities depends on their ability to raise capital in the future. Therefore, the use of valuation methodologies can be like a house built on sand—it looks sound until the ground shifts.

The reason projections for venture-stage companies are unreliable is that they often depend on innovative technology and business models to address markets that are new, competitive, and possibly fleeting. These are major links in a startup's value chain and the strength of a chain is defined by its weakest link.

So, the logic of the income approach is not its weakness. Rather, its weakness is the inability to reliably forecast income (or cash flows). And the projections are the basis for all that follows—if they are wrong, the discount rate doesn't matter.

A related problem is that key assumptions rely on judgment that can be altered to improve the results. Thus, applying the income approach can resemble a session with a Ouija game board.[3]

What of the market approach? It assesses valuation as price, not worth (asset and income approaches). Market prices can have a bipolar quality; climbing or falling in a manner that is disproportionate to what is happening. This clearly happens in the secondary market, where traders have a rule of thumb

---

[3] Ouija is a game played with a board that has letters and numbers on it. In a spiritual séance, players place their fingers on a small heart-shaped slider, taking note of where it points. Supposedly, the slider is guided by supernatural spirits that know the answer to questions the players ask.

that itself feeds volatility—buy on the rumor, sell on the news. In the private market, it can happen in a more dramatic, sudden-death manner because valuation comes up when the company itself needs money. If it's hot, the valuation will surge. If it's distressed, the valuation crumbles.

For these reasons, valuation experts are often no better than astute observers at explaining or forecasting prices.

> In 2013, Yahoo bought Tumblr for *$1.1 billion.* In 2016, Verizon bought Yahoo for $4.8 billion; in 2019, it sold Tumblr for less than *$3 million.*[D]

Rules of Thumb

Another way to evaluate a valuation is to utilize rules of thumb such as a multiple of revenue, earnings, or other proxies for value, like the number of customers. Some private investors insist on paying no more than a multiple of the valuation in the last round.

A multiple provides an approximation of value, albeit an arbitrary one, without elaborate effort; it provides a convenient way to consistently compare companies. In the secondary market, a price/earnings ratio may be the basis for a rule of thumb based on fundamental analysis, while trading patterns can reflect rules based on technical analysis. What the exact rule is will vary based on a company's industry, stage of development, location and, of course, who made the rule.

Non-Quantifiable Factors – the Power of Love, Reputation, and Charisma

Often, non-quantifiable factors affect how a valuation is evaluated. Caution can be thrown to the wind when the investor loves the idea and the entrepreneurs. This happens to individual investors, of course. Chapter 13 has an account from Bill Reichert reporting that it happens to VCs too, and David Kilpatrick has this anecdote in his 2011 book *The Facebook Effect:* [Bold added for emphasis]

> In venture capital deals…the investor usually forces the existing shareholders to dilute their ownership prior to the investment by adding a "pool" of shares that will remain unallocated, on the assumption that future employees will get some of their pay in stock options. The way it's calculated is complicated, but it has the effect of giving the VC more of the company and the entrepreneurs less. VCs typically insist that the existing shareholders of a company accept a pool of about 20 percent.

> But [a Facebook cofounder] had prepared [CEO Mark] Zuckerberg for this gambit, and it was clear at dinner the night before how badly [Accel Partners' Jim] Breyer wanted to invest. So Zuckerberg refused the 20 percent dilution. The two agreed on a 10 percent option pool instead. In addition, Zuckerberg would only accept half of that being applied to existing shareholders' ownership. So some of the dilution applied to Accel's money as well. "Mark negotiated really hard," concedes Breyer.

> They finally agreed on a deal that would value the company at slightly less than $98 million post-investment. Accel would invest about $12.7 million—a stunning sum for such a small company. It would own about 15 percent of the company. **"I knew the price was way too high," Breyer says now, "but sometimes that's what it takes to do the deal."** Breyer agreed to go on the board but asked if he could invest $1 million of his own money. The twenty-year-old and the VC shook hands. Zuckerberg left his office, and Breyer was elated.[E]

What causes an investor to fall in love with a prospective investment varies. The business opportunity plays a critical role but so does the strength of the executive team.

For some investors, the team is at least as important as the business. A saying captures this sensibility, "Bet on the jockey, not on the horse." It's a way of stating that a smart, savvy CEO will make a great business achieve its potential and make a not-so-great business better than it might otherwise be. Interestingly, investors may value a company more highly if a CEO has a reputation for delivering—a dream team makes investors more willing to accept a high valuation.

But the jockey effect can also hype a valuation, raising it without increasing the likelihood of success. Imagine *two companies with comparable prospects*. One is led by a star, the other by someone less accomplished. The one with the hot CEO may fetch a higher valuation than can be explained by reduced risk, a valuation premium based on a halo or celebrity effect. Investors think, "If so-and-so is on board, this will be big!" From a valuation perspective, this is both understandable and curious. Understandable, because it is reasonable to favor a star CEO over an unproven one. Curious, because it is questionable whether a star makes the opportunity bigger.

A set of stars may not make for an effective team, however. Some may have trouble sublimating their egos to achieve goals that require collaboration. Also, past success doesn't assure future success, as many can attest. That said, a CEO with a good reputation who puts the interests of others ahead of his or her own is the kind of jockey all investors want. Angel investor John Huston put it this way:

> The one commonality of the successful exits we've had is simply this: the team, led by the CEO, was successful in convincing our due diligence team that they would be profoundly, personally embarrassed if they couldn't give us our money back with a nice multiple in 5 years.**F**

In his 2011 book, *The Business of Venture Capital,* Mahendra Ramsinghani describes qualitative factors that VCs consider when they evaluate a company and its valuation. He writes that Geoff Smart, co-author of the 2008 book, *Who: The A Method for Hiring,* sought to discover what kinds of CEOs make money for investors. To find out, Smart teamed with Steven Kaplan, a professor of entrepreneurship and finance at the University of Chicago. Ramsinghani writes [bold added for emphasis]:

> [Smart and Kaplan] went on to conduct the largest study of CEO traits and financial performance. The results were compelling and controversial. Data from 313 interviews of [private equity-] backed CEOs were gathered and analyzed. Taking these assessments, the authors matched the CEO assessments with actual financial performance.

> Smart points out that investors have a tendency to invest in CEOs who demonstrate openness to feedback, possess great listening skills, and treat people with respect. "I call them 'Lambs' because these CEOs tend to graze in circles, feeding on the feedback and direction of others," he says. And he concludes that investors love **Lambs** because they are easy to work with and **were successful 57 percent of the time.**

> But Smart found that the desirable CEOs are the ones who move quickly, act aggressively, work hard, demonstrate persistence, set high standards and hold people accountable to them. (He called them "Cheetahs" because they are fast and focused.) **"Cheetahs in our study were successful 100 percent of the time.** This is not a rounding error. Every single one of them created significant value for their investors," writes Geoff. He and his

coauthor conclude that "emotional intelligence is important, but only when matched with the propensity to get things done."

Separately, Steve Kaplan's research leads to the same conclusion. In the study, "Which CEO Characteristics and Abilities Matter?" the authors assess more than 30 individual characteristics, skills and abilities. Surprisingly, the study showed that **success was not linked to team-related skills** and that such skills are overweighed in hiring decisions. **Success mattered only with CEOs with execution-related skills.[G]**

Ramsinghani addresses other reputational factors as well. He writes that integrity and honesty are fundamentally important qualities but hard to assess. With respect to experience, he references a study of serial entrepreneurs that concludes: [bold added for emphasis]

> All things equal, a VC-backed entrepreneur who has taken a company public has a **30 percent** chance of succeeding in his next venture. A failed entrepreneur is next in the pecking order with a **20 percent** chance of success and a first-time entrepreneur has an **18 percent chance**. Researchers assessed the cause of success and point out that successful entrepreneurs know how to launch companies at the right time, before the markets get crowded.[H]

This finding will be surprising to many people–it was to me–because it is thought that having an experienced, successful CEO (and other executives) on board suggests less risk, if not more potential, thus a valuation premium. While the evidence Ramsinghani cites indicates that is indeed the case, the difference isn't profound. What is? Market timing. Ramsinghani says that it "is important in entrepreneurs as well as investors. Consider the fact that 52 percent of computer startups founded in 1983 went public. In contrast, only 18 percent of those started in 1985 went public. The world had changed in 24 months by a factor of three!"

Nonetheless, a Silicon Valley veteran told me that "VCs value formation of a 'team' as a proxy for execution"–a valuation premium. Again, this seems intuitive. A sports team loaded with stars seems like it should be more valuable than one without an illustrious roster. But what if the stars don't deliver?

Does value flow from anticipation of performance or from the delivery of it?[4] Should valuations be a function of hope or performance?

I'd like to interject a point about the Fairshare Model. If you accept the idea that the past accomplishments of a management team can result in an outsized valuation premium, you have two camps to choose from.

- A large premium is undeserved: management should not be valued highly before it delivers results.

- A large premium is deserved because management's record suggests that their new company has less failure risk. It begs a corollary: the premium should go away if key team members leave.

---

4 There are limits to this analogy. The value of a sports franchise is based on revenue and profitability, not its winning record.

The second view captures how markets work better than the first one, but the Fairshare Model doesn't require one to choose. It melds the notion that little or no value should be placed on undelivered performance, with recognition that markets do exactly that. In a Fairshare Model IPO, the pre-money valuation reflects a return for the private capital raised and the performance achieved before the IPO. The Investor Stock price at IPO only reflects that, not anticipated performance.

Non-tradable Performance Stock is issued for future performance and issuers are likely to list a rise in the price of Investor Stock as a measure of performance for conversions. That means that any valuation premium awarded by secondary market investors can reward employees without any operational or financial performance. Thus, the benefits of a management halo effect on the market price of Investor Stock will be shared by both pre-IPO and IPO investors as well as by employees.

In other words, the Fairshare Model does not require one to proclaim whether value should be awarded when a team is formed or when it delivers. It can be both. Similarly, one need not argue that light is a wave, or a particle—it has the qualities of both. Contrast that with a conventional capital structure. When one is used, IPO investors don't benefit from the management halo effect because it is incorporated into the IPO's pre-money valuation.

Returning to entrepreneurial teams, Ramsinghani writes the following on the challenge of assessing the qualities of one:

> Do they understand their own limitations and weaknesses? Are they able to attract a team, and eventually, can they recruit their own CEO and replace themselves?" asks Lip-Bu Tan of Walden International.

> These qualities are fundamental but rare. After all, human beings suffer from insecurities. If they attract team members who are highly accomplished, they may end up looking like dwarves. Or get sidelined! And very few can overcome this innate and primal urge—most gravitate toward looking smart in a land of dwarves as opposed to looking stupid among giants.

> An investor needs to watch for traits where the founders or the core management team are able to attract star power. Most management teams will be replaced, either by choice or by sheer exhaustion in the travails of the startup journey. Team building can make an investment opportunity stronger. A simple question to consider: Is this person honest and bold enough to replace him-or herself at the right time or even become redundant?[1]

Charisma is another intangible that can affect how a valuation is evaluated. An investor charmed by a company's leadership will like it, even love it. This can lead to a valuation premium. However, as Susan Cain noted in her 2012 book, _Quiet: The Power of Introverts in a World That Can't Stop Talking,_ charisma is not strongly associated with performance.

> The essence of the Harvard Business School education is that leaders have to act confidently and make decisions in the face of incomplete information. The teaching method plays with an age-old question: If you don't have all the facts—and often you won't—should you wait to act until you've collected as much data as possible? Or, by hesitating, do you risk losing others' trust and your own momentum?

The answer isn't obvious. If you speak firmly on the basis of bad information, you can lead your people into disaster. But if you exude uncertainty, then morale suffers, funders won't invest, and your organization can collapse. The HBS teaching method implicitly comes down on the side of certainty. The CEO may not know the best way forward, but she has to act anyway.

Yet even at HBS there are signs that something might be wrong with a leadership style that values quick and assertive answers over quiet, slow decision-making. Contrary to the school's model of vocal leadership, the ranks of effective CEOs turn out to be filled with introverts.

"Among the most effective leaders I have encountered and worked with in half a century," the management guru Peter Drucker has written, "some locked themselves into their office and others were ultra-gregarious. Some were quick and impulsive, while others studied the situation and took forever to come to a decision.

"The one and only personality trait the effective ones I have encountered did have in common was something they did not have: They had little or no *charisma* and little use either for the term or what it signifies."

Supporting Drucker's claim, Brigham Young University management professor Bradley Agle studied the CEOs of 128 major companies and found that those considered charismatic by their top executives had bigger salaries but not better corporate performance.[J]

It is easier for an uncharismatic CEO to be effective in an established business than in a startup. After all, the vitality of the former is evident regardless of what the leader's personality is. In contrast, a startup CEO is like a magician or circus ringmaster, who asks an audience to imagine possibilities, to have the foresight to invest in, or work for, an unproven enterprise that plans to do something difficult, where the prospect for reward is questionable.

An opportunity that is preternaturally compelling will sell itself; CEO charisma is not critical. But for most startups, charm is necessary to get investors to pay attention, to see the potential, to believe that the team can achieve it, and to write a check. Beyond that, to get investors to accept a high valuation, the CEO must make them believe that he or she is a capable captain of the ship. The downside of charisma is that it can lead people, including the CEO, to be overly confident; there are subtle differences between a healthy ego and narcissism, which can be poison.

Quantifiable Factors for Evaluating Valuation

Many investors rely on rules of thumb and non-quantifiable factors to evaluate a valuation. The more sophisticated ones also calculate what the company's pre-money valuation *must be* if they are likely to make their target return. That is, they consider what a fair valuation might be but focus on the price that can get them what they want.

The calculation requires the investor to set a target rate of return for an investment with this expected risk, reward, and length. It also requires:

- expected value of the company at investor exit; and the
- expected size and timing of future capital raises (i.e., the amount of additional capital that will be needed, and the share of the company it will buy).

The computation works backwards; it starts with the estimated value at IPO or acquisition. From that, the expected dilution from future rounds is deducted to get the future value of today's ownership position. That value is discounted for the target rate of return. The result approximates the maximum pre-money valuation the investor can accept and make the target. The details are too technical for this book. Plus, it's not relevant; public investors don't negotiate a pre-money valuation, and they can sell in the secondary market before more capital is raised. The takeaway is that sophisticated investors establish the maximum valuation they are willing to pay.

How VCs Evaluate a Valuation

VCs routinely calculate the buy-in valuation they can accept. They are also extraordinarily plugged into what is driving valuations. They hear what other VCs are doing. Their network includes investment bankers, acquisition-minded executives and board members at companies that are interested in the type of startup they are looking at. They participate in events that provide them with insight from innovators who are at every point in the business development cycle.

So, they are expert assessors of valuation. But no one can know everything or reliably foretell the future. To protect themselves from overpaying, VCs rely more on getting attractive deal terms than on getting an attractive valuation. [See "Valuation Is a Challenge for VCs" in Chapter 13, "Valuation Concepts."]

That is, to secure a position in a deal they want, a VC will accept a high valuation if they get price protection provisions like anti-dilution, liquidation preference, dividends and/or board control. Such things create a bulwark against a valuation that reveals itself later to be too high. Terms can also secure the right to invest more when a deal looks like a winner.

How Angel Investors Evaluate a Valuation

Like VCs, angel investors use rules of thumb and non-quantifiable factors to evaluate a valuation. They also tend to invest in sectors that they understand. Those who are active in angel investor groups will also use their network to evaluate a deal. Angel investors who are not so networked are disadvantaged in all aspects of investment evaluation—screening, due diligence, deal structure, and valuation.

David S. Rose is CEO of Gust, an online platform (gust.com) that is a resource for angel investors as well as for entrepreneurs who want to pitch to them. In his 2014 book *Angel Investing: The Gust Guide to Making Money & Having Fun Investing in Startups*, Rose describes a variation of the calculation that was described on the prior page. He writes:[K]

How much money you make from your angel investing is determined by four simple numbers:

1. The value of the company when you invest.

2. The value of the company when you sell.

3. The number of years between these two events, which, taken together, give you your rate of return.

4. The rate of return, multiplied by the amount of money you invest, will determine your ultimate angel investing bottom line.

That first number, of course, is the pre-money valuation and Rose calls it "the single most important of the four simple numbers." He also says it is "the most confusing, debated and variable number in the world of angel investing."

Rose explains how angels can evaluate a valuation and estimate how much money they may make. One thing he says about the process is relevant to public investors. He feels a 25 percent rate of return is roughly what angel investors should target, which he points out is "a return that compares favorably to almost every other legal form of investment."[L] That rate may surprise those who earn far less on their money. In part, it reflects the valuation premium often awarded to companies when they go public.

Angel investors who correctly predict an exit value and the time it takes to get there can, nonetheless, vastly overestimate their return if they underestimate how much capital it will take to get there, and a VC is the source of the additional capital. That's because a VC's terms come at the expense of other shareholders. For example, say that angel investors own 20 percent of a company that they expect will be valued at $30 million at exit, when they expect to own 10 percent, worth $3 million. They can be right about the exit value, but very wrong about the value of their stake. They could end up with just 2 percent or $600,000—or even zero! How is this possible?

- An unplanned capital raise will dilute the position of early investors.

- A VC may evoke a "pay-to-play" provision for a new round. This requires all investors to invest in a new round to preserve their stake. If they do not, they lose it. In such a scenario, investors who want to retain their ownership position ("play") must invest more ("pay").

- A round at a pre-money valuation below the post-money valuation of the one before—a down round—will trigger VC price protection provisions that dilutes the position of the other investors.

- A VC with a liquidation preference is entitled to recover its investment, or a multiple of it, before other shareholders participate in the split of what remains.

- A VC may get shares for dividends owed and management fees to compensate for the time it spends on the company.

These glum possibilities are unlikely to affect how angel investors evaluate a valuation. If they want to invest, they are excited and optimistic enough to believe that things will go well. But down rounds happen, and they are never in the projections when investors invest.

The point is that even when a projected exit value is spot on, changes in the timing of a company's cash flows or shifts in the capital markets can drive it to raise money on terms that adversely affect angel investors. Such possibilities, in addition to the basic valuation challenge, shed light on why it is difficult for angel investors to evaluate "the single most important" number for an investment in a startup.

Valuation Evaluation – As Seen on TV!

In 2009, as the US worried about how get out of the Great Recession, the ABC television network debuted a show called *Shark Tank*.[M] It's like a talent show, but instead of singing or dancing for judges, contestants pitch their business idea to a panel of wealthy investors, who are called—oddly—the "Sharks." I say oddly, because such investors are normally called "angels." I suppose they are so-named because reality TV producers feel that the sense of conflict generates more viewer interest than kindness.

At any rate, novice entrepreneurs describe their concept, demonstrate the product, then say "I offer X percent of my company for Y dollars." The amounts seem to range from $30,000 to $300,000—a seed round size or early stage deal. What then follows is a bit of Q&A about the product, its sales history, prospects, and profitability. The Sharks then critique the pitch and announce whether they are out of the deal or willing to make an offer. Competing bids occur.

> It is remarkable to me that startup valuation is in pop culture! It was foreign matter to most people before *Shark Tank* raised awareness of deal terms.

Entrepreneurs always want the money and control. Counter offers are always for a lower valuation and often require control. For example, an entrepreneur may offer 20 percent of the company for $300,000, a $1,200,000 pre-money valuation.[5] But a Shark is likely to counter with 51 percent, a much lower $290,000 pre-money valuation, for the same amount of money.[6] Sometimes, a Shark's counter is equity plus a royalty on sales. The counteroffers can be hard for an entrepreneur to evaluate on-camera, particularly if a royalty is involved. Then there is the pressure—Sharks sometimes will shout: "Don't take that deal!" or "You have an offer—decide now!"

While the show is all about creating onscreen drama, it provides a glimpse into the dynamics of valuation and deal structure. Watch some episodes, and you'll see that the TV Sharks offer the lowest valuation they think they can get. They also look to secure at least one of these:

- ownership control, more than 50 percent;
- terms that enable them to recover their investment faster, such as a royalty on sales;
- leverage if the entrepreneur doesn't perform; debt, which can foreclose on the company.

As an aside, I feel royalty deals are a bad idea for a company, especially if profit margins are not high. By increasing its expense, royalties increase a company's need for capital and handicap its appeal to those who can provide it. Most angel investors and VCs don't require cash royalties because they understand that equity is mother's milk for venture-stage companies; taking cash out of a business that doesn't generate it weakens it.

Remember, a problem with a conventional capital structure is that voting power is tied to valuation. The entrepreneur must accept less control to offer an investor an attractive valuation. Conversely, to retain control, the valuation must climb. A multiclass capital structure can separate voting rights from valuation. Unfortunately, when one is used in an IPO, it is usually to give insiders control, even when investors pay a high valuation.

---

[5] ($300,000 investment/20% ownership) - $300,000 investment = $1,200,000 pre-money valuation

[6] ($300,000 investment/51% ownership) - $300,000 investment = $288,235 pre-money valuation

How Private Equity Investors Evaluate a Valuation

The types of professional investors that engage in venture capital investing have grown. Private equity (PE) firms also engage in it, but they evaluate a valuation differently than a VC.

VCs invest in companies that are creating a business. Like the entrepreneurs they back, many VCs are visionaries; they seek to create new markets or transform existing ones. Also, they finance companies with their fund's money—if there is any debt, it is for equipment leases. They are like athletes who create their own momentum, or gardeners who use seeds or sprouts.

PE firms invest at a later stage, where there is an established business, and assets that can serve as collateral for debt. More opportunistic than visionary, PE investors want to make something that is already in motion go faster—they aren't interested in funding an effort to create something new. Think of them as gardeners who put established plants in larger pots, then trim them to look better.

PE activity occupies a broad spectrum. At the early-stage end, PE favors companies with products for which there is an attractive market. The bet is that the company can accelerate its growth and improve its efficiency with the PE firm's capital, insight, and connections. On the mature end of the spectrum, PE invests in companies that could be worth a lot more with a makeover.

PE firms have advantages over VCs when it comes to assessing a valuation. One is that there is a historic trend to examine, much like an investor who can see a public stock's price trend, as well as valuation information for comparable companies. That helps them evaluate whether they may be able to help it rise faster or fix what's wrong and sell it at a profit. Another advantage is that, because there is an existing business, they can structure an investment as debt or, even better, can get others to lend the company money that can be used to buy the company: effectively, a mortgage.

Because cash flows are easier to project for an established business and repayment of debt plays a prominent role in building value, a PE firm pays a lot of attention to discounted cash flow analysis. As a result, their formula for success is a more precise version of the Next Guy theory than most investors use. It is one that is highly mindful of the cash that the PE investors may be at-risk for.

There are three strategies that a PE firm can use to increase the value of its equity stake in a company:

- Pay down the debt used to acquire the company by selling off assets (i.e., facilities or lines of business).

- Increase the multiplier applied to revenue or earnings by repositioning the business to focus on markets that have higher growth and/or are more lucrative.

- Improve income by increasing revenue and reducing expenses (i.e., cost reductions, drop low margin products, consolidate facilities, etc.).

How these strategies can pay off is presented next.[7]

---

[7] Tip of the hat to Brad Winegar of Salt Creek Capital, a leading private equity firm in the San Francisco Bay area, for providing this presentation.

The table to the right shows a company with income of $1 million that a PE investor acquires for $5 million. In other words, it is valued at a 5X earnings multiple.

To finance the purchase, the PE fund gets a lender to lend the company $4 million, based on its assets, income, and the PE investor's involvement. This allows the PE investor to buy a $5 million asset with $1 million of its own money; $4 million is borrowed by the company itself, not by the PE firm. The analog is that you buy a house for $100,000 using an $80,000 mortgage *borrowed by the house*, not by you–plus $20,000 of your money.

	Status at Acquisition
Earnings	$ 1M
Earnings Multiple	5.0 X
Enterprise Value	$ 5M
Debt	$ (4M)
Equity	$ 1M

The next table adds three columns to the one above, one for each way the PE investor can increase the value of its equity stake before it has an exit (i.e., an IPO or sale to another party).

	Status at Acquisition	Private Equity Strategies to Boost Valuation		
		Pay-Down Debt	Increase Multiple	Grow Income
Earnings	$ 1M	$ 1M	$ 1M	$ 2M
Earnings Multiple	5.0 X	5.0 X	6.0 X	6.0 X
Company Valuation	$ 5M	$ 5M	$ 6M	$ 12M
Debt	$ (4M)	$ 0M	$ 0M	$ 0M
Value of PE equity stake	$ 1M	$ 5M	$ 6M	$ 12M
% appreciation in stake		500%	600%	1,200%

Let's walk through the three strategies, assuming all are implemented, in the following order:

- The "Pay-Down Debt" column reflects the sale of assets that are not critical to the company's new strategy. The proceeds are used to retire the $4 million debt. As a result, the value of the PE firm's stake rises from $1 million to $5 million–500 percent appreciation. Note that the company's valuation itself is unchanged; the $5 million reflects the earnings and the multiple.

- The "Increase the Multiple" column shows the effect of increasing the earnings multiple, here, from 5X to 6X. This can occur by raising the company's profile with investors by focusing on fast-growing markets and public relations. The value of $1 million in earnings thus climbs from $5 million to $6 million (compare to prior column). With no debt, the PE stake is now worth $6 million, 600 percent more than at acquisition.

- The "Grow Income" column has the effect of higher earnings. It doubles from $1 million to $2 million. Since the multiple is 6X, the valuation is $12 million.

Achieving all steps drives the value of the PE investor's position from $1 million to $12 million; the appreciation is 12X or 1,200 percent. After deducting the $1 million investment, the return is 1,100 percent.[8] Since a PE investor can minimize its at-risk investment and has more ways to grow the value of its stake than a VC or angel investor, it may evaluate a valuation differently.

Evaluating the Valuation of a Company that Uses the Fairshare Model

Does the Fairshare Model change how a company's valuation is assessed? As they say in the American Midwest—you betcha! As they say in France—that's its *raison d'être* (or reason to exist). The premise, as you appreciate by now, is that it is hard to produce a reliable valuation for a venture-stage company. So, why have one that is likely to be wrong—more specifically, too high? This was touched on in Chapter 13, "Valuation Concepts."

In medicine, if there was an unreliable test for a condition where the treatment was consequential and had a high chance of being wrong, there would be clamor for a better way. It could be a better test, a way to delay treatment or, hopefully, a different treatment that may be better.

The analogy is this: absent a more reliable way to value a startup, shouldn't we explore ways to delay fixing the relative ownership interests of those who provide capital and those who provide ideas and labor? If you have made it this far in the book, you are clearly open to it.

So how should the valuation of a company be viewed when it uses the Fairshare Model? That's one of the discussions that will emerge. I think a valuation should be seen as something that

1. will change, possibly dramatically, based on the conversion rules and performance, and
2. is set for strategic reasons, not because of what it "should be" from an economic sense.

In a conventional IPO, an issuer will set a valuation 15 to 20 percent below what it expects it will trade at in the secondary market. This straight-forward approach rewards pre-IPO shareholders and IPO investors—as opposed to those who buy shares in the secondary market.

In a Fairshare Model IPO, if a Performance Stock conversion criterion is a rise in the price of the Investor Stock, an issuer's management has incentive to offer a much lower IPO valuation than in a conventional model. Here are considerations that various constituencies will have.

- *IPO investors:* A low IPO valuation encourages a Black Friday sale mentality that results in the offering being fully subscribed (or sold out) quickly.
- *Secondary market investors:* A low IPO valuation promotes secondary market trading.
- *Pre-IPO investors:* Those who have a long-term perspective will be unbothered by a low IPO valuation because it will be of fleeting significance if the market price climbs to that

---

[8] 1,100 percent return = [$12M value - $1M investment]/$1M investment)

of a conventional offering. Also, if the alternative is a private offering, a VC will seek a low valuation too. More significantly, it will require terms that could squeeze the position of the other investors. If those aren't reasons enough, an issuer might persuade pre-IPO shareholders to support a Fairshare Model IPO by issuing them sweeteners such as warrants on the Investor Stock or Performance Stock.

- *Employees:* a Fairshare Model IPO could appeal to the management team because:
  - ° Management defines the conversion criteria in its prospectus.
    Public investors need only approve changes to it.
  - ° If the team performs well, they can own more of the company's tradable stock than they would if the money came from VCs.
  - ° Their willingness to be capital structure innovators can attract interest in the company and its leadership. That can pay dividends in its business and increase demand for its stock.

A low IPO valuation is inconsequential if the Investor Stock climbs to the price it would be in a conventional IPO. Plus, it fosters broad-based good feeling. The company has the money it needs. IPO investors make money. Pre-IPO investors increase their wealth and have liquidity. Employees can earn a larger share of the company than if a VC provided the capital. The issuer is better positioned to acquire companies using its stock than when it was private. And, it has a remarkable tool to attract and motivate employees—Performance Stock.

Summation

How should one evaluate a valuation? It's a bit like evaluating a piece of art—opinions vary. The question reminds me of a poem by the 19th century American poet John Godfrey Saxe called, "The Blind Men and the Elephant." Inspired by fables from several religious traditions in the Indian subcontinent region, it illustrates the limits of analytical thinking, and the risks of fragmented knowledge.

Saxe tells of six learned men from Indostan (a term for the northern part of India) "who went to see the elephant, though all of them were blind." The one who feels its tail concludes that the elephant is like a rope. The one who feels its side proclaims the beast is very much like a wall. The one that grasps its feet declares it is clearly like a tree. The one that touches the ear says it's more like a fan. The one that strokes the tusk concludes a spear is more apt, while the one that encounters its trunk insists that the elephant is like a snake. The poem concludes:

And so these men of Indostan
Disputed loud and long,
Each in his own opinion
Exceeding stiff and strong,
Though each was partly in the right,
And all were in the wrong!

The story suggests how to assess a valuation: consider multiple perspectives, including the possibility that each is wrong. This moral inevitably leads one to question the appeal of a conventional capital structure, which demands a value for future performance when an equity investment is made.

Much advice is available to you elsewhere on how to evaluate a valuation. I hope this chapter encourages you to learn more. Do your research, seek out the most knowledgeable people you can, then find other sources. Persistently ask questions such as these: "How do you assess value?" "Why do you think that is the best way?" "How reliable is this approach?"

By the way, the way I evaluate a startup valuation is to consider the likelihood that the Next Guy will pay more. This assessment hinges on both external and internal factors. That is, the state of the market and the sector a company operates in, its projections, and the risks. I then estimate when the company will need more money and consider what conditions may look like then. I also consider whether the current investors seem likely to invest more and the likelihood that the company may be acquired.

What's Next?

The next chapter presents the case for a valuation disclosure requirement in offering documents.

Chapter Endnotes

Contextual references for material in this chapter appear as numbered footnotes on the page where the reference is made. **Source references** for material in this chapter appear below as endnotes with capital letter identifiers.

A Caldwell, Kyle. "Warren Buffett's Favorite Valuation Measure Says Stocks Are Overvalued." *Business Insider*. August 18, 2015. Accessed May 10, 2018. fairsharemodel.com/Buffett.

B Bernstein, Peter L. *Capital Ideas: The Improbable Origins of Modern Wall Street*. Hoboken, NJ: John Wiley & Sons, 2006. pages 117-118.

C All quotes and many of the ideas in this section about intrinsic value are from pages 149 to 162 of *Capital Ideas: The Improbable Origins of Modern Wall Street*, by Peter L. Bernstein.

D Southern, Matt. "Wordpress' Parent Company Acquires Tumblr for Shockingly Low Sum." *Search Engine Journal*. August 13, 2019. Accessed August 28, 2019. fairsharemodel.com/tumblr

E Kirkpatrick, David. *The Facebook Effect: The Inside Story of the Company That Is Connecting the World*. New York, NY: Simon and Shuster, 2012. pages 124-125.

F John Huston's video is no longer on Gust.com.

G Ramsinghani, Mahendra. *The Business of Venture Capital: Insights from Leading Practitioners on the Art of Raising a Fund, Deal Structuring, Value Creation, and Exit Strategies*. Hoboken, NJ: John Wiley & Sons, 2014. pages 182-183.

H Ibid, page 183.

I Ibid, pages 180-183.

J Cain, Susan. *Quiet: The Power of Introverts in a World That Can't Stop Talking*. New York, NY: Crown Publishers, 2012. pages 45-45 and 53.

K Rose, David S. *Angel Investing: The Gust Guide to Making Money and Having Fun Investing in Startups*. Hoboken, NJ: Wiley, 2014. page 94.

L Ibid. Page 96.

M *Shark Tank* episodes are on YouTube.

Chapter 16:

Valuation Disclosure

What's Included in This Chapter

- Introduction
- The Elephant in the Room
- Key Conclusions You Should Have in Mind
- The Case for a Valuation Disclosure Requirement
- What Valuation Disclosure Might Look Like
- What Disclosure of the Basis for the Valuation Might Look Like
- Valuation Disclosure – Why Hasn't It Happened Already?
- Summation
- What's Next?
- Chapter Endnotes

Introduction

This is an important chapter if you support any of the following:

- Market-based solutions
- Transparent investor disclosure (a.k.a. open, candid disclosure of significant information)
- The Fairshare Model

This chapter has a call to action—it asks you to petition policymakers to require that issuers of stock disclose their pre-money valuation in their offering document.

The Elephant in the Room

Dara Albright is a crowdfunding advocate who, in mid-2015, made an intriguing comparison between the 1971 Intel Corporation IPO and the 2014 IPO of the much-ballyhooed Alibaba Group.

	Intel Corporation	Alibaba Corporation[A]
Year of IPO	1971	2014
Number of pages in the Prospectus	38 pages	325 pages (39 pages of Risk Factors)
Amount raised	$7.5 million	$25 billion
IPO Valuation	$58 million	$170 billion
February 2015 valuation	$164 billion	$286 billion
Appreciation since IPO	282,659%	68%

For Alibaba's IPO investors to realize the same return as investors in Intel's IPO (who still hold the stock), Alibaba will need to trade at a $480 trillion market capitalization—six times more than the gross domestic product of every country on the planet combined!

Albright presents this table to argue that equity markets are in disrepair. That big financial institutions help channel immense amounts of capital to a few deals instead of modest amounts to small, job-creating businesses. And that investment banks allocate IPO shares in a manner that benefit privileged investors instead of average ones. She argues that this constitutes a misallocation of resources and that equity crowdfunding can help correct it.

Her table prompts me to contemplate these points as well:

- Is it possible to have a 38-page IPO prospectus anymore?
- Do offerings now emphasize risk disclosure to a brain-numbing degree?
- Why do disclosure requirements miss the proverbial elephant in the room, the valuation?

The Alibaba prospectus does not state that it set its IPO (i.e., pre-money) valuation at $170 billion. The references to valuation essentially said:

> Prior to this offering, there has been no public market for our shares. The public offering price has been determined by negotiation among us and the underwriters, based upon several factors.

Well, golly gee-whiz! Knock me over with a feather! That's such a meaningful disclosure! Seriously, if that's what will be said about a valuation—and it typically is—why bother saying anything?

Implicitly, Alibaba, like other issuers that similarly describe how their IPO price is set—virtually all of them—ask investors to view the matter as if it were the birth of Athena, the goddess of wisdom in Greek mythology.

Rather than emerging as an infant from a womb, she was born fully-formed, as an adult, springing out from the head of her father, Zeus. Perhaps it is not coincidental that Athena is also associated with purity, for she remained sexually chaste.

IPO issuers who make pronouncements like Alibaba's suggest that wisdom and purity guide where their valuation is set. The wisdom comes from its management and investment bankers. Purity is evoked in a virginal sense: the issuer's valuation is untested in the public market. So, goodness! Who can possibly know whether the IPO valuation makes sense or not?

Of course, just as Athena herself, these factors are based on myth. Greed has at least as much sway over the setting of an IPO valuation as wisdom. And all companies have a valuation history. Why it is considered irrelevant to public investors is a curious matter, indeed. After all, private investors routinely consider what a company's valuation trend is.

Non-disclosure of this data to IPO investors is simply unjust. It makes as much sense as non-disclosure of the private sector background of a first-time candidate for public office. But, when it comes to valuation, the apparent—albeit unspoken—rule for offering documents is: Don't Ask, Don't Tell. Investors should figure it out themselves.

For securities regulators, that seems, well, wrong-headed.

The remarkable birth of Athena

She burst out of the head of her father Zeus, as a fully formed adult.

Investors similarly must pull the basis for an IPO valuation out of their head.

Storytellers often incorporate myth to make a person or an event more compelling. Myth is also used to avoid a subject. Children are told that babies come from storks. Those promoting the stork story about birth might, when taking about a stock, similarly prefer fuzzy talk about its investment appeal. That is, they may favor talk about the company's technology, market, or management, over discussion about what the valuation is and whether it makes sense.

That makes valuation susceptible to magical thinking. Hans Christian Andersen's fable, *The Emperor's New Clothes,* satirizes group vulnerability to myth with a story about a magical cloth that is invisible to those who are unfit for their positions, stupid, or incompetent. It ends when a child cries out what others are afraid to say, that the emperor is wearing no clothes at all!

A valuation disclosure requirement, like that child, will encourage more people to engage in clear thinking about whether a valuation makes sense.

Key Conclusions You Should Have in Mind

Let's review some of the insights that I hope you've reached by now:

- Valuation is an important determinant of investor risk and upside.
- Investors who are valuation-unaware are more likely to make poorer decisions than those who are valuation-aware.
- The issuer and its investment bankers decide what the valuation will be.

- Comparable companies can choose significantly different valuations.
- Valuation is "price," but it can easily be misconstrued as a representation of "worth."
- Investors can better evaluate a valuation if they don't need to calculate it.
- Valuation is not stock price; stocks with the same price can have wildly different valuations.
- A simple calculation can determine a company's valuation; it is not rocket science.
- Many investors may feel uncomfortable computing an issuer's valuation—or neglect to do so.
- Venture-stage companies are difficult to reliably value. (If he were an investor, the protagonist in the movie *Forrest Gump* would compare them to a box of chocolates).[1]
- Startups are associated with economic growth, job creation and the good life. It follows that all three could be enhanced by improving entrepreneurial access to capital.
- Those who oppose allowing average investors to invest in high-risk companies should consider that venture-stage IPOs have been common for decades. And, that investors can invest in such companies in the secondary market.
- VCs can protect themselves from an excessive buy-in valuation, but public investors cannot.
- More venture-stage companies will be presented to public investors in the future.
- Notions of how established a company needs to be before it goes public are evolving.

With those points in mind, I'm about to make the argument for an additional conclusion—offering documents should disclose the issuer's pre-money valuation. At present, there is prominent mention of the price per share, but not the valuation.

The balance of this chapter is a call for social activism to provoke meaningful change in the equity capital market. What follows is an appeal for *your* help.

The Case for a Valuation Disclosure Requirement

The US Securities and Exchange Commission could help investors—both private and public—protect themselves from overpriced stock deals if it required companies to disclose the valuation that they give themselves in their offering documents.

Assume a scenario where a venture-stage enterprise, ABC Company, is raising capital at a $50 million pre-money valuation. How might an investor evaluate an investment? If she knows the valuation, she is likely to pose a question like this one:

> ABC Company has modest revenue and no profit, so why should I invest when it is valued at $50 million?

If the investor does not know the valuation, she might instead ask, "Why should I invest at $X per share?" But this is not meaningful. Many combinations of share price and shares outstanding can result in the same valuation. Both numbers are used to calculate a valuation, just as two hands are used to make the sound of a clap.

---

[1] In the 1994 movie, Forrest Gump declares "Momma always said, 'Life is like a box of chocolates, you never know what you're going to get.'"

The key question is, *"Why is ABC Company worth $50 million?"* and investors who fail to ask it are more likely to make a poor decision, even when they are right about the company's ability to achieve its potential. That's because one can overpay for a position in a successful company.

Valuation is a vital data point and investors should not, as they do now, have the burden of calculating it. Many do not know how to. Others may be uncomfortable doing so or forget to. Some may calculate it incorrectly. But if the amount is stated in an offering document, anyone can see what it is.

But the SEC does not require valuation disclosure. It assumes that investors can and will calculate it themselves. This is remarkable, given how important the figure is and how likely it is that an investor will fail to correctly calculate it. It is also odd, when one considers how many pages of an offering document are devoted to risk factors while a valuation can be expressed in a single sentence.

Venture capital and private equity firms know the valuation of companies they invest in. They also have insight on comparable valuations via their network and fee-based research services that rely on voluntary disclosure from private companies. Angel investors tend to know a company's valuation but have less market insight than VC and PE firms. In stark contrast, only a small fraction of a company's public investors is likely to know its valuation and few of them will know how it compares. This is not the hallmark of a healthy, open market.

The beneficiaries of a valuation disclosure requirement will be numerous. That's because data aggregation services can be counted on to harvest data points about private and public offerings from the regulatory database and use it to create rich content. For example, valuations could be associated with the amount raised and when, with an issuer's industry, location, financial data, and other factors. Such insight can enhance capital markets in ways that Zillow and Trulia benefit the real estate market.

Together, an issuer's valuation disclosure and access to robust market data will position any investor, not just the professional ones, to ask questions such as these.

- ABC Company appears to be like XYZ Company, which was recently valued at $40 million. What makes ABC worth $50 million?
- The average valuation for companies at ABC's stage of development is significantly different. What explains that?
- ABC's valuation is comparable to companies with backing from major VCs. Given that ABC doesn't have such support, shouldn't it be lower?

Such data can help companies avoid the problems of raising capital at excessive valuations. Doing so encourages arrogance about other people's money and naïveté about future raises of capital. The effects of either are bad and painful to recover from.

Companies that offer a below-market deal will benefit because more investors will recognize that one is offered. The data will also help investors evaluate an issuer's valuation trend—to compare its IPO valuation to what it was in its pre-IPO offerings. A result of such analysis will be the realization that much of the appreciation may not be explained by better performance or reduced risk, but by the notion that *public investors should pay (a lot) more* than private investors. That presumption is sure to be challenged as public investors wise up.

Valuation disclosure sets the stage for all these things to happen. Issuers will feel compelled to compete for investors much like merchants do for customers. Some in the investment business will scorn this prospect. It erodes the influence of clubby networks and seems, well, undignified. But competition is the cornerstone of capitalism and economies are more vibrant when they are as open as a bazaar.

Some believe, mistakenly, that the SEC approves an issuer's valuation. It doesn't. Rather, the agency assesses whether an issuer complies with disclosure requirements that caution *caveat emptor*.[2] A "buyer beware" tone makes sense, especially for valuation, because there is no reliable way to assess what one should be. Besides, in a market economy, prices are set in the market. But a Don't Ask, Don't Tell position does not make sense. If one doesn't know what valuation it is, how can it be judged?

There is a clear role here for government–the SEC–to promote transparency and competition. Absent a regulatory requirement, valuation disclosure will not be commonplace. Attorneys will advise issuers to not do it, citing concern that disgruntled investors might later argue the company represented itself as being worth the valuation. An issuer that is willing to disclose its pre-money valuation will find the task more complex than just providing the figure because the prospectus will also need to explain what valuation is.

The following concept formula summarizes why a disclosure requirement is needed.

No General Requirement to Disclose Valuation	=	Lack of Context for Voluntary Disclosures That Are Made	→	A Long Time Before Market Forces Lead to Voluntary Disclosures

Buyers in most markets–housing, clothing, food–know that there can be a difference between price and worth. Such items have utility, so it is easy to judge worth. It is harder to evaluate price versus worth for items that lack utility, like a stock. That's because it's hard for anyone to know what one is worth. Those who are valuation-unaware are further disadvantaged in making their judgment–they do not know the "real price."

Grocery stores demonstrate the potential benefit of valuation disclosure. Unit pricing helps shoppers evaluate and compare products. When it's not present, they must calculate the price per pound, per ounce, etc. Many don't because they are hurried or uncomfortable doing so. Absent unit pricing, food companies compete based on brand, advertising, packaging, and shelf position. With it, there is more emphasis on value for the price. Nutritional fact panels take the analogy further. Disclosure of ingredients and nutritional information encourages manufacturers to offer what consumers value–healthier foods. Similar dynamics are possible in the market for equity securities.

Skeptics of a valuation disclosure requirement might consider that more money has undoubtedly been lost by investors who overpaid for a stock than by fraud, which is a focus of regulators. Also, investors who are not valuation-aware are more susceptible to behavior that former US Federal Reserve Chairman Alan Greenspan dubbed "irrational exuberance."

In an online post, an investment advisor shared this humorous illustration of it:
> At the height of the dot-com boom, the stock of the stodgy Computer Literacy Inc. rose by 33% in a single day simply by changing their name to "fatbrain.com."

---

[2] Some states use their "blue sky" laws to evaluate an issuer's valuation, but, they lack authority over offerings that are registered with the SEC. More on this in Chapter 17, "Causes of Investor Loss: Fraud, Overpayment & Failure."

Funnier still is the tale of Mannatech, Inc., whose shares shot up 368% in the first two days following the initial public offering. Tech-crazed investors were keen to invest in anything to do with the internet and a company called Mannatech certainly sounded like it fit the bill.

The only problem was that Mannatech makes laxatives!

A similar expression of irrational exuberance was reported in December 2017. The microcap stock of Long Island Iced Tea Corp surged 500 percent after it announced it had changed its name to "Long Blockchain Corp."

The SEC's present position on valuation disclosure—no requirement to disclose—does nothing to inhibit such irrational market behavior.

Two things seem true. In the future, more venture-stage companies will offer stock to a larger pool of valuation-unaware investors. Also, markets benefit buyers when relevant information is readily available to them.

Valuation disclosure may sound esoteric, but it's not. The SEC requires issuers to disclose risk factors in offering documents. Frequently, the result is pages of eye-glazing prose. A requirement for valuation disclosure could be accomplished in a few sentences.

In and of itself, the figure would not necessarily mean much. As discussed in Chapter 15, "Evaluating Valuation," it is a challenge for anyone to evaluate a valuation. But one can't contemplate something unless they know what it is and engage in discussion with others attempting to evaluate it.

At a micro level, valuation disclosure will make it easier to ensure that investors and companies consider an important data point that has historically been in the closet. At a higher level, it will encourage market forces to work in capital markets as they do elsewhere—it promotes competition for buyers. A consequence of this will be better-informed investors. At an existential level, it promotes thinking about what constitutes value and how uncertainty is distributed.

All of this will lead market forces to improve how capitalism works.

A friend bemoaned to me that his son, who had been doing well in his computer science studies, had changed his major to philosophy, specifically existential philosophy. "What do they do all day?" he asked rhetorically. "Sit around asking, How high is up?"

Once it is understood that alternative capital structures are possible, philosophers will be among those who debate valuations. A conventional one will encourage IPO investors to emphasize potential over performance, which supports the axiom of secondary market investors—"buy on the rumor, sell on the news." The Fairshare Model will cause people to consider the extent to which value should be based on anticipation versus on delivery.

People can vacillate between the two ideas because each has appeal. They are a challenge to reconcile, however. Hence, the role for philosophic-minded folks. Physics offers a similar conundrum. Is light composed of waves, or particles, or both?

What Valuation Disclosure Might Look Like

What might a valuation disclosure requirement look like? The SEC calls for public comments before issuing a new rule, and respondents on this subject will surely have an array of views. Here are my thoughts.

To generate useful market data, the rule should apply to all equity offerings, both private and public. One might argue that the valuation in a private offering should not be public, but private companies are already required to inform securities regulators when they sell stock. Furthermore, a valuation is calculable from the information in many filings, but it will be easier to know the correct figure if the issuer states what it is. Another reason to include private companies is that some angel investors are uncomfortable calculating a valuation; just because they are rich enough to invest doesn't mean they will calculate the valuation. The cost of a full scope requirement is miniscule while the benefits are vast.[3]

Where should the disclosure appear in a prospectus? On the front page, where the price per share is displayed and in the section that summarizes key aspects of the offering.

What should the disclosure say? Something like the following:

> Based on the terms of the offering, we [the issuer] have given our company a valuation of $XXX. This is calculated by multiplying the shares outstanding at the time of the offering by the offering price per share.

An issuer should be allowed to offer a valuation that is calculated differently—if the explanation makes sense to the SEC. For example, a company may have good reason to exclude restricted shares from the calculation. A Fairshare Model issuer will exclude Performance Stock from its valuation and focus on the conditions that will trigger conversions to Investor Stock.

> "Take the two popular words today, 'information' and 'communication.' They are often used interchangeably, but they signify quite different things. Information is giving out; communication is getting through."
>
> –Sydney J. Harris
>
> "The single biggest problem in communication is the illusion that it has taken place."
>
> –Anonymous
>
> Both quotes provided by Dr. Mardy Grothe (drmardy.com)

What Disclosure of the Basis for the Valuation Might Look Like

A compelling case can be made for valuation disclosure. Should there be a requirement for an issuer to discuss how it arrived at the figure? I think companies should be encouraged to discuss the basis for a valuation but not be required to do so.

---

[3] Beginning in 2009, the SEC required companies to use a technology called XBRL in their regulatory filings that makes it easier for readers to find, extract and analyze data. Valuation disclosure follows that spirit as well as that of the so-called fintech movement, a term that applies to innovation in financial services.

Why? If management doesn't want to talk about it, they will say something like this:

> The initial public offering price of our common stock was determined through negotiations between us and our underwriters.

If valuation *must* be disclosed, issuers may want to say something about it. The following is an example of a more informative explanation:

> We estimate the fair value of our common stock using a discounted cash flow model and in consideration of the following factors:
>
> - the market value of comparable companies,
> - our historical results and forecasted profitability,
> - our market and liquidation value of our assets, and
> - other conditions that affect our business.

Issuers inclined to discuss their valuation in greater detail may struggle with what to say. Just as it's hard for an investor to evaluate one, it is a challenge for a company to explain why it set one where it did.

Here is a Top Ten list of candid explanations (i.e., not written by a lawyer) that one might see:

Top Ten Explanations for a Pre-Money Valuation You MIGHT See

10. We applied a multiple of 2.3X to our projected revenue for next year.

9. We applied a multiple of 8X to our projected income in three years.

8. We need $10 million, and our founders want 55 percent of the company, so that works out to a valuation of $12.2 million.

7. A valuation expert assessed our projections and risk factors, then used a sophisticated model to set a valuation range; we selected the midpoint.

6. We expect to be worth $40 million within three years, so we valued the company at $10 million to offer an attractive deal.

5. Our management team is worth it.

4. We created a five-year income projection and assumed a constant growth rate thereafter. To this, we applied a cost of capital of 18 percent to arrive at the present value of our company.

3. We met with lots of smart people and came up with a figure that made sense to everyone.

2. Firms in Silicon Valley and New York City are reportedly being valued at $500 million—we're based in the Midwest, so we offer a discount.

1. Our principal competitor has twenty times more customers than we do, but our product is better, so we should be valued at a premium.[B]

For fun, here are some explanations an issuer may have for a valuation that you'll *never see* in an offering document, especially one reviewed by an issuer's attorney:

Top 10 Explanations for a Pre-Money Valuation You Will NOT See

10. Beer pong.

9.   The size of our potential market is $6 billion; we expect to own one percent of that.

8.   VC backed companies are getting that.

7.   Consensus figure from our Ayn Rand book club.

6.   A formula: (Number of founders X $5 million) + (number of engineers X $2 million).

5.   We sense opportunity!

4.   Our business model is disruptive.

3.   We intend to be the top player in our space.

2.   We applied a multiple to our projected loss, then changed the negative sign to a positive.

1.   If all goes well, it's reasonable!

Valuation Disclosure – Why Hasn't It Happened Already?

Why doesn't an issuer's prospectus say something like, "our valuation is $X" or "our valuation is less than" that of comparable companies? The underlying reason is that many people associate valuation with worth. Plus, it is difficult to distinguish price from worth when dealing with stock.

As a result, an issuer's statement on what its valuation is and how it compares has rich potential to confuse people. That's why attorneys will discourage issuers from voluntarily discussing their valuation—it can foster misunderstanding.

There are other reasons why issuers don't compete for public investors by offering better terms. These four interlinked ones are in Chapter 5, "The Problem with a Conventional Capital Structure."

1. Public investors pay "retail" for venture-stage investments but don't know it.

2. They are not offered a better deal because they don't demand it.

3. They don't demand better deals because they are not valuation-savvy.

4. They aren't valuation-savvy because regulators don't require valuation disclosure, and, companies see no benefit from voluntarily stating what their valuation is and why they set it where they did.

Are these qualities the hallmarks of market-driven capitalism? Or, is it something else, a self-serving arrangement among those in positions of influence?

When you think about it, the dynamics affecting IPO valuations are peculiar. In most markets, sellers attract buyers by offering deals. So, why is price-based competition not prevalent in public equity? I'm hesitant to say it's because the market is rigged because that suggests a degree of intentionality that I'm uncomfortable with and more control than anyone probably has. It may be better to say that the market is tilted against public investors.

For competition to occur, investors must be valuation-aware. Market players are not eager to see that happen. Issuers don't want to compete on price. And investment banks benefit when investors are valuation-unsavvy. After all, an IPO is considered a success if there is a "pop" from the offering price. That translates into happy IPO investors who often flip their shares to those who lack the influence required to get shares from the issuer. There is a regenerative quality to this system; bankers who have a record of delivering a pop will attract customers who can help them secure new deals.

Fundamentally, issuers don't compete for average investors because they are not a market force; they rarely shape outcomes. They are rather, the target of market forces; they reside at the bottom of the capital market food chain. The eagerness of these buyers to compete for shares in the secondary market is the foundation of the system.

Government has an opportunity to encourage competition by requiring valuation disclosure. Why hasn't it? I have a two-part theory.

The first part deals with Congress, where many politicians raise campaign money from the financial services lobby. The CBS news magazine *60 Minutes* reports that several members of Congress have become "very, very wealthy" in office as a result of their ability to astutely trade stocks or get shares in hot IPOs.[c]

There are consumer-oriented legislators, of course, but many of them seem to have little interest in capital markets. They are more likely to oppose the ability of average investors to buy stock in risky companies than to find ways to make capital markets more competitive.

The second part deals with the SEC. I suspect the reason that it hasn't required valuation disclosure is because the financial services industry is certain to discourage it—and there is no political outcry for it. Since the agency is wholly dependent on Congress for its annual appropriations, this is a recipe for inaction on valuation disclosure.

In March 2012, former SEC chairman Arthur Levitt interviewed the then-current chairwoman of the SEC, Mary Schapiro, on his radio show. Concluding a discussion about the failure of the Congress to approve "self-funding" for the SEC, Mr. Levitt said the following. [Bold added for emphasis]

> I guess I can afford to be more cynical now, Mary. I think that the reason you didn't get self-funding was because Congress didn't want to give up the appropriation power over the agency. Because historically, it's **self-funding** for them in terms of campaign contributions. I can say it now. You probably can't.[D]

If the SEC were self-funded it would use the money that it collects in fees, fines, and settlements to cover its budget. Self-funded financial regulatory agencies include the Federal Reserve, the Federal Deposit Insurance Corporation, and the Office of the Comptroller of Currency. The only two that are not are the SEC and the Commodities Futures Trading Commission (CFTC).

Among those in favor of self-funding for them is the Systemic Risk Council, whose members include former SEC Chairman William Donaldson and former CFTC Chairwoman Brooksley Born. They argue that the difference between self-funding and the Congressional appropriations process is "enormous." [Bold added for emphasis]

> **Self-funding** helps agencies hire and retain good staff and **insulates them from political pressure exerted by the deep-pocketed institutions they regulate.** It also allows them to make and implement strategic decisions to adapt to changing markets and build needed information technology to become more effective and efficient, all which require multiyear budget certainty. The SEC and CFTC have none of these advantages.[E]

Of course, it may also be that the SEC staff just doesn't see this as an issue, even though the agency's motto is "The investor's advocate." After all, an investor just needs to pull two numbers out of the document and multiply them, something that would be obvious to those who work at the SEC. But, this logic is inconsistent with the lessons learned from unit pricing in grocery stores. That also requires a simple calculation that many shoppers are too uncomfortable or busy to make. Unit pricing empowers buyers to make wiser choices and encourages competition that benefits consumers.

Summation

I close out this section on valuation with a call for action by you. If you want to see market forces work for public investors, you and other like-minded people must do something. In Chapter 3, "Orientation," I wrote:

> Changing The-Way-Things-Are-Now always involves challenges. It has been observed that *change occurs when the pain associated with doing things differently is less than the pain of continuing to do it the way it's been done.* That suggests that public investors should channel Howard Beale—they should make their discontent known.

In the movie *Network*, Howard Beale is a news anchor who exhorts his viewers to go to their windows and yell out, "I'm mad as hell, and I'm not going to take this anymore!" Channel your inner Howard Beale. Then, in polite language, send the SEC chairman a message that conveys your support for a valuation disclosure requirement. If enough people do this, the matter is likely to capture the attention of the SEC staff. A simple message like this should suffice:

> *Dear SEC Chairman,*
>
> *I understand that the SEC does not require issuers of equity securities to make prominent disclosure in offering documents of the valuation that they give themselves. I urge you to change this. I hope the commission will make pre-money valuation a required disclosure for both private and public offerings.*
>
> *I support initiatives that encourage market forces to improve investor protections. If the SEC requires such disclosure, more companies may compete for investors by offering lower valuations and other favorable terms.*
>
> *Sincerely,*
>
> *[Your name and address]*

The commission provides this email address chairmanoffice@sec.gov for communications to the Office of the Chairman. The postal mail address is:

> Office of the Chairman
> Securities and Exchange Commission
> 100 F Street, NE
> Washington, DC 20549

Send your congressional representative and senators a similar message via their websites; those running for reelection are likely to pay attention. If you can speak to a new candidate for federal office, ask them to support valuation disclosure. Also, use social media to create awareness of the valuation disclosure movement. If you live outside the US, take similar action in your country. Equity crowdfunding is further along in Canada and Europe, so other countries might adopt valuation disclosure rules before the US.

Over time, valuation disclosure will encourage market forces to benefit non-professional investors. It will also shorten the time it takes for the Fairshare Model to emerge as a popular alternative for companies that raise venture-stage capital via an IPO.

For a perspective on how long it might take, see "The Concept Gap" at the end of Chapter 9, "Fairshare Model History & the Future."

Three Reasons Why Valuation Disclosure WILL HAPPEN

1. It is the right thing to do.

2. The cost to implement it is trivial.

3. Popular support becomes visible enough to policymakers that it counteracts the reasons why it will not happen, which are below.

Four Reasons Why Valuation Disclosure WILL NOT HAPPEN

1. It is not in the interests of powerful players in the financial sector.

2. Policymakers, possibly influenced by the preceding reason, don't perceive the absence of disclosure as a big problem—after all, anyone can calculate it.

3. Advocates of valuation disclosure lack the resources to effectively lobby policymakers.

4. Those who can benefit from valuation disclosure have a weak understanding of what valuation signifies.

What's Next?

This concludes Section 3. The chapters in the next section address fraud, failure, and the objections some people have to public venture capital.

Chapter Endnotes

Contextual references for material in this chapter appear as numbered footnotes on the page where the reference is made. **Source references** for material in this chapter appear below as endnotes with capital letter identifiers.

A Alibaba Group 2014 prospectus, page 62 and 267. Technically, the foreign-based Alibaba sold American Depository Shares that represent ordinary shares.

B Hesseldahl, Arik. "Domo's Josh James Defends His $2 Billion Valuation." *Recode.* April 29, 2015. Accessed May 16, 2018. fairsharemodel.com/Domos. Domo went public in June 2018–its IPO was among the worst performing of that year.

C "Insiders: The Road to the Stock Act" report, *CBS News, 60 Minutes,* aired Jan. 17, 2012, fairsharemodel.com/StockAct.

D "A Closer Look With Arthur Levitt: SEC's Mary Schapiro (Audio)", Mar. 23, 2012, *Bloomberg.* fairsharemodel.com/Levitt-Schapiro. Check out Levitt's other podcasts at fairsharemodel.com/Levitt-Podcast.

E Prial, Dunstan. "SEC: Self-Funding Vs. Congressional Appropriations." *Fox Business.* May 17, 2013. Accessed May 10, 2018. fairsharemodel.com/Self-funding.

SECTION 4:

Investor Loss

Entrepreneurs, and those most interested in seeing them succeed, tend to view the prospect of less expensive and burdensome requirements to raise capital from public investors as an angelic development.

But the very idea sends shudders down the spines of some policymakers, regulators, and opinion leaders. They see a potential demon that will bring harm to the wee villagers—average investors.

The JOBS Act led to changes in securities regulations that were cheered by the first camp and jeered by the other. That's because venture-stage companies typically raise capital in a private offering—the kind available only to accredited investors—and the changes made it easier to do so in a public offering. Some supporters of securities regulation liberalization believe more change is needed—like higher limits to the amount that can be raised in an IPO without a registration statement.

Those who oppose the JOBS Act reforms include people who want to see the income and wealth thresholds that define who is an accredited investor raised to adjust them for inflation. Doing that would make it *harder* for startups to raise capital because it would *shrink* the pool of accredited investors.

As a result, the debate is likely to be renewed. Those who oppose further liberalization of securities regulations focus on fear of fraud and argue that it is too difficult for average investors to make money in these types of investments.

This section considers the objections to making it easier for venture-stage companies to sell stock to average investors because such investments have inherent high failure risk.

Chapters in this section:

Chapter 17: Causes of Investor Loss: Fraud, Overpayment, and Failure

Chapter 18: Failure

Chapter 19: Other Objections to Public Venture Capital

Chapter 17:

Causes of Investor Loss:
Fraud, Overpayment, and Failure

What's Included in This Chapter

- Introduction
- The Anxiety
- Disclosure and Merit Review
- Registered and Exempt Offerings
- How Investors Lose Money
- Unpacking Fraud
  - Fraud Before the IPO
  - Fraud When IPO Investors Invest
  - Fraud After the IPO
  - Fear of Potential Fraud vs. Punishment of Actual Fraud
- Closing Thoughts on Fraud
- Investors Overpay
- Failure
  - A Prosecutor's Thoughts on Failure (and the Good Life)
  - A Regulator's Thoughts on the Need for Risk Tolerance
- What's Next?
- Chapter Endnotes

Introduction

The demon on the preceding page symbolizes investor loss writ large. Because we associate demons with darkness and shadows, our sense of them can be exaggerated: they evoke less fear in bright light.

Loss can occur in a variety of ways. Fraud, overpayment (i.e., overvaluation at buy in) and failure are the focus of this chapter because they are often used to describe the demon.[1] To help you place each of these causes in perspective, this chapter casts light on them.

I will argue that fear of fraud in an IPO from a venture-stage company is overblown, and that the most significant causes of loss are failure risk and valuation risk, which are discussed in Chapter 2, "The Big Idea and Thesis," and elaborated on in Chapter 20, "Investor Risk in Venture-Stage Companies."

The Fairshare Model lowers the risk of overpaying for a stock. So, if fear of fraud is exaggerated and valuation risk can be contained, investors' principal fear should be about failure—that a company they invest in will not achieve its operational goals.

Before getting to the causes of investor loss, let's consider the anxiety that surrounds efforts to make it less expensive for startups to sell stock to public investors, and the two approaches regulators use to protect investors—disclosure and merit review.

The Anxiety

Is the JOBS Act a liberalization of securities law that will stimulate economic growth and job creation? Or is it a weakening of safeguards that will harm average investors? It will take years to figure out the answer, but there are thoughtful people who fear its consequences.

One of them is Steven Rattner. He is a Wall Street financier who was lead advisor to the Obama administration's *Presidential Task Force on the Auto Industry,* which restructured the US auto industry. In 2013, before rules to implement the JOBS Act where created, he wrote the following in a *New York Times* op-ed called "A Sneaky Way to Deregulate."

> Slapping a catchy acronym like the JOBS Act [for Jumpstart Our Business Startups Act] on a piece of legislation makes it more difficult for politicians to oppose it – and indeed, that's what happened with the Jumpstart Our Business Startups Act. Its enticing acronym notwithstanding, the JOBS Act has little to do with employment. It's a hodgepodge of provisions that together constitute the greatest loosening of securities regulation in modern history.
>
> Most troublesome is the legalization of "crowd funding," the ability of startup companies to raise capital from small investors on the Internet. As soon as regulations required to implement the new rules are completed, people who invest money in startups through sites similar to Kickstarter will be able to receive a financial interest in the soliciting company, much like buying shares on the stock exchange. But the enterprises soliciting these funds will hardly be big corporations like Walmart or Exxon; they will be small startups with no track records.
>
> Picking winners among the many young companies seeking money is a tough business, even for the most sophisticated investors. Indeed, most professionally run venture funds lose money. For individuals, it's pure folly. Buy a lottery ticket instead. Your chance of winning is likely to be higher. Supporters say the amounts that can be lost will be limited. But an American earning $40,000 can still risk $2,000 per year.

---

[1] There are other causes of loss such as macroeconomic conditions, market manipulation and the fact that thinly traded stocks have poor liquidity.

To be sure, the Sarbanes-Oxley securities regulation law has overly burdened public companies and deterred initial public offerings. But the JOBS Act's update for "emerging growth companies" goes too far. Although 25 Democratic senators and one independent, Bernie Sanders, opposed the legislation, it had broad support from business groups and from some research organizations like the Kauffman Foundation. The Obama administration signed on, convinced that the need to encourage startup capital was great and that the legislation's shortcomings could be fixed during the implementation phase.

The largest number of jobs likely to be created by the JOBS Act will be for lawyers needed to clean up the mess that it will create.**A**

I wholeheartedly agree with Rattner that it is tough for anyone to pick a winning startup. I'll add that lottery tickets have odds that are far worse. And that a loss on a stock is tax-deductible but a loss on lottery tickets is not. Also, that the largest purveyors of lottery tickets are affiliated with government.

But I digress.

There are reasons to be anxious about making it easier for average investors to buy risky stocks. There are also reasons to experiment in this space; these types of companies are the engine for economic growth, job creation, and innovation. I call on critics of the JOBS Act to support ways to make investing less risky. One way to do this is to support a valuation disclosure requirement, the subject of the last chapter.

My appreciation of this anxiety is enhanced by my experience with Fairshare, Inc., a company I cofounded in 1996. To briefly recap what is in Chapter 9, "Fairshare Model History & the Future," Fairshare provided an online platform for investor education and interaction. One could say we tried to be a Facebook for investors years before there was Facebook. Our goal was to build a membership large enough to attract companies with a direct public offering (DPO). Once there, our plan was to let issuers pitch our members if they used the Fairshare Model, passed a due diligence review, and allowed members to invest as little as $100. We would be commission-free—an investor-oriented marketplace for DPOs.

Fairshare offered both free and paid memberships but said that paid members might not get more privileges than a free member. We also said that we were unsure if our plan would work. Essentially, our membership drive was a rewards-based crowdfunding campaign with lots of caveats. To solicit feedback, we posted our business plan on our website and mailed it to the SEC and other securities regulators.

The agencies that expressed concern allowed us to address them. The California regulator was the exception; it ordered us to cease and desist from offering memberships to California residents. The response from the California Department of Corporations was striking for three reasons.

1. It was premature: we said that it could take years to attract DPOs. In other words, the agency banned our product while it was early in research and development.

2. It was severe: other states engaged us in discussion, but California immediately responded in a harsh manner.

3. It utilized unique legal reasoning: it declared that a Fairshare membership was an investment contract; a position that other regulators explicitly rejected. Not only that, California said that a *free membership was an investment contract!* **2**

---

2 To form a contract, jurisdictions generally require that consideration—money or a promise to do something of value—must be exchanged. It is extraordinary to find that a contract can be formed without consideration.

So, California's enforcement action was premature, severe, and relied on novel reasoning. Its regulator was so alarmed by Fairshare's plan that it acted long before we identified a candidate company for an offering to our members. The agency sensed a demon and quickly took enforcement action. Fast-forward nearly two decades.

The JOBS Act is law and new rules have been issued by the SEC that alter the landscape of securities regulation. Nonetheless, the California Department of Corporations identifies its cease and desist order against Fairshare as a precedent-setting decision.

I see the California order as a manifestation of anxiety, expressed in this conceptual equation:

Internet + Venture capital + Average Investors = Something Bad

Steven Rattner and others might formulate the anxiety this way:

Public Venture Capital = (Hard to Succeed At + Vulnerable to Fraud) = Something Bad

Frankly, many people share the sentiments expressed in these equations.

Disclosure and Merit Review

Before addressing how average investors lose money in venture-stage investing—the demon—let's discuss some of the ways that government tries to protect investors. Of course, the "hair on fire" fear is fraud. Arthur Levitt, Jr., former chairman of the Securities and Exchange Commission, said this about the ability of regulators to prevent it.

By "government," I mean any level of it, as well as self-regulated organizations such as the Financial Industry Regulatory Authority (FINRA).

> I don't know of any government agency, any US attorney office [or] any district attorney that has been able to uncover a fraud until the fraud is perpetrated. So, the notion that the SEC is going to be there before the fraud happens is, I think, ridiculous.[B]

That said, securities regulation has broad anti-fraud provisions and government dedicates significant resources to enforcing it. To deter fraud, it relies on three basic strategies:

1. Help investors learn how to recognize and avoid questionable investments.
2. Make it difficult for suspicious offerings to clear the review process.
3. Investigate, prosecute, and punish wrongdoers to discourage others from acting similarly.

How the first and the third strategy are implemented is obvious—not so for the second one. That's because few people see the comment letter that a securities examiner sends to a company in response to disclosure documents a company files for a proposed public offering. Before it can solicit investors, a company must address (or clear) those comments to the satisfaction of the regulator.

The SEC and about twenty states rely on the disclosure standard for their review. Its goal is to ensure that an issuer's disclosures are full and fair. If a regulator suspects relevant information has been withheld or that disclosures are incomplete or misleading, the review process will take longer. If examiners think an offering is dubious, it is likely to be slow-walked. This makes it more expensive and discourages broker-dealers from agreeing to sell it. Ultimately, however, government relies on investors to assess an investment. As mentioned before, a former SEC examiner told me the premise, "You can sell stock in a dead horse, so long as you disclose that the horse is dead." Put another way, it is not fraud to sell stock in a dead horse if investors know, or should know, that it is dead.

A merit review goes further; government determines whether an offering is suitable for investors within its jurisdiction. It is used by about thirty states but not by the SEC. There isn't a uniform standard, however. The way it's applied can vary by state and even by examiner. If a merit review state finds that an offering is unfair, too risky, or otherwise unsuitable for its residents, it denies the issuer the right to sell it to them.

From an issuer's perspective, having multiple standards for suitability is vexing. It drags out the process and significantly increases the cost of capital.

Philip A. Feigin is a former Colorado securities commissioner who has led the North American Securities Administrators Association (NASAA), an organization that promotes uniformity in state securities laws, which are referred to as blue sky laws.[3] Feigin describes merit review this way:

> Merit review was the heart and soul of the original "blue sky" laws, the authority of state securities administrators to deny securities registration to an offering that, in the administrator's view, was "unfair, unjust or inequitable," or would "tend to work a fraud" on investors. At its height in the '70s and '80s, about 36 states applied merit review standards to new offerings already reviewed for disclosure by the SEC. While laudable in intention, making decisions based on those standards proved challenging to enforce and defend over the years.

> The goals of merit review are among the most misunderstood in American finance, by critics and perhaps state regulators both. Merit standards are intended to make an investment "fair" to the investor. It is not intended to be a predictor of profitability.

> Two classic examples of merit guidelines relate to repayment of principal loans and "cheap stock." Merit states place tight restrictions on issuers using investors' money, offering proceeds, to pay off prior loans made to the company by its principals. Instead, offering proceeds must be applied to the company's operations. Also under merit review, company insiders are required to place some or all of their promoters' shares a.k.a. "cheap stock" (shares they received from the company for nothing or at a price much lower than the price investors will pay for the registered shares) in escrow until such time as the overall value of the company has increased in an amount proportional to that "cheap stock"/public price differential.[c]

In addition to insider loans and cheap stock, some merit review states will consider an issuer's ability to pay fixed charges on debt—interest, principal, and fees—without the IPO proceeds, and whether the new stock's voting rights are inferior to that of already issued shares.

---

[3] An apocryphal explanation for the term "blue sky" is that these laws were to prevent someone from taking a sailor's britches and offering them to investors as "a piece of the blue sky." It's a poetic way to characterize a fraudulent or highly speculative business proposition. There is little uniformity among blue sky laws but about forty states utilize a shared model developed by NASAA.

Notwithstanding Feigin's statement that a merit review should not assess future profitability, states have been known to disqualify a public offering because little revenue had been generated, the prospect for near-term profitability was poor and/or the valuation is excessive relative to its tangible book value, earnings per share and/or financial condition.[D]

Of course, virtually all venture-stage companies have such characteristics, which led securities attorney Samuel S. Guzak to make the following observation.

> In 1980, the Apple Computer IPO became the poster child for what was wrong with allowing an additional layer of so-called state "blue sky" review. Massachusetts and more than a dozen other states barred non-institutional investors from participating in this IPO, viewing it as another "hot" IPO—too hot for the ordinary investor.[E]

Registered and Exempt Offerings

Harmonizing regulations can improve entrepreneurial access to capital and reduce its cost. The JOBS Act doesn't make regulations more uniform, but it makes it possible to raise a significantly larger amount of money without a merit review.[4] To understand how, we need to distinguish a registered offering from one that is exempt from registration.

When federal securities laws were created in the 1930s, the states ceded their authority over securities sold in their state to a new federal agency, the Securities and Exchange Commission, if it involved a "covered security." That's one that will trade on an SEC-approved stock exchange. The idea was that if an issuer met the criteria of such an exchange, its offering need only be reviewed by the SEC.

The vehicle for a review is a two-part registration statement prepared by the issuer.[F] Part I is the prospectus, which is the offering document that must be delivered to anyone who is offered or buys the securities. It describes the securities and the company's business, management, major shareholders, financial statements, and risk factors. Part II has information the issuer does not need to deliver to investors but must file with the SEC (i.e., contracts, patents, compensation agreements).

Registration is a complex, expensive process that requires audited financial statements and has ongoing reporting requirements (e.g., quarterly, and annual filings). Policymakers have long recognized that full registration was overkill for small public offerings and unnecessary in private ones because they are sold to accredited investors. As a result, some offerings are exempt—excused—from full registration.

Exempt offerings are subject to regulation, but the requirements are less demanding than those for a covered security. Also, state blue sky laws that don't apply to a registered offering may apply to an exempt one.

When the body of US securities regulation was formed in the 1930s, the SEC created an exempt offering called Regulation A or "Reg. A" for short. Some refer to it as a "mini-IPO" because, as Sam Guzak puts it, Reg. A "allowed small companies to sell their shares to the general public through an abbreviated SEC registration and review process which even dispensed with the need for audited financial statements and with no ongoing reporting obligations."[G] Significantly, a Reg. A offering is not subject to blue sky laws, hence, it is not subject to a merit review.

---

[4] I thank Sara Hanks of CrowdCheck for her insights. CrowdCheck (crowdcheck.com) provides due diligence and disclosure services for online alternative investments.

With the JOBS Act, the Congress authorized changes to Reg. A that are so substantial that it is now called Reg. A+. There are two forms of a Reg. A+ offering: "Tier 1" and "Tier 2." Each requires SEC review, the disclosure standard, and each result in tradable stock that can be sold to any investor. A Tier 1 offering can be used to raise up to $20 million *without audited financial statements, but it is subject to blue sky laws,* and a merit review state can require a Tier 1 issuer to provide audited financials. A Tier 2 offering *requires audited financials* and can be used to raise up to $50 million. It requires SEC review only; it is not subject to state blue sky laws.

Thus, the JOBS Act increased the amount that can be raised in a public offering that is not subject to state merit review from $5 million to $50 million. Reg. A+ was effective June 2015. Over time, it will present a laboratory for how to balance opportunity for both small companies and unaccredited investors against concerns about fraud. That is, it will test how well investors are protected without a merit review.

Other exemptions from registration exist. The JOBS Act also led to Rule CF, the crowdfunding exemption that is exempt from blue sky laws. A $10 million exemption was proposed to Congress, but investor protection concerns led it to be reduced to $1 million. Anyone can invest in one, but there is an annual limit on how much an unaccredited investor may invest. Unlike a Reg. A+ offering, there are restrictions on when shares can be resold and the options for secondary trading are not robust.

Another exemption affected by the JOBS Act is Regulation D (Reg. D), which affects private offerings.[5] The table below highlights some forms of offerings.

	Public Offerings				Private Offerings		
	Most public offerings	Rule CF: Crowdfunding	Reg. A+ Tier 1	Reg. A+ Tier 2	Reg. D Rule 504	Reg. D Rule 506b	Reg. D Rule 506c
Registered	X			X			
Exempt and not subject to state blue sky laws		X				X	X
Exempt but subject to state blue sky laws			X		X		
Who may invest	Anyone	Anyone, with limits for unaccredited investors			Anyone	Accredited investors and up to 35 financially sophisticated unaccredited investors	Accredited investors
Audited financials	Yes	No	No	Yes	No	No	No
Max. offering size	No limit	$1 million	$20 million	$50 million	$5 million	No limit	No limit

---

5 A Reg. D, Rule 506 offering provides a federal exemption from registration that supersedes state rules. A Reg. D, Rule 504 offering does not.

Exemptions for small public offerings have existed at the state and federal level for years, but they have not been used to significant effect to raise capital. Why?

- It is easier to target accredited investors because fewer of them are needed to fill out a round of financing–they can write big checks–and Reg. D offerings have few regulatory requirements.

- Small public offerings have an intermediary problem. To recap how it's described in Chapter 6, "Crowdfunding and the Fairshare Model," issuers with such an offering often lack an established following of investors to sell their stock to. Broker-dealers tend to be disinterested in selling small offerings and the investment platforms authorized by the JOBS Act have not proved to be particularly effective vehicles to market them.

How Investors Lose Money

How do public investors lose money on a venture-stage company? Three broad possibilities come to mind:

1. fraud,

2. investors overpay (i.e., buy-in at an excessive valuation), and/or

3. failure.

The ensuing pages consider each possibility separately, but they are not mutually exclusive–two or all can be present. For example, a failing company (#3) may engage in fraud (#1) to forestall collapse or benefit insiders. Or investors may overpay (#2) to invest in a company that eventually fails (#3), possibly because it was poorly managed or had little prospect of success. Then too, a company may engage in fraud (#1) to persuade investors to overpay (#2), then fail (#3), or not.

If a company is thinly traded, as many small-cap stocks are, there is yet another way for investors to lose money: lack of liquidity. That is, the stock price might be $2 if you are buying and $1 if you are selling. A stock with a wide spread between the buy and sell (or bid and ask) price is a "Roach Hotel."[6] It can be a significant contributor to investor loss, but I don't include it above because it is driven by an issuer's market, not by its business. Similarly, there are ways that a broker-dealer might engage in fraud, but I don't list them here because they are a function of the trading market, not the issuer.

Multiple perils face investors in venture-stage companies. However, the powerful, fear-inducing word–*fraud*–is frequently used by those who oppose making it easier for average investors to buy stock in them. I suspect that relatively few investor losses result from fraud. When an entrepreneurial team makes a sincere effort to create value but fails, it is wrong, silly, and derogatory to say that the loss is due to fraud.

It is hard to find data on the prevalence of issuer fraud, but opponents of equity crowdfunding and small-cap investing routinely evoke the specter of it when making their case. This can leave the other side tongue-tied and defensive. They can't credibly claim that fraud will not increase. All they can do is hope to put it in context.

---

6 Here, "Roach Motel" appropriates the tagline of the *Black Flag* Roach Motel insect control device– "Roaches check in, but they don't check out." Investors who have bought thinly traded stocks know there can be a big gap between the (bid) price to buy and the (ask) price to sell. Such stocks are vulnerable to "pump-and-dump" schemes.

Opponents of this investing activity may acknowledge its broad economic benefits yet believe it should be restricted to the wealthy because they can afford a loss of investment. Since they feel that average investors should be blocked or strongly discouraged from engaging in it, their motto for equity crowdfunding is *Just Say No!*

Despite such concerns, there is reason to believe that a sizeable number of average investors want better access to venture-stage investments, and that many more investors would like better information on valuation. And it is safe to assume that all investors would like deal structures that are friendlier to them. So, one might expect to see those who opposed JOBS Act reforms to support both a valuation disclosure requirement and the Fairshare Model.

Time will tell.

Unpacking Fraud

Opponents of efforts to make it easier for small companies to sell stock to average investors often center their argument on one word–fraud. When expressed like a shout of "Fire!," it encourages people to associate fraud with venture-stage investments that fail. That is unfair.

What constitutes securities fraud? It can occur in a variety of forms. To unpack concerns about IPO fraud with startups, however, let's focus on when one might occur:

- before IPO investors invest,
- when IPO investors invest, or
- after public investors invest.

The *when* question can shed light on the *what* question–what constitutes fraud?

That, in turn, can help us better explore the key question: *Is fraud more likely when companies raise venture capital via a public offering?*

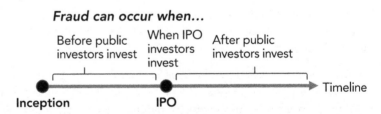

Fraud can occur when...

Before public investors invest   When IPO investors invest   After public investors invest

Inception   IPO   Timeline

Fraud Before the IPO

It takes a significant amount of time, effort, and money to conduct a public securities offering. Arguably, anyone who intends to engage in fraud is unlikely to form a company and file for an IPO. Fraudsters have other routes that are far less expensive and conspicuous.

Additionally, a stock offering requires disclosure, scrutiny, and collaboration among people who are mindful of their reputation. An inherently corrupt group will want to avoid the attention.

Can you tell if an offering is legal?

There is no obvious indication that an offering complies with securities regulations. The documents will not have a stamp, seal, or other official notation that indicates it is a legal offering.

To determine an offering's status, investors should contact their state's securities agency. An attorney, broker-dealer, or registered investment advisor can often provide insight.

Now, a scam might well be falsely presented as a lawful offering. That is, someone might represent that an offering is compliant with legal requirements when it is not. But relative to other scams, a stock offering is easier for authorities to detect and investigate. And those responsible for an unlawful offering can be required to return the money raised to investors, potentially, out of their own resources if the issuer lacks the funds to do so.

For these reasons, it seems unlikely that someone would attempt an IPO to pull off a fraud.

Fraud When IPO Investors Invest

Fraud when IPO investors invest occurs when an issuer fails to make important disclosures in a clear, truthful manner. When this happens, it may be intentional deceit. Or, it may be because management is highly confident they will succeed and/or wants to minimize negative thinking. Fraud connotes intentionality, but it can result from carelessness. Its form may be an overreaching assertion, a failure to disclose a conflict of interest, misleading data, or inadequate description of risk.

Is it fraud when a company uses faulty assumptions to value itself? Apparently not, so long as data isn't misrepresented. Bad projections are not clearly fraud. Besides, issuers have an out—as a risk factor, they say that their valuation is set arbitrarily.

Fraud can occur by omission or commission. When by omission, it may be the failure to take an action that one should take. A failure to disclose essential information is fraud via omission. Fraud via commission occurs when a wrong action is performed. For example, management may state or suggest that business is doing better than it is. Think of omission and commission as two sounds that can be combined to create bluster, overstatement, distraction, and the like.

Companies who are the target of a fraud complaint find it expensive, time consuming and emotionally draining to respond. And even if they prevail, their ability to attract new capital can be damaged. For anyone bent on deception, there are other ways to engage in fraud that have less risk.

I have no idea how often fraud occurs in a public offering, but I can point out dueling tensions on an issuer as it prepares for one. The pressure to sell the stock conflicts with the pressure to disclose why an investor should not invest. So naturally, issuers favor obtuse, boilerplate-like ways to satisfy the disclosure requirement and rely on investment banker networks, presentations, analysts, and favorable press to create the buyer demand needed to sell the offering and promote interest on the part of secondary market investors.

It can be the end of the company if regulators find that the offering was fraudulent. There are anti-fraud rules that, when violated, require an issuer to rescind or cancel an offering. That is, it can be required to send full refund checks to all investors in the offering, not just the ones who claim they were defrauded. If the company doesn't have the money to do this, its officers, directors, and significant shareholders may have to repay the money themselves.

Then, there is the potential for criminal charges.

The pressure to disclose appears to be a significant force to deter fraud at the time investors invest. If a company's management fabricates information or cherry-picks what to disclose, they face significant risks.

Again, if someone wants to engage in fraud, there are less conspicuous ways to do so than an IPO.

Fraud After the IPO

There are four points to bear in mind when considering the likelihood of fraud after an IPO:

1. If a company intends to engage in fraud before and at the IPO, it will likely continue after that. But, such a scenario is surely rare because there are more direct, less risky ways to conduct fraud. The anti-fraud provisions of securities law are broad, and the enforcement resources are significant. Using a public offering to purposely engage in fraud makes as much sense as booking a flight from San Francisco to Los Angeles by way of Denver. You could, but why would you?

2. There may be fraud before or at the IPO, but not afterwards because management is replaced or changes its behavior.

3. Fraud at the IPO seems unlikely to persist if it was unintentional.

4. Venture-stage companies present high failure risk, so adverse developments may not be due to fraud.

Given those considerations, what might fraud after the IPO look like?[H] Some basic categories are:

- misleading operational performance,
- misreported financial results,
- insider trading,
- pump and dump scams,
- undisclosed use of resources in a manner not intended to benefit the business,
- taking action that requires shareholder approval without obtaining it.

These actions run afoul of laws, rules, and regulations for anyone. Unless you believe that entrepreneurs are more intent on causing harm than other members of a community, it makes little sense to oppose steps that make it less expensive for them to raise public capital. By way of analogy, a teenager can be a licensed driver even though they are more likely to violate driving rules. They are simply subject to the same rules. For the same reason, startups can be subject to anti-fraud provisions of law that apply to established companies.

Fear of Potential Fraud vs. Punishment of Actual Fraud

Should we have barriers that make it difficult for all entrepreneurs to raise capital out of fear that some of them *might* engage in fraud? Government doesn't usually restrict activity out of fear that some will violate their responsibility in the future.[7] Rather, it pursues those suspected of doing wrong.

Closing Thoughts on Fraud

In a February 2013 panel discussion about crowdfunding, Stanford University law school professor Joseph Grundfest, a former SEC commissioner, told the audience that a presumption in securities regulation is that, "if you are wealthy, you are smart"—at least smart enough to evaluate an investment

---

[7] The idea echoes *Minority Report,* a science fiction novel by Philip K. Dick that was made into a 2002 movie, and then into a TV series in 2015. In it, futuristic police use psychic technology to detect who plans to commit a crime. Then, the police arrest the person before they can commit the crime.

and protect yourself from fraud. If you are not wealthy, the presumption is that you are not smart enough to do this. He observed that, in fact, many accredited investors are not that smart, and some unaccredited investors are. He suggested that a newly-minted Ph.D. in computer science is unlikely to qualify as an accredited investor but can expertly assess a software startup's technology. Nonetheless, securities law may not let him invest while it is a private company—he must wait until the company has a public offering.

Thus, the rules for selling securities to the wealthy are liberal while restrictive ones apply to everyone else. This construct has served society well in many respects. But a mélange of factors that include the internet, a desire to improve access to capital for young companies and rising general interest in entrepreneurial opportunities offer reasons to liberalize securities regulations that apply to average investors. Figuring out how to accommodate this while preserving investor protections is not easy.

The shortest distance between two points is usually the fastest. Similarly, a direct measure is better than an indirect one. Thus, a direct measurement of investor savviness would be better than an indirect one, like the accredited investor definition, which doesn't measure it at all. But government doesn't have a ready way to assess whether an investor understands an investment. So to minimize the number of people who can be harmed by a bad choice, the accredited investor rule provides an easy solution, albeit not a reliable one.

It has become increasingly clear, however, that there are smart, savvy non-accredited investors who want to engage in venture-stage investing. With two initiatives, the JOBS Act presents an experiment to see whether average investors profit in this investment sector by making it easier for small companies to sell stock.

- Unaccredited investors may invest in a Rule CF (crowdfunding) offering, which can be used to raise about $1 million. The shares are tradable after a year and there is an annual cap of on how much such an investor can invest in Rule CF offerings.

- The amount that can be raised in a Reg. A offering is increased from $5 million to $50 million. Some refer to such an offering, rechristened Reg. A+, as a "mini-IPO" because anyone can invest without restriction and the shares are immediately tradable.

These rules create qualms for those more interested in investor protection than liberalizing capital formation. To address their concerns about investor protections and spur innovation even further, I suggest that securities regulators require that all issuers of stock disclose their pre-money valuation. For the reasons described in Chapter 16, "Valuation Disclosure," this will encourage market forces to help all investors become better investors.

Investors Overpay

Investors can lose money when they overpay for an investment. My bet is that investors have collectively lost more money from overpriced IPOs than from fraud. It happens when the market price falls below the IPO price in the quarters that follow. Why does this happen? The key reasons are:

- Many investors are not valuation-savvy (i.e., they aren't sure what valuation is, how to calculate it, or how to evaluate one).
- It is hard to tell what a valuation "should" be.
- It is difficult for investors to get valuation history for an issuer or for comparable companies.
- Market forces are weak; issuers don't compete for investors based on valuation.

Earlier in this chapter, Steven Rattner likened an investment in a startup to a lottery ticket. It's a good analogy in that one is more likely to lose than win. But it is not a good analogy for pricing because it is easier to assess whether a lottery ticket is attractively priced than whether an IPO is. One can calculate the expected value of a lottery ticket by multiplying the prize value by the odds of winning (lotteries must disclose the odds). You can rank the appeal of different lotteries by comparing that value.

By comparison, it is tougher to evaluate an IPO valuation because:

1. There may not be a payoff at all (i.e., indefinite odds of a prize).

2. If there is a payoff, the amount is unknown (i.e., no certain prize value).

3. Investors don't have easy access to comparable valuations.

Equating an investment in a startup to a lottery ticket conveys the risk but does nothing to indicate that investors can overpay. So, let's try a different analogy.

Imagine that a significant percentage of new homes sold by developers regularly drops in value by ten percent or more. My guess is there would an outcry and that news reports would question how the price was set. Buyers expect that a new home will hold its value, especially since they take on debt to buy it. But a house resonates in our psyche in a way that a new stock does not, which makes homebuyers more sympathetic than IPO investors.

A good analogy for a new stock is hard to find. It occupies a unique space with respect to risk and price. Nonetheless, investors lose money (or opportunity for profit) when they overpay, and, public investors are the most likely to buy overvalued shares.

Why? In Chapter 5, "The Problem with a Conventional Capital Structure," I argue that weak market forces are a big reason. If they were stronger, issuers would compete for public investors by offering a better deal.

Failure

The causes of failure are explored in depth in the next chapter. Here, I simply posit that failure is a greater cause of investor loss than fraud and explore some high-level perspective on failure. To begin, consider these three points:

1. Failure is not fraud.

2. Fraud may occur in a failing firm, but it need not.

3. Fraud may be less likely to be noticed in a successful company.

Next, I'd like you to contemplate the relationship between innovation and failure at a macroeconomic level. It is uncontroversial to suggest that societies that tolerate failure are more likely to create innovative products and services than those that look down on those who try and fail.

In Chapter 10, I cite evidence of this provided by Edmund Phelps in his book *Mass Flourishing*. His research led him to conclude that societies thrive when they are economically dynamic because such dynamism spawns' growth and opportunity. It can also result in bad luck–that is, failure. For me, an important takeaway from his book is the idea that participants in a dynamic economy find a sense of purpose as they attempt to innovative. That is, its participants find greater meaning in their lives when they endeavor to create value for themselves and society—*even when the result is failure.***8**

Value is routinely measured by the income it generates, or the utility it provides. Ascribing it to an unsuccessful effort is a remarkable concept in economics, but a familiar one to philosophers and poets. Ralph Waldo Emerson said, "Life is a journey, not a destination" and Lord Alfred Tennyson penned, "Tis better to have loved and lost than never to have loved at all."

Phelps writes that modern beliefs, attitudes, and values are the foundation for a modern or dynamic economy, and that such an economy facilitates what Aristotle called the "good life."**9** Phelps argues that innovation is a byproduct of a dynamic economy and that the *pursuit of innovation* brings individuals and society meaning and vitality. Why? Because the pursuit encourages intellectual and moral growth, the *sine qua non* of human experience. You may recall the two conceptual equations I used to express Phelps's concept. They help us appreciate the upside of failure.

Modern Beliefs, Attitudes, and Values → Modern Economy → Aristotelian concept of "The Good Life"

The Good Life = The *intellectual growth* that comes from actively engaging the world + The *moral growth* that comes from creating and exploring in the face of great uncertainty

One can, therefore, say that at a macroeconomic level, the pursuit of innovation can contribute positive things to people and society, even when it results in failure.

Now, descend to the microeconomic level. How might one assess the effects of failure there? Let's consider the question from the view of entrepreneurial teams, suppliers, customers, and investors.

- **Founders:** Failure can be a badge of honor of sorts as it indicates a willingness to try to do something that demands sacrifice, talent, discipline, optimism, and pluck. A failure may exhaust them, but it can season them for other opportunities. Plus, they have the satisfaction that comes from having pursued something they were passionate about.

- **Other employees:** Employees of a failed enterprise will lose their jobs, but they can find that their experience helps them get new work and accelerate their career.

- **Suppliers:** The consequences for a supplier of a customer that fails can range from a learning experience to dire. Much depends on whether they were properly paid.

- **Customers:** The cost of a company's failure is inconsequential unless the customer was reliant on it for future services.

- **Investors:** The consolation prize for investing in a failure is a tax deduction, and a reminder to invest prudently and practice diversification.

---

8 A friend of mine, Nimish Gandhi, observed that "Entrepreneurs are different from most people. They don't view failure as defeat. Often, they find a way to come back and try again."

9 The good life is described in Chapter 10, "The Macroeconomic Context—Growth."

This breakdown presents a paradox. The *macroeconomic* benefits of failure are sensed, but it is hard to see them at a *microeconomic* level. How can there be societal level benefits to failure when it is hard to identify who the beneficiaries are?

One explanation is that the benefits of businesses that succeed more than offset the cost of those that fail. But that is unsatisfying. I've met many people who experienced failure, sometimes multiple ones, without an offsetting win. As a rule, they were happy, or at least content, to have taken the risks they did. Their pursuit of the good life enriched their lives in a way that a cautious path would not. In other words, there are people who do not have enough success to offset their failures, yet they derive satisfaction from the attempts.

> "You miss 100% of the shots you don't take."
>
> —Wayne Gretsky, hockey great

Another explanation is that an entrepreneurial culture encourages people to develop skills and attitudes that increase the skill and mobility of the economy's participants. Its failures plow and prepare the ground for new efforts. The lessons learned, directly and vicariously, enable entrepreneurial teams and the investors who back them to be more skillful the next time they try to succeed.

Then, too, failure is the shadow of a powerful emotion—hope. Where there is hope, the possibility of failure follows. That's because building a company is hard and deciding whether to invest in one is a challenge. All participants in a venture-stage ecosystem are imbued with hope. They seek to gain advantage, to make a mark, a difference, and profit. The collective hope of all these parties is the fuel of a dynamic, innovative economy.

Failure is the shadow of hope, and it is a major cause of investor loss.[10]

A Prosecutor's Thoughts on Failure (and the Good Life)

Preet Bharara is a former US Attorney for the Southern District of New York. Known for his prosecution of white-collar crimes on Wall Street and of elected officials in corruption cases, *Time* magazine named him one of the 100 most influential people in the world in 2012.

Below are excerpts from the commencement address he gave to the 2015 graduating class of the law school at the University of California-Berkeley.[1] They offer a fitting way to think about fraud because while his job was to prosecute it, he talks about failure and, without calling it that, the good life. [Bold added for emphasis.]

> The air is inevitably thick with expectations. Expectation of what kind of mark you graduates will make on the world. But if we're being honest, there is also inevitably some trepidation also. And not just when you think about how you are going to pay back your student loans. You may be asking yourself, "Did I make the right choice? Is this the right career?"
>
> So, let me start by offering a mildly radical suggestion. Promise yourself today that if you are not happy with your first law job, after giving it a genuine chance with genuine effort,

---

[10]In Greek mythology, Pandora's box explains the origins of human troubles. Pandora's curiosity leads her to open a forbidden box. That allows hardships and woes to escape and inflict themselves on humanity. She re-opens the box when she hears a small voice crying out within it. Out of the box flies what had been trapped inside, Hope.

and a genuine open mind, you will move on. And do that for every job you ever hold. If you don't like your job, because of the people, or the politics, or the hours, or the work, you can leave. You have worked too hard and invested too much to accept a long sentence in a job that you hate. I have seen in my years of practice too many people unhappy in a law job because they stayed too long, because they let inertia overwhelm their free will. Now, I'm generally not an advocate for being a quitter, but I am an advocate for being happy in your job. I believe you should grow, and mature, and learn, and derive joy, actual joy, from your work as a lawyer.

I know at this point there are parents saying "What the hell is Preet talking about? Does he know this is a law school graduation? We just paid $160,000 for this education. What do you mean: "Don't practice law?"

Now before you start throwing things at me, I should let you know that this happened in my own family. Not with me. My parents went through it with my brother, Vinny.

So my brother was a trained lawyer, but after a time he was bitten by the business bug. He felt the pull towards becoming an entrepreneur, so he left the law. His first dotcom business didn't do so well, but he recovered. In 2005, he started another e-commerce venture with his best friend from high school, this time, selling of all things, diapers. So basically, my brother—remember, this is a proud Indian-American family—my brother went from being a Harlan Fiske Stone scholar at Columbia Law School to selling diapers on the Internet under the slogan—and this is true—"We're Number One in Number Two!" I have the t-shirt, it's true. [Audience laughter.] You laugh.

My brother laughed too. Especially on the day that he sold his diaper company to Amazon for $540 million. Yes, my brother is now what plaintiff's lawyers call a "deep pocket."

My brother, by the way, is a fairly competitive guy. This is also his way of saying, "Hey bro, I see your whole US attorney thing and I raise you $540 million!"

There are reasons for America's enchantment with the tech and startup culture, and it does not, I think, have to do only with the gargantuan profit potential, though much of it is that. I think it also has to do with the spirit of energy and passion. It has to do, I think, also with the faith and possibility and attraction to the pioneering spirit.

Never mind that most new ventures fail. Each Silicon Valley success story can be seen as another example of the enduring example of the American Dream. And that is something very special.

But often **I wish we had more of that optimistic and visionary spirit in our legal community and in our own legal and government institutions.** Because law needs risk-takers too. The law needs entrepreneurs too. The law needs dreamers too.

And no matter what you decide to do in the law, I hope you find a way to inject some of that spirit because an idealistic lawyer can not only achieve the American Dream, but open up that dream to other people.

A Regulator's Thoughts on the Need for Risk Tolerance

This chapter closes with an excerpt from a May 2018 speech by SEC commissioner Hester M. Pierce on the need for risk tolerance in securities regulation.[J] [bold added for emphasis]

I worry that we can be too myopic when considering capital formation. Discussions often focus on the issuers, or maybe on the jobs the issuers might create, or on the money investors can earn. These things are extremely important to any discussion of capital formation, of course, but none is the reason we actually need robust capital formation.

We need it because of what the companies create. Perhaps it sounds a bit like an advertising slogan, but vibrant capital markets fund the good ideas that make life better. It's not too much to say that how well our markets work is a matter of life and death; markets fund new cancer drugs, car safety features, and medical devices.

When companies doing good things can't access the money they need, we lose out and we will never know just how much we're losing. We don't know what new invention was waiting to be created that now never will be. I realize this may be an obvious point, but I worry that it often gets lost in the conversation. Yet it is the reason that this discussion actually matters.

It matters especially here in the United States. While other countries depend heavily on the banking sector to fund business growth, we depend much more on our unparalleled capital markets. That's an excellent feature of our economic system. It opens the door to greater risk-taking by entrepreneurs, which allows more creativity and more opportunity for useful innovation.

Capital markets can fund an idea that may not meet a bank's underwriting standards but that will ultimately be a terrific success. Banks, the failure of which we have made a government matter, are looking for safe investments with predictable cash flows, not novel ideas with uncertain payouts. **Our reliance on capital markets brings a dynamism to our economy that's necessary for the economic growth we have enjoyed over much of the course of our history. This dynamism-growth combination has become increasingly important as Americans rely more and more on their own investments to fund their retirements.**

This is why I'm often puzzled when investor protection is presented as somehow in opposition to capital formation. The SEC's tripartite mission—to facilitate capital formation, protect investors, and maintain fair, orderly, and efficient markets—works as a cohesive whole.

No one mandate is in tension with another and focusing on one doesn't mean sacrificing another. While investor protection means deterring and punishing truly bad actors, it also means not erecting barriers that prevent investors from accessing investment. Facilitating capital formation means, in part, facilitating investor opportunity.

Facilitating both of these effectively requires some adjustments to our regulatory framework.

What's Next?

The next chapter will consider the causes of business failure.

Chapter Endnotes

Contextual references for material in this chapter appear as numbered footnotes on the page where the reference is made. **Source references** for material in this chapter appear below as endnotes with capital letter identifiers.

A Rattner, Steven. "A Sneaky Way to Deregulate." *The New York Times*. March 03, 2013. Accessed May 10, 2018. fairsharemodel.com/Sneaky.

B "A Closer Look With Arthur Levitt" radio show. Interview of SEC Chairman, Mary Shapiro. March 23, 2012. fairsharemodel.com/Levitt-Schapiro.

C Feigin, Philip A. "SEC's New Regulation A and the States' M Word (Merit Review)." *The National Law Review*. March 26, 2015. Accessed May 10, 2018. fairsharemodel.com/Merit.

D "Report on the Uniformity of State Regulatory Requirements for Offerings of Securities That Are Not 'Covered Securities.'" *US Securities and Exchange Commission*. October 11, 1997. Accessed May 10, 2018. fairsharemodel.com/Uniformity.

E Guzak, Samuel S. "Regulation A Packs a 'Punch' – So Too Congress and Title III Crowdfunding." *Corporate Securities Lawyer Blog–Samuel S. Guzik*. June 25, 2015. Accessed September 19, 2018. fairsharemodel.com/RegA.

F "What is a registration statement?" *SEC.gov*. Accessed May 07, 2018. fairsharemodel.com/Registration.

G Guzak, Samuel S. Ibid.

H An analysis of SEC enforcement actions for 2014 and first half of 2015 prepared by the Holland & Hart law firm is available here fairsharemodel.com/Enforcement.

I Preet Bharara's 2015 commencement speech at University of California-Berkeley. fairsharemodel.com/Bharara.

J Hester M. Pierce, "Tossing Fish and Catching Capital." Remarks at the 38th Annual Northwest Securities Institute CLE at the Washington State Bar Association. May 4, 2018. fairsharemodel.com/Pierce.

Chapter 18:

Failure

What's Included in This Chapter

- Introduction
- Perspective
- The Real Story of Silicon Valley Is its Tradition of Failure
- The Yin-Yang of Startups and Turnarounds
- Causes of Failure
- External vs. Internal Causes of Failure
  - When Is One-Man (or One-Woman) Rule a Good Idea?
- Seven Habits of Spectacularly Unsuccessful Executives
- The Startup Genome's Take on Failure
- Closing Thoughts on Failure
- What's Next?
- Chapter Endnotes

Introduction

The last chapter identified three broad categories of loss for investors in venture-stage companies: fraud, overpaying and failure. I have nothing to add about fraud, and much of this book deals with the risk of loss from buying in at too high a valuation. Failure deserves more discussion, however, and it is the focus of this chapter. Hope inspires an entrepreneurial team, its investors, customers, and suppliers, but the specter of failure is always lurking in the background. There are, after all, so many ways to fail.

Building a company is one of the most difficult challenges someone can take on and working for a startup can be similarly demanding, regardless of one's position in the organization.

Perspective

Just what is business failure? The answer will vary depending on whether you ask an entrepreneur, employee, creditor, or investor. Not achieving goals? Loss of control? Missing a window of opportunity? Bankruptcy? There are several possible answers. Here, I define it as investor loss due to a fraud-free failure of the business to achieve the projections implied in its offering document. The idea can be expressed in this conceptual equation:

Failure = Investor loss due to honest failure of the business

Honest failure can result from markets, product, competition, management, financial structure, etc. It can encompass things beyond management's control as well as those that could have been foreseen or responded to more effectively.

Inadequate access to capital limits the ability of companies to form and grow, which can lead to failure—but the emphasis here is on failure to sustain and grow operations, not failure to launch.

The Real Story of Silicon Valley Is Its Tradition of Failure

In the 1980s, while at the *San Jose Mercury News*, Michael S. Malone was one of the first reporters to regularly cover technology. His beat provided him exposure to movers and shakers and eventually led him to author several books on technology and business. Here is how he describes the role that failure has played in Silicon Valley. [Bold added for emphasis.]

> The standard history of Silicon Valley begins in the 1930s in Frederick Terman's laboratory at Stanford—where, in the first electrical engineering program west of the Mississippi [river], Terman instilled the love of innovation in the young Bill Hewlett, Dave Packard and Russ Varian. And they in turn, upon graduation, started companies in and around Palo Alto and kicked off the electronics age.
>
> As the story continues, the development of the technology and the region got a further boost in 1956, when William Shockley, co-inventor of the transistor, came home to Palo Alto, gathered the best and brightest young engineers and physicists in the USA, and founded Shockley Labs. Then, because Shockley was a terrible boss, this now-disaffected group of employees—the "Traitorous Eight"—walked out and founded the mother company of modern Silicon Valley, Fairchild Semiconductor. A decade late, Fairchild itself blew up and scattered dozens of chip companies all over the area—the birth of modern Silicon Valley.
>
> That's the story told and retold in books, museum exhibits, documentaries, and feature films. We like it because it is so simple: from Terman to the Packard garage to Fairchild; from Intel to Apple to Netscape; then from Google to Facebook and beyond. Part of this story's appeal is that it is so neat—not to mention that it reinforces our desire for the trajectory of this tale to be ever upward, from success to even bigger success.
>
> But the truth is that this accepted version is full of holes. For one thing, it ignores the reality that thousands of companies in the Valley were born, made important contributions, then died—often leaving little trace. Industry veterans know that **the real story of Silicon Valley is even more about failure than success. That is the cost of entrepreneurship and living on the bleeding edge of innovation.**[A]

Many policymakers and opinion leaders want to see more Silicon Valley-like environments because they associate it with economic growth and job creation.[B] Some of them, however, oppose JOBS Act reforms that aim to reduce the cost of capital for venture-stage companies.

As Malone points out, Silicon Valley is about failure. One might say that just as you can't make an omelet without breaking some eggs, you can't create a Silicon Valley-like environment without investor losses. To be sure, such an economy could happen without JOBS Act reforms but opposition to them can reinforce the idea that venture investing should be the preserve of the wealthy.

The Yin-Yang of Startups and Turnarounds

Startups and turnarounds are similar in ways that evokes the Chinese philosophical concept of yin-yang, which seeks to "describe how seemingly opposite or contrary forces are interconnected and interdependent in the natural world; and, how they give rise to each other as they interrelate to one another." [C]

Fundamentally, a startup or an established business in a turnaround situation are each in transition. A startup seeks viability while a turnaround seeks to avoid disaster. If they were airplanes, one needs to clear the ground while the other needs to avoid crashing into it.

A startup needs more capital than it can generate from operations and faces shifting conditions. A turnaround that needs capital may have an easier time raising it if it has assets to borrow against or an attractive underlying business. Its challenge is to recognize that it is in trouble and be able to respond in an appropriate and timely way. In both cases, to meet the challenges, management needs insight, honesty, courage, communication, commitment, and luck. The personalities of those drawn to such environments may also be attracted to work as firefighters or in a hospital emergency room.

Failure is not a topic that has been widely studied—there are oodles of books about success but comparatively few about failure. Makes sense, as it's a downer of a topic. Besides, everyone wants to know the secrets to success—few people care to learn the lessons of failure.

But prospective investors in venture-stage companies can learn much about how to minimize the bad investments they make by paying attention to what others have learned about failure. In the pages that follow, we'll look at conclusions reached by some students of business failure.

As you proceed, consider how the Fairshare Model might affect a public company that is at risk of failure. Ask yourself:

- Might a company's capital structure help it avoid tough times in the first place? If so, which is likely to be better: the Fairshare Model or a conventional one?

- Would investors in a company facing failure favor the Fairshare Model or a conventional capital structure?

- If a company with the Fairshare Model faces failure, how might the model affect the options that are pursued?

- Might a broad distribution of Performance Stock make it less likely that management will find themselves on the wrong track?

Of course, the answers to such questions are conjecture until the Fairshare Model is used several times in a turnaround situation. Nonetheless, an exploration of the causes of failure can help us contemplate some of the answers.

Causes of Failure

What causes companies to fail? For startups, the major reasons include loss of market, product shortcomings, unexpected competition, inadequate capital, and poor management. Loss of market is the least obvious of those. It is the failure of a market to develop as expected. It may not form at all, take longer to develop, or be shorter lived than hoped.

The Fairshare Model lowers these risks for IPO investors by not placing value on future performance. Thus, an IPO valuation will be a small fraction of what it would be with a conventional model. Think of the aggregate amount of capital raised in venture-stage IPOs in recent decades, then imagine that it was raised using the Fairshare Model. Many, many more companies could be funded with the same amount of money. In this way, the Fairshare Model reduces the macroeconomic risk of failure.

The causes of failure in established companies help us understand failure better because such companies were past the challenges that startups face. In 2002, Harlan and Marjorie Platt, both professors at Northeastern University, reported the following results from their research into the causes of failure in established companies.[D]

Causes of Business Failure in Established Companies

29%	Loss of Market
24%	Management Failure
18%	Finance
13%	Other
10%	Bad Debts
6%	Competition
100%	Total

Note that loss of market and management failure together account for more than half of the failures in established businesses. Loss of market can occur for a myriad of reasons—technology, cost, design, business model, shifts in economic conditions, etc.

Management failure refers to its failure to respond to the need for change. Potentially, the Fairshare Model makes it less likely that a company will be vulnerable to this. Why?

1. Management will have laser-like focus on the criteria to convert their Performance Stock. And if that criteria needs to change, say because of market shifts, it is a safe bet that management will seek approval from the Investor Stockholders to update the conversion rules to more relevant measures.

2. The Fairshare Model promotes management accountability by intensifying the interest that others have in the company's success. That's true whether an issuer distributes Performance Stock only to management, or broadly, to all employees and others (e.g., key investors, business partners, suppliers). All who can earn Investor Stock will be inclined to voice concern when they feel leadership is on the wrong track.

External vs. Internal Causes of Failure

Donald Bibeault is a particularly notable student of failure. In 1982, he literally wrote the book on how to manage a company in financial distress, *Corporate Turnaround: How Managers Turn Losers into Winners*, which emerged from his doctoral thesis at Golden Gate University. It relies on surveys, interviews of executives who had collectively led about 300 turnarounds, including sixteen accomplished "turnaround artists" and other management experts.

Bibeault studied established companies that had been at cruising altitude for years before encountering trouble, the kind that startups may face as they try to climb. When asked to rank the number one characteristic displayed by turnaround managers, 64 percent responded with "growth-oriented executive" or "entrepreneur."[E] *Corporate Turnaround*, therefore, sheds light on the challenges that any venture-stage company may face.

Bibeault examined how experienced turnaround managers—those brought in to fix a failure, not the managers that they replaced—analyzed the underlying reasons for the business failure, and, whether these turnaround pros thought it was due to *external* or *internal* reasons.

So, for example, if the cause of a failure was "loss of market," he wanted to know if the market loss was due to an external factor like the economy or technology, or if it was due to internal factors such as poor management. Thus, Bibeault teased out the difference between circumstances that were out of management's control—external factors—and the failure of management to respond to them.

It's a subtle, yet interesting point. Consider Lehman Brothers, the investment bank whose collapse sparked the Great Recession, because it frames the point nicely. As Charles H. Ferguson writes in his 2012 book, *Predator Nation* (which was made into a revealing documentary movie, *Inside Job*), Lehman's business model "was nearly totally dependent on short-term financing."[F] In autumn 2008, as sources of short-term capital "became increasingly nervous about the collapse of the bubble, they stopped lending to banks. When its lenders stopped accepting even its AAA mortgage paper as collateral, Lehman ran out of money, almost instantly."[G] It sank, and other businesses failed in the maelstrom that ensued.

The question that Bibeault pursued was: *Which failures are due to conditions management could anticipate?* Arguably, in Lehman's case, its business model, not the economy, led to its failure and so, Bibeault would characterize it an internal reason—management failure.

Lehman's CEO, Richard S. Fuld, Jr. admitted to internal mistakes but cited "uncontrollable market forces," rumors, and *other factors that were out of his control* as he laid the responsibility on government for not bailing Lehman Brothers out.[H] In other words, Fuld claimed that Lehman's failure was due to external factors that he and his leadership team could not reasonably anticipate.

When Fred Kofman, author of the 2006 book, *Conscious Business*, talks about having a victim mentality, he uses an analogy to draw a distinction between what is controllable and what is not. He asks an audience to imagine someone who comes in from the rain soaking wet. Then, he asks, "why is he wet?" Reliably, the first response is "It was raining." But Kofman solicits other explanations until he gets "He didn't have an umbrella."

He then makes the point that it takes two hands to make a clap sound—you can't make a clapping sound with one hand. In his story, the "clap" is that the guy is wet. One hand is an external factor that the fellow could not control—the rain. The other hand is an internal factor that he had control of—he could have had an umbrella!

From Corporate Turnaround: How Managers Turn Losers into Winners

"It is never sensible to push any analogy too far, but the collapse of a company is in some ways similar to the sinking of a ship. If a ship is in good condition and the captain is competent, it is almost impossible for it to be sunk by a wave or a succession of waves. Even if there is a storm, the competent captain will have heard the weather forecast and taken whatever measures are needed. Only a freak storm for which quite inadequate notice has been given will sink the ship."

–John Argenti, author of *Corporate Collapse: The Cause and Symptoms*

With the "clap" of business failure in mind, plus an appreciation for the complexity inherent in such a large topic, Bibeault identifies four external causes of business failure:[1]

1. changes in economic conditions (overall economy, interest rates, credit squeezes),
2. changes in competitive conditions,
3. changes in societal conditions (changes in attitudes and/or composition of a population), and
4. changes in technological conditions.

"Industries facing difficulties are comprised of survivors and failures. Since companies share exposure to the external factors, the internal factors often provide the best explanation as to why the business failed."

–Donald Bibeault

Bibeault also identified *two principal internal causes* of business failure–poor management, and a weak finance function. Each has multiple facets, which are listed below.[J]

1. Poor management (incompetence, narrow vision, misplaced priorities)
   a. dictatorship or one-man rule
   b. lack of management talent and depth
   c. lack of openness to change
   d. unbalanced top management team
   e. ineffective Board of Directors
   f. pursuit of inappropriate or high-risk strategy
   g. dishonesty or fraud

2. Weak finance function
   a. poor working capital controls
   b. excessive fixed assets
   c. excessive debt or "high financial leverage"
   d. inadequate equity capital
   e. excessive operating expenses

For each of these internal causes, Bibeault found that inadequate operating controls contributed significantly to the failure. These are the financial and accounting systems that deal with budgets, product cost, internal reporting, asset valuation, cash flow management, and internal controls.

After analyzing failure in this manner—whether due to external or internal causes—Bibeault concluded that failure due to internal causes was far more common than external causes. He put it this way:

> My opinion, based on surveys and discussions with over 100 turnaround leaders, is that in seven out of ten cases, decline is internally generated. In another 20 percent of the cases, internal reasons are partially responsible for decline. In broad terms, decline is therefore caused by internal factors about eight out of ten times.[K]

Bibeault concluded that the preeminent problem is management. "Internal constraints, such as unions, appear to be of minor importance as a cause of decline. Fraud and bad luck deserve no more than a passing mention."[L]

"We have met the enemy and he is us" is a famous line from Walt Kelly's cartoon strip, *Pogo*.[1] Pogo is an opossum, who lives in a swamp near the Gulf of Mexico. At the dawn of the environmental movement in the early 1970s, he makes that observation while looking at the pollution that fouls his bayou. It is often evoked in other contexts because, as *Wikipedia* states: "it perfectly describes [Kelly's] attitude towards the foibles of mankind and the nature of the human condition."

Might the Fairshare Model mitigate a principal cause of business failure—management itself? If employees have Performance Stock, they have a strong incentive to see that goals are met. It follows that they will be watchful of management and vocal when they feel it is on the wrong track.

When Is One-Man (or One-Woman) Rule a Good Idea?

One's answer to this question will reflect an instinctual view about leadership. If one's ideal is a dominating leader who personifies rugged individualism, it will seem like a bad idea to allow a substantial proportion of employees to vote on shareholder matters. If one's ideal is a collaborative leader who views employees as a vital stakeholder, a broad distribution of Performance Stock sounds like a terrific idea.

There is no shortage of opinion on what constitutes effective management. Chapter 15, "Evaluating Valuation," presents a few diverse thoughts on the subject. The Fairshare Model can accommodate any perspective. That's because its central goal is a better deal for IPO investors, not a style of leadership or corporate governance.

A company that narrowly distributes Performance Stock will have different dynamics than one that does it broadly. The same is true if an issuer has a class of super-voting Performance Stock for founders and another for other employees.

Ideas on how to administer Performance Stock will be considered by a range of experts on corporate governance once a critical mass of people signal interest in the Fairshare Model. Whether investors care how it is done is a question that will be tested by companies using different approaches.

For now, consider that Bibeault's research led him to conclude: "The success or failure of one-man rule depends on the size and organizational complexity of the company, problems of the industry, etc." He wrote [bold added for emphasis]:

---

[1] *Pogo* ran as a newspaper cartoon strip from 1948 to 1975.

One-man rule is necessary at the entrepreneurial stage but later causes problems. As Glen Penisten points out: "An entrepreneur has the personality of a creative individual. Very seldom does that personality type bring in disciplined management—a structure which listens to other people, has a board that sets policies. More often that entrepreneur nurtures a submissive management."

One-man rule is intended to describe chief executives who make decisions in spite of their colleagues' hostility or reticence; they allow no discussion, will hear no advice. They are autocrats. Not all autocrats are overambitious salesmen, so set upon hyper-successful performance that they cease to believe in the existence of failure. Some are relatively retiring people who impose their will by their superior knowledge.

One-man rule is not always bad and is sometimes needed. Thaddeus Taube says: **"One-man rule is a two-edged sword.** There's a lot of inbred lethargy in group management. Very strong one-man leadership can sometimes steer a business in the wrong direction.

Yet, it takes very strong leadership to steer a company in any direction. A company must tread a very fine line between imparting a great deal of authority and strength to a leader while hoping he will be responsive to advice from business associates.

[Bibeault concludes that] **It is the rare company that can prosper in the long run with one-man rule.** In extraordinarily complex organizations, it is essential to have management depth and permit managers to participate in decision-making. This is necessary for two reasons: first, one man cannot simply handle the complexity of running the organization single-handedly; second, it is essential that the company provide for management succession.**M**

Lawrence M. Miller is the author of a number of management books, including *Barbarians to Bureaucrats: Corporate Life Cycle Strategies* (1990). His blog has an entry that discusses a 2015 *New York Times* story that describes a stressful, demanding culture at Amazon.com. In it, Miller uses this chart to illustrate how an organization's decision-making style evolves over its life cycle.**N**

Life Cycle Stages and Leadership Styles

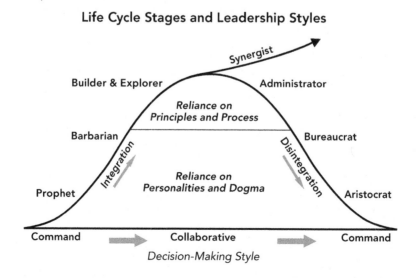

Miller associates a command style with the rise and the decline phases. In the beginning, the leader is the prophet with a vision. Growth creates complexity and so a barbarian personality emerges to create processes and integrate them. These stages are defined by the personalities of the leadership, and their views on how to conduct business. But as an organization matures, a builder/explorer style emerges that encourages decision-making based on shared principles and established processes. This is conducive to a collaborative culture.

The challenge is to continue that spirit and minimize a rule-based administrator mindset, which is associated with declining organizational vitality and can devolve into bureaucratic and aristocratic rule, each of which rely on command-based authority.

It is uncontroversial to assert that employees know when management is bad, and that they want effective leaders. It's debatable whether many public companies have ways for employees to express their concern about management without jeopardizing their jobs.

A premise of the Fairshare Model is that companies do better when employees have a stake in their company's performance that goes beyond their salary and benefits. So, it gives them a vote on shareholder matters, which may have a therapeutic effect on a leading cause of business failure—management failure.

Again, there will be variation on how issuers do this. Some will structure their Performance Stock in a manner that supports a command style of decision-making. That is, they may distribute it narrowly or have multiple classes of Performance Stock with different voting rights—more for some (founders, key investors, etc.) and less for others. Some will adopt a structure that supports a collaborative style of decision-making.

Seven Habits of Spectacularly Unsuccessful Executives

> "Truly colossal blunders don't come in isolation; they seem to come in clusters. Once a company has made a really bad misstep, it often seems as though it can't do anything right. How does this happen? Why, instead of fixing their mistakes, do business leaders regularly make them worse?"[O]

These are questions that Dartmouth College professor Sydney Finkelstein addresses in his 2003 book, *Why Smart Executives Fail: And What You Can Learn From Their Mistakes.* His research team sought "not only to understand why businesses break down, but to focus on the people behind these failures—not only to understand how to avoid these disasters, but to anticipate the early warning signs of failure."[P]

Finkelstein reports [bold added for emphasis] that some of the findings surprised his team in that **"many of the qualities that sound like the attributes of a dream enterprise turn out to be the basis for a business nightmare.** For managers, many of the qualities we aspire to emulate, or feel guilty for not having, turn out to be ones we're better off without. **For investors, many of the signposts of success that we strive to identify turn out to be markers for failure."[Q]**

The research spanned six years, from 1997 to 2003, and involved the study of approximately fifty companies that had suffered a large loss in market value because of failure. They were largely established

American businesses but included some non-US companies and some newly public companies. Data analysis and news reports were supplemented with nearly 200 interviews with executives and managers at the subject companies, competitors, journalists, industry experts, investment bankers, and the like. Finding and testing patterns that are reliably and repeatedly present in failure was the focus of the work.

Finkelstein wrote the following as the book went to press. The economy was recovering from the dotcom and telecom busts as well as the aftereffects of the 9/11 terrorist attacks of 2001.

> Over time, it became clear just how deep-rooted and relatively small in number the causes of failure actually were. **Businesses that at first appear to have nothing in common turned out to have failed for exactly the same reasons and in much the same way. Even the excuses that we heard from failed managers turned out to be the same in case after case.**
>
> Despite the vast number of things that could go wrong in something as complex as business enterprises, the really devastating failures turned out to have a surprisingly limited number of causes. Patterns of failure that could be applied not only to the scores of classic, almost common business breakdowns—think Rubbermaid, L.A. Gear, Barneys—but also to the Internet one-year wonders (e.g., Boo.com, eToys, Power Agent, Webvan) and the rogue companies that have dominated the news over the past two years (e.g., Enron, Tyco, WorldCom, Rite-Aid, Adelphia, ImClone Systems).[R]

Finkelstein points out that his book about failure is ultimately about human behavior—people who "run organizations into the ground." It did not reveal that tactical or organizational matters were a consistent cause, things that might be corrected by internal controls, a different organizational structure, or a set of best practices. He puts it this way [bold added for emphasis]:

> There's the young entrepreneur who makes it big and then proceeds to destroy everything he's built when he becomes convinced that he has all the right answers. There's the established big-time CEO who invests billions in a venture not because there's a truly compelling case for the venture, but because he wants to. There's the leadership team so in love with their product that they refuse to listen when their customers tell them, and tell them again, that something must change. There's the CEO who pursues acquisition after acquisition unencumbered by such pedestrian concerns as strategic logic and integration. **There's the group of executives who persist in self-destructive behavior, despite considerable evidence that such behavior can be toxic.**
>
> These people don't do these bad things on purpose. They want nothing more than to be successful, and oftentimes some of them were, to a grand degree. They also don't do these bad things by accident. Their actions, and inactions, while not intended to yield the disastrous results that they do, are also not random. It is not so-called "acts of God" that account for the stories of failure in this book, but rather "acts of men and women." And they don't do these bad things because they're not very smart. No, they are very smart, and very talented—often remarkably so—but do bad things nonetheless.[S]

Finkelstein identifies seven reasons that are popularly cited for business failure. They are listed in the box on the following page.

But he points out, **these reasons don't explain the failures.** Furthermore, they are incompatible with leaders who had established a track record of success over many years.[T]

Seven Popularly Cited Reasons for Failure Evaluated in *Why Smart Executives Fail*

1. The executives were stupid.

2. The executives couldn't have known what was coming

3. There was a failure to execute.

4. The executives weren't trying hard enough.

5. The executives lacked leadership ability.

6. The company lacked the necessary resources.

7. The executives were a bunch of crooks.

Each was found to be a weak explanation.

Source: Sydney Finkelstein

The real question was: how did the talented executives in this sample start getting everything wrong? That's because we fail to understand failure unless we can identify what caused it and, hence, how to avoid it.

Many of the failures Finkelstein studied were spectacular; they rendered world-renowned businesses nearly worthless. In the process, they caused thousands of people to lose their jobs and thousands of investors to lose their investments. These failures destroyed hundreds of millions or even billions of dollars of value.

So, he asks: "If these frequently offered explanations for failure don't reliably explain what happened, what does?"

Seemingly inspired by the popularity of Stephen Covey's book, *Seven Habits of Highly Successful People,* and fueled with a puckish sense of humor, Finkelstein writes that "to be spectacularly unsuccessful requires some very special personal qualities" in leadership, and he says there are seven of them.

It is possible to identify seven habits that characterize spectacularly unsuccessful people. Nearly all the leaders who preside over major business failures exhibit five or six of these habits. Many of them exhibit all seven. Even more remarkable, each of these habits represents a quality that is widely admired in today's business world. As a society, we don't just tolerate the qualities that make leaders spectacularly unsuccessful, we encourage them.

1. They see themselves and their companies as dominating their environments, not simply as responding to developments in those environments.

2. They identify so completely with the company that there is no clear boundary between their personal interests and their corporation's interests.

3. They think they have all of the answers, often dazzling people with the speed and decisiveness with which they can deal with challenging issues.

4. They ruthlessly eliminate anyone who isn't 100 percent behind them.

5. They are consummate company spokespersons, obsessed with managing and developing the company image.

6. They underestimate major obstacles, treating them as temporary impediments.

7. They stubbornly rely on the strategies and tactics that have made them and their companies successful in the past.[U]

Finkelstein also identifies warning signs of potential failure. The major ones are:

- unnecessary complexity,
- out-of-control spending,
- a CEO who is personally greedy and not focused on building company value,
- excessive hype and aggressiveness, and
- overconfident behavior that signals untrustworthiness.

The Startup Genome's Take on Failure

The failure researchers cited thus far in this chapter focused on established companies. Startups are vulnerable to many of the factors identified, but they carry additional risks that larger businesses don't. What makes startups succeed or fail? That is a question that a group of researchers affiliated with the University of California at Berkeley and Stanford University set out to answer in 2011 with the Startup Genome Compass project. They examined data from more than 3,200 high-growth technology startups, mainly internet-related, the type most likely to seek venture capital in an IPO.

Their March 2012 Startup Genome Report says "Most founders don't know what they should be focusing on and consequently dilute their focus or run in the wrong direction. They are regularly bombarded with advice that seems contradictory, which is often paralyzing."[V]

The researchers concluded that premature scaling was the chief cause of failure in startups. That is, spending money to grow or scale up a business before the product or strategy is attuned with what will succeed in the market. The spending is for headcount, marketing expense, facilities, inventory, and so on. Until the product appeals to customers and there is a sound strategy to acquire them, such expenditures are wasteful. If one thinks of entrepreneurs as soldiers, premature scalers are the ones who fire off their ammunition before they can clearly see the enemy. As the report put it: "They tend to lose the battle early on by getting ahead of themselves."[W] Other conclusions in the report are:

- Startups need two to three times longer to validate their market than most founders expect.
- Startups that haven't raised money over-estimate their market size by 100 times and often misinterpret their market as new.
- Startups that pivot or change direction once or twice have better user growth and are less likely to scale prematurely than those that pivot more than twice or not at all.
- Many investors invest two to three times more capital than necessary in startups that, in geek speak, "haven't demonstrated that they have reached a problem-solution fit" yet. That means that it isn't clear there is a problem for which they have a compelling solution.

- Founders overestimate the value of their intellectual property by 255 percent before "product-market fit" (i.e., before demonstrated market value).

Indirectly, the findings highlight why the defining characteristic of a conventional capital structure, the requirement that a value be set for future performance when new stock is issued, is a big problem for investors. It is difficult to do reliably well. As you know by now, in a private offering, investors can negotiate a valuation, and many of them secure price protection. But IPO investors are presented with the valuation that the issuer gives itself—and many of them are unlikely to know what the amount is, let alone be able to rationalize it. For those reasons, an IPO valuation is the product of weak market forces, where average investors are "at the back of the bus."

Closing Thoughts on Failure

Is it better for public investors to invest in failure-susceptible companies using a conventional capital structure, or the Fairshare Model? There are three overlapping dimensions to this question: employee motivation, corporate governance, and valuation. Here are some thoughts to contemplate:

- The Fairshare Model emphasizes reward for what employees can influence—operational results. In a conventional model, stock incentives are typically tied to the stock price, something employees have no control over. The Fairshare Model can more effectively focus incentives on operational results.

- Might a broad distribution of Performance Stock lower the risk of management failure by intensifying employee interest in their company's performance?

- How might a broad distribution of Performance Stock affect decisions about a course change? On the one hand, employees may object to a radical change in the business (e.g., closing or selling a line of business). On the other hand, it is uncommon for a CEO to produce a successful turnaround plan that lacks employee support.

- Might Apple's Steve Jobs, a dominating leader with obsessive qualities, have been attracted to the Fairshare Model? If not, is that bad? After all, Captain Ahab in Herman Melville's *Moby Dick* was dominating and obsessive too.

As you reflect on these points, also consider what Edward E. Whitacre, Jr. has to say about employee involvement. He was CEO of two iconic American corporations, AT&T and General Motors, as they underwent turnarounds. He wrote the following in his 2013 book, *American Turnaround: Reinventing AT&T and GM and the Way We Do Business in the USA.*

> Ninety-nine percent of the people out there want the exact same thing: to feel good about their lives, to feel that they're not failures, to feel like they're contributing and are part of something that is having a positive impact on their kids and families.

> That inner need to contribute and be a part of something good and positive is a powerful force. People want to be engaged and be listened to and taken seriously, they want to know that they matter.

> Employees are on the front lines every day, so they know, pretty much, how things are going. And if things aren't going so good, they can often tell you, with a high degree of accuracy, why that is.

> But they have to be engaged.[x]

Add to this mix an appreciation for the unique qualities of entrepreneurs who devote themselves to trying to make their company succeed in the face of daunting odds, giving far more of themselves than other employees. Also, add that the leadership qualities a business needs can change over time.

These and other issues will be explored by experts in securities, organizational development, and other areas in the next phase of the development of the Fairshare Model. That will happen after a critical mass of investors signal their interest in the model.

Again, the Fairshare Model envisions a broad distribution of voting Performance Stock among employees, but it need not be that way. A company might distribute it narrowly, to select employees. Another might do it broadly. They may differ in how they treat employees who leave the company–one may allow them to retain their interest–another may cancel it upon termination. Then too, a company might have multiple classes of Performance Stock with different voting rights; more for founders and/or key investors, and less for others. **The defining characteristic of the Fairshare Model is not corporate governance, it is IPO valuation.** But new thinking about corporate governance and employee motivation is a byproduct of its approach to valuation.

With respect to valuation, this book is replete with reasons why investors should be skeptical about the valuation venture-stage issuers give themselves. This chapter reports that one scholar of failure finds that loss of market and management failure were the causes of more than half of failures. Another concludes that internally-generated causes play a dominant role in failure. Yet another identifies qualities in leadership that might seem to presage success but instead, heighten the risk of failure. And the Startup Genome report finds that company founders are often unsure what their priorities should be, and the successful ones tend to have to pivot aspects of their strategy and vastly overestimate the value of their intellectual property.

> "Unicorn" startup Good Technology raised $388 billion over 13 private funding rounds. It was valued at $1 billion in April 2013; in September 2015, it agreed to be acquired for $425 billion, less than half its top valuation.
>
> –Source: *Marketwatch.com*

We also learned that founders are vulnerable to significantly misjudging where they are, what they need to do and, by extension, the value proposition that they offer investors.

An earlier chapter observed that ideas are worth nothing unless executed; execution is worth millions.

What's Next?

The next chapter considers other objections people have about making it easier for public investors to invest in young companies.

Chapter Endnotes

Contextual references for material in this chapter appear as numbered footnotes on the page where the reference is made. **Source references** for material in this chapter appear below as endnotes with capital letter identifiers.

A Malone, Michael S. "Silicon Valley Story." *Santa Clara Magazine.* Spring/Summer 2015. fairsharemodel.com/SiliconValleystory.

B Places with "Silicon" names. fairsharemodel.com/Silicon.

C "Yin and Yang." *Wikipedia.* Accessed May 10, 2018. fairsharemodel.com/YinYang.

D Platt, Harlan D. and Marjorie Platt. "Understanding the Renewal Profession: Results from a Survey." Pages 115-119, in *Turnaround Management, A Guide to Corporate Restructuring;* James E. Schrager, Editor, *Institutional Investor Journals,* New York, NY.

E Bibeault, Donald B. *Corporate Turnaround: How Managers Turn Losers into Winners.* Washington, DC.: Beard Books, 1999. page 372.

F Ferguson, Charles H. *Predator Nation: Corporate Criminals, Political Corruption, and the Hijacking of America.* New York, NY: Crown Business, 2012. page 220.

G Ibid.

H Puzzanghera, Jim. "Ex-Lehman CEO Blames Government for Firm's Collapse." *Los Angeles Times.* September 02, 2010. Accessed May 10, 2018. fairsharemodel.com/Lehman.

I Bibeault, Donald B. *Corporate Turnaround: How Managers Turn Losers into Winners.* Washington, DC: Beard Books, 1999. pages 27-33.

J Ibid, page 36.

K Ibid, page 35.

L Ibid.

M Ibid. Page 40.

N Miller, Lawrence M. "Amazon versus The New York Times." *Management Meditations.* August 18, 2015. Accessed May 10, 2018. fairsharemodel.com/Amazon.

O Finkelstein, Sydney. *Why Smart Executives Fail and What You Can Learn from Their Mistakes.* New York: Portfolio, 2004. page 8.

P Ibid. page 1.

Q Ibid. page 2.

R Ibid. Page 16.

S Ibid. pages 14-15.

T Ibid. pages 2-8.

U Ibid. pages 213-238.

V Marmer, Max, Bjoern Lasse Herrmann, Ertan Dogrultan, and Ron Berman. "Startup Genome Report: A New Framework for Understanding Why Startups Succeed." *Startup Genome Project.* March 2012. fairsharemodel.com/Genome. page 3.

W Ibid. page 5.

X Whitacre, Edward E., and Leslie Cauley. *American Turnaround: Reinventing AT & T and GM and the Way We Do Business in the USA.* New York, NY: Business Plus, 2013.

Chapter 19:

Other Objections to Public Venture Capital

What's Included in This Chapter

- Introduction
- Fraud vs. the Unethical
- Myths about Venture Capitalists
- How Scalable Are VC Funds?
- How the Fairshare Model Complements Angel Investing
- How Scalable Is Angel Investor Capital?
- Venture-Stage Investing Is Inappropriate for Average Investors Because…
  - We Are But Animals
- Companies Should Not Want Small Investors Because…
- Summation
- What's Next?
- Chapter Endnotes

Introduction

Fraud, overvaluation, and failure are the principal concerns for those opposed to seeing average investors involved in venture capital. But there are other, sometimes vaguely sensed, objections that led someone to say: "Let's leave venture capital investing to the VCs and angel investors." This chapter touches on matters relevant to that sensibility.

Fraud vs. the Unethical

I have a confession to make. I have trouble reconciling my twin advocacy for average investors and liberalization of securities law with my concern that unethical sales practices will result in vulnerable investors encountering the demon of loss.

It is as if I am Pandora of Greek mythology, but I'm not driven by curiosity to open a box of unknowns. Instead, I know there is something good in the box to release—a lower cost of capital for startups.

The problem is, I know there is something bad in the box too—unethical behavior. My dilemma is that I can't figure out how to release the good and contain the bad. Unethical behavior is likely to accompany the liberalization of securities laws because some people are prone to engage in it.

The fear of being caught doing something illegal inhibits unethical behavior. But there can be a difference between what is legal and what is right, and that is the worrisome territory. To illustrate, I'll tell you about my dear mother. She lives on a fixed income—her social security, and the modest assets she still has. She is a heavy consumer of cable TV news and gets loads of junk mail, so she's exposed to many appeals for money and pitches for dicey products and a variety of causes. She also fancies herself to be a far better investor than her track record suggests. All this—and the cognitive frailties of age—makes her vulnerable to unethical companies and sales people. People like my mother come to mind as I think about venture-stage companies selling stock to the public.

A few years ago, she bought gold coins from a dealer located in another state. After seeing a stream of advertisements and TV personalities exhorting the virtues of an investment in gold, she phoned in an order without any due diligence. She paid $11,000 for coins that were worth no more than $3,500 at the time. It was an awful, uninformed, and emotion-driven decision. I complained to the seller once I discovered what she had done. He offered to buy them back for $2,800. My mother refused. Accepting the offer would acknowledge that she had been foolish. Defiantly, she predicted they would go up in price.

Was the seller unethical? Certainly. He knew his price was excessive and could not have mistaken my mother's lack of sophistication. Was she a victim of a fraud? Yes, in the sense that she did not get what she expected—a competitive price. But it is not prosecutable because the coins *are* gold, apparently. Plus, she initiated the call and required nothing more than folksy assurance that she was making a wise choice. The seller did what was required to fulfil a legal contract that my mother initiated. Still, the operation reminds me of a "boiler room" where questionable investments are hawked.

If gold coins were a security, such behavior would more likely be punished. The securities regulator in my mother's state could use the broad, anti-fraud provisions of its blue-sky laws against the seller. And if the seller was a securities broker-dealer, the industry's self-regulatory organization, FINRA, might act. SROs exist in industries that are subject to government regulation such as securities, real estate, and medicine. They are trade associations with quasi-governmental authority that enables them to create rules for their members and discipline those who violate them. They can also protect the interests of their members, like a guild or union does.

FINRA has higher conduct standards for its members than government. For instance, it requires a member to evaluate the suitability of an investment for an investor when the SEC and state agencies do not. So, if gold coins were a security and the seller a broker-dealer, FINRA might require it to rescind the sale or refund a (larger) portion of it.

This suggests that unethical sales practices involving stocks are better policed if a broker-dealer is the seller. But what about direct public offerings? To require issuers to use broker-dealers to sell their stock is akin to requiring home owners to hire realtors to sell their properties.

One might wonder whether FINRA is an ideal organization to oversee the online platforms authorized by the JOBS Act. Its organizational mindset will reflect the highly profitable broker-dealer industry and may be ill-suited to the needs of an embryonic form of business that may have low margins and present a competitive threat to FINRA members. My concern is that FINRA members might use their influence to ensure that rules are created or enforced in a manner that handicaps online platforms. Often, organizations act to protect their members from competitive pressures.

Undoubtedly, you can think of examples, but I'll share one with you. Nowadays, it is unremarkable to find free, reliable valuation data about real estate online. In part, it is the result of the 2008 settlement agreement between the US Justice Department and the National Association of Realtors (NAR), the SRO for real estate broker-dealers.

It settled an antitrust lawsuit brought by the government that challenged NAR rules for its Multiple Listing Service (MLS) that inhibited competition. NAR agreed to "replace rules that discriminate against innovative brokers who use the internet to provide high-quality, low-priced brokerage services to consumers."[A]

Here's a related backstory. In 1991, I worked with a startup called PhotoBase that sought to innovate in the real estate space using 12-inch wide video laser discs, a now-obsolete technology. It took street view pictures of houses, much like those seen online today in a street view map. Those were coupled with information from real estate listings, property tax records, and other sources. The idea was to allow someone to view houses for sale and the adjacent properties without driving to them.

This effort was hindered by NAR's restrictions on MLS data that protected the interests of its members. PhotoBase's prospects would have been brighter if these anticompetitive rules, which took nearly a quarter of a century to be overturned by the government, did not exist to begin with.

I don't know if FINRA will similarly impede innovations that can reduce paychecks for its members, but I will be surprised if it does not. My skepticism is based on human nature and on behavior I have observed from similar organizations. The ancient Roman poet Juvenal put the challenge of ultimate oversight this way: "Who will guard the guards themselves?"

That said, consider how a conventional capital structure itself can encourage unethical selling practices. A value must be placed on future performance and "possibility thinking" is a pixie dust that can dazzle investors. There is no need to value future performance in the Fairshare Model, so unethical sales practices could be less of a problem—time will tell. As you ponder the challenge of unethical selling practices for securities, here are two questions to think about.

1. What information might help investors better protect themselves? I make a case for valuation disclosure in Chapter 16. What else might help?

2. Is there a role for investor certification? Instead of relying on income and wealth to establish investor suitability, might regulators define a class of investor based on knowledge and sophistication, setting purchase restrictions on those who fail to meet the standard?

Another response to the challenge of protecting vulnerable investors is to ask: "Is innovation in venture capital even necessary?" Why not rely on the professionals in the VC industry to meet the needs of young companies? That line of thinking ignores the fact that venture capital has been raised in public offerings for decades. And it is elitist to presume that average investors are incapable of being savvy. Nonetheless, the balance of this chapter considers this question further.

Myths about Venture Capitalists

"Six Myths about Venture Capitalists" appeared in the May 2013 issue of the *Harvard Business Review*. In it, Diane Mulcahy, director of private equity at the Kauffman Foundation and a former VC herself summarizes a report that she co-authored: *We Have Met The Enemy And He Is Us: Lessons from Twenty Years of the Kaufman Foundation's Investments in Venture Capital Funds and The Triumph of Hope Over Experience.*[B] The report is written from the perspective of a limited partner—an investor in VC funds.

"The myths surrounding venture capital can be powerful," Mulcahy writes. To provide a realistic sense of the industry and what it offers, she challenges six of the most common myths:[C]

Myth 1: Venture Capital Is the Primary Source of Startup Funding
VC financing is the exception for startups. Historically, less than 1 percent of US companies have raised capital from VCs, and the VC industry is contracting. But less venture capital does not mean less startup capital since non-VC sources, such as angel capital, are growing.

Myth 2: VCs Take a Big Risk When They Invest in Your Company
VCs take risks with investors' money, not their own. The typical VC commits only 1 percent of partner capital to a fund while investors commit the remaining 99 percent. The VC revenue model that generates guaranteed and cumulative management fees regardless of investment performance insulates VC partner personal compensation from the risk of poor returns.

Myth 3: Most VCs Offer Valuable Advice and Mentoring
VCs differ in how much effort they put into these nonmonetary resources, and the quality of advice and mentoring from VCs can vary widely, so founders who want more than capital from their investors should conduct due diligence on a VC firm they are considering.

Myth 4: VCs Generate Spectacular Returns
The VC industry underperforms on the returns it generates for its investors.

Myth 5: In VC, Bigger Is Better
The contrary is true for both the industry and individual funds. Industry and academic studies show that VC fund performance declines as fund size increases above $250 million.

Myth 6: VCs Are Innovators
VCs may be well known for funding innovation, but the VC industry and business model have not seen significant innovation in two decades. The VC fund structure, fund life, and economic terms have remained the same for more than 20 years." Mulcahy has a note for the VC industry: "Increasing the standard 2 and 20 compensation model to 2.5 and 25 is not innovation." *[Note: The first figure is the annual percentage fee on capital committed by limited partners. The second figure is the percentage of the profit on an investment that general partners get, it is known as the "carried interest" or the "carry."]*

How Scalable Are VC Funds?

There are people who support better access to capital by young companies but oppose making it easier to raise it from average investors. Some of them favor more government involvement but, in the US at least, there is little prospect for that. Most who have this point of view expect the money to come from VC funds, the source the Kauffman report de-mythologizes.

A fundamental question emerges—is reliance on VCs a healthy and sustainable strategy for funding the economy's entrepreneurs? Or, to put it in VC-speak, are VC funds a scalable idea? Here are some reasons to believe they are not.

- VCs tend to invest in companies located no more than 90 minutes from their office. Since most cluster in certain areas, VCs do little to expand the geographic supply of capital.

- VCs congregate around sectors that are hot—they all want to take the same dates to the dance. Thus, they may not provide capital to companies that are not in a popular category.

- VCs tend to invest in male entrepreneurs and/or those who went to a small set of universities. That may reflect a bias by VCs toward entrepreneurs they share an affinity with. A 2018 report shows that 82 percent of VCs are male, 70 percent of them are white, and 40 percent attended Harvard or Stanford.◻ The pool of entrepreneurial talent is far more diverse than the pool of VCs.

- An increase in the number of VCs may not achieve the goals of this option. Individual VCs vary significantly in their skills, wisdom, and operational backgrounds; it takes years for one to be seasoned by a range of situations and economic cycles. It also takes time for a new partner to be accepted by his/her partners.

- At a personal level, individual VCs may be too time-constrained to significantly expand the number of deals that they invest in. They have demanding jobs; there is fund-raising, networking, deal screening, due diligence, and monitoring of portfolio companies—some of which may require their intense attention. Individually, they naturally aspire to have the best work-life balance they can. Therefore, as funds increase in size, VCs are more likely to pursue deals where more can be invested versus an increase in the number of deals.

- VC firms risk becoming institutional as they scale. This is a high-touch, high-risk business—you can't just grow in size and expect the quality of outcomes to remain stable. Think big banks—big anything.

- Innovative opportunities may be shunned in favor of safer deals.

- VC money is "on the meter," which can generate pressure on portfolio companies to scale prematurely.

- Increasingly, limited partners—who provide 99 percent of the capital in a VC fund—are disgruntled with the compensation model for the general partners.

The biggest reason to oppose preservation of venture capital as a province for VCs is that it perpetuates the idea that average investors *should play the role of the Next Guy,* relegated to paying high valuations for risky ventures. This is unfair, and it continues an unfortunate tradition of weak market forces, as described in Chapter 5, "The Problem with a Conventional Capital Structure."

How the Fairshare Model Complements Angel Investing

Angel investors will absolutely benefit if IPOs are a viable alternative for capital provided by VCs. An IPO option may have more appeal than a VC deal. Having one can also help the company negotiate a better deal with a VC. Companies that don't have VC interest will have an alternative path to consider. It is good for angel investors when the companies they invest in have more funding options.

To be sure, VCs will remain the principal source of capital because they offer many advantages. However, VC capital is not particularly scalable, and it can ultimately be unfriendly to angels. Furthermore, VCs don't support the range of opportunities that angels do. Therefore, an IPO alternative to a VC round complements the interests of angel investors.

Angels invested in a company planning an IPO may prefer a conventional capital structure because it is traditional. But would that be better for them than the Fairshare Model? The answer depends on whether they intend to sell or hold their shares. If they plan to sell, angel investors will favor a conventional model because the IPO valuation will be higher. Those who plan to hold will view the IPO as another venture round. They may favor the Fairshare Model because Performance Stock can turbo-charge the company's performance, hence, the long-term profitability of the investment.

Intriguingly, one can view a Fairshare Model IPO as a hybrid of a private VC round and a conventional IPO.

- If the IPO is priced as a private VC round, the price of Investor Stock may well pop in secondary trading to one that anticipates future performance. Secondary market investors who are enthusiastic about an issuer could easily push the price higher because the pool of tradable shares will be smaller than if a conventional model is used.

- Angel investors can reduce their at-risk capital by selling some of their Investor Stock.

- Performance Stock could be issued to a company's pre-IPO investors, creating additional long-term upside for supporting a Fairshare Model IPO.

- Unlike VCs, public investors will not "pick the pocket" of angel investors.

Another angle of interest to angel groups is that they can build a reputation among public investors as a source of quality deal flow. The group's involvement with a company can suggest a level of quality akin to the *Good Housekeeping* magazine seal of approval.[1]

To be sure, this can also happen when the companies use a conventional capital structure, but with greater reputational risk for the angels because there will be greater valuation risk for public investors. If IPO investors fail to do well on IPOs backed by an angel group, its involvement will not be a reliable indicator of quality for public investors.

Angel groups that affiliate with IPOs that use the Fairshare Model will be better positioned to foster a favorable impression with public investors because their involvement can connote lower failure risk and the Fairshare Model will ensure far less valuation risk.

---

[1] *Consumer Reports* magazine and online sites like Yelp offer comparable forms of information for buyers.

How Scalable Is Angel Investor Capital?

The amount of capital invested by angel investors has grown significantly in recent decades and this source is scalable. The SEC estimates that 12 million US households, less than ten percent of the total, met the wealth and income standards to be accredited investors in 2013.[E]

The Center for Venture Research at the University of New Hampshire estimates that in 2014, there were 316,600 active accredited investors in the US who invested $24 billion in entrepreneurial ventures. By these measures, less than three percent of those who qualify to be accredited investors engage in angel investing. So, there is clear potential for angel capital to be more abundant.

The top of the following table has data on US VC firms compiled by the National Venture Capital Association for 1994, 2004, and 2014. The bottom has data on US angel investors from The Center for Venture Research for 2004 and 2014. It has no data for 1994, as activity was embryonic.

Number of Venture Capital and Angel Investors in the US	1994	2004	2014
Venture Capital Firms[F]			
- VC firms	385	985	803
- VC funds (i.e., a firm may have multiple funds)	635	1,803	1,206
- Professionals in VC firms	3,735	8,964	5,680
Angel Investors[G]			
- Active angel investors	n/a	222,500	316,600
- Women angels	n/a	11,250	82,600
- Minority angels	n/a	8,100	25,300

The 2014 data indicates there are about 400 angel investors for every VC firm and 55 angels for every professional at a VC firm. Angels are inclined to collaborate—more so than VCs who can be competitors or have competing interests. In contrast, angels share insight on how to invest, how to screen deals and how to perform due diligence on them.

In many ways, they operate with a hive mentality and due to JOBS Act reforms, they are better connected—accredited investors can connect via online funding portals. The capabilities of angel groups are sure to grow in the years ahead. Thus, there are reasons to view angel investors as a scalable source of venture capital.

> The number of angel investors in the US will surely reach half a million before there are 10,000 professionals in VC firms.

Angel investors are a diverse group, much more so than VCs, according to many reports. Note that the number of women and minority investors climbed significantly between 2004 and 2014. During that time the number of VCs shrank, making them more vulnerable to criticism that their industry is dominated by white males who share a similar background.[H]

Now, of course, VCs can apply far greater firepower to an opportunity than angel investors. They can respond to the need for capital faster and with fewer complications than angels—especially as the offering size grows. VCs can write multimillion-dollar checks.

Angels write much smaller ones; amounts from $20,000 to $50,000 are common. So, it takes longer to close an angel round of financing.

Still, interestingly, as the table below shows, the aggregate amount of angel investing in 2004 and 2014 ($22.5 billion and $24 billion, respectively) approximates what VC firms raised in those years ($17.6 billion and $29.9 billion, respectively).

Venture Capital and Angel Investor Activity in the US	1994	2004	2014
Venture Capital Firms (amounts in billions)			
- VC capital raised this year	$ 7.6	$17.6	$29.9
- VC capital under management (includes amounts raised earlier)	$33.2	$271.1	$156.5
Angel Investors (first figure in billions, second in thousands)			
- Angel capital invested this year in billions[1]	n/a	$22.5	$24.0
- Average annual investments per angel in thousands[2]	n/a	$100.0	$75.8

The table before the one above shows that the number of angel investors increased from 2004 to 2014, from 225,000 to 316,000, or 41 percent. The one above shows that the amount invested by angels increased from $22.5 to $24 billion, just 6.6 percent. That indicates the average annual investment per angel fell from $100,000 in 2004 to $75,800 in 2014.

Since less than three percent of households that qualify to be accredited investors engage in angel investing, this source of capital has greater potential to scale than VC firms. One can imagine it growing to $50 billion by 2019 based on present growth and because, in 2015, the SEC allowed funding portals to facilitate angel investments without being a broker-dealer. Private offerings have never been so easy for accredited investors to find, compare and perform due diligence on. Therefore, the number who invest in them is likely to climb.

Angel investors have a relevant range for deal size–they can fund early rounds–$2 million scratches the limit in many places. Whatever the ceiling, there may be amounts that are tough for a company to raise from angels.

VCs are well-positioned to fund large, expansion rounds. But as pointed out in Chapter 8, "The Tao of the Fairshare Model," VCs secure terms that enable them to effectively pick the pockets of angel investors with respect to ROI–sometimes, they take their pants too! So, there is a risk to angels when their company takes VC money–they may benefit far less than the VC, even though they invested before it did.

That insight leads to a question: Might the angel investor ecosystem benefit if an IPO becomes a viable alternative for companies to raise rounds of venture capital?

---

[2] The number of active angel investors increased nearly 41% from 2004 to 2014, from 225,000 to 316,000. Yet the amount invested increased just 6.6%, from $22.5 to $24 billion. What gives? The average annual investment fell from $100,000 to $75,800. Possibly, this was due to the Great Recession and an increase in caution.

Venture-Stage Investing Is Inappropriate for Average Investors Because...

Let's shift perspective and focus on the opposition to JOBS Act reforms. It is rooted in fear of the demon of investor loss. The considerable risk—and the concern about unethical sales practices—can naturally lead one to conclude that it is best if accredited investors are the sole source of venture capital.

Opposition to making it easier to raise it from average investors reflects the sense that it is simply too difficult for them to make money on their investments. The feeling can be expressed in a sentence that begins:

"Venture-stage investing is inappropriate for unaccredited investors because...[insert argument]."

The table below has arguments that could complete that sentence as well as alternative solutions that could make average investors less vulnerable to loss.

Venture-stage investing is inappropriate for unaccredited investors because...	
Argument	**Alternative solution to banning such investments**
Average investors cannot absorb the losses associated with venture-stage investing.	Deter investors from investing more than a modest amount in small, high-risk ventures in a year. The equity crowdfunding provisions of the JOBS Act have such limits.
Average investors are not positioned to perform due diligence.	Allow average investors to join groups that pool due diligence and provide other non-commission-based services. Accredited investors can do this already. Average investors in investment clubs can do it for stocks that trade in the secondary market. But as discussed in Chapter 6, "Crowdfunding and the Fairshare Model," some regulators oppose allowing anyone other than a broker-dealer to offer average investors such services in connection with an IPO. This has the effect of preserving the broker-dealer franchise.
Average investors are not knowledgeable enough to assess the risk.	Securities regulators could require issuers to disclose the valuation they give themselves (discussed in Chapter 16). This would encourage investors to be more valuation-savvy, therefore reducing the likelihood that they lose money because they overpay. It would also encourage issuers to compete for investors by offering better terms.
Average investors are not knowledgeable enough to assess whether a startup has reasonable prospect for success.	Promote investor education about the ways an investment in a company can result in a loss. If done in conjunction with the solutions above, average investors will be better able to protect themselves.
Scams abound where small companies and small investors connect.	Authorities should enforce the law when fraud is suspected.

Collectively, these solutions foster a balance of investor protection and opportunity with better access to capital for entrepreneurial companies.

We Are But Animals

As I just suggested, average investors are disadvantaged with respect to performing due diligence: their ability to assess risk, and a new venture's prospects for success. An unkind way to express that concern is to say that they are not smart or savvy enough to be successful at this type of investing.

Put aside for a moment the fact it is a hard area for anyone to succeed at venture-stage investing, as well as the notion that there are other benefits that accrue from investing in early-stage companies (i.e., it is fun, leads one to engage the world in good ways, and it contributes to an entrepreneurial culture). Let's focus on the whether an online collective of average investors might be up to the task. To begin, let's concede that virtually all individuals know far less about venture-stage companies than an individual VC.

Next, consider whether collectively, using the dynamics of a network, they might acquire capabilities that increase the odds of making a well-considered decision to invest or not. There are several online communities devoted to increasing investor savvy about traded stocks (e.g., The Motley Fool, Seeking Alpha). It seems inevitable that, if allowed, similar communities would form to enhance the ability to assess small company IPOs. After all, it's nature!

PBS's *Nova Science Now* has an episode called "What Animals Are Thinking" that examines collective intelligence in animals like bees, fish, and even slime mold.[J] Those who fear the worst for average investors may take heart from research that shows that slime mold, which has no brain or nerve system at the individual cell level, can, as a collective, find food on the other side of a maze. It does this by communicating along the colony's collective body—composed of thousands of individual slime cells.

By working together, these simple cells can do some smart things. In the program, researcher Iain Couzin notes: "It completely blows away this idea that you have to be smart to solve problems. We used to think of intelligence as having one large brain, whereas now we realize you can build intelligence in other ways." The program's narrator adds:

> For example, slime molds can find the shortest route through a maze towards a piece of food. First, the slime mold extends its tendrils through every corridor, essentially mapping the entire maze. It then retracts every tendril that didn't find food, leaving behind a trail of slime that acts as a kind of external memory.

> The trail reminds the slime mold that certain corridors are dead ends. It avoids these areas and grows exclusively along the shortest path from the beginning of the maze to the tasty treat.

> But that's not all. After scientists placed food in the relative position of major cities and urban areas, slime molds accurately recreated the rail system of Tokyo, and the major roadways of England, Canada, Spain, and Portugal. In other words, this one cell animal solved a real-world problem that it took teams of engineers to figure out.[K]

This bit of insight suggests that average investors can develop surprisingly effective ways to protect their collective interests.

Companies Should Not Want Small Investors Because...

Here's one final shift in perspective. Some opponents of average investors in early-stage companies base their arguments on the interests of companies, not investors. They say it is better to raise venture money from a VC because there is less fuss and you get the "VC value-add." There are good arguments for this, three of which are below, along with rebuttals.

Argument 1: Such companies need oversight from investors who can ensure management is held accountable or make changes in management when necessary. Average investors are not well-positioned to do this.

Rebuttal
- To be in such a situation is one of the most painful scenarios that a company can go through, and it can devolve into civil war between entrepreneurs and their investors.
  - For entrepreneurs, it brings out the "dark side" of the VC value-add—the bright side being money, advice, network, etc. And the impetus for conflict may not be performance-related.
  - For angel investors, this oversight can cut both ways. If changes are called for, it can be helpful to have a VC manage it. But when things are not going well, a VC may squeeze angel ownership.
- Ideas on how to deal with management discipline/change will be explored in the second phase of the Fairshare Model's development, after interest in the model is apparent.

Argument 2: Early-stage companies benefit from investors who can facilitate alliances with other businesses. Small investors lack such a network, so a company that relies on them for capital is less likely to be successful, even if its product is good. They simply can't run fast enough to succeed.

Rebuttal
- A company can attract influential investors at or after the IPO. Plus, for some businesses, having many small investors might help it market its product.

Argument 3: Average investors are unlikely to provide the future capital needed, and large investors who can provide it will shy away from a company with small investors.

Rebuttal
- An issuer that adopts the Fairshare Model could raise additional capital via a secondary offering or a private offering (i.e., Private Investment in Public Equity or PIPE).
- If stock warrants are attached to IPO shares, the issuer can be positioned to raise more capital.[3] For example, one can structure a $5 million IPO with a series of warrants that can result in $20 million in additional capital being raised at higher valuations over time.

The point is, there are ways to address such concerns.

---

[3] What stock options are to employees, stock warrants are to investors. Warrants are discussed in Chapter 21, "Blockchain and Initial Coin Offerings."

Summation

There are good reasons to be concerned about the involvement of average investors in venture capital. The high valuation risk associated with a conventional capital structure is the most significant reason to me, but the Fairshare Model addresses that. This chapter discusses some of the concerns that others raise. It offers two important thoughts to consider.

One is that VC funds and angel investors cannot provide all the capital that an innovative economy requires. There is a role for average investors and it shouldn't necessarily be as the Next Guy, those who may only invest at the retail price, not the lower wholesale price.

The second thought is that average investors may be more capable as venture-stage investors than many people assume. That's especially true when they can share due diligence.

What's Next?

This concludes Section 4. The next—and final—one is called "Advanced Topics."

Chapter Endnotes

Contextual references for material in this chapter appear as numbered footnotes on the page where the reference is made. **Source references** for material in this chapter appear below as endnotes with capital letter identifiers.

A "US v. National Association of Realtors." *United States Department of Justice.* October 27, 2015. Accessed July 24, 2018. fairsharemodel.com/Realtors.

B Mulcahy, Diane, Bill Weeks, and Harold S. Bradley. "We Have Met the Enemy—And He Is Us." *Ewing Marion Kauffman Foundation.* May 2012. Accessed May 10, 2018. fairsharemodel.com/Enemy.

C Mulcahy, Diane. "Six Myths About Venture Capitalists." *Harvard Business Review.* May 2013. Accessed May 10, 2018. fairsharemodel.com/Myths.

D Kirby, Richard. "Where Did You Go to School?" *Noteworthy-The Journal Blog.* July 30, 2018. Accessed August 01, 2018. fairsharemodel.com/School.

E Alois, JD. "The Number of Accredited Investors." *Crowdfund Insider.* December 21, 2014. Deck by Rachita Gullapalli; US SEC Division of Economic and Risk Analysis. Accessed May 10, 2018. fairsharemodel.com/Accredited.

F 2015 Yearbook. National Venture Capital Association. page 9.

G Sohl, Jeffrey, "The Angel Investor Market in 2014" and "The Angel Investor Market in 2004", *Center for Venture Research.*

H Cutler, Kim-Mai. "Here's A Detailed Breakdown of Racial and Gender Diversity Data Across U.S. Venture Capital Firms." *TechCrunch.* October 06, 2015. Accessed May 10, 2018. fairsharemodel.com/VCdiversity.

I Sohl, Jeffery. "The Angel Investor Market in 2004: The Angel Market Sustains a Modest Recovery." *Center for Venture Research.* March 22, 2005. fairsharemodel.com/2004Angel.

J "What Are Animals Thinking?" *PBS Nova.* November 7, 2012. Accessed May 10, 2018. fairsharemodel.com/NovaAnimals.

K "Slime Mold Smarts." *PBS Nova.* November 08, 2012. Accessed May 10, 2018. fairsharemodel.com/Slime.

SECTION 5:

Advanced Topics

This last section discusses subjects that will interest some—but not all—of my target audience. It elaborates on the Big Idea that underlies the thesis of this book, that there are two fundamental risks for investors in venture-stage companies—failure risk and valuation risk.

It also discusses the Fairshare Model from the perspective of game theory, behavioral finance, and secondary market investors.

Finally, it considers blockchain technology and initial coin offerings, concluding with an example of how a company might use both a Fairshare Model IPO and initial coin offerings (ICOs).

Chapters in this section:

Chapter 20: Investor Risk in Venture-Stage Companies

Chapter 21: Game Theory

Chapter 22: Blockchain and Initial Coin Offerings

If these topics don't interest you, proceed to the Epilogue.

Chapter 20:

Investor Risk in Venture-Stage Companies

What's Included in This Chapter

- Introduction
- A 2:3 Paradigm for Investor Risk
    - Analytics Path
    - Cohort Path
    - Structure Path
- Applying the 2:3 Paradigm to Valuation Risk
- The Problem with Public Venture Capital
- Valuation Risk Reduction for Public Investors
- Summation
- What's Next?
- Chapter Endnotes

Introduction

This chapter presents the overarching theme of this book in greater depth, which is that heightened valuation awareness by public investors can lead to better investment outcomes and generate profound benefits for the economy. It also explains why I hold opposing views about the JOBS Act. I am enthusiastic about innovations that improve access to capital for entrepreneurs—the people who promote economic vitality—but I fear that average investors will fare poorly when a conventional capital structure is used.

A 2:3 Paradigm for Investor Risk

How might one evaluate an investment in a venture-stage company? That is, one that presents substantial risk of failure and will require more money from investors in the future to survive.

It is a tough question, one that isn't just the province of investors in private offerings—it affects average investors, and anyone concerned that they may be imprudent in their investment choice. I offer you a high-level framework to address it—a 2:3 Paradigm for Investor Risk.

The "2" refers to the two fundamental risks for investors: failure and valuation. The first is that the venture will fail to meet expectations, from an operational perspective–say, less revenue or profit. The second is that the investor will overpay for a position, something that can happen even if the company fully meets operational expectations.

These risks underpin all others. Those related to market, technology, and management are a blend of these two. It is true for fraud as well, for it is a serving of failure and valuation risk, garnished with false or inadequate disclosure.

Failure risk is omnipresent in a venture-stage investment. Due diligence can help investors avoid it if it causes them not to invest. If they do invest, there isn't much most investors can do to affect failure risk because their ability to affect corporate governance is weak. That said, if the company is public, they can sell–if it is private, they are strapped in for the ride.

Valuation risk lurks as well. An investor may invest in a company that is a success but lose money (or make less than expected) because the buy-in valuation was too high.

The "3" in the title–A 2:3 Paradigm for Investor Risk–indicates that there are three paths to address the two fundamental risks–analytics, cohorts, and structure.

The three paths can be combined for a variety of effects. The following table shows that investors use two of these paths–analytics and cohorts–to mitigate failure risk and that there isn't a structural solution for failure. In contrast, all three paths are potentially available to investors to mitigate valuation risk.

2:3 Paradigm for Risks in a Venture-Stage Investment		3 Pathways to Mitigate Risk		
		Analytics	Cohorts	Structure
2 Fundamental Risks	Failure	X	X	
	Valuation	X	X	X

Analytics Path

Analytics refers to data that one can independently assess. Established companies have a lot of it. Young companies don't, and what they do have has dubious predictive value, especially if they utilize novel technologies or business models.

In 1968, Edward Altman, a finance professor at New York University, devised an algorithm to predict whether a public company would be bankrupt within two years. It weighed measures of profitability, working capital, and market value for indications of weakness. Altman dubbed the result a "Z-Score."

Could there be a forward-looking measure for early-stage companies? One that assesses the potential for success, not failure? It is a challenge that Nimish Gandhi at Invesights (invesights.com) has tackled. A former finance professor who has studied small companies, he has a methodology to predict the viability of early-stage and established companies. Invesights's algorithm generates a score that Gandhi calls the "Investment Outlook Score (IOS)." It is akin to a FICO score that measures a person's creditworthiness. Like a Z-Score, an IOS seeks to portend the future. Unlike the Z-Score, it measures business vitality.

Independent of such a system, analytics can screen for failure risk by identifying questionable assumptions. It can also be used to evaluate competitive advantage and a company's need for future infusions of capital.

Analytics is central to valuation analysis and discounted cash flow (DCF) is its cornerstone.[1] Theoretically, it is appealing; the present value of an enterprise is the sum of its future cash inflows, discounted for the time value of money (interest rate) and risk. In practice, it is only as helpful as the earnings projections, which can be unreliable for established companies and are routinely so for startups. Computer scientists have an expression that fits: garbage in, garbage out.

DCF can suggest a valuation when an investor's anticipated exit is via acquisition of the company. But there are problems here too–the valuation is based on an outcome that may never happen. Then too, a purchase price may be based on the company's strategic value to the acquirer, not its cash flow, and that can vary based on who the buyer is, and what the company's market position is. Either is hard to reliably anticipate.

Multiples offer another analytic approach to valuation. Public stock analysts look at the multiple the market applies to a company's earnings per share–its price/earnings ratio. Acquirers and private equity (PE) firms value companies using a multiple of sales, profits, or other indicators of value such as the number of customers. When a valuation exceeds a multiple's norm, valuation risk climbs.

Multiples are not particularly useful to VCs for they invest in new technologies and disruptive business models–it can be hard to identify relevant multiples for such opportunities.

Bottom line: in theory analytic tools offer a compelling way to establish a valuation for a company–but in practice, they have significant shortcomings, especially when applied to venture-stage companies.

Cohort Path

A cohort is a group whose members share a common characteristic, and here it refers to those who influence an investor's assessment of a company. Since one need not have a personal relationship with someone to be influenced by them, the pool of potential cohorts is large.

Virtually everyone heeds what others say or do. That makes the cohort path the most popular way to assess failure and valuation risks. As social creatures, investors ask: "What do others think of a company? Is it likely to go up in value?"

VC and private equity firms use cohort networks to help them evaluate both failure and valuation risk in private companies. Angel investors do this too when they approach due diligence as a team sport, coordinating it with others.

In contrast, investors evaluating a public venture-stage company have poor access to cohorts with quality insight. Financial advisors sensibly discourage such investments because of their high failure and valuation risk, but that doesn't prevent someone who wants to take a chance from doing so.

Venturesome public investors are left with media reports, press releases, and online postings. These can help assess failure risk, but they often offer notoriously poor information about valuation risk.

---

[1] DCF and valuation multiples are discussed in Chapter 13, "Valuation Concepts."

Some of these cohorts put out misleading information for their own gain. They seek to spur demand for shares as part of a pump and dump scam or crash the price in order to profit from short sale positions.

Access to the cohort path for investors in venture-stage companies is evolving. In 2013, the SEC began to let certain websites share information about private offerings with accredited investors. In 2016, it allowed other types of websites to provide information on certain small public offerings. Such developments are recent and suggest dynamism for the cohort path in the years to come.

Structure Path

The structure path is about the terms of an investment. A capital structure facilitates deal terms, hence the name, structure path.

Deal terms don't reduce failure risk, but they can limit valuation risk. Put another way, the structure path does not help investors avoid a failure, but it can keep them from overpaying for a position.

The smartest, best networked investors in the venture space—VC and PE firms—are skilled at using the analytics and cohort paths to reduce failure risk. But since it's hard for anyone to know the "right valuation" for a company, analytics are of limited value when assessing valuation risk. The cohort path is similarly handicapped because everyone has this problem. Therefore, while these investors use analytics and cohorts to evaluate valuation risk, *they rely on the structure path to control it.*

More precisely, VC and PE firms use the structure path to secure deal terms that can reduce the significance of the buy-in valuation they agree to—effectively, a valuation safety net.

A price ratchet clause is a basic way to do this. It is an antidilution deal term that will retroactively reduce an investor's effective price per share if later investors get a price that is low enough to trigger the provision. If that happens, the issuer must give the protected investor additional shares—for free. And of course, free shares reduce the average price per share of an investor's position, so it lowers the buy-in valuation.

Another form of price protection is a liquidation preference clause, which entitles an investor to a preferential return relative to other shareholders, and it is activated if the company is acquired or otherwise liquidated. A 3X liquidation preference, for example, entitles an investor to receive three times its investment from the proceeds before sharing what's left with others.

These, and other forms of price protection are the structure path. It allows VC and PE investors to tell entrepreneurs: "Give me my terms and I'll give you your valuation." That is, they can simultaneously give entrepreneurs what they want—an attractive pre-money valuation—while protecting themselves from accepting one that reveals itself to be too high.

Theranos Inc. offers a case study in risk for venture-stage investors. The now-kaput medical device startup was a high-profile Silicon Valley unicorn. Formed in 2003, it raised $400 million in venture capital and was valued at $9 billion before reports emerged in 2015 that it had misrepresented the effectiveness of its blood-testing technology.[A]

Fraud hindered the ability of investors to use the analytics path to evaluate failure risk. In a blog post, Jean-Louis Gassée, former chief technology officer for Apple, suggests that investors were sloppy, since some simple due diligence would have revealed inconsistencies in blood test results and made the failure risk clearer.

Later investors in Theranos favored the cohort path: the reputations of other investors and members of the board of directors—none of

> **Thought Experiment**
>
> If Theranos had gone public earlier, it would have used a conventional capital structure. It would have raised money at a far higher valuation than pre-IPO investors paid. Therefore, public investors would have the same failure risk that the VCs had, but far more valuation risk.

whom were apparently aware of the fraud allegedly perpetuated by the CEO and the COO. Gassée speculates that investors were guided by herd instinct, saying that once the CEO "bagged a couple of high-visibility marks, the rest made the easy decision to follow. Getting those first few investors—that was [the CEO's] real magic."[B]

As it turned out, mitigation of valuation risk was for naught as the deal was overwhelmed by the realization of failure risk. The SEC charged Theranos's CEO and its former COO with fraud in March 2018. The company formally dissolved a few months later.

Applying the 2:3 Paradigm to Valuation Risk

Before considering how the three pathways address valuation risk, let's touch on how a valuation is established.

Three are three approaches—asset, income, and market. The asset approach looks at the value of a company's assets. The income approach estimates the present value of its future earnings and possibly, its future value to an eventual acquirer. The market approach uses the valuation of comparable companies as a marker. A valuation results from weighing input from all three approaches.

This table shows how the three valuation approaches intersect with the three paths investors can take to mitigate the risk that it is too high—the analytics path, cohort path and structure path .

Valuation: Ways to Set the Amount and Mitigate the Risk		Mitigate Risk		
		Analytics Path	Cohort Path	Structure Path
Establish the Amount	Asset Approach	X	X	
	Income Approach	X		
	Market Approach		X	

Explanation:

- The asset approach is on the analytics and cohort paths because asset valuation can reflect independent assessment and/or the opinion of others.
- The income approach is on the analytics path as it relies on independent assessment of DCF analysis, valuation multiples, or similar metrics.
- The market approach is on the cohort path because it evaluates what others think.

Note that no valuation approach utilizes the structure path. That's because structure does not set a valuation. Rather, it protects against a bad one. It can protect new investors from a valuation that proves to be too high. In an acquisition, clawback terms allow the buyer to retroactively reduce its purchase price if certain conditions are not met. In a private offering, VC and private equity firms modify a conventional capital structure to effectively do the same thing. Structure can also protect *current shareholders* from a too-low valuation from new investors. In an acquisition, the seller may have earn-out clauses that requires the buyer to pay more if certain conditions are met.

There are two key points here:

1. Valuations based on the asset, income, and market approach can be unreliable for established companies and they are virtually always unreliable for a venture-stage company. That is not an indictment—it is merely an acknowledgement that it is difficult to get reliable data.

2. Structure can make a valuation elastic—conditioned on subsequent events.

The final table shows that the structure path is available to private investors but not to public ones.

Access to Paths	Analytics Path	Cohort Path	Structure Path
Private (pre-IPO) investors	X	X	X
Public investors	X	X	

This raises the question that pervades this book. **If companies offer pre-IPO investors price protection, why don't they offer it to IPO investors too?**

Fundamentally, it is because IPO investors don't demand it, so issuers have little incentive to offer it. Undoubtedly, public investors don't demand similar treatment because so many are valuation-unaware. After all, if you are unsure what a valuation is, how to calculate it, or how to evaluate one, why would you call for protection from buying in at an excessive one?

Then too, The-Way-Things-Are works well for valuation-savvy IPO investors who trade out of their position soon after they get shares. Rather than buy and hold, they buy and flip. For them, valuation protection comes from being a favored client of the underwriter, able to get an "IPO pop" of fifteen percent or more. If you doubt that, ask yourself: If Wall Street banks allocated IPO shares in a lottery, how long would it take privileged investors to call for price protection for all investors?

If public investors signal interest in terms that reduce valuation risk, will issuers offer it? Surely, yes, for it is the nature of markets to respond to demand.

If they wanted to do so, how would companies offer it? They would have a multiclass capital structure—a modified conventional capital structure or the Fairshare Model—when they have an IPO. This would allow a corporation to treat IPO investors differently from other shareholders. A single-class capital structure—a conventional capital structure—requires that all shareholders be treated the same.

VC- and PE-backed companies always have a multiclass capital structure when they are private. Employees get a different stock than investors (i.e., employees get common stock and investors get preferred stock). When there are multiple rounds of financing, investors in each round have a unique class of preferred stock that specifies their deal terms.

Typically, when such a company has an IPO, its multiclass capital structure converts to a single class structure—a conventional capital structure. The different classes of preferred stock convert to the common stock held by employees in accordance with their terms and new common stock is issued to IPO investors. (See "What Leads a Capital Structure to Change?" in Chapter 4, "Fairshare Model Q&A.")

However, IPO issuers need not have a single class of stock. When Ford Motor went public in 1956, it sold Class A shares to the public while certain insiders held Class B shares with super-voting rights. Nearly fifty years later, the Class B shares represented about 2 percent of Ford's total shares but controlled 40 percent of the vote. In 2004, Google took a similar approach with its IPO; the Class A it sold to the public had one vote per share, and the Class B shares held by some pre-IPO shareholders had 10 votes per share. Since then, several companies have used a multiclass structure to similar effect in their IPO. The most extraordinary example, surely, is Snap, which sold non-voting shares in its $3.4 billion 2017 IPO.

Note the irony of The-Way-Things-Are. *Private companies adopt a multiclass capital structure to protect new investors from insiders—employees and earlier investors. But IPO issuers use one for the opposite effect—to protect insiders from new investors.*

The Problem with Public Venture Capital

I opened this chapter by saying I'm supportive of initiatives that make it less expensive for young companies to raise venture capital from public investors. At the same time, I fear that average investors will lose money when they invest in them, but not because of failure risk. Over time, I suspect many will learn how to evaluate that risk themselves or through cohorts.

The problem is valuation risk. Average investors who invest in a company with a conventional capital structure will be exposed to a full dose of it for two reasons.

1. Companies value themselves much higher when they sell stock to public investors than to private ones.

2. Public investors have poor access to good cohort data and virtually no access to the structure path.

Valuation Risk Reduction for Public Investors

This book promotes two ideas to help public investors reduce their exposure to valuation risk:

1. A valuation disclosure requirement for offerings, which is discussed in Chapter 16, "Valuation Disclosure." The idea is that all investors, *private and public,* could reduce their valuation risk if the SEC were to make it easier to use the cohort path. It can do this by requiring *all issuers* of equity securities, whether private or public, to disclose the valuation implicit in their offering. This will enhance the competitiveness of capital markets by making it easy for data aggregation services to provide two key data points: the valuation of comparable companies, and the valuation trend line for the issuer.

2. The Fairshare Model. It uses the structure path to reduce valuation risk for IPO investors —to treat public venture capital with the respect given to private venture capital.

Summation

There are two risks that investors in venture-stage companies assume: failure risk and valuation risk. Failure risk is pervasive, whether the company is private or public. Valuation risk is higher if the company is public because IPO investors don't get the price protection terms that VC or PE investors get when they invest; plus, IPO investors buy-in at far higher valuations.

What's Next?

Game theory provides an interesting way to consider how the Fairshare Model relates to capital markets.

Chapter Endnotes

Contextual references for material in this chapter appear as numbered footnotes on the page where the reference is made. **Source references** for material in this chapter appear below as endnotes with capital letter identifiers.

A Loria, Kevin. "This Woman's Revolutionary Idea Made Her A Billionaire–And Could Change Medicine." *Business Insider.* September 29, 2014. Accessed May 22, 2018. fairsharemodel.com/Holmes.

B Gassée, Jean-Louis. "Theranos Could Have Been Stopped." *Medium.* May 20, 2018. Accessed May 22, 2018. fairsharemodel.com/Gassee.

Chapter 21:

Game Theory

What's Included in This Chapter

- Introduction
- Behavioral Finance and Game Theory
- Applying Game Theory to Capital Formation
- Why an IPO Pop Is Vital to Wall Street
- The Dutch Auction Model for IPO Valuation
- The Fairshare Model's Game – Pareto Optimization
- IPO Valuation Game – Conventional vs Fairshare Model
- Employee Stock Options
- Short Selling
- Thin Trading Markets – A Roach Motel
- Stock Buybacks
- Valuation as a Game of Hot Potato
- What's Next?
- Chapter Endnotes

Introduction

In Chapter 3, "Orientation," I suggest that you think of capital structures as art. This chapter presents a new perspective on capital structures–game theory.

Behavioral Finance and Game Theory

The dismal science of economics is being influenced by disruptive thinking that goes beyond formulas or grand theories of human nature to consider the behavior of individuals and groups. This school of thought, which has emerged in recent decades, is known as behavioral finance or behavioral economics.

Game theory inhabits this field of study. Research focuses on how people interact rather than on mathematical games of chance. What economists call game theory, psychologists call the theory of social situations as it can frame problems in a manner that allows for different viewpoints and identifies strategies to bridge them. That's because games can apply solutions to problems that are based on competition, cooperation, or a combination of both.

Here's how Princeton University professor Avinash Dixit and Yale University professor Barry Nalebuff explain game theory:

> Game theory is the science of strategy. It attempts to determine mathematically and logically the actions that "players" should take to secure the best outcomes for themselves in a wide array of "games." The games it studies range from chess to child-rearing and from tennis to takeovers. But the games all share the common feature of interdependence. That is, the outcome for each participant depends on the choices (strategies) of all.
>
> Games are fundamentally different from decisions made in a neutral environment. To illustrate the point, think of the difference between the decisions of a lumberjack and those of a general. When the lumberjack decides how to chop wood, he does not expect the wood to fight back; his environment is neutral.
>
> But when the general tries to cut down the enemy's army, he must anticipate and overcome resistance to his plans. Like the general, a game player must recognize his interaction with other intelligent and purposive people. His own choice must allow both for conflict and for possibilities for cooperation.**A**

In the Cold War era, interest in game theory grew out of a desire to explore options for conflict resolution when adversaries had nuclear weapons. A zero-sum game is one where only one side can "win"–there is a winner and a loser. The idea that there could be a "winner" when the game was Mutually Assured Destruction–the apt acronym is "MAD"–was brilliantly satirized in the classic 1964 movie *Dr. Strangelove.* Less consequential exercises abound in politics, sports, lawsuits, labor negotiations, etc. There are a variety of alternatives to a zero-sum game. What they have in common is that the gain of a player need not come at the expense of another.

Some conflicts will always be zero-sum games because they are resolved via contest. The winner of a political race assumes office, the loser doesn't. Other examples are sports championships and legal matters that are decided by a court. Many conflicts are resolved via negotiation, however. The parties may have a zero-sum mindset but decide that it will not produce the best solution.

A more effective strategy may be to identify what's important to the other party but not critical to you–then offer a deal that maximizes their satisfaction or minimizes their dissatisfaction. Better yet, minimize the conflict and find ways to align interests. Say you want a raise and your boss is unsupportive. If this conflict is cast as a contest, someone will win, and someone will lose.

Casting it as a negotiation can result in one of you granting the other more flexibility on when you work, or whether you can work from home. Or better yet, if your boss is concerned about a measure of organizational performance (sales, responsiveness, quality) or conditions (attitudes, training, safety), offer to make an extra effort to improve those areas in exchange for the raise.

When a decision is framed using game theory, one can acquire a fresh perspective on it. Jeff Bezos favors one that he calls "regret minimization framework." Here is how he says he applied it in 1994, when he decided to leave a secure job to start Amazon.

So, I [Bezos] wanted to project myself forward to age 80 and say: "Okay, now I'm looking back on my life. I want to have minimized the number of regrets I have."

I knew that when I was 80, I was not going to regret having tried this. I was not going to regret trying to participate in this thing called the internet that I thought was going to be a really big deal. I knew that if I failed, I wouldn't regret that, but I knew the one thing I might regret is not ever having tried. I knew that that would haunt me every day, and so, when I thought about it that way, it was an incredibly easy decision.

And, I think that's very good. If you can project yourself out to age 80 and sort of think, 'What will I think at that time?' it gets you away from some of the daily pieces of confusion. You know, I left this Wall Street firm [his employer] in the middle of the year. When you do that, you walk away from your annual bonus.

That's the kind of thing that in the short-term can confuse you, but if you think about the long term then you can really make good life decisions that you won't regret later.[B]

Applying Game Theory to Capital Formation

Valuation is usually thought of as the result of a process, but it can be viewed as a game. One that relies on the analytics approach, like discounted cash flow analysis—or the cohort approach, which relies on canvassing the opinion of others.[1]

Valuation-setting can be viewed as a zero-sum game, where a gain for one player is a loss for the other. Insiders may want a high valuation, for instance, because it maximizes their control, wealth, and ego gratification—it is a point of pride to be able to say that your startup is worth a lot. On the other hand, new investors will want a low valuation, as that maximizes the profit they might make.

Valuation can also be a win-win game. A company may be happy to offer a deal to an investor whose prestige or expertise can boost the valuation beyond what it might otherwise be in the future.

Mostly, though, it is a zero-sum game, in which there is uncertainty about what the valuation should be.

That dynamic is expressed in the following concept formula:

Valuation = (Zero-Sum Game X Uncertainty Factor)

Another factor—orchestration—can influence a valuation. There are so many forms of it that it is simpler to identify its effect, which is to promote Fear Of Missing Out or FOMO. In a private offering, orchestration is managed by a company's management, existing shareholders, and its investment banker—if there is one. In a Wall Street IPO, orchestration is managed by the investment banker, who needs to *make it profitable for the IPO investors to buy shares,* thus making it is easier for the banker to attract investors to other deals it has.

---

[1] My experience is that valuation experts are never relied upon by sophisticated parties in private venture-stage technology deals. Their tools are a point of reference for corporate M&A dealmakers and investment bankers, but the answers they provide are hardly determinative, which explains why acquirers frequently offer amounts for companies that are widely different from the so-called market value.

The share allocation process is the most powerful tool in the IPO orchestration toolbox. It enables a broker-dealer to reward its best customers with shares that they can, in turn, sell to eager, less valuation-savvy public investors. This tool plays a critical role in the ability of an underwriting syndicate to promote conditions that create a valuation pop for IPO investors to sell into.

Accordingly, a FOMO factor can be added to the basic concept formula:

Valuation = (Zero-Sum Game X Uncertainty Factor) X FOMO Factor

Zero-sum games make it difficult to align interests. So, VC and PE firms prefer to secure price protection over having a hard contest over valuation. With the right terms, the valuation fades in significance. Price protection doesn't change the game, however. It recasts interests in ways that obscure and defer a valuation to a time when there is less uncertainty. Thus, price protection terms are added to the concept formula as it applies to a private offering:[2]

Private Offering Valuation = [(Zero-Sum Game X Uncertainty Factor) X FOMO Factor] + Price Protection Terms

Two changes must be made to the concept formula for a valuation in a private offering to make it apply to an IPO:

1. Remove investor protection terms from the concept formula.

2. Add an exponential notation(i.e., "n") to the FOMO variable to account for the greater number of investors who buy shares.

    a. Chapter 5, "The Problem with a Conventional Capital Structure," describes the effect of a "bigger neighborhood" on pricing, which this concept formula shows:

More Potential Buyers = Higher Potential Demand = Higher Potential Price

   The other reason to make the FOMO factor exponential in IPO valuation is that many of the investors are valuation-unaware and/or valuation-unsavvy—and they can define the secondary market valuation for several quarters.

With those two changes, the concept formula for an IPO valuation is as follows:

IPO Valuation = (Zero-Sum Game X Uncertainty Factor) X $FOMO^n$

Thought Experiment
(From Chapter 11, "The Macroeconomic Context – Income Inequality.")

Imagine that, starting tomorrow, shares in Wall Street IPOs are allocated by lottery, not by wealth, privilege, or based on connections. Will investors who have routinely been able to get shares at the IPO price be content with a conventional capital structure?

If, starting tomorrow, they must buy shares in the secondary market—from those who win the lottery—might these well-connected investors clamor for a different approach to valuation? *A different game?*

---

[2] See Chapter 8, "The Tao of the Fairshare Model."

Why an IPO Pop Is Vital to Wall Street

If you haven't considered IPO valuation as game theory, contemplate how important a valuation pop is to broker-dealers. A November 6, 2013 report on NPR's *Morning Edition* about the then-upcoming Twitter IPO provides a glimpse behind the curtain. It references the 2012 Facebook IPO, which was panned by some for not having an IPO pop. Indeed, the stock fell significantly and remained below what it was at IPO for over a year. Here is the transcript [bold added for emphasis].**c**

Renee Montagne, Host: What makes an initial public offering a success? Twitter is going the old school route, pricing its shares modestly in hopes of a pop in early trading. The company will go public on Thursday, and the banks they've hired to help are some of the oldest and most well-established in the country.

It's *Morning Edition*, from NPR News. Good morning. I'm Renee Montagne.

Steve Inskeep, Host: And I'm Steve Inskeep. Twitter is going public tomorrow, an initial public offering of stock—an IPO. And if there's one message the company's executives want to get across in the lead-in to that IPO, it's this: Twitter is not Facebook. NPR's Steve Henn reports.

Steve Henn: In many ways, Twitter is planning **an old-school IPO.** Unlike Apple, Microsoft, and Facebook, it's not going to be listed on the tech-heavy NASDAQ. Instead, it's going with the staid New York Stock Exchange. The banks Twitter's hired to take it public are some of the oldest and most well-established in the country. And when Twitter first proposed a price for its IPO, it signaled to investors it was looking for a first-day pop.

Neil Stewart: Well, the **holy grail of equity capital markets is a nice pop on opening day.**

Henn: Neil Stewart's the research director for *Investor Relations* magazine. A pop is when a newly IPO'ed stock shoots up on its opening day of trading. These pops were what made Internet IPOs so appealing back in the days of the dot.com boom. **For investment bankers, a pop is a pretty helpful thing.**

John Kolz: Hi. My name is John Kolz. I'm a managing director at Credit Suisse, in equity capital markets.

Henn: **Kolz's job is to drum up investor interest in new IPOs. He approaches the same big investors before shares start selling to the public again and again. These relationships are the bread and butter of his business. And a nice, predictable pop on opening day keeps big investors happy.** But Facebook fizzled.

Stewart: Yeah, it was botched.

Henn: Neil Stewart says Facebook sold so many shares at such a high price, it glutted the market for its stock.

Stewart: It was in shambles, in the end. It took a year to climb back to its IPO price. It disappointed a lot of people. It was probably pretty hard within Facebook to keep their heads down, working away, when all of that was going along.

Henn: Recently, Mark Zuckerberg was asked if he had any advice for Twitter on the eve of its IPO.

Mark Zuckerberg: See, that's funny on its surface because I'm kind of like, the least—the person you would want to ask last how to make a smooth IPO.

(LAUGHTER)

Henn: Zuckerberg jokes about it now, but it's probably not fair to call Facebook's IPO a complete failure. The company raised billions of dollars, on great terms. And today, its investors—assuming they held onto their stock—are doing great. In fact, **there's a school of thought—especially on the West Coast, and especially among entrepreneurs—which believes that a big, old-school pop on the opening day of an IPO is actually a really bad thing.**

Bill Hambrecht: When I try to think—When did I first start questioning the system?—to be honest, the first time it really—someone brought it home to me, was in the initial pricing of Apple Computer, in 1981.

Henn: Bill Hambrecht is an investment banker based in San Francisco. He's been helping tech companies go public for years, including Apple, Amazon, Genentech, and Google. **He says a pop doesn't benefit tech firms. It benefits Wall Street.**

Hambrecht: Steve Jobs figured out very quickly how Wall Street worked. And he really questioned: Hey, why do you price it at 18 when you know it's going to sell at 28? And why do you charge me a 7 percent commission? And, you know, who gets that stock at 18? I mean, you know, why not my friends? Why your friends? I mean, he questioned the whole process.

Henn: When founders underprice an IPO, money that could flow into a fledgling company to finance growth goes to Wall Street insiders instead. And in the last year, five companies that went public saw their stock price shoot up more than 100 percent on the opening day of trading. Hambrecht says that's not a sign of success. It's a disaster.

Hambrecht: To me, we've been trying to say, hey, you should really approach this as anybody would who's selling any asset. Find the fair price.

Henn: Hambrecht says imagine for a second that you sold your house to a friend of your real estate broker. And then you found out afterward that guy flipped your house, less than an hour later, for twice the price.

Hambrecht: You'd probably want to send the broker to jail, particularly if you found out he got part of that profit back in other business.

Henn: Too often, Hambrecht says **that's how so-called successful IPOs actually work.** So, he says if Twitter's stock price shoots to the moon tomorrow, it's actually a sign Twitter lost out. Steve Henn, NPR News, Silicon Valley.

The Dutch Auction Model for IPO Valuation

The preceding NPR transcript cast the valuation game as a contest between the issuer and its investment bankers. And the person who charged that issuers are short-changed by investment bankers, Bill Hambrecht, is one himself. In fact, he is a penultimate insider at the junction of Silicon Valley and Wall Street.

The predecessor of his eponymous investment bank, W.R. Hambrecht and Company, was Hambrecht & Quist. Founded in 1968, H&Q was an early player in the technology sector; one of its leaders, Q.T. Wiles, is mentioned in earlier chapters. Hambrecht is also well-known for promoting the use of a "Dutch auction" to set IPO pricing. "Auction" comes from the Latin word *auctionem:* "a public sale by increasing bids." In a traditional auction, the price starts low and goes up, and the winning bid is the highest one. But there is variation in how auctions are constructed.

One variant is called a Dutch auction. In one, the price starts high and falls. Imagine a marketplace where growers gather to sell tulips to resellers. It is inefficient to have all buyers and sellers negotiate individually. Plus, doing so would result in unfair outcomes for some. The Dutch auction solution is to begin taking orders at a high price. If there isn't enough demand to sell all the tulips, orders are accepted at progressively lower prices until enough additional orders are received to sell all of them. The lowest price is applied to all orders, even those submitted earlier, at a higher price. This form of auction facilitates the sale of all tulips at a single price that occupies the intercept of market supply and demand.

When a Dutch auction is used for an IPO, the IPO price is the highest one that ensures all shares are sold. In the chart below, a company offers a percentage of its ownership, represented by 1 million shares, in a Dutch auction. The open question is, what will it get for them? It has bids for 100,000 shares at $10.00 per share, 200,000 shares at $9.50 per share and so on. Demand increases as the price drops. At $8.50 per share, cumulative demand meets the supply of shares and so, all 1 million shares are sold at $8.50, raising $8.5 million.

Dutch Auction Chart — Price setting in a Dutch Auction IPO

IPO price set where aggregate demand buys total supply

Shares offered in IPO		1,000,000 shrs
Bid Price	# Bids	Cumulative Bid
$ 10.00	100,000 shrs	100,000 shrs
$ 9.50	200,000 shrs	300,000 shrs
$ 9.00	300,000 shrs	600,000 shrs
$ 8.50	400,000 shrs	1,000,000 shrs
$ 8.00	500,000 shrs	
$ 7.50	600,000 shrs	

IPO shares	1,000,000 shrs
IPO price	$ 8.50 per shr
IPO raise	$ 8,500,000

In September 2014, public radio station WBUR's *Here & Now* program interviewed Bill Hambrecht for a report called "Dutch Auctions May Offer 'More Democratic' Way to Launch IPO." Here is a portion of the report:[D]

"IPOs have always been handled by traditional investment banks, and essentially it's sort of an insider's game–goes back 120 years, really," Hambrecht says.

When a firm like China's Alibaba wants to go public, it usually picks a traditional investment bank to do the legwork. The bank, which is the underwriter, helps set the price per share, and then makes those shares available at a discount to its own customers first.

So, if you want a piece of Alibaba, you will have to wait until big institutional investors get a chance to snap it up first. "So, the public is excluded from it, and the price is depending on, effectively, the underwriter deciding the price," Hambrecht says. "And I felt it was a lot fairer to open up the market to every investor. And number two, do it at a market price."

Hambrecht says the big investment banks have an incentive to set the original price low, so the stock will jump on the first day of trading and make early investors a lot of money.

That's why Hambrecht goes against the grain with his auction IPOs. He says Boston Beer, the maker of Sam Adams, pioneered the idea in the mid-1990s. The financial research firm Morningstar used a Dutch auction in 2005.

"The best example, and the best one we did of course, was Google," Hambrecht says. Hambrecht's firm was one of about 30 investment banks involved when Google went public a decade ago. "They wanted to tell all their users—and at that point there were 100 million of them—that if you want to own our stock you have access to it through an auction, and if you want to buy our shares, you can do it by bidding," Hambrecht says. "And that's what they accomplished."

Bill Hambrecht's firm has taken a company public with an auction 24 times, and the two he has in the works now are small companies trying to raise less than a $100 million.

The *Here & Now* report includes criticism of the Dutch auction that might explain why it hasn't been widely adopted. Namely, that it is complex to manage and can result in an issuer raising less money than it might otherwise. That sounds like balderdash.

I think the real reason a Dutch auction isn't used more often is because it messes with the business model of investment banks. Complexity? Orchestrating an IPO to ensure all shares are sold and a valuation pop is sustained is complex! And less money raised? A Dutch auction can deliver a *better deal for issuers* by rerouting the profit earned by investors who flip shares to the company's coffers. And a wee portion of the advertising budget of investment banks could make what's unfamiliar to investors look attractive. But they aren't going to do that because a Dutch auction will take the fizz out of an IPO pop.

The Fairshare Model is a different form of innovation in IPO pricing. *Whereas a Dutch auction provides a better deal for IPO issuers, the Fairshare Model delivers a better deal for IPO investors.* A valuation pop is unimportant because the IPO places no value on future performance. The valuation grows more in response to performance than to orchestrated expectations. That said, it is likely that a Fairshare Model IPO will deliver a valuation pop—one that is bigger than a conventional IPO. That's because secondary market investors are likely to bid up the valuation to where it approaches that of comparable companies that have a conventional capital structure. If that occurs, the pop benefits IPO investors, just like a conventional IPO. But it also benefits employees if the market capitalization of the issuer is a measure of performance (i.e., the share price of Investor Stock multiplied by the number of shares of investor Stock).

Like a Dutch auction, however, the Fairshare Model is likely to get a cold shoulder from Wall Street because it messes with the business model of entrenched interests.

The Fairshare Model's Game – Pareto Optimization

You may be familiar with the "80/20 rule," the idea that, for many events, 80 percent of an effect is explained by 20 percent of the causes. The 80/20 rule was first known as "Pareto's Rule."

Vilfredo Pareto was an Italian engineer, sociologist, economist, political scientist, and philosopher who died in 1923. "His legacy as an economist was profound. Partly because of him, the field evolved from a branch of moral philosophy as practiced by British economist Adam Smith into a data intensive field of scientific research and mathematical equations. His books look more like modern economics than most other texts of that day: tables of statistics from across the world and ages, rows of integral signs and equations, intricate charts and graphs."[E] Pareto made important contributions to the understanding of income distribution and decision science. The 80/20 principle results from his finding that 80 percent of the land in Italy was controlled by 20 percent of the families. He discovered that criminal activity followed a similar distribution: 20 percent of the people were responsible for 80 percent of crimes.

His observation about unequal distributions led others to notice that the relationship was apparent in other areas. In business, 80 percent of a company's sales might be explained by 20 percent of its products or by 20 percent of its customers. In an organization's workforce, some may sense that 80 percent of the value is created by 20 percent of the employees. This assessment has even been applied to relationships! Some say that people get about 80 percent of what they want from a relationship with another person—total fulfilment is rare.

Pareto's work led to a framework for analytical thinking about tradeoffs faced by a decision-maker with conflicting objectives. For example, the term "Pareto optimality" describes a set of solutions for which resources are allocated to optimize the expected result for all parties. This model is what managers use, consciously or not, when they seek to make decisions that balance the interests of their investors, the company, its employees, and customers. It is also used in government, engineering, healthcare, and education—virtually anywhere there is an effort to arrive at a solution that maximizes everyone's expected benefit or expected utility.[F]

In game theory, a Pareto optimal solution is the most efficient one possible for all players. Such a solution cannot be changed without hurting at least one other player. A simple expression of the concept was expressed in 1789 by British philosopher Jeremy Bentham, the founder of a school of thought known as Utilitarianism. He said the goal of government ought to be policies that offer "the greatest good for the greatest number." The Fairshare Model is a Pareto optimal solution that offers the greatest good for all those willing to participate in the funding and building of a company. That's because it offers something attractive to employees, pre-IPO investors, and IPO investors.

IPO Valuation Game – Conventional vs Fairshare Model

Game theory can "illustrate the potential for, and risks associated with, cooperative behavior among distrustful participants."[G] So, let's contemplate this game of IPO valuation, a contest for how best to raise public venture capital!

- **Game:** Value a company that raises venture capital via an IPO.
- **Two teams:**
    - one to use a conventional capital structure (i.e., the conventional model)
    - one to use the Fairshare Model
- **Players on each team:**
    - issuer (company selling new shares)
    - issuer's pre-IPO investors whose shares are eligible to trade—for the conventional model team, this includes employees
    - IPO investors
    - Performance Stockholders (Fairshare Model team only)
    - secondary market investors

- **Game goal:** Optimize the benefit of all the players.
- **Goals by player:**
  - Issuer
    - Raise the capital it needs.
  - Pre-IPO investors
    - If planning to sell, set the highest valuation possible.
    - If planning to hold, goals are the same as the issuer.
  - IPO investors
    - Buy shares at lowest valuation possible.
  - Performance Stockholders (Fairshare Model team only)
    - Convert Performance Stock to Investor Stock.
  - Secondary market investors
    - Buy shares at lowest valuation possible.
- **Rules:**
  - Conventional Model: set IPO valuation 15 to 20 percent below what it is expected to be in secondary market trading.
  - Fairshare Model: establish and manage criteria for converting Performance Stock.
- **Strategies:**

Player	Conventional Model	Fairshare Model
Issuer	Promote prospects; describe deal structure.	Describe prospects; promote deal structure.
Pre-IPO Investors	Hold shares or sell them to secondary market investors.	Same as conventional model.
IPO Investors	Accept valuation for actual and expected performance.	Accept valuation for actual performance and rules for Performance Stock conversions.
Performance Stockholders	Not applicable	Achieve requirements for Performance Stock conversions.
Secondary Market Investor	Trade based on expected performance, or how valuation compares to comparable companies.	Same as conventional model.

- Key risk:

Player	Conventional Model	Fairshare Model
Issuer	Overly optimistic expectations may create challenges for corporate governance.	Performance.
Pre-IPO Investors	Duration of the IPO price pop.	Whether valuation will rise to what it would be with a conventional model.
IPO Investors	The size and duration of the valuation pop; will performance be strong enough to sustain it?	Issuer's long-term performance will not cause the price of Investor Stock to climb.
Performance Stockholders	Not applicable	Employees feel inadequately rewarded for their performance.
Secondary Market Investor	Expected performance is overvalued, or will not be achieved.	Performance Stock conversions cause the price of Investor Stock to drop.

- Expected outcomes:

Player	Conventional Model	Fairshare Model
Issuer	Capital is raised from investors who pay up front for expected performance. IPO valuation is substantially higher than what it is using the Fairshare Model. Insiders' ability to affect corporate governance is high. Ability to offer employees stock options that are likely to pay off diminishes as stock price climbs.	Capital is raised from investors who don't pay for expected performance. IPO valuation is substantially lower than what it is using a conventional model. Insiders' ability to affect corporate governance is significant, at minimum. Options on tradable stock more likely to pay off for employees for the above reasons. There's an ability to offer interest in Performance Stock for at least a decade.
Pre-IPO Investors	Liquidity option at higher IPO value than Fairshare Model.	Liquidity option at a lower IPO value than conventional model.
IPO Investors	Liquidity option	Same as conventional model.
Performance Stockholders	Not applicable	Employees have tremendous incentive to meet criteria for Performance Stock conversions.
Secondary Market Investor	Liquidity option	Same as conventional model.

I bet that an 80/20 break in favor of the Fairshare Model will emerge because it benefits more people than a conventional model.

When the conventional model prevails in this game, the consequences are likely to include the following:

- Average investors will be less likely to make money when they invest in a venture-stage company because they will assume much higher valuation risk than pre-IPO investors.

- The types of companies that raise private capital from VCs will fit into a narrower band—those likely to attract interest from large numbers of public investors. Figuratively, it will be akin to having all movies produced by major Hollywood studios.

- Overvalued public companies will find it difficult to use stock options to motivate employees.

- Investors in small public companies will be vulnerable to pump-and-dump schemes where promoters orchestrate short-term demand for a stock, then sell their shares. A conventional model is very vulnerable to this because tradable shares are issued for future performance; they can include shares issued to promoters for little or no money as an incentive to get the price up.

On the other hand, when the Fairshare Model wins the game, the consequences will probably include the following:

- Average investors will be more likely to invest in venture-stage companies because, with far less valuation risk, they are more likely to profit when they invest in a company with high failure risk.

- Private capital will be more inclined to back the equivalent of independent movie studios because the Fairshare Model provides a viable liquidity option. This will encourage greater diversity in the types of companies that get funded. For example, there will be those whose markets are too small to capture VC interest, but they may attract public investors. They will find it easier to raise private money because of the improved prospects for raising more money later in an IPO. The same will be true for companies that have social/sustainability goals as part of their purpose.

- Companies will be less likely to be overvalued in the secondary market because of the nature of the Fairshare Model. That is, tradable shares are not issued for performance before it has been delivered. However, it is possible that Fairshare Model companies will be overvalued—because markets do that. But when it happens, Performance Stock will help them do a better job of aligning the interests of investors and employees than companies that use a conventional capital structure.

- Companies will be less vulnerable to promoter-driven pump-and-dump schemes because the ranks of Investor Stockholders will be comprised of those who bought stock with a long-term perspective or earned it via performance. Such shareholders are unlikely to be short-term investors.

Employee Stock Options

A stock option gives an employee the right to buy a company's stock at the grant price–typically, the common stock at the market price on the grant date. The employee can exercise the right once vested to do so, which often takes three to five years of employment.

In theory, work performed during the vesting period will cause the stock price to rise. Since options have delivered substantial wealth to many people, they are widely viewed as an effective way to motivate employees, to align their interests with those of investors.

This conceptual equation captures the high-level premise:

$$\text{Work} = \text{Reward}$$

Game theory can provide a fresh view on options as it prompts one to consider the perspective of the players. The question is: How effective are they at motivating employees? The answer is that it depends. With stock options, the connection between work and reward is weaker and more situational than you might expect.

To understand why the connection between work and reward is weak, consider the following table, which shows how the terms are defined and measured in a stock option program.

The Work and Reward Connection – When Stock Options are the Reward		
	Work	**Reward**
Defined as	Value created by the employee during the option's vesting period.	The right to a portion of the increase in the company's value due to the employee.
Measured by	The increase in the value of the company's stock during the option's vesting period.	Increase in stock price between the option grant date and when employee is fully vested, gaining the right to exercise the option. *Multiplied by* Number of shares in option grant
Principal weakness	The connection between work and reward is indirect.	
Reasons for Principal Weakness	• It is impossible to reliably forecast the quality and quantity of an employee's work. • It is impossible to assess the effect of an employee's work on the price of a stock.	The reward principally reflects: • when an employee is hired (i.e., the stock price when option is granted), and • their ability to negotiate the number of shares in the option grant The reward has a weak connection to the actual value of the work performed.

The table identifies the weakness of options—the indirect connection between work and reward. It is indirect because employees don't get stock for work—a direct connection. Rather, they get the right—the option—to buy stock later at the exercise price. If the stock appreciates during the vesting period, that price is a bargain.

It's a risk-free decision for the employee to exercise an option to buy the stock. If it is profitable to do so, they reap an immediate gain. For example, someone who can buy stock for a dollar a share that is worth ten dollars reaps a nine dollar per share profit if they immediately sell after exercising the option.

If it isn't profitable, the employee doesn't lose because they have no money at-risk. It's like a game: think of a coin flip where "heads" means the stock is higher than the exercise price and "tails" means it is below it. For an employee with a vested option, head's mean profit while tails mean nothing—no gain or loss. That's because an option is free to the grantee: money is only paid to exercise an option, not to receive it.

The table also identifies why the connection between an option and work is indirect:

1. It is impossible to forecast an individual employee's contributions when the grant is made, and
2. it is impossible to identify the effect of that employee's work on the stock price.

Something else is indirect also—the connection between an option and reward. The reward depends on something the employee doesn't control—the stock price when the option is granted and when it can be exercised. The magnitude of the potential upside is based on something employees may be able to influence by negotiating the number of shares in the grant. The problem is that an employee's negotiating ability can have little to do with the value of their future work.

There's another reason for the weak relationship between the reward provided by an option and the work an employee performs. If the stock appreciates during the vesting period, good and mediocre work are equally rewarded: if the stock price is flat or falls, terrific work gets nothing—there is no stock reward.

So, the reward provided by a stock option is not directly connected to work. What is it directly connected to? Employment during a period when the value of the stock climbs.

The collective value of employee work is a significant factor—a stock is more likely to rise when valuable work is delivered. However, the role of luck and timing in the reward is at least as significant. Comparable work delivered by workers at a different company, or at the same company at another time, can be rewarded very differently.

Why is the effectiveness of stock options as a tool for motivating employees situational? The chart on the following page indicates that their incentive power depends on whether the company is private or public, and if its valuation is high or low relative to its actual performance.

The reference to "high" and "low" valuation measures employee belief, not the assessment of outsiders. Options motivate employees if they *believe* the stock price will rise during their vesting period. It need not be a well-founded belief, it need only exist.

The chart shows why options are not an effective motivator when the company is public and highly-valued. In that situation, employees have easy access to what the company's valuation is and the opinions of others about its attractiveness.

It also provides a reminder that the Fairshare Model applies only to companies that use it to go public.

In a private company, *believing* that the valuation will go up can be an article of faith, based on the reputation of options and optimism about the potential for an IPO or acquisition. Where such optimism exists, it need not reflect an *assessment* of the

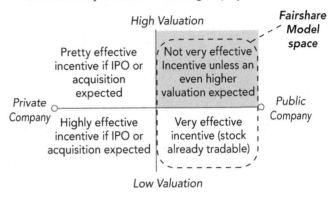

Stock Options Plans

When are they effective at creating employee incentive?

valuation. Few employees may know what it is because private companies are loath to discuss it. One reason is to avoid sowing confusion–after all, the figure can be a mirage. Convertible debt can muddle the picture, as can the deal terms investors have. Chapter 8, "The Tao of the Fairshare Model," discusses some of them.

That said, employees with options from a private company need not rely just on signs of forthcoming prosperity to believe their option can pay off–they have a structural reason for optimism. Their option is for common stock, which is cheaper than the preferred stock investors buy. Generally, the exercise price for grants on common stock begin at 70 to 80 percent below the current value of the preferred stock. So, for example, when investors in a private company pay $1.00 for a share of preferred stock, employees stock options are likely to be granted with an exercise price between $0.20 and $0.30. The discount shrinks as a liquidity event approaches. When one occurs, the preferred stock converts to common, which causes the value of the common to rise. (See "What Leads a Capital Structure to Change" in Chapter 4, "Fairshare Model Q&A.") Thus, even if the hopes held by employees with options for the company are not fully realized, they can still profit nicely.

The dynamics differ if the company is public when an option is granted–the exercise price is usually the current price of the common stock. So, in a structural sense, the upside is less than for an option issued by a private company. That's because a company is usually worth more when public than private. The opportunity to profit from the step-up in valuation associated with going public isn't there.

However, there are advantages to an exercisable option on a public stock. One is that the stock is easily converted to cash. The other is that a public stock is often more volatile in price than a private stock. An adverse event or news story can cause it to plunge. If the company resets the exercise price when the market price is low, the option's incentive is invigorated because the price may well be higher later, even without substantial improvement in operating performance. Public stocks often do that.

However, stock options granted by a public company that is highly-valued provide a weak incentive if employees feel the stock price is unlikely to climb much. This can happen with an established company as well as with an overvalued startup.

Ironic, isn't it? Stock options are least effective as a motivator when a company needs performance and has more investors than ever before! That is, when it has the largest number of investors! In that situation, the stock option incentive can get screwed up.

It makes one wonder: Is there a better way to structure employee stock incentives?

Frankly, Fairshare Model issuers will play this same game when they grant employees options on Investor Stock. But there will be two differences between stock options issued by companies that use the Fairshare Model versus a conventional capital structure:

1. The IPO valuation of a Fairshare Model issuer will not consider future performance.

   a. However, investors in the secondary market may do so, which can cause the price of Investor Stock to rise.

2. Fairshare Model issuers will have a powerful complement to stock options to offer employees—Performance Stock, which can create a direct connection between work and reward.

   a. Interests in Performance Stock will be granted based on actual, not anticipated, performance.

   b. Employees will be motivated to deliver valuable work regardless of whether the Investor Stock is highly-valued or not. This, in turn, ought to make it more likely that options on Investor Stock will be "in the money" for employees.

Short Selling

With a conventional IPO, future performance accounts for a high proportion of a company's valuation. When a stock climbs in the secondary market, some investors value undelivered performance even more richly. The reasons are discussed in Chapter 5, "The Problem with a Conventional Capital Structure."

Valuing future performance leads to a peculiar game—short selling. It allows an investor to profit when a stock falls in price. In the nomenclature of Wall Street, an investor who buys a stock takes a "long position" and money is made if it rises in value. When taking a long position, an investor takes a positive, long-term perspective, even when the stock is held briefly. For instance, flip-oriented investors who invest in an IPO take a long position in the sense that they expect the shares to appreciate.

However, an investor can sell a stock he doesn't own. The opposite of a long position is a short one; "selling short" is the opposite of "buying long." An investor who sells a stock short expects it to fall in price. It's a more complex trade. The investor borrows shares from a broker-dealer, pledging collateral and paying interest on the value borrowed. If the stock falls, the investor's profit is the difference between the value of the shares when they were shorted and when he returns them to the broker-dealer. If the stock does not change, the investor's loss is the interest charge. If it goes up, the investor's loss is the interest *and* the appreciation, because he must buy the shares to replace those borrowed in the market.

To illustrate this without considering interest and transaction expenses, assume an investor shorts 1,000 shares valued at $10,000; the market price is $10 per share. If it falls to $7, the investor replaces the borrowed shares by buying them in market for $7,000 and profits $3,000 (1,000 shares X

[$10 per share borrowed minus $7 per share to repay the loan]). The investor loses if the price rises. If it goes to $12 per share, the investor suffers a $2,000 loss when the position is closed (1,000 shares X [$10 per share borrowed minus $12 per share to repay the loan]).

The details can be confusing, but the point isn't. Short-selling is a way to place a bet that a stock price will fall. Thus, an investor can make money by thinking positively (long) or negatively (short) about a stock's prospects.

This sets up a contrast to contemplate. In a conventional capital structure, the value of future performance is reflected in the IPO price and speculated on in secondary market trading. In the Fairshare Model, no value is placed on future performance in the IPO valuation. Investors in the secondary market may place a value on future performance, however.

Short-selling is fueled by negative energy. It's the bane of any company but has a corrective effect for markets. Venture-stage companies are more vulnerable to it because their future performance is difficult to assess, and their performance is often unsteady. That's why their price is so volatile.

Negative energy has its place. But, isn't it be better to have positive energy when it comes to companies as they struggle to find their way? Companies that use the Fairshare Model may be less vulnerable to short-selling as the value placed on future performance is unlikely to be excessive enough to attract short-sellers.

Why? It isn't in the IPO valuation to begin with. Plus, Performance Stock conversions dilute the holdings of Investor Stock when performance is delivered. And that may dampen the effect of expectations in the secondary market.

Also, the Fairshare Model is likely to attract investors with supportive attitudes and long-term perspectives. They may generate demand for Investor Stock if it slips in price. Such buying pressure can make it less likely that a short position will pay off–discouraging attention from "The Shorts."

Thin Trading Markets – A Roach Motel

Valuation is an important consideration when you buy a stock because it establishes a critically important determinant of your eventual return–your buy-in price. The other, your exit price, can be affected by the depth of the trading market.

Companies that do not trade on a major exchange like NYSE or one of the NASDAQ platforms are likely to have a thin pool of investors interested in buying the stock in the secondary market. Market makers play a vital role in facilitating market liquidity.

You want to buy 100 shares of a stock in the secondary market? A market maker will sell it to you if it has it in inventory. If not, it will try to buy it from someone who has 100 shares by raising the bid– or buy–price. Once the market maker has the 100 shares, it will sell them to you at a higher ask, or sell, price. The difference, called the spread, is earned by the market maker for being the middleman.

A challenge for investors in venture-stage companies with thinly-traded secondary markets is that when they want to sell stock, the price can drop significantly. That is, if you have 100 shares to sell, and the market bid price is $10 per share, you are likely to get $10 per share. But if you want to sell 1,000 shares, the price may well be lower than $10, and you will get a sharply lower price than that if you seek to sell 10,000 shares.

Market forces determine the price you get by matching supply and demand for the stock. That price is not just a matter of the company's operational performance, it's influenced by investor awareness of the stock and enthusiasm about its potential. This adds a game element—a trap for investors in small cap stocks—regardless of what the issuer's capital structure is.

One reason to be cautious about investing in small venture-stage companies is that it may be hard to get the quoted bid price because there aren't many investors eager to buy. A reason public companies hire investor relations firms is to promote their visibility in the market. Publicists perform a similar function for celebrities, movies, books, and music.

Stock Buybacks

I suspect that issuers that use the Fairshare Model are less likely to engage in stock buybacks than those that use a conventional capital structure. In part, that's because startups rarely, if ever, have a buyback—they have better uses for their cash. But my surmise flows from the nature of the two capital structures, not the average size of the companies that will use the Fairshare Model.

A stock buyback is the repurchase by a corporation of its own shares trading in the secondary market—it buys stock from shareholders willing to sell. Companies conduct them when they have more cash on hand than they can profitably deploy in their business and it feel that a reduction in the number of shares outstanding provides more value to shareholders. The idea is that if the company has fewer shares, the remaining ones will rise in price—same demand for shares, less supply.

In August 2018, the PBS *NewsHour* reported that stock buybacks are expected to hit a record $1 trillion that year, nearly 50 percent higher than in 2017.[H] The cash used to fund them could be distributed to shareholders as a dividend, but it's more appealing for executives with stock options to use it for a buyback. Doing so can increase the stock price for a longer time than a dividend. A buyback can therefore profit executives with stock options more than a dividend—which makes it topical for game theory.

In August 2018, Senator Elizabeth Warren introduced a bill in the US Senate called the Accountable Capitalism Act. A provision requires that shares received by executives as pay must be held for five years after they are received, and at least three years after a share buyback. That is evidence of political interest in making stock compensation less of a game and encouraging executives to have a long-term perspective. Given how political power is distributed in 2019, it is unlikely to become law, however.

Nonetheless, it is interesting to consider how use of the Fairshare Model might influence a company with excess cash. I suspect it will be less likely to engage in stock buyback because:

- Few will think that a Fairshare Model issuer has too many tradable shares—it will likely have fewer than if it had a conventional capital structure.

- The price of Investor Stock might not climb significantly if a rise will cause conversions of Performance Stock conversions.

- Investor stockholders are unlikely to support a stock buyback if it can result in Performance Stock conversions. And if conversions will not result from a buyback, management is unlikely to pursue one—they will view it as a stupid use of cash. A dividend will make more sense, especially if it is a trigger for a Performance Stock conversion, as it should be.

Of course, if a Fairshare Model issuer does have a buyback or dividend that results in Performance Stock conversions, employees will participate in any wealth generated for the Investor Stockholders.

Valuation as a Game of Hot Potato

The final game theme I'll leave you with is older than game theory: Hot Potato. Played by children, an object is rapidly tossed from one player to another—like a hot potato. Whoever holds it when time is called is removed from the game. It is repeated until there is a single winner.

The valuation of a conventional stock in the secondary market reminds me of Hot Potato, which is the Next Guy theory on steroids. Expectations play a critical role in valuation, and they can be volatile, which encourages short-term trading. Individuals who engage in this in an extreme manner are called day traders. Investment firms that do it are called hedge funds.

In his 2014 book, *Flash Boys*, Michael Lewis described how some hedge funds went to extraordinary expense to rig the ultra-short-term game of high-frequency trading so that they could see incoming orders before they appeared in the exchange's execution queue. The funds then inserted trades micro-seconds ahead of them that allowed them to profit from knowing what the next order was.

Short-termism begets more short-termism. Corporations find it harder than in decades past to justify decisions that endanger quarterly results. The attention of the players—management, investors, analysts—is on the hot potato. It's understandable because the incentives are set up to reward a short-term focus. But sometimes, incentive systems are flawed; they reward behavior that really isn't beneficial to a system at-large.

Perhaps capitalism can benefit from adoption of the philosophy of the slow food movement, the idea that we can have food that is healthier and more delicious by changing how we produce and prepare it. The essential elements of capitalism, such as market-based transactions and pricing, would remain unchanged. But key aspects of the result might be different.

Examples include:

- ownership interests
- corporate governance
- the relationship between capital and labor
- corporate purpose
- market volatility, and
- overall economic vibrancy.

Fundamentally, the Fairshare Model offers a way to set incentives to achieve diverse, long-term values. It encourages a view of valuation that is like slow food—developed over time and based on substance. It encourages a form of capitalism that is less like a game of Hot Potato.

What's Next?

The final chapter, which covers something new that has sprung onto the capital formation stage—blockchain-related initial coin offerings (ICOs).

Chapter Endnotes

Contextual references for material in this chapter appear as numbered footnotes on the page where the reference is made. Source references for material in this chapter appear below as endnotes with capital letter identifiers.

A Dixit, Avinash, and Barry Nalebuff. *Thinking Strategically: A Competitive Edge in Business, Politics, and Everyday Life.* New York: W. W. Norton, 1991.

B "Jeff Bezos - Regret Minimization Framework." YouTube. Accessed May 10, 2018. fairsharemodel.com/Bezos.

C Henn, Steve. "Twitter's IPO Managed Differently Than Other Tech Stocks." NPR *Morning Edition.* November 06, 2013. Accessed May 10, 2018. fairsharemodel.com/Twitter-IPO.

D O'Dowd, Peter. "Dutch Auctions May Offer 'More Democratic' Way to Launch IPO." WBUR *Here and Now.* September 09, 2014. Accessed May 10, 2018. fairsharemodel.com/Dutch.

E *Wikipedia* entry for Vilfredo Pareto.

F "Pareto Efficient and Pareto Optimal Tutorial." *Economics Wiki.* August 13, 2012. Accessed May 10, 2018. fairsharemodel.com/Pareto.

G Smith, M. Shane. "Game Theory." Beyond Intractability Knowledge Base Project. Conflict Information Consortium, University of Colorado, Boulder. Eds. Guy Burgess and Heidi Burgess. August 2003. Accessed May 10, 2018. fairsharemodel.com/Game.

H Solman, Paul. "Why Recent Stock Market Gains Might Not Benefit the Economy." PBS *NewsHour.* August 23, 2018. Accessed August 24, 2018. fairsharemodel.com/Stock-market-gains.

Chapter 22:

Blockchain and Initial Coin Offerings

What's Included in This Chapter

- Introduction
- Whatevers for Whatchamacallits
- Quick Definitions
- Functional vs. Investment Tokens
- Blockchain and Cryptocurrencies
  - Bitcoin Economics
  - Where Bitcoins Come From
- I Don't Know Much About Whatchamacallits, But I Know This…
- What Is a Security?
- What Is an ICO?
- What Is the Appeal of an ICO to Issuers and Investors?
- ICOs Expand the Potential for Fraud
- Regulation Will Be Good for the ICO Market
- If a Token Is a Security, How Does One Value It?
  - If a Token Conveys No Ownership Interest
  - If a Token Provides an Ownership Interest or Income Stream
- Valuing an Investment Token for a Non-Cryptocurrency Project
- Why the Fairshare Model Approach to Valuation Makes Sense for ICOs
- Why an Issuer Might Prefer a Fairshare Model IPO to a Conventional ICO
- Stock Warrants Can Turbocharge an IPO
  - Stock warrants
  - Exploding stock warrants
  - Integration
- A Scenario That Uses a Fairshare Model IPO and ICOs
- What's Next?
- Chapter Endnotes

Introduction

This chapter discusses blockchain technologies and how two offshoots—cryptocurrencies and initial coin offerings (ICOs)—expand the definition of securities and present a valuation challenge. Many people are aware of these terms but have trouble explaining them. Comedian John Oliver says cryptocurrencies combine everything you don't know about money with everything you don't know about computers.

There is a lot to absorb about this space. It is easy to feel disoriented as it is new, complex, and evolving. In their early days, PCs, the internet, and mobile/social computing spawned similar feelings. I am no expert in blockchain, cryptocurrencies, or ICOs, but I have delved into them enough to be informed. I share insights that I've acquired to orient you, should you be *cryptocurious* enough to dive deeper into this world.

After providing an overview of blockchain and cryptocurrencies—Bitcoin, in particular—I discuss why the Fairshare Model offers an appealing way to raise equity capital for a blockchain venture. Regardless of whether the money is raised using an IPO or ICO, such a venture-stage company is difficult to reliably value at the time an equity investment is made.

So, ICOs simply provide a different venue for the battle that has been described throughout this book—the one between a conventional capital structure and the Fairshare Model. The fundamental question is the same: Should public investors be content buying-in to a valuation for future performance when they invest, or should they demand price protection, like VCs get?

The chapter closes with an intriguingly illustration of how a venture might use *both* a Fairshare IPO and one or more ICOs.

Whatevers for Whatchamacallits

For about a decade, I have lived in Oakland, California. The city has a long history as a site for demonstrations about wars, elections, civil rights, and economics. It's next to Berkeley, after all.

Starting in December 2017, as I contemplated how to approach this chapter, Bitcoin is the rage, but mysterious to most people, some of whom want to invest in anything related to blockchain. I imagine demonstrators on Broadway enthusiastically proclaiming support for ICOs with signs that include "Whatevers for Whatchamacallits."

I'll explain.

Classic thinking is that a company's stockholders are its owners; that a share represents a voice in governance, and a share of distributed profits or any value that remains in a liquidation, after creditors are paid. The notion that some shareholders are more equal than others was advanced in a notable way in 1956, when Ford Motor Company went public.

The dominant practice then was for public companies to have a single class of voting stock (i.e., a conventional capital structure). Ford broke with tradition by concentrating voting and dividend rights in a separate class of shares held by insiders (i.e., a modified conventional capital structure). It was unusual, but then Ford had a strong record of performance. The idea was resurrected by Google in its 2004 venture-stage IPO. These adverse terms didn't dampen investor interest, so other companies adopted it too. Some even sold stock with no voting rights.[1]

The trend raises a question: if a stock need not have voting rights, what is the defining quality of one? Seemingly, it is just a residual claim on assets. That is, upon liquidation, stockholders have the right to the value that remains after creditors are satisfied. That's it. Voting rights are optional.

But if a stock lacks voting power, should it be called something different? The 1980s gave us "junk bonds," the moniker for bonds issued by companies with speculative ability to repay the debt. We may need a name for stocks that have little or no voting rights. Junk stock? Silent Partner shares? Investment chips?

What about what is sold in an ICO? Digital coins or tokens might as well be called "whatchamacallits" because people have trouble describing what they are to begin with.

"Whatevers" is a fitting way to refer to those who invest in whatchamacallits because most don't have ownership in the organization that issues them, nor a vote in governance. For that reason, ICO investors are best viewed as donors or contributors.

But, as we'll see, the SEC has signaled that it views many tokens to be securities. If that is the case, and a token lacks ownership rights, it makes little sense to call investors "shareholders," and they aren't "creditors" if the issuer isn't obligated to repay them.

So just what is a "token holder"? Eventually, we will have a name for those who own a token that *is a security,* and another for those who own one that *isn't a security.* Those terms are explained next. But know now that there is a shapeshifter aspect to tokens. One can be part investment, part not. And, what a token "is" can change with circumstance–it is a "thingamajig."

It's so confusing that perhaps we should just call token holders "whatevers."

This chapter departs the well-mapped land of stocks and enters the wild, unexplored territory of "whatchamacallits." There is no perfect way to begin, but a useful one is to learn some terms.

Quick Definitions

When an area is new and evolving, as the digital token world is, one often sees different terms used to refer to essentially the same thing. While the terms in the chart on the following page are explained in this chapter, it can be helpful to see them in table format.

---

[1] Google sold Class C no-vote stock in 2014 and Snap's 2017 IPO was for no-vote stock.

Thingamajig	=	Digital Token (or Coin)	=	Virtual Token (or Coin)	=	A bundle of rights
Cryptocurrency	=	Virtual or digital currency	=	Bitcoin & 1,000+ others		
Dollar, Euro, Yen, Pound, Renminbi, etc.	=	Regular money	=	*Fiat* currencies		
Token	=	A functional or utility token (not regulated as a security)	OR	An investment token (regulated as a security)	OR	A token with functional & investment qualities
Tokens	*Rarely*	Provide ownership rights	*While*	Stocks almost always do		
Tokens	*Rarely*	Provide voting rights	*While*	Stocks almost always do		
Initial Coin Offering (ICO)	=	Initial Token Offering (ITO)	=	Security Token Offering (STO)		
Utility ICO (or ITO)	=	ICO of functional tokens	*Which is*	Not regulated as security	*Which is*	Not well-understood
Security ICO (or ITO or STO)		ICO of investment tokens (ITO) a.k.a. security tokens	*Which is*	Regulated as a security	*Which is*	Controversial & subject of regulatory interest

Another blockchain related term is "smart contract"—a software program that acts like an escrow agent. Once parties enter the terms they agree on into the program, the smart contract automatically executes as milestones are met. For example, if a buyer and seller agree that the buyer's bank account will be charged when an order is placed, and that the seller will be paid when it ships, a smart-contract can be created to administer it. Effectively, the program is a self-executing contract—one that does not require human intervention to trigger a reciprocal action.

Conceptually, the Fairshare Model is a smart contract between investors and employees: Performance Stock converts to Investor Stock based on measures agreed to by the two classes of stock.

Functional vs. Investment Tokens

Gifts are tokens of affection. In Old English, "token" means sign, symbol, or evidence. A token can be a surrogate for money, such as a bus token or casino chip, both of which resemble a coin. On computer networks, a digital token provides evidence of identity. In an investment context, a digital token represents a bundle of rights that the issuer and investor have agreed to.

Securities regulators have *two categories for digital tokens:* investment tokens and functional tokens. A *functional token* has utility, the ability to authenticate identity, signify rights, track activity, obtain a product, or a discount on one. An *investment token* may have functionality, but its appeal is its potential to rise in value. In practice, it can be difficult to place a token in either camp for the same reason it is difficult to classify real estate, art, jewelry, exotic cars, or fine wines as purchased for consumptive value, or as an investment. So, **a token may be partly functional and partly an investment.**

Some other points:

- Functional tokens are not regulated (in the US), *but that could change.*

- Investment tokens are sold to fund a project (i.e., product/service, cryptocurrency) or an enterprise. They are subject to regulation, but just how is not fully settled. Likely, an investment token will be regulated as a security, but it could be as a commodity, a forward contract or something else.

- Regulators, not issuers, decide if a token is a security. A tripwire for determining this is whether investor interest is based on an expectation that it will rise in price, say when the project is complete. If that is a material motivation for buyers, the token is security.

- An investment token must satisfy disclosure requirements before it can be sold in a regulator's jurisdiction.

- More than a thousand cryptocurrencies have been issued. Measured by market capitalization (i.e., number of tokens times the market price of one), Bitcoin is the largest.

- Often, a token doesn't convey ownership rights in the issuer or its technology, nor a vote in governance. The difference between a token and a no-vote stock is that a stock has a residual claim on assets. If the issuer is acquired at a price that exceeds its liabilities, there is a payoff for a stockholder. If that happens to a token issuer, there may not be an investor payoff because a token usually has no claim on its assets.

- Thus far, cryptocurrencies have been issued by private organizations, but some governments—Singapore, Russia, Israel, Switzerland—have considered issuing their own digital money—a fiat cryptocurrency.

- Cryptocurrencies exist only on computer networks, but not as a file. "There are no bitcoins, only records of bitcoin transactions. There are only records of transactions between bitcoin addresses. Every transaction that ever took place is stored in a vast public ledger called the blockchain. If you want to work out the balance of any bitcoin address, the information isn't held at that address; you must reconstruct it by looking at the blockchain."[A]

- Those who buy investment tokens take on a heavy dose of failure risk and valuation risk.

Blockchain and Cryptocurrencies

Blockchain is a software technology that could influence every society in the decades ahead. Think of it as an operating system for network interactions. One that enables shared, concurrent, verifiable records that are not controlled by any one entity.

Moses Ma is managing partner of FutureLab, a consulting firm that applies agile development principles to innovation initiatives. In his 2017 book, *Blockchain Design Sprint,* Ma calls blockchain the "fifth major disruptive computing paradigm in the history of the Information Age, following mainframes, PCs, the internet and mobile/social computing."[B]

Historically, trusted third parties—government, institutions, companies, lawyers, accountants, notaries—have been relied on to validate and verify records, to provide authoritative evidence of

> "All commerce is based on trust, verification of identity, and undisputed ownership of assets. In the omnidirectional, internet-enabled global marketplace, these factors are burdened by approaches and an infrastructure well-suited to industrialism, but not [how] we do commerce today, or the ways we will do it tomorrow.
>
> The emerging, digital-enabled, globalized economy is still burdened by critical deficiencies, and blockchains are attractive precisely because they can address every single one of these factors more efficiently than previously possible.
>
> The blockchain [therefore,] is a technology for disrupting business models, one that is quite likely to disrupt markets far beyond Bitcoin digital currency.
>
> Ignoring the blockchain [is] akin to saying, around 2000, 'Do we really need a website?' Or in 2008, 'Isn't it safer to wait and see if this smartphone thing is for real to develop a mobile app?'"
>
> —Moses Ma, *Blockchain Design Sprint*

what is so. But a single-source of information can be wrong; a transaction may be missing, falsified, or incorrectly recorded. Plus, it is not subject to confirmation by anyone else.

Blockchain cures that defect with cryptography: complex mathematical methods to securely store and transmit data. The technology makes possible a single shared source of truth using a network of distributed ledgers that rely on time-stamped transactions that are verified and validated using consensus among the other ledgers.

Along with robotics, machine learning and other forms of artificial intelligence, blockchain promises to transform life in profound ways.

It is a potential game changer for transactions and record keeping because it can:

- dramatically reduce the time required to update records:
- reduce costs by removing overhead and middlemen or other intermediaries; and
- reduce the risk of forgery, tampering, and collusion.

Potential applications of blockchain include:

- proof of identification, existence, ownership, and authenticity of assets;
- contract administration (i.e., "smart contracts" perform escrow administration);
- process monitoring,
- financial records,
- health records; and
- voting.

Blockchain also enables new forms of money: digital currencies known as cryptocurrencies or alt-currencies—shorthand for alternative currencies. Money issued by countries is known as *fiat currencies* because governments declare what its legal tender is (*fiat* is Latin for *it shall be*).

The first alt-currency, Bitcoin, launched in 2009, shortly after a whitepaper described how blockchain could be the basis for a form of money not controlled by a government. A whitepaper is a document that presents a problem and a proposed solution. The author of the Bitcoin whitepaper, Satoshi Nakamoto, is a mysterious figure who has not been identified. Is he a real person? Is the name a *nom de plume* for one or more computer scientists? Nobody seems to know.

Interest in Bitcoin grew for technical and social reasons. Marc Andreessen, a VC who co-developed the popular Mosaic web browser in the early 1990s, describes the technical reasons this way:

> Bitcoin is the first practical solution to a longstanding problem in computer science called the Byzantine Generals Problem. To quote from the original paper defining the B.G.P.:

> [Imagine] a group of generals of the Byzantine army camped with their troops around an enemy city. Communicating only by messenger, the generals must agree upon a common battle plan. However, one or more of them may be traitors who will try to confuse the others. The problem is to find an algorithm to ensure that the loyal generals will reach agreement.

> More generally, the B.G.P. poses the question of how to establish trust between otherwise unrelated parties over an untrusted network like the internet.

> The practical consequence of solving this problem is that Bitcoin gives us, for the first time, a way for one internet user to transfer a unique piece of digital property to another internet user, such that the transfer is guaranteed to be safe and secure, everyone knows that the transfer has taken place, and nobody can challenge the legitimacy of the transfer. The consequences of this breakthrough are hard to overstate.

> What kinds of digital property might be transferred in this way? Think about digital signatures, digital contracts, digital keys (to physical locks, or to online lockers), digital ownership of physical assets such as cars and houses, digital stocks, and bonds—and digital money.[C]

The social drivers of Bitcoin have roots in distrust of central authority, which is age-old. The 1970s witnessed it with the Pentagon Papers and the Watergate scandal. The cyber punk movement gave it identity in the 1990s. More recently, the Great Recession eroded confidence in governments and banks, and spawned provocative thinking about assets, power, and accountability.

Interest in alt-currencies rose from skepticism of the motives and the competence of institutions. Idealism played a role too; a desire to improve accountability, reduce fraud and corruption; to lower the cost and increase the efficiency and security of transactions for people in less developed countries.[2]

In 2017, another social factor—speculation—defined interest in Bitcoin, in an explosive way.

Bitcoin Economics

The software to create a cryptocurrency is open-sourced, which means it is available for anyone to use. By early 2019, more than 1,600 cryptocurrencies had been created and more were being created each week.[D] A handful of them—Bitcoin, Ether, Litecoin and Bitcoin Cash—have been recognized by regulators as digital currencies and, therefore, they are not considered securities.[E]

---

[2] Idealism is common early in the adoption cycle of something new. In their time, plastics, television, fast food, PCs, the internet, and social media all were talked up as having a positive effect on people and society.

The economics of Bitcoin, the one with the highest capitalization, provides insight into how many of them are created and used. There is no central authority for Bitcoins, no central bank or owner. What there is instead, is a protocol that defines how many Bitcoins can be created, about 21 million in total, and the rate at which they will be created over a 20-year period, from 2009 to 2029.

The following chart has actual and projected data about the supply of Bitcoins and its growth rate. The number of Bitcoins is the solid line and its values are on the left vertical axis; zero in 2009 and nearly 21 million in 2029. The dotted line is the year-over-year growth rate in the number of Bitcoins and the right vertical axis measures it.

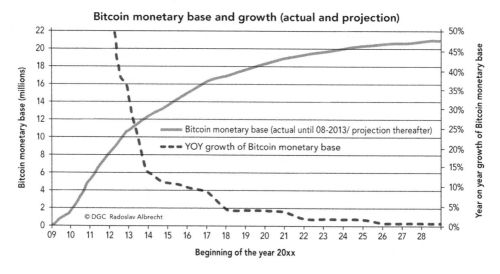

Bitcoin monetary base and growth (actual and projection)

There are two takeaways. One is that the supply of Bitcoin has grown rapidly since 2009, but the growth rate is slowing, and it will completely stop growing in 2029.**F** The other takeaway is that the growth rate began to drop in 2013 and falls thereafter. That dynamic fosters a sense of increasing scarcity.

Over the first seven years of its existence, Bitcoin traded at nominal prices—around $100. The next chart shows how the price changed from late 2013 through 2018. In 2013, it jumped to just under $1,000,

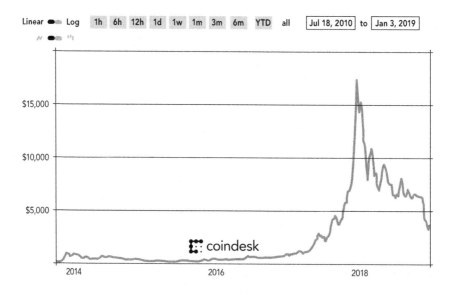

then slowly descended to less than half that before climbing back to about $1,000 in 2016. The price exploded in 2017–jumping to $19,100, an 1,810% increase in one year! A year-long decent followed. It closed out 2018 at $3,880, down 80% from its high.

What explains the amazing rise in the price of Bitcoin in 2017? Not a reduction in supply; according to the prior chart; it grew 10 percent in 2017. It isn't that it became more attractive as a medium of exchange; it's easier, faster, and cheaper to transact with fiat currencies–at least in developed economies.

Nor did Bitcoin become a safer store of value than dominant forms of fiat money or asset classes like government notes, corporate bonds and stocks, real estate, precious metals, or gems, etc. Its volatility undermines that; if it appreciates quickly, it can fall quickly.

I think the price shot up because Bitcoin is a new thing with intriguing potential and limited supply. Given the mounting attention blockchain attracts, more people began to pay attention to its early fruit–Bitcoin. Rising awareness of something often drives demand for it. Bitcoin could turn out to be to asset classes what Le Beaujolais Nouveau is to wine. That's the name of the first Beaujolais wine sold each year. Routinely mediocre, it is nonetheless marketed with enough panache to make it a thing to buy.

At the end of 2017, Yale professor Robert J. Schuller, winner of a Nobel Prize in economics, assessed Bitcoin's price performance this way.

> The Bitcoin market is a marvelous case study in ambiguity and animal spirits. It is providing invaluable information about how millions of human brains process stimuli coming from public acceptance, imagination, and innovation in surrounding cryptocurrencies. This is fascinating from a psychological and neurological perspective, but it isn't grounded in solid economics.**G**

"Money is worth only what someone else is willing to give you for it."

–Niall Ferguson,
The Ascent of Money: A Financial History of the World

Where Bitcoins Come From

It's easier to say what a Bitcoin *isn't* than to describe what it *is*. It isn't a physical thing; images of them are props. Also, it isn't controlled by a government, a bank, or any other entity that is accountable, in a traditional sense.

What *is* a Bitcoin? It is software that functions as a chit. A chit is a piece of paper that shows how much someone owes or has paid. Bitcoin is software that manages and tracks all Bitcoin transactions in a manner that relies on consensus among a majority of ledger-keepers, the record-keepers. Bitcoins exist in a "distributed," or decentralized, network of ledgers known as the Bitcoin blockchain. Marc Andreessen describes it this way: [bold added for emphasis]

> **[Bitcoin is] an internet-wide distributed ledger.** You buy into the ledger by purchasing slots [blocks in the blockchain], either with cash or by selling a product or service for Bitcoin. You sell out of the ledger by trading your Bitcoin to someone else who wants to buy into the ledger. Anyone in the world can buy into or sell out of the ledger any time they want–with no approval needed, and with no or very low fees.

The Bitcoin "coins" themselves are simply slots in the ledger [blocks in the blockchain], **analogous in some ways to seats on a stock exchange,** except much more broadly applicable to real world transactions.

Bitcoin is a digital bearer instrument. It's a way to exchange money or assets between parties with no pre-existing trust. The sender doesn't need to know or trust the receiver or vice-versa. Related, there are no chargebacks[3]—this is the part that is literally like cash—if you have the money or the asset, you can pay for it; if you don't, you can't.

"Mined" is the term for how a Bitcoin is created and "miners" are those who compete to earn a slot in the Bitcoin ledger network, a block in the Bitcoin blockchain. [I prefer "ledger-keepers" as it is more descriptive of what miners do, and it makes more sense when talking about digital tokens.]

Instead of picks and shovels, Bitcoin miners use computers optimized to perform complex cryptographic calculations to compete to solve a mathematical puzzle. A new puzzle is created every ten minutes and the winner is awarded Bitcoins. The number began at 50 in 2009, halved to 25 in 2012, halved to 12.5 in 2016, and will halve to 6.25 in 2020. When Bitcoin was $15,000, the prize was worth nearly $200,000. The winner also gets to manage a ledger/slot/block in the Bitcoin network. The size of the network is equal to the number of Bitcoins. There were 16 million ledgers at the end of 2017—it will peak at 21 million in 2029.

I think of the Bitcoin network as a franchise because ledger-keepers can charge users fees when they buy into or sell out of the ledger (i.e., use Bitcoin for a transaction).[H] An article in *The Balance* describes the mining process this way:

As more people learn about Bitcoin and get interested in mining, and as the bitcoin price increases, more people are using their computers to mine bitcoins. As more people join the network and try to solve these math puzzles, you'd expect each puzzle to be solved sooner, but that doesn't happen.

The software that mines Bitcoin is designed so that it will always take ten minutes for everyone on the network to solve the puzzle. It does that by varying the difficulty of the puzzle depending on how many people are trying to solve it.

How do you calculate the electrical energy used to power the bitcoin network? One way to do it is to look at how many sums are conducted every second to solve bitcoin's mathematical puzzles, and then to find out how much electrical energy it takes to do each sum.

These individual sums are called hashes, and there are vast numbers of them—so many, in fact, that we have to think of them in terms of millions of hashes (known as megahashes) or billions of hashes (gigahashes) to make any sense of them.[I]

The power required to mine Bitcoins will grow because the puzzles become more complex as more miners compete to solve them. One observer writes:

The sad truth is, only those with specialized, high-powered machinery are able to profitably extract bitcoins nowadays. While mining is still technically possible for anyone, those with underpowered setups will find more money is spent on electricity than is generated through mining. In other words, mining won't be profitable at a small scale unless you have access to free or really cheap electricity. [JK]

---

3 A charge disputed by a credit card provider is a chargeback for the merchant (i.e., reverse transaction).

Since electricity is a major cost, miners set up shop where it is inexpensive. Cheap power is why more Bitcoins (and other cryptocurrencies) are mined in and exported from China than any nation.[L] It's ironic, as China sharply restricts the use of cryptocurrencies because they have been used to evade its currency exchange rules.

Worldwide, some miners operate as power parasites: "employees with high-level network privileges and the technical skills needed [have turned] their company's computing infrastructure into a currency mint."[M]

A December 2017 report indicates that the power used to mine and verify Bitcoin transactions approximates what is used by Denmark and growing at 25 percent a month.[N] That underscores how important electricity is to Bitcoin.

Cryptocurrencies that require less power, process transactions faster, or are more profitable for miners could threaten Bitcoin. Competition may well come from an alt-currency that will grow in supply as demand climbs, which would make it less volatile. It could also come from established payment systems that use less power (i.e., a credit/debit card transaction requires miniscule power).

I Don't Know Much About Whatchamacallits, But I Know This…

I understand two things about blockchain-related projects.

First, a web of community support plays a vital role for making a project successful. Without it, even the best technology will have trouble getting the market traction it needs. Marc Andreessen describes the key constituencies for Bitcoin this way:

> Bitcoin is a four-sided network effect. There are four constituencies that participate in expanding the value of Bitcoin as a consequence of their own self-interested participation. Those constituencies are:

1. consumers who pay with Bitcoin,

2. merchants who accept Bitcoin,

3. "miners" who run the computers that process and validate all the transactions and enable the distributed trust network to exist,[4] and

4. developers and entrepreneurs who are building new products and services with and on top of Bitcoin.[O]

Andreessen does not list investors, probably because Bitcoin didn't raise public capital and because he is a VC who can write a big check. Blockchain projects that raise money via an ICO will certainly have investors on their list of key constituencies.

The second thing I know about blockchain projects is that regulatory gravity is pulling ICOs into a yet-to-be-settled orbit around the established body of securities law. The fundamental question to wrestle with is whether an ICO is a security offering or a form of rewards-based crowdfunding.[5]

---

4   I wonder how artificial intelligence or machine learning will affect blockchain implementations. Will the ledger-keepers be machines that are controlled by machines? If so, will they share the same instructions?

5   Crowdfunding is discussed in Chapter 6, "Crowdfunding and the Fairshare Model."

What Is a Security?

The definition of a security is not limited to stocks and bonds. The US Supreme Court has said it:[P]

> ...was meant to include "the many types of instruments that in our commercial world fall within the ordinary concept of a security...It includes ordinary stocks and bonds, along with the countless and variable schemes devised by those who seek the use of money of others on the promise of profits..."

> Thus, the [definition of the term "security"] is not limited to instruments traded at securities exchanges and the over-the-counter markets but extends to uncommon and irregular instruments. We [the Court] have repeatedly held that the test "is what character the instrument is given in commerce by the terms of the offer, the plan of distribution, and the economic inducements held out to the prospect. Moreover, we are satisfied that Congress, in enacting the securities laws, did not intend to provide a broad remedy for all fraud."

While the definition is broad, just what is a security is subject to interpretation. Chapter 9, "Fairshare Model History & the Future," illustrates that with the story of Fairshare, Inc. memberships. California's regulators said they were a security—an investment contract—while those from three other states and SEC rejected that idea.

In July 2017, the SEC released a report that provides insight into its perspective on ICOs. It describes the result of its investigation into a plan to offer tokens to US residents by an internet-based entity called "The DAO" (for Distributed Autonomous Organization) which was affiliated with a German corporation, Slok.it.[Q] The money raised would fund blockchain projects and token holders would share in the earnings they generated. The report is significant because it describes why the token could be a security; it met a test for an investment contract: "The presence of an investment in a common venture premised on a reasonable expectation of profits to be derived from the entrepreneurial or managerial efforts of others." It signals that the SEC will view comparable tokens as securities.

Some in the cryptocurrency community raise technical points to say that the SEC's reasoning is faulty. Their arguments don't matter, for two reasons. One is that courts give regulators wide berth when it comes to defining a security. Second, when authorities see behavior that concerns them, they often decide what they want to do, then figure out how to justify it.

And, ICOs are on the regulatory radar. SEC Chairman Jay Clayton signaled that in November 2017, with the following statement:

> I have yet to see an ICO that doesn't have a sufficient number of hallmarks of a security. [Moreover], there is also a *distinct* lack of information about many online platforms that list and trade virtual coins or tokens offered and sold in initial coin offerings.[R]

In a November 2017 blog post with the foreboding title, "The SEC and ICOs: Winter is Coming," John Reed Stark, former Chief of the SEC's Office of Internet Enforcement, predicts regulators plan an "upcoming effort to enforce financial regulations in the ICO space, placing ICOs and other cryptocurrency-based transactions under greater scrutiny than ever before." He adds:

> My take is that the federal and state regulatory onslaught in store for the purveyors of ICOs is imminent and will ensnare a broad range of ICO market participants. No one is likely to escape the SEC's reach – as well as the reach of state regulators, and the litany

of other federal regulatory and criminal prosecutorial agencies who will surely (and eagerly) follow the SEC's lead.[S]

Such words suggest hostility toward ICOs, but that's not what Chairman Clayton wants to convey. In December 2017, he said: [bold added for emphasis]

I believe that **initial coin offerings**—whether they represent offerings of securities or not—**can be effective ways for entrepreneurs and others to raise funding,** including for innovative projects. However, any such **activity that involves an offering of securities must be accompanied by the important disclosures, processes, and other investor protections that our securities laws require.**

A change in the structure of a securities offering does not change the fundamental point that when a security is being offered, our securities laws must be followed. Said another way, replacing a traditional corporate interest recorded in a central ledger with an enterprise interest recorded through a blockchain entry on a distributed ledger may change the form of the transaction, but it does not change the substance.

We at the SEC are committed to promoting capital formation. The technology on which cryptocurrencies and ICOs are based may prove to be disruptive, transformative and efficiency enhancing. I am confident that developments in fintech will help facilitate capital formation and provide promising investment opportunities for institutional and Main Street investors alike.

I encourage Main Street investors to be open to these opportunities, but to ask good questions, demand clear answers and apply good common sense when doing so. When advising clients, designing products, and engaging in transactions, market participants, and their advisers should thoughtfully consider our laws, regulations, and guidance, as well as our principles-based securities law framework, which has served us well in the face of new developments for more than 80 years.[T]

What Is an ICO?

Initial Coin Offerings inhabit the center of the whatchamacallit jungle. The first one was conducted in 2013, and 2017 was a boom year for them. Market interest in ICOs significantly receded in 2018, however.[U] ICOs have been used by companies, and by nebulous organizations like The DAO (see earlier in this chapter), and they can be used to fund anything (e.g., a cryptocurrency, business, product, real-estate project, a cause) using contributions, debt, royalties, or equity. ICOs epitomize ambiguity.

Where an ICO can be sold is an issue. If an issuer wants to sell tokens, it must comply with regulatory requirements for where the investor resides. Regulators in the issuer's country can impose requirements on an issuer too. Tokens are a new thing and countries vary in how they are approaching them. US investors who invested in an ICO did so before the SEC's unfolding approach was in effect, or they told the issuer they were not a US resident.

Nowadays, ICOs must run a gauntlet before they can be offered in the US. Regulatory and related matters need to stabilize. Issuers and investors need to understand them better. My guess is that it will take years before SEC-compliant ICOs will not routinely appear.

Chapter 9, "Fairshare Model & Future," concludes by describing the Concept Gap that the Fairshare Model must cross before early adopters try it. ICOs face similar challenges plus an additional one—a regulatory framework. The Fairshare Model doesn't require that—it simply extends established practice for private offerings to an IPO. While both have legal, accounting, and tax issues to resolve, ICOs have more.[6] If investor interest is evident in the Fairshare Model, there may be a Fairshare Model IPO before there is a SEC-compliant ICO.

Even if I'm wrong on the timing, I don't doubt that ICOs have potential—billions of dollars have been raised with them. Such interest augurs well for the Fairshare Model, for it indicates investor receptiveness to alternative capital structures.

So, an ICO is an organization's initial public offering of digital tokens; money for a bundle of rights. Tokens are sometimes called "coins" because tokens were first used to fund cryptocurrency projects and calling one a coin is a play on Bitcoin, the first cryptocurrency.

It's confusing, but deceptive names appear in the arts, finance, politics, and religion too. For example, if you can explain why the late music star, Prince, changed his name in 1993 to the symbol to the right, saying he henceforth wanted to be called "The artist formerly known as Prince," you will have little difficulty explaining what an ICO is. Maybe.

An organization may be able to have multiple ICOs, which sounds odd. If an offering is the first of its kind, how can those that follow also use the word "initial?"

The answer may be that ICOs rarely offer equity in the sponsoring (or parent) organization. Rather, they finance a project using debt or rewards-based crowdfunding. So, an organization with multiple projects might have an ICO for different ones. But if a token provides an ownership interest in something, a subsequent offering should be called a secondary coin offering because it will not be the first.

So, *what* is an ICO? In the pre-regulatory era, which ended in late 2017, one began with an organization (not necessarily a legal entity) describing on the internet a project that it wanted to develop in a whitepaper. If there was investor interest, it created an ICO and web pages to accept investments. If the minimum amount needed was collected, the ICO closed and buyers got tokens that entitled them to whatever rights were provided.

ICOs have largely been used to fund a project in exchange for the right to some of what will be produced or a discount on it (a "pre-sale"), but they can used to finance *anything* (i.e., equity, real estate, investment fund, contribution, etc.) and the rights conveyed can vary widely; tokenholders can be entitled to income from the funded project, ownership in it, or nothing at all—a contribution. Tokens have no inherent rights.

Some blockchain enthusiasts have been critical of ICO structures, arguing that a pre-sale signals that a project is weak, or that an attractive one shouldn't require a discount to attract support. Another critique is that a discount undermines alignment of interests among supporters if flip-oriented investors are involved. In fact, pump-and-dump scenarios have been frequent; projects were hyped to stir up demand, then early buyers sold their tokens to new investors at a profit.

---

[6] For example, the SEC has said that Bitcoin and a few other cryptocurrencies are a currency, not a security. But the Internal Revenue Service indicates it views a cryptocurrency as property, not money, which suggests that profit realized from holding one is taxable as a capital gain. It also raises a question, will localities that tax personal property such as inventory also tax holdings of cryptocurrencies? Will it be subject to sales and use tax?

Similar arguments are made about stocks, of course; IPO investors can be driven by short term interests that are not aligned with those of the issuer and long-term investors.

At this writing, one can't say what a regulatory-era ICO will look like, but one thing is certain. The disclosure document that accompanies an ICO will include information that many whitepapers omitted in the pre-regulatory era, such as the address of the issuer, the name and background of the principals, information about their compensation, use of proceeds, financial data, and risk factors.

Potentially, ICO issuers will be required to disclose and discuss the valuation of the project. If so, that may create pressure to require similar disclosures for IPOs.[7]

What Is the Appeal of an ICO to Issuers and Investors?

Pavel Kravchenko is a cofounder of Distributed Lab, a Ukrainian company that develops blockchain protocols. With a PhD. in cryptography, he is an expert in the technology. He is also an advocate for entrepreneurial ventures in the space.

In a July 2007 article published in *ICO Crowd* magazine, "The Ins and Outs of an ICO," Kravchenko poses a rhetorical question, Why are startups seeking investors via ICOs? His answer is astonishingly frank:

> It seems like an easy way of making money without getting into long discussions with investors. On top of this, there are no legal consequences for a startup if it fails.[v]

While his second sentence hasn't been robustly tested, Kravchenko captures the sentiment of many ICO enthusiasts. Frequently, ICOs provide little credible information about the principals. I would add that another appeal for issuers is that investors have been undemanding–as a result, few ICOs provide ownership or voting rights.

Kravchenko then poses another question: Why are people investing in ICOs? He offers the four reasons listed below, and also provides the remarkably candid analysis that follows:

1. the desire to make money while the wave is on;
2. the effect of the crowd–"other people are investing, I will too;"
3. a desire to feel like an investor; and
4. a belief in startups.

The premise of the ICO investment is that tokens will "pump up" the startup, as will the expectations of other investors. A significant percentage of those in the market, or those who are eager market observers, remain certain that the old-style model of venture investment (with its negotiations, traction requirements, and due diligence) is dying out.

In fact, it's not uncommon that investors with no strong feelings about putting their money into a startup will leap at the chance to participate in its ICO. I [Kravchenko] feel this can only be explained by them really believing in the existence of significant numbers of people who'll buy at a higher price."

---

[7] A flip-oriented investor seeks to profit from holding an investment briefly, just like many IPO investors do.

ICO skeptics will be surprised, no doubt, to see a blockchain enthusiast share observations that echo their concerns for investors. Kravchenko, apparently, is a straight-talking analyst.

Those with opposing views will argue that an ICO can offer investors ownership and voting power, and that they can create financing options that appeal to both issuers and investors. But, while they can do that, few have.

ICOs Expand the Potential for Fraud

In 2017, nearly $28 million was raised in an ICO by a project called DADI with a whitepaper plagiarized from another ICO issuer, SONM. When discussed on Twitter, one investor expressed indifference to DADI's fraud, saying "I don't care, I'm here to make money."

Failure risk and valuation risk are higher in an ICO than in an IPO. Why?

As of this writing, virtually all ICOs have been used to finance blockchain projects and no blockchain business has had an IPO. Blockchain, as promising as it might be, is fraught with failure risk as winning strategies for a blockchain venture are not yet clear. Talent-wise, it is a muddle. People with modest achievements present themselves as expert in ICOs, blockchain technology, and on how to build a blockchain-based business. It's also difficult to assess regulatory matters than can affect business operations and market conditions. For these reasons, a blockchain project or venture is at substantial risk of not achieving what investors are encouraged to expect.

With respect to valuation risk, it is too early to assess what a blockchain project or venture might be worth if it achieves its operational goals. Indeed, it may have trouble articulating what its goals are in a meaningful, measurable manner. Thus, it is even more difficult to determine what one might be worth that achieves less than it says it will.

In Chapter 20, "Investor Risk in Venture-Stage Companies," I describe fraud as "a serving of failure and valuation risk, garnished with false or inadequate disclosure." Chapter 17, "Causes of Investor Loss: Fraud, Overpayment and Failure," describes why fraud seems unlikely in an IPO. ICOs are different; fraud risk is higher. That's because:

- Few ICOs have been reviewed by regulators before being pitched to investors. Until that changes, it is safe to assume that whitepapers will omit vital information or have false or misleading statements. That's because whitepapers are *selling documents;* their goal is to create investor interest. Disclosure documents can do that, but they emphasize why someone *might not want to invest.* They do that to raise a defense against potential claims by disgruntled investors that they were misled into investing. Whitepapers haven't done that because ICO issuers haven't been concerned about being sued or prosecuted for false or misleading statements.

- Investors have been willing to invest in ICOs with sparse information. This attracts fraudsters the way honey attracts bears.

- It can be more difficult for law enforcement to identify the principals behind an ICO, let alone hold them accountable for any misdeeds. That encourages fraudsters too.

- Eager investors are unlikely to perform due diligence.[8] Since ICO investors have been eager, they have been more prone to back projects that are unlikely to succeed, run by entrepreneurs who spend foolishly or for self-enrichment.

- Secondary trading markets for tokens are highly vulnerable to pump-and-dump manipulations.

For these and other reasons, a report on the Financial Crypto 2018 Conference in Curaçao, Venezuela stated there are "no shortage of strange ways users can lose money in the cryptocurrency Wild West."[W]

> "The ICO market is a market where telling investors the truth is the exception rather than the rule."
>
> —Irwin Stein, blogger at *Law and Economics in the Capital Markets*

There are many reasons to be skeptical of investments in the crypto space. If you are considering making one, check out Tone Vays' "CryptoScam" videos on YouTube. "CryptoScam #9–Crypto Hedge Funds," (fairsharemodel.com/Vays) provides a primer on the background of those in some crypto funds.

At the four-minute mark, Vays interviews the managing partner of a self-described $12 million crypto hedge fund—one that has plans for an ICO. During the segment, the scantily-clad executive discloses that she was homeless before meeting the fund's founder at the Burning Man festival the year before.

After the interview, Vays goes on to demonstrate how one might begin to perform due diligence on some other crypto funds.

Regulation Will Be Good for the ICO Market

The ICO market will benefit from regulation, just as other financial markets have. Standard disclosures, reviewed by disinterested parties, will promote investor confidence, and encourage institutional investors to participate. Exchanges that are subject to oversight will be more honest than those that are not.

If regulatory compliance isn't overly burdensome, issuers who endeavor to deliver a project that meets investor expectations are unlikely to object to it. Issuers that pass scrutiny will distinguish themselves from those that are suspect or too weak-kneed to do the same. If you are interested in investing in an ICO and the issuer asserts that its token is not a security, request an opinion letter to that effect from its securities attorney. If one is not provided, beware. The issuer may be at-risk of legal peril, and the cost it incurs to respond to enforcement actions can damage the token's value.

---

[8] Investors who are inclined to perform due diligence are unlikely to know how to evaluate a blockchain venture because the space is so new. That makes it very difficult to screen for failure and valuation risk. And that makes ICO investors more vulnerable to fraud.

As ICOs are regulated, how might they change? The next two tables show a set of variables to consider. The first table characterizes the ICO landscape before late 2017, when full regulatory oversight began. The lettered columns identify four different attributes of an ICO—what it funds, who provides the money, how it is structured, and how future performance factors into valuation—and the options for each attribute.

[A] ICO money will fund a...	[B] Source of ICO money	[C] ICO structured as...	[D] Effect of future performance on ICO valuation
A project without a legal entity sponsor	Public supporters & investors from anywhere in the world	Contribution (donation-based crowdfunding)	Value placed on future performance (like an IPO based on a conventional capital structure)
A legal entity (i.e., corporation)		Pre-order (rewards-based crowdfunding)	
A project sponsored by a legal entity		Revenue/income share (annuity)	

- Column A indicates that many ICOs have been for projects without a legal entity sponsor; often, the identity of the principals was unclear. To be sure, ICOs were issued by legal entities or sponsored by one, but the number of ICOs from nebulous organizations was striking.

- Column B shows that public supporters and investors were the source of much of the money raised from ICOs.

- Column C states that ICOs were structured as donation- or rewards-based crowdfunding affairs. That is, they did not provide an investor with an equity interest or any income from the project.

- Column D points out that ICO valuations reflected the anticipated performance of the project.

The table on the following page shows how these variables are likely to change now that ICOs are regulated as securities.

[A] ICO money will fund a...	[B] Source of ICO money	[C] ICO structured as...	[D] Effect of future performance on ICO valuation
A legal entity (i.e., corporation)	Private and foreign investors	Debt	Value placed on future performance (conventional model)
A project sponsored by a legal entity	Public supporters & investors based in jurisdictions where the ICO is legal.	Equity (ownership interest)	No value placed on future performance (Fairshare Model)
		Contribution (donation-based crowdfunding)	
		Pre-order (rewards-based crowdfunding)	
		Revenue/income share (annuity)	

- Column A shows that ICOs from amorphous entities with anonymous principals will not be allowed. ICO issuers will be a legal entity or a project sponsored by one, and the principals will be identified.

- Column B has public investors as a source of ICO funds, but the challenges of forming a legal ICO will encourage issuers to raise capital from private and/or foreign investors. The idea may be to raise the money to build the project from lightly or non-regulated sources, then have a public ICO once the regulatory landscape is more hospitable.

- Column C points out that ICO deal structures will be include debt or equity (i.e., the structural options will expand beyond just contributions, pre-orders, and annuities), as well as the forms that existed before late-2017.

- Column D anticipates that most issuers will place a value on their performance when they price their ICO because it is conventional to do so, and investor interest in this space is strong. However, some ICO issuers that offer equity might use the Fairshare Model, which places no value on future performance when the money is raised.

A point that will be made in the ensuing pages is that IPOs and ICOs have the potential to be used together: an IPO to sell ownership in the parent and ICOs to fund projects that it sponsors.

If a Token Is a Security, How Does One Value It?

How might one assess the valuation of an ICO? Chapter 15, "Evaluating Valuation," describes the pillars of valuation analysis—the asset, market, and income approaches. They provide a framework for thinking about the worth of an ICO issuer or a blockchain project. Below, I contemplate how to apply them to:

- tokens that provide no ownership interest and
- tokens that do provide an ownership interest.

If a Token Conveys No Ownership Interest

Frequently, ICOs have not provided investors with an ownership interest in anything, which leads to an interesting question. What determines what one might pay for such a token? Bitcoin provides a launch point for the answer because it is well-established, and a Bitcoin does not convey an ownership interest in anything other than the token itself.

- *Asset Approach:* In terms of intrinsic asset value, Bitcoin doesn't have one since it isn't backed by a government nor does it have an intrinsic value. It is trusted by blockchain enthusiasts, however. They value the ability of a cryptocurrency to be a medium of exchange and a store of value. Some see value in the ability to mask the identity of parties to a transaction. While that appeals to those who want more anonymity than bank networks allow, it's a negative for those who value transparency.

> **Thought Experiment**
>
> Might an increase in the supply of other cryptocurrencies reduce demand for Bitcoin and cause its asset value to drop even more?

- *Income Approach:* The income approach is not a relevant measure of value for Bitcoin investors because it doesn't generate income for them. It does so only for ledger-keepers who record and verify transactions. For them, the income-related value of a Bitcoin is the present value of the fees they can earn on managing records, after the cost of equipment and electricity. Whatever that is, it didn't change significantly in 2017, when the price skyrocketed.

- *Market Approach:* The market price of a Bitcoin is better explained by the Next Guy theory (see Chapter 5, "The Problem with a Conventional Capital Structure") than by its asset or income value. Bitcoin closed at $13,800 in 2017; weeks earlier, it peaked at nearly $19,100. In January 2018, it was $9,700, down 56 percent in a month. By the end of that year, it was as low as $3,180.

The three valuation approaches suggest very divergent values for Bitcoin. How they might apply to an ICO for a new cryptocurrency? Potentially, this way:

- The *Asset Approach* will emphasize why the cryptocurrency is better than Bitcoin. It may be program features, lower operating costs, or the business model. Whatever advantages are touted, its value at the point of the ICO will be speculative.

- The *Income Approach* will be applied one way if the token generates income only for ledger-keepers, like Bitcoin, and another way if generates income for investors. This formula has the variables for a token that generates income only for ledger-keepers.

$$\text{Value of cryptocurrency for ledger-keepers (miners)} = \text{Expected income from using token} - \text{Cost to use token}$$

It simply indicates that, from an income perspective, there are two ways to increase the value of a cryptocurrency for ledger-keepers.

1. *Increase their income.* This can happen with greater transaction volume. It can also happen with higher fees, but that may discourage usage and make the cryptocurrency vulnerable to competition. That might be avoided by charging fees to the party who benefits the most, as credit cards do (i.e., they charge merchants, not consumers).

2. *Reduce their cost to operate.* This might be done by making it easier to become a ledger-keeper or by using cryptographic methods that require less power to process.

Those two things, which only benefit ledger-keepers, can enhance the value of a cryptocurrency for investors, from an asset perspective. That's because if ledger-keepers are happy, the currency's utility as a medium of exchange is improved.

- The *Market Approach* will suggest a valuation based on other cryptocurrencies. This value measure may be as infused with speculation as Bitcoin's is. If the basis for valuing something is the value of something else that is speculative, that feeds a valuation bubble.

  ◦ In a blog post, investment analyst Vitaliy Katsenelson: "Wall Street strategists have a way to model and value Bitcoin. 'If only X percent of the global population buys Y amount of Bitcoin, then due to its scarcity it will be worth Z.' On the surface, these types of models bring apparent rationality and an almost businesslike valuation to an asset that has no inherent value. You can let your imagination run wild with X's and Y's, but the simple truth is this: Bitcoin is un-valuable."

An important influence on a new cryptocurrency's market value will be its supply. If it doesn't expand with usage, price increases in the cryptocurrency are likely, as happened with Bitcoin before 2018. If that is associated with volatility, like Bitcoin is, the money's acceptance as a medium of exchange and as a store of value is undermined.

Bitcoin Fails as a Stable Medium of Exchange (and Store of Value)

On December 7, 2017, Kevin O'Leary of TV's *Shark Tank* fame shared an anecdote on CNBC that reveals how Bitcoin's volatility undermines its asset value as a medium of exchange and a store of value. O'Leary sought to settle a $200,000 transaction. The European party said it would accept Bitcoin if he guaranteed the value of the payment against the US dollar. Bitcoin's price fluctuated 20 percent as he evaluated how to pay, so he decided to use dollars, and concluded that Bitcoin doesn't work as a currency.

O'Leary said "If neither side thinks [Bitcoin] is stable enough to transfer in one minute, and they don't even want to take one minute of risk, it is not a currency. The fact is, it is so unstable—volatility is both directions, it's up and it's down—that nobody in a substantive transaction will take that risk. So, it is a long way from being a currency. However, is it an asset? Yes. It is one of the most successful assets on the planet right now because it's a global speculation. I have no idea what its value is, and neither does anybody else. The volatility makes it very difficult for me, as an investor, to put that into a portfolio. So, to me, it is a speculation."

If a Token Provides an Ownership Interest or Income Stream

A token will be valued differently if it provides investors an ownership interest in the issuer or project, or a source of income such as interest, a dividend, or royalty.

If the ICO funds are used to acquire something of value, say a tangible asset like real estate or an intangible one like intellectual property, the asset approach will be more of a factor than it is with a cryptocurrency.

If there is potential income for investors, the token's value, using the income approach, is the present value of the expected revenue stream or potential acquisition value. In that scenario, what ledger-keepers earn will be relegated to *a business model matter;* it will affect the token valuation by affecting the credibility of the business projections. That is, it will indicate whether the token has the ability to attract the supporting infrastructure it needs to become popular. For token valuation, however, what ledger-keepers earn will not be as important as what token holders can.

The market approach will reflect what others might pay for the asset and projected income, and that will be subject to the winds of the market.

Valuing an Investment Token for a Non-Cryptocurrency Project

A cascade of blockchain projects will be financed in the years ahead that do not involve a cryptocurrency. That becomes apparent when one recognizes two things about the opportunity:

1. Blockchain technology competes with centralized systems, and since centralized systems are ubiquitous, there are many potential blockchain projects.

2. Centralized systems that perform similar functions in multiple organizations may be most vulnerable to being replaced with a blockchain solution. That's because the cost of a comparable distributed ledger network is bound to be less than the aggregate cost of each organization's discrete system.

In other words, businesses that provide centralized solutions and perform similar functions in separate organizations may be those most threatened by blockchain. To illustrate, consider how the technology might benefit local government. There are about 3,000 counties in the US and nearly all have an assessor's office that manages records of real estate ownership and property tax using their own computer system. The cost to support a network of ledger-keepers who provide the same data to all counties is likely to be less than the aggregate cost of the separate systems.

If such a project is financed via an ICO, and investors are repaid with interest, the project's tokens will be valued, from an income approach, as a revenue bond. If investors have an ownership interest and receive income, the tokens will be valued as a dividend-earning stock. If they are not to be repaid, have no ownership, but receive fees, the token will be valued as an annuity. The deal structure will determine how the income approach is applied. These ideas apply to any blockchain project.

Why the Fairshare Model Approach to Valuation Makes Sense for ICOs

In Chapter 3, "Orientation," I suggest that you consider capital structures as art. In that vein, think of ICOs as an artistic style in which a new financial instrument, tokens, can be used to finance projects, companies or causes. A token can represent equity, debt, a contribution, or something else.

Thus far, mania has defined valuations but eventually, investors will evaluate them like other securities, and that will affect how ICOs are constructed. In the case of a stock-like token, issuers will project a value for future performance and offer ICO investors a discount from what it expects investors in the secondary market will pay for it.

> An ICO based on a conventional model will focus on the value of potential performance. One based on the Fairshare Model will focus on defining the criteria for actual performance.

This makes the Fairshare Model relevant to ICO issuers that offer investors an equity interest, for it presents an alternative approach to value a stock-like token–value performance *after* it is delivered, not before. Replace "stock" with "token" and you have a Fairshare Model ICO. Investors get tradable Investor Tokens and insiders get an interest in a pool of non-tradable Performance Tokens that convert to Investor Tokens based on milestones.[9]

The Fairshare Model's approach to valuation makes sense for an ICO because it is no easier to reliably forecast performance for a blockchain project than it is for a venture-stage company. For an issuer, the challenge presented by the Fairshare Model is the same for an ICO as it is for an IPO–how to define and measure performance.

The ones I've proposed for an IPO are market capitalization (i.e., for an ICO, that means the number of Investor Tokens times the market price of one), developmental milestones, financial measures, and even measures of social good.

Earlier, this chapter discussed how community support is important to a blockchain project. The Fairshare Model facilitates building a web of support by providing the issuer a tool to create alignment between investors and employees, as well as with suppliers and strategic partners. For an IPO, that tool is Performance Stock–with an ICO, it would be Performance Tokens. Both can promote long-term thinking within a community of support for a company or a project.

The Fairshare Model also encourages investors to accept the failure risk associated with a project because it reduces their valuation risk, which increases the likelihood that investors will make money. That, in turn, promotes investor interest in other projects/ventures with high failure risk.

A few examples to get your imagination going are projects that involve blockchain, healthcare, drug discovery, mining/oil, environmental, construction, movies, or a business in a geographic area that you care about. Such ventures can lead to innovation and economic vitality. Therefore, reducing their valuation risk for public investors is a good thing![10]

The alternative to a Fairshare Model ICO is a "conventional ICO." It's conventional in the sense that it will, like a conventional IPO, place a value for future performance in the ICO valuation when it raises equity capital for an issuer/project. The conventional model enables insiders to profit when public investors don't–the Fairshare Model does not.

---

9 Voting rights are not an issue here because ICO issuers generally don't offer them to investors.

10 Chapter 17, "Causes of Investor Loss," closes with a discussion about the economic benefit derived from supporting risky entrepreneurial ventures; it points out the upside of failure.

Why an Issuer Might Prefer a Fairshare Model IPO to a Conventional ICO

This book considers capital structures from the perspective of the public investor. The balance of this chapter does something different. It examines, from an *issuer's perspective*, two things:

1. why a Fairshare Model IPO may be more appealing than an ICO and,
2. how a Fairshare Model IPO might be used in conjunction with an ICO.

To begin with, in the following three scenarios, an issuer will prefer an ICO to an IPO, regardless of how it is structured:

- Investors will not have an ownership interest in the project.
- Investors will have an ownership interest in the project, but not in the sponsoring (parent) organization.
- Investors will have no ownership interest in the project, but they will have a financial interest in it, earning a royalty or interest.

If, however, a company seeks *equity capital for itself,* not just funding for a project, a Fairshare Model IPO may better suit its needs than an ICO that provides an ownership interest. Why?

ICOs are without precedent. Thus, they will encounter barriers that take time and money to overcome. The Fairshare Model is a new thing too, but it is an innovation, not an invention; it adapts well-established practices in private stock offerings to an IPO. It may have hurdles to overcome, but not as many or as challenging as those ICOs face.[11]

Thus, an equity-raising issuer may favor a Fairshare Model IPO because:

1. The Fairshare Model is designed to comply with US securities law. So far, ICOs have been designed without regard to it, or to avoid it. If an ICO doesn't comply with US securities law, it can't be sold to US investors.
2. ICOs will require more legal work than an IPO. Guidelines are scant, precedents are rare, and regulators will take more time to examine them than an IPO. That means more billable hours from professional service providers who are dealing with new requirements, learning as they go.
3. It is more difficult for investors to understand a token offering than a stock offering. The Fairshare Model capital structure requires explanation, but not as much as an ICO.
4. Trading platforms or exchanges for stocks are better developed than those for tokens.
5. Effective employee incentives are easier to develop with the Fairshare Model (i.e., stock options and Performance Stock) than with an ICO. Employees will have difficulty understanding how they benefit from earning tokens, which can be volatile in price, and awkward to convert to another currency.

---

[11] A significant one for cryptocurrencies is that tax authorities have signaled they view a token as property, not money. This can result in an income tax liability when tokens are sold at a profit and possibly a liability for state and local personal property taxes on tokens that are held (i.e., an inventory tax assessment).

Stock Warrants Can Turbocharge an IPO

This chapter concludes with an illustration of how the Fairshare Model might be used by a company that *also has an ICO*. Before we get to it, a few words about stock warrants is called for.

For an issuer, warrants set the stage to raise additional capital after the IPO closes—at a higher price, without the need for a new offering.

For investors who feel the stock could climb above the exercise price, a warrant provides incentive to invest in the offering by conveying the right to secure that appreciation without risking money upfront. And if the warrant is transferrable, the investor can sell it and effectively reduce the cost of their stock.

Stock Warrants

When an issuer uses warrants to enhance the investor appeal of its stock offering, shares and a warrant are bundled and sold as a "unit."

For an investor, the allure of a warrant is similar to what stock options are for employees. For example, if the price of a stock is $5, and the investor believes it could double within three years, a three-year warrant to buy shares at $8 can result in an additional $2 profit ($10 - $8 = $2). A warrant is like an inverse insurance policy. An insurance policy limits loss from adverse events. A warrant provides opportunity to profit from a favorable event.

An option and a warrant both convey the right to buy a stock at a pre-established price in the future.[12] How are they different? A company grants options to employees and issues warrants to non-employees (i.e., investors, service providers, and strategic partners). Also, an option is not transferable, but a warrant can be.

Another difference is where the exercise price is set. For an option, it is usually the value of the stock when the option is granted. The exercise price can be lower, but it is never higher because the goal is to create incentive for the employee to work in ways that can make the stock rise. In contrast, the exercise price for a warrant is generally higher than the stock when the warrant is issued, but lower than what it might be with the resources that the warrant holder provides.

With investors, that resource is equity capital. With lenders, it is credit. When they extend credit to companies backed by VC or private equity firms, lenders like to secure warrants as part of their compensation, in addition to interest and fees. That's because they know such investors are driven to exit at a higher valuation via acquisition or IPO. The practice was pioneered in the 1980s by Silicon Valley Bank, which leveraged it to become a major financial institution. The resources being rewarded can also be services. Attorneys often get warrants in addition to their fees.[13] Strategic partners, be they customers or suppliers, sometimes get warrants for their services too.

Another difference is the duration of the exercise period. Options tend to vest over two to five years of employment and must be exercised while the grantee is employed. Warrants need not vest—they can often be exercisable immediately, and the exercise period is often longer—three to ten years.

---

[12] Put and call options are a different kind of stock option that involve someone who owns a public stock and someone who doesn't (i.e., the company isn't involved).

[13] A company's auditor cannot get warrants because they must be independent, with no conflict of interest.

Potentially, warrants could be used in an ICO. Instead of a token, the issuer offers a unit made up of tokens and a warrant to buy more tokens at a higher price. If investors believe the token will climb above the exercise price before the warrant expires, the warrant will have appeal. If the warrants are exercised, the ICO issuer will raise more capital at a higher price without an additional offering.

A variant of this idea is for the ICO issuer to offer a warrant for tokens in a *different ICO*. Assume ABC is an aggregator of patents and other intellectual property (IP). Rather than offer equity in itself, ABC uses ICOs to fund different projects that utilize its IP. As a sweetener to invest in one project, ABC might attach a warrant to obtain tokens in another ICO sponsored by ABC.

This is what warrants do—stimulate interest for someone to provide a resource to the issuer. If a token is regulated as a security anyway, the issuer might want to add another security—a warrant.[14]

Warrants can be highly effective in a Fairshare Model IPO. The valuation will be low, relative to comparable companies, because no value is placed on future performance. The prospect for a higher valuation will therefore be good. For example, if similar companies are valued at $100 million, a Fairshare Model issuer's IPO valuation will be far lower, say $30 million. That's because a low IPO valuation makes Performance Stock conversions more likely, assuming that a rise in the price of Investor Stock is a measure of performance. Also, because secondary market investors will see that the issuer's employees are highly motivated to deliver performance.

So, warrants priced above the IPO price are likely to be exercised. If they are, the result is more capital to the company at higher valuations, along with happy IPO investors.

Exploding Stock Warrants

An "exploding warrant" is a warrant with a twist. Ordinarily, a warrant is exercised once, like a grocery coupon. The investor buys shares at the exercise price and the warrant is canceled. End of story.

An exploding warrant is different. When exercised, the investor gets shares at the exercise price, just like a regular warrant, *plus another warrant to buy more shares at an even higher price.*[15] When the second warrant is exercised, the investor gets the shares and *another warrant to buy yet more shares at a higher price.* Conceptually, it is like an inverse set of Russian nesting dolls. Ordinarily, opening a doll reveals another, smaller one. Similarly, the exercise of an exploding warrant reveals another one, but at a higher price.

To illustrate, assume XYZ's IPO is for units comprised of 10 shares of stock at $5 per share (i.e., 10 shares for $50) plus a warrant to buy 10 more shares at $10 per share (i.e., 10 shares for $100). If it is an exploding warrant, in exchange for the $100 to buy the shares, XYZ issues 10 shares plus another warrant to buy, say, 10 more shares at $20 per share (i.e., 10 shares for $200). The exercise of those warrants can result in issuance of another warrant at a higher price.

---

[14] A variant of this concept is a "rights offering," where stock is preferentially offered to existing shareholders.

[15] An investor will only exercise a warrant if it is for a price that is below the market price.

An issuer whose stock has good potential to rise in value can turbocharge its IPO with exploding warrants. Similarly, an ICO issuer whose token has good potential to rise in price have can use them to turbocharge its ICO.

Integration

An issuer may not sell securities to unaccredited investors in the US unless they are registered or exempt from registration. A traditional SEC registration statement, like a Form S-1, can be used to raise any amount of money. Exemptions exist to make capital formation for small companies less burdensome. Rule CF is the crowdfunding exemption that can be used to raise about $1 million from public investors. Reg. A+ is an exemption that can be used to raise up to $50 million. Prior to the JOBS Act reforms, offerings above $5 million had to be registered—now that requirement kicks in above $50 million.

A concept in securities law called "integration" can apply when an issuer has more than one offering that relies on an exemption from registration. If the size and scope of separate public offerings indicate that they are, effectively, a single offering that does not qualify for the exemption, it is unavailable to the issuer. Thus, an issuer may be unable to have a Reg A+ offering that uses warrants if the total amount that could be raised exceeds $50 million.

But that may not be a big deal. A startup with little history may find that registration isn't much more expensive than an offering that relies on an exemption.[16] The benefits of registration include the ability to raise any amount of money, better access to broker-dealers, market makers, and exchanges. It can also facilitate efforts to utilize ICOs in creative ways.

Securities law is complex so anyone contemplating a strategy to raise money for a company or a project should seek guidance from an experienced securities attorney. That said, the following pages describe an idea designed to spark your imagination.

A Scenario That Uses a Fairshare Model IPO and ICOs

This chapter concludes with an illustration of how a Fairshare Model IPO might be used with ICOs. They are not mutually exclusive; a company can use both. That is, it can use the Fairshare Model to raise equity capital with stock and ICOs to fund projects with tokens. Below, is an example as to how this might work.

XYZ Ventures seeks to be a publicly traded "business accelerator," a venture capital platform that intends to incubate startups in exchange for an ownership stake.[x] As it prepares to launch, XYZ has an IPO and two ICOs. Highlights are as follows:

- XYZ has a Fairshare Model IPO to raise $10 million to fund operations. Nine million is raised from 50 accredited investors who invest to secure preferred access to the private offerings of startups that XYZ sponsors. The remaining one million is raised from 10,000 average investors who each invest $100. It takes weeks to attract that many investors so there are multiple closes; XYZ has 10,050 investors as of the final one. [17]

---

[16] A registration statement requires that the issuer's financial statements for the previous five years be audited. If a company has less history, then that must be audited. Thus, a two-year-old startup need only have two years audited—it need not have five years of history.

[17] To keep the focus on the public offerings, this scenario assumes no pre-IPO investment.

XYZ Ventures, a publicly-traded business accelerator			
	Accredited Investors	Non-Accredited Investors	Total
Capital raised via Fairshare Model IPO	$9,000,000	$1,000,000	$10,000,000
Number of investors	50	10,000	10,050
Investment size - average	$180,000	$100	$995
Source of capital	90%	10%	
Sharehold composition	0.5%	99.5%	100%

- IPO investors get Investor Stock and an exploding warrant, constructed in a manner that could result in another $90 million being raised over the next five years at higher valuations. The initial warrant is likely to be exercised because the IPO valuation is low (i.e., no value placed on future performance). Subsequent warrants, at ever higher exercise prices, are likely to be exercised if XYZ's performance is good enough to cause the stock price to rise.
- Before commencing operations, XYZ has two ICOs, one for a utility token, which is not a security, and another for an investment token, which is a security.[18]
  - The utility token entitles the holder to preferred access to any IPO or ICO that emerges from XYZ's system.[19] Attached to the token, which has a nominal price of $1, is a five-year exploding warrant that works this way:
    - When the token is redeemed, in addition to the shares or tokens purchased from a XYZ startup, the investor gets a new warrant that ensures an allocation of shares in *two other offerings* that XYZ sponsors. Each warrant, once exercised, returns *two* more.
    - The warrant is transferable, so the warrant holder can sell or give it away, just like a food counter ticket dispenser.
    - The warrant rewards those who invest in an XYZ-sponsored IPO or ICO in the first five years with preferential access to others. If investors in the early offerings make money, there will be interest in other ones that XYZ sponsors.
  - The investment token is sold in a separate ICO and it funds XYZ's $20 million venture fund, which will invest in companies in its system. This token is sold only to accredited investors in order to minimize regulatory issues.
- To develop a pipeline of opportunities for XYZ's stakeholders, it uses the $10 million it raised in the IPO to screen and support companies that could be candidates for an ICO

---

[18] If the utility token is deemed to be a security, it will be subject to registration.

[19] How "preferred access" is defined isn't an issue here. It can be like a placeholder ticket at a deli counter.

and/or a Fairshare Model IPO. XYZ takes its compensation from the startups in the form of fees or equity.

- To promote entrepreneurial and investor interest in offerings it might sponsor, XYZ provides general education on valuation and deal structures.

- For issuers, the allure is XYZ's diverse and growing base of followers. There are accredited investors capable of taking large positions and, possibly offering other options (e.g., private offering, acquisition, or conventional IPO). For those who have an IPO or ICO based on the Fairshare Model, XYZ has a base of average investors interested in access to screened deals. The combination helps an issuer to:
  - maximize the amount raised,
  - minimize the expense to market an offering,
  - minimize the time it takes to close an offering,
  - attract investors with a long-term perspective,
  - acquire enough shareholders to qualify for a desirable exchange[20], and
  - spur awareness of its Investor Stock or Investor Token, which can increase secondary market demand and cause the price to rise.

XYZ Ventures shows how the Fairshare Model and ICOs can be used to create an array of financing strategies—just as a few notes can create all manner of music.

What's Next?

Epilogue

Chapter Endnotes

Contextual references for material in this chapter appear as numbered footnotes on the page where the reference is made. **Source references** for material in this chapter appear below as endnotes with capital letter identifiers.

A "How Do Bitcoin Transactions Work?" *CoinDesk.* January 29, 2018. Accessed May 10, 2018. fairsharemodel.com/Transactions.

B Ma, Moses. *Blockchain Design Sprint: Implement an Agile Design Sprint for Your Blockchain Business.* Createspace Independent Publishing Platform, 2017. Page 7.

C Andreessen, Marc. "Why Bitcoin Matters." *The New York Times.* January 21, 2014. Accessed May 10, 2018. fairsharemodel.com/BGP.

D In a March 2018 segment of his HBO show *Last Week Tonight,* called "Cryptocurrencies," John Oliver reports the 1,500 cryptocurrencies include names like Titcoin, Trumpcoin, Jesuscoin, Insanecoin, Electroneum, Wax, Particle, and Deep Onion. fairsharemodel.com/Oliver.

E Testimony of Mike Lempres, chief legal officer of Coinbase, before the US House Committee on Financial Services, Subcommittee on Capital Markets, Securities and Investment on March 14, 2018. fairsharemodel.com/Lempres

[20]NYSE and NASDAQ exchanges have minimum shareholder base requirements.

F A company that makes Bitcoin analysis software, Chainalysis, estimates that about 20 percent of Bitcoins are out of circulation. For some, it's because the owner cannot access the "digital wallet" where the cryptographic code is stored, so their money is like lost cash. Malone, Kenny. "Finding Your Lost Bitcoins." *NPR Morning Edition.* January 18, 2018. Accessed May 10, 2018. fairsharemodel.com/LostBitcoin.

G Schiller, Robert J. "What Is Bitcoin Really Worth? Don't Even Ask." *The New York Times.* December 15, 2017. Accessed May 10, 2018. fairsharemodel.com/Schiller.

H Chaparro, Frank. "Bitcoin Miners Are Making a Killing in Transaction Fees." *Business Insider.* August 24, 2017. Accessed May 10, 2018. fairsharemodel.com/Fees.

I Bradbury, Danny. "Here Is a Look at How Much Power It Takes to Create a Bitcoin." *TheBalance.com.* October 5, 2017. Accessed March 17, 2018. fairsharemodel.com/Power.

J Tuwiner, Jordan. "Is Bitcoin Mining Profitable or Worth It in 2017 & 2018?" *Buy Bitcoin Worldwide.* June 13, 2007. Accessed May 10, 2018. fairsharemodel.com/Profitable.

K "Bitcoin Energy Consumption Index." *Digiconomist.net.* Accessed May 10, 2018. fairsharemodel.com/Energy.

L Patel, Hetal. "Three Countries With the Largest Number of Bitcoin Miners." *Iq Blog.* January 8, 2017. Accessed May 10, 2018. fairsharemodel.com/#Miners.

M Orcutt, Mike. "Secret Software Is Spreading across the Internet that Hijacks Your Computer to Mine Cryptocurrency." *MIT Technology Review.* October 05, 2017. Accessed May 10, 2018. fairsharemodel.com/Hijack.

N Jezard, Adam. "In 2020 Bitcoin Will Consume More Power than the World Does Today." *Medium–World Economic Forum.* December 17, 2017. Accessed May 10, 2018. fairsharemodel.com/Power-suck.

O From Andreessen's *New York Times* article cited earlier in this chapter.

P Rosenblum, Robert H. *Investment Company Determination Under The 1940 Act: Exemptions and Exceptions.* Chicago, IL: American Bar Association, 2003. Chapter 2: Definition of a Security. fairsharemodel.com/Security.

Q SEC's July 2017 report on "The DAO" fairsharemodel.com/DAO.

R Vigna, Paul. "SEC Chief Fires Warning Shot Against Coin Offerings." *The Wall Street Journal.* November 09, 2017. Accessed May 11, 2018. fairsharemodel.com/SECwarning.

S Stark, John Reed. "The SEC and ICOs: Winter Is Coming" *LinkedIn.* November 10, 2017. Accessed May 11, 2018. fairsharemodel.com/Winter.

T Clayton, Jay. "Statement on Cryptocurrencies and Initial Coin Offerings." *SEC.gov.* December 11, 2017. Accessed May 11, 2018. fairsharemodel.com/Statement.

U Williams-Grut, Oscar. "Only 48% of ICOs Were Successful Last Year - but Startups Still Managed to Raise $5.6 Billion." *Business Insider.* January 31, 2018. Accessed June 27, 2018. fairsharemodel.com/ICOraise.

V Kravchenko, Pavel. "The Ins and Outs of an ICO." ICO Crowd. July 2007. Accessed May 11, 2018. fairsharemodel.com/InOut. Pages 6-7.

W Hertig, Alyssa. "Ponzis and Death: The Stranger Ways to Lose Crypto." *Coindesk.* March 12, 2018. Accessed May 11, 2018. fairsharemodel.com/LoseCrypto.

X In their Global Accelerator Report 2015, the funding platforms Gust and Fundacity report that 400 accelerators that collectively invested $200 million in 9,000 startups. fairsharemodel.com/Accelerators2015.

Epilogue

Each chapter has closed with a heading "What's Next?" That question is a fitting way to conclude this book. The answer depends on readers like you.

At the end of Chapter 4, "Fairshare Model Q&A," I said that if the Fairshare Model is going to be put into practice in a meaningful manner, those who like it need to make their support for it apparent on social media, in blog posts and articles, as well as on radio and television.

A LOT of you need to make a little bit of noise like the tiny residents of Whoville in Dr. Seuss's children's book, *Horton Hears a Who!*

Many voices are needed to create buzz that will cause others to take note and join in.

People who like the Fairshare Model must combine their small voices and shout....

We Are Here!

We Are Here!

We Are Here!!

We Are Here!!!

Entrepreneurs will consider using the Fairshare Model only if there is clear and growing investor interest in it. That, in turn, will lead attorneys and others with expertise in capital markets to take a sharp look at how to apply the Fairshare Model to the needs of clients. They will be joined by experts in corporate governance, compensation, tax, and financial reporting. Angel investors, VCs, investment bankers, and stock exchanges will weigh in on it too.

The big questions that must be addressed include:

- How might performance be defined?
- Who should define performance?
- How might it be measured?
- Who should measure it?
- How should rewards of performance be allocated?
- Who should administer the Performance Stock, and how?

Those who have studied marketing are familiar with a product lifecycle curve. It maps the trajectory of market acceptance for new products. It starts with customers who are innovation-minded—enthusiasts for the latest thing. Then the early adopters get on-board—a larger group of people who are visionary when it comes to seeing the product's appeal. Next, pragmatists must accept the product—they constitute an early majority of a market. Then there are the late adopters, who are conservative market participants. Finally, there are the laggards who are skeptical of new things.

The Fairshare Model faces a similar adoption curve, which appears below. The opportunity was identified decades ago. This book defines the concept further, but it now faces a gap—a concept

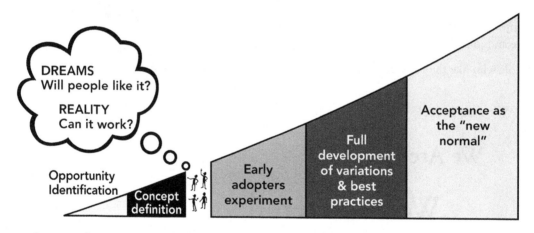

gap—that must be crossed before early adopters will try it. To do that, you and others need to make your interest in the Fairshare Model palpable to others. Once enough of you do that, early adopters will begin to experiment with the Fairshare Model.

Over time, implementations of the Fairshare Model will be developed for a variety of situations, and best practices will begin to be defined. My sense is that in a generation or two, the Fairshare Model will emerge to be the normal way companies raise venture capital in the public market. That's because price protection—the mitigation of valuation risk—is a mainstay feature in the private capital market. If it works well for private offerings, it should for public ones as well.

This effort to re-imagine capitalism will take work and time. There will be failures and setbacks because the Fairshare Model involves risky companies and a new way of thinking, on multiple fronts.

But, the reward may be worth it, don't you think?

Acknowledgements – Fairshare Model

In general, I want to acknowledge those who supported Fairshare, Inc. from 1996 through 2001, be it as a member, an investor, or as a worker. That venture laid the foundation for this book in two ways.

First and foremost, it led me to look at capital formation from the perspective of IPO investors, and that led to the insights that this book offers. Secondly, I'm also thankful for one bit of feedback I received on the content I was creating for the Fairshare website and newsletters. Someone who hadn't studied finance before told me: "What you're writing seems important, but it's boring!" That led me to rethink how to write—how to present complex ideas in a manner that is more inviting to read. That goal influenced everything in this book—the topics, how they are organized and discussed, the illustrations and how pages are laid out.

In particular, I thank Karen Poeschel for setting up my website, and Robin Rose for her insightful feedback on drafts of chapters. I also thank Erica Freeman for her developmental editing, Ruth Schwartz—a.k.a. The Wonderlady—for being the book's midwife, Henry White for his illustrations, Lorna Johnson for the book's design, Matt Hinrichs for the cover design, and the inimitable Irwin Stein for his foreword.

I also thank those who reviewed the draft material and the readers of my blog posts who encouraged me to press on.

Finally, I acknowledge two groups for teaching me about indie publishing: the Bay Area Independent Book Publishers Association (BAIPA), and the Independent Book Publishers Association (IBPA).

About the Author

A Detroit-area native, Karl Sjogren graduated with high honors from Michigan State University with a BA degree in business/pre-law and an MBA in finance. He is registered as a certified public accountant in Illinois and credentialed in turnaround management. After working for large manufacturers for a decade, he worked for 25 years as a consulting chief financial officer for early-stage companies in northern California.

From 1996 to 2001, he was co-founder and CEO of Fairshare, Inc., which sought to build an online community of average investors interested in investing in early-stage companies.

Fairshare was a forerunner for what is now called "equity crowdfunding," but with a twist. It sought to popularize the use of a novel performance-based capital structure for companies that raised venture capital from its members via an initial public offering.

Before it went under in 2001, Fairshare had 16,000 opt-in members and attracted many more visitors than that to its website, which provided education about deal structures and valuation.

Karl Sjogren resides in Oakland, California.

Appendix: Pre-Money Valuation Tables

Chapter 14, "Calculating Valuation," describes two methods for calculating pre-money valuation, the price to buy the entire company, given the terms of an offering. The percentage method requires two inputs: the offering size and the percentage of ownership that it buys.

The following tables make it easy to see the pre-money valuations under several scenarios. The columns show investments that range from $0.5 million to $26 million in increments of $0.5 million. The rows show ownership levels that range from one percent to a hundred percent, in one percent increments.

If the scenario you are interested in is outside this range, use the following formula to calculate a company's pre-money valuation.

$$\text{Valuation} = \left(\frac{\text{Investment Amount}}{\text{Percentage of the Company Bought}} \right) - \text{Investment Amount}$$

A few takeaways that you can take from scanning the tables:

- When half of a company is sold, its pre-money valuation is equal to the investment.
- When a quarter of a company is sold, its pre-money valuation equals three times the investment.
- Rules of thumb don't work well for other scenarios; don't try to estimate the pre-money valuation, calculate it. The chart on the following page shows that the relationship between pre-money valuation and the percentage of the company purchased is not linear.

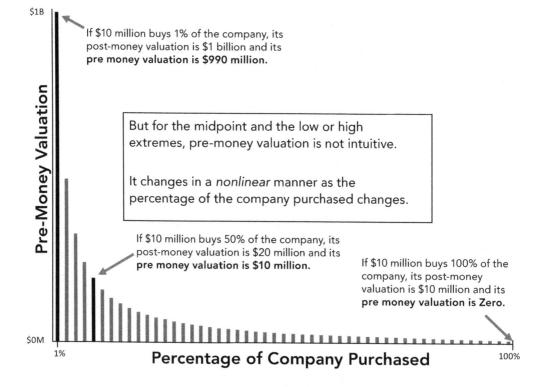

If $10 million buys 1% of the company, its post-money valuation is $1 billion and its **pre money valuation is $990 million.**

But for the midpoint and the low or high extremes, pre-money valuation is not intuitive.

It changes in a *nonlinear* manner as the percentage of the company purchased changes.

If $10 million buys 50% of the company, its post-money valuation is $20 million and its **pre money valuation is $10 million.**

If $10 million buys 100% of the company, its post-money valuation is $10 million and its **pre money valuation is Zero.**

Pre-Money Valuation

$1B

$0M

1%   **Percentage of Company Purchased**   100%

Pre-Money Valuation Table

Examples: If a $500,000 investment buys 1% of a company, its pre-money valuation is $49,500,000
If a $1,000,000 investment buys 10% of a company, its pre-money valuation is $9,000,000

Investments in millions (i.e. $0.5M equals $500,000)

	$0.5M	$1.0M	$1.5M	$2.0M	$2.5M	$3.0M	$3.5M	$4.0M	$4.5M	$5.0M	$5.5M	$6.0M	$6.5M
1%	49.5	99.0	148.5	198.0	247.5	297.0	346.5	396.0	445.5	495.0	544.5	594.0	643.5
2%	24.5	49.0	73.5	98.0	122.5	147.0	171.5	196.0	220.5	245.0	269.5	294.0	318.5
3%	16.2	32.3	48.5	64.7	80.8	97.0	113.2	129.3	145.5	161.7	177.8	194.0	210.2
4%	12.0	24.0	36.0	48.0	60.0	72.0	84.0	96.0	108.0	120.0	132.0	144.0	156.0
5%	9.5	19.0	28.5	38.0	47.5	57.0	66.5	76.0	85.5	95.0	104.5	114.0	123.5
6%	7.8	15.7	23.5	31.3	39.2	47.0	54.8	62.7	70.5	78.3	86.2	94.0	101.8
7%	6.6	13.3	19.9	26.6	33.2	39.9	46.5	53.1	59.8	66.4	73.1	79.7	86.4
8%	5.8	11.5	17.3	23.0	28.8	34.5	40.3	46.0	51.8	57.5	63.3	69.0	74.8
9%	5.1	10.1	15.2	20.2	25.3	30.3	35.4	40.4	45.5	50.6	55.6	60.7	65.7
10%	4.5	9.0	13.5	18.0	22.5	27.0	31.5	36.0	40.5	45.0	49.5	54.0	58.5
11%	4.0	8.1	12.1	16.2	20.2	24.3	28.3	32.4	36.4	40.5	44.5	48.5	52.6
12%	3.7	7.3	11.0	14.7	18.3	22.0	25.7	29.3	33.0	36.7	40.3	44.0	47.7
13%	3.3	6.7	10.0	13.4	16.7	20.1	23.4	26.8	30.1	33.5	36.8	40.2	43.5
14%	3.1	6.1	9.2	12.3	15.4	18.4	21.5	24.6	27.6	30.7	33.8	36.9	39.9
15%	2.8	5.7	8.5	11.3	14.2	17.0	19.8	22.7	25.5	28.3	31.2	34.0	36.8
16%	2.6	5.3	7.9	10.5	13.1	15.8	18.4	21.0	23.6	26.3	28.9	31.5	34.1
17%	2.4	4.9	7.3	9.8	12.2	14.6	17.1	19.5	22.0	24.4	26.9	29.3	31.7
18%	2.3	4.6	6.8	9.1	11.4	13.7	15.9	18.2	20.5	22.8	25.1	27.3	29.6
19%	2.1	4.3	6.4	8.5	10.7	12.8	14.9	17.1	19.2	21.3	23.4	25.6	27.7
20%	2.0	4.0	6.0	8.0	10.0	12.0	14.0	16.0	18.0	20.0	22.0	24.0	26.0
21%	1.9	3.8	5.6	7.5	9.4	11.3	13.2	15.0	16.9	18.8	20.7	22.6	24.5
22%	1.8	3.5	5.3	7.1	8.9	10.6	12.4	14.2	16.0	17.7	19.5	21.3	23.0
23%	1.7	3.3	5.0	6.7	8.4	10.0	11.7	13.4	15.1	16.7	18.4	20.1	21.8
24%	1.6	3.2	4.8	6.3	7.9	9.5	11.1	12.7	14.3	15.8	17.4	19.0	20.6
25%	1.5	3.0	4.5	6.0	7.5	9.0	10.5	12.0	13.5	15.0	16.5	18.0	19.5
26%	1.4	2.8	4.3	5.7	7.1	8.5	10.0	11.4	12.8	14.2	15.7	17.1	18.5
27%	1.4	2.7	4.1	5.4	6.8	8.1	9.5	10.8	12.2	13.5	14.9	16.2	17.6
28%	1.3	2.6	3.9	5.1	6.4	7.7	9.0	10.3	11.6	12.9	14.1	15.4	16.7
29%	1.2	2.4	3.7	4.9	6.1	7.3	8.6	9.8	11.0	12.2	13.5	14.7	15.9
30%	1.2	2.3	3.5	4.7	5.8	7.0	8.2	9.3	10.5	11.7	12.8	14.0	15.2
31%	1.1	2.2	3.3	4.5	5.6	6.7	7.8	8.9	10.0	11.1	12.2	13.4	14.5
32%	1.1	2.1	3.2	4.3	5.3	6.4	7.4	8.5	9.6	10.6	11.7	12.8	13.8
33%	1.0	2.0	3.0	4.1	5.1	6.1	7.1	8.1	9.1	10.2	11.2	12.2	13.2
34%	1.0	1.9	2.9	3.9	4.9	5.8	6.8	7.8	8.7	9.7	10.7	11.6	12.6
35%	0.9	1.9	2.8	3.7	4.6	5.6	6.5	7.4	8.4	9.3	10.2	11.1	12.1
36%	0.9	1.8	2.7	3.6	4.4	5.3	6.2	7.1	8.0	8.9	9.8	10.7	11.6
37%	0.9	1.7	2.6	3.4	4.3	5.1	6.0	6.8	7.7	8.5	9.4	10.2	11.1
38%	0.8	1.6	2.4	3.3	4.1	4.9	5.7	6.5	7.3	8.2	9.0	9.8	10.6
39%	0.8	1.6	2.3	3.1	3.9	4.7	5.5	6.3	7.0	7.8	8.6	9.4	10.2
40%	0.8	1.5	2.3	3.0	3.8	4.5	5.3	6.0	6.8	7.5	8.3	9.0	9.8
41%	0.7	1.4	2.2	2.9	3.6	4.3	5.0	5.8	6.5	7.2	7.9	8.6	9.4
42%	0.7	1.4	2.1	2.8	3.5	4.1	4.8	5.5	6.2	6.9	7.6	8.3	9.0
43%	0.7	1.3	2.0	2.7	3.3	4.0	4.6	5.3	6.0	6.6	7.3	8.0	8.6
44%	0.6	1.3	1.9	2.5	3.2	3.8	4.5	5.1	5.7	6.4	7.0	7.6	8.3
45%	0.6	1.2	1.8	2.4	3.1	3.7	4.3	4.9	5.5	6.1	6.7	7.3	7.9
46%	0.6	1.2	1.8	2.3	2.9	3.5	4.1	4.7	5.3	5.9	6.5	7.0	7.6
47%	0.6	1.1	1.7	2.3	2.8	3.4	3.9	4.5	5.1	5.6	6.2	6.8	7.3
48%	0.5	1.1	1.6	2.2	2.7	3.3	3.8	4.3	4.9	5.4	6.0	6.5	7.0
49%	0.5	1.0	1.6	2.1	2.6	3.1	3.6	4.2	4.7	5.2	5.7	6.2	6.8
50%	0.5	1.0	1.5	2.0	2.5	3.0	3.5	4.0	4.5	5.0	5.5	6.0	6.5

Percentage of Ownership

Pre-Money Valuation Table

Examples: If a $500,000 investment buys 100% of a company, its pre-money valuation is zero
If a $4,000,000 investment buys 70% of a company, its pre-money valuation is $1,714,300

Investments in millions (i.e. $0.5M equals $500,000)

	$0.5M	$1.0M	$1.5M	$2.0M	$2.5M	$3.0M	$3.5M	$4.0M	$4.5M	$5.0M	$5.5M	$6.0M	$6.5M
51%	0.5	1.0	1.4	1.9	2.4	2.9	3.4	3.8	4.3	4.8	5.3	5.8	6.2
52%	0.5	0.9	1.4	1.8	2.3	2.8	3.2	3.7	4.2	4.6	5.1	5.5	6.0
53%	0.4	0.9	1.3	1.8	2.2	2.7	3.1	3.5	4.0	4.4	4.9	5.3	5.8
54%	0.4	0.9	1.3	1.7	2.1	2.6	3.0	3.4	3.8	4.3	4.7	5.1	5.5
55%	0.4	0.8	1.2	1.6	2.0	2.5	2.9	3.3	3.7	4.1	4.5	4.9	5.3
56%	0.4	0.8	1.2	1.6	2.0	2.4	2.8	3.1	3.5	3.9	4.3	4.7	5.1
57%	0.4	0.8	1.1	1.5	1.9	2.3	2.6	3.0	3.4	3.8	4.1	4.5	4.9
58%	0.4	0.7	1.1	1.4	1.8	2.2	2.5	2.9	3.3	3.6	4.0	4.3	4.7
59%	0.3	0.7	1.0	1.4	1.7	2.1	2.4	2.8	3.1	3.5	3.8	4.2	4.5
60%	0.3	0.7	1.0	1.3	1.7	2.0	2.3	2.7	3.0	3.3	3.7	4.0	4.3
61%	0.3	0.6	1.0	1.3	1.6	1.9	2.2	2.6	2.9	3.2	3.5	3.8	4.2
62%	0.3	0.6	0.9	1.2	1.5	1.8	2.1	2.5	2.8	3.1	3.4	3.7	4.0
63%	0.3	0.6	0.9	1.2	1.5	1.8	2.1	2.3	2.6	2.9	3.2	3.5	3.8
64%	0.3	0.6	0.8	1.1	1.4	1.7	2.0	2.3	2.5	2.8	3.1	3.4	3.7
65%	0.3	0.5	0.8	1.1	1.3	1.6	1.9	2.2	2.4	2.7	3.0	3.2	3.5
66%	0.3	0.5	0.8	1.0	1.3	1.5	1.8	2.1	2.3	2.6	2.8	3.1	3.3
67%	0.2	0.5	0.7	1.0	1.2	1.5	1.7	2.0	2.2	2.5	2.7	3.0	3.2
68%	0.2	0.5	0.7	0.9	1.2	1.4	1.6	1.9	2.1	2.4	2.6	2.8	3.1
69%	0.2	0.4	0.7	0.9	1.1	1.3	1.6	1.8	2.0	2.2	2.5	2.7	2.9
70%	0.2	0.4	0.6	0.9	1.1	1.3	1.5	1.7	1.9	2.1	2.4	2.6	2.8
71%	0.2	0.4	0.6	0.8	1.0	1.2	1.4	1.6	1.8	2.0	2.2	2.5	2.7
72%	0.2	0.4	0.6	0.8	1.0	1.2	1.4	1.6	1.8	1.9	2.1	2.3	2.5
73%	0.2	0.4	0.6	0.7	0.9	1.1	1.3	1.5	1.7	1.8	2.0	2.2	2.4
74%	0.2	0.4	0.5	0.7	0.9	1.1	1.2	1.4	1.6	1.8	1.9	2.1	2.3
75%	0.2	0.3	0.5	0.7	0.8	1.0	1.2	1.3	1.5	1.7	1.8	2.0	2.2
76%	0.2	0.3	0.5	0.6	0.8	0.9	1.1	1.3	1.4	1.6	1.7	1.9	2.1
77%	0.1	0.3	0.4	0.6	0.7	0.9	1.0	1.2	1.3	1.5	1.6	1.8	1.9
78%	0.1	0.3	0.4	0.6	0.7	0.8	1.0	1.1	1.3	1.4	1.6	1.7	1.8
79%	0.1	0.3	0.4	0.5	0.7	0.8	0.9	1.1	1.2	1.3	1.5	1.6	1.7
80%	0.1	0.3	0.4	0.5	0.6	0.7	0.9	1.0	1.1	1.3	1.4	1.5	1.6
81%	0.1	0.2	0.4	0.5	0.6	0.7	0.8	0.9	1.1	1.2	1.3	1.4	1.5
82%	0.1	0.2	0.3	0.4	0.5	0.7	0.8	0.9	1.0	1.1	1.2	1.3	1.4
83%	0.1	0.2	0.3	0.4	0.5	0.6	0.7	0.8	0.9	1.0	1.1	1.2	1.3
84%	0.1	0.2	0.3	0.4	0.5	0.6	0.7	0.8	0.9	1.0	1.0	1.1	1.2
85%	0.1	0.2	0.3	0.4	0.4	0.5	0.6	0.7	0.8	0.9	1.0	1.1	1.1
86%	0.1	0.2	0.2	0.3	0.4	0.5	0.6	0.7	0.7	0.8	0.9	1.0	1.1
87%	0.1	0.1	0.2	0.3	0.4	0.4	0.5	0.6	0.7	0.7	0.8	0.9	1.0
88%	0.1	0.1	0.2	0.3	0.3	0.4	0.5	0.5	0.6	0.7	0.7	0.8	0.9
89%	0.1	0.1	0.2	0.2	0.3	0.4	0.4	0.5	0.6	0.6	0.7	0.7	0.8
90%	0.1	0.1	0.2	0.2	0.3	0.3	0.4	0.4	0.5	0.6	0.6	0.7	0.7
91%	0.0	0.1	0.1	0.2	0.2	0.3	0.3	0.4	0.4	0.5	0.5	0.6	0.6
92%	0.0	0.1	0.1	0.2	0.2	0.3	0.3	0.3	0.4	0.4	0.5	0.5	0.6
93%	0.0	0.1	0.1	0.2	0.2	0.2	0.3	0.3	0.3	0.4	0.4	0.5	0.5
94%	0.0	0.1	0.1	0.1	0.2	0.2	0.2	0.3	0.3	0.3	0.4	0.4	0.4
95%	0.0	0.1	0.1	0.1	0.1	0.2	0.2	0.2	0.2	0.3	0.3	0.3	0.3
96%	0.0	0.0	0.1	0.1	0.1	0.1	0.1	0.2	0.2	0.2	0.2	0.2	0.3
97%	0.0	0.0	0.0	0.1	0.1	0.1	0.1	0.1	0.1	0.2	0.2	0.2	0.2
98%	0.0	0.0	0.0	0.0	0.1	0.1	0.1	0.1	0.1	0.1	0.1	0.1	0.1
99%	0.0	0.0	0.0	0.0	0.0	0.0	0.0	0.0	0.0	0.1	0.1	0.1	0.1
100%	0.0	0.0	0.0	0.0	0.0	0.0	0.0	0.0	0.0	0.0	0.0	0.0	0.0

Percentage of Ownership

Pre-Money Valuation Table

Examples: If a $7,000,000 investment buys 1% of a company, its pre-money valuation is $693,000,000
If a $8,000,000 investment buys 10% of a company, its pre-money valuation is $72,000,000

Investments in millions (i.e. $7.0M equals $7,000,000)

	$7.0M	$7.5M	$8M	$8.5M	$9.0M	$9.5M	$10.0M	$10.5M	$11.0M	$11.5M	$12.0M	$12.5M	$13.0M
1%	693.0	742.5	792.0	841.5	891.0	940.5	990.0	1,039.5	1,089.0	1,138.5	1,188.0	1,237.5	1,287.0
2%	343.0	367.5	392.0	416.5	441.0	465.5	490.0	514.5	539.0	563.5	588.0	612.5	637.0
3%	226.3	242.5	258.7	274.8	291.0	307.2	323.3	339.5	355.7	371.8	388.0	404.2	420.3
4%	168.0	180.0	192.0	204.0	216.0	228.0	240.0	252.0	264.0	276.0	288.0	300.0	312.0
5%	133.0	142.5	152.0	161.5	171.0	180.5	190.0	199.5	209.0	218.5	228.0	237.5	247.0
6%	109.7	117.5	125.3	133.2	141.0	148.8	156.7	164.5	172.3	180.2	188.0	195.8	203.7
7%	93.0	99.6	106.3	112.9	119.6	126.2	132.9	139.5	146.1	152.8	159.4	166.1	172.7
8%	80.5	86.3	92.0	97.8	103.5	109.3	115.0	120.8	126.5	132.3	138.0	143.8	149.5
9%	70.8	75.8	80.9	85.9	91.0	96.1	101.1	106.2	111.2	116.3	121.3	126.4	131.4
10%	63.0	67.5	72.0	76.5	81.0	85.5	90.0	94.5	99.0	103.5	108.0	112.5	117.0
11%	56.6	60.7	64.7	68.8	72.8	76.9	80.9	85.0	89.0	93.0	97.1	101.1	105.2
12%	51.3	55.0	58.7	62.3	66.0	69.7	73.3	77.0	80.7	84.3	88.0	91.7	95.3
13%	46.8	50.2	53.5	56.9	60.2	63.6	66.9	70.3	73.6	77.0	80.3	83.7	87.0
14%	43.0	46.1	49.1	52.2	55.3	58.4	61.4	64.5	67.6	70.6	73.7	76.8	79.9
15%	39.7	42.5	45.3	48.2	51.0	53.8	56.7	59.5	62.3	65.2	68.0	70.8	73.7
16%	36.8	39.4	42.0	44.6	47.3	49.9	52.5	55.1	57.8	60.4	63.0	65.6	68.3
17%	34.2	36.6	39.1	41.5	43.9	46.4	48.8	51.3	53.7	56.1	58.6	61.0	63.5
18%	31.9	34.2	36.4	38.7	41.0	43.3	45.6	47.8	50.1	52.4	54.7	56.9	59.2
19%	29.8	32.0	34.1	36.2	38.4	40.5	42.6	44.8	46.9	49.0	51.2	53.3	55.4
20%	28.0	30.0	32.0	34.0	36.0	38.0	40.0	42.0	44.0	46.0	48.0	50.0	52.0
21%	26.3	28.2	30.1	32.0	33.9	35.7	37.6	39.5	41.4	43.3	45.1	47.0	48.9
22%	24.8	26.6	28.4	30.1	31.9	33.7	35.5	37.2	39.0	40.8	42.5	44.3	46.1
23%	23.4	25.1	26.8	28.5	30.1	31.8	33.5	35.2	36.8	38.5	40.2	41.8	43.5
24%	22.2	23.8	25.3	26.9	28.5	30.1	31.7	33.3	34.8	36.4	38.0	39.6	41.2
25%	21.0	22.5	24.0	25.5	27.0	28.5	30.0	31.5	33.0	34.5	36.0	37.5	39.0
26%	19.9	21.3	22.8	24.2	25.6	27.0	28.5	29.9	31.3	32.7	34.2	35.6	37.0
27%	18.9	20.3	21.6	23.0	24.3	25.7	27.0	28.4	29.7	31.1	32.4	33.8	35.1
28%	18.0	19.3	20.6	21.9	23.1	24.4	25.7	27.0	28.3	29.6	30.9	32.1	33.4
29%	17.1	18.4	19.6	20.8	22.0	23.3	24.5	25.7	26.9	28.2	29.4	30.6	31.8
30%	16.3	17.5	18.7	19.8	21.0	22.2	23.3	24.5	25.7	26.8	28.0	29.2	30.3
31%	15.6	16.7	17.8	18.9	20.0	21.1	22.3	23.4	24.5	25.6	26.7	27.8	28.9
32%	14.9	15.9	17.0	18.1	19.1	20.2	21.3	22.3	23.4	24.4	25.5	26.6	27.6
33%	14.2	15.2	16.2	17.3	18.3	19.3	20.3	21.3	22.3	23.3	24.4	25.4	26.4
34%	13.6	14.6	15.5	16.5	17.5	18.4	19.4	20.4	21.4	22.3	23.3	24.3	25.2
35%	13.0	13.9	14.9	15.8	16.7	17.6	18.6	19.5	20.4	21.4	22.3	23.2	24.1
36%	12.4	13.3	14.2	15.1	16.0	16.9	17.8	18.7	19.6	20.4	21.3	22.2	23.1
37%	11.9	12.8	13.6	14.5	15.3	16.2	17.0	17.9	18.7	19.6	20.4	21.3	22.1
38%	11.4	12.2	13.1	13.9	14.7	15.5	16.3	17.1	17.9	18.8	19.6	20.4	21.2
39%	10.9	11.7	12.5	13.3	14.1	14.9	15.6	16.4	17.2	18.0	18.8	19.6	20.3
40%	10.5	11.3	12.0	12.8	13.5	14.3	15.0	15.8	16.5	17.3	18.0	18.8	19.5
41%	10.1	10.8	11.5	12.2	13.0	13.7	14.4	15.1	15.8	16.5	17.3	18.0	18.7
42%	9.7	10.4	11.0	11.7	12.4	13.1	13.8	14.5	15.2	15.9	16.6	17.3	18.0
43%	9.3	9.9	10.6	11.3	11.9	12.6	13.3	13.9	14.6	15.2	15.9	16.6	17.2
44%	8.9	9.5	10.2	10.8	11.5	12.1	12.7	13.4	14.0	14.6	15.3	15.9	16.5
45%	8.6	9.2	9.8	10.4	11.0	11.6	12.2	12.8	13.4	14.1	14.7	15.3	15.9
46%	8.2	8.8	9.4	10.0	10.6	11.2	11.7	12.3	12.9	13.5	14.1	14.7	15.3
47%	7.9	8.5	9.0	9.6	10.1	10.7	11.3	11.8	12.4	13.0	13.5	14.1	14.7
48%	7.6	8.1	8.7	9.2	9.8	10.3	10.8	11.4	11.9	12.5	13.0	13.5	14.1
49%	7.3	7.8	8.3	8.8	9.4	9.9	10.4	10.9	11.4	12.0	12.5	13.0	13.5
50%	7.0	7.5	8.0	8.5	9.0	9.5	10.0	10.5	11.0	11.5	12.0	12.5	13.0

Percentage of Ownership

Pre-Money Valuation Table

Examples: If a $7,000,000 investment buys 70% of a company, its pre-money valuation is $3,000,000
If a $10,000,000 investment buys 92% of a company, its pre-money valuation is $870,000

Investments in millions (i.e. $7.0M equals $7,000,000)

	$7.0M	$7.5M	$8M	$8.5M	$9.0M	$9.5M	$10.0M	$10.5M	$11.0M	$11.5M	$12.0M	$12.5M	$13.0M
51%	6.7	7.2	7.7	8.2	8.6	9.1	9.6	10.1	10.6	11.0	11.5	12.0	12.5
52%	6.5	6.9	7.4	7.8	8.3	8.8	9.2	9.7	10.2	10.6	11.1	11.5	12.0
53%	6.2	6.7	7.1	7.5	8.0	8.4	8.9	9.3	9.8	10.2	10.6	11.1	11.5
54%	6.0	6.4	6.8	7.2	7.7	8.1	8.5	8.9	9.4	9.8	10.2	10.6	11.1
55%	5.7	6.1	6.5	7.0	7.4	7.8	8.2	8.6	9.0	9.4	9.8	10.2	10.6
56%	5.5	5.9	6.3	6.7	7.1	7.5	7.9	8.3	8.6	9.0	9.4	9.8	10.2
57%	5.3	5.7	6.0	6.4	6.8	7.2	7.5	7.9	8.3	8.7	9.1	9.4	9.8
58%	5.1	5.4	5.8	6.2	6.5	6.9	7.2	7.6	8.0	8.3	8.7	9.1	9.4
59%	4.9	5.2	5.6	5.9	6.3	6.6	6.9	7.3	7.6	8.0	8.3	8.7	9.0
60%	4.7	5.0	5.3	5.7	6.0	6.3	6.7	7.0	7.3	7.7	8.0	8.3	8.7
61%	4.5	4.8	5.1	5.4	5.8	6.1	6.4	6.7	7.0	7.4	7.7	8.0	8.3
62%	4.3	4.6	4.9	5.2	5.5	5.8	6.1	6.4	6.7	7.0	7.4	7.7	8.0
63%	4.1	4.4	4.7	5.0	5.3	5.6	5.9	6.2	6.5	6.8	7.0	7.3	7.6
64%	3.9	4.2	4.5	4.8	5.1	5.3	5.6	5.9	6.2	6.5	6.8	7.0	7.3
65%	3.8	4.0	4.3	4.6	4.8	5.1	5.4	5.7	5.9	6.2	6.5	6.7	7.0
66%	3.6	3.9	4.1	4.4	4.6	4.9	5.2	5.4	5.7	5.9	6.2	6.4	6.7
67%	3.4	3.7	3.9	4.2	4.4	4.7	4.9	5.2	5.4	5.7	5.9	6.2	6.4
68%	3.3	3.5	3.8	4.0	4.2	4.5	4.7	4.9	5.2	5.4	5.6	5.9	6.1
69%	3.1	3.4	3.6	3.8	4.0	4.3	4.5	4.7	4.9	5.2	5.4	5.6	5.8
70%	3.0	3.2	3.4	3.6	3.9	4.1	4.3	4.5	4.7	4.9	5.1	5.4	5.6
71%	2.9	3.1	3.3	3.5	3.7	3.9	4.1	4.3	4.5	4.7	4.9	5.1	5.3
72%	2.7	2.9	3.1	3.3	3.5	3.7	3.9	4.1	4.3	4.5	4.7	4.9	5.1
73%	2.6	2.8	3.0	3.1	3.3	3.5	3.7	3.9	4.1	4.3	4.4	4.6	4.8
74%	2.5	2.6	2.8	3.0	3.2	3.3	3.5	3.7	3.9	4.0	4.2	4.4	4.6
75%	2.3	2.5	2.7	2.8	3.0	3.2	3.3	3.5	3.7	3.8	4.0	4.2	4.3
76%	2.2	2.4	2.5	2.7	2.8	3.0	3.2	3.3	3.5	3.6	3.8	3.9	4.1
77%	2.1	2.2	2.4	2.5	2.7	2.8	3.0	3.1	3.3	3.4	3.6	3.7	3.9
78%	2.0	2.1	2.3	2.4	2.5	2.7	2.8	3.0	3.1	3.2	3.4	3.5	3.7
79%	1.9	2.0	2.1	2.3	2.4	2.5	2.7	2.8	2.9	3.1	3.2	3.3	3.5
80%	1.8	1.9	2.0	2.1	2.3	2.4	2.5	2.6	2.7	2.9	3.0	3.1	3.2
81%	1.6	1.8	1.9	2.0	2.1	2.2	2.3	2.5	2.6	2.7	2.8	2.9	3.0
82%	1.5	1.6	1.8	1.9	2.0	2.1	2.2	2.3	2.4	2.5	2.6	2.7	2.9
83%	1.4	1.5	1.6	1.7	1.8	1.9	2.0	2.2	2.3	2.4	2.5	2.6	2.7
84%	1.3	1.4	1.5	1.6	1.7	1.8	1.9	2.0	2.1	2.2	2.3	2.4	2.5
85%	1.2	1.3	1.4	1.5	1.6	1.7	1.8	1.9	1.9	2.0	2.1	2.2	2.3
86%	1.1	1.2	1.3	1.4	1.5	1.5	1.6	1.7	1.8	1.9	2.0	2.0	2.1
87%	1.0	1.1	1.2	1.3	1.3	1.4	1.5	1.6	1.6	1.7	1.8	1.9	1.9
88%	1.0	1.0	1.1	1.2	1.2	1.3	1.4	1.4	1.5	1.6	1.6	1.7	1.8
89%	0.9	0.9	1.0	1.1	1.1	1.2	1.2	1.3	1.4	1.4	1.5	1.5	1.6
90%	0.8	0.8	0.9	0.9	1.0	1.1	1.1	1.2	1.2	1.3	1.3	1.4	1.4
91%	0.7	0.7	0.8	0.8	0.9	0.9	1.0	1.0	1.1	1.1	1.2	1.2	1.3
92%	0.6	0.7	0.7	0.7	0.8	0.8	0.9	0.9	1.0	1.0	1.0	1.1	1.1
93%	0.5	0.6	0.6	0.6	0.7	0.7	0.8	0.8	0.8	0.9	0.9	0.9	1.0
94%	0.4	0.5	0.5	0.5	0.6	0.6	0.6	0.7	0.7	0.7	0.8	0.8	0.8
95%	0.4	0.4	0.4	0.4	0.5	0.5	0.5	0.6	0.6	0.6	0.6	0.7	0.7
96%	0.3	0.3	0.3	0.4	0.4	0.4	0.4	0.4	0.5	0.5	0.5	0.5	0.5
97%	0.2	0.2	0.2	0.3	0.3	0.3	0.3	0.3	0.3	0.4	0.4	0.4	0.4
98%	0.1	0.2	0.2	0.2	0.2	0.2	0.2	0.2	0.2	0.2	0.2	0.3	0.3
99%	0.1	0.1	0.1	0.1	0.1	0.1	0.1	0.1	0.1	0.1	0.1	0.1	0.1
100%	0.0	0.0	0.0	0.0	0.0	0.0	0.0	0.0	0.0	0.0	0.0	0.0	0.0

Percentage of Ownership

Pre-Money Valuation Table

Examples: If a $13,500,000 investment buys 1% of a company, its pre-money valuation is $1,336,500,000
If a $15,000,000 investment buys 50% of a company, its pre-money valuation is $15,000,000

Investments in millions (i.e. $13.5M equals $13,500,000)

		$13.5M	$14.0M	$14.5M	$15.0M	$15.5M	$16.0M	$16.5M	$17.0M	$17.5M	$18.0M	$18.5M	$19.0M	$19.5M
	1%	1,336.5	1,386.0	1,435.5	1,485.0	1,534.5	1,584.0	1,633.5	1,683.0	1,732.5	1,782.0	1,831.5	1,881.0	1,930.5
	2%	661.5	686.0	710.5	735.0	759.5	784.0	808.5	833.0	857.5	882.0	906.5	931.0	955.5
	3%	436.5	452.7	468.8	485.0	501.2	517.3	533.5	549.7	565.8	582.0	598.2	614.3	630.5
	4%	324.0	336.0	348.0	360.0	372.0	384.0	396.0	408.0	420.0	432.0	444.0	456.0	468.0
	5%	256.5	266.0	275.5	285.0	294.5	304.0	313.5	323.0	332.5	342.0	351.5	361.0	370.5
P	6%	211.5	219.3	227.2	235.0	242.8	250.7	258.5	266.3	274.2	282.0	289.8	297.7	305.5
e	7%	179.4	186.0	192.6	199.3	205.9	212.6	219.2	225.9	232.5	239.1	245.8	252.4	259.1
r	8%	155.3	161.0	166.8	172.5	178.3	184.0	189.8	195.5	201.3	207.0	212.8	218.5	224.3
c	9%	136.5	141.6	146.6	151.7	156.7	161.8	166.8	171.9	176.9	182.0	187.1	192.1	197.2
e	10%	121.5	126.0	130.5	135.0	139.5	144.0	148.5	153.0	157.5	162.0	166.5	171.0	175.5
n	11%	109.2	113.3	117.3	121.4	125.4	129.5	133.5	137.5	141.6	145.6	149.7	153.7	157.8
t	12%	99.0	102.7	106.3	110.0	113.7	117.3	121.0	124.7	128.3	132.0	135.7	139.3	143.0
a	13%	90.3	93.7	97.0	100.4	103.7	107.1	110.4	113.8	117.1	120.5	123.8	127.2	130.5
g	14%	82.9	86.0	89.1	92.1	95.2	98.3	101.4	104.4	107.5	110.6	113.6	116.7	119.8
e	15%	76.5	79.3	82.2	85.0	87.8	90.7	93.5	96.3	99.2	102.0	104.8	107.7	110.5
	16%	70.9	73.5	76.1	78.8	81.4	84.0	86.6	89.3	91.9	94.5	97.1	99.8	102.4
	17%	65.9	68.4	70.8	73.2	75.7	78.1	80.6	83.0	85.4	87.9	90.3	92.8	95.2
o	18%	61.5	63.8	66.1	68.3	70.6	72.9	75.2	77.4	79.7	82.0	84.3	86.6	88.8
f	19%	57.6	59.7	61.8	63.9	66.1	68.2	70.3	72.5	74.6	76.7	78.9	81.0	83.1
	20%	54.0	56.0	58.0	60.0	62.0	64.0	66.0	68.0	70.0	72.0	74.0	76.0	78.0
	21%	50.8	52.7	54.5	56.4	58.3	60.2	62.1	64.0	65.8	67.7	69.6	71.5	73.4
O	22%	47.9	49.6	51.4	53.2	55.0	56.7	58.5	60.3	62.0	63.8	65.6	67.4	69.1
w	23%	45.2	46.9	48.5	50.2	51.9	53.6	55.2	56.9	58.6	60.3	61.9	63.6	65.3
n	24%	42.8	44.3	45.9	47.5	49.1	50.7	52.3	53.8	55.4	57.0	58.6	60.2	61.8
e	25%	40.5	42.0	43.5	45.0	46.5	48.0	49.5	51.0	52.5	54.0	55.5	57.0	58.5
r	26%	38.4	39.8	41.3	42.7	44.1	45.5	47.0	48.4	49.8	51.2	52.7	54.1	55.5
s	27%	36.5	37.9	39.2	40.6	41.9	43.3	44.6	46.0	47.3	48.7	50.0	51.4	52.7
h	28%	34.7	36.0	37.3	38.6	39.9	41.1	42.4	43.7	45.0	46.3	47.6	48.9	50.1
i	29%	33.1	34.3	35.5	36.7	37.9	39.2	40.4	41.6	42.8	44.1	45.3	46.5	47.7
p	30%	31.5	32.7	33.8	35.0	36.2	37.3	38.5	39.7	40.8	42.0	43.2	44.3	45.5
	31%	30.0	31.2	32.3	33.4	34.5	35.6	36.7	37.8	39.0	40.1	41.2	42.3	43.4
	32%	28.7	29.8	30.8	31.9	32.9	34.0	35.1	36.1	37.2	38.3	39.3	40.4	41.4
	33%	27.4	28.4	29.4	30.5	31.5	32.5	33.5	34.5	35.5	36.5	37.6	38.6	39.6
	34%	26.2	27.2	28.1	29.1	30.1	31.1	32.0	33.0	34.0	34.9	35.9	36.9	37.9
	35%	25.1	26.0	26.9	27.9	28.8	29.7	30.6	31.6	32.5	33.4	34.4	35.3	36.2
	36%	24.0	24.9	25.8	26.7	27.6	28.4	29.3	30.2	31.1	32.0	32.9	33.8	34.7
	37%	23.0	23.8	24.7	25.5	26.4	27.2	28.1	28.9	29.8	30.6	31.5	32.4	33.2
	38%	22.0	22.8	23.7	24.5	25.3	26.1	26.9	27.7	28.6	29.4	30.2	31.0	31.8
	39%	21.1	21.9	22.7	23.5	24.2	25.0	25.8	26.6	27.4	28.2	28.9	29.7	30.5
	40%	20.3	21.0	21.8	22.5	23.3	24.0	24.8	25.5	26.3	27.0	27.8	28.5	29.3
	41%	19.4	20.1	20.9	21.6	22.3	23.0	23.7	24.5	25.2	25.9	26.6	27.3	28.1
	42%	18.6	19.3	20.0	20.7	21.4	22.1	22.8	23.5	24.2	24.9	25.5	26.2	26.9
	43%	17.9	18.6	19.2	19.9	20.5	21.2	21.9	22.5	23.2	23.9	24.5	25.2	25.8
	44%	17.2	17.8	18.5	19.1	19.7	20.4	21.0	21.6	22.3	22.9	23.5	24.2	24.8
	45%	16.5	17.1	17.7	18.3	18.9	19.6	20.2	20.8	21.4	22.0	22.6	23.2	23.8
	46%	15.8	16.4	17.0	17.6	18.2	18.8	19.4	20.0	20.5	21.1	21.7	22.3	22.9
	47%	15.2	15.8	16.4	16.9	17.5	18.0	18.6	19.2	19.7	20.3	20.9	21.4	22.0
	48%	14.6	15.2	15.7	16.3	16.8	17.3	17.9	18.4	19.0	19.5	20.0	20.6	21.1
	49%	14.1	14.6	15.1	15.6	16.1	16.7	17.2	17.7	18.2	18.7	19.3	19.8	20.3
	50%	13.5	14.0	14.5	15.0	15.5	16.0	16.5	17.0	17.5	18.0	18.5	19.0	19.5

Pre-Money Valuation Table

Examples: If a $15,000,000 investment buys 60% of a company, its pre-money valuation is $10,000,000
If a $15,000,000 investment buys 75% of a company, its pre-money valuation is $5,000,000

Investments in millions (i.e. $13.5M equals $13,500,000)

	$13.5M	$14.0M	$14.5M	$15.0M	$15.5M	$16.0M	$16.5M	$17.0M	$17.5M	$18.0M	$18.5M	$19.0M	$19.5M
51%	13.0	13.5	13.9	14.4	14.9	15.4	15.9	16.3	16.8	17.3	17.8	18.3	18.7
52%	12.5	12.9	13.4	13.8	14.3	14.8	15.2	15.7	16.2	16.6	17.1	17.5	18.0
53%	12.0	12.4	12.9	13.3	13.7	14.2	14.6	15.1	15.5	16.0	16.4	16.8	17.3
54%	11.5	11.9	12.4	12.8	13.2	13.6	14.1	14.5	14.9	15.3	15.8	16.2	16.6
55%	11.0	11.5	11.9	12.3	12.7	13.1	13.5	13.9	14.3	14.7	15.1	15.5	16.0
56%	10.6	11.0	11.4	11.8	12.2	12.6	13.0	13.4	13.8	14.1	14.5	14.9	15.3
57%	10.2	10.6	10.9	11.3	11.7	12.1	12.4	12.8	13.2	13.6	14.0	14.3	14.7
58%	9.8	10.1	10.5	10.9	11.2	11.6	11.9	12.3	12.7	13.0	13.4	13.8	14.1
59%	9.4	9.7	10.1	10.4	10.8	11.1	11.5	11.8	12.2	12.5	12.9	13.2	13.6
60%	9.0	9.3	9.7	10.0	10.3	10.7	11.0	11.3	11.7	12.0	12.3	12.7	13.0
61%	8.6	9.0	9.3	9.6	9.9	10.2	10.5	10.9	11.2	11.5	11.8	12.1	12.5
62%	8.3	8.6	8.9	9.2	9.5	9.8	10.1	10.4	10.7	11.0	11.3	11.6	12.0
63%	7.9	8.2	8.5	8.8	9.1	9.4	9.7	10.0	10.3	10.6	10.9	11.2	11.5
64%	7.6	7.9	8.2	8.4	8.7	9.0	9.3	9.6	9.8	10.1	10.4	10.7	11.0
65%	7.3	7.5	7.8	8.1	8.3	8.6	8.9	9.2	9.4	9.7	10.0	10.2	10.5
66%	7.0	7.2	7.5	7.7	8.0	8.2	8.5	8.8	9.0	9.3	9.5	9.8	10.0
67%	6.6	6.9	7.1	7.4	7.6	7.9	8.1	8.4	8.6	8.9	9.1	9.4	9.6
68%	6.4	6.6	6.8	7.1	7.3	7.5	7.8	8.0	8.2	8.5	8.7	8.9	9.2
69%	6.1	6.3	6.5	6.7	7.0	7.2	7.4	7.6	7.9	8.1	8.3	8.5	8.8
70%	5.8	6.0	6.2	6.4	6.6	6.9	7.1	7.3	7.5	7.7	7.9	8.1	8.4
71%	5.5	5.7	5.9	6.1	6.3	6.5	6.7	6.9	7.1	7.4	7.6	7.8	8.0
72%	5.3	5.4	5.6	5.8	6.0	6.2	6.4	6.6	6.8	7.0	7.2	7.4	7.6
73%	5.0	5.2	5.4	5.5	5.7	5.9	6.1	6.3	6.5	6.7	6.8	7.0	7.2
74%	4.7	4.9	5.1	5.3	5.4	5.6	5.8	6.0	6.1	6.3	6.5	6.7	6.9
75%	4.5	4.7	4.8	5.0	5.2	5.3	5.5	5.7	5.8	6.0	6.2	6.3	6.5
76%	4.3	4.4	4.6	4.7	4.9	5.1	5.2	5.4	5.5	5.7	5.8	6.0	6.2
77%	4.0	4.2	4.3	4.5	4.6	4.8	4.9	5.1	5.2	5.4	5.5	5.7	5.8
78%	3.8	3.9	4.1	4.2	4.4	4.5	4.7	4.8	4.9	5.1	5.2	5.4	5.5
79%	3.6	3.7	3.9	4.0	4.1	4.3	4.4	4.5	4.7	4.8	4.9	5.1	5.2
80%	3.4	3.5	3.6	3.7	3.9	4.0	4.1	4.2	4.4	4.5	4.6	4.7	4.9
81%	3.2	3.3	3.4	3.5	3.6	3.8	3.9	4.0	4.1	4.2	4.3	4.5	4.6
82%	3.0	3.1	3.2	3.3	3.4	3.5	3.6	3.7	3.8	4.0	4.1	4.2	4.3
83%	2.8	2.9	3.0	3.1	3.2	3.3	3.4	3.5	3.6	3.7	3.8	3.9	4.0
84%	2.6	2.7	2.8	2.9	3.0	3.0	3.1	3.2	3.3	3.4	3.5	3.6	3.7
85%	2.4	2.5	2.6	2.6	2.7	2.8	2.9	3.0	3.1	3.2	3.3	3.4	3.4
86%	2.2	2.3	2.4	2.4	2.5	2.6	2.7	2.8	2.8	2.9	3.0	3.1	3.2
87%	2.0	2.1	2.2	2.2	2.3	2.4	2.5	2.5	2.6	2.7	2.8	2.8	2.9
88%	1.8	1.9	2.0	2.0	2.1	2.2	2.2	2.3	2.4	2.5	2.5	2.6	2.7
89%	1.7	1.7	1.8	1.9	1.9	2.0	2.0	2.1	2.2	2.2	2.3	2.3	2.4
90%	1.5	1.6	1.6	1.7	1.7	1.8	1.8	1.9	1.9	2.0	2.1	2.1	2.2
91%	1.3	1.4	1.4	1.5	1.5	1.6	1.6	1.7	1.7	1.8	1.8	1.9	1.9
92%	1.2	1.2	1.3	1.3	1.3	1.4	1.4	1.5	1.5	1.6	1.6	1.7	1.7
93%	1.0	1.1	1.1	1.1	1.2	1.2	1.2	1.3	1.3	1.4	1.4	1.4	1.5
94%	0.9	0.9	0.9	1.0	1.0	1.0	1.1	1.1	1.1	1.1	1.2	1.2	1.2
95%	0.7	0.7	0.8	0.8	0.8	0.8	0.9	0.9	0.9	0.9	1.0	1.0	1.0
96%	0.6	0.6	0.6	0.6	0.6	0.7	0.7	0.7	0.7	0.7	0.8	0.8	0.8
97%	0.4	0.4	0.4	0.5	0.5	0.5	0.5	0.5	0.5	0.6	0.6	0.6	0.6
98%	0.3	0.3	0.3	0.3	0.3	0.3	0.3	0.3	0.4	0.4	0.4	0.4	0.4
99%	0.1	0.1	0.1	0.2	0.2	0.2	0.2	0.2	0.2	0.2	0.2	0.2	0.2
100%	0.0	0.0	0.0	0.0	0.0	0.0	0.0	0.0	0.0	0.0	0.0	0.0	0.0

Percentage of Ownership

Pre-Money Valuation Table

Examples: If a $20,000,000 investment buys 20% of a company, its pre-money valuation is $80,000,000
If a $24,000,000 investment buys 40% of a company, its pre-money valuation is $36,000,000

Investments in millions (i.e. $20.0M equals $20,000,000)

	$20.0M	$20.5M	$21.0M	$21.5M	$22.0M	$22.5M	$23.0M	$23.5M	$24.0M	$24.5M	$25.0M	$25.5M	$26.0M
1%	1,980.0	2,029.5	2,079.0	2,128.5	2,178.0	2,227.5	2,277.0	2,326.5	2,376.0	2,425.5	2,475.0	2,524.5	2,574.0
2%	980.0	1,004.5	1,029.0	1,053.5	1,078.0	1,102.5	1,127.0	1,151.5	1,176.0	1,200.5	1,225.0	1,249.5	1,274.0
3%	646.7	662.8	679.0	695.2	711.3	727.5	743.7	759.8	776.0	792.2	808.3	824.5	840.7
4%	480.0	492.0	504.0	516.0	528.0	540.0	552.0	564.0	576.0	588.0	600.0	612.0	624.0
5%	380.0	389.5	399.0	408.5	418.0	427.5	437.0	446.5	456.0	465.5	475.0	484.5	494.0
6%	313.3	321.2	329.0	336.8	344.7	352.5	360.3	368.2	376.0	383.8	391.7	399.5	407.3
7%	265.7	272.4	279.0	285.6	292.3	298.9	305.6	312.2	318.9	325.5	332.1	338.8	345.4
8%	230.0	235.8	241.5	247.3	253.0	258.8	264.5	270.3	276.0	281.8	287.5	293.3	299.0
9%	202.2	207.3	212.3	217.4	222.4	227.5	232.6	237.6	242.7	247.7	252.8	257.8	262.9
10%	180.0	184.5	189.0	193.5	198.0	202.5	207.0	211.5	216.0	220.5	225.0	229.5	234.0
11%	161.8	165.9	169.9	174.0	178.0	182.0	186.1	190.1	194.2	198.2	202.3	206.3	210.4
12%	146.7	150.3	154.0	157.7	161.3	165.0	168.7	172.3	176.0	179.7	183.3	187.0	190.7
13%	133.8	137.2	140.5	143.9	147.2	150.6	153.9	157.3	160.6	164.0	167.3	170.7	174.0
14%	122.9	125.9	129.0	132.1	135.1	138.2	141.3	144.4	147.4	150.5	153.6	156.6	159.7
15%	113.3	116.2	119.0	121.8	124.7	127.5	130.3	133.2	136.0	138.8	141.7	144.5	147.3
16%	105.0	107.6	110.3	112.9	115.5	118.1	120.8	123.4	126.0	128.6	131.3	133.9	136.5
17%	97.6	100.1	102.5	105.0	107.4	109.9	112.3	114.7	117.2	119.6	122.1	124.5	126.9
18%	91.1	93.4	95.7	97.9	100.2	102.5	104.8	107.1	109.3	111.6	113.9	116.2	118.4
19%	85.3	87.4	89.5	91.7	93.8	95.9	98.1	100.2	102.3	104.4	106.6	108.7	110.8
20%	80.0	82.0	84.0	86.0	88.0	90.0	92.0	94.0	96.0	98.0	100.0	102.0	104.0
21%	75.2	77.1	79.0	80.9	82.8	84.6	86.5	88.4	90.3	92.2	94.0	95.9	97.8
22%	70.9	72.7	74.5	76.2	78.0	79.8	81.5	83.3	85.1	86.9	88.6	90.4	92.2
23%	67.0	68.6	70.3	72.0	73.7	75.3	77.0	78.7	80.3	82.0	83.7	85.4	87.0
24%	63.3	64.9	66.5	68.1	69.7	71.3	72.8	74.4	76.0	77.6	79.2	80.8	82.3
25%	60.0	61.5	63.0	64.5	66.0	67.5	69.0	70.5	72.0	73.5	75.0	76.5	78.0
26%	56.9	58.3	59.8	61.2	62.6	64.0	65.5	66.9	68.3	69.7	71.2	72.6	74.0
27%	54.1	55.4	56.8	58.1	59.5	60.8	62.2	63.5	64.9	66.2	67.6	68.9	70.3
28%	51.4	52.7	54.0	55.3	56.6	57.9	59.1	60.4	61.7	63.0	64.3	65.6	66.9
29%	49.0	50.2	51.4	52.6	53.9	55.1	56.3	57.5	58.8	60.0	61.2	62.4	63.7
30%	46.7	47.8	49.0	50.2	51.3	52.5	53.7	54.8	56.0	57.2	58.3	59.5	60.7
31%	44.5	45.6	46.7	47.9	49.0	50.1	51.2	52.3	53.4	54.5	55.6	56.8	57.9
32%	42.5	43.6	44.6	45.7	46.8	47.8	48.9	49.9	51.0	52.1	53.1	54.2	55.3
33%	40.6	41.6	42.6	43.7	44.7	45.7	46.7	47.7	48.7	49.7	50.8	51.8	52.8
34%	38.8	39.8	40.8	41.7	42.7	43.7	44.6	45.6	46.6	47.6	48.5	49.5	50.5
35%	37.1	38.1	39.0	39.9	40.9	41.8	42.7	43.6	44.6	45.5	46.4	47.4	48.3
36%	35.6	36.4	37.3	38.2	39.1	40.0	40.9	41.8	42.7	43.6	44.4	45.3	46.2
37%	34.1	34.9	35.8	36.6	37.5	38.3	39.2	40.0	40.9	41.7	42.6	43.4	44.3
38%	32.6	33.4	34.3	35.1	35.9	36.7	37.5	38.3	39.2	40.0	40.8	41.6	42.4
39%	31.3	32.1	32.8	33.6	34.4	35.2	36.0	36.8	37.5	38.3	39.1	39.9	40.7
40%	30.0	30.8	31.5	32.3	33.0	33.8	34.5	35.3	36.0	36.8	37.5	38.3	39.0
41%	28.8	29.5	30.2	30.9	31.7	32.4	33.1	33.8	34.5	35.3	36.0	36.7	37.4
42%	27.6	28.3	29.0	29.7	30.4	31.1	31.8	32.5	33.1	33.8	34.5	35.2	35.9
43%	26.5	27.2	27.8	28.5	29.2	29.8	30.5	31.2	31.8	32.5	33.1	33.8	34.5
44%	25.5	26.1	26.7	27.4	28.0	28.6	29.3	29.9	30.5	31.2	31.8	32.5	33.1
45%	24.4	25.1	25.7	26.3	26.9	27.5	28.1	28.7	29.3	29.9	30.6	31.2	31.8
46%	23.5	24.1	24.7	25.2	25.8	26.4	27.0	27.6	28.2	28.8	29.3	29.9	30.5
47%	22.6	23.1	23.7	24.2	24.8	25.4	25.9	26.5	27.1	27.6	28.2	28.8	29.3
48%	21.7	22.2	22.8	23.3	23.8	24.4	24.9	25.5	26.0	26.5	27.1	27.6	28.2
49%	20.8	21.3	21.9	22.4	22.9	23.4	23.9	24.5	25.0	25.5	26.0	26.5	27.1
50%	20.0	20.5	21.0	21.5	22.0	22.5	23.0	23.5	24.0	24.5	25.0	25.5	26.0

Percentage of Ownership

Pre-Money Valuation Table

Examples: If a $24,000,000 investment buys 60% of a company, its pre-money valuation is $16,000,000
If a $24,000,000 investment buys 80% of a company, its pre-money valuation is $6,000,000

Investments in millions (i.e. $20.0M equals $20,000,000)

Percentage of Ownership

	$20.0M	$20.5M	$21.0M	$21.5M	$22.0M	$22.5M	$23.0M	$23.5M	$24.0M	$24.5M	$25.0M	$25.5M	$26.0M
51%	19.2	19.7	20.2	20.7	21.1	21.6	22.1	22.6	23.1	23.5	24.0	24.5	25.0
52%	18.5	18.9	19.4	19.8	20.3	20.8	21.2	21.7	22.2	22.6	23.1	23.5	24.0
53%	17.7	18.2	18.6	19.1	19.5	20.0	20.4	20.8	21.3	21.7	22.2	22.6	23.1
54%	17.0	17.5	17.9	18.3	18.7	19.2	19.6	20.0	20.4	20.9	21.3	21.7	22.1
55%	16.4	16.8	17.2	17.6	18.0	18.4	18.8	19.2	19.6	20.0	20.5	20.9	21.3
56%	15.7	16.1	16.5	16.9	17.3	17.7	18.1	18.5	18.9	19.3	19.6	20.0	20.4
57%	15.1	15.5	15.8	16.2	16.6	17.0	17.4	17.7	18.1	18.5	18.9	19.2	19.6
58%	14.5	14.8	15.2	15.6	15.9	16.3	16.7	17.0	17.4	17.7	18.1	18.5	18.8
59%	13.9	14.2	14.6	14.9	15.3	15.6	16.0	16.3	16.7	17.0	17.4	17.7	18.1
60%	13.3	13.7	14.0	14.3	14.7	15.0	15.3	15.7	16.0	16.3	16.7	17.0	17.3
61%	12.8	13.1	13.4	13.7	14.1	14.4	14.7	15.0	15.3	15.7	16.0	16.3	16.6
62%	12.3	12.6	12.9	13.2	13.5	13.8	14.1	14.4	14.7	15.0	15.3	15.6	15.9
63%	11.7	12.0	12.3	12.6	12.9	13.2	13.5	13.8	14.1	14.4	14.7	15.0	15.3
64%	11.3	11.5	11.8	12.1	12.4	12.7	12.9	13.2	13.5	13.8	14.1	14.3	14.6
65%	10.8	11.0	11.3	11.6	11.8	12.1	12.4	12.7	12.9	13.2	13.5	13.7	14.0
66%	10.3	10.6	10.8	11.1	11.3	11.6	11.8	12.1	12.4	12.6	12.9	13.1	13.4
67%	9.9	10.1	10.3	10.6	10.8	11.1	11.3	11.6	11.8	12.1	12.3	12.6	12.8
68%	9.4	9.6	9.9	10.1	10.4	10.6	10.8	11.1	11.3	11.5	11.8	12.0	12.2
69%	9.0	9.2	9.4	9.7	9.9	10.1	10.3	10.6	10.8	11.0	11.2	11.5	11.7
70%	8.6	8.8	9.0	9.2	9.4	9.6	9.9	10.1	10.3	10.5	10.7	10.9	11.1
71%	8.2	8.4	8.6	8.8	9.0	9.2	9.4	9.6	9.8	10.0	10.2	10.4	10.6
72%	7.8	8.0	8.2	8.4	8.6	8.7	8.9	9.1	9.3	9.5	9.7	9.9	10.1
73%	7.4	7.6	7.8	8.0	8.1	8.3	8.5	8.7	8.9	9.1	9.2	9.4	9.6
74%	7.0	7.2	7.4	7.6	7.7	7.9	8.1	8.3	8.4	8.6	8.8	9.0	9.1
75%	6.7	6.8	7.0	7.2	7.3	7.5	7.7	7.8	8.0	8.2	8.3	8.5	8.7
76%	6.3	6.5	6.6	6.8	6.9	7.1	7.3	7.4	7.6	7.7	7.9	8.1	8.2
77%	6.0	6.1	6.3	6.4	6.6	6.7	6.9	7.0	7.2	7.3	7.5	7.6	7.8
78%	5.6	5.8	5.9	6.1	6.2	6.3	6.5	6.6	6.8	6.9	7.1	7.2	7.3
79%	5.3	5.4	5.6	5.7	5.8	6.0	6.1	6.2	6.4	6.5	6.6	6.8	6.9
80%	5.0	5.1	5.2	5.4	5.5	5.6	5.7	5.9	6.0	6.1	6.2	6.4	6.5
81%	4.7	4.8	4.9	5.0	5.2	5.3	5.4	5.5	5.6	5.7	5.9	6.0	6.1
82%	4.4	4.5	4.6	4.7	4.8	4.9	5.0	5.2	5.3	5.4	5.5	5.6	5.7
83%	4.1	4.2	4.3	4.4	4.5	4.6	4.7	4.8	4.9	5.0	5.1	5.2	5.3
84%	3.8	3.9	4.0	4.1	4.2	4.3	4.4	4.5	4.6	4.7	4.8	4.9	5.0
85%	3.5	3.6	3.7	3.8	3.9	4.0	4.1	4.1	4.2	4.3	4.4	4.5	4.6
86%	3.3	3.3	3.4	3.5	3.6	3.7	3.7	3.8	3.9	4.0	4.1	4.2	4.2
87%	3.0	3.1	3.1	3.2	3.3	3.4	3.4	3.5	3.6	3.7	3.7	3.8	3.9
88%	2.7	2.8	2.9	2.9	3.0	3.1	3.1	3.2	3.3	3.3	3.4	3.5	3.5
89%	2.5	2.5	2.6	2.7	2.7	2.8	2.8	2.9	3.0	3.0	3.1	3.2	3.2
90%	2.2	2.3	2.3	2.4	2.4	2.5	2.6	2.6	2.7	2.7	2.8	2.8	2.9
91%	2.0	2.0	2.1	2.1	2.2	2.2	2.3	2.3	2.4	2.4	2.5	2.5	2.6
92%	1.7	1.8	1.8	1.9	1.9	2.0	2.0	2.0	2.1	2.1	2.2	2.2	2.3
93%	1.5	1.5	1.6	1.6	1.7	1.7	1.7	1.8	1.8	1.8	1.9	1.9	2.0
94%	1.3	1.3	1.3	1.4	1.4	1.4	1.5	1.5	1.5	1.6	1.6	1.6	1.7
95%	1.1	1.1	1.1	1.1	1.2	1.2	1.2	1.2	1.3	1.3	1.3	1.3	1.4
96%	0.8	0.9	0.9	0.9	0.9	0.9	1.0	1.0	1.0	1.0	1.0	1.1	1.1
97%	0.6	0.6	0.6	0.7	0.7	0.7	0.7	0.7	0.7	0.8	0.8	0.8	0.8
98%	0.4	0.4	0.4	0.4	0.4	0.5	0.5	0.5	0.5	0.5	0.5	0.5	0.5
99%	0.2	0.2	0.2	0.2	0.2	0.2	0.2	0.2	0.2	0.2	0.3	0.3	0.3
100%	0.0	0.0	0.0	0.0	0.0	0.0	0.0	0.0	0.0	0.0	0.0	0.0	0.0

Index by Name

Page numbers followed by *n* indicate notes.

Index by Subject

Page numbers followed by *n* indicate notes.

Made in United States
North Haven, CT
14 May 2022

19146133R00239